CLASS AND ECONOMIC CHANGE IN KENYA

The Making of an African Petite Bourgeoisie
1905–1970

GAVIN KITCHING

Yale University Press
New Haven and London

Designed by Caroline Williamson and set in Monophoto Times.
Printed in the United States of America

Published in Great Britain, Europe, Africa, and Asia (except Japan) by Yale University Press, Ltd, London. Distributed in Australia and New Zealand by Book & Film Services, Artarmon, N.S.W., Australia; and in Japan by Harper & Row, Publishers, Tokyo Office.

Library of Congress Cataloging in Publication Data
Kitching, G   N
   Class and economic change in Kenya.

   Bibliography: p.
   Includes index.
   1. Kenya—Social conditions. 2. Kenya—Economic conditions.
3. Kenya—Colonial influence. 4. Social classes—Kenya.
5. Marxian school of sociology.
I. Title.
HN793.A8K57   309.1'676'2   79-21804

ISBN 978-0-300-02929-1

For my father, and Abel Msario

Contents

Part Two: Some Economic Origins of Mau-Mau 1905–1952
B. African Trade and Business, Pastoralism and Labour

Part Three: Kenya's 'Agrarian Revolution':
Myth and Reality 1952–1970

List of Figures

Abbreviations used in Footnotes and Text

AAD	African Affairs Department *Annual Report*
ADC	African District Council
CKAR	Central Kavirondo District Annual Report
CNAR	Central Nyanza District Annual Report (Central Kavirondo after 1947)
CPAR	Central Province Annual Report
CPEK Paper	Paper given to a Conference on 'The Political Economy of Kenya 1929–52', held at Trinity College, Cambridge, 26–29 June 1975.
DagAR	Dagoretti Annual Report
DagHOR	Dagoretti Handing Over Report
DAR	Department of Agriculture *Annual Report*
EAISR	East African Institute for Social Research (annual conference papers 1952 to 1966)
ES	Republic of Kenya, Ministry of Finance and Planning, Statistics Division, *Economic Survey* (annual 1960 to 1977)
FHAR	Fort Hall District Annual Report
GaAR	Garissa District Annual Report
IDS	Institute for Development Studies, University of Nairobi (Discussion Papers and Working Papers)
ILO Report	*Employment, Incomes and Equality* (ILO, 1972)
IsAR	Isiolo District Annual Report
KAR	Kikuyu (later Kiambu) District Annual Report
KajAR	Kajiado District Annual Report
KeAR	Kericho District Annual Report
KHOR	Kiambu District Handing Over Report
KisAR, KisQR	Kisii District Annual and Quarterly Reports (South Kavirondo District before 1918)
KisuAR, KisuQR	Kisumu District Annual and Quarterly Reports (Central Kavirondo before 1929)
KLC-R	Kenya Land Commission *Report* 1934
KLC E & M I-III	Kenya Land Commission, *Evidence and Memoranda*, Volumes I to III

KPAR	Kikuyu Province Annual Report
LC	Reports on African *Labour Census* 1946–8
LDAR	Labour Department *Annual Report* (1943–64)
LNC	Local Native Council
MaAR	Machakos District Annual Report
MasAR	Masailand Annual Report
MLAR	Ministry of Labour *Annual Report* (1965–70)
NAD	Native Affairs Department *Annual Report*
NAR	Nyeri District Annual Report
NaAR	Nandi District Annual Report
NKAR	North Kavirondo District Annual Report
NkAR	Nakuru District Annual Report
NLC	*Report of the Native Labour Commission* 1912–13
NNAR	North Nyanza District Annual Report (North Kavirondo after 1947)
NyeriHOR	Nyeri Handing Over Report
PCSS	Provisional Council for Social Sciences (East Africa) (annual conference papers 1970–2)
QR	Quarterly Report (various districts pre-1918)
SA	Colony and Protectorate of Kenya (later Republic of Kenya) *Statistical Abstract* (annual 1955 to 1976)
SKAR	South Kavirondo District Annual Report
SNAR	South Nyanza District Annual Report (South Kavirondo after 1947)
UPAR	Ukamba Province Annual Report
USSC	University (of East Africa) Social Science Council (annual conference papers 1968 and 1969)
WaAR	Wajir District Annual Report

A Note on Money

Kenyan pounds and pounds sterling were at strict parity up until Independence (1963). Since then rates of exchange have fluctuated but are of no importance in the discussion here. For convenience Kenyan pounds are identified as K£ throughout.

Acknowledgements

I gratefully acknowledge the following for permission to quote material from other sources: Makerere Institute of Social Research for permission to quote text and tables from H. Fearn's *An African Economy*; Professor Simeon Ominde for permission to use maps from his *Land and Population Movements in Kenya*; the *Review of African Political Economy* for permission to quote from Kerstin Leitner, 'The Situation of Agricultural Workers in Kenya' and from my 'Modes of Production and Kenyan Dependency'; Oxford University Press for permission to quote from J. Forbes Munro's *Colonial Rule and the Kamba*; A. D. Peters and Co Ltd, agents for Dr Kenneth King, for permission to quote from his *The African Artisan*; Northwestern University Press for permission to quote from Bohannan and Dalton (eds) *Markets in Africa*; *The Eastern Africa Journal of Rural Development* for permission to quote from W. Chipeta, 'The Roles of Customary and Modern Money in the Exchange Economy of Malawi'; Martin Secker and Warburg Ltd for permission to quote from Jomo Kenyatta's *Facing Mount Kenya*; Dr David Parkin for permission to quote from his *Palms, Wine and Witnesses*; Dr Jean Hay for permission to quote from her Ph.D. dissertation 'Economic Change in Luoland: Kowe 1890–1945'; the Controller of Her Majesty's Stationery Office for permission to quote from the *Kenya Land Commission, Evidence and Memoranda* Vol. 1, and from *Colonial Research Publication No. 3—African Labour Efficiency Survey 1947*; the International Labour Office for permission to quote from *Employment, Incomes and Equality*; Dr Anthony Clayton for permission to quote from his Ph.D. thesis 'Labour in the East Africa Protectorate 1895–1918'; Routledge and Kegan Paul Ltd for permission to quote from J. G. Peristiany, *The Social Institutions of the Kipsigis*. Lines quoted on pages 121–6 are taken from Jeanne Fisher *The Anatomy of Kikuyu Domesticity and Husbandry*, Crown copyright reserved. Finally, I would like to thank my friend and colleague Mike Cowen for permission to quote from his work on Central Province, to which, like all serious students of Kenya, I am enormously indebted.

Preface

A small area of Oxford and the period of the late sixties and early seventies are inextricably linked in my mind with the names and faces of a host of people with whom and from whom I learned, and whose contributions to the ideas worked out in this book are not any the less for not being precisely calculable. I would therefore like to thank the following friends and comrades from whom I learnt far more than any lecture or seminar ever taught: Frank Snowden, Charles van Onselen, Belinda Bozzoli, Mark Harrison, Barbara Smith, Dick Holt, Liz Glass, Sarah Graham-Brown, Rick Johnson, Diane Elson, Alexander Ador, and Gay Weber. I owe a particular debt to Stan Trapido who taught me the value of painstaking historical research, and who continued to help and encourage me long after his formal responsibility as my doctoral supervisor had ended. In particular I wish to thank Joanna de Groot who shared these years and this learning experience with me, and to whose knowledge of history I shall always be indebted. During the more recent period in which this book was written, I owed a great deal while in Oxford to John Harrison who provided a mixture of sympathetic support, acute criticism and alcohol in perfect proportions, and while in Swansea to Francis Clarke, who has provided friendship and constant intellectual stimulus. Would that all academics had his breadth of interest and vision Above all I have owed to Angela Reidy a companionship which has meant far more than any mere formal acknowledgement could ever express. Finally, it needs to be said that the echo of Edward Thompson in the sub-title of this work is quite deliberate. Although I now have many theoretical disagreements with Thompson's approach to Marxism, his strong sense of the ethical issues involved in being a Marxist in a post-Stalin world and his conviction that we need to create a Marxism expressed in the English intellectual idiom have remained powerful influences on my work.

As well as its profound debt to individuals, this book owes a great deal to institutions. The archival work and field research in Kenya on which it is based were begun when I was Research Officer at Queen Elizabeth House in Oxford (1971–4), and as well as the help and support of academic colleagues there, I also had the benefit of the services of its Librarian, Bob Townsend, whose knowledge of the development studies literature and willingness to share it make the catalogue which sits in front of his desk largely redundant. I also owe a profound debt to Mr F. E. Leese and his staff at Rhodes House Library, who showed endless patience and graciousness in allowing a rather chaotic researcher and his assistants to plunder their marvellous archive. Whilst I was in Kenya, the Institute for Development Studies, University of Nairobi, provided an excellent base from which to venture forth. Rather later a generous grant from the Social Science Research Council allowed the archival work on which this book is mainly based to be completed, and Zareer Masani and David Staton in particular did a great deal of the invaluable 'digging'. Last but by no means least, I must thank Professor Charles Elliott and all my other colleagues at the Centre for Development Studies, University College of Swansea, for their help and support in this enterprise. They bore an extra load of work when I took sabbatical leave to write this book, and both before and since that time have been unstinting in their interest and encouragement. I hope that the finished product may be some recompense for their friendship. Needless to say, neither they nor anyone else other than myself is responsible for the faults in what follows, and to that extent it is all my own work.

Gavin Kitching
Swansea
January 1980

Introduction

This book is an attempt to make a contribution to two areas of study which to their mutual impoverishment have been quite distinct in the literature on underdevelopment. On the one hand it is a study of the impact of colonialism and imperialism on the internal structure of a dominated economy and society, and in particular on patterns of stratification within that society. On the other hand it aims to make a contribution to the development of Marxist theory and in particular to explore some of the central theoretical problems which arise when an attempt is made to apply the Marxist perspective to non-capitalist societies and economies. It thus aims to make a contribution both to the economic and social history of an underdeveloped country, Kenya, and to Marxist theory.

I have not seen these two aims as antagonistic or contradictory. On the contrary, I believe that good history requires a theoretical perspective both implicit and explicit and that Marxist theory not informed by a detailed empirical grasp of historical development is in the end always arid. Yet inevitably this book will be read by teachers, students, and I hope by some of the African people involved in the struggle for liberation in Kenya. They will see it from at least two perspectives. There are those who will seek insights in it into the history of Kenya and of Africa which they can use for their own work and struggle, and there are others whose prime interest will be in the theoretical issues it explores. Moreover, if my experience is anything to go by, the criteria of judgement which these two groups will bring to the book will be rather different. For those whose primary interest is historical there will be greater interest in the detail of the historical account, and in finding parallels and dissimilarities with their own work. Those whose primary interest is in theory will perhaps be willing to take a lot of the historical detail as given, and will seek within it for the essential theoretical points. Obviously it is my hope that both groups will be satisfied with the book as they find it, but I am inclined to think that both will be critical, from somewhat different perspectives, and that in aiming for synthesis the book may be convicted of being a somewhat unsatisfactory compromise.

Thus I should say that I regard this book as primarily a work of theory and not of history. There are two senses in which this is true. In the first place, as originally conceived, it was supposed to provide a theoretical overview on the basis both of social and economic history and of contemporary sociological and economic study (particularly of rural stratification) which had been done by others. It was only when I discovered that the volume and quality of empirical work on Kenya which I required did not exist in the early seventies (this was particularly true of the historical work) that I commenced primary historical research on my own account.

In the second place, and much more substantially, my telling of the historical tale has been influenced throughout by my concerns as a theorist. As the sources I used yielded up one fascinating story after another, some of them still little explored in Kenyan historiography (such as the Somali stock trade, the role of Local Native Councils in African trade and business, the changing role of bridewealth, the effect of labour migration on the sexual division of labour within different types of household, and so on), I was constantly tempted to explore these themes in more and more detail. Each time however, even when I felt that other published sources might have revealed more, I turned away from further exploration at the point where I felt that enough had been said to support the generalisation which for one theoretical reason or another it was important to develop. In some cases it was necessary to turn away even before that point, because it was fairly clear that only oral evidence would be likely to take one further. In such situations, where a degree of indeterminacy remains in the evidence (such as whether the control of male household heads over their wives was as strong in poor households in which the head was a migrant as in poor households where he was not), I have simply noted that indeterminacy and left it. While I have been writing this work, the first oral-based social and economic history of Kenya has begun to emerge in the work of Miracle, Hay, King, Furedi, Waller and Newman among others, and I have found this material invaluable. It is my hope that in return for its debt to their work this study will open up further avenues for oral enquiry, avenues which open at the point where many of the documentary sources fall silent.

The specific role of the historical narrative in this work is also indicated by one omission. For this is a history of Kenya between 1905 and 1970 which uses the year 1952 as an end-point of one part of the narrative, and yet fails to discuss Mau-Mau itself (as distinct from the 'agrarian revolution' supposedly produced by it) or even its impact on the developing pattern of stratification. I shall state the reason for this here, as I do not do so anywhere else. In my view Mau-Mau was an interregnum which essentially left the pattern and trend of stratification which had preceded it largely intact. Those who benefited from Mau-Mau were essentially 'loyalist' and their interests were well protected and indeed enhanced by the colonial regime during the Emergency, while the poor, who had lost out badly in the preceding period, made up the majority of the forest fighters and in the end gained very little economically for their sacrifices. No doubt more detailed research will discover certain marginal alterations in the overall pattern of stratification made by Mau-Mau, but I am inclined to think that they will be precisely that: marginal. Therefore I have treated post-Emergency trends as largely a continuation of those of the pre-Emergency period, so far as differentiation of the African population of Kenya is concerned.

Thus this book will have failed if the reader, even in the midst of what may seem a great deal of empirical detail, does not feel him or herself pulled back repeatedly to the lead strings of theoretical inquiry which run through it. As far as its historical chapters (I to XII) are concerned, the prime theoretical aims are to describe and analyse the social and economic mechanism producing stratification of the African people of Kenya and the forms of exploitation to which that mechanism led. In essence, I found that the central mechanism involved— the use of off-farm income to expand landholdings and commercialise agricultural production—had many and varied ramifications once it was 'unpacked' into its various dimensions, and the historical chapters of the book trace out some of those ramifications and look at the mechanism from different points of view. But in the end, the reader only has to accept that the mechanism which I isolate was of considerable importance in producing stratification and inequality, and that a rather curious social structure and pattern of stratification has resulted from it. For the historical narrative, detailed though it is, is only intended to demonstrate these two propositions in a manner which may seem reasonably convincing. From then on, in chapters XIII, XIV and the appendix, I am concerned to explore the theoretical problems which Marxists face in explaining and conceptualising this pattern of stratification, and the structure of production and circulation which underlies it.

This accounts for a rather curious characteristic of the book which I am sure many readers, and particularly those whose primary interest is historical, will very readily observe. It has no historical conclusion. By this I mean that when I have taken the time-based narrative and analysis to the point which I feel will suffice for my purposes (1970), I simply end it, and then commence on the theoretical discourse. At intervals throughout the narrative there are summings-up and generalisations from the data offered, but there is no component of this type for the overall narrative, such as one would expect to find in a conventional work of history. Instead there is a jump to the beginning of the theoretical discourse. The reason for this is that given my particular purposes this discourse does sum up the historical work so far as I am concerned. Or rather it is its recapitulation from a theoretical perspective which essentially takes a point in time and looks at certain logical and structural relationships within the economy and society at that point (*circa* 1970). In addition there is an attempt to state what I take to be structural transformations wrought in that economy and society by historical change, and the problems which these pose (or rather which their incompleteness poses) for a theoretical grasp of contemporary Kenya. Of course to call these transformations 'incomplete' is not metaphysically to predicate history with a predetermined end (something which is constantly condemned outside and inside Marxism as 'teleology'), but to say something about Marxism as a theoretical problematic, and in particular to say something about the set of logical relationships between concepts within it which gives each of them their meaning and reference. I shall be concerned especially with such central concepts as 'class structure', 'class struggle', and 'exploitation', and with problems posed by the limitations of the total theoretical context within which they are embodied. Those limitations are revealed by Kenya as a 'hard case', a case which generates certain theoretical puzzles. The point of the final two chapters and the appendix is to explain how and why those puzzles are generated, and to discuss how best to come to terms with them theoretically. In this case, 'coming to terms' means assessing different propositions and concepts in Marxism from the point of view of their generality and their dependence on contingent historical conditions. In particular I suggest that certain concepts of 'class' and 'class struggle' in Marx presuppose certain empirical conditions which are not universally met with, and that the essence of the concept of exploitation,[1] which I argue is much more central to Marxism than 'class analysis' as such, is maintainable under a less restricted range of historical conditions, and can embrace the Kenyan case.

I also argue that the structural preconditions of the concepts of value and surplus value are similarly restrictive, and are only met with in historical conditions which are still untypical even within the capitalist world. But the concepts of 'socially necessary labour time', 'surplus labour', 'surplus product', 'use value', 'exchange value', 'commodity production', and 'circulation of commodities' as well as 'exploitation' cover a much broader historical range and can encompass the Kenyan case, generating important explanatory propositions about that case and, I am sure, about many other similar cases in the Third World.

The end result of all this is that I reject the concept of 'pre-capitalist modes of production' and of a 'mode of production in general' as having any explanatory value in the post-capitalist world.[2] Outside of the socialist bloc, there is only one mode of production in the world today, the world capitalist mode of production of which Kenya and other Third World economies are an integral part. In this regard I concur with A. G. Frank, though for rather different reasons.[3] In addition however I wish to suggest explicitly here (since I only do so implicitly elsewhere) that the single major theoretical impediment to the effective analysis of actual production in the Third World is the concept of a 'mode' of

1. 'Exploitation' in this work will be taken to be the transfer of the product of its labour power from one class in society to another either through the process of production of commodities, or through the circulation process.
2. For an attempt to give these concepts a highly rigorous formulation see B. Hindess and P. Q. Hirst, *Pre-Capitalist Modes of Production* (London, 1975).
3. See A. G. Frank, *Capitalism and Underdevelopment in Latin America* (Harmondsworth, 1971).

production. Reification of this concept (and indeed of 'social formation') has been one of the most negative legacies of Althusserian work on Marxist theory. Abandonment of it does not lead to an aconceptual empiricism, for the concept itself (or rather the concept of a capitalist mode of production, which I would argue is the only concept of a mode of production ever theoretically developed by Marx) can be unpacked into a number of lower-level concepts of much greater generality and specificity. These concepts include 'mode of the appropriation of nature', 'mode of the appropriation of surplus labour', 'division of labour', 'intensity of labour', and 'circulation' (of commodities and money), which have the merit, as E. J. Hobsbawm observed a long time ago,[4] of being applicable to any historical situation in which commodity production occurs, and at the same time of allowing questions to be formulated (e.g. 'What is the mode of appropriation of nature?'), whose answers lead to important and highly specific propositions about that situation.

A fixation on 'modes' of production has led to a comparative neglect of these lower order concepts which has in its turn led to a rigidity of theoretical formulation. For these neglected concepts have a degree of flexibility, both of reference and of combination, which the concept of a 'mode' of production or of an 'articulation' of modes within a single 'social formation' does not have. This is simply another way of saying that those lower order concepts assume a less restricted set of historical conditions than do the higher order ones.[5]

However, these conclusions did not come to me simply from an analysis of the logical relationships between concepts. They came to me as the result of theoretical reflection on historical reality. I found that I could analyse that reality using these concepts whilst I could not use the higher order concepts on which Althusser and Balibar invite us to focus.[6] The presence of a detailed historical narrative within this work is meant to make that point and thus to be in itself an exemplification or expression of a particular theoretical perspective. It is because the economic history within the book has itself a theoretical role

4. E. J. Hobsbawm, 'Introduction' to K. Marx, *Pre-Capitalist Economic Formations* (London, 1964), especially p. 16. The 'mode of the appropriation of surplus labour' is simply the means by which a product over and above a labourer's subsistence is obtained from him (e.g. by rent, taxes or through profit of enterprise). The 'division of labour' and 'circulation' of commodities and money are largely self-explanatory concepts, while 'intensity of labour' refers to the productivity of a given expenditure of labour power which depends not merely upon the length of time the labourer works or the enthusiasm and concentration with which he works, but also upon the extent to which his labour is aided by capital, especially machinery.
5. This view is rather similar to that adopted in Hindess and Hirst's 'Auto-Critique' (B. Hindess and P. Q. Hirst, *Mode of Production and Social Formation: an auto-critique of 'Pre-capitalist Modes of Production'*, London, 1977), but was derived not from deductive logic alone but from the deductive/ inductive dialectic which I take to be the centre of Marxist method. See further brief remarks on the philosophical position of the Althusserians below.
6. L. Althusser and E. Balibar, *Reading Capital* (London, 1975).

to play (a role in which its simple presence is almost as important as its content) that a work of fourteen chapters, twelve of which are devoted to economic history, can still claim to be primarily a work of theory.

If it were particularly relevant to an understanding of this book, I would go on to argue that the central weakness of the Althusserian tradition in Marxism, of which the problems I have encountered are just one example, is that it abandons the philosophical realist position of which Marx's own thought is one of the finest examples. It is not possible, other than at the level of assertion, to maintain within the Althusserian problematic the view that reality is independent of our perceptions of it. To be sure such a view must involve a leap of faith (since by definition we only have those perceptions by which to know it), but in my view it is a leap of faith whose logical consequences are less contradictory than is the so-called 'theoretical realist' position to which the Althusserians are committed, and which is in fact not a philosophical realist position at all but a kind of idealism.[7] If this assertion makes me an 'empiricist' I am happy to be such, and certainly I feel that I am in the company of Marx in this matter.

I am straying further from the path of relevance than an introduction to a study of Kenya between 1905 and 1970 warrants. I will therefore commend myself to the reader's mercies with one final comment. It was my hope, as I have said, to bring together history and Marxist theory in a fashion which would make their interdependence obvious, and which would be of equal interest to the professional historian, the student of African history, the Marxist theoretician, and to anybody interested in the problems of underdevelopment. In the end such a satisfactory synthesis of narrative and theory has been beyond me, and I have felt increasingly that the book should be judged above all, by Marxists, as a work of Marxist theory, though I am hopeful that it will still be of interest to others. One aspect of my failure which intrigues me is the grinding change of gear between the historical and theoretical parts of the book. By this I mean not only that there is a partial change of focus and perspective from chapter XII to chapter XIII, but that there is a marked change in the very vocabulary, grammer and syntax at that point. Such a change occurs from time to time even inside the historical narrative, when I attempt to draw out the theoretical implications of a historical trend. I suspect that this is because historical narrative is time-bound (and this is reflected in its syntax and tense structure), whilst theory is timeless and proceeds in a sort of eternal present, which in turn forces syntactical changes on one. It seems that this is one problem caused by the fact that Marxism (and especially Marx's *Capital*) represents an exploration, within social reality, of the relationship between formal logic and the passage of

7. For what I believe to be an essentially correct statement of the epistemological basis of Marxism, and, by implication, a devastating critique of the Althusserians and other idealist tendencies in Marxism, see D. H. Ruben, *Marxism and Materialism: A Study in Marxist Theory of Knowledge* (Hassocks, 1977).

time. I am told by a friend that this relationship remains of perennial fascination to mathematicians and logicians and generates some of the most important theoretical puzzles in both disciplines. If this is the case, Marxism might benefit from an understanding of these puzzles arising in other areas. Certainly I feel that such an exploration might throw more light on Marx's few explicit epistemological and methodological prescriptions, and above all on 'dialectics'. But such an exploration is beyond me; I will leave the matter there.

Chapter I
Colonial Change
and the Distribution of Labour Time

> Individuals producing in society—hence socially determined individual production—is, of course, the point of departure. Karl Marx, *Grundrisse*, p. 83

I wish to begin by attempting to draw an 'ideal typical' picture of production and the division of labour as it was in pre-colonial Kenya, approximately in the period 1880–1905. The use of such an ideal type is open to all the usual objections. It treats as static what was in fact a changing historical situation, and in offering an essentialist description drawn from all the peoples of pre-colonial Kenya it does not provide an accurate or comprehensive description of any one of them. But the use of this device is necessary here, as in so many studies, in order to provide a sort of rough historical bench-mark for the description and analysis of social and economic change in the colonial period which will take up most of this work. Without such a bench-mark it would be impossible to analyse the structural transformation which took place in production and in the division of labour among Africans in colonial Kenya. Thus much of the point of this work, which is designed to show the really profound changes which came over the African way of life in Kenya in what was in historical terms a staggeringly short period of time, would be lost.

1. The Pre-Colonial Work Pattern—An Ideal Type

The patterns of work in most of the small-scale societies of pre-colonial Kenya seem to have been very similar, and much like those in other parts of Africa. In the more sedentary societies in which pastoralism was combined with shifting cultivation, men were responsible for the initial clearing of forest or bush (which, since cultivation was shifting, was a regularly recurring task), and for the initial turning of the earth so cleared. Groups of men usually built houses and other buildings. Married women planted, weeded and harvested the food crops on which everyone depended, and were assisted in this by their unmarried daughters. Small boys herded the cows, sheep and goats which were kept near the homestead, and both adult men and women milked them when this was required.

8

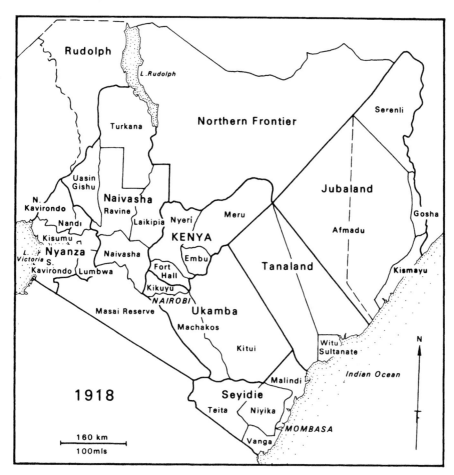

Figure I:1. Districts and Provinces, East African Protectorate, 1918.

Unmarried youths were generally engaged in hunting, stock raiding and in inter- or intra-tribal fighting, and were directed in these activities by older unmarried males and younger married males (generally all men up until their late thirties). Domestic work was invariably the preserve of married women assisted by their daughters; in pre-colonial Africa such work probably consisted mainly of the preparation, storage and cooking of food.

Both men and women were engaged in trade, the women generally being restricted to those kinds which could be practised near to the homestead, the barter of foodstuffs and of home-made beer being the two most common. Men seem to have monopolised the long-distance trade in both livestock and food-

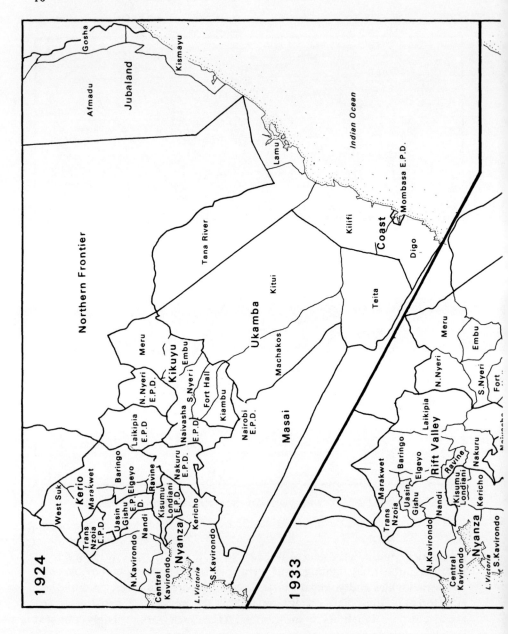

1924

Gosha
Jubaland
Afmadu
Kismayu
Northern Frontier
Indian Ocean
Lamu
Tana River
Kilifi
Mombasa E.P.D.
Coast
Digo
Teita
Meru
Kitui
Ukamba
N.Nyeri E.P.D.
Kikuyu
Machakos
Kiambu
Fort Hall
Embu
S.Nyeri E.P.D
Naivasha E.P.D
Laikipia E.P.D
Nairobi E.P.D.
Masai
Baringo
Nakuru E.P.D.
Ravine
Elgeyo
E.P. D.
Uasin Gishu
Kerio
Marakwet
West Suk
Trans Nzoia E.P.D
Nandi
N.Kavirondo
Kisumu Londiani E.P.D
Kericho
Nyanza
Central Kavirondo
S.Kavirondo
L. Victoria

1933

Meru
N.Nyeri
Embu
S.Nyeri
Fort
Laikipia
Rift Valley
Nakuru
Ravine
Baringo
Elgeyo
Marakwet
Trans Nzoia
Uasin Gishu
Nandi
Kisumu Londiani
Kericho
N.Kavirondo
Central Kavirondo
Nyanza
S.Kavirondo
L. Victoria

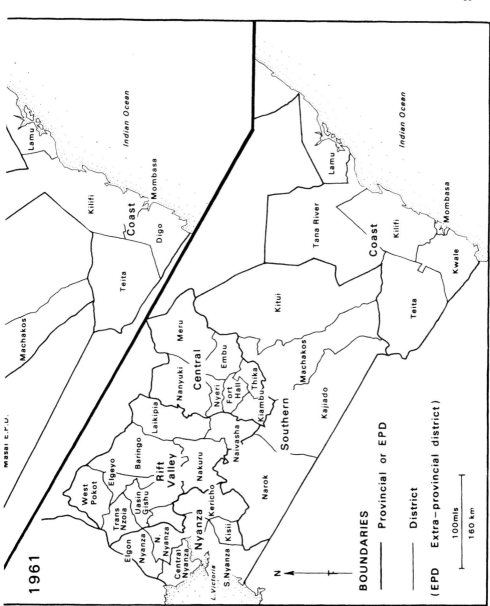

Figure 1:2. Districts and Provinces, Kenya Colony, 1924, 1933 and 1961.

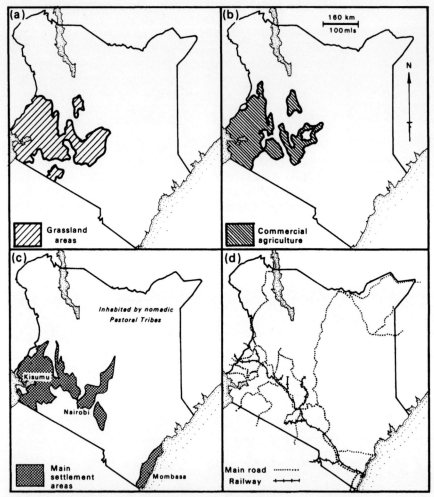

Figure 1:3. Distribution of highland grass, commercial agriculture, population and communications, Republic of Kenya, 1970.

crops, largely because of the need for such trade to have military protection.[1] However 'long-distance' here is historically a very specific term, since in pre-colonial Kenya the distance which men might venture from their homesteads without fear of attack could in many cases be quite short: one or two miles in the case of those living on the boundaries between disputing ethnic groups.

Apart from the sexual division of labour, there seems to have been some

1. P. Marris and A. Somerset, *African Businessmen: A Study of Entrepreneurship and Development in Kenya* (Nairobi, 1971), pp. 30–43; R. M. A. van Zwanenberg with Anne King, *An Economic History of Kenya and Uganda 1800–1970* (London, 1975), pp. 147–59; J. Forbes Munro, *Colonial*

further development of specialisation within each sex. Certain clan[2] groups of men, for example, were known for their skills as iron founders and smiths, and traded their products both within their own tribe, and over longer distances.[3]

Among other specialists, Hay mentions producers of wood carvings, leather, harps and baskets among the Luo, and among the Abaluhya specialist producers of baskets and pots, as well as the famous blacksmithing clans of Samia. Among the Gusii there also seem to have been specialist producers of pipes and vases carved from soapstone.[4]

Short-distance trade seems to have been a non-specialist occupation for the greater part of the nineteenth century, since at its simplest all that was required was the ability to carry a basket of millet, a gourd of beer, or three or four pots to the homes of neighbours or, in a limited number of cases, to a generally recognised trading point. However, there is some evidence that, particularly in the late nineteenth century, long-distance trade was becoming more organised

---

Rule and the Kamba: Social Change in the Kenya Highlands 1889–1939 (Oxford, 1975), pp. 23–6; F. E. Bernard, *East of Mount Kenya: Meru Agriculture in Transition* (Munich, 1972), pp. 37–41; Marvin Miracle, 'Economic Change among the Kikuyu 1895–1905' (IDS Working Paper No. 158 1972), pp. 7–19 and 21–3; L. S. B. Leakey, 'The Economics of Kikuyu Life', *East African Economic Review*, Vol. 3, 1956, pp. 165–80. Leakey suggests that the Kikuyu trade with the Masai was actually monopolised by women, and the view is supported by Muriuki: G. Muriuki, *A History of the Kikuyu 1500–1900* (Nairobi, 1974), p. 107. However, these general assertions are at odds with the one detailed study of a part of the trade which we have (Marris and Somerset's account of the trade between Mahiga location in the present-day Nyeri district and the Purko Masai). Leakey also notes that men monopolised trade with the Kamba (ibid. p. 173). In this rather confused state of the literature on the Kikuyu (which clearly demands further research), and in view of the evidence on male dominance of long-distance trade on other areas of Kenya and East Africa I have left this generalisation untouched. Also of course in the nature of historical accounts in general and oral research in particular the distinction between 'short' and 'long' distance is bound to be a shifting and fuzzy one.

2. The sources are often vague about what is meant by 'clan', and in any case the term was often used as a translation of African vernacular terms with quite different meanings. All the reader needs to assume is a number of male household heads linked together by a claim (real or fictive) to be the descendants of the same male ancestor usually through the male line (i.e. fathers' sons or fathers' brothers' sons). Clan groups proper were larger and 'deeper' in kinship terms than lineages and might go back four generations or more.

3. See van Zwanenberg with King, op. cit., pp. 115–19 and also Leakey, op. cit., p. 170, who distinguishes separate 'guilds' of Iron Smelters and Metal Workers among the pre-colonial Kikuyu, and also a 'Guild of Ornament and Bead Workers' who made ornaments in 'brass, copper, iron and so on'. Each guild it appears was endogamous for the men within it. He also mentions a 'guild of miners' (of iron ore) and one of 'merchants of soda'. The concept of a guild here is obviously being used as a rather loose analogy, and it seems doubtful if any of these organisations (which were clearly clan or kin groups as well as occupational categories) possessed the full panoply of rules and functions identified with guilds in medieval Europe, for example.

4. Margaret Jean Hay, 'Economic Change in Luoland: Kowe 1890–1945' (Univ. of Wisconsin Ph.D. 1972), p. 105; Günter Wagner, *The Bantu of Western Kenya: With Special Reference to the Vugusu and Logoli* (London, 1970), Vol. II, pp. 9–16; SKAR 1916, p. 16 and 1917, p. 4. See also Bernard, op. cit., p. 43 on the specialist production of pots, baskets and mats among the Meru.

and specialised, with Africans adopting the 'caravan' form of organisation pioneered in the area by the Arabs and Swahilis, and using it for the barter trade between the Kikuyu and Masai, Kamba and Masai and in the salt trade from Lake Magadi.[5]

Nonetheless the overall picture of pre-colonial Kenya which we get from the limited historical evidence currently available is one in which the sexual division of labour in production was very marked, but in which beyond this there was comparatively little specialisation in production in the region as a whole, except perhaps in iron founding and smithing, basketwork, and pottery. Even here the specialisation was by clan or sub-clan group within tribes rather than by individual producer. There was also a limited degree of specialisation in the sphere of circulation, especially perhaps in the long-distance circulation of livestock, food crops, iron goods and pottery and salt. It is my view that this society was one which had a very considerable degree of underutilised labour time and indeed that major developments in colonial Kenya are inexplicable unless this is recognised.

2. The Underutilisation of Labour Time in Colonial Kenya

Labour time in pre-colonial Kenya was underutilised in two different senses. It was underutilised firstly in the quantitative sense that labour time was simply not expended in material production for a large part of the working year. This was particularly true of male labour time. Younger men were engaged in fighting, in stock raiding or in the pursuit of stock raiders from other groups, or they were hunting. Hunting of course added to the food supply of the group, whilst expansion of the holdings of livestock or the defence of current holdings represented the preservation of the group's principal use and exchange values. Such activities were therefore necessary to the social formations inside which production occurred. But they were not directly productive activities, in the sense of adding directly to the stock of use values, so that once many of them had been made otiose or impossible by the colonial presence, a great deal of young male labour time was released for expenditure in other ways. Similarly, there was a great deal of underutilised male labour time among older married males, by which one means men of thirty-five to forty or older, since in the pre-colonial situation their fighting and hunting were by this age largely replaced by ritual and judicial functions and to a lesser extent by trading. Since death came early, with few men surviving beyond sixty, this phase of seniority may have been shorter than one supposes, but, especially after the development of colonialism and the lengthening of life which it brought, there was a considerable stock of potential labour time in this group too.

5. Van Zwanenberg with King, op. cit., pp. 152–3.

Among women, domestic and childrearing tasks, plus the more regular cultivating tasks, meant that a labour day or year was probably fuller than that of a man. But nonetheless there was still considerable underutilisation. This arose principally because agricultural production in pre-colonial Kenya was restricted almost entirely to the production of annual cereal crops, mainly millets and eleusine. These crops are distinguished by their resistance to low rainfall short of total drought, and by their ability to yield regularly with a minimum of husbandry. In a situation of land abundance, and with shifting cultivation guaranteeing a soil of reasonable fertility, a subsistence crop would grow from a specified cultivated area with a minimum of labour input. In fact, planting and harvesting and a little weeding represented the principal tasks, and yields found low by colonial agricultural officers would have been perfectly adequate when storage facilities were non-existent and trade outlets minimal. Within the home, domestic tasks were restricted to child rearing, which could be shared with older daughters, and the preparation of food. Slack periods in the agricultural year were occupied with handicraft production, but these were activities for which market purchase could be substituted when market outlets expanded in the colonial period.

I have no wish to revive the colonial stereotype of 'the lazy African', let alone to suggest that pre-colonial life was easy. Disease, drought and locusts brought frequent and widespread suffering, as late-nineteenth-century accounts show. However, it was precisely because of this that the necessary labour input into production was so limited. Given a minimum labour input and good fortune with weather, health (of animals and people) and pests (above all the locust), a fairly regular subsistence living could be obtained. Extra labour input into production would simply have created undisposable surpluses, so that labour time was far better spent carrying out ceremonies and sacrifices which might bring the needed good fortune. For if bad fortune befell, crops withered or animals died, no extra labour input of the type and efficacy available in pre-colonial Kenya would have sufficed to alter or avert the suffering which came. The best that could be done was to ameliorate the situation by trading what one had left with other peoples whose crops or livestock had fared better.

However, if labour time and labour power were underutilised in a simple quantitative sense (i.e. a great many days and hours were not spent in materially productive effort), they were also underutilised in a qualitative sense. A great deal of the labour power which was expended was unaided by or unintensified by anything other than very simple technology. This is not to deny that labour power was informed by knowledge and skill. Apart from the skills of the special-ist artisan, most men developed skills in hunting, herding (and animal husbandry in general[6]) and house-building, whilst women used well the simple agricultural

---

6. It was only fairly late in the colonial period that some understanding emerged of the rationality and skill of African animal husbandry (for long lambasted by colonial officials), and this only after

technology available to them, and developed a variety of handicraft skills. But in comparison with the agricultural technology which became available to Africans in the colonial period, as well as the artisanal and manufacturing techniques which they learned then, the production technology available even at the end of the pre-colonial period was rudimentary.

This meant of course that in the colonial period it was possible, at least in some areas of the country and in some areas of production, to intensify the labour power expended, so that (schematically) one hour of 1914 cultivating labour time in Kiambu district was worth two hours of 1890 labour time. 'Worth' here of course refers to physical output per hour of labour expended.

This intensification in turn allowed for the release of labour power from agricultural production and allowed the formation of the specialist wage labour category whose emergence and stratification we will examine in a later chapter. It also allowed for more labour time (and labour power) to be released into artisan, service and repair activities and into trade, whilst increasing the volume and range of products to be traded.

Thus, the quantitative and qualitative underutilisation of labour time and labour power in pre-colonial Kenya allowed the African population to adjust in two ways to the demands made by a colonial and settler presence. In the case of quantitative underutilisation it was possible to redistribute labour time within the population so as to create a new pattern of production and a new division of labour. In the case of qualitative underutilisation it was possible to intensify or raise the productivity of the labour power expended so as to obtain increased production from the same labour time. The latter increase in productivity allowed Africans cultivating the land to compensate for the transferral of labour power to other forms of production. However the process schematically outlined above was in reality complicated by a number of factors, including uneven chronological and geographical development (especially as between sedentary and nomadic groups), the sexual division of labour, and the squatter phenomenon. We shall now examine these complications.

3. Redistribution and Intensification of Labour Power in Colonial Kenya

As we shall see, the period 1905–18 saw the slow emergence of:
(a) an African labour force not engaged in agriculture, pastoralism, traditional hunting and fighting or other traditional productive activities. This new labour force was engaged in colonial administration, in teaching, clerking and service

the ecological and disease problems of animal husbandry in the tropics came to be appreciated. For an interesting account, see R. L. Tignor, *The Colonial Transformation of Kenya: The Kamba, Kikuyu and Maasai from 1900 to 1939* (Princeton, 1976), pp. 310–24.

activities, and in semi-skilled and unskilled manual labour on the railway, in water transport and road construction. All these occupations were 'new' occupations to the African labour force and required some amount of formal or informal exposure to the colonial education system, especially for the more skilled or responsible positions. With the small exception of some aspects of domestic service, all these occupations were performed by men.

(b) an African labour force undertaking agricultural production on land now alienated to Europeans. Part of this labour force was permanently resident on the settler farms and plantations ('squatters'), and another part was contracted on short term, usually monthly, contracts for (in this period) about three months every year. The type of concrete labour performed on the farms was in some cases very similar to that which Africans had undertaken in the pre-colonial period, so for the majority of unskilled labourers there was no need for formal or informal education or skills not already possessed. This was certainly the case where the farms were in effect sheep or cattle ranches. In other cases however where new crops were involved (maize, coffee, sisal), a learning process (always informal) was involved. In addition of course there were a number of 'new' skilled artisan, driving and domestic service jobs on nearly all farms, as well as a number of 'labour control' positions, and these would require a degree of formal and informal instruction. In the case of the squatter labour force, the labour power of men, women and children was expended. Non-resident labour on the other hand was almost entirely adult male.

(c) an expanded and altered African trade and business labour force. Up to 1918 this group was engaged in a much expanded form of stock trading (involving Somalis, Sudanese and Swahilis who had entered Kenya either with the colonial administration or with the Imperial British East Africa Company), and the very first beginnings of maize milling, butchering, the sale of food and drink, and small-scale retailing in Nairobi and southern Kiambu. All the latter were 'new' forms of trade, while the expansion of the range and scale of stock trading had been made possible by the *pax Britannica*. In addition, traditional itinerant barter traders had new commodities to sell, and the *pax Britannica* itself began to undermine late nineteenth-century 'caravan' trading and organisation among Africans. Before 1918 very few African artisans had left wage employment to set up 'on their own behalf'. But it is possible that, for a while at least, some of the traditional blacksmiths found an increased demand for an expanded range of products.

It is almost impossible to give quantitative dimensions to these three categories, and in particular I have come across no official attempt to assess the size of the squatter population before 1923 (when it was put at 13,773 'heads of families',[7] i.e. some 60–70,000 people). Clayton and Savage suggest that in 1918 'The government employed some 3,000–5,000 in the Public Works Department,

7. *NAD* 1923, p. 34.

and some 7,000 on the Railway (including contractors). The private sector raised the total employed at peak seasons to approximately 110,000.'[8]

Most of these 110,000 would have been men, women and children employed on farms and estates at peak periods. In 1918 there were probably no more than 10–15,000 people employed in all forms of non-farm wage employment (excluding the armed forces and the carrier corps). It is clear nonetheless that the emergence of these three categories of 'new' labour represented a major redistribution of labour time, and that it was essentially male labour time which was withdrawn from hunting, herding and fighting and redistributed into these new forms of production and exchange. However, squatter labour represents a partial qualification of this pattern for it is clear that initially (1905–25) most male squatters entered European farms with the intention of maintaining the old distribution of labour time intact. That is to say, with the alienation to Europeans of land which they were already occupying, many Africans found themselves to be squatters overnight. Others moved on to farms in the Rift Valley to escape demands for compulsory labour in the Reserves, impressment into the wartime Carrier Corps, or simply because, being large stock owners, they wished to have access to the fine grazing of the Rift Valley, so long denied them by the Masai, but now opened up by the settlers.

Insofar as the squatter phenomenon was initially conservative in motivation, it was largely successful, at least up to about 1925. Until then, most squatters succeeded in living a distinctly 'pre-colonial' life on the huge, largely undeveloped tracts of land which the Administration was pleased to call 'farms', 'ranches' and 'plantations'. Just as before, young men concerned themselves with hunting, raiding and fighting, and older men with the acquisition of stock and wives, and with their judicial, sacrificial and ceremonial duties. Young boys herded the stock, and women and girls undertook the domestic work and the cultivation for domestic consumption. It is clear from the report of the 1912–13 Native Labour Commission that settler calls on squatter labour for farm or ranch work were very occasional, easily evaded, and sometimes non-existent.[9]

Thus the section of the African population which was most affected by the new colonial presence before 1918 was that which contributed labour power on a 'non-squatter' basis: those households which lost labour power (usually male) for part or all of the year, in circumstances where that labour power was unable to return when required, being physically very distant. In general this was the minority of the African labour force before 1918 which was either engaged full-time or part-time in non-agricultural wage employment, or constituted non-resident labour on farms and estates.

8. Anthony Clayton and Donald C. Savage, *Government and Labour in Kenya 1895–1963* (London, 1974), pp. 64–5.
9. *NLC*, pp. 6, 12, 13, 20, 229, 238, 240 and 272. See also Rebman M. Wambaa and Kenneth King, 'The Political Economy of the Rift Valley: A Squatter Perspective' (Historical Association of Kenya Annual Conference Paper, 1972, pp. 1–2).

Even in the latter case, however, it is likely that before 1930 the majority of this genuinely non-resident male labour power on farms was supplied from the Luo and Abaluhya areas of western Kenya, since many of the Kikuyu classified as 'non-resident' farm labour before that date were actually squatters, as indeed were the bulk of other groups supplying formally non-resident or contract farm labour (e.g. the Nandi, 'Lumbwa' or Kipsigis, and the Kamba[10]). In fact only a minority of labourers who were living immediately adjacent to farms were in any genuine sense non-resident, in that their families remained in the Reserve and they returned to their homes on the completion of a day's work. Moreover, even those Luo or Abaluhya households whose young men were long-distance migrants rarely needed to replace the labour lost, since up to 1918 (and indeed up to 1930), it involved those household members who had been least involved in household production (cultivation and animal husbandry) even in the pre-colonial period.

In fact, the only households who might have needed to replace labour were those who lost heads of households to 'permanent' employment, and these were very rare in the pre-1918 period, since most of the young educated (who held clerks' or teachers' jobs outside the Reserve) were unmarried at this time.[11] The labour of the few married men involved in this category could be replaced by that of brothers or growing sons.

In short, before 1930 the demands of the colonial economy for a redistribution of African labour time had hardly begun to utilise the 'spare capacity' inherent in the pre-colonial division of labour. Such demands as were made could be met simply by redistributing a small part of the quantitatively under-utilised male labour time toward wage and farm employment, and since the functions traditionally performed by the men involved were either historically otiose (certain forms of military protection) or increasingly difficult for a variety of reasons (hunting and stock raiding) such labour time could easily be spared and did not even need to be replaced. The recurrent tasks of cultivation and food preparation for domestic consumption had always been the preserve of women and this remained the case, both in the Reserve and on the settler farms. At this stage a qualitative improvement or intensification of this female labour had barely begun, because before 1930 it was hardly necessary.

Everything above refers to the sedentary pastoralist peoples of Kenya in the period before 1930. As far as the nomadic pastoralists are concerned, one may say that there were effectively no changes in the internal division of labour within the nomadic household or tribe in the period 1905–30. What did occur was an intensification of the trading links both between agricultural and pastoral peoples (centred on the traditional exchange of grain for livestock and livestock products) and between different pastoral peoples (centred on the exchange of

10. See Clayton and Savage, op. cit., pp. 51–4 and *NLC*, op. cit.
11. See for example Hay, op. cit., pp. 172–3.

different types of livestock), and in this latter development the Somalis played a central part. In the course of time both types of trade were to alter their form and have profound effects on the pastoral economies, and this will be discussed briefly in chapter VIII.[12]

4. Theoretical and Explanatory Implications

It is important that the phenomenon of underutilised labour time in pre-colonial and early colonial Kenya be grasped, since otherwise it is impossible to explain astonishing inter-war developments which are very often presented as unproblematic by historians of the period. I refer to the fact that despite massive population losses in Kenya in the decade 1890–1900 (from plague and other diseases, starvation due to losses of cattle through rinderpest, and drought) and the death of some 150,000 men in the first world war and the influenza epidemic that followed, the African population of Kenya was able to provide a continual expansion of the farm and non-farm wage labour force up until the late 1920s or early 1930s and at the same time expand the cultivated area within the Reserves quite massively. With the depression of the 1930s much male labour returned to the Reserves to aid the women, but the fact remains that in the period 1905 to 1930 it was the quantitative expansion of women's labour time which was primarily responsible for such commercialisation of African agriculture as occurred. Since this process was geographically uneven, and was restricted in the 1920s almost entirely to Kikuyuland and Nyanza, women in these areas were able to hire in labour (from less commercialised areas both within and outside Kenya) to partially replace the departed men. But in the main they filled the gap by an expansion of the amount of their own labour time devoted to agricultural production, and by beginning to use labour-saving technology both in cultivation and in associated processes. Both in the hiring of replacement labour power, and in the purchase of improved agricultural implements, women were aided by remittances of wages earned by the departed men.

The expansion of the cultivated area in the 1920s, at least in Central and Nyanza Provinces, and the considerably increased volume and value of the crops produced, in turn made possible the expansion of increasingly specialised labour (generally male) in the sphere of circulation. This labour power was involved in the purchase, transportation and sale of crops, and their exchange (often in the form of barter, until *circa* 1930) with other crops, imported consumer goods, various services, and livestock. The beginning of this continuing

12. This brief discussion anticipates a more detailed analysis in that chapter. See especially pp. 202–3 for a justification of the term 'sedentary pastoralist' to describe the Kikuyu, Luo Kamba and Abaluhya peoples of Kenya in the pre-colonial and early colonial periods.

story appears in the next chapter, but here it is simply presented as a testimony to the degree to which African labour time and labour power were underutilised in the period 1890–1918. The extent to which this must have been the case is brought home most powerfully if we consider that all this occurred despite the fact that in all probability the African population of Kenya actually fell, in absolute terms, from 1890 to 1921 or 1923, and had probably only recovered its level of 1900 by 1931.[13]

With this schematic model of structural change in production in mind, we may now turn to examine in detail developments in the African economy of Kenya between 1905, when systematic district records began, and 1952, when the onset of the Mau-Mau Emergency signalled a crisis in the colonial political economy, whose resolution required a planned 'revolution' in African agriculture. In this analysis a disproportionate amount of space is accorded to changes in agricultural production and their implications both for the sexual division of labour within African households and for relations between households. I take four chapters to describe and analyse these changes, whilst other sectors are dealt with in a single chapter covering the entire forty-seven-year period, except for the section on the Local Native Councils which proceeds from their foundation in 1925.

This allocation of space represents my notion of the comparative importance of the phenomena being dealt with. This does not mean that I posit a simple one-way causality in which changes in production and the relations of production in agriculture cause changes in trade and business, or in pastoralism, or produce the phenomenon of a wage labour force. Rather, there was the familiar interaction in which for example an expansion of the agricultural surplus to a certain point was the prerequisite for the emergence of a stratum of specialised produce traders; the improved circulation of products brought about by such traders in turn stimulated further expansion of the marketed surplus. A decision to accord priority to the explanation of production and production relations does not have to spring from any simple linear notion of causal priority. I accord priority to agricultural production because it was through this activity that the majority of men and women obtained their subsistence, i.e. produced and reproduced the means of their own existence throughout most of the period considered. As chapter VIII indicates, this was not the case at the beginning of the period. But a history of the years 1905–52 in Kenya is in large part the story of how agriculture replaced pastoralism as the major mode of production for subsistence and exchange.

Thus a collapse of African agricultural production, or even its failure to expand output in line with population expansion, would threaten human life in Kenya in a very direct way, and it did so regularly in the period considered. It was the perception of many African households from 1930 onwards that their

13. Van Zwanenberg with King, op. cit., pp. 10–13.

landholdings were inadequate to provide subsistence for the people dependent on them, which induced many more men to seek wage employment.

In my view Marx's injunction to historical materialists to 'begin with production'[14] represents nothing more than a recognition of this simple but overwhelmingly important truth, that life and the reproduction of life are threatened by the breakdown of production in any society, and that conversely, whilst a highly productive economy is by no means a sufficient condition of universal material prosperity, it is a necessary condition of such prosperity. Thus all societies must be organised so as to produce, and this organisation, the distribution of human beings among the various forms of production, represents the base of the social structure. This was as true of colonial Kenya as of any other society. But of course the forms or patterns which these 'relations of production' take, can be, and have been, enormously varied in history. From this diversity Marx himself abstracted a number of ideal types, and the three of these to which he gave most attention, he termed the 'feudal', 'petty commodity', and 'capitalist' 'modes of production'. This work aims both to describe and analyse the organisation of production in Kenya in the period 1905–70 as accurately as possible, and also to consider how the pattern which emerges from such an examination compares with the ideal types which Marx identified—notably 'petty commodity production' and 'capitalism'.

14. See Marx, *Grundrisse. Foundations of the Critique of Political Economy (Rough Draft)*, Harmondsworth, 1973, pp. 83–100.

PART ONE

SOME ECONOMIC ORIGINS OF MAU-MAU 1905–1952

A. AGRICULTURE

Chapter II

Agricultural Development and the Quantitative Expansion of Labour Time: Kikuyuland and Nyanza 1908–1918

1. Nyanza Province

The colonial administration's attempt to encourage the growth of 'economic' crops by Africans would begin haphazardly in a particular area, almost from the moment the infrastructure of an administration was set up there. Initially almost everything was tried, including industrial crops such as sesame[1] (introduced in central and southern Nyanza in the period 1908–10), improved varieties of food crops such as maize, beans and peas, and crops with both industrial and domestic uses such as groundnuts and wattle. Thus, to take one of many examples, a Kisumu quarterly report for 1909 noted that 'groundnuts, sim-sim [sesame] and maize, and small quantities of rose coco and white beans were issued over the year, and the results up to date show promise'. It also noted however that cotton seed had been issued 'from time to time', but the results up to date were 'nil'. Similar issues were made in the following year, and by then the District Officer felt that 'the new economic crops are now mainly producing the hut tax', and instanced the decline in stock sales at the tax collection period as proof.[2] Whether he was justified in this optimistic assertion or not, the remark clearly goes to the root of the initial motivation for the introduction of new crops—which was simply to generate a cash income for the African from which he might pay 'his' tax. Apart from the broader objective of making the new colony self-supporting, and in particular justifying the enormous expenditure on the construction of the Uganda railway,[3] such a policy was also thought to have local advantages in ending the practice of paying taxes in livestock, of which the Administration then had to dispose.

In southern Nyanza the District Officer tried out 'mountain rice, wheat and

---

1. Sesame was in fact both a food crop and an industrial crop (used as a source of vegetable oil). For the first see, for example, Wagner, op. cit., Vol. II, p. 67. For the latter use, see for example *DAR* 1938, p. 82.
2. KisuQR to Dec. 1909, p. 15 and to June 1910, p. 20.
3. See M. F. Hill, *Permanent Way: The Story of the Kenya and Uganda Railway* (Nairobi, 1950), pp. 242–3.

oats' on a small plot near the newly established administrative headquarters in 1908, and also encouraged the planting of small quantities of groundnuts and Hickory King maize.[4] Up to 1918, and indeed, according to Fearn, up to 1931, the results of these administrative efforts in the Nyanza Province were minimal.[5] And indeed there is no doubt that, compared with production increases occurring from the late 1920s on, achievements up to the end of the first world war were rather limited. Failures were due, as Hay shows, to the low returns available on some crops chosen (above all cotton), to an inadequate knowledge of the soil and the rainfall conditions in the area, and to the methods used for first introducing crops, which nearly always involved a degree of coercion on the part of chiefs and headmen.[6]

Nonetheless, these efforts were not entirely without success. In the first place, as Hay also demonstrates, in trying 'everything' colonial officers did hit upon some crops which were suitable to local conditions, could be integrated with the labour process required for domestic production, and were sufficiently remunerative to be attractive. As a result, crops which may have obtained a negative or minimal response under administrative pressure were very often taken up again by local innovators in the 1920s, and spread much more rapidly thereafter. In terms both of volume and of value, there is no doubt that the most significant of these crops was maize, which effectively displaced local millets as the indigenous staple, and provided the main African cash crop from surplus production.

But even up to 1918, results were not negligible. For example, a list of exports from the South Kavirondo district for 1919–20 shows that in that year the district exported some 259 tons of sesame seed, forty-seven tons of groundnuts, twenty-one tons of maize and fifteen tons of wheat. This was in addition to exports of hides, skins, eggs and dairy products.[7]

Figures for the North Kavirondo district for 1917–18 show that 550 tons of maize and 305 tons of sesame seed left the district in that year,[8] and Fearn presents the figures in table II:1 for exports from the whole of Nyanza Province from 1908/9 to 1917/18.

With the exception of some produce re-exported from Nyanza, but originating in Uganda, the difference between these provincial export figures and those district figures cited for North and South Kavirondo is an indication of the early dominance of the Central Kavirondo (at this period Kisumu) district in Nyanza's commercial agricultural production. This early lead was probably due to the district's proximity to the railhead at Kisumu.

4. KisQR to July 1908, p. 2. See also KisQRs to Dec. 1908, p. 5; and to June 1909, p. 3.
5. Hugh Fearn, *An African Economy: A Study of the Economic Development of the Nyanza Province of Kenya 1903–53* (Nairobi, 1961), pp. 63–90.
6. Hay, op. cit., pp. 129–34.
7. SKAR, 1923, p. 25.
8. NKAR, 1917, p. 22.

Table II:1. *Principal local country produce exported from various stations and lake ports in Nyanza province, 1908/9 to 1917/18 (tons)*

Commodities Exported	Year ended 31 March										Total tonnage over ten years
	1909	1910	1911	1912	1913	1914	1915	1916	1917	1918	
Indigenous Products											
(a) Crops											
Beans	47	182	327	268	471	—	109	242	1,366	187	3,199
Groundnuts	42	77	59	254	590	386	118	94	167	169	1,956
Maize and Maize Flour	469	2,024	3,254	8,510	8,594	11,882	7,165	12,108	14,192	5,689	73,887
Mtama and Mtama Flour	1,770	997	1,039	1,210	1,457	462	986	772	99	19	8,811
Sweet Potatoes	26	52	58	30	26	7	10	14	34	32	289
Simsim	394	1,447	1,661	3,951	3,991	3,155	1,085	2,981	3,324	983	22,972
(b) Animal Products											
Eggs	8	9	9	—	—	—	—	—	—	—	26
Ghee	53	67	111	178	195	82	74	87	194	147	1,188
Hides	165	383	346	437	768	856	592	771	1,107	1,102	6,527
Skins	71	145	92	89	113	119	92	109	176	59	1,065
Ivory	35	29	34	—	—	—	—	—	—	—	98
Introduced Products											
(a) African-Grown											
Lint Cotton								{189	330	314	833
Seed Cotton	—	2	1	125	166	—	89		78	27	383
								{133			238
(b) Asian-Grown											
Jaggery	25	46	21	66	19	29	17	109	116	217	665
Rice	—	—	—	34	158	87	88	55	46	—	468
(c) European-Grown Wheat and Wheat Flour	1	49	422	41	62	42	27	12	3	37	696
Coffee	—	2	3	2	4	—	1	24	509	467	1,012
Rubber	2	20	21	2	—	—	—	—	—	—	45

These figures have been extracted from the *Annual Reports* of the Provincial Commissioner, Nyanza Province and have been rounded to the nearest ton.

Source: Fearn. op. cit., p. 79.

The implication of Fearn's figures would be that Kisumu district produced perhaps 4,500 to 5,000 tons of maize and maize flour for export in 1917–18, and perhaps 400 tons of sesame seed. The district must certainly have produced the bulk of the 73,887 tons of maize and maize flour leaving Nyanza Province in the period 1909–18: no small response to these first attempts to commercialise African agriculture.

Moreover, figures for exports outside the Province (themselves probably an underestimate) seriously understate total production for sale in this period, since they do not include expansion of production for trade within and between districts within the Province, and we know that both were quite considerable.[9] As a result, the available figures are no guide to the extent of expansion of the cultivated area, which is remarked on constantly in all the district reports for the period.[10]

Fearn's table also strongly suggests that there was a marked expansion in the production of maize, beans and sesame just before and during the first world war, and this is confirmed from the district reports.[11]

The initial expansion of the cultivated area in the period 1909 to 1918 in Nyanza owed something to improvements in the cultivating technology available. Thus Hay notes that while a wooden form of hoe was still in use in Kowe in 1900, by the 'early 1900s' a hoe with an iron blade (called *Nyarlte* or *Kasiri*) had been introduced and by 1918 somewhat stronger iron-bladed hoes (known as *Opanga*) were obtainable from Indian traders. She notes however that the 'modern' form of African hoe (or *Jembe*) did not appear in Kowe until 'the 1920s'.[12] It may be that in areas of Central Kavirondo nearer to Kisumu the process was more advanced by 1918, at least among chiefs and headmen and the tiny educated elite. For example the Kisumu district report for 1913–14 notes that '30,000 English hoes' were sold in Kisumu, and that among the record quantities of imported goods purchased by Africans were 'hoes and slashers'.[13]

It is clear why expanded production should be concentrated on food crops, surpluses of which were then sold for cash or, more commonly at this period, bartered. In concentrating on food crops women cultivators were able to raise their standards of domestic consumption, make an attempt at increased security of food supply for their dependents in the event of natural disaster, and create an increased stock of 'exchange values' with which other products might be obtained. This of course partly explains the initial and continuing unpopularity

9. See KisAR 1907, p. 5; KisuQR to March 1910, p. 8; and to Sept. 1911, p. 17; SKAR 1912, pp. 5 and 9; 1913, p. 11; and 1916, pp. 15–16. See also Wagner, op. cit., Vol. II, pp. 162–5 and Hay, op. cit., pp. 106–10.
10. KisQR to July 1908, p. 2 and to March 1912, p. 2; KisuQR to March 1910, p. 19 and to March 1911, p. 1; KisuAR 1913, p. 4. (See also 1912, p. 10.)
11. SKAR 1915, p. 5; CKAR 1914, p. 5. See also CKAR 1917, p. 4.
12. Hay, op. cit., p. 149.
13. KisuAR 1913, p. 15.

of cotton, because apart from other problems which it introduced, it was an inedible or 'pure' cash crop, and thus commitment of land and labour power to it did not carry the element of built-in security inherent in the production of increased food crop surpluses. It is probably the case that the desire to obtain tax revenue without recourse to the sale of livestock, plus the desire to obtain increased 'exchange' access to livestock through the production of greater surpluses were the most powerful initial stimulants to the expansion of production.[14]

2. Kikuyuland

District records appear at first sight to suggest that the origins of expanded food crop production in the Kiambu, Fort Hall and Nyeri districts of Central Province were not, in general terms, very different from those in Nyanza Province. It stemmed from the Administration's desire to have some products which might fill the empty rail wagons returning to Mombasa, and to stimulate a source for payment of taxes in cash rather than livestock. Thus, just as in Nyanza, from the inception of District Reports, we hear frequent reference to official 'issues' of Hickory King or 'white' maize seed, to replace the supposedly lower-yielding African 'yellow' maize, as well as issues of rose coco beans and several varieties of white beans.[15]

However, African cultivators had begun to produce food crop surpluses for the Nairobi market well before the Administration began to offer such encouragement. Thus in the earliest extant District Report for the 'Kikuyu' (subsequently Kiambu) district, the officer is already able to say that 'It is impossible to gauge with any degree of accuracy the trade of this District owing to the fact that almost all the saleable products from Kikuyu go into Nairobi which is outside this district', and by the following year he is noting that there is 'more food planted' for sale in Nairobi, and that 'here and there poultry are being kept', clearly also for the same market.[16] The production of potatoes at Escarpment or Limoru is first mentioned in a report for 1912–13, but had clearly been going on for some time before this, and obviously also without much in the way of official support or encouragement.[17]

In fact, as Marvin Miracle has shown, some Kikuyu were growing potatoes for the Nairobi market from as early as 1900, though the main adoption seems to have taken place between 1902 and 1905, i.e. within five years of the establishment of the railhead at Nairobi.

14. See SKAR 1912, pp. 4–5; KisuQR to Dec. 1910, p. 20; SKAR to Dec. 1910, p. 2; KisQR to Sept. 1910, p. 2; SKAR 1912, p. 26.
15. See for example UPAR 1906, p. 3; MaAR 1909, p. 3; UPQR to June 1910, p. 2; KAR 1910, p. 8; KAR 1912, p. 3; DagAR 1913, p. 2.
16. KAR 1907, p. 1; and 1908, p. 3.
17. DagHOR 1912, p. 14.

Oral tradition—[indicates]—that in the Kiambu area Fort Smith was the centre from which this new crop spread and that Swahili employees stationed at the Fort were the principal agents of change. In addition to the garden for European residents at Fort Smith, the Africans stationed there—largely Swahili and Nubian [Sudanese] apparently—were allowed to make gardens of their own and some of them grew Irish potatoes which they gave or sold to Kikuyu labourers they employed and others. Some informants say that thefts from Fort Smith's gardens also contributed to Kikuyu supplies of the new crop.[18]

As in Nyanza, so in Kiambu, the output of maize and beans increased massively in the period from 1905 to 1918. Again Miracle indicates that the new varieties of maize (including the high-yielding Hickory King) had reached some Kikuyu growers some time before the Administration began to issue seed, and once again the Fort Smith gardens seem to have been the source.[19] However, the spread of maize and beans among large numbers of growers may have owed as much to government efforts as to informal channels. It is clear that from the beginnings of regular reporting on Kiambu district (1907–8) the cultivated area under potatoes, maize and beans spread rapidly. By the time of the Dagoretti Handing Over Report for 1912–13 it is reported that in this area (of southern Kiambu) there were five acres of land 'to each woman, three acres of which may be said to be in use and two in fallow'.[20] The rapidly increasing density of population in southern Kiambu in the period 1905–18 was primarily due to the alienation of land to settlers, and to the migration of people from the Kikuyu districts to the north, attracted by work prospects in Nairobi and by the opportunities for market production. But from the point of view considered here, the most remarkable feature, if the Dagoretti report is even remotely accurate, is the very small amount of uncultivated land within southern Kiambu at this date, especially when we consider that a decade before the Kikuyu in this area were in all probability still involved in a land-extensive form of shifting cultivation combined with pastoralism.[21] It is not surprising that in these circumstances households holding large quantities of livestock began to move out.[22]

By 1915–16 the District Commissioner in Kiambu was unambiguous about the trend. Of the low-lying areas of the district, from which nearly all the maize and beans came, he noted 'land will shortly be unobtainable'; everywhere pastures were being broken up. He felt that those wanting more land would either have to go to higher land where previously 'the struggle against bracken' had disheartened them, or they would have to leave the district.[23]

18. Miracle, op. cit., p. 24.
19. Ibid., p. 27.
20. DagHOR 1912, p. 20.
21. See the evidence in *KLC E & M* I (extensively referred to later, chapter X).
22. Wambaa and King, op. cit., pp. 1 and 2. See also DagAR 1917, pp. 5–6.
23. KAR 1915, p. 42.

However, it was not only in southern Kiambu that the cultivated area and output expanded massively. In Nyeri district too, somewhat later, the area of land under maize began to expand in response to the demand of settlers to the north and west for maize flour to feed their resident labour. Dundas drew attention to this phenomenon in a particularly perceptive Handing Over Report written in 1914, in which he argued that the previous policy of not encouraging African agricultural production in Nyeri district was ill-advised and in any case futile. Both the European desire for, and use of the land 'teaches the Kikuyu that land has a value' and this was clearly instanced in the growing trade in African-grown maize to settler areas. 'What therefore the farmer may encourage the trader will promote' and 'evidence is not lacking that the Kikuyu is awakening to all this... about Limuru and Escarpment the Natives do a lively trade in potatoes, almost half the maize in Kikuyu is now native... in Nyeri potatoes are grown, and in most parts imported beans are comparatively plentiful, even wheat is grown'.[24]

Marris and Somerest state that the export of African-grown maize from Nyeri to the settler farms of the Rift Valley began *circa* 1909–11, and noted how the Kikuyu traders operating in this area were very often the same men who had previously been engaged in more traditional exchanges with the previous occupants of the Rift Valley—the Masai.

Unfortunately, since all the marketed production of Kikuyuland in this period found its way through 'informal' marketing channels into inter-district or intra-district trade (i.e. into channels organised by African producers and traders and Indian traders), there are no production statistics, however inadequate, available for these years. What is clear is that here, just as in Nyanza, the cultivated area and production developed with increasing rapidity towards 1914 and then massively during the war itself.[25] This latter increase was clearly a response to the demand generated by the armed forces and by the greatly swollen population of Nairobi, which produced large price increases for stock and for basic foodstuffs. Moreover, at the start of the war at least, and probably throughout it for some sections of the African military force, this demand was 'effective' because of (a) the high level of carrier corps wages at the beginning of the war, and for certain categories of carrier and troops even after 1915, (b) the greatly increased numbers of men who through army service received cash wages for the first time in their lives and (c) the ability of many men to save from even meagre wages while serving in the corps, because of a lack of opportunity for expenditure during campaigns.[26] In these circumstances it is not surprising that the first Kikuyu-owned shops trading a restricted range

24. NyeriHOR 1914 ('Memorandum of Native Agriculture'—appended to report—p. 3.)
25. See for example DagAR 1917, p. 3; KAR 1914, p. 20; and 1915, p. 2.
26. For details on this see my forthcoming 'The Rise of an African Petite-Bourgeoisie in Kenya 1905–18'.

of consumer goods and exchanging them for maize, beans and other food crops (which would thus be 'bulked up' for sale in Nairobi or to larger Indian traders) appeared in the Kiambu reserve in 1916.[27] Their emergence is the physical indication, as it were, that the surplus product being produced by Africans in one part of Kenya was now sufficiently large to allow some 'local' Africans, as well as Indians, Somalis, Swahilis and Sudanese, to obtain a share of the profit in the sphere of circulation. I will argue later that the initial capital to start these pioneering enterprises (and indeed the majority of their successors in the 1920s and 1930s) was obtained through access to the power of the colonial state and to its wage fund. However what we must note here is that this development was only possible because in a geographically limited area the proportion of surplus to necessary labour had grown to a significant extent.

This was in fact the principal distinction between developments in Nyanza and in southern Kiambu at this date. In Nyanza the aggregate surplus product was being obtained by small-scale shifts in the quantitative and qualitative labour time of each cultivating household, and in particular of adult women. In southern Kiambu (though probably not in Nyeri or Fort Hall at this date) there had been considerably more marked internal shifts in the quantitative distribution of female labour time towards cultivation. In all probability too (though we have as yet no evidence to confirm it), qualitative intensification of labour power by the use of better implements and higher-yielding seed had also occurred in Kiambu on a more marked scale than elsewhere. Since this process was occurring in a geographically and socially more restricted area, which had a large market for the realisation of the surplus product near at hand, the state had no need to intervene (as it had to in Nyanza) to bulk up this relatively thinly-spread surplus product and ensure its transportation to urban areas and more distant 'export' markets in the colony. It was this greater proportion of surplus product per unit of labour time and of land, and the spatial concentration of its circulation, which allowed a greater number of traders to live off a share of the profit accruing to the sphere of circulation. The war years finally ensured that this increased number of traders would be significant enough to embrace even a few Africans at its margin.

27. KAR 1916, p. 19.

Chapter III

Further Expansion and the First Qualitative Intensification of Labour Power: Kikuyuland and Nyanza 1918–1930

1. Kikuyuland

It was not until Fazan's 'Economic Survey of the Kikuyu Reserves' in 1932[1] that there was even the roughest attempt to estimate the land under crops in Central Province, and even he made no attempt to trace its historical rate of growth. Yet there is no doubt, both from oral sources and from the district records for that period, that the years 1920–30 (Fazan's survey was for the year 1931) saw a very considerable increase in the land under crops both in Kiambu and in the two northern Kikuyu districts. Indeed it was precisely the speed and scale of this expansion, with the concomitant rapid reductions in the area of natural 'communal' grazing, which was one of the factors generating the rising Kikuyu unease over land in this period, and led to the appointment of the Kenya Land Commission, for whom Fazan prepared his survey. All oral and written sources confirm that it was during the 1920s that out-migration from Kikuyuland to settler farms rose from a constant trickle to a flood. Wambaa's evidence for example indicates that this flood was made up both of large 'traditionalist' stock owners (who viewed the expansion of the cultivated area, and thus the decline of grazing, with alarm) and increasingly of insecure or dispossessed *ahoi*.[2]

The *ahoi* were those Kikuyu households and individuals in the Reserve who occupied land not by right of first clearance or by descent from such a 'pioneer' but as the result of a client relationship with the lineage landholders (or *mbari*). In older areas of Kikuyu settlement when land was abundant and labour to work it scarce, this form of clientage had not been very onerous. Effectively it involved total rights of occupancy of whatever land a household could effectively cultivate or graze for as long as they wished, in exchange for occasional transfers of livestock, beer or crops. However as the areas of natural Kikuyu expansion became 'blocked' by alienation of land to settlers, and as the cultivated area

---

1. S. H. Fazan, 'An Economic Survey of the Kikuyu Reserves', *KLC E & M* I, pp. 971–1039.
2. Wambaa and King, op. cit., pp. 1–5. See also KAR 1919, p. 4 and 1922, p. 3; DagAR 1925, p. 16; KPAR 1922, p. 3.

within the block of land now designated as 'native Reserve' increased, so some *ahoi* came under increasing pressure from the lineage head and his dependents (themselves increasingly short of land) to cede rights now seen as 'weaker' than those of the *githaka* or land 'holders', as they became known.[3] It appears that in the 1920s (and indeed on into the 1930s and 1940s), *ahoi* coming under such pressure, or fearing that they might experience it, departed the Reserve to become squatters in the Rift Valley.

It is fortunate that this indirect evidence for the expansion of the cultivated area in Kikuyuland in the period 1920–30 is so strong, because the direct evidence is exceedingly meagre. District Officers in all three districts make occasional references to increases in the production of this or that crop, or the appearance of a new crop (such as wattle in Dagoretti in 1928, or wheat in Fort Hall in 1926 or of vegetable growing there in 1929). In addition lists of crop prices appear occasionally (in Kiambu from 1918 to 1922), and there is the odd, obviously estimated figure for crop exports (such as the 440 tons of maize which left Fort Hall in 1922). But in general there are very few direct references to cropland expansion, and what there are pattern out in a rather interesting way. They seem to indicate that whilst really dramatic increases in the area under crops occurred in Fort Hall in the mid-1920s, the process was delayed in Nyeri until the late twenties (from about 1926 onwards), and in Kiambu there would appear to have been only a gradual increase in the area under crops until about 1928–9 when a greatly increased area was planted to potatoes and wheat, and most noticeably to wattle.[4]

What this suggests is that by the early twenties there was little uncultivated land left in the lowland locations of southern Kiambu immediately adjacent to Nairobi, so that further expansion of the cultivated area in the district had to take the form of movement on to higher land and the clearance of forest. This was a labour-intensive form of development which may not have appeared worthwhile until the appearance of wattle in the late twenties.

On the other hand, the expansion of cultivation from what was probably a very low base was clearly much more spectacular in Fort Hall in the mid-1920s. The slow improvement of roads was opening up the Nairobi market to areas more distant than Kiambu, and production of surplus food crops was expanding in order to gain access to the livestock of the Kamba in particular. Production of vegetables in the areas immediately adjacent to Fort Hall town seems to have followed in the late twenties.[5]

Nyeri district lagged just a little behind Fort Hall, with poor roads (and inadequate transport generally) both to Nairobi and the North Nyeri farms preventing large increases in output. However, the arrival of the Thika–Nyeri

3. See below, chapter X, for a more detailed discussion of Kikuyu land holding and its development.
4. KARs 1918–22; FHAR 1922, p. 2; FHAR 1924, pp. 3 and 5; 1925, p. 32; 1927, pp. 7 and 23; DagAR 1928, p. 3; NAR 1926, pp. 4 and 34; KPAR 1928, p. 40; and 1929, p. 40.
5. FHAR 1929, p. 25.

railway line at Karatina seems to have marked some sort of turning point, since in that year (1926) the District Officer noted 'an increase, nine-fold of sales and other products to Indians—much of it goes to European farms of Fort Hall and North Nyeri'.[6]

Price data are almost entirely lacking for this decade, and in fact are restricted to a few figures from Kiambu showing the high level of food prices at the end of the war, the precipitate fall in prices during the well-documented period of post-war depression (1920–2), and their sharp recovery thereafter. Impressionistic data from Central Province, plus somewhat fuller price data from Nyanza and elsewhere, indicate a buoyant price level for nearly all food crops from 1923 onwards, through a series of generally good harvests. When these ended (in 1928 and 1929) with two periods of drought, growers in Nyeri and Fort Hall, which were less affected by the drought, were able to make a killing from the rise in prices, and in particular from the dramatic shift in the barter terms of trade between their food crops and the livestock of the drought-stricken nomadic pastoralists. As a result the District Officer noted a definite increase in the live-stock and cash incomes of Nyeri cultivators, a prosperity reflected in increased numbers of African-owned shops and flourishing trade in the markets.[7] In this case, the quantitative expansion of the agricultural surplus product occurred not because of the expansion of the total product, but because of a proportionate increase of the component exchanged in response to a dramatic increase in its exchange value. I shall deal with this issue extensively in a later chapter. But it may be said here that in a production complex in which natural disaster formed a powerful and continually present factor disrupting the 'supply' side of the market, opportunities for such shifts of the surplus/subsistence boundary within total production occurred regularly, and were invariably taken.

We come now to Fazan's survey. His work undoubtedly represents the most careful study available of Kikuyu agriculture as it was at the end of the 'boom' decade of the 1920s. It also shows the acute limitations on the data available at that time, and nearly all the criticisms which can and have been levelled at the survey spring from these data deficiencies, rather than from lack of care in their use on Fazan's part.

Fazan determined the total area of 'Kikuyu Proper' (Kiambu, Fort Hall and Nyeri) to be 822,400 acres, of which in 1931 267,461 (or 32.5 per cent) were cultivated, 208,689 acres (25.4 per cent) were not cultivable under the conditions then prevailing, and 301,826 acres (36.7 per cent) were 'cultivable but not culti-vated'. A further 44,424 acres were cultivated but under fallow. He then esti-mated the division of the total and cultivated area between the three districts as in table III:1.

Subsequent data presented by Fazan on the production of nine major crops

6. NAR 1926, p. 34.
7. NAR 1929, p. 5. See also FHAR 1929, p. 16.

*Table III:1. Acreage and utilisation showing acreage of 'Kikuyu proper'
and the extent to which it is cultivated*

District	Sub-Division	Cultivated	Necessarily fallow	Cultivable but not cultivated	Non-cultivable	Total
Kiambu	North and Central Divisions.	55,974	9,666	67,996	33,404	167,040
	Dagoretti	26,595	4,593	2,128	7,004	40,320
	Ndeyia	Negligible		6,400	40,960	47,370
Kiambu total		82,569	14,259	76,524	81,368	254,720
Fort Hall		119,095	19,577	158,459	75,989	373,120
Nyeri (less Keruguya)		65,797	10,588	66,843	51,332	194,560
Total for the area under review (Kikuyu proper)		267,461	44,424	301,826	208,689	822,400

Source: Fazan, op. cit., p. 984.

in the Province, and on the volume and value of exports of those crops outside the district, have allowed the construction of table III:2. This shows the physical ('use value') size and proportions of the 'socially necessary' and 'surplus product' of the three districts of Central Province at the end of the 1931 season.

Putting the data on cultivated areas together with those on production and exports, a number of interesting conclusions emerge.

Counting land under fallow as 'cultivated' land, it appears that Kiambu had 96,828 acres of land under crops in this year, which was very nearly 60 per cent of the land in the district deemed cultivable by Fazan. But Fort Hall had a much greater absolute area cultivated (138,672 acres), and even Nyeri had some 76,385 acres in cultivation, which was 53 per cent of its cultivable land. Once again it is clear that Kiambu's nearly half share in the total exported surplus product must have been due to the greater part of its cultivated area devoted to commercial production. This confirms that commercialisation of African agriculture involved internal shifts in the proportion of a given volume of production marketed, as much or perhaps more than expansion of that volume (and the cropped area). Obviously this is particularly likely to be the case where one is dealing primarily with the commercialisation of food crop production. This emerges clearly in table III:3. Thus the 'average' Kiambu household was not noticeably more productive than its Fort Hall or Nyeri counterpart in 1931 (indeed, the general level of productivity per household member was very low in

Table III:2. The 'socially necessary' and 'surplus' product of Kikuyuland 1931, by crop and district, in tons of agricultural produce[8]

Crop	Kiambu				Fort Hall				Nyeri			
	Socially Necessary Product	%	Surplus Product	%	Socially Necessary Product	%	Surplus Product	%	Socially Necessary Product	%	Surplus Product	%
Maize	5,646	28.5	14,159	71.5	6,223	27.3	16,552	72.7	4,390	41.5	6,194	58.5
Beans and Other Pulses	2,818	45.6	3,366	54.4	4,667	63.7	2,657	36.3	3,292	85.9	540	14.1
European Potatoes	3,767	30.6	8,543	69.4	3,111	72.7	1,170	27.3	2,195	89.4	260	10.6
Sweet Potatoes	5,646	68.6	2,580	31.4	12,446	86.2	2,000	13.8	8,780	94.6	500	5.4
Millets	939	100	0	0	4,668	85.4	800	14.6	3,217	99.4	20	0.6
Yams, Arrowroots, Vegetables, Cassava	1,073	92.9	81	7.1	1,773	91.7	160	8.3	1,250	51.0	1,200	49.0
Sugar Cane	23,117	93.8	1,531	6.2	38,189	95.5	1,800	4.5	26,935	96.9	850	3.1
Wattle	0	0	4,071	100	0	0	4,166	100	0	0	780	100
Bananas	2,404	90.3	258	9.7	3,972	95.0	210	5.0	2,801	97.2	80	2.8
Total	45,414	56.7	34,625	43.3	75,049	71.8	29,515	28.2	50,059	82.7	10,424	17.3

8. Constructed from table in Fazan, op. cit., p. 981. The 'socially necessary' product is the estimated directly consumed subsistence product of the three Kikuyu districts, and the 'surplus product' is that product exported from the three districts, either to other areas in Kenya or abroad. See also p. 39 below.

Table III:3. 'Household' Production of all Produce
and of Exported Produce by district of
Kikuyuland 1931

District	'Household' Production of All Produce	'Household' Production of Exported Produce
Kiambu	3.6 tons	1.6 tons
Fort Hall	3.2 tons	0.9 tons
Nyeri	3.2 tons	0.5 tons

Source: Constructed from tables in Fazan, pp. 975 and 984.

absolute terms over the whole Province); it simply sold more of what it produced.

From these figures it appears that the 'average' household in Central Province in 1931 (consisting of 5.3 persons) was producing a little over 3.3 tons of produce per annum, of which a little less than one ton was exported. This works out at a little over twenty-two pounds of produce per household member per week or just slightly more than half a pound of exported produce per household member per day. Clearly this sort of arithmetic is no guide to the actual return to labour time at this period, since we have no figures available for farm and crop labour inputs, but by their very meagreness they serve to show the low level both of the productivity of labour power and of the commercialisation of agriculture in this period. If we add that Fazan's estimate of household size is almost certainly too small, then both these volume figures and his calculation of average household income from produce sales (Shs. 200) are put in perspective.

However, whilst Fazan's survey shines a rare beam of quantitative light in the gloom of District Commissioners' estimates and impressionistic generalisations, one should be very much aware of its limitations. Fazan was clearly a well-informed and interested spectator of agricultural development in Kikuyuland, and this emerges clearly in many of his comments and notes on methods of production and on the inaccuracy of official statistics. Moreover, in obtaining his acreage and production figures he clearly spent some time visiting African farms and interviewing both cultivators and traders.[9] Nonetheless, he was still very much at the mercy of the contemporary state of knowledge, and he clearly had neither time, opportunity, nor means to check all the data on which he had to rely. Thus in compiling his population estimates and projections he was forced to use the hut counts made for tax purposes and the conventional assumptions about the ratios of men to women and of adults to children which the Administration used for a variety of purposes. In the 1948 census the population figures for 1947 derived from such measures were found to be underestimated

9. See for example the Notes on pp. 980 and 984 and Appendix II of the Survey, pp. 1036 and 1037.

by twenty-five per cent![10] Assuming that matters were not significantly better in 1931 than in 1947, it is clear that Fazan's family and household sizes are both too small, so that his figure for the 'acreage available per household' may be overestimated by as much as twenty to twenty-five per cent. In addition a close examination of Fazan's notes to his tables detailing cultivated areas, crop mixes and sales, indicates just how much he had to rely on 'estimates' and 'assumptions', either his own or other people's. Moreover, while he clearly did make an attempt to assess directly the volume and value of production marketed through the 'informal' (i.e. uncontrolled by Government) trade network of Kikuyuland, it must have been almost impossible for him to undertake even the most remotely comprehensive survey. Finally, we should note that in 1931 agricultural production in Kikuyuland was adversely affected by a locust invasion.[11]

For all these reasons it is highly likely that the figures for the total cultivated area are significantly underestimated (and that for uncultivated land correspondingly overestimated), whilst both the surplus product and the socially necessary product derived from his figures are probably too small. In addition it is likely that he underestimated the size of off-farm earnings quite substantially. Moreover, whilst he tried persistently to correct any falsely egalitarian impressions given by his use of 'average' figures (by pointing up the differences between what he took to be the 'typical' Kikuyu household and the statistical 'average'), he provided no guide to the actual distribution of cultivated land or surplus product between households, though he did note that some households were considerably more involved in commercial production than others.

There is one final theoretical point in this regard. The figures provided for the 'surplus product' of Kikuyuland in 1931 refer to the surplus product of the whole population, and its proportion to the subsistence or socially necessary production of the whole population. The proportion between these two magnitudes would of course be very different were actual (as against 'average') household figures available, and would almost certainly have shown that some households had significantly greater total production, together with significantly greater surplus production and larger ratios of surplus to necessary product. In this context, Fazan's category of 'sales' is rather misleading, since some part of the production consumed in the Reserve (and treated by him as unsold) would of course have been sold by some Kikuyu households and purchased by others.

2. Nyanza Province

The Nyanza districts experienced a post-war pattern of events much like that in Kikuyuland. Widespread drought in 1918–19 produced a marked increase in

10. Van Zwanenberg with King, op. cit., pp. 7–8.
11. KAR 1931; FHAR 1931; and *DAR* 1931.

prices for the reduced food surplus available. Once again however, both in Kisumu district and in South Kavirondo, the impact of the drought seems to have been sufficiently localised for less-affected areas to have profited. Thus the District Officer in Kisumu reported that the 'famine' of 1918 had been particularly bad in the Luo locations of Nyakatch, Kadimu and Uyoma, and that the people of those locations 'have had to sell a lot of their stock to purchase food in other locations'. These 'other locations' were in fact the 'Bantu' (or Abaluhya) locations further north, away from the rain shadow area of the Lake Victoria shore, which were 'rolling in wealth owing to the amount of food they sold at high prices'. I am sure that the 'selling' here referred to was in fact barter, and that the pattern of events noted in the earlier section on Nyeri had occurred again here, as it was to do time and time again in this period.

Indeed in South Kavirondo in the same year (1918), there was a similar pattern of drought in the lakeland 'Luo' locations, while in the highlands of Kisii 'the Kisii [who] had a lot of surplus food ... became rich by supplying the wants of the Kavirondo [Luo] in exchange for livestock and rupees'.[12]

However, this brief localised price boom did not last long, and by 1920 the post-war depression was being felt. Thus the Kisumu District Officer lamented that in that year 'magnificent crops of *mtama* [millet] and maize, sim-sim, chiroko beans and groundnuts were raised throughout the year. Owing however to the depression they realised poor prices.'[13]

However, as in Kikuyuland, prices rose toward the end of 1921, and though this came too late to raise the prices of a 'poor crop' of maize and millet, by 1922, in Kisumu at least, the District Officer reported a very good maize crop, large-scale planting of sesame in the short rains, and 600 acres planted with cotton.[14]

By 1923 it seems that rapid expansion of the cultivated area was under way in all three Nyanza locations, in response to the price recovery of 1921–2. An initially good growers' price for cotton of 25–30 cents per pound stimulated the planting of some 5,000 acres in the Uyoma, Asembo, Seme, Samia and Ugenya locations of Kisumu district, while in North Kavirondo a similar amount of planting occurred in the western locations near the Uganda border.[15] In South Kavirondo, at this date, cotton planting had barely begun, but the District Officer provided some figures to demonstrate the progress in agricultural production and exports since 1919–20, as shown in table III:4. In addition, North Kavirondo exported 100 tons of maize from 'the district north of the Nzoia river', which was to become the main area of African maize production in the coming years, and about 250 tons of sesame seed and twenty tons of rice 'grown near Mumias and the western part of the district'.[16]

12. KisuAR 1919, p. 21; and SKAR 1918, p. 21.
13. KisuAR 1920, p. 22. See also SKAR 1920, p. 23.
14. KisuAR 1922, p. 26.
15. KisuAR 1923, p. 16 and NKAR 1923, p. 28.
16. NKAR 1923, p. 27.

Table III:4. Agricultural Exports from South Kavirondo district 1920 and 1923. Principal items by quantity and value

Commodity	1920		1923	
	Quantity (Tons)	Value (Shs.)	Quantity (Tons)	Value (Shs.)
Eleusine	19.9	5,436	92.3	7,973
Maize	21.7	2,972	806.3	62,225
Sesame	260.0	157,880	963.4	362,496
Sorghum	11.1	2,082	0.3	19
Beans	4.2	794	24.7	2,608
Groundnuts	47.4	29,264	778.8	241,540
Onions	0.03	24	8.6	4,286

Source: Based on a table in SKAR 1923, p. 25.

By 1924 the development of planting and production in North Kavirondo had emerged clearly. For despite hail damage the district exported 4,000 tons of maize and 600 tons of groundnuts. In the same season, South Kavirondo exported 1,282 tons of sesame seed, and 603 tons of groundnuts, no figures being provided for maize or beans, which at this period seem to have been a smaller part of the district's exports than either of the former—a rather unusual situation.[17]

At this point in all three districts we enter a period of steady expansion during which (as was normal) District Officers apparently lost interest. Estimates of food crop exports and production disappear from the reports, to be replaced by an almost exclusive concern with the problems of cotton. However, since the Administration's attempt to promote cotton production in Nyanza Province did not reach full intensity until the 1930s, when it became one of many policies designed to raise the colony's foreign-exchange earnings in the depression, detailed consideration of it can be left until that point.

It is clear then that, despite administrative indifference, a sustained expansion of food crop surplus production and export continued until 1930 in all three districts, with a boom in prices for maize, beans and sesame throughout late 1928 and 1929 as a result of the drought in a large area of central Kenya from the Rift Valley to Ukamba, and even parts of Coast Province. Before this, in 1927, the upland areas of South Kavirondo (Kisii) and North Kavirondo had once again been able to benefit from drought in the Lake Shore areas, and the familiar exchange of livestock for grain (which clearly had a long pre-colonial history) occurred once more, much to the advantage of the grain cultivators.[18]

We may now turn to the 'economic surveys' of the three Nyanza districts presented to the Kenya Land Commission by their respective Agricultural or

17. NKAR 1924, p. 18 and SKAR 1925, p. 8.
18. NKAR 1927, p. 27; SKAR 1928, pp. 1–2; and KisuAR 1929, p. 13.

Table III:5. Socially Necessary and Surplus Product of North Kavirondo 1931

Crop	Zone I				Zone II				
	Socially Necessary	%	Surplus	%	Socially Necessary	%	Surplus	%	Socially Necessary
Maize	23,759	78.5	6,509	21.5	1,109	80	277	20	226
Beans etc.	11,667	93.5	811	6.5	3,494	86.3	553	13.7	1,355
Millets	11,391	100	0	0	16,189	100	0	0	4,268
Sweet Potatoes and Cassava	8,950	100	0	0	16,344	100	0	0	8,669
Bananas	9,774	98.9	107	1.1	122	100	0	0	248
Sesame	0	0	0	0	0	0	1,109	100	0
Cotton	0	0	0	0	0	0	0	0	0
Total	65,541	89.8	7,427	10.2	37,258	95.1	1,938	4.9	14,766

District Officers. As in the case of Fazan's survey they purport to outline the general production situation in these districts at the end of the 1931 season. Unlike Fazan's report however, there is some attempt to disaggregate the figures on a sub-district basis, and as we shall see, this does serve to highlight very considerable intra-district differences and to point out the dangers of working with district-level statistics. In the case of the Central and North Kavirondo surveys the divisions used are the different 'zones' identified as ecological and agricultural entities by the Department of Agriculture as part of its new programme of 'zone development planning' for African agriculture.[19] In the case of South Kavirondo the division adopted is between the highlands of the south-east inhabited by the Kisii and Bakoria people ('Kisii–Bakoria') and the north and western lowland locations of the Lake Victoria shore inhabited overwhelmingly by Luo people ('Luo–Abasuba').[20]

The general picture of Nyanza agriculture at the end of the 1920s which emerges from these surveys is of a province only just beginning to feel the impact of commercialisation. As tables III:5–III:7 show, export production was mainly restricted to surpluses of maize and beans, with a small amount of cotton production in the Samia area of Central Kavirondo and in the westerly locations of North Kavirondo. North Kavirondo, with 37 per cent of its cultivable land under crops, was agriculturally the most developed Nyanza district. But even this figure mainly reflected the influence of its densely populated southern zone, where over 77 per cent of the cultivable land was either under crops or fallow even in 1931. This was a higher proportion than any of the Kikuyu districts except Dagoretti (94 per cent according to Fazan's figures),

19. See below, chapter IV.
20. See *KLC E & M* III, pp. 2206–7, 2247–9 and p. 2352.

by Zone (in Tons of Agricultural Produce)[23]

Zone III			Zone IV				Zone V			
%	Surplus	%	Socially Necessary	%	Surplus	%	Socially Necessary	%	Surplus	%
66.6	113	33.4	580	83.3	116	16.7	279	100	0	0
85.9	223	14.1	3,483	92.1	298	7.9	3,346	96.8	110	3.2
100	0	0	11,610	100	0	0	7,467	100	0	0
100	0	0	22,349	100	0	0	17,402	100	0	0
100	0	0	639	100	0	0	613	100	0	0
0	266	100	0	0	58	100	0	0	111	100
0	0	0	0	0	108	100	0	0	564	100
96.1	602	3.9	38,661	85.5	6,580	14.5	29,107	97.3	785	2.7

but of course this zone was a smaller part of the total district. The proportions in the other zones (21–38 per cent) thus brought the overall percentage down markedly. In comparison Central Kavirondo had a mere 18 per cent of its cultivable land under crops in 1931 and South Kavirondo with 8 per cent was barely cultivated at all.[21]

Generally speaking the areas with the largest proportion of their land under crops were also those producing most of the exported product. Given that the major African 'cash crops' at this date were in fact food crop surpluses, this is as one would expect, but it has the odd result that areas producing the largest absolute amounts of maize or beans for export might nonetheless have a smaller proportion of their production exported than a less intensively cultivated area. Thus for example the southernmost zone of North Kavirondo produced 6,500 tons of maize for export in 1931 compared with the central locations of Central Kavirondo which produced only 4,125 tons, but while the former figure was only 21 per cent of its total estimated production, the latter figure accounted for 47 per cent of total output.[22]

One can see this as an interesting pointer for the future, for it suggests that the rate of expansion of 'commercial' production of food crops was constrained by the degree of subsistence pressure on the land. This in turn suggested that if less densely populated zones further away from Kisumu and the railway could be opened up for commercial food crop production they would be able to expand their surplus product much faster than areas like Maragoli. The key to doing this was either to improve roads and transportation to the railhead

21. Ibid., pp. 2214, 2258, 2352 and 2365.
22. Ibid., pp. 2210 and 2256.
23. Ibid., p. 2256 (Source for table).

Table III:6. Socially Necessary and Surplus Product of Central Kavirondo 1931 by Zone (in Tons of Agricultural Produce)[24]

Crop	Zone A				Zone B				Zone C			
	Socially Necessary Product	%	Surplus Product	%	Socially Necessary Product	%	Surplus Product	%	Socially Necessary Product	%	Surplus Product	%
Maize[+]	1,219	71.4	489	28.6	4,709	53.3	4,125	46.7	7,884	80.7	1,886	19.3
Beans					803	84.8	144	15.2	620	85.6	104	14.4
Millets and Sorghum	7,428	100	0	0	8,150	100	0	0	13,140	100	0	0
Sweet Potatoes, Cassava and Vegetables	6,194	100	0	0	6,497	100	0	0	10,512	100	0	0
Bananas	175	100	0	0	261	100	0	0	421	100	0	0
Sugar Cane					230	100	0	0	376	100	0	0
Groundnuts					233	73.7	83	26.3	730	96.7	25	3.3
Oils	0	0	134	100	0	0	269	100	0	0	135	100
Cotton[†]	0	0	0	0	0	0	0	0	0	0	485	100
Total	15,016	96.0	628	4	20,883	81.8	4,621	18.2	33,683	92.7	2,635	7.3

[+]Maize, includes maize flour in Zone B.

[†]'Cotton' includes cotton seed in Zone C.

24. Ibid., p. 2210 (Source for table).

Table III:7. Socially Necessary and Surplus Product of Southern Kavirondo 1931 by Zone (in Tons of Agricultural Produce)[25]

Crop	Zone Kisii-Bakoria				Zone Luo-Abasuba			
	Socially Necessary Product	%	Surplus Product	%	Socially Necessary Product	%	Surplus Product	%
Maize and Maize Flour	5,146	91.5	475	8.5	8,577	96.8	282	3.2
Beans and other Pulses	1,600	87.9	219	12.1	4,764	98.4	76	1.6
Sweet Potatoes	4,723	100	0	0	12,590	100	0	0
Cassava					3,560	100	0	0
Millets	19,211	99.2	136	0.8	10,240	99.5	45	0.5
Bananas	971	100	0	0				
European Potatoes	0	0	15	100				
Groundnuts					0	0	675	100
Sesame					0	0	1,353	100
Total	31,651	97.3	845	2.7	39,731	94.2	2,431	5.8

(since maize and beans were both low value/high weight crops), or to find new markets nearer these remote zones. Both developments were to occur in the thirties, but there are some indications of the latter solution even in 1931. In North Kavirondo the settler farm areas of Uasin Gishu and Trans-Nzoia provided a *'posho'*[26] market for some maize and beans for small areas immediately abutting onto them, though due to the preponderance of 'squatter maize' on these Afrikaaner farms, this market was always to be quite small. In South Kavirondo the opening of the Kericho tea estates in the late 1920s was just beginning to be reflected in the nearly 700 tons of maize and beans exported from Kisii in 1931.[27]

Aside from maize and beans production for local (Kenyan) markets, one other feature of commercial production in Nyanza stands out, and serves to distinguish the province from Kikuyuland. Firstly, the Memorandum on Central Kavirondo makes it clear that in 1931, twenty-six per cent of its maize production had been exported not merely outside the district, but outside Kenya.[28] In addition, all this district's sesame production (the main crop in the category 'oils') and of course all of its nascent cotton crop went abroad. The somewhat greater orientation of commercial African production in Central

25. Ibid., p. 2364 (Source for table).
26. *Posho* was the Swahili term for the food rations provided to workers on farms, estates and other industries. Their main ingredient was maize flour, to be made into a stiff maize porridge (*ugali*) with beans as a relish and (very occasionally) meat.
27. *KLC E & M* III, p. 2354.
28. Ibid., p. 2209.

Kavirondo towards foreign exports, compared with Kikuyuland up to the early thirties, reflects the slightly different origins of commercialisation in the district, so bound up with the arrival of the Kenya–Uganda railway at Kisumu, and the search for some traffic to take down rail to Mombasa. That orientation was to be continued in respect of sesame and strengthened in respect of cotton as the thirties wore on, but it would be challenged in the Province as a whole and especially in North Kavirondo by the ever-growing importance of the domestic market for maize.

However in the province as a whole in 1931, and in South Kavirondo in particular, the majority of the land in the majority of locations remained under natural grazing or was not used at all. It still awaited fuller utilisation. Levels of output *per capita* and per acre in the province were far lower even than the minimal levels reached in Kikuyuland. In Central Kavirondo for example output per acre was 40 per cent lower than in Kiambu and Nyeri and 30 per cent lower than in Fort Hall, whilst overall *per capita* output in Kikuyuland was about two and a half times that of Central Kavirondo in 1931.

It should be restressed however that as indices of the level of development of agriculture in Nyanza these figures should not be taken too seriously. Most obviously the exceedingly dubious nature of the statistics in the various Kenya Land Commission memoranda warrant extreme caution, and in addition, given the enormous fluctuations in natural conditions, one season's figures are hardly an adequate basis for inter-area comparisons. Also, precisely because of the localised and uneven nature of the commercialisation process, it is to some degree inaccurate to assess its impact on rural households simply by citing statistics of land cultivated or proportions of zonal or district production being exported outside their boundaries.

For within a highly developed and/or highly commercialised zone (such as the southern locations of North Kavirondo or central Central Kavirondo, or parts of the Kisii Highlands), particular households might be much more involved in market relations both as buyers and sellers than these aggregate statistics suggest. Most notably, households with above average landholdings and production might be both producing more and making a far greater absolute contribution to marketed production than their neighbours, whilst poorer households, with less land and much smaller total production, might need to have much more frequent recourse to the market for subsistence consumption. This latter point is particularly important because it indicates that the volume of marketed production within any location, zone or district could be markedly in excess of its exported production. That is, marketed production was made up of exported production and subsistence production exchanging between households through the market. In turn this 'subsistence marketed production' would be made up both of produce which was genuinely 'surplus' production of some households (i.e. produce surplus to subsistence needs) and of produce placed on the market by other households who needed cash for other subsistence purposes, or hoped to take advantage of terms of trade in the food market by selling dear and buying in later more cheaply. That these reflections are not merely speculative will be clear from the section which follows.

We may now examine such evidence as we have on changes in the objects of labour, the implements of labour, and the labour process in Nyanza in this period, with particular reference to Hay's work on Kowe in Central Kavirondo. She notes that in the period from 1910 to 1930 the following new crops were raised by Kowe cultivators (the list is in broad chronological order):

1. White maize (both Hickory King and 'Kitale' varieties)
2. Cotton
3. New sorghum varieties
4. Cassava
5. Groundnuts
6. New varieties of beans (Canadian Wonder and Rose Coco)
7. 'European' vegetables (notably onions, cabbages and tomatoes)
8 Fruit and wood trees (guava, papaya, mango, eucalyptus and *cassia florida*).[29]

Prior to 1920, Kowe cultivators had been restricted almost entirely to traditional sorghum varieties and millet, and indeed most households continued with the production of the latter, whilst preferring the new varieties of sorghum to white maize for domestic consumption. The adoption of vegetable growing came only at the end of the 1920s, and then only among a small group of the most innovative households. So up to 1930 agricultural innovation mainly took the form of the expansion of the cultivated land under cereals, a more continuous and possibly less 'peaked' labour presence in the field, and the adoption of the new iron-bladed hoe (especially the *Opanga)* in place of the less hard-wearing *Nyarlte* iron hoe and of the traditional wooden hoe. In addition the new varieties of sorghum adopted probably had higher yields per unit of land and labour time, while Kowe, unlike some other areas of Kenya, appears to have moved straight into the growing of white maize, not having been a maize-growing area before the end of the first world war. Since the taste of white maize was initially disliked (as in Kikuyuland up to the middle or late twenties, where varieties of 'yellow' maize were preferred for domestic consumption), the limited number of growers of maize in Kowe in 1930 traded the whole crop, aside from the following year's seed.

Ox-drawn ploughs, or to be precise one ox-drawn plough, had been introduced into Kowe by 1928, it having been bought by Thadayo Obara from the profits of long-distance cattle trading. It was however hired out to other households, as was the hand gristing mill for maize which he introduced in 1929.

The overall picture in the period up to 1930 in Kowe is the quantitative

29. Hay, op. cit., p. 130. The account which follows is based entirely on chapter V (pp. 122–51) of this work.

extension of the cropped area, the introduction of white maize and beans, and the continued predominance, in the total sown area, of sorghum, in the form of higher-yielding varieties. To work the enlarged cultivated area there was an increased labour input (probably with a slightly 'flattened' labour profile over the year), but the quantity and quality of digging and weeding per unit of labour time was probably increased by the new iron hoe. This represented one aspect of the qualitative intensification of labour power (going along with its quantitative extension) in this period. Another aspect of intensification was embodied in the new varieties of maize and sorghum themselves. They 'intensified' the labour of the cultivator in the sense that they produced higher output per unit of time expended, but they were only able to do this because of the quality of labour power (of the microbiologist, agronomist etc.) embodied in them during their development.

Hay believes that up to 1930 the pre-colonial sexual division of labour remained largely unchanged, and this for interesting reasons to do with the pattern of male labour migration. She notes that the latter began in Kowe in 1914, when a handful of men left the sub-location for jobs in Kisumu, Nairobi, and Nakuru, and on sisal plantations in Coast Province.[30] By 1930, Hay estimates, about 10–15 per cent of Kowe men had worked outside the sub-location in one form or another of wage labour. However, nearly all were unmarried and aged between fifteen and twenty when they left, and 'more than half' of them stayed away for periods of fifteen to twenty years! This long-stay group in turn divided into two: (a) sons of prominent men, who had obtained some education, usually at the Church Missionary Society school at Maseno, and obtained 'good jobs'—by which is meant 'white-collar' employment—with Government or private firms; and (b) sons of poorer families, or orphans, who had little claim on land or stock, and little prospect of inheriting much of either, for whom 'long term wage labour provided a chance to improve their economic position, acquire stock for bridewealth, or to purchase consumer goods which ordinarily would have been beyond their means'.[31] Of the genuine short-term labour migrants who began to emerge in the years up to 1930, again nearly all were young men, those who would have been warriors or herdsmen, and they generally timed their absences to coincide with low demand for labour on the farm.

Hay thus believes that up to 1930 this emergent pattern of labour migration had had almost no impact on the sexual division of labour because the extra labour demands in cultivation were still rather small and could be met from the stock of underutilised women's labour time; the young males who had left were those who had been least involved in cultivation in any case; and although in pre-colonial Kowe the 'theory' had been that men tended livestock, cleared and

30. Ibid., p. 171.
31. Ibid., pp. 172–3.

broke up fields and did the building and fighting while women were responsible for housework, child care, most of the cultivation and the food supply, 'In practice, the man's role in agriculture varied a great deal from one individual to the next. Generally wealthier men—particularly those with many wives—would scorn work in the fields, while poorer ones would often help their wives with almost all of the agricultural work.'[32] Hay believes that this pattern continued up to 1930, so that although women continued to provide most of the labour power in agriculture, the extra demands on them were not great, and they were aided by the new implements and crops. In poorer families, women continued to have the help of their husbands, and in richer ones, which provided the 'educated' long-stay migrants, missionary influence may have increased male labour input.

Nonetheless from 1928 to 1930, in the adoption of the plough and the hand gristing mill, there is the first indication of a rather different pattern of labour use, which was to become far more marked in the 1930s and 1940s. For in this latter period, male labour migration from Kowe increased markedly, and with it came the need to find new ways both of replacing male labour and of utilising female labour more intensively. In brief, this was done through cash remittances from men to their wives (for both the hiring of ploughs and labour), and by further improvements both in hoes and crops. But this process will be examined in the next chapter.

It is probable that the pattern of change observed in Kowe was reproduced in other areas of Nyanza and in Kikuyuland in the period up to 1930. However, there were also differences, deriving largely from the different 'times' of the process from area to area. In southern Kiambu for example it is probable that the 'time' of crucial transitions was as much as a decade ahead of their equivalents in Kowe. Thus while a broader range and improved varieties of crops mainly 'hit' Kowe in the late 1920s, similar processes were clearly at work in Kiambu from 1916 or 1917 on a large scale, and had begun somewhat earlier.[33] Similarly in Nyanza, locations nearer Kisumu certainly had larger numbers of males in labour migration before 1930, and this may have brought forward the increased pressure on female labour which Hay dates from the 1930s. One crucial variable about which we need to know much more is the precise pattern of male labour migration. Hay suggests that in later years poorer long-term migrants usually became squatters on farms and estates, so that if they married, or when they married, they took women and children with them out of Kowe. In this case of course the question of finding ways of replacing male labour, or of intensifying the wife's labour on the home plot, would not arise, since the home plot would effectively have been abandoned. The problem of the replacement of lost labour would of course arise for the community, but not

32. Ibid., p. 102.
33. See Miracle, op. cit., especially pp. 23–9.

for the household involved, which would simply be reconstituted on settler land. Such evidence as we have suggests that the 'problem' was usually solved through the acquisition of the land by the community's better-off families, and an increase in ploughing, hiring in of labour, etc.

I shall argue in a later chapter that Hay's findings are not at all untypical, and that a great deal more labour migration was long-stay migration than is commonly believed, even in the 1920s and 1930s. Mistaken impressions about this have I believe largely derived from the exceedingly misleading labour statistics for these years.[34] It is unclear what proportion of long-stay migrants were in a position to take their families with them. Obviously those who obtained positions as 'squatters' which were reasonably secure were able to do so, and did so, but in the 1930s and 1940s in particular this became increasingly difficult. In any case it is clear that some long-term male migrants changed work and residence with bewildering rapidity, and may never have been in a position to have their wives and families join them, or in a position to acquire a stable wife or wives and family. It was probably the wives, and the other adult women in the family of origin of this sort of male migrant, who felt the full weight of the loss of male labour. For they would not have been in a position to replace that labour power with 'money' (as were the women agnates or affines of educated or skilled long-term male migrants) nor to reconstitute the traditional division of labour on the settler farm (as would women attached to 'stable' squatters). It is probable that their response was to maintain labour input on the farm at a minimal subsistence level, while supplementing this with casual farm labour for others. These women were in fact the losers in the transition toward an increasingly commercialised agriculture.

Other Areas of Kenya

The phenomenon of the uneven 'times' in the process of commercialisation in Kenya is not simply restricted to the provinces of Nyanza and Kikuyuland. In the middle and late 1920s, cultivators in other areas of the colony began to expand their cropped areas in response to the demand for food crop surpluses. Two areas in particular commenced the process which had had its origin in southern Kiambu before the first world war—Machakos district and the Kipsigis area of the Kericho district. In the period up to 1930 the development of these two areas was very similar. In both, development occurred in response to the demand of nearby settler farms for maize meal to feed their resident workforce, and thus both areas concentrated heavily, indeed almost exclusively, on the cultivation of maize, and to a lesser extent beans. In both areas it was the 'European' white maize which was adopted, and in both areas the major factor

34. See below, chapter IX.

in the very rapid expansion of the cultivated area from the mid-twenties onwards was the use of the ox-drawn plough.

In the case of Machakos district, the expansion of maize production was not the first form of commercialised food production. Kamba people living within twenty miles or so of Nairobi had traded poultry, eggs, bananas, sugar cane, and some maize and beans to Nairobi, both before and during the first world war. By 1921 the Ukamba Province Annual Report recorded that the trade in poultry and eggs had 'reached remarkable proportions'. Some of the first owners of ploughs in Machakos had earned the money to buy them through this earlier form of trade, while others, just like Thadayo Obara in Kowe, had been involved in the cattle trade.[35] There were perhaps 200 ploughs operating in the Machakos district in 1930, and most of them were hired by their owners to others. There is no doubt that they allowed a rapid expansion of the cultivated area, and of maize production. The Kenya Land Commission *Report* of 1933 estimated that with the iron hoe 'a man and his wife' had cultivated some one and-three-quarter acres of good land and two to two-and-a-half acres of poorer land, while with the ox plough it thought that each 'owner' tilled about four acres.[36]

In the case of the Kipsigis, it was the rapid expansion of the nearby tea estates in Kericho (in 1930 they were reported to be employing 11,000 labourers, 8,000 of them on a regular—i.e. resident—basis) that rapidly expanded the market for maize and maize flour. In 1920 the district report records the sale of 20,119 loads of maize at the post-war depression price of 1 rupee per load to Indian and European traders in the towns and trading centres. By 1923 a 'large amount' of maize was being sold, and by 1925 'the area under maize has increased enormously in recent years', whilst by 1927 'the maize planted in Belgut [was] considerably more than ever before'. Belgut location was in fact the earliest growth point of maize production in Kipsigis, and it was here that the first plough was introduced by arap Bargochat. Belgut was, as one might expect, strategically situated near to the Kericho plantations. By 1930 there were 266 ploughs operating in Belgut, 124 in the adjacent Buret location and ten in Sotik, a location much further south and adjacent to a number of European maize farms and ranches. By 1930 too, there were seventy-three Kipsigis-owned water mills for the grinding of maize into flour, whereas there had been only one in 1921, twenty-two in 1926 and sixty-nine in 1929.[37]

35. UPAR 1921, pp. 13–14; J. Newman, 'First Steps in Rural Capitalism: Machakos Before the Second World War' (CPEK Paper); Hay, op. cit., pp. 155 and 171.
36. *KLC-R*, p. 205.
37. All the above data are from Robert A. Manners, 'Land Use, Labor and the Market Economy in Kipsigis Country', in P. Bohannan and G. Dalton (eds.), *Markets in Africa* (Evanston, 1962), pp. 493–526, esp. p. 502. But see also J. W. Pilgrim 'Land Ownership in the Kipsigis Reserve' (*EAISR*, June 1959), especially for the important role played by the African Inland Mission (with its headquarters in Buret location) in the beginnings of commercial agriculture among the Kipsigis.

Some data on the organisation of Kipsigis agricultural production at this date are available from the ethnographic work of Peristiany.[38] His account, though seriously limited, demonstrates clearly that the commercial production of maize introduced some changes into the organisation of Kipsigis agricultural production. Traditional production had divided the cultivated land into two types of field. The first was the *kabungut*, the wife's vegetable garden, adjacent to her hut, and cultivated exclusively by the wife and her daughters. In addition there was the *imbaret a mossop* (or 'field of the house') in which the millet which provided the staple food for the entire household was grown.

> The work in this field is done by the wife with the assistance of resident relatives and even of her husband in such things as sowing or erecting a fence. Beer is also given for the people to come and help in the digging, weeding, harvesting etc. The produce of the *imbaret a mossop* is stored in the *tobot* (granary) on the second storey of the hut over the sleeping quarters.[39]

In a subsequent detailed description of the opening-up and cultivation of the millet fields, Peristiany makes it clear that in fact the bulk of the work, with the exception of the harvesting, was done by women (and thus the 'resident relatives' referred to above would all be female). In polygynous households each wife had her own *imbaret a mossop* which was cultivated 'with hoes of European make', and over the produce of this field 'the husband has no authority. He cannot take some of it to give beer to his friends, or to feed his sweethearts. It has one purpose, to feed the household, and from this purpose no member of the family can divert it.'[40]

At this point however we are introduced to a third type of field—the *imbaret ab soi—kapande*, which 'in contradistinction to the *imbaret a mossop* is the field over which the husband has complete authority'. Before the introduction of maize it was sown with peek (a type of eleusine) or millet, 'but nowadays ... maize preponderates'. The maize is stored separately from the produce of the *imbaret a mossop* and is mainly traded with the Indian shopkeepers, and used by the man to 'pay his poll tax, buy spears, cloth and cattle', all purposes for which he could not, apparently, use the produce of the *imbaret a mossop*.[41]

At this point however Peristiany's account becomes somewhat vague. He analyses the labour process on the *imbaret a mossop* in some detail, but devotes much less attention to the maize fields, and what he does say is rather contradictory. Thus we are told that 'all the work in the *imbaret ab soi* and *kapande* is done by the owner and by paid helpers. His wife and daughters are not asked to help him, as their energies are devoted to the family plot.' However, this does not turn out to mean a great deal, since the women do 'help' with the

38. J. G. Peristiany, *The Social Institutions of the Kipsigis* (London, 1939).
39. Ibid., p. 129.
40. Ibid., pp. 129–30.
41. Ibid., pp. 130–1.

harvesting of maize, and his short account of the cultivation of maize makes clear that very little manual labour was undertaken in the maize fields between ploughing and harvest, aside from broadcast sowing and very occasional weeding (when the women may 'rarely' help).[42] At this point we come to an impasse, since Peristiany does not tell us anything about the mode of payment of the helpers, nor their sex. There is some indication however that the mode of payment at this date was mainly beer, and the helpers of both sexes, from the *Kokwet* (or small group of neighbouring huts).

He does however provide some interesting detail on the hiring of ploughs, on plough owners, and on the growing individualisation of tenure. We are told for example of the fencing of both maize and household millet fields at this time, and of the *kapande* fields he remarks: 'The cultivation of the fields of maize is a man's own concern. There is no reciprocity here, no help given by the kokwet, and the field may be sold by the husband without any previous consultation with his family—altogether a very sophisticated and un-Kipsigis state of affairs.'[43] And of ploughs and plough owners he says:

> People who have sold a few cows to buy a plough have made large profits by this transaction, as they hire out the plough at a very high rate, the normal charge being 12s. for three to four days for a plough and six bullocks, or 8s. with only three bullocks, and 5s. for the plough alone. In three days a field 100 ft. by 40 ft. can be ploughed. Sometimes money is not demanded, but the man to whom the plough is lent is asked to assist the owner in ploughing or weeding his fields . . . A. Seuer's fields were the largest in his part of the village, as he was the only owner of a plough and by hiring it out he could have men to work his fields gratis. Arap Seuer and Arap Maina . . . were the only two owners of ploughs in the whole of Kipkoybon, and certainly the wealthiest men in their kokwet.[44]

Developments in Machakos and Kericho district among the Kamba and Kipsigis in the late 1920s mirror those in North Kavirondo and Nyeri district in the early 1920s, in that they represent a response to a market created by neighbouring European farms and plantations. Something very similar was to happen in Nandi district in the 1930s. However, there is a crucial difference between this pattern of commercialisation and that which had preceded it and continued alongside it in southern Kiambu, Fort Hall or Central Kavirondo. That difference lay in the almost universal adoption of the ox plough in Machakos and Kericho district, and the concentration on a land-extensive monoculture of white maize. This was a pattern of cultivation learnt from direct or indirect contact with European farms, many of which were monoculture maize

42. Ibid., pp. 139–40.
43. Ibid., p. 140.
44. Ibid., p. 147.

producers in the 1920s. Its essential prerequisite was a low population density on the land, and the abundance of uncultivated flattish land over which ox-ploughs could be manipulated. This was available in the northern locations of North Kavirondo and Nyeri, in parts of Machakos district, and very widely in Kericho and Nandi, but it was not available in sufficient quantities, even in the early 1920s, in Central Kavirondo, southern Kiambu or southern Nyeri. Therefore adoption of plough technology was more difficult, since small and fragmented plots produced problems of social organisation in the use of ploughs. This will be seen clearly when we come to analyse developments in Kowe in the 1930s and 1940s. Since maize was a low-value crop with a small return per acre and per unit of labour time, profitability depended heavily on production and sale of comparatively large quantities, particularly as with plough cultivation costs per acre decline rapidly with increased acreage.

The consequence of this was that cultivators growing maize commercially on small areas of land with a hoe technology found the profits per acre and per unit of labour time low, certainly yielding a net income much below what could be earned per unit of labour time even in unskilled wage employment. What was clearly required in these more densely populated African areas was a crop with a much higher return per acre, and to a degree such a crop emerged in the 1930s in Kikuyuland with the adoption of wattle growing.[45] However, a suitable crop of this sort was not found for Central Kavirondo in this period, with the result that male labour migration increased markedly even during the low wage years of the depression (1930–7) in Kenya. As a result of both these developments the low density 'plough' districts (and particularly North Kavirondo) came to dominate commercial African growing of maize in the 1930s.

One final point about the emergence of plough technology in African areas should be noted. If the data on Kipsigis presented by Peristiany are at all typical of the other maize-growing areas, it is probable that in these areas the benefits of plough adoption accrued overwhelmingly to male heads of households. For in these land-abundant areas ploughs did not replace or supplement the expenditure of hoe labour power by women, but were simply introduced alongside it on separate areas of land, the product of which the male household head appropriated for his own use. The household's 'socially necessary labour time' was expended in one place and with a labour-intensive technology (the hoe), whilst the 'surplus' labour time was expended elsewhere using a more capital-intensive mode of breaking up the land. Moreover, it appears that women were not able to confine the use of their labour time entirely to the 'household' gardens, and were called upon to help in the maize fields, with what must have been an expanded amount of weeding and harvesting. The crucial question of course is how much labour time the male household head could appropriate in this way before facing demands for some share in the

45. See below, chapter IV.

product or in the commodities acquired through its exchange, and this is certainly a subject requiring research.[46]

Clearly the manner or mode whereby a household entered commercial production is a crucial variable here. Where women entered into commodity production before or at the same time as the men (by expanding cultivation in their own gardens), one would expect them to have had greater bargaining power when the open land frontier closed and decisions had to be made about the division of land and labour power between 'subsistence' and 'surplus' production and about the division of the surplus product so obtained. Where however, as in Kipsigis, entry into commercial production was a discrete, spatially separated step with a completely different labour process controlled by the household head, his decision-making power might not be challenged to the same extent, and access of wives to the proceeds of the surplus product would be more on a grace-and-favour basis, e.g. payment of school fees or bridewealth for the children of the favoured wife of a polygamist.

Another variable of course was the presence or absence of the household head. If a man was a monogamist and a long-term labour migrant, then he was forced to make his wife into an effective 'farm manager' in his absence, and in this case she would have a great deal more decision-making power in her hands (this clearly happened very widely in Kowe in the 1930s and 1940s). It is noticeable that in Kipsigis men generally took up extensive maize-growing as an alternative to migrating.

Summing up, then, we may say that by 1930 both Central and Nyanza Provinces of Kenya, and at least two other districts of Kenya, contained a large number of cultivating households that had expanded their cropped area, and entered increasingly into the commodity production of surplus food crops and (rather reluctantly) of cotton. This was mainly achieved through the quantitative expansion of women's cultivating labour time, and to a degree from the 1920s onwards by the qualitative intensification of the labour power expended in that time.

Within these areas, male labour time had played only a marginal role in this development, since many males were absent either in wage employment or in its pursuit, or (as we shall see in later chapters) engaged in itinerant trading (sometimes of crops produced, sometimes of livestock, sometimes both). Many men however remained in the Reserve, and in the poorer, monogamous households assisted their womenfolk in cultivation. Another large category however were those who left the Reserves altogether and 'squatted' on European-owned land. Finally toward the end of the 1920s the emergence of the plough in the cultivation of maize enabled male appropriation of the surplus product to increase, whilst only marginally increasing the amount of male labour time expended in cultivation.

46. See below, chapter IV.

In the 1930s and 1940s, as we shall see in the next chapter, things changed somewhat. A precipitate fall of the number of men in off-farm wage employment enforced a return of some men to the Reserve, and a greater contribution of male labour to Reserve cultivation. In addition the colonial administration made a much greater effort than ever before to increase African commercial agricultural production, and this further intensified the labour expended. Thus there was a steady continuation, and even acceleration in some areas, of the trends towards commercialisation which had got under way in the 1920s. This trend was finally massively reinforced by high wartime prices for crops.

Chapter IV

Depression and the State:
The Directed Expansion of African Agriculture
1930–1940

The previous chapter has suggested that, through a series of reasonably good harvests and buoyant food prices, African cultivators expanded the area that they cultivated and made small-scale but important improvements in their techniques of production in the period 1918–30, especially in the period 1923–8, after the post-war depression produced by both local and international factors had passed away. In October 1929, however, the world depression hit Kenya, and between then and the end of the year the prices of maize, sesame seed, groundnuts, hides and ghee fell by fifty per cent, and this despite droughts in 1928 and 1929, which as we have already seen, had driven up prices in the earlier part of 1929. The dramatic effect of this price fall can be seen from table IV:1, showing the value of domestic exports from Kenya in the period 1928–34.

The effect of the depression on the settler economy is extremely well known, and in broad terms well documented. Since the overwhelming proportion of settler production went to export, and since by 1930 over fifty per cent by value of these exports were accounted for by one crop, coffee, the effect of the depression was catastrophic.[1] A number of settler farms and estates went bankrupt, and many more would have done so had not the colonial state stepped in, first with a whole series of refunds, rebates and loan subsidies on exports, and in 1931 with the formation of the Land Bank (with an initial loan capital of K£500,000) to tie further farm lending to a process of crop diversification, particularly on monocrop maize farms which had been hit particularly hard.[2]

Despite these and other measures of support, the cultivated area on settler

---

1. Between 1929 and 1932 the world price of wheat fell from Shs. 16/78 per bag to Shs. 8/05 and maize from Shs. 11/10 to Shs. 5/06 (and to Shs. 3/30 in 1933). Butter prices fell less precipitately from Shs. 0/56 per lb in 1931 to Shs. 0/47 in 1935.
2. See R. M. A. van Zwanenberg, 'Primitive Colonial Accumulation in Kenya 1919 to 1939. A study of the processes and determinants in the development of a wage labour force' (Ph.D., Univ. of Sussex, 1971), pp. 64–7. See also his 'The Agricultural History of Kenya' (Historical Association of Kenya Papers No. 1, Nairobi, 1972), pp. 17–20.

Table IV:1. Value of Kenyan
domestic exports 1928–34

Year	Value of Domestic Exports
1928	K £3,266,403
1929	K £2,745,910
1930	K £3,422,571
1931	K £2,343,874
1932	K £2,280,982
1933	K £2,247,000
1934	K £1,910,000

Source: *Trade Reports* 1928–34.

farms fell from 644,000 acres in 1930 to 502,000 acres in 1936.[3] This of course went hand in hand with a sharp fall in African employment, first on farms and then, as depression spread through the economy, in other areas of the private and public sector. Between 1929 and 1932 the average number of Africans registered monthly as being in employment fell from 160,076 to 132,089. Moreover, even those Africans who remained in employment suffered severe wage cutting, estimated at between fifteen and fifty per cent 'in all industries', according to the 1931 Native Affairs Department *Report*.[4]

Now since the largest proportion of African agriculture's surplus product (made up overwhelmingly of maize and beans before 1930) had found a market as *posho*, or food rations supplied to workers on farms and plantations and in private businesses and the public sector, one would expect such an 'export-led slump' to have marked ramifying effects on domestic crop prices, and in the official statistics at least this occurred.[5] Nonetheless, it appears that despite the depression both the cultivated area and the total and marketed output increased in all the districts of Kikuyuland and central Nyanza during the decade 1930–40. In other areas such as Kericho, north Nyanza and Machakos, where expansion had just begun in the late twenties, there was a similar trend (and perhaps even a faster rate of acceleration from a low base in both districts, than in Kikuyuland or central Nyanza), while in the same period new districts such as Nandi and Teita came into commercial agricultural production for the first time. Moreover the range of inedible and edible African 'cash' crops increased during this decade; there was the marked expansion of wattle acreage in Kikuyuland and of

3. The bulk of this being wheat and maize land, see E. A. Brett, *Colonialism and Underdevelopment in East Africa* (London, 1973), p. 184.
4. See *NAD*s 1929–32, especially 1931, p. 118. See also I. D. Talbott, 'The Politics of Agriculture: Rural Development Planning in the 1930s' (CPEK Paper, 1975), pp. 1–2, and Sharon Stichter, Labor and National Development in Colonial Kenya' (unpublished Ph.D., Columbia University, 1972), pp. 129, 132 and 134.
5. Official internal prices were those paid to settlers. They are an inadequate guide to African producer prices. See below pp. 70–3.

the cultivated area under cotton in Nyanza Province, more growing of vegetables, and the first cautious experiments with African growing of coffee and
tobacco.

This is the paradox to be explained in this period, and the explanation must
be multi-variant. Firstly, we should note that recovery from the depression came
somewhat earlier (in at least a limited way) in Kenya than in some other areas
of the world. Thus from a low of 132,089 in 1932, the average number of Africans
in monthly employment rose to 141,000 in 1933, and thereafter increased
steadily to reach 183,000 in 1937 and 208,000 in 1941.[6] This was partly due to
the marked expansion of the settler acreage under pyrethrum from 1935 onwards and partly to the employment provided by the discovery and exploitation
of the Nyanza goldfields from 1932 onwards.[7] There was a partial recurrence
of depression in 1938–9, but this came to an end shortly after the outbreak of
war.

Secondly, though the money prices of food crops fell continuously from late
1929 to 1934, the prices of livestock fell even more dramatically during the
same period. This was due to a series of droughts and locust infestations from
1928 to 1934 which affected pastoral areas particularly badly. The cumulative
effect of these disastrous years for the pastoral areas of Kenya was to raise the
'livestock price' of surplus food crops from the agricultural zones dramatically,
just as their 'modern money' prices were slumping. The net result was a massive
influx of stock into Kikuyuland and (to a lesser extent) into Nyanza and other
food-producing districts, as cultivators took full advantage of the dramatic
improvement in the traditional barter terms of trade. By the time this 'boom'
began to peter out (in 1935–6), the demand from settlers for maize for their
workers had begun to expand once again, and a new government policy designed
to encourage an increase in African agricultural production was in operation.

The genesis of this policy was complex, as indeed was its effect, and a certain
amount of debate surrounds both. As already noted, nearly all settler production of food and other crops found its way to the export market before 1930.
With the slump in world prices, exports of maize, wheat and dairy products
became uneconomic because unit prices fell below production costs.[8] The first
response of the colonial government was to provide export subsidies, as we have
seen, but it quickly became apparent that the cost of these would soon be
beyond a government whose revenue was falling rapidly. A second two-pronged
strategy was therefore devised, in which government-sponsored cartel arrangements were designed to give settlers a monopoly of the domestic food market,
whilst at the same time it was hoped to divert increased quantities of African
production on to export markets. It was assumed that African producers with

6. *NAD* 1932–41.
7. For this, see Fearn, op. cit., pp. 123–150.
8. See Paul Mosley, 'Protecting the core of the settler economy: pricing and marketing policies for
wheat, maize and dairy produce 1929–52' (CPEK Paper, 1975).

much lower production costs would be able to get under depression level export prices and still show a profit. Expansion of African production, and its direction on to export markets was also thought likely to have a double pay-off. On the one hand it would increase export earnings and foreign exchange reserves which the government could either use directly or as collateral for the amount of borrowing required to fund the Land Bank and other measures necessary to keep settler agriculture afloat. On the other hand, increased incomes accruing to African producers would allow them to buy the high-priced food which settlers were hoping to be able to sell to them as well as to Europeans and Asians in Kenya, Uganda and Tanganyika.

Now clearly this strategy involved nothing less than a total reversal of pre-1930 policies. Up to that date, African producers, with little or no coordinated assistance from central government, had expanded production and the market-ed surplus primarily as a low-cost input into settler production, which in its turn had come to dominate the export market in food crops. Now it was pro-posed to reverse the whole process, and it was recognised that this would involve the diversion of money and manpower into the improvement of African agri-culture. However, the production and consumption of maize soon emerged as a major problem. Whereas the European producers of wheat, barley, oats, rye, butter and cheese were few and African competition effectively non-existent (and thus a government cartel organised through the Kenya Farmers' Associa-tion was not difficult to set up), it soon became clear that though European producers dominated the marketed production of maize, African production was increasing rapidly, and its producers were far too many to be effectively cartelised.[9] Government response to this was to bring in 'marketing rules' for maize which attempted to force African producers to sell in regulated markets (rather than to a plethora of small traders) and to meet certain quality standards guaranteeing a higher price; maize not meeting these standards was supposed therefore to be unsaleable. At the same time the Kenya Farmers' Association became a purchaser in these markets, and was supposed to dispose of the maize so purchased either on domestic markets at a price which would be profitable for European producers, or on export markets. Unfortunately, there has been no systematic study of the effectiveness of this strategy cooked up by government and settlers for the rescue of settler agriculture, and therefore there are a great many elements in it which remain obscure. Settler food crop producers did remain in being, but this may have owed as much to agreements between banks and government to prevent foreclosure on debts, as to effective capture of domestic markets.[10] Since our concern is with the African side of things, this obscurity is of limited significance, and on the African side one or two things may be ventured with some certainty.

9. Ibid., p. 4.
10. This is certainly van Zwanenberg's view. See 'The Agricultural History of Kenya', op. cit., pp. 15–30.

First of all, there was clearly never any chance that African producers could be turned overnight into major contributors to export earnings, let alone into consumers of high-priced wheat, butter and cheese! In fact by 1938, when the depression was over, African producers still only contributed thirteen per cent of exports by value. Had such a policy been seriously meant to succeed, it would have required the commitment of considerable amounts of money and man-power to African agriculture for many decades, and of course once the depression showed signs of abating, neither settlers nor government accorded it anything like this level of priority. Secondly, it is clear that the maize strategy was almost a complete failure, since, in the face of rapidly increasing African production, the Kenya Farmers' Association never had the funds, the organisation or the storage space to purchase the quantity of maize which would have been required if the base of domestic maize prices was to be lifted. In fact, as Mosley shows, domestic prices continued to fall until 1933, rallied a little in 1934 (probably due far more to a particularly bad locust invasion than to the efforts of the Kenya Farmers' Association), and then continued to fall again until 1937.[11] By this time of course the depression in Kenya had already passed its worst.

Failure here had other dimensions. Clearly it was almost impossible for the Administration to prevent 'illegal' sales of low quality maize through African and Asian traders, and, as I shall attempt to show, such sales were probably massive both at this period and later (when 'regulation' of marketing became even more total). Moreover, both coffee and tea plantation interests had been opposed to the introduction of maize marketing regulations, since they were the major agricultural purchasers of African-grown maize, and did not want to see their labour costs rise at a time of falling export prices. Regulations were passed in any case, other sections of the European agricultural lobby winning out, but one can imagine that this split must have been of considerable assistance to African growers and to Asian and African traders in evading the regulations.[12] In contrast to other writers therefore, I do not believe that the maize regulations were efficacious in making Africans 'pay' (either as producers or consumers) for the tribulations of European agriculture. It seems more likely that Africans continued to pay for it much as they had always done, through the tax system, with the maize regulations having an entirely marginal effect.[13]

11. Mosley, op. cit., Appendix tables A-1 to A-3.
12. What this shows of course is that the European agricultural interest in Kenya was never mono-lithic, and thus in the depression both the motivations for and the effects of the 'rescue strategy' were very diverse. M. G. Redley, 'Power and Authority in the Colonial Society 1929–40: The White Case' (CPEK Paper, 1975) brings the politics of these intra-European disputes out clearly, but the analysis is not related to any economic dimension.
13. For the manipulation of the tax system in Kenya see van Zwanenberg, 'Primitive Colonial Accumulation', op. cit., pp. 226–8; and E. A. Brett, op. cit., pp. 190–9. For the general failure of the maize strategy, see Mosley, op. cit. ; and also M. Yushida, 'The historical background to maize

The desperation and lack of realism of the government's depression strategy, and its inefficacy with regard to maize, does not mean that it had no effect on African agricultural production. In fact throughout the 1930s the first serious efforts were made to obtain systematic information about African agriculture, to devise a strategy for its improvement and expansion and to inaugurate research and extension efforts at least at a minimal level.

The centre of this new positive strategy toward African agriculture was 'zone development planning'. By the end of 1932 the Department of Agriculture had divided all the African areas of the colony into five climatic and ecological zones. Plans for the expansion of existing crops or for new crop production were then drawn up for each zone. Subsequent development of this idea produced zonal plans for each district.[14]

In addition, between 1932 and 1936 the Department initiated plant-selection and cross-breeding programmes designed to increase yields from existing African crops, to provide crops more resistant to drought for agriculturally marginal areas regularly threatened by famine, and to breed up varieties of food crops more suitable for growth under African conditions. In addition, influenced by increasing administrative worries about soil erosion in the Reserves, the Department attempted to design smallholder 'mixed farming' combinations of grass leys (for intensive pasturing of livestock), 'cash' and 'subsistence' crops (in rotation), which by balancing nutrient demands on the land and providing organic manure would increase production, raise nutritional levels and safeguard soil fertility.[15]

As we are about to see, only a part of this programme was ever implemented, if only because during the four years taken by the Department to complete the plans, African cultivators had already put a large amount of the 628,000 acres which it had calculated were available for expansion under a rather more limited range of crops (notably maize and wattle). But nonetheless the strategy was not without its effects, notably in the spread of cotton and cashew production in the coast Province, the expansion of cotton production in Nyanza, and the introduction of drought-resistant and other improved varieties of crops.

1. Agricultural Production in Kikuyuland 1930–1940

The best data on the structure of African agricultural production in Kikuyuland as it was at the beginning of the thirties comes from Fazan's survey. According

marketing in Kenya and its implications for future marketing reorganisation' (Makerere, Economics Dept. Research Paper 91, 1966).
14. For details, see Talbott, op. cit., pp. 7–8 and *DAR* 1936, p. 60.
15. Ibid., pp. 8–13. For other accounts of the strategy, see 'Memorandum on Native Agricultural Development in the Native Reserves' (Kenya, Dept. of Agriculture, 1937) and also the 'Memorandum' by the Director of Agriculture (Mr Alex Holm) to *KLC, E & M* III, pp. 3065–72.

to that survey, in 1932 a total of 265, 560 acres was under annual crops, of which the bulk (150,394 acres or 57 per cent) was maize and 76,295 acres or 29 per cent was beans. In fact the total under these two crops alone was 72 per cent of the cultivated area, and they accounted for 28 per cent of the total production of the Province by volume and 30 per cent by value. Of the perennial crops, sugar cane dominated if measured by its proportion of the total volume of production (37 per cent), but bananas represented a greater proportion of the Province's exports by value (K£243,125 or 34 per cent). Of other perennial crops, wattle had hardly made its mark in the production structure of Kikuyuland agriculture in 1931, coming a long way second to sugar cane in terms both of volume and of value in Kiambu and Fort Hall whilst in Nyeri, where at this date its production was least developed, the volume of its production was somewhat less than that of yams, arrowroots, vegetables and cassava, and only 2.8 per cent of sugar cane production. For the Province as a whole the value of wattle 'sold' (all of which was exported abroad either as bark or extract) was in 1932 only 11 per cent of the value of maize, 24 per cent of beans, and a mere 6 per cent of the value of bananas.[16]

All this had changed by 1938, by which time the value of wattle exports from the Province had increased by almost 600 per cent. Table IV:2 shows the growth of sales of dried and green wattle bark from the Central Province as a whole in this decade. Unfortunately we do not have any comparable figures for the expansion of the area under wattle or for the volume of production, though from district, agricultural, and native affairs reports from the period it is clear that both were startling. For example, in the Native Affairs Department *Report* for 1935 it is stated that the acreage under the crop had risen from 45,000 acres in 1934 to 100,000 acres in 1935, and that it was planned to add a further 50,000 acres in 1936.[17] It is clear in fact that there was an organised campaign for the expansion of wattle acreage (especially in 1935–6) and the forces behind this will be examined shortly. But even before this the Kiambu District Officer had reported an increase in output in 1932, a 'rapid growth' in 1933 (by which time Kiambu was producing half of all the Central Province's output of wattle), while by 1936 it was reported that Kiambu district had 25,000 acres of land under wattle (producing 3,697 tons of dried and 2,279 tons of green wattle bark) and in 1937 27,000 acres. In subsequent years African cultivators cut down their sales of green bark, in response to a marked price differential, so that in 1937 Kiambu produced 3,595 tons of dried and 1,954 tons of green, and in 1938, 3,496 tons of dried and 556 tons of green.[18]

In Fort Hall the District Officer was reporting big increases in wattle acreages in the 'higher regions' as early as 1931. This increase continued in 1932 and by

16. Calculations from data in Fazan, op. cit., p. 983.
17. *NAD* 1935, p. 100.
18. KARs 1932–7; *NAD* 1937, p. 141; and *DAR* 1938, p. 116.

Table IV:2. Wattle Sales in the Central Province 1929–38 (Tons)

Year	Dry Bark	Green Bark
1929	900	—
1930	6,170	—
1931	9,600	—
1932		
1933	10,800	—
1934	12,900	3,780
1935	13,095	8,435
1936	11,975	8,309
1937	16,025	5,202
1938	11,649	2,500

Source: *DAR* 1929–38.

Table IV:3. Wattle bark passed through inspection centres —South Nyeri 1936–40

Year	Tons
1936	4,327
1937	3,006
1938	1,325
1939	3,716
1940	4,472

Source: Humphrey. 'The Relationship. . .', op. cit., p. 6.

1933 the crop had assumed 'undreamt of proportions'. In 1936 alone some 3,000 acres were planted to wattle and produced 10,277 tons of bark which sold for some K£15–20,000. In 1937 some 8,705 tons of dried bark and 3,248 tons of green were passed through produce inspection centres, and in 1938 the figures were 5,620 tons of dried and 1,944 tons of green bark. Finally in 1939, receipts for the crop were put at K£34,000, and a further 1,509 acres were planted under the crop for the 1940 season.[19]

In Nyeri in 1930 only 65 tons of wattle bark were exported through Karatina railway station, and the District Commissioner noted that 'this trade has only recently started in this district'. By 1937 however a Department of Agriculture Memorandum estimated that there were 24,000 acres in the district under the crop (compared with 44,000 acres in Fort Hall and 15,000 acres in Kiambu). Humphrey presents figures showing the pattern of production in the district in the years 1936 to 1940 in table IV:3.

The expansion of wattle production on smallholdings in the thirties was the product of a complex interaction of forces involving a U.K. multinational (Forestal) engaged in the manufacture of tannin extract for the world leather industry, the colonial state in Kenya (and in particular the Department of Agriculture) and the production and consumption imperatives of the small-holders themselves. The full, complex story of wattle production in Kenya has

19. NAR 1930, p. 5, 'Memorandum on Native Agricultural Development . . .', op. cit., p. 8; and N. Humphrey, 'The Relationship of Population to the Land in South Nyeri' in *The Kikuyu Lands* (Nairobi, 1945). Figures from 1936 probably represent reasonably accurate approximations for wattle bark output, since the way the latter was marketed guaranteed that most of it had to pass through inspection centres. Figures before this refer only to bark railed from Karatina and may well understate total output. However, since wattle wood could also be sold as firewood, charcoal and buildings poles, these figures certainly understate its exchange value to the Nyeri smallholder (see below).

been told by Cowen.[20] But here we need only note that after a slow expansion of wattle growing in the 1920s, restricted almost entirely to the holdings of chiefs, headmen, clerks and teachers, production was expanded markedly from 1932 with the purchase by Forestal of the British East Africa Wattle Estates and Extract Company at Kikuyu. The aim of Forestal in entering the Kenya industry had been to attempt to reconstitute its control of the production of tanning resins in Argentina and Paraguay, which it had dominated up to 1930, but which it had lost with the onset of the depression. At that time the Argentinian government had forced the company to abandon its policy of operating production well below plant capacity to keep up prices, and attempted to force Forestal instead to capture a larger share of a shrinking world market by price cutting. In entering wattle extract production in Kenya and South Africa from 1930 onwards, Forestal aimed to undercut Argentinian and Paraguayan production and to force producers there back into the price-fixing pool. It was aided in its attempts to do this by the fact that the bark of the wattle (or mimosa) tree was in general richer in tannins than that of the South American tree (known as *Quebracho*) with which it was competing.[21]

Forestal's initial goals in Kenya therefore were twofold. Most obviously it wished to expand output and exports of wattle extract as quickly as possible to bring pressure to bear on the South American producers, but in addition it wished to make sure that as large a part as possible of Kenyan wattle production took the form of extract. For various reasons the colonial state was keen to assist in the first objective, and indeed the Department of Agriculture was keen to expand wattle production on smallholdings at this period because this policy was not opposed by settlers,[22] and because it was believed that 'costless' household labour would enable smallholders to compete in a world market of falling prices in a way in which estate producers could not. Collaboration between Forestal and the Department of Agriculture on this reached its height in 1935 when the Department's wattle planting campaign in Central Province increased the planted acreage from 45,000 acres to 100,000 acres in one year.

Forestal's second goal was more problematic. It brought the multinational into conflict both with local Indian and European merchant capital (which from the 1920s had been engaged in exporting estate-produced and other bark for conversion into extract by tanners abroad), and with sections of the colonial state who resented what they saw as Forestal's demands for a monopoly over Kenyan production, which they feared would eventually lead to lower prices for both European and African producers.[23] More importantly from our point of view it also brought the company into continual conflict with African produc-

20. M. P. Cowen, 'Wattle Production in the Central Province: Capital and Household Commodity Production 1903–64' (mimeo MS, Nairobi, July 1975).
21. Ibid., pp. 22–5 and 29.
22. Ibid., p. 40.
23. Ibid., pp. 38–41.

Table IV : 4. Prices per ton, maize, beans, potatoes and wattle bark 1931 and 1937[25]

	1931 (mean price)	1937 (mean price)	1937 (maximum price)
Beans	K£3.85	K£6.16	—
Maize	K£2.75	K£3.81	K£5.12
Potatoes	K£2.20	K£3.11	K£4.17
Wattle	K£1.75	K£2.66	K£5.12

ers, since the latter's reasons for growing wattle were somewhat at odds with Forestal's priorities.

It is clear that the Department of Agriculture's planting campaign in the early thirties was taken up so eagerly by many Kikuyu producers at least in part because wattle, as a tree crop, had a unique combination of use and exchange values for its producers. Its wood could be used for building purposes on the holding and could also be sold for such purposes, and as colonial forestry policies restricted access to natural wood sources (both for building and firewood) ever more stringently, this was of increasing importance. As well as being sold to extract factories or for export, the wood could be burnt and sold as charcoal, widely used in heating and cooking in urban and rural areas. Cowen notes the problems caused for Forestal during the war years and afterwards by the high price of logs for charcoal, and the greater quantity of 'under grade' bark reaching the extract factories as a result of the felling of what (from the point of view of the extract producer) were still 'immature' trees. But as early as 1935 the Kiambu District Officer was noting that 'Natives all agree that an acre of wattle trees brings in more money for the charcoal than it does for the bark.'[24] Even this combination of use and exchange values possessed by wattle would not perhaps have attracted smallholders to its production had it not been for other factors. For price data for these years indicate that the unit price of wattle bark to producers was never above and was usually below that of Central Province's principal food crops. And this is true whether we consider maximum or mean prices as table IV:4 shows. It was two other characteristics of wattle which attracted smallholders, and in the context of our overall argument, these two factors are very significant, for they indicate the major constraints which were beginning to affect smallholder agriculture in the Central Province in this period, i.e. a shortage (at prevailing levels of technique) of both land and labour.

By the mid-thirties the most densely populated areas of southern Kiambu, western Fort Hall, and southern Nyeri had large numbers of medium and small holdings on which the extensive farming of maize or beans was impossible, even where the terrain allowed the use of the plough.[26] In these areas a crucial

24. KAR 1935, p. 34.
25. Sources: KAR, FHAR and NAR 1931; and *NAD* 1937, p. 141. For more comprehensive data, see table IV:7 below.
26. See KAR 1934, p. 42.

factor in the adoption of any crop was its yield per unit of land, and as a tree crop wattle had an advantage in this respect. To put it simply, a ton of maize or beans might have fetched more for their producer in 1937 than a ton of wattle bark, but they would also have taken much more land on which to grow. The volume of output from an acre of wattle trees simply exceeded the volume of output from any available alternative crop by a margin which more than counterbalanced any difference in unit prices. This was always an important factor in the mind of any smallholder with limited land resources, especially when considering the adoption of a crop which had no direct use value to the household. We shall see shortly how it constantly told against the adoption of cotton in Nyanza Province.

Secondly it is clear that wattle had the appeal of being very much a non-labour-intensive crop to grow. To quote Cowen, 'Between establishment and maturity, without spacing and thinning, wattle required no cultivation and only labour power for harvesting.'[27] It was thus perfectly adapted for production by households experiencing increased constraints on labour power by the departure of ever more male labour into wage labour migration. As the Senior Agricultural Officer for Central Province put it, 'Many natives have discovered that wattle trees keep growing while they are sleeping and therefore are an ideal source of direct revenue and a comfortable life. They plant wattle, tend it for a year, go to Nairobi and know that when they return their "bank" has grown to be worth many shillings without the owner doing much work.'[28] Because wattle production was comparatively so little demanding of labour time, it is very probable that the returns per unit of labour time, as well as per unit of land, were significantly higher for this crop than for any alternative available to smallholders in Central Province at this time.

So much for wattle production. Table IV:5 provides some clue to the general structure of Kikuyuland agriculture in the 1930s. Looking at the matter more closely, and taking 1937 as a not untypical year, we see that although at this period the Central Province contained Embu and Meru districts as well as Kikuyuland, all but 719 tons of the wattle came from Kikuyuland, with the major producing district being Fort Hall (11,953 tons or 58 per cent of total Kikuyu production), then Kiambu (27 per cent) and Nyeri (15 per cent); 54 per cent of the maize (105,891 bags) came from the Kikuyu districts, with Fort Hall again being the largest producer (52 per cent) followed by Nyeri (35 per cent) and Kiambu (13 per cent). Kiambu had maintained its traditional dominance over potato production (66 per cent of all 'Central Province' production and 67 per cent of all Kikuyu production), with Nyeri producing the remainder. Finally in the production of legumes (beans), Fort Hall again dominates Kikuyu production, followed by Nyeri and Kiambu.[29]

Though accurate (or even inaccurate) statistics are lacking for this period,

27. Cowen, op. cit., p. 63.
28. Ibid., p. 63.
29. Calculated from table in *NAD* 1937, p. 141.

Table IV :5. Volume and value of major crops marketed in Kiambu, Fort Hall and Nyeri 1930–40

Year	Maize		Beans		Potatoes		Vegetables		Cotton*	
	Vol. (Tons)	Value (K£)	Vol. (Tons)	Value (K£)	Vol. (Tons)	Value (K£)	Vol. (Tons)	Value (K£)	Vol. (Bales	Value (K£)
1930										
1931										
1932										
1933										
1934										
1935	25,144	—	1,674	—	4,737	—	—	1,256	223	—
1936	16,108	—	2,942	—	5,436	10,872	—	—	1,486	—
1937	17,254	65,083	3,651	22,492	3,434	10,683	—	6,000	1,540	15,400
1938	24,034	106,102	3,118	37,584	9,724	4,584	—	6,000	1,019	11,209
1939										
1940										

*All cotton figures include production from Embu and Meru districts as well as Fort Hall.

Source: *DAR* 1930–8.

there is also abundant impressionistic evidence in the reports of the continued expansion of the cultivated area.[30] Nor was expansion of the cultivated area restricted to maize, beans, potatoes and wattle (though these are the crops for which the most data are available, because of the imposition of marketing rules on them). Kikuyu growers certainly continued to grow millet, sugar cane,

30. 1931 'The acreage under potatoes and beans has been greatly increased.' (KAR). 'The planting of wattle has increased tremendously throughout the higher regions of the district.' (FHAR).

1932 'In spite of the low price of cereals the natives have very appreciably increased the acreage under cultivation and their short rain crops are in excellent condition.' (FHAR).

1933 'The wattle industry is already very considerable and is growing rapidly ... This district at present produces about half the wattle which comes from the 3 Kikuyu districts.' (KAR).

1935 'There was a large increase in native production. 1935 was generally a slump year but South Nyeri has been an exception to the rule. Prices were low but there was a great increase in the quantities sold; never before has the district been so prosperous.' (NAR). 'The growth of the wattle bark industry in the higher areas of Central Province has been spectacular ... the area under cultivation went up from 45,000 acres to 100,000 acres and it is intended to add a further 50,000 acres,' (*NAD*).

1936 '3,000 acres of additional land were placed under wattle.' (FHAR).

1937 'The acreage under wattle is believed to have increased from 25,000 to 27,000 acreas.' (KAR).

1938 '1,380 acres were planted to cotton, an increase of 553 acres.' (FHAR).

1940 '... a larger acreage than usual was put under pigeon peas ... it is estimated that a further 2,000 acres were placed under wattle.' (FHAR). 'It was decided to put a stop to the gradual infiltration of Kikuyu into the (Ndeiya) grazing grounds which had increased greatly of recent years. A line was fixed, west of which no cultivation could be allowed, and east of which cultivation would only be allowed on permit from the District Commissioner.' (KAR).

bananas and staple subsistence crops like yams, arrowroot, cassava and sweet potatoes. We know nothing definite about what happened to the cultivated area under these crops in this period, and little about the volume of their production, or changes in their value. However there is abundant impressionistic evidence to indicate that the Kiambu–Nairobi trade in bananas, vegetables and a number of other products continued throughout the thirties, and indeed expanded in 1939 with the outbreak of war. Among innovations was the introduction in the early thirties of onions into the Kandara area of Fort Hall district for sale in Thika town, and the introduction of improved strains of millet into the same district in 1936. In fact both onions and millet figure continuously in the agricultural prices quoted for the district for 1934–6, and exports of both clearly continued after this date.[31]

In short, there is a great deal of evidence, albeit of a diffuse and impressionistic kind, to suggest that in the 1930s the parameters of the Kikuyuland surplus product shifted to embrace small quantities of crops like millet which had previously been produced entirely for domestic consumption, whilst output of other crops grown for sale from the first (such as vegetables) expanded. In addition, sales of other products such as firewood and charcoal expanded with the wattle acreage, and the sale of poultry and eggs probably increased because of administrative measures (in Kiambu district among other places) making improved poultry strains available to Africans. There was also some increase in pig raising, and in the keeping of grade dairy cows.[32]

Finally two completely new cash crops—cotton and tobacco—were introduced into Kikuyuland in this period, in quite small quantities. The production of cotton was restricted to a small area of Fort Hall district and appears to have begun in 1935 as a small offshoot of an intensified cotton-planting campaign for African areas. It commenced with the planting of 178 acres by 711 cultivators, and this expanded to 627 acres in 1936, and 1,380 acres in 1937. In 1936 the first crop sold amounted to 23,878 pounds of A and B grade cotton, and in 1937 this had risen to 50,956 pounds. In 1938 the price dropped sharply, and this, together with weather damage, reduced the area under the crop to 166 acres by the end of the year. So apparently ended an always limited experiment.[33]

Tobacco was rather more of a success. Although only really introduced in Fort Hall in 1938 when 25 acres were put under the crop (again as part of a deliberate official campaign), it was noted to be 'growing in popularity' by 1939, when K£446 worth of tobacco was sold at a 'return per grower' of Shs. 32/50 an acre, while by 1940, 99,823 pounds of tobacco had been cured, 'practically all' of it from Fort Hall. However by 1940 the size of the experiment was still

31. KAR 1931, p. 6; 1934, p. 27; 1937, p. 18; and 1942, p. 3; FHAR 1933, p. 31; 1936, p. 40.
32. NAR 1938, p. 6. 'Memorandum on Native Agricultural Development . . .', op. cit., p. 12; KAR 1934, p. 27; and 1937. p. 18. FHAR 1936, p. 42; and 1937, p. 34.
33. FHARs 1935–8. Also *DAR* 1935, p. 87; 1936, p. 63; and 1938, p. 77.

·very small (probably with less than 100 acres under the crop), and as yet of only marginal significance to the Kikuyuland agricultural economy.[34]

Prices and the Penetration of Capital

Table IV:6 brings together a rather disparate collection of data on the growers' prices of maize, beans, potatoes and wattle. There are both single figures (which usually are presented as 'average' prices in the sources) and price ranges, the latter being more useful since they show the minimum and maximum prices reached in local markets in any one season. A glance at this table shows the tremendous volatility of all crop prices; this was true not merely of Central Province in this period, but of all areas of Kenya throughout the colonial period, and indeed subsequently. This volatility within one area from month to month, and from one comparatively small area to another at all seasons, makes price means useless, since the deviations from those means were clearly so persistent and so large.

The principal factors behind these variations were major changes in the supply of crops caused by weather and other 'natural' hazards such as locusts as well as by more predictable seasonal fluctuations.[35] Thus we see that even at the height of the depression in 1932 maize prices in Fort Hall could still reach Shs. 8 per bag. This occurred in January and February of that year as a result of the destruction of the 1931 long rains maize crop by locusts, and the failure of the short rains in 1931 to make good the losses. A further indication of how complex the impact of meteorological conditions could be is provided by a section of the Fort Hall report for 1933:

> There was an excellent short rain crop of maize, beans and millets. But there was an almost complete failure of long rain crops in the lower locations, and on the poorer *shambas* [plots] in the middle and higher locations.
>
> The bean crop failed practically everywhere, but above 5,000 feet a maize crop about 50% of normal was obtained and between 4,000 and 5,000 feet about 30%. This with a fair crop from pigeon peas and the quantities of food in store arrested any season's food shortage.[36]

It is small wonder the same report commented that 'prices have fluctuated considerably'!

Or again, while in 1938 Fort Hall had almost optimum conditions for the production of maize and beans, and produced a record crop for the former

34. FHARs 1935–8. Also *DAR* 1937, p. 65; and 1938, pp. 87–8.
35. By this I mean the marked fluctuations in prices deriving from harvest and non-harvest periods with food prices generally falling in the former and rising in the latter. In particular in many parts of Kenya food crop prices were often high in March and April when domestic stores from the short rains crop (November–December) were at a low point or exhausted, but the long rain crop had not yet come in.
36. FHAR 1933, p. 27.

Table IV:6. Unit prices of maize, beans, potatoes and wattle sold in Kikuyuland 1930–40 (in Shs.)

Year	Kiambu				Fort Hall				Nyeri			
	Maize	Beans	Potatoes	Wattle	Maize	Beans	Potatoes	Wattle	Maize	Beans	Potatoes	Wattle
1930				45–60				45–60	5/80	8/00	4/03	40–60
1931	4/80	6/80	3/60	35	4/80	6/80	3/60	35	4/80	6/80	3/60	35
1932				62	3–8			40–50	3/00			
1933												
1934				50	3/30–13	4–25	3–12	29–31			3–6	30
1935				35	1/70–6	4–5	3–6	30–39				
1936					2/10–9/25	4–11/50		39/20–48/18	2/50–3/75	4–5/50	4/50–9	28–44
1937	6–10	11	2/50–7	45/92–72/80	6/80	11		max. 79/52	2–6	5–6		
1938			1–2/75				5	61/60	6/80		3–7	39–66
1939	5/40–10	5/40–10	1/20–10		4/50–6/40	7–10/20			4/50	7/50	1–2/75	58/2
1940												

All prices are in Kenyan shillings. Prices for maize and beans are per 200 pound bag, for potatoes per 180 pound bag and for wattle (dried only), per ton.

Sources: Fazan, op. cit., and *NAD*s and District Reports 1930–40.

and a 'very good' crop of the latter, the District Officer in Kiambu was reporting the failure of his long rain crops in Dagoretti and an export ban on maize and beans from the whole district.[37]

A year later, the Fort Hall District Officer had invoked the food export ordinance due to 'the failure of the rains', whilst the Kiambu District Officer was lamenting that 'The long rains were a partial failure and the short rains a complete failure. This was the culmination of four poor seasons and as a result reserves have been used up and an actual shortage of food was general except in the higher zones where potatoes are grown.'[38] And he went on to relate this to the large fluctuations in Kiambu food crop prices noted in table IV:6 for 1939.

Moreover it is clear that the district is far too large a unit of analysis to allow one fully to appreciate the extent of these fluctuations. The quotation from the Kiambu District Officer states implicitly, and that from the Fort Hall report explicitly, that harvests could vary enormously within districts according to the effect of altitude, soil conditions, and even wind direction (a major determinant of locust distribution). A quite extraordinary example of intra-district variation is provided by Fort Hall in 1939 where the imposition of a ban on food exports is reported in the same paragraph as the news that the district had had an all-time record marketed surplus of beans![39] Clearly we are dealing here either with a marked variability by area within the district, or the unsuitability of that season's rainfall and other conditions for some crops but not for beans (not an uncommon pattern).

Examples of these meteorological variations could be multiplied many times since they are a feature of every district report.[40] But enough has been said to suggest that, acting as they did on the supply of food and other crops, they were a powerful determinant of price fluctuations. Indeed I have no doubt that were the data complete enough to support such an exercise, a multivariant regression would show rainfall changes (for example) to be a much more powerful determinant of 'short term' price fluctuations (i.e. fluctuations both within seasons and from one season to the next) than any demand side factor. District and Native Affairs reports only locate 1935 as the year when 'the depression' eased in Kenya because a generally excellent harvest had not resulted in an across-the-board fall in minimum prices in the period immediately after the harvest.

The predominance of factors affecting supply is particularly strong in any situation in which advances in the technology of agricultural production have been so few, or so underutilised, as to render producers defenceless in the face of climatic and other changes. The penetration of capital in the form of improv-

37. KAR 1938, p. 51.
38. KAR 1939, p. 4.
39. FHAR 1939, p. 8.
40. See also the evidence in van Zwanenberg, 'Primitive Colonial Accumulation . . .', op. cit., pp. 179–80.

ed seeds and hardier varieties, disease and pest control, and irrigation can begin to reduce this defencelessness somewhat, and indeed it was in the 1930s that such a penetration (directed by government policy) began to occur. But by 1940 it had hardly begun to reduce risks for cultivators, the major form of capital improvements being in technology which increased output on the assumption of optimum rainfall and other conditions. This finds its reflection at the price level in the more or less total domination of price movements for food crops by ecologically dictated fluctuations in harvests.

Conclusions

The 1930s in Kikuyuland have conventionally been seen as the 'era of wattle', and indeed in terms of the rate of expansion of the cultivated area under this crop, vis-à-vis others, this is so. This was not due to the tremendously high value of wattle as bark, but more because of its wide range of use values, and its additional exchange values in the form of charcoal and firewood. In addition, its higher rate of return per unit of land and per unit of labour time made it attractive to small and medium land holders in the crowded locations of southern Kiambu, southern Nyeri and western Fort Hall, where the altitude and soil type also suited it.

The absence of any coherent sets or series of statistics on cultivated area and output make it impossible to trace accurately the progress of agricultural production in Kikuyuland during this decade, but all the impressionistic evidence is of an expansion in production of all crops. The partial exception is maize, the marketed surplus of which probably increased overall but commercial production of which became concentrated in a few, less densely populated, lowland locations;[41] that is, the maize surplus product of smaller landholders in the more densely populated upper locations may have been reduced in favour of wattle. The insistent direct evidence of the expansion of output and of the cultivated area is powerfully supported by evidence relating to an increase in the number of land disputes (resulting from land shortage) by the marked increase in outright sales of land to richer households (see chapter X), and by the abundant evidence of the decline of grazing land. In the latter case the situation had become so acute that by the late thirties an area of 'communal' grazing (*ndeiya*) added to the Kikuyu Reserve as a safety valve by the Kenya Land Commission had already begun to be used for cultivation.

2. Nyanza Province

Agricultural statistics for this period are sufficiently full to justify an attempt at tabulation, and tables IV:7 to IV:12 show acreages, output, marketed output

---

41. See *Food Shortage Commission of Inquiry Report 1943* (Nairobi, 1943), p. 29.

Table IV:7. Output, acreage and marketed production of selected crops 1930–40

Year	Cotton			Maize			Beans			Acreage
	Acreage	Output	M.P.[1]	Acreage	Output	M.P.	Acreage	Output	M.P.	
1930										
1931										
1932		175			5,486			441.4		
1933					11,314.1			748.7		
1934					11,161.5			405.2		
1935		808			10,439.0			192.8[2]		
1936	40,000 'up by 100%'	2,719	9,350		8,451	33,500[2]		371.8		10,300
1937	+ 4,000	2,596.1								
1938					10,089.3					
1939					8,928.6					
1940										

and prices by district. The data in all three districts are much fuller for cotton and maize than for other crops, and this is simply a reflection of the interest taken in them by District Officers, the easier availability and reliability of cotton statistics (given that virtually all output was sold, and was marketed exclusively at government-controlled 'buying posts'), and the attempted control of maize marketing from 1935. Fortunately, it also reflects economic priorities, in that these two crops undoubtedly accounted for the major part both of the cultivated area and of the agricultural income accruing to Nyanza Province in this decade.

A much more insistent government cotton-planting campaign than anything attempted in the 1920s began in 1930/5, and centred at first on South Kavirondo, before spreading to other districts. It intermeshed with the Administration's 'zoning' policy, with the Province being divided into three cotton production zones each with their own production targets, seed distribution system, etc. As a result of this policy and of a steady increase in the price of cotton from 1933 to 1935, cotton output for the Province as a whole expanded from the minimal figure of 410 tons in 1931 to over 10,000 tons in 1937 and 1938. In 1939 production dropped drastically to under 5,000 tons, largely as a result of hailstorms.[42]

The progress of maize production in this decade is much more difficult to plot with any accuracy, since official reports up to 1937 relied on statistics showing the amount of the crop exported from the Province by rail from certain stations. From the 1920s onwards, a smaller and smaller proportion of the Province's exported produce left by rail, so that, for example, the apparently

42. See the account in Fearn, op. cit., pp. 72–8 and pp. 194–5. See also *DARs* 1934 to 1938.

Central Kavirondo district (tons)

Sesame		Groundnuts			Rice			Tobacco		
Output	M.P.	Acreage	Output	M.P.	Acreage	Output	M.P.	Acreage	Output	M.P.
1,264.8			59.8							
1,993.9			4.6							
662.0			10.0							
212.5			9.4		23.5	41				
476.8	1,500		0.9		775	166				
2,938										
1,575		294.6				409		Trials		
					581	60.0		45	3.5	3.5

1) In the case of cotton, output and marketed production are treated as identical.
2) All legumes

Source: CKAR 1930–40

declining maize exports from Central Kavirondo district over the years 1933 to 1936 (table IV:7) are much more a reflection of this fact than of anything else. This shortcoming is most important in the case of North Kavirondo, since a much smaller proportion of its production left by rail than did that of Central Kavirondo. This emerges clearly from 1937 onwards when inspection centre figures become available. In that year 3,393 tons of maize left the North Kavirondo district by train. But we know from other sources that 7,142 tons passed through inspection centres in the district, and Humphrey, using statistics presumably collated later, puts official (i.e. 'inspected') exports of maize and maize meal for 1937 at 10,893 tons. This later figure is still only about a quarter of the 40,000 tons which the senior Agricultural Officer offered to Günter Wagner as his best estimate of total district production.[43]

Thus, even making generous allowance for consumption within the district, it appears that most of the maize and maize meal leaving North Kavirondo over the decade went uninspected, and in all probability went to the neighbouring settler farming areas of Trans-Nzoia, Uasin Gishu and Kisumu–Londiani. There is not doubt that by 1937 North Kavirondo was producing the bulk of the maize exported from Nyanza Province. In that year the Agricultural Department *Annual Report* estimated that out of some 22,321 tons of maize 'sold out' of the Province 'in a normal year', 16,071 tons came from North Kavirondo.[44]

It should be noted that although by the late thirties the district was being

43. NKAR 1937, p. 6. N. Humphrey, *The Liguru and the Land: Sociological Aspects of some Agricultural Problems* (Nairobi, 1947), p. 5. and Wagner, op. cit., Vol. II, p. 36. See also *DAR* 1937, p. 67.
44. Van Zwanenberg, 'Primitive Colonial Accumulation . . .', op. cit., p. 199.

Table IV:8. Producer prices of selected crops 1930–40 in K£ per ton—
Central Kavirondo

Year	Cotton	Maize	Beans	Sesame	Groundnuts	Rice	Tobacco
	Unit Price	Unit Price	Unit Price	Unit Price	Unit Price	Unit Price	Unit Price
1930							
1931	11.8	1.9					
1932		1.2–1.4					
1933	10.1	2.5	5.6	7.2–7.7.	5.4		
1934				6.9–8.7	7.2–7.7		
1935							
1936							
1937	19.0		6.1	10–11.1			
1938	7.8	2.4–4.3	4.2–5.3	7.5–8.7			24.6–35.8
1939	('about the same as 1938' until Oct., when rose)						
1940							

Source: ibid.

referred to somewhat hyperbolically as the 'granary of Kenya', output expanded only slowly between 1931 and 1937 (from 33,000 to 40,000 tons), and that the really major expansion both of cultivated area under maize and of marketed production came with the war years and the guaranteed prices of the Maize and Produce Board (see chapter V).

Nonetheless, Wagner's figures on the expansion of production in South Kitosh show a very rapid growth of exported production (from a very low base) in the years 1931 to 1936. His figures are reproduced in table IV: 13. By 1936 South Kitosh accounted for nearly all of North Kavirondo's maize exports, though the more densely populated southern locations probably still dominated the district's total production, and perhaps even its total marketed production if intra-district trade ('subsistence marketing') is taken into account. This suggests of course that the subsistence pressure on the land in the southern locations (and particularly in Maragoli) was taking its toll of its surplus product.

Statistics on the cultivated area under crops are too meagre to reveal anything of substance. Once again impressionistic remarks in all the reports indicate a continual expansion of the cultivated area, certainly after the droughts and locusts of 1931–4 had departed, but the only figures are for cotton acreage in North Kavirondo, provided by Wagner, which suggest that the area under the crop rose 600 per cent in six years.[45]

45. Wagner, op. cit., Vol. II, p. 36.

The price data also suggest that Nyanza Province differed from Kikuyuland in this period in having a cash crop—cotton—whose value per unit of output was significantly in excess of that of maize or beans. It will be noted for example that in 1936, when cotton prices fell below 10 cents per pound, the value of some 3,000 tons of marketed output was still over four times greater than that of an almost identical amount of maize.[46] We clearly have to explain the failure of cotton output to expand at the rate which the Administration desired, and such an explanation cannot rest on prices, though much conventional discussion has revolved round this issue. Though prices did decline rapidly through the late twenties, they stabilised in the 1930s, and there is no evidence that thereafter output falls were related to price movements.[47] Indeed, given the enormous price differential between cotton and the other crops being grown by Nyanza Province cultivators in this period, any other trend would be surprising, since price rises would presumably only encourage output increases, whilst price falls would have to have been catastrophic to bring cotton down to the level of maize or beans. Why then did output rise so comparatively slowly in the period 1931–6 and why were the large output increases of 1937 and 1938 not sustained?

A major part of the answer lies simply in climatic conditions in the Province. As early as 1932 the Director of Agriculture had remarked that his department's programme for improving African agriculture had 'two fundamental and considerable problems to contend with . . .'

> The three areas to which services are given are the Kikuyu, Kavirondo and Coast Reserves. The first and second of these, so far as natural conditions go, are in the main highly productive areas with large populations . . . however there is an obvious inferiority. This is due to the lack of large areas suitable to relatively high-priced crops such as cotton, groundnuts and rice. Kikuyu and Kavirondo produce large quantities of relatively low-priced crops such as maize, millets, beans and potatoes. They are except for small areas of the lower altitudes, too high and damp for cotton and groundnuts, and suitable for rice only in small localised spots.[48]

And Hay notes that when in 1937, 'fully thirty years after they had first begun to encourage cotton cultivation in Nyanza', a programme of experimental cotton plots was begun, they revealed the general unsuitability of Nyanza's soil and rainfall conditions for cotton.[49]

In addition cotton seems to have remained unpopular over many areas of Nyanza which could grow alternative food/cash crops like maize or beans be-

46. Ibid. p. 36.
47. Fearn, op. cit., p. 76.
48. Quoted in *NAD* 1932, p. 94.
49. Hay, op. cit., p. 940.

Table IV :9. Output, acreage and marketed production of selected crops 1930–40

Year	Cotton			Maize			Beans			Acreage
	Acreage	Output	M.P.	Acreage	Output	M.P.	Acreage	Output	M.P.	
1930										
1931	5,015	672		33,000						
1932										
1933		1,088.2			410.7					
1934		2,121.3			964.3					
1935	'extended consider- ably'	2,730		'greater'	2,544.6					
1936	25,000	3,115		48,000	3,259	31,500[1]				6,270 'acreage increas- ed'
1937	31,000	4,206.7		40,000	10,893				412.9	
1938		4,079.8			11,785		'crops have been good'		410.9	
1939		1,914.2			12,108				160.7	
1940		1,512.2			25,670				22.1	

cause for the small peasant farmer its low weight yields per unit of land meant that in terms of net returns its higher unit price simply was not realisable as a worthwhile cash income for the small farmer. The micro-economics of this are discussed in detail in the next chapter, but suffice it to say here that cotton was unpopular as a source of cash income for exactly the same reasons which made wattle popular. Wattle was adopted eagerly because it had a variety of use and exchange values for the smallholder and in addition it had a high weight yield per unit of land in areas of Central Province where land was becoming scarce (at prevailing intensities of use). The densely populated locations of Central and southern North Kavirondo were in much the same land-scarce situation, and they were being pressed to grow a crop which only had one exchange value and no use value at all to the farmer; it was not even edible.

It followed then that cotton was only likely to succeed in locations which were unsuitable for the growing of any heavier-yielding food/cash crop (because of aridity), and in fact, as far as one can tell, these were the conditions prevailing in the lake-shore locations of Central and Southern Kavirondo. Cotton production was pushed heavily by the Administration in these locations during

—*North Kavirondo (tons)*

	Sesame		Groundnuts			Rice			Tobacco		
	Output	M.P.	Acreage	Output	M.P.	Acreage	Output	M.P.	Acreage	Output	M.P.
						starts					
									starts		
							5			14,000 lb	
			300	450			11			19,200 lb	
	744.8			420			102				
	397.1			'decreas-ed'		107.1	42		6.8	6.8	
						'destroyed by locusts'					
'up on 1939'	268.8			+ 600			21.8	70	9.1	9.1	
	844.3						36.0				

1) All legumes.
Source: NKARs 1930–40.

the 1930s, Agricultural Officers feeling that cultivators could derive a double benefit from the adoption of cotton growing. On the one hand they would raise their incomes with what, as we have seen, was undoubtedly the highest-priced crop available to Africans in the period, and on the other hand this income would provide a safeguard against food-crop failure by providing a higher-than-average income from which to purchase food in time of shortage.[50] Unfortunately, we have no micro-study of cotton adoption in these locations through which to assess responses to this programme, though the persistent expansion of the acreage under the crop, and of output, in these locations of Central and Southern Kavirondo would seem to indicate that the response was generally positive.

The introduction of small-scale Arabica coffee planting into the Nyaribari

50. See SKARs 1935, 1936 and 1937; and *DAR* 1934, p. 90; 1935, pp. 94–6; 1937, p. 55; and 1938, p. 75, for the cotton campaign in South Kavirondo and grower response. See also SKAR 1938, p. 25, for what amounts to an open confession of the continued need to use coercion in some areas. Cotton growing was also seen as a famine prevention measure in other areas, notably Kitui District and parts of Coast Province.

Table IV: 10. Producer prices of selected crops 1930–40 in K£ per ton—
North Kavirondo

Year	Cotton	Maize	Beans	Sesame	Groundnuts	Rice	Tobacco
1930							
1931							
1932	10.1						
1933					5.4		
1934	12.8						
1935	14.5	0.8 to 1.7					
1936	3.4 to 14.5	0.6 to 3.7					
1937	16.8 'minimum'	3.3 'average' to 5.6 'maximum'	5.6 'average'	11.0		6.2 'average'	
1938	14.5 'average'	2.9 'average'	4.5 'average'	8.4		5.6 'average'	16.8 to 22.4
1939	9.0						
1940							

1939—Total value of all produce marketed = K£ 64,381

1940—Total value of all produce marketed = K£ 116,800

Source: ibid.

and Kitutu locations of Kisii from 1934 seems to have owed a great deal to the persistence of District Commissioner Buxton, who overcame the strong opposition of the Department of Agriculture. It was restricted at the beginning to a few progressive chiefs and their friends and relatives. As table IV:11 shows, it remained on a very small scale up until the outbreak of war (and indeed through and after the war, until the early 1950s), and though it undoubtedly brought substantial incomes to one or two classic representatives of the African petite bourgeoisie (especially Chief Musa Nyandusa of Nyaribari), it was generally of minimal significance in this period. With hindsight it may be seen (along with similar experiments in Embu and Meru districts) as a harbinger of the future. In the latter regard the figure for the unit price of coffee in 1938 given in table IV:12 goes a long way towards explaining the insistent demand by representatives of the petite bourgeoisie (in Local Native Councils and elsewhere) to be allowed to grow coffee, a demand which began in this period. In 1938 a ton of coffee berries was worth over two and a half times a ton of cotton to a smallholder, over three times a ton of sesame, over five times a ton of groundnuts and nearly fourteen times a ton of maize. Just as importantly, it was a crop with a high weight yield per unit of land. Small wonder that to many of the ambitious it seemed the key to wealth, or at least to comfort, through agriculture. However, toleration of these small elite experiments in Kisii, Embu and Meru betokened no weakening of the Department of Agriculture's general support for the European position of denying Africans access to coffee growing.

Table *IV:11. Acreage and marketed production of selected crops 1930–40 — South Kavirondo district (tons)*

Year	Wattle Acreage	Wattle M.P.	Cotton Acreage	Cotton M.P.	Maize Acreage	Maize M.P.	Beans Acreage	Beans M.P.	Groundnuts Acreage	Groundnuts M.P.	Sesame Acreage	Sesame M.P.	Millet Acreage	Millet M.P.	Coffee Acreage	Coffee M.P.
1930																
1931																
1932						1,190		284		1,744		584		320		
1933			3,500	31.7		1,288		90		462		1,153		603		
1934				384		973		226		179		619		884	8	
1935	1,000			770		777		58		522		683		872		
1936	5,000		16,700	2,232		772		83	8,000	2,065	9,500	1,564		631	50	
1937	'9–10,000'			2,232		2,378		163		3,235		1,336		341	76	
1938	15,000			1,742		1,260		205		1,444		951		770	91	3
1939																
1940																

Source: SKARs 1930–40

Table IV: 12. Producer prices of selected crops 1930–40 in K£ per ton—
South Kavirondo district

Year	Wattle	Cotton	Maize	Beans	Gdnuts	Sesame	Millet	Coffee
	Producer Price	Producer Price	Producer Price	Producer Price	Producer Price	Producer Price	Producer Price	Producer Price
1930								
1931								
1932								
1933								
1934		11.2	1.17	5.6	6.93	7.15	3.47	
1935		8.46	2.2	9.5	10.1	10.1	3.92	
1936		11.2	2.48	3.28	10.8	11.34	3.6	
1937		8.96	3.57	4.37	7.8	10.44	4.6	
1938		10.38	2.2	4.75	5.5	9.09	4.49	28.6
1939								
1940								

Source: ibid.

Indeed they were only tolerated because the areas involved were some distance from European plantations, and on the understanding that the experiments were to remain small-scale.[51]

The Labour Process in Nyanza Agriculture in the 1930s

Wagner provides a fairly detailed picture of 'traditional' agricultural practices among the Logoli of Maragoli and the Vugusu of South Kitosh as he observed them in the period 1934–8, and he also presents a fairly detailed description of the Logoli method of land holding. However, as is common in social-anthropological monographs of this period, he provides considerably less detail for the effects of the commercialisation of agriculture on the labour process and on the use of land (as opposed to its effects on land tenure norms).

Wagner reports that among the Logoli the male household head apportioned the land cultivated to his wife or wives. If the family involved was monogamous and poor it would cultivate only two garden plots, of which one would be allocated to the wife. If the family was somewhat better off and had four or six such plots then two would be allocated to the wife, and in either case this plot or plots would be tilled by the wife 'on behalf of the family household'. In the case of polygynous households,

> Each wife is apportioned a separate field, the *olumini gwa guga* [land inherited by the household head because he was the eldest son in his family of origin]

51. The account here is essentially derived from R. M. Maxon, 'Cash Crop Innovation among the Gusii in the 1930s' (CPEK Paper, 1975). For more details on the role of Musa Nyandusi, see below chapter X.

*Table IV: 13. Increase in the production
of maize for export—South Kitosh*[46]
1931–6

Year	Maize exports (tons)
1931	116
1933	418
1934	982
1935	2,593
1936	3,325

usually being allotted to the great or senior wife and plots of decreasing size to the junior wives, although adjustments would later be made in accordance with the number of children in each house.[52]

In Maragoli in 1934–8 the garden plots so allocated varied considerably in shape and size 'but about one acre for each garden may be taken to be a fair average'. Thus in the case of a monogamous family holding four acres of land in cultivation, it would appear that the husband would allocate two or possibly three acres of land for his own use, while the wife would cultivate the other for family consumption. It appears that the wife's (or wives') plots were not distinguished in any way within the labour process of cultivation, nor in terms of crop mix.[53] The distinction appears to have lain simply in the end use to which produce or income from the respective plots was put. That is to say, the plots allocated to the wife were meant to feed the family. There is however an ambiguity involved in this account. The household head had an exclusive right of disposal of the land occupied by the household, and more importantly he had sole power to dispose of the produce of the land not allocated to his wife and to use income in cash or kind ensuing from that disposal as he wished. In all cases this was the major part of the household's cultivated area.[54] But the reservation of the wife's/wives' garden to the 'feeding' of her husband and children could mean either that the produce of that garden was all directly consumed, or that it might be sold or bartered but that the income from such sale or barter was so reserved. Wagner's silence on this topic is particularly unfortunate because it seems likely that one effect of the commercialisation of agriculture was precisely to bring about such a transition. Both the male household head and his wife or wives would at first barter and then sell increased proportions of their produce, but the proceeds from these transactions would in one case be at the disposal of the household head, in the other at the disposal of the wife. This division was probably also reflected in a division of labour in trade, with the

52. Wagner, op. cit., Vol. II, p. 86.
53. Ibid., p. 21.
54. Ibid., p. 86.

wife trading the produce of her garden whilst the male household head traded the produce of the rest of the land.

In assessing the impact of the commercialisation of agriculture on the political economy of the family, a great deal turns on how the extra land which was cultivated as the cropped area expanded was controlled. If it was simply annexed to the husband's estate, then clearly he would control a gradually increasing part of the household's production. If however wives' gardens tended to grow or multiply in proportion to the household's cropped area, which Wagner's account at one point appears to suggest, then a balance of power within the household—in the sense of power of decision over the disposal and use of the surplus agricultural product—may have been maintained.

It has already been suggested that in the case of the Kipsigis such a balance of power was not maintained; the ploughed maize fields were annexed to the husband's estate, an annexation rendered easier by the fact that women were excluded from the actual ploughing process, though taking part in harvesting and weeding. A comparison of the impact of the commercialisation of agriculture through the 'plough' monocropping of maize in South Kitosh with the situation of Maragoli could have been illuminating on this point; but this is not provided for us, since Wagner's overall treatment of 'modern developments in agriculture' is so generalised for both cases and his analysis of land holding and working arrangements within the family is entirely restricted to the Logoli.

His account of 'tillage' in Maragoli however makes it clear that most of the labour time expended in cultivation was women's labour time, and that after 'commercialisation' (which mainly took the form of an increased acreage under maize plus the barter or sale of increased proportions of other food crops such as sorghum, peas, beans, sweet potatoes, cassava and bananas) cultivation remained exclusively hoe cultivation, with nearly all of the hoeing being done by women. As in Kowe, so in South Maragoli (and indeed it would appear in all the southern locations of North Kavirondo); by 1934 the traditional wooden and iron hoes had been superseded by imported 'European hoes' or *jembes* (called *amajembe* by the Logoli),[55] but this remained the sole technical advance in the instruments of labour, because South Maragoli and all the southern

---

55. In fact Wagner's account of the process of transition to 'European' hoes is very interesting and accords closely with the process described for Kowe by Hay. He says, 'There are two types of traditional native hoe. One of them (*embago*) has an iron blade attached to a knee-shaped wooden handle.' This appears to be the *Nyarlte* or *Kasiri* described by Hay for Kowe. 'The other one (*elihaya*) has a wooden blade fastened to the same kind of handle and is used chiefly in the stony soil prevailing in some parts of South Maragoli.' Hay also mentions a 'wooden hoe' in Kowe which was in use around 1900 and that the adoption of the *jembe* in Kowe in the 1920s was preceded by the spread of a stronger iron blade (*apanga*) obtainable from Indian traders in 1918 'for one large basket of grain'. She indicates that this form of hoe was still predominant in Kowe in the 1920s, and was not really superseded by the *jembe* on most holdings until the late thirties. If this is so, and Wagner's *amajembe* was not Hay's *apanga*, then clearly South Maragoli had progressed further in implement change than Kowe. See Wagner, op. cit., Vol. II, p. 25; and Hay, op. cit., pp. 149–50.

locations of North Kavirondo were too densely populated, and landholdings too fragmented, to allow for the widespread adoption of the plough. Moreover, by the late thirties the colonial administration was actively discouraging the use of ploughs in this area because of worries about sheet erosion induced by ploughing up and down the sides of rides.[56]

In the previous chapter we noted that in the 1920s the expansion of the surplus product in North Kavirondo had mainly taken the form of the addition of the hoe cultivation of maize to a previous cropping pattern and that the increased surplus product so produced came overwhelmingly from the more densely populated southern locations; Maragoli, Bunyore, Kisa, Bidakho, South Marrama, North and West Tiriki and South and West Kakamega.

Moreover, in this chapter I have already suggested that from Wagner's own figures, the northernmost and westernmost areas of North and South Kitosh (the present Elgon Nyanza) were making only a marginal contribution to North Kavirondo's maize production before the war. The expansion of maize production in the 1930s must therefore have come from North Kavirondo's zones 2 and 3,[57] involving a mixture of hoe and plough cultivation, with the balance in any given area being dictated by terrain and population density. If women were able to maintain their bargaining power in the process of commercialisation much better in a situation in which expansion of the cropped area was through the hoe rather than the plough, then the northward spread of maize production in North Kavirondo in the thirties would make a fascinating set of local case studies to substantiate this. Without such studies the nature of the labour process in Maragoli and South Kitosh in the mid-thirties can only be deduced from Wagner's accounts. From his descriptions of the sexual division of labour and the agricultural calendar of South Maragoli, it appears that in that location (and apparently in all the other southern locations of North Kavirondo) there were in the mid-thirties two maize crops, two sorghum crops and one crop each of beans and sweet potatoes. In addition there were seven different periods of sowing or planting, four different harvests, three periods of weeding and two different periods of hoeing or turning over land in preparation for planting. Women were responsible for all these tasks, sharing only a small proportion of the planting duties and the harvesting of maize with men. There can be little doubt that in these locations women's labour input into cultivation far exceeded that of men.

In apparent contrast to this, Wagner reports that in the 'plough' maize-growing area of South Kitosh both the weeding of all grain crops and the threshing of maize was being done by men. It is also clear from Wagner's account of South Kitosh that the cultivated area on all ploughed holdings had expanded

56. Wagner, op. cit., Vol. II, p. 35.
57. Zone 2 was made up of Waholo, Wanga, North Marama, Mukulu, Kakalewa and Watsotso locations and zone 3 of Kabras, North, West and East Kakamega and North and East Tiriki. *KLC E & M* III, pp. 2247–49 ('Memorandum' by M. H. Grieve, District Agricultural Officer).

rapidly from the early thirties. With a much larger amount of land under maize, the amount of harvesting and weeding work would have increased considerably, and it is interesting therefore that men were doing most of it, as well as threshing the maize (but not other grains). Either women had been able to insist on this, making men take responsibility for these tasks, especially the unpopular task of weeding, as a prerequisite of female assent to plough cultivation, or (and this seems more likely) male labour input had increased in order to ensure male control of the expanded surplus product of the household.[58]

Thus expansion of the cropped area and increased commercialisation of production in the southern locations had entailed a considerably increased work load for women there,[59] while further north, where the plough rather than the hoe form of commercialisation was predominant, men were sharing the extra burden of work, at least up to the mid-thirties.

The crucial question is whether or not these different patterns of commercialisation implied differences in who controlled the surplus product which was generated. That is, if women's labour time made a greater contribution to the creation of the surplus product, did women thereby acquire a greater say in its disposal? This is a subject which must await research, but it may be that in the end it made little difference. For it may be that the crucial point was the ability of male household heads to assert their right of control over the produce of all land other than that from the plot or plots accorded to his wife/wives. For this power, going hand in hand with the power to decide the size and location of the wife's plot within the total holding, may have meant that in both cases male household heads were able effectively to arrogate the bulk of the land cultivated to their own control, leaving their wives with an increasingly marginal subsistence holding.

It should not be forgotten that household heads with larger land holdings were more easily able to allocate an adequate subsistence plot to their wife or wives, whilst at the same time being less dependent on them for field labour which they could hire for beer or (later) cash. They may thus have been much more able to marginalise the wife's role in commercialisation. But this is not all. 'Richer household heads' is itself an ambiguous phrase. The richer household heads in northern areas of Kavirondo like South Kitosh were probably men wealthy in stock who could use that stock to obtain both wives and ploughs. They would have been, at least at this date, both polygynous and non-christian. In turn the

58. Wagner, op. cit., Vol. II, pp. 21–9.
59. A large part of this work load was accounted for by the greater amount of planting, weeding and threshing necessitated by the double cropping of maize in South Maragoli. On the other hand, by the mid-thirties cultivators there had access to the new higher-yielding white maize (*Zea mays*) being pushed by the Department of Agriculture in these years in place of older yellow varieties, and as we have seen the quality of hoes was also improving. See Wagner, op. cit., Vol. II, p. 35; *DAR* 1938, p. 80; and C. L. A. Leakey (ed.), *Crop Improvement in East Africa* (Farnham Royal, 1970), pp. 22–6.

wealth generated by large-scale maize farming allowed them to stay out of the wage labour market, and living at home they had full control over production decisions, and over the use to which the income from the surplus product was put.

In South Maragoli, it appears that many more male household heads were absent from their land for various periods of time, and some of these men must have been skilled manual or white-collar employees. In short these were the sort of 'richer household heads' who might be absent for long periods of time, or who for one reason or another took little or no part in agricultural production. In such cases of course their wives would have had somewhat greater freedom in making production decisions and perhaps in utilising the surplus, and would also have been able to relieve themselves of their extra load of labour by means of hiring in.

The whole dimension of stratification among households remains completely unexplored in Wagner's work, as indeed does the issue of the implications of labour migration for agricultural production, even though Wagner himself notes that the rate of migration increased during the 1930s: 'In 1932 about 20% and in 1937 about 30% of the adult male population of the District (and probably an even higher percentage among the Logoli) was at any given time of the year away from the Reserve.'[60] For an exploration of this whole issue we must turn to Hay's work on Kowe in Central Kavirondo.

Kowe and Maragoli Compared

Hay's account of developments in the Kowe sub-location of the Seme division of Central Nyanza after 1930 can be usefully compared with Wagner's findings on South Maragoli. According to Armitage's memorandum to the Kenya Land Commission in 1932, South Maragoli had a population of 22,581 men, women and children living in an area of fifty-two square miles. The population density was thus 434.25 persons per square mile, or in acreage terms an average of 6.47 acres per family of 4.39 persons. In the same year according to his calculations the population of Seme was 30,051, living in an area of 123 square miles which worked out at 244 persons per square mile, or in acreage terms 12.59 acres per family of 5.35 persons.[61] Treating these figures with caution, as indicating general orders of magnitude only, we have a picture of a markedly higher population density in South Maragoli, inducing a generally smaller household size, and with the 'average' household having a much greater proportion of its 'available' acreage under crops (45 per cent against 19 per cent in Seme). From the data provided by Wagner and Hay we have the following crops being raised in Maragoli and Kowe in the mid-1930s:

South Maragoli (North Kavirondo): maize, beans, eleusine, sorghum, sesame, sweet potatoes, bananas.

60. Wagner, op. cit., Vol. II, p. 94.
61. *KLC E & M* III, pp. 2220 and 2272.

Kowe (Central Kavirondo): maize, beans, sorghum, cassava, groundnuts, sesame, pumpkins, barley, vegetables, cotton, fruit and wood trees (i.e. guava, papaya, mango, eucalyptus, *cassia florida*).[62]

As far as acreages under these different crops are concerned, Hay does not attempt to provide any figures for this period, while Wagner simply refers to Grieve's 1931 statistics. In any case the whole point of Hay's analysis is to suggest that specific crops spread unevenly during the 1930s, so that for example by the end of the period virtually all households were growing some maize, but some households were growing much more than others. In this connection, it is to be noted that it was only during the late 1930s that the double cropping of maize became common in Kowe, whilst the general tenor of Wagner's account is to suggest that this had been common practice in Maragoli at least from the beginning of the decade and probably earlier.[63] Both accounts thus confirm that in densely populated areas of central Nyanza Province double cropping was the main way of expanding maize output, with population pressure acting as a 'trigger'; at a certain point, if subsistence production and the surplus product were to be maintained in the face of increasing subsistence pressure, double-cropping had to be adopted. With the end of shifting cultivation and rapidly declining amounts of fallow land, this was likely to have deleterious effects on soil fertility.

The absence of cassava and groundnuts in Maragoli may reflect the unsuitability of climatic and/or soil conditions, but a number of contingent factors also seem to be at work here.[64] Cotton was grown in Kowe but not in Maragoli, though climate and soil conditions were no more suitable for cotton in Kowe than they were in Maragoli. However Kowe was unfortunate enough to be included in an agricultural production zone deemed suitable for cotton growing while Maragoli avoided this fate. As a result the cultivators of Kowe came under increased administrative pressure to plant cotton in the 1930s, pressure which encountered strong passive resistance, but which continued until 1942 when a series of local trials by the Agricultural Department confirmed the unsuitability of local conditions for the crop. Hay also notes that cotton was unpopular in Kowe because it markedly increased peak period demands for labour input, since it had to be planted during the long rains in April, when the major part of Luo food crop planting was also taking place.[65]

We may now turn to the central issue of historical change in agricultural production in this period, and outline Hay's general findings for Kowe.

62. Sources: Wagner, op. cit., Vol. II, p. 24; and Hay, op. cit., p. 130.
63. Wagner, op. cit., Vol. II, pp. 24–5 and 34–5 and Hay, op. cit., pp. 204–25.
64. Particularly in the case of cassava the Department of Agriculture appears to have pushed the crop heavily in Kowe in the early thirties as a famine crop after the area had been very badly hit by locusts. Hay, op. cit., p. 209.
65. Ibid., pp. 138–40 and pp. 194–203.

Kowe 1930–40

Hay notes two closely linked tendencies in the agricultural history of Kowe in this decade. On the one hand there was the slow expansion of the new crops and technology which were being introduced in the late 1920s, and on the other hand there was a notable increase in the level of male labour migration from the area. She does not attempt to quantify this latter phenomenon, but seems to feel that Wagner's estimate of an increase from 20 per cent to 30 per cent of the adult male population leaving Maragoli in the period 1932 to 1937 is about right for Kowe too. She accounts for this development with reference to three different stimuli operating during the 1930s. Firstly, there was the failure of cotton in Kowe. The importance of this derived from the far higher price levels for cotton than for other crops, since once its unsuitability for Kowe had been established it became clear that returns to labour in agriculture could never equal those from wage employment. Secondly, there was the opening up of a goldmine in Kowe in 1934 which markedly increased opportunities for local wage employment, not only for men but for women and children as well. This introduced a much greater proportion of Kowe's population to wage labour, and in addition (since goldmines generally paid slightly better wages even to unskilled employees than did farms, estates or government) may have produced a rather inflated impression of the monetary advantages of wage earning. Hay suggests that many of the men who gained their first experience of wage labour at the Kowenje goldmine went on to other forms of work both in Nyanza and elsewhere. Thirdly, an increase in demands on men for unpaid communal labour in the Reserve, which began in the late thirties and only ended in 1947 (when the Local Native Council began to pay wages), led many to prefer to leave and work for wages elsewhere.[66]

Hay's account of the way in which this process intermeshed with trends in agricultural production is interesting. She suggests that its overall effect was to marginalise agricultural production, which increasingly came to be regarded as a 'holding operation' to provide a basic subsistence, whilst households in Kowe looked to wage earning to increase their income and provide a means of accumulation. The spread of maize, and of hand gristing and water-powered maize mills in Kowe, helped in this process since double maize cropping 'flattened' the crop labour profile and spread labour demands more evenly over the year, whilst hand gristing and maize milling mills cut down the labour time invested in food preparation. 'The labour saved in this way was then reinvested in other activities judged to be more productive, namely wage employment outside the district and trading.'[67]

The considerable increase in (perhaps even the actual beginning of) regular

66. Ibid., pp. 226–32.
67. Ibid., pp. 211–12.

trading by women in Kowe was once again related to the opening and expansion of the goldmines, which provided a buoyant market for foodstuffs. This is treated in more detail in a later chapter.

This general account of the marginalisation of agriculture in the 1930s is not totally consistent with some of the evidence provided by Hay, and in particular the much more rapid spread of the use of the ox plough in this period. If Hartley's estimate of the amount of uncultivated land available for cultivation in Seme in 1931 was anything like accurate, there was room in Seme (and thus in Kowe) for this development at the onset of the 1930s, certainly far more room than there was in Maragoli. Hay's account confirms that it occurred and that it spread in the 1930s particularly among 'labour migrants' who remitted money to the Reserve to make up for the absence of their own labour power.

Now this development is presented by Hay as being labour-saving for the wife 'since a plow team could dig up in a day or two the amount of land that a man and his wife could have hoed for many weeks',[68] but clearly whilst there was a net saving in hoeing, and possibly in agricultural work overall (since hoeing was a labour-intensive activity), this would have been at least partially offset by increases in labour input for sowing, weeding and harvesting. The evidence from Wagner and Peristiany (and indeed from all modern farm economic survey data) confirms that the adoption of ploughing does increase labour demands in these respects. It is difficult therefore to believe that in the 'minority' of households who had adopted ploughing by 1940, agriculture was being marginalised in the general way suggested, and indeed her mention of the wives of some labour migrants hiring labourers with money remitted also confirms this.

My own view is that the contradictions in the evidence and interpretation provided by Hay can be resolved if the households in Kowe between 1930 and 1940 are disaggregated, and indeed, once again some of her evidence suggests, albeit obliquely, how to do this. Disaggregation into their various types would take the following form:
1. Wife at home on the plot. Male migrant in long-term, better-paid wage or salary employment away from the Reserve. Remittances above average, adoption of ploughing, hiring in of labour. Wife as effective farm manager. Probable purchase of land 1930–40.
2. Wife at home on plot, husband in better-paid wage or salaried employment within the Reserve. Plough bought from husband's salary, also hiring of labour but possibly less than in (1) above. Husband as farm manager. Land purchasing 1930–40.
3. Husband and wife in full-time employment on the plot throughout period, probably no plough, and almost certainly no labour hiring. Adoption of more maize, use of hand gristing mill and of better hoes, but much smaller expansion

68. Ibid., p. 230.

of cropped area than (1) and (2) above. Probably no land purchase. Increased labour input on farm by husband. Wife increasingly involved in trading.

4. Husband and wife depart Kowe on long term labour migration—squatting etc. Land purchased by groups (1) and (2) above.

5. Husband departs on long-term labour migration but as unskilled labourer and with frequent change of job. Wife at home on plot, no remittances or only small remittances. No adoption of ploughing, much less land under crops than (1), (2), (3) or (4), and certainly much less land under maize. Restriction of production by wife to minimum subsistence more heavily biassed toward sorghum and cassava. Husband's labour input on plot nil, and wife's decreasing.

6. Husband in short-term labour migration, returns at times of peak period labour demands. Probably no ploughing, limited adoption of maize, but use of hand gristing mill, better hoe etc. Very small expansion of cropped area. Possible tendency of husband to longer and longer spells of migration. Wife increasingly involved in trading.

Hay's evidence, though offering abundant confirmation of the general hierarchy of households involved, is certainly not detailed enough for one to be sure of the precise boundaries and the activities of particular types. Type (6) may have been rather uncommon, since if pre-1930 trends were continued the bulk of short-term migrants would have been unmarried men, in which case married male migrants would have been either of type (4) or type (5). However, with goldfield employment so nearby, some of the married male migrants must have been of type (6) in this period, even if after the goldmines closed (and they went further afield) they became type (5).

By 1940 the bulk of male labour migrants from Kowe were of types (5) and (6), with type (1) as a small but privileged minority. It is also likely that with restrictions on squatting in this period the number of new migrants of type (4) was falling. Even by 1940 the majority of households in Kowe were probably still of type (3), i.e. households where the head had no experience of labour migration. Over time (that is from 1930, and even more markedly from 1945 onwards) this type of household in Kowe may have tended to decline in numbers, becoming of type (5) or (6), while a tiny minority were 'upwardly mobile' and joined 'elite' types (1) and (2). Insofar as the decline of male and female farm labour input (with a household's transition from type (3) to types (5) and (6)) was the quickening trend of events in Kowe in 1930–45, then Hay is right to characterise the period as one in which agriculture became 'marginalised'. But this was certainly not so for households of the elite types (1) and (2), and in the case of type (1), labour migration, far from being an alternative form of accumulation to agriculture was a mode of accumulation in agriculture (as well as in other sectors).

Turning back to South Maragoli for a moment, it is fascinating to speculate about the household structure of that location in 1940 using the schema developed above from Hay's work. It may well have been that since general levels of migration (and thus off-farm earnings and remittance levels) were probably higher in Maragoli than in Kowe by 1940, the proportion of households of type (4) was smaller, the dominance of households of types (1) and (2) over Maragoli's land and surplus product proportionately greater, and the number of agriculturally marginalised households of types (5) and (6) also proportionately greater.

Conclusions

The detailed picture of the labour process in agriculture and of the changes in the process occurring over the decade obtained through the work of Wagner and Hay is frustrating only because in revealing so much their studies also invite further questions and speculations which their data cannot answer. However a number of general points, some positive, some negative, can be made on the basis of these two studies. Firstly, in showing the major differences in crop mix, cultivating practices and indeed in land availability in these two areas, they make clear the inadequacy of data drawn from provincial or even district level surveys when dealing with the process of commercialisation. We may take two important examples to illustrate this point.

Firstly, in Kowe one imponderable factor in the movement toward increased labour migration was the failure of cotton: a failure which I have suggested (though Hay is more ambiguous) was primarily due to the unsuitability of the area and its low returns to labour and land, rather than to price as such, or, initially at least, to labour availability problems. Is it therefore the case that throughout Nyanza at this period labour migration was greatest from locations either in which cotton could not be grown at all or in which land and population densities made the plough cultivation of maize impossible and the returns to cotton minimal? I think that detailed research might show that this was the case. However this hypothesis cannot be generalised to Kikuyuland because of a number of complications, notably the introduction of wattle and the development of the boom market of Nairobi.

Secondly, we have seen that the presence of a goldfield nearby acted as a powerful stimulus to wage labouring for many men who had not previously entered the labour market, and that from there they went on to other jobs. Now gold discoveries were not of course restricted to this area, but occurred throughout western Nyanza Province and at the height of the gold rush (1934–9) employed some 10–15,000 African males in mining and ancillary occupations. Most of these men were recruited from the locations immediately adjacent to the mines, so a number of locations around Kakamega, Kisumu and Kisii must have had similar experiences to Kowe in this period.[69] Although the 14,000 or so men who were employed in goldmining did not constitute a large proportion of the

---

69. See Fearn, op. cit., p. 130 and pp. 137–8.

Province's adult male population, nonetheless in densely populated locations where cotton could not be grown and where commercial production of maize was impossible for all except the most privileged, the gold boom of Nyanza may have left behind one lasting legacy in taking labour migration over a threshold at which for many Nyanza men it became, in Hay's words, 'a way of life'.

Our survey of South Kitosh, Maragoli and Kowe has suggested that in the latter two densely populated locations expansion of production and of the surplus product involved an increased input of female labour in this decade, particularly when the household was restricted to a hoe technology (a feature probably more general in Maragoli than in Kowe by the late thirties, as a result of greater population pressure). But by the 1930s two further factors had begun to cut across the gradually increasing pressure on female labour which we have noted as a general feature of commercialisation since the early twenties. The first of these was the increasing practice of using ploughs and hiring labour in the richer households, and the second is an apparent process of withdrawal from agricultural labour on their own land by women in poorer households. The implications of the adoption of the plough for the overall input of women's labour into agriculture are unclear, but it may be the case that in the modernising christian households of Kowe and of other locations of central Kavirondo and of southern North Kavirondo where this was occurring, the wife withdrew from field labour into a farm management role, whilst extra labour input required by the plough was provided by the women of poorer households. The latter, without the assistance of male labour power, and lacking remittances, or remittances on a scale to make 'working with money' possible, kept the cropped land on their own plots static or expanded it only slowly, and concentrated on subsistence rather than surplus production. Cash for school fees and other purposes was thus obtained from occasional wage labour on the land of others and from meagre remittances.

However in these densely populated locations of central Nyanza Province it is likely that even by 1940 the majority of households still had the male head resident on the plot, and where this was the case it appears that the male share of labour input, at least in the production of maize and of cotton, was increasing. It would not by 1940 have been anything like equal to that of women.

In more lightly populated areas like South Kitosh, commercialisation had only got under way in the late thirties, and involved a form of monocrop maize production using the plough and relying entirely on expansion of the cultivated area to increase output. It appears that the pattern in this area was very similar to that observed in the case of the Kipsigis maize producers of Kericho, with commercialisation involving a major expansion of male labour input and total male control over the disposal and use of the surplus product in either its natural or its monetised form. Whether male control was any greater in this sort of area, where female labour input into the surplus product may also have been less than in the 'hoe' areas, it is difficult to say. It is possible that male control over all household land resources meant that there was little difference in the two types of area in the end.

The marked differences between those three locations should serve as a warning of the dangers of generalisation from small areas to the regional level. The variations in natural conditions (and thus the population density and the crop mix), and in the spread and availability of education (and thus in the income of the labour migrants from area to area and within areas) all make for a complexity of local conditions, and an even greater complexity of the provincial picture. I have attempted to do no more than suggest some crucial parameters and to offer some hypotheses for further empirical research.

3. Developments in Other Areas of Kenya 1930–1940

Machakos and Kipsigis

Maize production in Machakos and in the Kipsigis Reserve expanded considerably over this decade, and in fact the trend toward land-extensive maize monocropping using the plough, having got under way in the late 1920s, spread markedly over this decade. Unfortunately there is no readily available statistical material on the expansion of the cropped area in these districts, nor is there any monograph material dating from this period which can throw light on changes in the labour process and its effects on the political economy of the household. As noted, Peristiany's work in Kipsigis probably concerns the situation in the late twenties or early thirties.

In the absence of such material one must rely on impressionistic evidence, which is rather more abundant for both districts. The number of ploughs in use in Machakos district rose from less than 20 in 1926 to over 600 in 1934, and as elsewhere these ploughs were both used by their owners and hired to others. By 1938, 3,750 tons of maize was being exported from the Machakos district by Indian traders alone, together with 652 tons of beans and peas,[70] whilst in the Kipsigis district of South Lumbwa as early as 1934 the District Commissioner was expressing concern that

> A situation is arising in this district which may well prove a matter for anxiety in a year or two. A number of the more advanced Kipsigis are plough-owners and as the tribe has no system of land tenure other than as a community, these plough-owners tend to cultivate very large areas indeed, thus reducing the available amount of grazing. If at any time the squatters are removed from the Sotik farms, and have to return with their cattle to the Reserve the overstocking question may arise here.[71]

'The overstocking question' had arisen in Machakos in a very acute form by

70. Forbes Munro, op. cit., p. 169 and Appendix C, p. 254.
71. Quoted in *NAD* 1934, p. 105.

Table IV:14. Population densities in
Machakos district 1931 and 1939[76]
(per square mile)

Location	1931	1939
Iveti	252	302
Kangundu	249	314
Matungulu	199	231
Kiteta	192	203
Mbooni	185	208

1938, and it is clear that a major factor bringing pressure on grazing in the district by the end of the decade was the expansion of the cultivated area. Forbes Munro notes the leading role taken in this process by 'younger Kamba improvers' who had taken up plough cultivation. He suggests that communal grazing (*weu*) had largely disappeared from Iveti location by 1930, and from all the northern areas of Machakos by 1939.[72]

The net result of all this was that the colonial administration came to believe that the remaining communal grazing land in Machakos was seriously overgrazed, and that this had produced a soil erosion problem by the late 1930s of crisis proportions.[73] This conviction produced, among other things, an attempt at compulsory destocking in 1938, an attempt which met with such fierce resistance that it had to be abandoned.[74] Nonetheless the expansion of the cropped area in the north and west of Machakos district must have been considerable and rapid over the 1930s.

How far the geographical and household division between plough commercialisation and hoe commercialisation noted for both Central Province and North Kavirondo also applied to Machakos is not clear. The Land Commission *Report* had estimated that in 1931 the population density in the district as a whole was 110 per square mile, and that out of a total of 1,386,240 cultivable acres a mere 15 per cent (210,000 acres) was cultivated, with this latter figure encompassing 70,000 acres of fallow land.[75] In 1931 and 1939 the most densely-populated locations of the district were as in table IV:14. Comparing these figures with those for South Maragoli and Seme it appears that even the most densely populated locations of Machakos (Iveti and Kangundu) were not as crowded in 1939 as Maragoli had been a decade earlier, whilst Mbooni, Kiteta and Matungulu were probably about as densely populated as Seme both in 1931

72. Forbes Munro, op. cit., pp. 200–1.
73. Ibid., pp. 207–8.
74. Ibid., pp. 208–23 and pp. 224–46. See also Tignor, op. cit., pp. 310–54.
75. *KLC-R*, pp. 204–5.
76. Calculated from statistics in *KLC E & M II*, p. 1318 and Forbes Munro, op. cit., Appendix F, p. 257.

and 1939. Iveti and Kangundu however both appear to have been more densely populated than Seme in 1931 and 1939.

Were we to extrapolate Nyanza findings then we might expect plough cultivation to have declined in Iveti over the decade and to have become more prevalent in Matungulu by the end of the decade. We might also expect it to have spread through Kiteta and Mbooni, for example, in the 1940s (when according to Newman plough cultivation spread outside Iveti and Matungulu). We should also expect of course that the extent of ploughing and thus of the cropped area and surplus product was markedly uneven from household to household, and indeed this is clearly implied in Newman's work, though he does not examine any one location in detail, as does Hay.[77]

Some limited support for this speculation is forthcoming from material in both Munro and Newman concerning the 'market gardening' of vegetables in southern Iveti (for the Machakos market) spreading through the whole location and into Kangundu and Matungulu in the 1920s and 1930s as the Nairobi market was made more accessible through improved transport facilities. In addition, on the steeper hill areas of Kilungu and Mbooni wattle growing commenced with a government campaign in October 1936.[78]

In the light of what we know about Kikuyuland and Nyanza, two interesting speculations open up. Firstly were the 'market gardening' households of Iveti or Kangundu and Matungulu also plough cultivators of maize or wheat, or were they, as one might suspect, households without the land to make the former possible, going in for a hoe form of commercialisation with higher value crops such as onions, potatoes, strawberries and oranges? Secondly, were the wattle growers, as appears from Newman's account, those households living in high and steep locations where the plough was difficult to use and the rainfall levels too high for successful maize growing?[79] If so, then it is clear that the plough/ hoe distinctions in the pattern of commercialisation noted for Kikuyuland and Nyanza would indeed be observable here too, both from location to location and between households within locations. Looking at the matter on a district level, however, it is likely that a far higher proportion of Machakos households were using a plough in 1940 than for example in Kiambu or Nyeri.

As far as the relationship between commercialisation and the labour supply is concerned, it is impossible to say whether in Machakos the same sort of stratification of households existed as in Kowe since no research of this in detail has been done. There are a number of suggestive pieces of evidence however. Firstly it is clear that in Machakos, just as in Kowe, the first plough owners and hirers were from the small nucleus of 'mission' families who had attended mission schools. Also, as in Kowe, some of these plough owners had been

---

77. Newman, op. cit., pp. 8–11.
78. Ibid., pp. 16–17 and Forbes Munro, op. cit., pp. 170–2.
79. Newman, op. cit., p. 16.

engaged in the cattle trade before moving into commercial farming.[80] Secondly we know that the level of labour migration, though significantly lower than in the central locations of Nyanza—it had only reached 16 per cent of adult males in 1937—does seem to have increased markedly from the late twenties and to have been highest in those locations where the commercialisation of agriculture was most advanced. Munro, much like Hay, interprets this as a 'Kamba' response to the acute limitations placed on commercialisation by the growing shortage of land for crop expansion and declining maize yields due to mono-cropping. He also suggests, no doubt rightly, that restriction of commercialisation to maize production in most of the district encouraged the turn to wage labour because of its relatively low returns per acre and per unit of labour time.[81]

But once again it seems that such an interpretation is too generalised and must be disaggregated, both into different types of labour migration (to highly paid or skilled employment or to unskilled employment) and with reference to the uses to which wage incomes were put. If, as in Kowe, a minority of male household heads used better-paid wage employment to expand investments in land and in cultivation, whilst a much larger and expanding minority turned to labour migration because the expansion of the cropped area and production of the agricultural surplus product was being dominated by elite households, then one would expect this larger minority to have used much lower wage incomes for investments outside of agriculture (especially for the education of children), while unsupported female labour power working a small cropped area was marginalised in the agricultural process, as in Kowe. There is no doubt that in Machakos, as in Nyanza or indeed in Kikuyuland, the majority of migrants were unskilled workers going to occupations paying low wages. But the statistical dominance of this group should not be allowed to mask the structural importance of the elite labour migrants and their households both in the process of commercialisation, and indeed in inducing 'poor' labour migration.

In Machakos in 1940 however, just as in Kowe, 'the majority of Kamba were still members of what may be described as a middle-level peasantry owning their land from which they obtained subsistence and a little surplus for sale',[82] i.e. the majority of households were of the type (4) identified for Kowe, households in which the male head was resident on the plot and where his labour input into cultivation had increased in support of, but not in equality with, that of his wife.

Nandi District 1930–40: More Maize Monocropping
In 1931 the Land Commission reported that the Nandi practised agriculture 'on a small scale' but the cropped area was both in absolute and relative terms so small that not even an estimate of it was available to the Commission. Thus

80. Ibid., pp. 4–8.
81. Forbes Munro, op. cit., pp. 208–9. See also chapter IX below (pp. 250–51).
82. Forbes Munro, op. cit., p. 204.

they treated the entire Nandi people (in the Reserve) as though inhabiting un-
interrupted natural grazing land.

It will be noted that the density of population in the Nandi Reserve at the
beginning of the 1930s—sixty-two per square mile—was almost identical to
that in North and South Kitosh at the same time, and indeed the Commission
categorised it in the same way—'Stock country, large open grazing areas, and
thinly scattered population'.[83]

Developments in Nandi district seem moreover to have followed a very similar
path to those in Kitosh in this decade, though in relying on district reports we are
once again working with impressionistic data. In 1930 it was reported that the
Nandi Local Native Council's 'scheme' for ploughs and water mills had to date
met with little success. In the former case the Council was hiring ploughs to any
cultivator who could put together a team of oxen, but in that year only four had
been taken up. In the latter case the Local Native Council was providing advances toward the construction of water mills but there had been no takers at all,
despite the fact that only five mills were operating in the Reserve at that date.
However, there was one light in the darkness; E. W. arap Boit, 'a sub-headman
in Location 7', was reported to have put 'large areas' under cultivation, and
had received a grant from the Local Native Council for the purchase of a
harrow.[84]

By 1931 six ploughs had been 'issued' by the Local Native Council, and it was
noted that 'Our native partnership near Kapiyet put a considerable area under
cultivation, but suffered considerably from locust. Arap Boit of Location 7 and
Sam of Location 8 are two others who are annually extending their acreages
under the plough.'

By 1932 a further acceleration of the process had been noticed. A 'record area'
was now under maize, twenty-five ploughs were operating under the Local
Native Council's scheme, 'one man returned from working on a farm and
brought his own plough with him', and 'One enterprising member of the Talisi
clan erected a water wheel and a power mill during the year', which apparently
was the first water mill in the Reserve in African hands.[85]

By 1934 the District Officer was able to enthuse that 'For the first time known,
the Nandi had a real surplus of maize and sold an appreciable quantity.' There
was no doubt that agriculture was 'slowly but steadily extending', and that the
Shs. 1,000 spent annually by the Local Native Council on its plough scheme
was a major factor in this. The trade figures confirmed this, showing that 181
tons of maize had been exported from the district, as against thirty-eight tons
in 1933 and a mere fifteen bags in 1932. By 1935 the figure had increased to 202
tons and the District Officer was reporting that 'There are some Nandi who

83. *KLC-R*, pp. 271–3. The density in Kitosh in the same year was 61.4 per square mile.
84. NaAR 1930, p. 37.
85. NaAR 1931, p. 26; and 1932, p. 34.

grow maize on a fairly extensive scale, their farms running up to forty acres or so.' There were fifty-one ploughs in operation.[86]

At this point a hitch was encountered. The average price for a bag of maize had apparently been Shs. 6 in Nandi in 1934, but at the end of 1935 the price fell sharply, and the District Officer noted that Nandi maize was also facing 'stiff competition' from maize grown by Kikuyu squatters on nearby settler farms. In addition in 1936 the price of livestock exported from the Reserve turned up sharply, and heavy rain ruined a great deal of the maize crop. As a result the amount of maize exported from the Reserve by Indian traders fell to twenty-one tons. This was only a small proportion of the maize actually exported in that year, but production did drop sharply.[87]

From this point the district reports are of little help in charting the progress of maize production, because a very great deal of the maize produced, particularly in Ndalet in the north of the district, was sold through channels for which district statistics were not available. Thus in 1937, despite a reportedly excellent year for crops, a mere seventy-five bags are listed as having been exported, while the two succeeding seasons, both of which seem to have had good weather, produced respectively a mere twenty-one tons and thirteen tons of maize formally exported.[88]

However, even allowing for the increasing unreliability of the trade statistics over the period, it seems likely that if in later years Nandi production had continued to increase dramatically this would have registered to some degree in the figures for formal exports. It is clear then that by the outbreak of war the marked progress which had been registered in Nandi maize production in the mid-thirties had not been sustained, and as we shall see it took the high and guaranteed prices of the wartime Maize and Produce Board, plus a markedly increased administrative effort, to encourage further expansion.

In the light of previous analyses of Kipsigis and Kitosh it is interesting to speculate why this was. A number of obvious factors suggest themselves including climatic and soil conditions and the low prices of maize, but it seems that these can be discounted. Climatic conditions appear to have been no bar to expansion in later years, and though they were clearly not optimum (Nandi was in general too wet for maize), it is clear that they were not markedly different from Kitosh or Kipsigis. Secondly, prices seem to have been very little better or worse in Nandi than in the other two areas, and as already indicated the whole point of extensive maize growing was to compensate for low unit prices with large volume—the great advantage of producing maize by plough rather than by hoe.

The declining curve of Nandi maize production over the latter part of the decade must have been due to other factors, and three suggest themselves as pos-

---

86. NaAR 1934, pp. 41, 43 and 52; and 1935, p. 46.
87. NaAR 1935, p. 46; and 1936, pp. 6, 23, 28 and 29.
88. NaAR 1937, p. 27.

sibilities. In the first place production appeared to expand most rapidly in the early thirties when grain prices were lower but grain/stock barter terms were very favourable. The initial motivation of at least some cultivators may therefore have been the increase of livestock holdings through highly advantageous barter trading with stock. It certainly seems significant that after stock prices rose in 1936 and production fell due to climatic factors, production then did not recover even in subsequent good seasons.

Secondly, in comparison with Kipsigis, Nandi producers lacked a buoyant and expanding local market for maize and maize flour, on the lines of the huge Kericho tea estates. Both the local Nandi farms and the farms of Uasin Gishu and Eldoret seem to have become increasingly self-sufficient in maize and maize flour for their non-resident workers, largely through the efforts of Kikuyu squatters. Nandi's other market, North Kavirondo (the District Officer noted that 'thirty per cent' of Nandi maize had been purchased by *dukas* (shops) on the North Kavirondo border in 1933) was also increasing its own production over this decade and may thus have been a declining outlet.[89]

Thirdly (and here we are really speculating) it is clear that in comparison with Kipsigis, Machakos or even Kitosh, the Nandi Reserve was an area of massive labour out-migration during nearly all of this decade. In 1931 the District Officer noted that 90 per cent of all adult males were at work outside the Reserve in November of that year, and the average for the whole year had been 69 per cent. In 1935 the average figure had increased to 73 per cent with 40 per cent of all adult Nandi males being squatters on the farms of Uasin Gishu, and in 1937 the District Officer was still asserting that the Nandi statistics for the proportion of adult males out at work were the highest for any area in the entire colony.[90]

Now it is equally clear that these percentages were exaggerated due to the sort of persistent underestimation of the population which we have already noted elsewhere, but nonetheless, even if we assume an exaggeration of 20 per cent, it is clear that a very considerable proportion of all adult male labour power was absent from the Nandi Reserve for long periods of the agricultural season. In this situation the extra sowing, weeding and harvesting implied by extensive plough cultivation would have fallen almost entirely on the female labour force, and it may be that the refusal or inability of wives and adult daughters to shoulder this extra burden of labour placed a marked constraint on the extension of the cultivated area in this period. The major alternative to greater female labour input, 'beer work', i.e. the hiring of the male and female labour power of neighbouring households, would have been constrained by this same factor. It certainly seems significant that Nandi maize production again resumed its exponential growth in a period—1941–5—when a great deal of Nandi

89. NaAR 1933, p. 35; and 1935, p. 46. See also G. W. B. Huntingford, *Nandi Work and Culture* (HMSO, 1950), pp. 61–3.
90. NaAR 1931, p. 10; 1935, pp. 29–30; and 1937, p. 17.

squatter labour was being compulsorily returned to the Reserve from the Uasin Gishu farms.[91]

The combination of high wartime prices plus the new availability of Nandi male labour power together produced the sort of explosive expansion of the cropped area and of marketed production in Nandi in the forties which had occurred in Kipsigis in the late twenties and early thirties. The really massive expansion of extensive maize cultivation in Kitosh and Elgon Nyanza in general also required the stimulus of high wartime and post-war prices, but how far labour out-migration had acted as a constraint in Kitosh before this it is difficult to say. It is unlikely that it was a major factor in that case, since the level of out-migration was clearly so much lower.

4. The Administrative Programme for the Expansion of Agricultural Production in Kenya 1930–1940: Structure and Effects

Although there has been some study of the origins and motivations of the increased interest and support shown by the colonial state to African agriculture in Kenya in the 1930s,[92] to date we are without any systematic study of the precise structure of the programme or, more importantly, its effects.

From a survey of annual district reports and Department of Agriculture memoranda and reports and other sources in the period, it seems that structurally the programme was composed of the following elements:

1. An increase in the number and size of Local Native Council seed farms and demonstration plots on which crops deemed suitable for a particular area (under the production zones policy) were tested and propagated among the local African population.

2. The posting of a European Agricultural Officer to every district of major African production and an increase in the number of staff working under him on extension and instructional work. Local Native Councils seem to have borne the major part of the cost of this latter increase in the number of 'native instructors'.

3. The propagation of famine-resisting crops in areas which had been particularly plagued by drought and locusts (this was a primary preoccupation in the years 1930–4).

4. The issuing of higher-yielding varieties of African food crops, which had been developed in Department of Agriculture experimental horticultural centres—notably the Scott Agricultural Laboratories at Kabete in Kiambu, and the centres at Bukura in North Kavirondo district and at Kibarani in the

---

91. See below, chapter V, pp. 146–8.
92. Talbott, op. cit.

Coast Province. The varieties developed at these centres were then tested further for suitability for more local conditions at Local Native Council seed farms and then issued to cultivators either directly from the farm, or through agricultural instructors, chiefs and headmen, or even missionaries.

Among important crop innovations the development of the new white maize variety (*Zea mays*) was central. It had a much higher yield per unit of land than any of the indigenous varieties of 'yellow' maize, or earlier forms of white maize like 'Hickory King'. In addition, cross-breeding produced a variety of cassava with a higher protein value and a greater resistance to drought, and higher-yielding varieties of sorghum, millet and beans.

5. A greatly expanded campaign for cotton cultivation in all districts of Nyanza Province, in the drier low-lying areas of Fort Hall, Embu and Meru, in Kitui district and in all the districts of the Coast Province. In the Coast Province, Kitui and in Nyanza, cotton was encouraged in areas which had regularly known famine, and the campaign combined the planting of cotton with cassava, and (in the Coast Province) with cashew nuts.[93] By the end of the decade very small beginning had been made with the planting of other 'pure' cash crops by African farmers, notably tobacco (Northern and Central Kavirondo, Embu, Kitui and Fort Hall) and robusta and arabica coffee (Southern and Northern Kavirondo, Embu and Meru).

6. From 1935 onwards a strong campaign to encourage wattle production particularly in Central Province, but also in north-western Machakos, Kisii and North Kavirondo. In addition, from the beginning of the decade increased quantities of gum tree seedlings were issued to cultivators in the highland locations of Central Province, Machakos, Kisii and North Kavirondo. They seem to have been very popular in all these areas. Like wattle they provided a quick-growing source of construction timber and firewood at a time when the decline of natural forests and colonial forestry regulations had made them difficult and expensive to obtain. Other tree seedlings issued included fruit trees (especially mangoes and pawpaws) eucalyptus and *cassia florida*.

7. The encouragement of the growing of high-value fruit and vegetable crops. These required a much more intensive form of cultivation than grain crops but realised high prices per unit of weight and high returns per unit of land. This was particularly 'pushed' in agriculturally rich areas bordering or having access to an urban market such as southern Kiambu, and north-western Machakos (for Nairobi), but also occurred in Teita (for the Mombasa market) and in locations around Kisumu, Kakamega, and Kisii. In addition to potatoes, other crops

---

93. 'The cashew nuts were designed to supplement cotton by providing a long term investment, whereas the fiber crop (cotton) could bring an annual return to farmers. Cashew nuts thrived on the light sandy soils of the Coast, and could be interplanted with cotton. Cashew nuts formed an important contribution to Coastal farming by acting as a windbreak and reducing losses due to wind erosion and monsoon rains', Talbott, op. cit., p. 11.

mentioned in reports under this heading include cabbages, onions, tomatoes, ginger, oranges, lemons and cauliflowers.

8. The systematic encouragement of the spread of improved instruments of production, notably the 'European' hoe (or *jembe*), in place of wooden-bladed hoes or earlier forms of indigenous iron-bladed hoes, and of the ox plough in areas considered to be suitable.

9. The encouragement of improved planting practices (notably 'proper' spacing of crops), earlier planting and sowing, crop rotation, more regular and thorough weeding, and growing some crops (notably maize and beans) in single rather than mixed stands.

10. A series of measures towards the end of the decade designed primarily to reduce or prevent soil erosion. These included encouraging the increased use of organic manure and of compost heaps, stone terracing and the planting of trees on steep slopes and wash stops on the tops of hills, as well as contour plough- ing and ditching on slopes. This policy culminated in a programme to encourage 'mixed farming' among the most 'advanced' cultivators in both Central Province and Nyanza Province at the end of the decade. The aim of these mixed farming schemes (which were designed at Kabete and Bukura) was simultaneously (a) to increase yields and prevent soil erosion by the use of organic manure, (b) to improve diet and the marketed surplus by adding the production of meat and dairy products to a wider variety of food crops, and (c) to ensure an ecologically balanced use of the land on intensively cultivated smallholdings.

All sorts of problems arise in any attempt to assess the efficacy of this pro- gramme, of which the three most serious are the total lack of agro-economic surveys in this period from which one could assess the impact on yields and farm incomes, the difficulty of knowing when adoptions of new crops and practices were due to the programme and when they would have occurred 'spontaneous- ly' in any case, and the highly varied pattern of implementation of the pro- gramme from district to district.

Even without detailed research on the matter a number of broad conclusions seem possible. Firstly, it seems that all the tree planting campaigns were very successful, and that whilst the growth of the wattle 'industry' in Central Province had made limited progress before 1935, the boom in the area under the crop after that date owed everything to the conjunction of the cultivators' wish to grow the crop and a campaign which made the seedlings far more easily avail- able. The popularity of all the tree seedling issues seems to have been due, as al- ready noted, to the many use values of timber as well as to its exchange value, and the desire of cultivators to have wood sources on their land if they could not have free access to the forests of the colony.

Secondly, administrative pressure may have increased the rate of adoption of the 'European' *jembe* so that by 1940 it was probably being used by the majority of cultivators at least in Central Province, Nyanza and Machakos. This prob- ably did not amount to much more than the acceleration of a process which would have occurred in any case. For administrative action does not appear to have consisted of much more than encouraging importers to carry larger stocks of the *jembe* (and also of the *panga* or machêtê-like knife, used for a variety of farm work), and encouraging traders to sell them. In the case of ox ploughs however the matter is rather different, since in Nandi, and in nearly all districts, Local Native Councils played a vital role in encouraging the early use of ploughs, particularly in the extensive maize-growing areas of Kipsigis, Machakos, Elgon Nyanza and Nandi. They were not the sole source of plough adoption in any of these areas, but in Nandi at least the Local Native Council was clearly the most important source; and by making ploughs available in the early years to any cultivator who could provide an ox team, the Local Native Council subsidised an early pattern of plough use which later turned into individual plough purchase by particular household heads. Ironically the Agricultural Department came somewhat to regret its own success in this area in the late thirties when worries about soil erosion began to mount, and at that time some Local Native Councils were bulldozed by District Officers into passing local ordinances outlawing or restricting the use of ploughs on hill land.

Thirdly (and lastly in the case of fairly unambiguous 'successes') it seems that measures to encourage vegetable growing for local markets (whether urban centres or Nyanza goldmines) were nearly always successful when they identified cultivators with the right quality of land and when such cultivators had or could be provided with a market and transport. And indeed measures in this area seem often to have done no more than add to the variety or quality of fruit or vegetables which strategically situated market gardeners were already growing.

In short, the major part of the programme to encourage African agriculture during the 1930s was fairly successful and did much to increase the productivity of cultivators' labour time. This was done mainly by improvements in the objects of labour (new and improved varieties of crops, and crops more suited to local conditions) rather than in the instruments of labour, since there was no qualitative advance in the latter in this period but simply a quantitative expansion of the improvements introduced in the previous decade. Nonetheless this spread in itself must have contributed to the increase in aggregate output and to the raising of the productivity of labour. Because of the absence of farm data, it is almost impossible to say how great was the increase in productivity in the decade. Wagner quotes an 'estimate' that in North Kavirondo in 1937–8, as a result solely of the issue of improved seed, the yield per acre had increased by 40 per cent for maize, sesame and beans, and by about 30 per cent for sorghum and eleusine.[94] This is impressive if it is at all accurate, but it must be remembered that it represented improvement from an abysmally low base. In 1931 the Agricultural Officer for North Kavirondo had submitted estimates to the Kenya Land Commission that the highest maize yields being obtained in the district

94. Wagner, op. cit., Vol. II, p. 35.

amounted to a little over half a ton per acre and the lowest to less than a third of a ton. The yield for beans was put at a quarter of a ton, while that for sesame was a mere 400 pounds per acre.[95] Fazan was offering yield estimates of a very similar sort for Central Province at that date.

Moreover it is highly unlikely that over the colony as a whole anything like Wagner's annual rate of improvement was maintained over the decade. Apart from weather and locusts (which we have suggested were the prime determinants of changes in supply and thus in prices over the decade) there were other factors working against the improvements in the objects and instruments of labour in this period. Two in particular stand out. Firstly there was the tendency towards declining yields of maize in some areas due to monocropping or double-cropping combined with inadequate rotation and manuring, and secondly there was the persistently small price advantage accruing to cultivators for quality improvements. This was markedly the case for the low-value food crops like maize and beans. But even for cotton (where the price for A quality lint was consistently double the price of B quality) it is probable that much more than double the labour input was required to increase the quality from B to A.

Both these factors highlight by implication the areas where the Administration's 'new' policy of the 1930s was a failure. These were in making any substantial impact before 1940 on traditional planting, weeding and manuring practices; and in improving the marketing arrangements for African-grown crops; and in particular in 'rewarding' increased quality of production through the price mechanism.

Although the number of agricultural extension personnel working in the African reserves was markedly increased in absolute terms over the decade, they were still very thinly scattered. For example the number of agricultural field staff employed by the Department of Agriculture in North Kavirondo increased from twelve in 1933 to sixty-seven in 1937,[96] but the latter figure still only amounts to one instructor for every 5,291 persons (if we use the almost certainly underestimated official district population figures for 1937). Each of them was responsible for very nearly thirty-nine square miles of the district and would be fortunate if in 1937 they had even a bicycle to get round it.

Even if the extension service had been greatly expanded, it is unlikely that its work would have had very much effect at a time when Africans were still mainly restricted to the growing of low-value food crops, and when women, who we have suggested were still providing the bulk of farm labour input in 1940, had come under increasing pressure over the decade simply through expansion of the cultivated area. Women would have had to increase their labour input into cultivation still further and to have been assisted by men to a much greater

95. *KLC E & M* III, p. 2257.
96. Wagner, op. cit., Vol. II, p. 30. The 'Memorandum on Native Agricultural Development', op. cit., p. 3, outlines the general progress in staffing between 1923 and 1937.

extent if 'improved' cultivating practices were to be adopted. The monetary return from such an increased input would have had to have been considerable, and women would have had to have had a greater say in the use and disposal of the increased surplus product so produced.

It will be seen in chapter VI that the question of women's control over an increased surplus product was a non-issue, since the colonial administration was never able to deliver the necessary monetary return. This was because of the general failure of its marketing strategy in African producing areas.

5. Conclusions

Despite the depression and the years of locusts and drought, the decade 1930–40 saw a very considerable expansion of the cropped area in Kikuyuland, Nyanza, Machakos, Kipsigis, Nandi and in the Coast Province. This expansion was partly a continuation of earlier trends. But it was also profoundly affected by the intervention of the colonial administration into the commercialisation of agriculture. This intervention took the form of raising the productivity of labour in cultivation by ensuring the spread of improved instruments of labour, and, probably more importantly in this period, by improving the objects of labour by the systematic addition of scientific (biological and horticultural) labour power. In addition some new crops were introduced to Africans on a very small scale (tobacco and coffee) and others which had taken up a much smaller proportion of the colony's cropped area (cotton and wattle) were immensely expanded.

Although some increase in the productivity of agricultural labour was thereby accomplished (shown in particular in increased yields of food crops) these were gains from a very low base, and output increases continued to come overwhelmingly from the expansion of the cropped area, rather than from rising output per unit of land or labour time. The major part of the labour time invested in agriculture continued to be provided by women who continued to increase the proportion of their total labour time invested in cultivation. The 'pressure' on women's labour now came to assume a stratification dimension, with the situation varying markedly between types of household. In this variation the degree and type of male labour migration away from the plot was a crucial variable. It is probable that both at the top and bottom of the hierarchy of households which was emerging in commercialising areas a minority of wives were stabilising or cutting their investment of labour time on their own plots, though for very different reasons.

There is one more theoretical point of note concerning developments in these years. The continued expansion of the cropped area through the depression, and the very minimal or possibly non-existent relationship between the movement of food crop prices in the Reserves and the movement of world prices are both indicative of the very limited extent to which African agricultural production in Kenya had been penetrated by international capital. For had this occurred to any substantial extent, the predominance of localised supply conditions (particularly climate, rainfall and pests), and of localised exchange conditions (particularly the barter terms between crops and livestock) in the determination of price levels and production decisions would not have been nearly so marked. Indeed, one of the effects of the capitalisation of production is to minimise the effect of such local variations on output to the maximum possible extent. In the case of non-agricultural commodities the tendency is for price and profit levels to attain a certain uniformity across more and more sectors of production as they are penetrated by capitalism.

Such a total penetration and homogeneity in the conditions of production and of price levels has always been much more difficult in agriculture because of the continued uncontrollability of the weather, but the massive variations in price and profit levels from one area to another characteristic of Kenyan agriculture at this time indicate that the Colony was at the beginning of the continuum of capitalist penetration rather than at the end.

This issue is examined in rather more theoretical detail later, but at this point it should be noted that despite this general characterisation African agriculture in Kenya did move along the continuum in two respects in the decade 1930–40. In the first place cultivators became increasingly dependent on instruments of production which had to be imported and bought with money and could not be made locally, and they also became the focus for the first time of a plant technology which was imported and not indigenous.

Secondly, as we shall see in chapter VI, with the near universalisation of exchange transactions in money, African agriculture in Kenya had reached the stage which is the prerequisite for the expansion of commodity production. For without a universal equivalent, a means of exchange which can operate in all types of transactions and which is indifferent to the various types of products or use values being exchanged, differentiation of the number of products produced for exchange and a large increase in the number of such exchanges is impossible. It may be indeed that the emergence of money exchange in local markets and the increase in the number of women involved in handicraft production (see chapter VI) were related developments. Paradoxically, as we shall also see, it was the massive influx of livestock into Central Province and Nyanza (as a result of the turn of barter terms in favour of the agriculturalists in 1930–4), which guaranteed the universalisation of modern money in exchange transactions. For as the stock so acquired overflowed the ever more limited grazing available to them, and as for a variety of reasons their use value to cultivators narrowed in range, so the limitations of livestock 'money' became apparent. The livestock boom of the early 1930s was the last of its kind, and from then on modern money was king, at least as a means of exchange of commodities.

Chapter V

War and Aftermath
1940–1952

The outbreak of war was a great boon to African agricultural producers in Kenya. The presence of troops from South Africa, India and Britain expanded the domestic market for foodstuffs, whilst the colonial government's brief in the war effort was to expand food exports, particularly for the provisioning of troops in the Middle East campaign. This stress on production led to the rapid abandonment by the Administration of its concern with soil erosion, which had been coming increasingly to the fore in the late thirties. Africans, like settlers, were encouraged to put every available acre under crops.[1]

Unfortunately, while all district reports speak in general terms of the wartime 'boom', statistics of production vary from district to district depending, as always, on the interests of officers and partly too on the situation in the district. The war quickly revealed, more sharply than at any previous time, the difference between districts like Kiambu, Fort Hall and Nyeri on the one hand, and those like North Kavirondo or Kericho on the other. In the former, the effect of market forces was strong enough to produce rapid expansion of output and sales, for being within striking distance of Nairobi these districts (above all Kiambu) were the first to experience the increased demand for all types of foodstuffs deriving primarily from the military presence. Their response was immediate.

In the case of districts like Kericho or North Kavirondo, the problem was a slightly different one. As we have already seen, these districts depended almost entirely on the export of maize cultivated by hoe or plough. As a low-value and high-weight crop, maize suffered from high transport costs, increased by the bad state of many roads. Thus the spread of production away from railheads or from the immediate market (e.g. the tea estates in Kericho) was impeded by the lower producer prices which rapidly escalating transport costs tended to involve. We have already seen that even in the late thirties the bulk of North Kavirondo maize was still being produced in the densely populated southern locations with a hoe technology, despite the availability of abundant land in the north-west of the district suitable for plough monocropping, and this transport factor had played a part in inhibiting expansion in North and South Kitosh.

1. *NAD* 1939–45, p. 37.

108

If this sort of blockage was to be overcome, and maize production maximised in all suitable areas (which included not only North and South Kitosh, but other areas of Kericho further from the tea estates, and districts like Nandi), then it was important to give these more remote producers the full benefit of high wartime prices.

The creation in May 1942 of the Maize and Produce Control was meant to solve this problem, though, as with so many interventions by the Administration into agricultural marketing it owed more to settler pressures than to any concern with African maize production. It introduced what the settler mixed farmers had always wanted—a guaranteed minimum price.

Nominally this price was set at the same level (initially Shs. 8/50 per 200 pound bag) for both European and African producers, but in practice differential pricing operated, since from the African producer's price it was proposed to deduct the cost of the provision of bags, transport charges, a traders' commission, and a 'cess' (or tax) on each bag, to be paid into an Agricultural Betterment Fund (the latter to be used for the improvement of 'native' farming). Together these deductions brought the first season's price to the African producer down to Shs. 4/90. These deductions were not made from the European price, on the grounds that the settler farmer provided his own bags, transport, etc.[2] A 'transport pool', i.e. an equalising of transport costs between all producers (whether near to or remote from markets and buying posts) went along with the guaranteed price as a way of solving the distance problem already noted.

Now the Maize and Produce Control faced the same problem with maize marketing (and indeed with other crops as they were declared 'controlled' for various reasons during the war) as does any form of statutory state intervention in agricultural markets. This was on the one hand to set prices which would satisfy both producers and consumers (which turned out to be an impossible task), and on the other to stop massive leakages of produce out of control and into the black market in response to free market prices. The general impression left by the sparse literature on the subject, and by the reports, is that the latter problem in particular was more severe in the immediate hinterland of Nairobi than it was elsewhere, because Nairobi free market prices were almost invariably higher than those set by the Control. Most officers felt that the 'transport pool' idea in particular had been a trump card in the more remote districts like North Kavirondo, and that by offering a single price to all producers irrespective of distance from the Maize and Produce Control buying post, the Control had come up with an incentive which kept the bulk of produce off the black market. In Central Province, where distances to Nairobi were shorter, the roads better, and the black market price differentials considerable, even allowing for transport costs, most reports tended to treat the notion of controlled

2. See *Food Shortage Commission*, op. cit., pp. 11 and 48.

prices somewhat wryly and to make it clear that far more produce found its way on to the black market than ever passed through control. The most extreme case of this type was Kiambu, as one might expect, which is why officers rarely even attempted estimates of produce marketed out of that district during the war.[3]

How far this distinction between 'controlled' Nyanza Province and effectively 'uncontrolled' Central Province was a real one is difficult to say. There is some evidence from North Kavirondo, for example, that when bad harvests in local areas provided high prices for unaffected or less affected producers in adjacent areas, those opportunities were invariably taken and the leakage from the Control even in that district would be considerable.[4] On the other hand, the districts in Kenya which experienced food shortages during the war—notably Masailand, Machakos and Kitui (at intervals from 1939 and almost continuously from 1943–5)[5]—were all remote from Nyanza, and thus the transport factor would have intervened. The Control monopolised the railway, and lorry transport costs over the 200 or so miles involved would have been enormous. It could well be therefore that district and provincial officers were correct in believing that in Nyanza at least the leakage from the Control was marginal.

In Central Province the proximity of Machakos and Kitui was just one more factor making the 'official' figures for marketed production and price trends exceedingly questionable.[6] We will now turn to an analysis of those figures and their limitations in delineating production trends in Kikuyuland in these years.

1. Kikuyuland

Such figures as are available for marketed output and after 1942 for 'official' prices appear in tables V:1–V:3. The data are much fuller for Fort Hall and for Nyeri than for Kiambu. Generally the Fort Hall data show a general trend of price rises from 1940 to 1952 for maize, beans, wattle, bananas and millet, with the intervention of the Maize Control in the maize market being signalled by the sharp rise in maize prices between 1942 and 1945 (from Shs. 39/20 per ton to Shs. 81/46 per ton). The statistics for 'fruit' and for 'fruit and vegetables' from Fort Hall indicate the high unit prices of these horticultural crops, in which Kiambu in particular specialised, and they serve to indicate why there appears to have been such an expansion of vegetable production in all three districts of Central Province both during the War and after it.[7] It is also note-

3. See for example NAR 1942, p. 19; and 1943, p. 14; KAR 1944, p. 46; FHAR 1942, p. 2; and FHAR 1944, p. 21. Also *Food Shortage Commission*, op. cit., p. 28.
4. NKAR 1943, p. 18.
5. *NAD* 1939–45, p. 4; and *DAR* 1945, pp. 1–6.
6. FHAR 1944, p. 21; and *NAD* 1939–45, p. 37.
7. See for example *Food Shortage Commission*, op. cit., p. 29.

worthy that with the steep rise in wattle prices from 1942 onwards, wattle producer prices did begin to exceed those of maize and continued to do so even after the imposition of the Control's minimum prices had lifted the official maize price. Unit prices of wattle in Fort Hall continued to exceed official maize prices until 1952. This may well have been the position only so far as official prices were concerned. There were droughts in Machakos and/or Kitui in 1943–4, 1944–5 and 1948–50 and in Fort Hall in particular full advantage was taken of these shortages, producers selling at much higher prices than the Control was offering.

District Officers frequently berated cultivators who took advantage of such prices by 'overselling' and thereby producing food shortages at a later period when the harvest, and the boom, was over. Normally they responded to such shortages, or anticipated shortages, by the imposition of bans on food exports, which would simply be breached at the next harvest, if there were other shortages to be capitalised upon.[8]

Cultivators were probably not 'thriftlessly' overselling in the way constantly suggested by the reports, but were taking a calculated risk that with the money realised from the sale of cereals which would have gone to subsistence, a greater quantity of cereals could be obtained in the market by purchasing imports from other areas whose harvest was at a different time.[9] In this way they could purchase the product of more labour time than the labour time expended in the production of the cereals which they were selling.

Now this 'speculative' selling by the household head of produce defined as 'subsistence' clearly represents a first step on the road to a more regularised situation in which more and more of a household's subsistence is obtained in the market, and in Kiambu, and in particular in southern Kiambu nearest to Nairobi, this trend was well advanced. Thus the District Commissioner reported in 1942 that 'Kiambu eats maize and rice but grows very little of either. The supply comes from elsewhere and is paid for by cash obtained in Nairobi by the sale of firewood, charcoal, potatoes, eggs etc., which the Nairobi people need, and things that people in other parts need too—labour, wattle and timber.' Now as the District Commissioner went on to observe, 'This economy is normally sound enough, but when during a war imports are restricted by lack of shipping, while the basic foodstuffs in the country are scarce through over-export or failure of rains, Kiambu is in the unhappy position of having plenty of money and nothing to eat.'[10] So the question arises why, if cereal prices could rise as sharply in times of shortage as I have suggested (and indeed shortages did occur in 1942 and 1943), there was a persistent tendency for the cropped area under maize in Kiambu to fall? The answer I think is that the smallest landholders in

8. FHAR 1944, p. 21; NAR 1943, p. 14; 1944, p. 1; and 1945, p. 16; and *DAR* 1950, p. 37.
9. On the multiple harvests in Kenya see *Food Shortage Commission*, op. cit., p. 11.
10. KAR 1942, pp. 7–8.

Table V:1. Volume and value of marketed produce 1940–52 in tons and Kenyan

Year	Wattle Bark		Charcoal		Fuel and Poles		Maize		Potatoes	
	Vol	Val.	Vol.	Val.	Vol.	Val.	Vol.	Val.	Vol.	Val.
1940										
1941										
1942										
1943		28,327	15,750			12,960				
1944		28,532	18,000	54,000		16,200				
1945										
1946										
1947										
1948										
1949	20,672	197,476	40,000				536	9,000*	9,608	93,864*
1950										
1951		135,673								
1952										

Kiambu believed that if higher-value crops were grown on the densely populated land (wattle, and above all fruit and vegetables), the terms of trade between vegetables and cereals on the free market were so advantageous to the vegetable growers in most years that cereals would cost less labour time if obtained through exchange than if grown in sufficient quantity on the plot. Thus in southern Kiambu during the war years cultivators deliberately switched 'subsistence' land and labour time exclusively to cash crops, and used part of this extra marketed production to exchange for part of their subsistence.

Now this represented a qualitative break, in that prior to this period nearly all African cultivators in Kenya had generally sought to assure their own subsistence from their own land (i.e. outside the market) before marketing for cash or in barter. In this sense marketed surpluses had genuinely been so, i.e. were defined as 'surplus' by the household head. It is a qualitative change because it is a markedly different phenomenon from the barter or sale of subsistence crops from the wife's garden for other subsistence crops or for home-produced pottery or handicrafts, which had also been happening in parts of Kenya from the thirties. For in the most densely populated parts of southern Kiambu such 'separate' gardens had effectively ceased to exist, and all the household's land resources were treated as one productive unit, the entire output of which would be disposed of as determined by the male household head. When in such circumstances the crop mix was weighted heavily in favour of high-value cash crops for sale in Nairobi or elsewhere, so that the household was not directly producing most, or even any of its subsistence product, it was necessarily much more dependent on the market for its subsistence than had previously been the case.

pounds, Kiambu district

	Peas		Bananas		Onions		Flowers and fruit		Pyrethrum		Green vegetables	
	Vol.	Val.	Vol.	Val.	Vol.	Val.	Vol.	Val.	Vol.	Val.	Vol.	Val.
								1,000				120,960
								5,000				125,000
	89.3	1,402*	150	15,000		3,000			2.42	270	8,000	80,000
											10,000	

Source: KARs 1940–52.
*Prices for maize, potatoes and peas are free market prices, all prices are estimated 'averages' for a season.

No doubt this was a minority phenomenon in Kiambu, even by the end of the period here considered (1952), and was concentrated in the areas of southern Kiambu closest to Nairobi, but it is signalled in the reports by the persistent if scattered evidence of declining cereal output in the district as a whole. The effect in district terms, as already noted, was to make Kiambu a net importer of cereals, principally from the other two Kikuyu districts to its north, but also from Embu and Meru.

This is still a very different situation from that of the industrial worker whose product may be inedible or of no use for his family's subsistence, or who does not produce a whole commodity at all but only a tiny part of one. A family relying overwhelmingly on vegetable and wattle production could still build with the wattle poles, cook or warm themselves with the wood, and eat the vegetables if they could not sell them at a profit. But nonetheless, once house-hold production has become this specialised, there arises, for example, the possibility of a markedly unbalanced diet, if other foodstuffs cannot be obtained through the market. Once production switches to a crop with a minimal food content and with a very narrowly defined use value (such as coffee or tea), then of course so long as the household continues to concentrate its land and labour time on the production of such crops, dependence on the market for subsistence is almost total.

Turning now to other points which emerge from an analysis of the frag-mentary data in these tables, one sees once again the dominant influence on output of supply conditions, and particularly the weather. Thus the marketed output of maize (Fort Hall and Nyeri), wattle bark (Fort Hall and Nyeri) and tobacco (Fort Hall), for which fairly complete series are available, rise and fall

Table V:2. Volume and value of marketed produce 1940–52 in tons and Kenyan

Year	Maize		Beans		Potatoes		Sorghum		Millet		Pigeon peas	
	Vol.	Val.	Vol.	Val.	Vol.	Val.	Vol.	Val.	Vol.	Val.	Vol.	Val.
1940	—	20,066	—	3,915	180	1,787	1.3	7	99	1,106	—	1,295
1941	9,296	20,824	1,361	9,908							69.5	584
1942	12,041	23,600	1,351	11,348								
1943	—	—	—	—								
1944	—	—	—	—								
1945	982	4,000	—	—								
1946	0	0	—	—								
1947	6,849	41,094	—	—								
1948	1,797	13,028	46	437			1.3	7	99	1,106		
1949	1,797	14,016	214	2,007					78	875		
1950	125	2,290	295	4,785								
1951	3,035	—	—	—								
1952	—	58,928	—	18,191								

without any discernible relationship to price movements, but with a strong relationship, as district reports always make clear, to weather conditions. This is not to say that producers did not respond to price rises. All the comments from the reports show strong responses in terms of increases in cropped areas of various crops. Thus for example, the Kiambu report for 1941: 'wattle grow-ing ... has extended far beyond its reasonable limits' and for 1942, 'the increased production of food, especially vegetables, has been enormous ... That the Kikuyu have made a good deal out of the black market there is no doubt...'[11] And in Fort Hall the report noted in 1940 'increased acreages' under potatoes and pigeon peas and a further 2,000 acres under wattle, and in 1941 an increase of the acreage under tobacco. Subsequent reports note the continued boom in vegetable production and the impossibility of effectively controlling the rapidly increasing wattle acreage with growers' permits (due to widespread infraction and the growth of a black market in permits!).[12]

The problem therefore was not lack of the response of expanding the cropped area (where this was possible) or shifting the crop mix (where it was not). The problem was simply, as observed repeatedly in earlier chapters, that a crop sown was not a crop harvested, and that weather conditions were perfectly capable of

11. KAR 1941, p. 12; and 1942, p. 2.
12. FHAR 1940, p. 3; 1941, p. 10; 1944, p. 21.

pounds—Fort Hall district

Bananas		Charcoal		Firewood		Tobacco		Fruit and vegetables		Wattle bark	
Vol.	Val.	Vol.	Val.	Vol.	Val	Vol.	Val.	Vol.	Val.	Vol.	Val.
						45	143			—	31,809
—	3,000				—	3,500	—	165.5			10,997	32.271
—	7,000				—	4,000	—	150			13,265	41,121
										13,281	48,662
—	7,000				—	7,000	163	708			10,442	49,594
					—	8,000	97	438			11,904	68,906
						123	383			9,739	80,468
160	12,000	40,000 bags	3,000	36,500	22,000	163	915	10	280	11,701	117,256
150	11,250	40,000 bags	4,000	36,300	31,018	163	886	23	478	15,351	157,632
160	20,000	40,000 bags	5,000	86,500	32,850	84	413	204	2,290	16,681	169,279
						89	—	—	—	9,000	134,622
		—	5,781			—	170	—	11,683	—	183,702

Source: FHARs 1940–52. All value figures based on estimated 'average' prices over the year.

turning an expanded acreage into a reduced marketed surplus, and often did so.

Thus increased reliance on the market for subsistence was indeed a risky business, and it is clear that it was forced on many of the smaller producers in Kiambu by land shortage, and by the inability of a household, with the cereal yields then available, to obtain an adequate subsistence directly from the land at its disposal. On the other hand, one aim of concentrating on the production of relatively high-value crops like fruit and vegetables, in southern Kiambu, was to use the wartime boom to accumulate funds in order among other things to buy more land.[13] Thus increased risks in the short term were expected, or hoped, to lead to greater security in the long term. Some indication of the extent of the land shortage prevailing in parts of Central Province by the end of the war is provided by Humphrey's study of southern Nyeri in 1944.[14]

Humphrey's work is of particular interest because it can be compared with Fazan's survey of 1931, and indeed Humphrey himself uses Fazan's study as a base for his own survey. According to Fazan's estimates, the population density of Nyeri in 1931 was 398.7 per square mile, in a district of 307 square miles. Dividing the total population by the figure for the total number of married men, Fazan had found the 'average' household in Nyeri to consist of 6.05 persons

13. See KAR 1941, p. 8; 1942, p. 10; 1943, p. 22; and *DAR* 1948, pp. 71–2.
14. Humphrey, 'The Relationship...', op. cit.

Table V:3. Volume and value of marketed produce 1940–52 in tons and Kenyan pounds—Nyeri district

Year	Maize		Beans		Wattle bark		Potatoes		Vegetables		Onions		Bananas		'Native' tobacco		Charcoal	
	Vol.	Val.	Vol.	Val.	Vol.	Val.	Vol.	Val.	Vol.	Val.	Vol.	Val.	Vol.	Val.	Vol.	Val.	Vol.	Val.
1940	1,521		75		4,472		233											
1941	2,354		582		3,326		1,471		349		1.74		612		104		1,042	
1942	1,355		441		2,624		161		1,054		34.16		659		48		1,312	
1943	72		0.63		2,453		3.45		1,500		107.8		245		27		1,054	
1944	48	266	256	2,010	4,013	18,000	332	2,200	6,000	21,000	130	1,700	658	3,000	58	2,125	887	1,700
1945																		
1946																		
1947																		
1948																		
1949						48,947												
1950																		
1951						72,600												
1952																		

Source: NARs 1940–52. All value figures based on estimated 'average' prices over the year.

Table V:4. Cultivated land in Nyeri district 1931 and 1944

	1931	1944	% Increase
Annual Crops	40,070 acres	54,141 acres	35
Perennial Crops	13,423 acres	24,880 acres	85
Proportion of cultivable land cultivated (including fallow and homestead land)	53.2%	76.1%	22.9%

who had at their disposal 9.71 acres of land. Of this in 1931, 3.80 acres were under crops (including fallow) and 5.91 acres were still held as part of the communal grazing. This statistical 'average' household had just under 40 per cent of 'its' land under crops in 1931.[15]

Using the population estimates for 1943, Humphrey found that population increase had reduced the size of the 'average' household to 5.68 persons holding 6.86 acres of which he estimated 3.72 acres were under crops (including fallow) and 2.78 acres were held as grazing, i.e. 57 per cent of its land was now under crops.[16]

Fazan had broken this average household acreage down by crop, and though Humphrey does not do this he suggests that each household in Nyeri had 1.85 acres under annual crops (maize, millet, beans, potatoes, sweet potatoes, yams, cassava) in 1944 as against two acres in 1931, but that the acreage under perennial crops had increased to 0.85 acres in 1944 (from 0.67 acres in 1931). Most of this increase was due to wattle planting. Since Humphrey estimated there to be 29,271 households in Nyeri in 1944, as against 20,035 in 1931,[17] the gross acreage increases work out as in table V:4. Thus we see that on Humphrey's estimates the cultivated area of Nyeri district had increased by 23 per cent over thirteen years (an annual rate of increase of 1.77 per cent), with the largest part of this increase being accounted for by wattle production. Since this method of averages completely excludes distributional differences either by area or by household, and since, as we shall see, Humphrey's estimate of the population of Nyeri in 1944 was far too low, his figures very much understate the density of population on the land, and very much overstate the actual mean holding size, particularly in the most densely populated locations of southern Nyeri.

In fact the first proper census of the African population of Kenya in 1948 showed that the African population of Nyeri district on 23 August 1948 was 183,057,[18] which compares with Humphrey's estimate of 166,440 for 1944. Thus

15. Fazan, op. cit., table 4, p. 975 and table 1, p. 989.
16. Humphrey, op. cit., pp. 7 and 51.
17. Ibid., p. 7, Appendix C, pp. 12 and 10.
18. *Geographical and Tribal Studies* (Source, East African Population Census 1948), East African Statistical Dept: Sept. 1950, p. 12.

*Table V :5. Available and cultivable acreage of households in
Nyeri district, 1931, 1944 and 1948*

Year	No. of households	Available acreage per household	Cultivable acreage per household
1931	20,035	9.71	7.15
1944	29,271	6.86	4.89
1948	32,193	6.04	4.45

we can repeat the calculation undertaken by Humphrey (and Fazan) on the basis
of the 1948 census figures. Taking the area of the district as 307 square miles, the
density for 1948 is 596.3 per square mile, an increase of almost 50 per cent over
Fazan's 1931 figure and of nearly 10 per cent over Humphrey's 1944 figure.
Since unfortunately the 1948 census did not enumerate the number of married
men, we are forced to use the percentage figure (17.5 per cent of the total
population) used by Humphrey and Fazan. On this basis there would have been
32,193 'households' in Nyeri in 1948. We thus obtain the comparison shown in
table V :5. The number of households in the district increased by 61 per cent over
seventeen years (3.6 per cent per annum on a linear basis) whilst in the same
period the available and cultivable acreage per household fell by 38 per cent.
Again it is likely that this understates the population density and pressure on
land, because densities were undoubtedly much higher than the district average
in some locations, and in addition there would have been quite a number of
households without a male head, notably those consisting of widows alone or
with their children. In addition, as we saw, Fazan made the unlikely assumption
that all land in the district which was not cultivable was available for use as
grazing. The actual situation on the ground, then, is much more likely to be
captured in the figures showing cultivable acreages per household than in the
available acreages statistics, i.e. 4.45 acres to support 5–6 household members.
And when farm survey data did become available for the district in the early
1960s, they broadly confirmed that this situation (less than one acre under
crops for each household member) must have been the situation of the average
household in Nyeri in the late forties.

Finally, it is interesting to compare Fazan's 1931 survey with what may be
gleaned about the situation in 1948 from the census results in Kiambu and Fort
Hall.[19] The results of such a comparison are summarised in tables V :6, V :7 and
V :8.

19. By 1948 Dagoretti had ceased to exist as an administrative entity, and the mode of presentation
of the statistics in the 1948 census did not allow it to be reconstructed for the purpose of this analysis.
I have therefore simply taken the proportion of the district population in Dagoretti in 1931 and
transferred this to the 1948 population figure. This procedure almost certainly understates the
population density in southern Kiambu in 1948 because it makes no allowance for the large number
of people, particularly those working in Nairobi, who migrated to the area between 1931 and 1948.
The rate of migration to this area probably outstripped that into Kiambu as a whole in this period.

Table V:6. Available and cultivable acreage of households in Dagoretti (S. Kiambu), 1931 and 1948

	Population	Density (p.s.m.)	No. of households	Available acreage per household	Cultivable acreage per household
1931	38,822	610.2	8,201	4.92	4.06
1948	96,265	1513.1	20,331	1.98	1.63
Increase or Decrease	+ 148%	+ 148%	+ 148%	− 59.7%	− 59.7%

Source: East Africa *Population Census*, 1948, p. 4 and Fazan, op. cit., table 4 p. 975 and table E, p. 984.

Table V:7. Available and cultivable acreage of households in Kiambu, 1931 and 1948

	Population	Density (p.s.m.)	No. of households	Available acreage per household	Cultivable acreage per household
1931	104,028	258.8	21,976	11.59	7.88
1948	258,085	642	54,508	4.67	3.18
Increase or Decrease	+ 148%	+ 148%	+ 148%	− 59.7%	− 59.7%

Source: East Africa *Population Census* 1948, p. 4 and Fazan op. cit., table 4, p. 975 and table E., p. 984.

Tables V:6–V:8 clearly suggest that as one might expect, Kiambu district was the most densely populated of the three Kikuyu districts by the late forties, with something over half an acre of cultivable land available for every man, woman and child in the district. In Dagoretti the figure was down to one-third of an acre of cultivable land for every household member, and this is almost certainly an overestimate due to the method of calculation. These levels of density do a great deal to explain the movement out of low-yielding low-value cereals and into wattle and fruit and vegetable growing which had been going on in Kiambu in the 1930s and 1940s. They also suggest that in southern Kiambu at least, even with the production of higher-value crops, the 'average' household would have needed to supplement its farm income with off-farm income sources, and of course this happened. By 1948 40 per cent of the adult male population of the district was working outside the district for wages for all or part of the year, and of course a number would also have been employed for wages within the district. The land shortage varied markedly by household, as later farm

Table V:8. Available and cultivable acreage of households in Fort Hall, 1931 and 1948

	Population	Density (p.s.m.)	No. of households	Available acreage per household	Cultivable acreage per household
1931	171,852	291.9	32,671	11.42	9.1
1948	303,646	515.8	57,723	6.46	5.14
Increase or Decrease	+ 77%	+ 77%	+ 77%	− 43.4%	− 43.4%

Source: East Africa *Population Census* 1948, p. 4 and Fazan, op. cit., table 4, p. 975 and table E, p. 984.

surveys were to show, and it is probable if not certain that a minority of households were cultivating less than an acre each even in 1948. Many of these households would have had one or more members employed, probably in Nairobi, and would be using their household plot for little more than to supplement a diet whose major constituents were purchased from wages. Some areas of southern Kiambu had effectively become dormitory suburbs of Nairobi.

So rapid had been the rate of population growth in Kiambu over the seventeen years since 1931 (8.7 per cent per annum) that by 1948 both the available and cultivable acreages per household in the district were less than in Nyeri and Fort Hall (a reversal of the 1931 situation). Kiambu's rate of population growth over this period was double that of Fort Hall (4.4 per cent) and almost treble that of Nyeri (3.0 per cent) which, even allowing for Fazan's underestimate of population in 1931, is an eloquent testimony to the rate of in-migration to Kiambu over this period. The majority of this migration was accounted for by a drain of population southwards from the two northern districts. By the mid-thirties households migrating in this way must consistently have been obtaining less land than they had possessed in their districts of origin, and this is in itself suggestive of the preference for wage labour, especially in the high pay area of Nairobi, over marginal returns to labour time in cultivation.

There are no figures for cash income from the land for this period which can be compared with Fazan's estimates for 1931, though Humphrey presented an estimate that in 1944 the average household in Nyeri would have required some 6.5 acres under crops and five acres of permanent grazing in order to have an adequate diet plus a cash income of K£18–20 per annum.[20] Since on his own calculations the average household in Nyeri at that date only had 3.72 acres under crops and 2.78 acres under permanent grazing, he concluded that there were some 14,000 'surplus' households on the land.[21] Now it is clear that such

20. Humphrey, 'The Relationship. . .', op. cit., p. 9.
21. Ibid., p. 10.

estimates are very sensitive to assumptions about the nature of an 'adequate diet', to yield estimates etc.,[22] and they are also rendered largely valueless in this case since Humphrey takes no account of off-farm earnings, which in Nyeri, as elsewhere in Central Province, were considerable. But nonetheless it is clear that by the late forties population pressure on the land (certainly in the most densely populated parts of Kiambu, Nyeri and Fort Hall) had effectively reduced the average household farm income over the seventeen years from 1931.[23]

The Labour Process in Kikuyu Agriculture
Some data on the labour process in Kikuyu agriculture as it was in the early 1950s are found in the work of Jeanne Fisher. Her account *Kikuyu Domesticity and Husbandry* is based on fieldwork carried out between 1950 and 1952 mainly in Fort Hall and Kiambu, and is in the author's own words 'the first field study of an East African people to be made with special reference to the women'.[24]

Fisher presents data on the sexual division of labour, and also three agricultural calendars for three altitude zones of Kiambu and Fort Hall. She identifies a low zone (under 5,000 feet), a middle zone (5,000–6,000 feet) and a high zone (over 6,000 feet). The calendars in particular reveal the massive predominance of female labour in Kikuyu agriculture by the early fifties. Each of the zones had at least two periods of hoeing and preparation of plots, two periods of planting and two harvests, and each had one period of weeding, usually of long duration. Since women were responsible for nearly all the hoeing, all of the harvesting, and most of the planting (indeed they virtually monopolised the care of all the annual food crops with which the bulk of the acreage on the farms she surveyed were planted), this predominance comes out clearly.[25] Fisher states that this predominance had increased 'under modern economic conditions' because 'A large percentage of the younger men now take paid employment, generally leaving their wives and families in the tribal territories . . .' and 'Education along European lines has had a tendency to lead to a change in the men's attitude to agriculture . . .' There is much less attention given in Fisher's study to the cultivation of perennial crops, presumably because they took up so much less of the labour time on the farms in any given year. She does note however that in the case of wattle trees 'Men fell wattle trees and women strip the bark, although it is not uncommon to see women also engaged in felling.'[26] In other words, it appears that in the case of wattle trees as well the bulk of

22. I shall argue later that Humphrey's yield estimates were probably too low.
23. See below, pp. 150–2.
24. Jeanne M. Fisher, *The Anatomy of Kikuyu Domesticity and Husbandry* (Dept. of Technical Cooperation; bound cyclostyled report, 1954?), Preface, p. 1.
25. Ibid. pp. 261–3 and 264–6. See also the detailed observations pp. 237–54. The low, middle and high zones identified by Fisher correspond broadly to the Star Grass, Kikuyu Grass and High Bracken zones of the Kenya Highlands identified by geographers. See S. H. Ominde, *Land and Population Movements in Kenya* (London, 1968), pp. 40–4.
26. Fisher, op. cit., p. 265.

the labour input on the farm was female, although whether this was also true of other processes, i.e. drying the bark and transporting it to a trader, is not clear.

Because of her particular interests, Fisher devotes a great deal of attention to the 'rights' of men and their wives and to the control of produce and of agricultural activity with reference to the sexual division of labour in agriculture. Despite this her account is ambiguous in a number of respects, and these ambiguities are revealing.

In general she asserts that a women on marrying has a 'right' to land from her husband's estate in order 'to grow food for the household', and that a responsibility to provide such land is primary. If he had little land then this provision of land to his wives might mean that he would be unable to have gardens of his own. Nonetheless, he was 'expected' to provide land for his wife even if this was the result.[27]

Once land had been allocated to her, a wife it appeared was free to decide what should be grown on such land: 'she decides what to plant, the period of fallow, and what surplus food there is for sale or for making gifts to relatives and friends.'[28] The cereals grown on the wife's gardens were stored in her granary and Fisher recounts that a woman's rights over the granary were jealously guarded, even to the point of denying her husband the right to enter it.[29] For his own part the husband would also have a separate granary, and this would be used to provide food for visitors and secondarily for the household 'when his wife's supplies begin to run low'.[30]

However, this straightforward account is undermined by internal evidence. Firstly, Fisher does not provide any coherent analysis of what alterations had been made in these norms by the advent of cash cropping, though it is clear that both men and women grew inedible cash crops in 'their' gardens, as well as trading surpluses of food crops. However some insight into what may have been happening is provided in a fascinating footnote which it is worth quoting in full:

> It is considered shameful for a husband to interfere in matters concerning his wife's gardens. An elder in discussing marital relationships and garden management said: 'If a woman does not cultivate well her husband may beat her. If a woman wants to plant millet in a garden, and maize and beans in another, then he will not refuse. There is no war of the wife with the husband.' On the same subject, a woman remarked: 'A woman can plant whatever she likes in her gardens, but some men tell their wives they must plant a certain crop in a certain garden, that is to say, wattle in one and sweet potatoes in another, and the wife must obey. If she does not he may beat her.

27. Ibid., p. 212.
28. Ibid., p. 213.
29. Ibid., p. 273.
30. Ibid., p. 274.

If a woman wants to plant coffee she can tell her husband, but if he does not want that garden to be planted with coffee he tells her it is not good, but it is good that she plants tea. Then she must obey and plant tea there.'[31]

Moreover, it turns out that in practice a woman's rights over her gardens were by no means total since 'if she is lazy (*kiguta*) or a poor cultivator he may, with some justification, make use of some of her gardens'.[32] Similar ambiguities arise when Fisher is discussing wives' 'rights' to trade surplus produce from their gardens:

Provided a woman ensures there is always sufficient food for her husband and children, she may sell any surplus either in the market or in private transactions, but she has no right to sell the whole of her crops. Normally she is not expected to hand over the proceeds to her husband, but is free to spend them on the purchase of household utensils, implements and seed, clothes, gifts for relatives and friends, or occasionally a few luxury foods or perhaps an ornament for herself.[33]

However, once again it turns out that 'Some men object to their womenfolk going to market to buy or sell, or simply to sight-see. Needless to say, the women occasionally seize the opportunity to sneak off, dressed in their best, when their husbands are away from the homestead or else a trusted friend may sell their produce for them.' When a husband traded produce from his garden or gardens the proceeds were used 'as a rule, for the running expenses of the household'. But again it turns out that such proceeds could prove insufficient and, 'Although he normally has no say over the disposal of his wife's crops, should he require money for a specific purpose (e.g. to buy stock or clothes, to pay school fees) he may tell her to sell some of her crops so that he may "see the money" for these things.'[34] Once all these infractions of the norms have been admitted, it is difficult to see how Fisher can unambiguously conclude as she does that

The women exercise almost complete control over the management of their gardens and the disposal of the crops therefrom.[35]

The 'almost' here is inadequate to deal with the scale of infractions of 'the norm' which Fisher herself presents, and in fact it seems that the problem with her entire account derives largely from the theoretical assumptions which underly it. That is, Fisher, much like many social anthropologists of her generation, is concerned to lay bare a set of 'tribal' or 'traditional' norms which have

31. Ibid., footnote 128, p. 273.
32. Ibid., p. 213.
33. Ibid., p. 275.
34. Ibid., p. 276.
35. Ibid., p. 285.

guided, are guiding and presumably will for ever guide, conduct among the theoretical entity known as 'the Kikuyu'. Thus, matters which were clearly the focus of perennial and possibly bitter dispute within households, and which may in fact have been more and more disputed as the volume and value of the household surplus product grew, are presented by Fisher as timeless norms known presumably to all 'Kikuyu' and particularly their 'elders'. She persists in her pursuit of such norms, even when her own informants show clearly, albeit by implication, that they did not exist, or rather that, like all norms, they served only to regulate dispute, or to be the focus of conflict. One can imagine for example the wide variety of circumstances in which a man might have reason to claim that his wife was 'lazy' and thus that he could take back land from her!

If then we free her account from this fixation with 'tribal' norms, what does it suggest? It seems that by the early 1950s most Kikuyu male household heads had managed to achieve a position in which their wives (and daughters) undertook the major part of the labour in cultivation but in which the male heads had virtually untrammelled power of disposal over the product of that labour power.

From Fisher's account it appears that the balance of sexual labour input was not markedly different from the wives' gardens to the husbands'. The annual calendars presented by her applied equally to both types of garden. It seems that the sole distinction between the wives' and husbands' gardens lay in a loose presumption that the produce of the wives' gardens was earmarked for the subsistence of the household. But by the early 1950s (and probably, as we have noted elsewhere, for some time previously), this presumption had been rendered of minimal practical import because produce for exchange was grown in both types of garden. Thus in practice the product of the totality of the family's land was partly directly consumed and partly traded, and both parts were a focus of intra-family debate, negotiation and dispute. In this dispute, it appears that wives in general were endeavouring to maintain a distinction between the two types of garden, so that they might maintain the power of disposal over at least some part of the household production for which they were mainly responsible. The tendency of Fisher's account is to suggest that, on balance, women were not being successful in this attempt.

In putting the matter in this way, one is in danger of falling into Fisher's theoretical problematic in which an undifferentiated entity called 'the Kikuyu' was experiencing this conflict over male and female rights. In practice it is likely that the sexual balance of power within households varied markedly between households with the crucial variables being: the presence or absence of male household heads from the farm; the level of male labour input (which probably varied considerably even within households with male heads at home); the size of land holding; and the extent of hiring in of labour (which Fisher confirms was happening at this date, the majority of labourers being women).

Generally speaking a male household head with abundant land resources (and therefore large gardens of his own), who was present on the farm for at least part of the year, and who could afford to hire in labour, would be likely to control a much larger proportion of the household's surplus product, than a man on a smallholding who was semi-permanently absent, and entirely dependent on his wife's labour for production on the plot. However, it may be (this would require further research) that paradoxically such men in a weak 'strategic' situation—so far as the control of surplus product disposal was concerned—may have been more motivated to try and assert their 'rights'. How far they were being successful in such an assertion no doubt varied, with the personalities of husband and wife being as important as any other variable in deciding the outcome.

At any rate Fisher's account does seem to confirm that the focus of dispute was the extent to which the household's land was to be regarded as one domain so far as disposal of produce was concerned (it seems already to have become one domain in Kikuyuland so far as the labour process was concerned), and how far women could keep production and disposal separate. In this dispute, one norm, the household head's apparently undisputed status (by early 1950) as 'owner' of all the household land, may have worked in his favour, since it enabled him to argue from 'ownership' of the land to 'ownership' of its usufruct. Since this very concept of land 'ownership' was itself a product of the colonial experience, and, in the case of the Kikuyu people, of an experience of massive land loss to Europeans,[36] it is clear that this dispute within Kikuyu households was predicated on norms which were the product of a particular historical experience, and were not the timeless, indigenous, tribal values, for which Fisher constantly searched. In this regard it is interesting to note that she also reports that women themselves were purchasing land:

> In former times, women did not buy land unless, as the Kikuyu remark, they were widows of wealthy men. The transactions were conducted on their behalf by their adult sons or by brothers of the late husband, and legally the land belonged to their sons. Modern times provide a contrast. Many women now buy gardens although male relatives still conduct the transactions and mark the boundaries. One informant in Fort Hall, an intelligent vivacious woman, summed up the position as follows: 'In the past women did not buy gardens or cattle or *mburi* (goats), but in these days, when they have money, women buy gardens for cultivation, cattle and *mburi*.' She concluded her remarks by saying that now women had 'wisdom', but formerly they were fools of women (*irumu cia atumia*).[37]

In the light of previous speculations the growing tendency of women to buy land would make a great deal of sense. Since I have suggested that male household

---

36. See below, chapter X.
37. Fisher, op. cit., p. 187.

heads were increasingly claiming to monopolise decisions about the usufruct of the entire household landholding on the grounds that they 'owned' the land, one obvious way for women to maintain some landholdings whose usufruct they could deny to the husband would be to purchase land, since then the husband's argument could be stood on its head.

One other point of interest emerges from Fisher's account of 'Kikuyu' agriculture in this period. In her account of cultivation, she makes mention of an important change in connection with seed corn:

> Formerly, at harvest time most women put aside a seed reserve (*kigiina*, plural *igiina*) for the following season. The modern position is rather different. It is true there is the group of women consisting of old ladies, the more conservative of the young women, and women who have no children to feed, who continue to keep seed reserves, but perhaps the majority of cultivators, either because it is easier, or because they have large households for which to provide, now buy their seed supplies in the market or 'beg' them from kin and friends.[38]

This piece of information can be put together with another to provide some sort of fragmentary picture of the mechanisms and consequences of differentiation among Kikuyu households in this period. Elsewhere Fisher says:

> There are three main incentives in agriculture. The first, and most important, is the production of food; the second is the prestige acquired by skill in cultivation; and the third is the production of cash crops. According to aged informants, in former times most families were self-sufficient in foodstuffs and exchanged any surplus in the market or through private barter for other commodities or foodstuffs which they did not grow themselves or for which they had a predilection. Nowadays, in contrast, production often falls below subsistence level with the result that many housewives have to buy food at some time during the year, though it is considered a 'bad thing' to do so. One woman who frequently went to market to buy food for her family of five, when discussing the subject, said of a friend who had an even larger family to feed, 'She does not need to buy food. She has gardens of yams, bananas, Colocasia and English potatoes to produce food in the time of hunger.' There is no doubt that to the progressively-minded Kikuyu the cultivation of cash crops is a great incentive to improve their agricultural techniques. But to conservative cultivators who have neither the means nor the desire to break with traditional practices cash crops are a ready and easy source of money, and only too often are planted in land which would otherwise be devoted to food crops.[39]

38. Ibid., p. 239.
39. Ibid., p. 281.

What was happening in at least some areas of Fort Hall and Kiambu in this period seems to have been the following. For various historical reasons land-holdings had become markedly unequal. Consequently in those households with little land, concentration on the production of cereals alone by the women culti-vators would have produced a considerable risk, or perhaps even a certainty (where landholdings were very small) of failing to meet socially determined subsistence requirements. In this situation the proportion of directly consumed production was reduced, and land planted to 'cash crops' (probably wattle, some vegetables, and perhaps, by the early fifties, some coffee or tea), and an increased proportion of domestic food requirements (in cereals and legumes) was purchased in the market. As already suggested, this would be because the terms of trade between wattle and vegetables and cereals in the market were favourable to the cash crop grower, and (in the case of wattle) because of its higher weight (and value) yields on a small amount of land, and its multifarious use and exchange values.

However this movement in the crop mix toward greater dependence on the market for subsistence entailed some risks, including sudden rises in the prices of cereals at times of local or general harvest failure, and the failure of one's own crops. One symptom of the change was the sale of seed corn by households on smaller holdings, and the consequent dependence on markets or on larger scale cultivators for this input. When because of the small size of the landholding and/or shifts in crop mix away from cereals, cereals output was below annual subsistence requirements, sale of most, or even all, of one's cereals at a time of price rises or at a time of need for cash was rational (even if one needed to buy in again at a later date) so long as the general terms of trade between cereals and other cash crops remained favourable. It did entail considerable risks because of the marked fluctuations in the prices of cereals caused principally by the weather. Where households had very small landholdings they probably had no choice but to adopt this high-risk strategy.[40]

On larger holdings, and particularly on the largest, cash crops could be grown in excess of subsistence production, and almost certainly in far greater volume than on smaller holdings. Thus cash cropping entailed far less risk; for example, one was not dependent on the market for cereals seed. Farm profits per acre and per unit of labour time were almost certainly larger, even though output per acre or per 'man' hour might be lower. In addition, as already suggested, many of the larger landholders would have had larger than average off-farm incomes as well (this in fact is mainly how they came to have the larger than average

40. 'Nowadays . . . since food crops . . . have a cash value, it is not uncommon for people to sell part of their harvest in order "to see money", which may be urgently needed for a specific purpose, despite the fact that the stores will be depleted and foodstuffs will almost certainly have to be purchased at higher prices later in the year', ibid., p. 273.

holdings)[41] and this provided an extra insurance against harvest failure and the need to buy in food.

Conclusions

Fisher's is the only participant observation study of the labour process and agricultural production in Central Province which pre-dates the widespread adoption of coffee and tea, and thus captures the agricultural system as it was at the end of the thirty years or so of persistent change whose outlines were traced in earlier chapters. In general it does seem to confirm the picture of the mechanisms and effects of those changes which were derived from the fragmentary data of earlier years.

Fisher's particular interest in the domestic and agricultural roles of women, and her apparent success in winning their trust as informants, allowed her inadvertently to portray the struggle over the control and disposal of the agricultural surplus which was going on in many households, and which derived from declining land resources, from the adoption of higher-value cash crops, and from the marketing of increased proportions of the total product (the latter representing the increasing 'commoditisation' of the household labour product).[42] Particularly in households with small total holdings, this struggle took the form of the attempt of the male household head to assert complete control over the use and disposal of the usufruct of the entire landholding, and to reduce the distinction between wives' gardens and husbands' (or household) gardens to a purely formal level. At the time of Fisher's fieldwork this issue was by no means resolved in most households, and most wives maintained separate granaries, and endeavoured to assert their 'rights' over the produce of 'their' gardens, 'rights' derived from an earlier situation of relative land abundance. It does seem however that in many households male heads had, by the early 1950s, successfully managed to assert their right to dispose either of the produce of wives' gardens or of the money or other produce obtained from its exchange.

This was probably because in situations where a household's total landholdings were very small, if the returns from the sale of the produce in the husband's gardens were inadequate to meet (say) the total bill for school fees for children, or the total clothing bill, the wife's refusal to agree to the use of 'her' money for these purposes would mean her children dropping out from school, being in-

---

41. See below, chapter XI.
42. On the other hand it may be that her greater concentration on women informants misled her in one respect. Her general conclusion that women maintained their 'right' of disposal over 'their' produce in 'their' gardens, may reflect the ideological preference of many Kikuyu women at this period, i.e. clearly in a situation where their husbands were endeavouring to assert complete control over the usufruct of the entire landholding it would be in the interests of the women to assert the 'traditional rights' of wives to the prior allocation of land, total control over the usufruct of their land etc. This is not to deny of course that at an earlier period a situation approximating to this might have existed.

adequately clad, etc. In monogamous households (and they were certainly the majority in Central Province by this period) such considerations would be likely to be powerful ones in the merging of the household's land and labour into one unit of production and consumption. In polygynous households the matter might be more complex, especially if a husband attempted to use income from one wife's plot to pay (for example) school fees for the children of another wife.

The salience of the question of the distribution of land between households in this entire matter makes it even more regrettable that Fisher's discussion abstracts totally from the issue of differentiation between households, except by implication in respect of discrete observations. In particular it means that one cannot be certain about the situation in elite monogamous households where land was relatively abundant. One possibility would be that in these households wives would have found it easier to maintain 'their' gardens as separate consumption units even if here, as in other households, production was effectively merged. On the other hand of course, since the husband would under these circumstances retain large holdings of land for himself, it may be that it was in 'his' gardens that the bulk of cash crop production went on, with the husband maintaining control over the income from them. Another crucial variable here of course would be the use of hired labour. But Fisher is silent about this, save for noting that it existed by this period and that the labourers were mainly women: 'Usually, only older women who have no children at home, or women who have few plots of their own, are willing to work as paid gardeners.' She notes that the rates of pay at this period were about seventy cents for seven hours' weeding, and eighty cents 'for the harder work of hoeing or clearing bush'.[43] However she says very little about who the hirers were, save that, as one might suppose, they were those whose landholdings were in excess of their household labour resources.[44] The reference to some of the labourers as 'women who have few plots of their own' does suggest that there might have been some processes in train in Central Province parallel to those analysed for Kowe, in which some households' landholdings were so small that even the 'cash-crop-substitution-for-food-crop' strategy was not feasible, and with their husbands absent in low-paid employment (or perhaps dead) such women were left with no alternative but to labour for others.

The general picture of growing crisis in Kikuyu agriculture in the late forties and early fifties which emerges from the fragmentary colonial data is confirmed by Fisher, and it is also confirmed that this crisis was affecting the poorer households above all. It must be remembered that her fieldwork was carried out at a time when the prices of maize and wattle were at a peak (but before the widespread introduction of coffee, tea and pyrethrum) and yet she still reports that 'for many cultivators ... production has fallen below subsistence level',

43. Fisher, op. cit., p. 269.
44. Ibid., p. 268.

and there can be little doubt that these 'many' were the smaller landholders. In addition however she reports that 'some farmers' could earn up to Shs. 3,000 per annum from the sale of 'all kinds of cash crops'.[45] These are the sort of differentials which lay behind the 'averages' so beloved of the colonial administration, and which had dominated analyses of African agriculture from the Kenya Land Commission onwards. The mechanisms of this differentiation are examined in chapter XI.

2. Nyanza Province

Marketed output and price data both for the Province and for its constituent districts for this period are presented in tables V:9–V:12. Once again they are exceedingly varied in continuity and comprehensiveness, being most complete for North Nyanza[46] district, and much less so for Central and South Nyanza.

The statistical detail is a fairly accurate reflection of the relative importance of the constituent districts of the Province in the eyes of the Administration. With the very considerable expansion of the cotton and maize output of North Nyanza from 1940 onwards, the district came to dominate the Province's agricultural production. Thus in 1944 North Nyanza produced 38 per cent of the Province's total output of cotton, and 51 per cent of its maize. By 1945 the percentages were 48 per cent of the cotton and 50 per cent of the maize.[47]

Moreover, as we have already noted, North Nyanza was the district where the Administration felt that the Maize and Produce Control worked best, and for which indeed it was largely set up. Before proceeding however to an analysis of the much fuller data available for this district, some analysis of trends in Central and Southern Nyanza is in order.

Central Nyanza
The most remarkable feature of the Central Nyanza statistics is the continued downward trend of marketed surpluses of food from the end of the war until 1952. This is true for maize, eleusine and sorghum. In fact only cotton, from 1949, and rice, from the same season, show any upward trend. Conclusions of this sort from the few figures available would be extremely tenuous were they not supported by a number of observations in the reports. Thus in 1943 the District Officer noted a 'decrease' in the marketed surplus, and in 1945 he reported that the quantity of cereals available for export was 'not great'.[48] Moreover it is noticeable that throughout the war years the district reports concentrate almost entirely on the provision of livestock and labour as being the district's contri-

45. Ibid., p. 138.
46. All the districts of Nyanza Province were renamed in 1948.
47. See Humphrey, *The Liguru* . . ., op. cit., table IV, p. 5; and DAR 1945, p. 18.
48. NKAR 1943, p. 2; and 1945, p. 8.

Table V:9. Volume and value of marketed produce 1940–52 in tons and Kenyan pounds—Central Nyanza district

Year	Maize		Beans		Cotton		Eleusine		Sorghum		Cassava		Rice		Groundnuts	
	Vol.	Val.	Vol.	Val.	Vol.	Val.	Vol.	Val.	Vol.	Val.	Vol.	Val.	Vol.	Val.	Vol.	Val.
1940																
1941																
1942																
1943																
1944																
1945																
1946	4,690				530				272				275			
1947	3,842				1,112		31		149				48		57	
1948	3,000								108				18			
1949	2,616	49,266	25	311	2,895	106,304	5	49	98	588	936	3,774		3,774	104	1,884
1950	2,588	17,754			2,081		18	162	107	606	67	28	169	2,086	9	175
1951	3,385	40,617	4	75	3,243		18	200	100	830	1,150	4,828	505	7,052	10	190
1952																

Source: CKARs, CNARs and DARs 1940–52.

Table V:10. Volume (tons) and value (K£) of marketed production—South

Year	Cotton		Maize		Wattle		Beans		Millet		Sorghum	
	Vol.	Val.	Vol.	Val.	Vol.	Val.	Vol	Val.	Vol.	Val.	Vol.	Val.
1940												
1941	870.9	11,704	2,678				625		2,321		1,607[1]	
1942	1,400 bales		5,357				893		1,786		1,696	
1943	—		7,500				17.8		535		2,857	
1944	670											
1945	297		5,654						2,068[2]			
1946			11,036[3]				259.3[3]		3,446[3]		1,712[3]	
1947	—		8,817	2,937	29.605[4]		7		772		3	
1948			8,159		1,060		—		900.5		508.5	
1949			11,887				11.8		965		474.1	
1950												
1951												
1952												

bution to the war effort. By 1952, the African Affairs Department annual report is unequivocal: 'Central Nyanza is becoming a consuming area to which possibly two thirds of the Kipsigis maize crop found its way through black market channels.'[49]

Bearing in mind Hay's analysis of trends toward the marginalisation of agriculture in Kowe in this period, this decline of the Central Nyanza district as a food surplus producer is not perhaps surprising, especially since by 1951 (and probably for some years before that) some 62 per cent of the district's adult male population were reported to be working all or part of the year outside the district.[50] Moreover the 1948 census revealed that nine out of the fifteen locations making up the district had cropland densities in excess of five hundred per square mile,[51] so clearly land shortage, together with an acceleration through the war of the trends toward stabilisation or reduction of both male and female labour time in agriculture, would explain this decline in general terms, even if the implications of this process from household to household were markedly varied.

One must assume that in this period the group of middle-level households, using both male and female labour power in cultivation, was further reduced, first by conscription into the army and into farm work elsewhere, and then by the continuation of this trend towards ever-increased labour migration.

49. *AAD* 1952, p. 5.
50. CNAR 1951, p. 7.
51. S. H. Ominde, 'Land and Population in the Western Districts of Nyanza Province' (Makerere University College Ph.D., (1963), p. 315.

Nyanza district 1940–52

Sesame		Groundnuts		Coffee		Rice		Potatoes		Wheat	
Vol.	Val.	Vol.	Val.	Vol.	Val.	Vol.	Val.	Vol.	Val.	Vol.	Val.
982.1			2,500	—		4.6					
982.1			2,679	—		13.3		24.1			
89.2			893	—		44.6		177.4		89.2	
				27.6							
				16.5⁵							
30.1³			1,179³	19.9⁵				120.7³		177.9³	
—			1,355	14.8⁵		1,438		1		29	
2			998.6	22.1⁵						32	
11.5			758.9							38.2	

Source: CKARs and SNARs 1940–52 and *DAR*s 1940–52.

1) Forcibly requisitioned.
2) *DAR* 1946, p. 8.
3) *DAR* 1946, p. 38—bags inspected.
4) Calculated from price data *DAR* 1947, p. 7.
5) Parchment figs. *DAR* 1948, p. 33.

Certainly here, as in the other two Nyanza districts, the wartime reports bear witness to the high level of remittances from army recruits being sent back into the district, and it was this money which to a very large degree funded the food imports after the war.[52] Nor should the steady increase in cotton production from 1947 to 1951 be seen as a major source of revenue for the district as a whole, since nearly all this cotton came from one location—Samia.[53]

Thus there is a parallel between developments in Central Nyanza and in Kiambu, but a parallel which reveals much through its limitations. In Kiambu pressure on land had made for difficulties in maintaining direct production of the socially given subsistence, but this was offset to some degree by the proximity of the Nairobi market and the possibility of growing 'high value' fruit, vegetables and wattle on small areas of land, and trusting to the market to provide one's subsistence. Labour migration also occurred here, but over far shorter distances, and probably a greater proportion of it to higher-income occupations in Nairobi. In Central Nyanza the absence of a high-value cash crop which would give high yields from a small acreage meant that long-distance labour migration had become the sole mechanism for raising household incomes. In both Central Nyanza and Kiambu a minority of households earned higher incomes from migration and invested those incomes in land, agriculture and trade, but the minority was probably larger in Kiambu, due to the dominance of this area in providing skilled and white collar employees (see chapter IX).

52. CKAR 1942, p. 1; and 1946, p. 2; NKAR 1942, pp. 7–8; 1943, p. 16; 1944, p. 11; SKAR 1945, p. 13.
53. Ominde, 'Land and Population', op. cit. (1963), p. 234.

North Nyanza

As will be seen from tables V:11 and V:12, the production and price data on North Nyanza (or North Kavirondo, as it had once been known) are much fuller than for the other two Nyanza districts. As already suggested the main reason for this is the dominance of this district over the total marketed production of the Province, and the concentration of the Maize and Produce Board upon this district, now firmly established as the 'granary of the Colony'.[54]

It owed this title, as can be seen, to the startling increase in maize production in this district from the onset of the war. In 1939 formally marketed production of maize and maize meal from the district was 12,108 tons. By 1940 in response to wartime prices and the Administration's production campaign it was 25,570 tons, an increase of 111 per cent in one season. Thereafter it rose to 27,653 tons in 1941, and remained around this level throughout the rest of the war, except for 1943 when a drought cut back production seriously here, as in other parts of Kenya. It was the colony-wide food shortages resulting from this drought which helped to secure the guaranteed price policies associated with the introduction of the Maize and Produce Control. The effect of these policies appears in the steadily rising 'official' prices of maize reflected in the second column of table V:12, and in Fearn's graph and bar chart reproduced in figure V:1.

Even these steadily rising domestic prices failed to satisfy European producers of the crop, for the simple reason that, from the onset of war, world maize prices rose sharply, and this buoyant price level was maintained after the war due first to the disruption of American production, and then to the onset of the Korean War boom in commodity prices. Therefore, despite steady increases, the domestic prices offered by the Maize and Produce Control remained some 25 per cent below world prices. Settler pressure on the Administration finally culminated in 1951 in a Commission of Enquiry into the prices of both maize and wheat. The Troup Commission report predictably recommended a sharp increase in domestic maize and wheat prices.[55] The startling effect of the implementation of these proposals is seen in the price rises for maize from 1952 onwards (i.e. at the end of the period considered here). The North Nyanza producers, who despite continuing deductions from their producer prices also benefitted from the Commission report, were unable to take full advantage of the massive price increases immediately, due to a series of bad or indifferent harvests between 1951 and 1954.

At the same time that maize prices were showing a steady and then dramatic

54. *NAD* 1939–45, p. 4.
55. *Report: Inquiry into the 1951 Maize and Wheat Prices and to Ascertain the Basis for the Calculation Annually of a Fair Price to the Producer for Maize, Wheat, Oats and Barley and Other Farm Products the Prices of which are Controlled by the Government* (Troup Report—L. G. Troup, Commissioner, Nairobi, 1952). See pp. 10–11 for data on world cereal prices during and after the war.

Table V:11. Volume and value of marketed produce 1940–52 in tons and Kenyan pounds—North Nyanza district

Year	Cotton Vol.	Cotton Val.	Maize Vol.	Maize Val.	Sesame Vol.	Sesame Val.	Rice Vol.	Rice Val.	Beans Vol.	Beans Val.	Sorghum Vol.	Sorghum Val.	Eleusine Vol.	Eleusine Val.	Vegetables Vol.	Vegetables Val.	Firewood Vol.	Firewood Val.
1940	2,325		25,570		854		36											
1941	2,954	28,256	27,653	52,508	841	7,539	121	905	736	1,010					400		6,000	
1942	1,789	17,538	25,635	70,205	1,316	14,765	266	1,985	612	2,860	1,532				350		7,000	
1943	863	13,422	16,307	68,716	121	1,522	1,052	11,004			2,278	8,928	44					
1944	1,092	20,792	29,786	140,115	15	188	1,480	12,800			2,987	13,800	35					
1945	1,249	20,855	28,237	133,098	125	1,541	1,483	13,786			1,977	2,120	18					
1946																		
1947	1,043	22,009	29,233	154,599	85	1,031	243	3,477			126		132	1,015				
1948	1,204	18,325	17,143	108,901	48	806	1,258	12,657			16	80	152	1,494				
1949	1,655	118,748	7,589?						5									
1950	1,539	130,207	14,285						21									
1951	1,913	216,588	9,375						350									
1952	2,718	344,232	6,964															

Source: NKARs and NNARs 1940–52.

Table V:12. Unit prices (K£ per ton) of marketed produce 1940–52—North Nyanza

Year	Cotton	Maize	Sesame	Rice	Beans	Sorghum	Eleusine
1940							
1941	9.56	1.89	8.96	7.48	1.37		
1942	9.80	2.74	11.20	7.46	4.67		
1943	15.55	4.21	12.57	10.46		3.91	
1944	19.04	4.70	12.53	10.46		4.62	
1945	16.70	4.71	12.32	9.30		1.07	
1946							
1947	21.10	5.29	12.12	14.30			7.67
1948	15.22	6.35	16.79	10.06		5.00	9.82
1949	28.00	6.46					
1950	31.36	6.85					
1951	42.56	7.64					
1952	50.40	12.78					

Source: ibid.

increase through the war years and afterwards, cotton prices were also buoyant as can be seen from the first column of table V:12. As will be seen, throughout the period, and despite the Troup Commission increases in 1952, cotton remained a much more valuable crop than maize. In fact its unit producer price was regularly about four times that of maize throughout the period, and double that of the next most valuable crop grown in North Nyanza district—rice, whose production increased markedly with Control-guaranteed prices from 1943 onwards. And yet cotton production pursued a distinct and continuous downward path from 1940 until 1948 when the District Officer instituted a campaign to revive what he termed the 'moribund' cotton production of the district.[56] Why was this?

Cotton in North Nyanza was grown in a series of locations on the western fringes of the district, notably Malakisi, Itesio, Buhayo, Marach and Buholo (this same cotton-growing area extended into Samia, North and South Ugenya and Alego in Central Nyanza).[57] None of these locations was particularly densely populated,[58] so it is unlikely that cultivators here felt the need to stop production of an inedible cash crop in order to go into food production due to declining land resources. Moreover, cultivators in these locations were clearly not switching away from cotton into maize over the war years, since maize did not grow well on the soils of these locations.[59] The answer seems to lie in a

56. NNAR 1948, p. 31.
57. For details see Ominde, 'Land and Population', op. cit. (1963), pp. 230–4.
58. All fell in Ominde's density categories II and III. Malakisi, Itesio and Buhayo had less than 200 people per square mile in 1948, Marach had 272 and Buholo 307. This compares with Maragoli's 976, Bunyore's 825 or Teriki's 763. See ibid., pp. 126, 129 and 133.
59. See ibid., pp. 246 and 251.

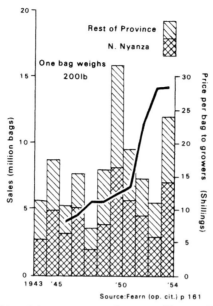

Figure V:1. Maize prices and output, Nyanza Province.

combination of factors. Firstly it is possible that not all the areas of those locations which were planted to cotton during the Administration's big cotton-growing drive of the mid-thirties were in fact suited to the crop, so some areas probably went out of production once the administrative pressure was relaxed with the onset of war. Secondly, although maize will not grow well on 'black cotton' soil, some other crops such as sorghum, groundnuts, cassava and beans will do so; and the level and stability of the prices of these crops appears to have improved after they too came under the purview of the Maize and Produce Control. However, it is unlikely that switches to these other crops would have been made in areas suitable to cotton had it not been for one further factor. This was that the yield of a cotton bush is extremely low in weight terms, which means that the returns per unit of land are also extremely low, and with smallholder production this is likely to be a determining factor in the cultivator's choice of crop mix.

Fearn presents a table of comparative crop profitabilities from North Nyanza in 1955 which makes this point clearly. Since cotton required levels of labour input comparable to other crops (see table V:13) returns per unit of labour time in cotton production were just as unfavourable as the comparative returns per unit of land. Thus the apparent high value of cotton relative to other crops, when the matter is looked at in terms of producer prices, failed to impress the cultivator when in order to harvest a ton of cotton lint she would have needed (in 1955) to have had 11.2 acres under the crop, whereas she could obtain more

*Table V:13. Comparative crop profitability table—North Nyanza
1955 plantings*

Produce	Yield per acre	Price to Grower	Costs at Shs. 1.50 per day	Inducement return per acre
		Shs.	Shs.	Shs.
Maize	18 bags	512/40	75/00	437/40
Cassava	60 bags	309/00	139/50	169/50
Groundnuts	4 bags	288/00	90/00	198/00
Mixed paddy (irr)	12 bags	230/40	172/50	57/00
Simsim	2 bags	144/00	97/50	46/50
Rose coco beans	3 bags	136/80	64/50	72/30
Mtama* white	5 bags	110/00	72/00	38/00
Cotton	200 lb.	100/00	75/00	25/00

Source: Fearn, op. cit., p. 198.

Crop	Days work (per acre)	Yield in lbs.	Inducement return per acre
			Shs.
Cotton	50	200	75/00
Maize	50	3,600	437/40
Mtama*	48	1,000	38/00
Groundnuts	60	800	198/00

Marketing Officer, Nyanza Province. *Comparative Crop Profitability Table* 1955, Planting—North Nyanza 1955.

*Sorghum
Source: Fearn, op. cit., p. 77.

than a ton and a half of maize, or half a ton of sorghum, or 5.35 tons of cassava from an acre even if she could not grow maize. Against these yield differentials the producer price differentials pale into insignificance, since clearly comparatively few cultivators in any of these locations would have had holdings large enough to put 11.2 acres under cotton. And even where they had, the cost of the extra labour required to tend the crop (should any of it have had to be hired) would have meant that the total return from those 11.2 acres would have been equivalent to 65 per cent of that from one acre of maize or about 40 per cent more than one acre of cassava![60]

Given these disparities the apparently irrational pattern of price and produc-

60. Fearn's table does not make it clear what is being counted in the production costs of Shs. 1/50 per day but I have assumed that it is either family labour given an imputed price equivalent to the daily cost of hired labour, or actual hired labour. These figures are for 1955 and it will be remembered that Fisher was quoting rates of 70–80 cents per day for hired labour in Central Province in 1952. If they do refer to hired labour, Shs. 1/50 would therefore appear to be the equivalent of two labour

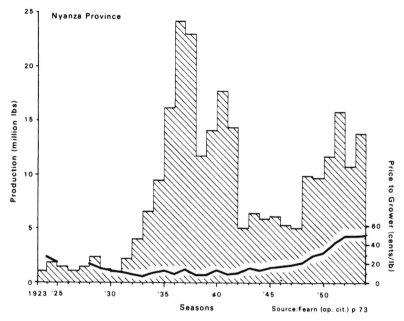

Figure V:2. Cotton prices and output, Nyanza Province.

tion figures for cotton in the entire Province from the early thirties to the mid-fifties shown in Fearn's graph and bar chart (figure V:2) also becomes explicable. To take it at its most extreme, provincial output of cotton in the season 1951–2 was only 65 per cent of the record output figure of the 1935–6 season, even though the producer price had increased by 300 per cent! Clearly the major difference is that in 1935–6, under strong administrative pressure, every acre which was suitable (and some which were not) was being planted to cotton, and this, plus a suitable season in weather terms, produced a record output. By 1951–2 the administrative pressure was back on again, but this time in a rather more discriminating fashion (more now being known about which areas could grow the crop and which could not). At neither point however were cultivators enthusiastic about cotton, and so, left to themselves (1939–48), they withdrew from its production in ever-increasing numbers, or at least put less and less of their land under the crop. In addition it must be remembered that cotton was entirely inedible so one could not hope to 'cash in' on others' shortages from the growing of cotton, nor did it provide any insurance against one's own food shortage. Thus once cassava and drought-resistant sorghum varieties were available, cotton had little to commend it to a cultivator, even in arid areas. It is this, rather than the higher prices for crops like sorghum, cassava

---

days per acre, but it may be that hired labour rates were somewhat lower in North Nyanza than in Central Province.

or groundnuts offered by the Maize and Produce Control, which made these other crops more appealing to the cotton cultivator of Nyanza Province. As we have seen, these guaranteed minimum prices though stable continued to be well below free market prices in times of shortage.

What all this suggests is that, unless yields and prices could be massively increased and/or costs reduced, the sheer 'weight' problem of cotton was likely to make it a consistently unsuccessful crop for smallholder production.[61]

A comparison of the price and output data for the other main crops of the North Nyanza district for this period indicates the general trend of rising prices for rice and sesame during the war years and immediately afterwards, with, in the case of rice, a rising output to accompany the prices. In the case of sesame, marketed output of the crop fell consistently from 1940 to 1948 despite steadily rising prices, which is probably some indication both of land shortage and declining soil fertility in its growing areas, since it was generally grown on land fresh from fallow, and was not inter-cropped.[62] The figures on other crops are too sketchy for any safe conclusions to be drawn, though the generally declining marketed production of sorghum should be noted. It may be that this decline also reflected its generally much lower returns per acre in comparison with maize.[63]

The Labour Process in North Nyanza 1945

Humphrey's study of North Nyanza agriculture[64] at the end of the war was mainly motivated by revived official concern about soil erosion as the result of maize monocropping. He ranges far wider than this, and provides some important data on the labour process. He provides an agricultural calendar for Marama location for example which shows that there was still no second crop of maize in that location in 1941, by which time Maragoli had been double-cropping for at least a decade.[65] This stark difference was clearly related to the population densities in the two locations. At the 1948 census Maragoli had 976 persons per square mile and Marama 334. Humphrey does not present a formal listing of the sexual division of labour by task, preferring to treat this sketchily in the text, but he does present the following outline of what he calls a 'specimen day's work' for men and women. As will be noted, the table is headed 'North Kavirondo' but the context leaves the strong impression that the observations mainly refer to Marama.

61. It is worth noting in this connection that the most conspicuously successful scheme for the production of 'smallholder' cotton in Africa—the Gezira scheme in the Sudan—is so organised that production is in fact on a large scale block basis. See for example Anthony S. Barnett, *The Gezira Scheme: on illusion of development* (London, 1977).

62. See Wagner, op. cit., Vol. II, p. 23. *DAR* 1947, p. 8 also notes the replacement of sesame by 'more highly priced legumes'.

63. In any case it seems to have been grown primarily as a food crop. See *DAR* 1949, p. 9; and 1950, p. 9.

64. Humphrey, *The Liguru...*, op. cit.

65. Ibid., p. 32.

Specimen Day's work—North Kavirondo[66]

Approximate Time	Man	Woman
6.0–7.0 a.m.	Goes out to *shamba* and begins work.	Cleans house, puts on cooking pots and perhaps feeds children. A small child is left at home with an older sister or girl of near kin, whilst the mother is in the field. It may be brought out to the *shamba* about 9.0 a.m. to be fed by its mother.
7.0–11.0 ,,	Works in *shamba*.	In *shamba*, having brought husband's food (probably gruel).
11.0–1.0 p.m.	Miscellaneous tasks according to season, *e.g.*, collecting building materials, weeding and cultivating, hunting, etc.	Continues working in *shamba*.
1.0–2.0 p.m.	In modern families second meal of day but may be only a snack in the *shamba*.	
2.0–3.30 ,,	Water cattle, collects ants.	Collects wood and vegetables. Brings water.
3.30–5.0 ,,	Passes the time.	Shells corn, grinds grain, prepares vegetables and cooks the big evening meal.
5.0–6.0 ,,	Evening Meal.	
6.0 ,,	Prepares evening fire, puts cattle in kraal, talks with friends round fire retiring about 9.0 p.m.	Prepares sleeping quarters and perhaps talks before going to bed.

This method of approaching the sexual division of labour certainly has some advantages over the more conventional task lists of the social anthropologists, in that it leaves a clearer impression of a lived day in the life of a household. On the other hand, given the necessarily seasonal nature of agricultural work, it is difficult to know exactly of what and when this 'specimen' day is meant to be

66. Ibid., p. 39.

typical. The general impression left by the timetable, of men doing no agricultural or animal husbandry work from the early afternoon until the early evening may have been typical of many households in Marama in off-peak periods, but was it typical of any during peak periods and especially during harvests? Moreover, we have already suggested that the level of male labour input would have been markedly varied from household to household depending on the presence or absence of the male from the farm (and the precise timing of those absences), and depending too on the farm size.

In this connection Humphrey makes some interesting remarks which seem to indicate that in his view the level of the male contribution to farm labour time when the man was at home was much greater in general in Maragoli than in Marama. One might expect this of course given the greater pressure on land in Maragoli and the presumably smaller mean holding size. In this case, and down to a minimum holding level, modern farm survey data would lead us to expect that output could only be increased by greater intensity of cultivation, and that the man or men resident on the farm would have had to have made their contribution to this. On the other hand, below this minimum threshold the alternative of long-term male labour migration might be taken up, and the woman left at home might stabilise her own labour input to the minimum for subsistence, or even transfer labour time to working for others. All this must be speculation.

Less speculative is a further comparison between the situation in Marama and Maragoli in 1945 made by Humphrey. So relevant is this comparison to issues raised by Fisher's study in Central Province that it is worth quoting at length:

> Nevertheless, there is in the trend towards idleness an inherent danger that the men will lower the status of the women in the same way as has undoubtedly occurred amongst the Kikuyu. It is perhaps not too much to think one can detect this already in Maragoli, and as an example I quote the different attitudes of the men there and in Marama in regard to food stores. In Marama we find three types of store. There is firstly the 'family' store, which is in the charge of the wife and is used by her for day to day necessities. Only when it comes to the disposal of any surplus must she seek her husband's approval. Within her hut are the pots which, again, are in her charge and probably contain such foods as simsim, beans and groundnuts. Quite distinct are the man's personal stores. These often contain *wimbi* and are primarily a food reserve; as such they are entirely the man's affair. Once he knows they are not needed for that purpose any longer, he is free to dispose of their contents as he thinks fit, possibly by sale, possibly by use in beer making. In general, however, whilst the man is the final arbiter, a wife has a very definite say in matters concerning the utilization and disposal of food and much obviously depends on her good management.
>
> In Maragoli, on the other hand, I was told that the men regarded women as

incapable of managing food economically and in need of protection against their own incapacity. Consequently, all the external stores from whatever source the grain comes, are under the man's control completely. The pots on the food shelf in the hut contain the grain for daily use; when they are emptied, a woman must ask her husband for more grain to fill them. There seems, in fact, to be much greater stress laid on the position of the woman as a mere user. Nor was this an unsupported instance and it seemed to me that the theoretical dominance of the man as *Owe lidala*, which normally allows a wife much scope in her own domain, is being emphasized increasingly in Maragoli and marks a trend towards female subservience, similar to that which is so characteristic today of much of Kikuyu life.[67]

Clearly the significant observation here is that in Maragoli as against Marama 'all the external stores from whatever source the grain comes, are under the man's control completely'. In short, the struggle which we inferred was going on within the Kikuyu households observed by Fisher is seen as having ended with the victory of the household head in Maragoli by 1947. It is also noticeable that the justification used by the male household head for this assumption of total control over the household surplus product was his position as '*owe lidala*' (which Humphrey elsewhere translates from the Logoli as 'owner of the homestead'), and this again would appear to confirm that the imported concept of 'ownership' was being used ideologically in a struggle for resources within the African household, as well as in the wider struggle among Africans in general.

What is puzzling is that by the tenor of his general observations both here and elsewhere Humphrey leaves the strong impression that he believes Maragoli simply to be following in the footsteps of events in 'Kikuyu'. Thus we have

First impressions . . . are definitely favourable after being in Kikuyu country. One may see a man and his wife digging together in their *shamba* or women swinging along with comparatively modest loads balanced on their heads and a long pipe dangling from their lips, full of life and cheerful and probably on their way to join a chattering mob at a near-by market. No greater contrast to the Kikuyu drudge could be imagined . . .[68]

Now this may simply be an example of the phenomenon of tribalism to which many colonial officers were prey,[69] but it may also be that the different impression left by Humphrey in comparison with Fisher's rather later account is due

67. Ibid., p. 40.
68. Ibid., p. 38.
69. The most famous case in Kenya of course being attitudes to the Masai who were either the last and greatest example of the noble savage maintaining intact their proud, aristocratic and martial culture, or backward, conservative primitives with no conception of the demands of progress, according to taste.

to the different areas of Central Province in which the two observers were working. Humphrey had just completed a study of agriculture in Nyeri district before going to North Nyanza, [70] and it is this study in Nyeri he is thinking about. Fisher, on the other hand, worked in an unspecified area of Fort Hall and Kiambu districts.

Since his report on Nyeri was primarily concerned with the effects of population pressure on the land, Humphrey would certainly have concentrated his field-work in the most densely populated southern locations. Fisher on the other hand leaves the distinct impression of having concentrated her investigation on households with larger than average landholdings.[71] If this is so, then the contrast between Marama and Maragoli locations of North Nyanza may have been mirrored in the contrast between south Nyeri and these frustratingly unspecified areas and households of Kiambu and Fort Hall. That is, in areas in which the population pressure was heaviest, the process of the 'centralisation' of control over the household surplus product and of the effective disappearance of a functionally separate sphere of control centred on the 'wife's garden' would have been most advanced, with the decline of the woman's economic independence being mirrored in a decline of her status vis-à-vis the household head. In addition southern Nyeri and Maragoli were both areas of high out-migration by men, and this too would have increased the general work load on women, certainly in those cases (and they would be the majority) in which the migrants were poorly paid and the amount of 'working with money' (remittances) which could be done was limited.

Conclusions

Humphrey's studies of Nyeri and North Nyanza, put together with Fisher's work on Kiambu and Fort Hall, allow us to take a little further the typology of households which was derived from Hay's work in Kowe. For most of the Central Province, and for at least the most densely populated locations of southern North Nyanza, Central Nyanza and parts of South Nyanza, as well as for the most densely populated areas of Machakos, we may identify the following types of household as having clearly emerged by 1952.
1. Wife at home on the plot. Male migrant in long-term better-paid employment away from the district. Remittances above average, used for the purchase of land and for the hiring of labour. Wife as effective farm manager but crucial decisions on the use of farm income probably in the hands of the husband.
2. Wife at home on the plot, husband in better-paid wage or salaried employment and/or in trade or business locally. Hiring of wage labour and purchase of land. Husband with more control over day-to-day managerial decisions than in (1) above, but wife probably retaining own land within the estate and power of

70. Humphrey, 'The Relationship. . ., op. cit.
71. Fisher, op. cit.

disposal over income from its produce. She may however have had the help of hired labour in working her own gardens.

3. Husband and wife permanently resident on the plot. Husband's labour input into cultivation considerably in excess of (1) and (2) above but still less than that of wife. Very limited or no hiring of labour, possibly some buying of land but on a smaller scale than (1) or (2) Wife probably still maintaining effective control over a proportion of the household's land holding, but conflict over this increasing.

4. Husband long-term labour migrant in low-paid employment. Wife at home on plot but few or no remittances received. No hiring of labour, no land purchase. Probable sale of land to meet short-term cash needs or through lack of labour to work it effectively. Strong conflict over control of land and over disposal of income, with an attempt by the husband to centralise such control, wife's resistance based on her actual control over day-to-day managerial decisions. Probable shift of crop mix to 'high risk' strategy noted earlier (in contrast to types (1), (2) and (3) where cash crop production is largely additional to subsistence production). On the smallest landholdings increased adoption of work as hired labourers, by the women involved.

5. Husband in short-term labour migration, at home at various points in the agricultural calendar. Therefore male labour input into cultivation in excess of (4) above, but considerably less than (3). Centralisation of control over farm land and income probably advanced or complete with total loss of wife's autonomy (certainly on the smallest holdings). No land purchase or hiring of labour, possible loss of land as in (4) above, also adoption of high-risk crop mix strategy as in (4) above.

By the early fifties, migrating squatter households (noted for Kowe in the 1930s) would effectively have disappeared as this option would now be closed. By this time in both Central Province, parts of Nyanza and other squatter areas like Nandi and Kipsigis, the compulsory repatriation of squatters from the farms was producing an in-migration of gigantic proportions.

This typology and stratification of households represents reasonably accurately the major parameters of the situation in Kenya's agricultural districts by the early fifties, but it must be noted that the proportion of each household type in any given location would vary markedly at any one time. Thus, very broadly, in the most densely populated locations (of southern Nyeri, Central Nyanza and southern North Nyanza) it is probable that by the early 1950s the majority of households would be of types (4) and (5), with types (1) and (2) a growing but small minority, and type (3) in continuous decline from a previous majority position. In less densely populated areas however, household type (3) probably still was in a majority in 1952, with types (1), (2) and (4) growing but not statistically dominant. The contrast between Marama and Maragoli locations exemplifies this difference clearly and so I suspect would the contrast between southern Kiambu or southern Nyeri and other parts of Kiambu, Nyeri and Fort Hall district. In addition, as already pointed out elsewhere, it is probable that in Kiambu far more of the male labour migrants would have had better-paid jobs than in, say, the main out-migration locations of Central Nyanza.

Further, in addition to differences between areas at one time there would be differences within areas at different times. That is, as already noted, there would be a general tendency up to 1952 in all areas for households of type (3) to decline relatively and for households of the 'elite' and 'impoverished' types to be 'recruited' from it, as it were. But also individual households would change types through time. Thus, not only might the educated son of a household type (3) come to head a household of type (1) or (2), but one man might in the course of his adult life shift his household from type (1) to type (2) and then (on his retirement from work or business) to type (3).

We see then an enormously complicated mosaic of household stratification with pronounced spatial and temporal differences and continuous internal movements within small groups of households. Clearly a more settled pattern of stratification within the most 'advanced' areas could only come about when household types could be held through generations, for example when the sons of elite households, types (1) and (2), could themselves feel fairly sure, in their turn, of heading elite households. I will argue later that from the 1920s onwards there was a tendency, growing in strength over time, for this stabilisation to occur. The major mechanism of this stabilisation was continuous privileged access to education (and thus to higher wage or salaried incomes) within families.[72]

Developments in Nandi District

The war years and after in Nandi district saw a marked expansion of maize monocropping with the plough. Table V:14 shows the quantities of maize formally marketed from the district over these years. As will be seen this increase in marketed output was by no means a smooth and linear process, there being frequent downturns due to droughts, and in certain years (1943, 1948, 1949 and 1952) the district became a net importer needing to purchase food to feed both people and livestock. Nonetheless, despite the familiar discrepancy between intention and outcome in tropical agriculture, it is clear from observations in the district reports and from the occasional mention of increases in the number of ploughs in the Reserve that the area under maize in Nandi increased markedly over these twelve years. By 1946 as Nandi squatters and their livestock began to return from the alienated farms of Uasin Gishu and other areas, the District Officer was so concerned at the reductions in the area of 'communal' grazing caused by large extensions of ploughed land that he had the Local Native Council pass a motion restricting the issue of ploughs to two for each *kokwet*,

72. See below, chapter IX.

Table V:14. Marketed output of maize,
Nandi district 1940–52

Year	Maize Marketed output (tons)
1940	94.6
1941	277.6
1942	316.9
1943	? —probably small or nil— drought
1944	1,785.7
1945	2,678.5
1946	357
1947	806.1
1948	? —drought
1949	—
1950	3,928.5
1951	1,785.7
1952	? —drought

Source: NaARs 1940–52.

or parish, of the district.[73] Huntingford, writing in 1950, reported that 'In 1939 there were some 250 ploughs in the Reserve and the number has increased to such an extent that in some places the elders of the *kokwet* have had to restrict the area under cultivation.'[74]

It does not seem that such restrictions were efficacious however, for by 1949 the District Officer was reporting that, in addition to ploughing, 'the more advanced natives' were beginning to fence their land and that the Local Native Council had decided to endeavour to control but not to prevent this 'inevitable' trend.[75] By 1952 these attempts at control of individual holdings had taken the form of Local Native Council rules laying down maximum acreage and attempting to prevent uneconomic subdivision of holdings by inheritance. There were also attempts to control rights of land disposal or sale.[76] In short by the late forties or early fifties the same processes which had taken root in Kericho in the mid-thirties were firmly established in Nandi as well. Moreover this appears to have happened largely in response to 'free market forces'.

Thus in 1942 the application of Maize Control regulations in Nandi was said to have created a 'flourishing black market'.[77] In 1948 there appears an account of the familiar situation in which a bad harvest had produced a food

73. NaAR 1946, p. 15.
74. G. W. B. Huntingford, op. cit., p. 61.
75. NaAR 1949, p. 12.
76. NaAR 1952, pp. 21–2.
77. NaAR 1942, p. 3.

shortage in the district because of heavy selling the previous year. Due to shortages, black market prices had reached Shs. 35 a bag (K£19.6 per ton, or over three times the Control buying price in that year).[78] As well as sales within the district when cultivators with a surplus sold to those without, it also seems clear that a great deal of unregulated or black market export of maize to both North and Central Nyanza occurred, particularly from the late forties. This seems to have run parallel to the export of cattle to these districts in the same years, and was clearly on a fairly large scale,[79] so once again we can be fairly sure that the statistics for maize formally marketed through the Control represent only a proportion of that produced and sold.

The level of exports to Central Nyanza, which seems to have increased in the immediate post-war period, confirms evidence reviewed earlier concerning the decline of this district as a food producer and its reduction to the status of a regular importer both from Nandi and, on an even larger scale, from Kipsigis. Exports to North Nyanza are more puzzling, but it may be that at times of good harvests (such as 1944 and 1945 in Nandi) maize was cheap enough to bear the costs of transport to North Nyanza for sale at a profit either to the Control or (more probably) to free market buyers.

3. Other Developments

The principal new departure in African agriculture from 1950 onwards was the initially slow but—after the Emergency—rapidly quickening encouragement of African production first of pyrethrum, then of coffee and tea. This happened not only in the three Kikuyu districts, but in North, Central and South Nyanza, Embu and Meru districts (where it had begun in a small way in the thirties but was now expanded) and in Teita in Coast Province. The entry of Africans into high-value export crop production, which marked a major new stage in small-holder agricultural development in Kenya, has been the focus of much study and analysis, and is discussed in depth in chapter XI. It had hardly begun however by the time of the Emergency, and so is not treated here.

In fact, 1952 can be taken as a rough bench-mark of the end of a process of commercialisation of African agriculture begun in earnest in the twenties and focussed overwhelmingly on the production of cereals, and then in the thirties of wattle, cotton and (on a much smaller scale) of vegetables as well. By the early 1950s that pattern had been imprinted not only on Central and Nyanza Provinces, Machakos district, and the Nandi and Kericho districts, but had begun to support small outposts in other parts of the colony. Thus by 1949 there appears to have been some plough cultivation of wheat among the previously entirely

78. NaAR 1948, p. 13.
79. See NaARs 1943, p. 3; 1945, p. 14; 1946, p. 8; 1948, p. 27; 1949, p. 27; and 1950, p. 27.

*Table V:15. Crop yields in Nyeri district
1931 and 1944 by major crop.*

	1931	1944
Maize	600 lb per acre	1800 lb per acre
Millet	700 lb per acre	700 lb per acre
European Potatoes	1½ tons per acre	2 tons per acre
Beans	500 lb per acre	600 lb per acre
Wattle Bark	6.6 cwt per acre	11.4 cwt per acre
Bananas	400 bunches per acre	320 bunches per acre

Sources: Fazan, op. cit., table D, p. 2212 and Humphrey, 'The Relationship...',
table XV, p. 9.

pastoral Elgeyo of the Rift Valley Province, and in 1950 Gulliver counted seventeen ploughs in operation among the Jie of the Northern Province.[80]

Both these cases can be seen as 'repeats' of processes which had already happened in Kipsigis and Nandi, whereby peoples who had previously relied overwhelmingly on animal husbandry for their subsistence were being moved into agricultural production by the innovations of a small minority. As this process was now occurring in districts which because of their aridity were more marginal for the growing of cereals, agriculture developed with more difficulty than in Kipsigis or Nandi.

We must now consider how most African households caught up in this process had fared as a result of it by 1952. Unfortunately this is where reliable data is at its most scanty, whether we are considering the movements in physical output per acre or per 'man' hour over this period of twenty-five years or so, or whether we are concerned with trends in real farm incomes. Consider for example the comparison in table V:15 of physical crop yields in Nyeri district, taken from Fazan and Humphrey.

It will be seen that Humphrey's estimates (from which he derives his income figures for Nyeri in 1944) show only very small increases of yields for all crops over these thirteen years, with the exceptions of maize where his estimates represent a threefold increase, and bananas where he shows an absolute fall! There is little doubt that Humphrey's estimates are too low, certainly for maize, and probably for the other crops as well. Crop surveys in North Nyanza eleven years later showed maize yields double those quoted by Humphrey,[81] and Huntingford's estimate of Nandi yields for the middle or late forties put them at the same level (1800 lbs per acre) as Humphrey's estimate for Nyeri.[82] Since Nyeri was a much more densely populated district than Nandi, and maize

80. Pamela Gulliver and P. H. Gulliver, *The Central Nilo-Hamites* (London,1953), p. 31; and *AAD* 1949, p. 17.
81. Fearn, op. cit., p. 198. See below.
82. Huntingford, op. cit., p. 65.

*Table V:16. Crop yields in Nyeri
district 1944—corrected*

Maize	2,400 lb per acre
Millet	933 lb per acre
Potatoes	2.66 tons per acre
Beans	800 lb per acre
Wattle Bark	15.2 cwt per acre
Bananas	426 bunches per acre

was raised by the more intensive hoe method rather than by the plough, one would expect yields in Nyeri to have been generally higher at this time. It is probable that Humphrey was here misled by his own semi-obsession with soil exhaustion, and also by a field visit conducted just after a bad year of drought in Nyeri.

If, therefore, shooting in the gloom, we raise all Humphrey's yield estimates by a third, we obtain the picture given in table V:16. If on the basis of these output figures we repeat Humphrey's income calculations we find that the 'average' household in Nyeri in 1944 would have had a cash income from all sources (including poultry and a cow as well as crop produce) of Shs. 382/53 in 1944. This is an increase in money terms of some 89 per cent over the Shs. 202 which Fazan had calculated for 1931.

This compares with Fisher's estimates of between '1,000 and 3,000 shillings' per season as the income of 'some farmers' in Kiambu and Fort Hall in 1952. However these figures do not seem very reliable because they appear to refer, at least at the Shs. 3,000 end, to elite households with large landholdings, and her expenditure data suggest patterns of spending in poorer households which would amount to Shs. 1,000 per annum at the most. Moreover we must remember that there was consistent and accelerating inflation in Kenya between the onset of war and the early fifties, and that therefore this Shs. 1,000 would have to be deflated. I have constructed a cost of living index for African income earners based on data provided by Stichter and the 1950 Cost of Living Commission in Kenya. Using this index (or indices, since for the late forties two alternative sets of statistics are available), a measure of real money farm incomes for African farmers in Central Province is provided using the fragmentary data provided by Fazan, Humphrey and Fisher. In the case of Humphrey both his original estimates and my corrected estimates are used for purposes of comparison.

4. Conclusions

It will be seen that taking these 'average' figures, farm incomes rose steadily over this period, being some 178 per cent higher in 1952 than they had been

Table V:17. A cost of living index[83] *for farm households in Central Province 1931–52 and the effect on real farm incomes*

Cost of living indices for Africans in Kenya (1931 = 100)			Real value of 'average' farm cash incomes of African farmers in Central Province (1931 estimate used as base)	
1931	100		1931	Shs. 202 (Fazan)
1932	93.5			
1933	85.6			
1934	83.4			
1935	88.2			
1936	86.1			
1937	90.8			
1938	87.2			
1939	86.4		1939	Shs. 229/06 (real value of 1931 figure)
1940	—			
1941	—			
1942	—			
1943	134.7			Humphrey (original) Shs. 260/8
1944	139.7		1944	Humphrey (corrected) Shs. 273/8
1945	139.8			
1946	142.5			
1947	148.2	171.1		
1948	157.6	178.8		
1949	161.6	178.8		
1950	171.0	193.5		
1951	162.4			Fisher (1) Shs. 562/4
1952	177.8			(2) Shs. 516/7[1]

Sources: Sharon Baker Stichter, 'Labor and National Development in Colonial Kenya' (Columbia University, unpublished Ph.D., 1972), table 3.4, p. 188. Colony and Protectorate of Kenya, *Cost of Living Commission Report*, (Nairobi, 1950), pp. 3 and 4, and *Report of the Cost of Living Committee* (Nairobi, 1954).

[1] Fisher (1) and (2) takes her Shs. 1,000 figure as an average for all smallholders in Kiambu and Fort Hall and deflates it to 1931 equivalents using the two alternative price indices. This provides exceedingly optimistic estimates of real farm incomes in 1952.

83. In the case of the indices for 1951 and 1952 taken from the Cost of Living Committee *Report*, comments in the report on the construction of the index show that food and drink were weighted at 38.23, whereas a survey of African household expenditure in 1950 put the weight for Africans at 71. Since the report went on to suggest that food price rises (and in particular rises in the price of maize) had been mainly responsible for the post-war inflation in Kenya, the much higher weight which would have needed to be given to food in an African index would (as the Mombasa figures for 1947–50 suggest) have meant much higher levels of inflation for African consumers. See *Report of the Cost of Living Committee*, op. cit., pp. 5–8.

twenty-one years earlier. But there is no doubt that these averages are mislead-ing, both because Fisher's 1952 estimates are especially questionable, and also because all the base figures for income abstract totally from the issue of dis-tribution. As we shall see in chapter XI, when reliable farm income data on Central Province first became available in 1963, they strongly suggested that the real incomes of the mass of small farmers in the Province had actually fallen from the end of the war to the early sixties. Fisher's figures in particular are much more a reflection of how the larger farmers fared in the early fifties than they are of the typical situation in Kiambu and Fort Hall.

However it is possible that the massive price rises in maize, cotton and wattle in the war and post-war period (maize was 700 per cent above its pre-war level in 1952) buoyed up the cash incomes of even the smallest farmers above the general rise in the cost of living. When this boom petered out in the early fifties, the basic structural problems of the Central Province economy, and indeed of the African smallholding economy in general, reasserted themselves. I shall now restate the roots of these problems.

Pressure of population on the Reserves had been building up during the thirties, albeit in localised areas, but relief had been afforded by the departure of entire households to take up residence on settler farms as squatters. However in the late thirties and through the forties settler pressure to reduce squatter numbers had produced a flood of returning immigrants to those areas which were least able to absorb them, and their attempts to obtain land produced an enormous amount of bitter social conflict, only the tip of which surfaced in land litigation. But the essential problem was not one of 'population pressure on the land'. There was no simple demographic determinism involved. The crisis in the smallholding areas of Kenya in the early fifties derived rather from the combination of low crop yields, restriction of Africans to crops which for one reason or another had a low exchange value, and markedly and increasingly unequal distribution of land between households.

It is unlikely that any of these three factors alone would have produced a crisis, but their combination was guaranteed to do so. In particular the highly unequal distribution of land between households meant that the low exchange value of African cash crops 'mattered' in a way in which it would not have done had there been equal land distribution or some form of collectivised produc-tion. For in that case the conventional description of 'the native farmer' by col-onial officials as a 'man' who had 'his' subsistence assured and only sold 'surpluses' would have been a broadly accurate universal description, apart from the assumption about the farmer's sex. As it was, it was partially but crucially inaccurate, in that the households with the smallest landholdings were increasingly being forced to obtain their subsistence on the market. In Marxist terms, a rising proportion of the social necessary labour time of these house-holds was being expended in the production of commodities rather than in the production of directly consumed use values. In the case of the very smallest households (which most often consisted of women alone without any source of labour power to replace that of the husband) a part of this labour time was actually being expended in wage labour on adjacent smallholdings, and landholdings would often actually have been reduced, through incapacity to utilise total holdings combined with the need to raise money quickly, often for subsistence purposes.

The relatively low exchange value of African crops in combination with their low yields had had another effect. Colonialism had introduced a number of new use values including cotton clothing, other cheap consumer durables, and formal education, to which access was only possible with modern money. In addition it had introduced and regularly raised tax liabilities and had demanded from the earliest possible moment that they should be met with modern money. This meant that African households were required to make a calculation not only of the use value returns to labour time, but also of the monetary returns, and it is clear that from the early thirties onwards an increasing number of households decided that the monetary returns to labour time in wage labour were markedly better than those in agriculture, despite slowly rising farm cash incomes. It is clear too that the greatest number of the households making this decision came from the areas experiencing greatest population pressure on land, i.e. those areas where small landholdings in combination with low yields increasingly loaded the equation against cultivating labour time.

But even this conceptualisation (which is the conventional one of Kenyan historiography) is inadequate and inaccurate if left in this form. It is inaccurate because, firstly, 'households' did not make this decision about 'their' labour time. Male household heads made this decision about their labour time, while for the wife such a decision was structurally precluded. She simply remained behind on the plot. The reason why the division 'wage labour time/cultivating labour time' became coterminous with the sexual division of labour needs some discussion. In a later chapter I shall argue that it was due to the sexual division of labour in the pre-colonial period and the sexual balance of production and labour use at that time, which when the issue of wage labour versus cultivation came to be posed, structurally predisposed it to be answered in this 'sexual' fashion.

Secondly, the conceptualisation is inaccurate because it abstracts from the whole issue of differentiation among households. The migration of male household heads to unskilled wage labour was the response of those households who had least land and who thus felt the constraints of low yields most acutely. The return even to low-paid wage labour time was superior to cultivating labour time for such households because these constraints were so severe. Moreover, and just as importantly, once this decision had been made, reliance on wage labour income by the household became more and more complete, because labour input into already small landholdings itself declined and with it the farm income.

At the other end of the spectrum, the migration of a male household head from a larger landholding to a much more highly-paid skilled or white-collar post provided the means to purchase both more land and the labour power with which to work it. However, the delineation of these two paradigmatic 'richest' and 'poorest' household situations only marginally illuminates the complexity of household differentiation in these areas. For not only were there many middle-level households where the male remained on the plot and increased his labour input, as did his wife, but even among labour migrants wage incomes were enormously varied both at one time and through time, since (as we shall see in chapter IX), the African labour force in colonial Kenya was stratified by a myriad of finely-graded wage scales. Thus the most accurate way of conceptualising household differentiation in Kenya by the early fifties is not in terms of wide-layered strata, but as a finely-graded spectrum stretching from richest to poorest with the closely intertwined and interdependent criteria of size of off-farm income and size of landholding as the twin axes around which that differentiation revolved.

However, it seems likely that the effect of war and post-war inflation in Kenya was to put a very much increased proportion of the households in the bottom end of this spectrum under strain, for wages were increasingly unable to compensate for low farm incomes in raising or stabilising total household incomes. But in addition, as from the early forties cost of living increases began to outpace wage rises for the first time, and, albeit temporarily cash returns to agricultural labour exceeded those to low-paid off-farm wage labour, the hardest hit were those in low wage occupations who had lost access to land, i.e. precisely those squatters and low-paid agricultural labourers whom we know made up the bulk of the forest fighters in Mau-Mau,[84] and who must have bitterly resented their inability to find land in the Reserve at a time of agricultural boom.

It should be noted, in this context, that the fact that the 'Abaluhya' and Luo peoples of Nyanza did not join with the Kikuyu in Mau-Mau is no indication of the absence of a crisis in those areas. This crisis in Nyanza was most severe in southern North Nyanza and in Central Nyanza, where there is every indication that physical output on most farms had actually been falling, and where the differentiation between households was probably just as marked as in Central Province. The crisis in Nyanza however was 'solved' temporarily by two developments: the movement of many Luo and Luhya migrants into better-paid employment lost by Kikuyu males during the Emergency, and minimum wage legislation which came into force in a period when Luo and Abaluhya were dominant in the wage labour force. In the longer term the crisis in Nyanza was 'solved' in precisely the same way in which it was solved in Central Province. What was this solution?

---

84. See for example, F. Furedi, 'Olenguruone in Mau Mau Historiography' (Paper to a Conference on the Mau Mau Rebellion, Institute of Commonwealth Studies, London, March 1974).

In one sense the solution was clearly implicit in the problem. A way had to be found both of raising the productivity of cultivator labour on African farms, and of raising the exchange value of the crops produced in that more productive labour time. It was particularly necessary to do this on the smallest farms. The 'solution' as everybody now knows was the introduction of the much higher value crops (pyrethrum, arabica coffee and tea) on to African small-holdings, combined ultimately with the excision of a small amount of land from the settler farm areas for settlement by Africans. This latter was essentially a holding operation to take population pressure off the land, whilst the other measures were given time to come to full fruition. Parallel with the introduction of these higher-value crops, a programme of land consolidation took place which had the effect of increasing the proportion of the labour day which could actually be devoted to cultivation (rather than being expended in moving from one land fragment to another). In addition there was a marked rise in real wages for at least part of the African wage labour force.

All these developments took place in the period after 1952 and were continuous from the colonial to the post-colonial period. They were essentially complete by 1970, and are examined in chapter XI.

Looked at from the perspective of 1952, such a programme (whose outlines had begun to be sketched even at that time) clearly required a massive investment of money and manpower in African agricultural production. There arose the question of the agency which would undertake this. In fact the 'question' was hardly a 'question' at all. Within the economic structure of colonial Kenya in 1952, the colonial state was the only agency which was willing or able to undertake the task, and the determination and resources to do so were only forthcoming when the eruption of Mau-Mau threatened to undermine the whole colonial political economy.

SOME ECONOMIC ORIGINS OF MAU-MAU 1905–1952

B. AFRICAN TRADE AND BUSINESS, PASTORALISM AND LABOUR

Chapter VI

African Trade and Business
1918–1952

I shall be overwhelmingly concerned in this chapter with the emergence of African-owned businesses purchasing crops from cultivators, and selling manufactured commodities to them; with those African businesses engaged in the further preparation of surplus food crops by the addition of a labour process (the milling of maize and the manufacture of jaggery from sugar cane); and with service and repair businesses provided by Africans for African cultivators —above all the provision of transport. The development of the African trade in and for livestock will be dealt with in chapter VIII, when the history of Kenya's pastoral areas before Mau-Mau is analysed. I deal with the matter in three historical periods.

1. 1918–1930

Some crude statistical material is available on the expansion of African business enterprise in the years just before and after 1918, since the emergence of such businesses at first took District Officers by surprise, and so were a feature of some interest and comment. Then in later years, as the numbers expanded, they became something of an index of 'progress' in the various African reserves so far as the Department of Native Affairs was concerned. However, the reports themselves reveal little or nothing about the way in which the capital to start such businesses was accumulated, and detail on such matters comes largely from more recent oral sources.

Tables VI:1 and VI:2 present statistics culled from the annual reports on the number and type of such businesses in the six districts of Nyanza and Kikuyu-land in the period 1918–30. Where a figure is not provided in a report, but some relevant remark is made, this is quoted. These two tables indicate perfectly the nature of colonial economic statistics. The numbers involved, despite their apparent specificity, are almost all national, whilst given the absence of any detailed categorisation of data in reports, figures appear and disappear from year to year on the basis of the interests of the District Officer. The unusually full set of figures for Fort Hall, for example, indicates the presence of a Commissioner with a more than usual interest in economic matters. Moreover the categories

Table VI:1. African business enterprises in Central Province 1918–1930

Year	Kiambu			Fort Hall			Nyeri		
	Shops	Flour mills	Lorries	Shops	Flour mills	Lorries	Shops	Flour mills	Lorries
1918	'becoming very popular'	2	—	—	—	—	—	—	—
1919	—	2	—	—	—	—	—	—	—
1920	—	—	—	—	1	—	—	—	—
1921	—	—	—	—	1	—	—	—	—
1922	—	—	—	—	2	—	—	—	—
1923	30? (trade licences)	—	—	—	4	—	—	—	—
1924	49	6	—	70	6	—	'quite a considerable no.'	—	—
1925	57	6	1(?)	126	12	—	—	—	—
1926	—	15	—	150	18	—	—	—	—
1927	—	21	7	144	37	6	60	42	5
1928	'very large numbers'	—	—	208	—	—	—	—	—
1929	—	—	—	154	40	4	—	—	—
1930	—	—	—	—	—	—	—	—	—

Source: KARs, FHARs and NARs 1918–30.

Table VI:2. African business enterprises in Nyanza Province 1918–30

Year	N. Kavirondo			C. Kavirondo			S. Kavirondo		
	Shops	Flour mills	Lorries	Shops	Flour mills	Lorries	Shops	Flour mills	Lorries
1918	—	—	—	—	—	—	—	—	—
1919	—	—	—	—	—	—	—	—	—
1920	—	—	—	—	—	—	—	—	—
1921	—	—	—	—	—	—	—	—	—
1922	—	—	—	—	—	—	—	—	—
1923	—	—	—	—	—	—	—	—	—
1924	'nearly 40'	—	—	'a number . . . opened'	1	—	—	—	—
1925	'no. considerably increased'	—	—	'decreased' —poor management	9	—	—	—	—
1926	—	—	—	69	34	27	—	'several started'	—
1927	220	102	—	'less than last year'	34	—	'some established'	9	2
1928	—	—	—	—	34	—	—	'some closed'	—
1929	—	—	—	—	—	—	—	3	—
1930	—	—	—	—	—	—	—	—	—

Source: NKARs, CKARs and SKARs 1918–30.

used are rather vague, and fluctuate from year to year and from area to area. In the case of maize mills, for example, by the late 1920s three different models were in use: a hand powered 'gristing' mill for use on the farm for the hulling of the maize, and actual flour mills powered by either water or diesel engine. In North Kavirondo in 1927, in addition to ninety-six water-powered and six diesel-powered mills, there were apparently 209 hand-powered gristing mills, and similarly in Fort Hall in 1929 there were eighteen hand mills in addition to the forty water-powered mills entered in the table.[1] In the case of shops, it is fairly clear that at this time, and for many years afterwards, many African-run retail shops selling a small range of simple consumer goods would also function as what the reports call 'tea shops' or restaurants selling food and drink. Thus some reports refer to 'shops and tea shops', but leave it unclear when the two functions were combined, and where (if at all) there was specialisation. Finally, before the emergence of African-owned lorries, used for the transport of goods and people, there was a consistent expansion of the number of African-owned ox carts. Thus Chief Koinange of Kiambu had an ox cart as early as 1918 (and in fact owned a plough and one of the two flour mills operating at this date as well). 'Native owned ox carts' were transporting produce from markets in Kiambu in 1925, and 'a large number' of natives were running them by 1927. A first count in 1928, in fact, showed that there were 117 such 'waggons'. In 1927 there were twenty-three 'carts and waggons' in Fort Hall district, which rose to seventy-six in 1928 and eighty-two in 1929.[2]

Shop and restaurant keeping, maize milling and the provision of transport do not exhaust the range of African-owned businesses commencing in the two provinces over this decade. Chief Kinyanjui and Chief Kioi had requested government permission to open up two maize mills and two sugar presses as early as 1910.[3] The fate of their application is unknown, but it is clear that mills for the preparation of jaggery from sugar cane (the jaggery then being used for the distillation of alcohol) was a business operating in Kikuyuland in this period and later. By 1927 in fact the District Commissioner of Fort Hall had become so concerned about the level of drunkenness in the district that he forced a resolution through the Local Native Council to 'abolish' African-owned sugar mills in the district. The resolution he records was passed only by eleven votes to nine as 'several of the Council members are sugar mill owners', and in addition the Kikuyu Central Association had also offered bitter opposition to the implementation of the resolution, 'many' of its members being mill owners.[4]

In addition there were an increasing number of African tailors making their appearance in these years, setting up their sewing machines in the open air in

---

1. NKAR 1927, p. 29; and FHAR 1929, Appendix XVII.
2. KHOR 1918, p. 4; KAR 1925, p. 10; 1927, p. 4; 1928, p. 12; FHAR 1927, p. 25; and FHAR 1929, p. 16.
3. KAR 1910, p. 11.
4. FHAR 1927, p. 3.

front of a shop or tea room. There were seventy-two such 'sewing machines' in Central Kavirondo in 1926 and seventy-six in 1928, and we know that they were spreading over Kikuyuland at this period as well.[5]

In addition the reports mention a number of specific businesses in each district, including the quarrying and transportation of sand for building purposes at Sagana in Fort Hall, the sale of firewood and manure in Kiambu, and the supply of fish (as employees' food) to a sugar estate in Miwani, Central Kavirondo, by Chief Daniel Odindo, which seems to have started in 1926. This is aside from the continuation of more traditional trading in pottery, salt, soapstone pipes and pots, and blacksmithing.[6]

Nor, as in the case of the commercialisation of agriculture, were developments restricted to the Central and Nyanza Provinces. There were five Kamba-owned shops operating in the trading centre at Kangundu in Machakos district in 1928, and 'many more' in the Reserve. Eight African-owned lorries were also operating, and we have already noted the very rapid expansion of maize mills in Kipsigis in the middle to late 1920s, so that the number in that district in 1930 was greater than that in Fort Hall.[7]

However, the organisation and pattern of capital accumulation for this expansion of business enterprise are far more interesting topics than mere numbers, and here we have to rely primarily on oral evidence. First of all it is clear, even from the district reports, that many if not all of the shops and water-powered mills, and even carts, were not owned by individuals, but were under some form of group or collective ownership. Thus for example the first maize-grinding mill in Central Kavirondo was described as being 'established by Chief Ogada at Yala River with a small syndicate',[8] and the 1929 Fort Hall report states that 'A contract to supply the Railway Extension at Naro Moru with 2,000 tons of sand was secured by Petro Kigondo [at this time the senior African clerk in the district administration] and his group of cart-owners and is now being excavated at the rate of 100 tons per month.'[9] As far as shops are concerned the Kikuyu Province Annual Report for 1926 noted that Kikuyu shopkeepers had problems deriving from their inability to buy goods on wholesale terms and from the fact that 'in too many cases an attempt is made to support five or six people on one shop, where there is only room for one, or at most two'.[10]

It is clear that the need to have some form of group ownership stemmed from

5. CKAR 1927, p. 14; and 1928, p. 16.
6. FHAR 1927, pp. 25–6; KAR 1928, p. 4; and CKAR 1926, p. 15; SKAR 1917, p. 12; NKAR 1917, p. 8. Wagner, op. cit., Vol. II, pp. 9–14 and 166–71; and van Zwanenberg with King, op. cit., pp. 151–2.
7. UPAR 1928, p. 38. Forbes Munro, op. cit., p. 171, cites 85 Kamba-owned shops in the Reserve in 1929 and 169 by 1932. Manners, op. cit., p. 502, reports that there were 73 Kipsigis-owned water mills by 1930 compared with 40 in Fort Hall.
8. CKAR 1924, p. 13.
9. FHAR 1929, p. 16.
10. KPAR 1926, p. 8.

the limited amount of money which any one man could raise to invest in fixed and working capital. But if more modern Kikuyu practice is anything to go by, the partnerships involved would be centred round a major investor who would act as manager and be regarded as the owner, whilst small quantities of supporting capital would come from friends and family. Marris and Somerset's survey of small Kikuyu businessmen seems to indicate that, in retail trade in particular, later generations of owners preferred to eschew partnerships altogether, principally because partners were likely to think themselves entitled to unlimited credit. And it may be that such attitudes reflect the hard experiences of these early years. Certainly both in the late twenties and thirties, District Officers noted the tendency of shops to appear and disappear with great frequency, and the instability of partnerships.[11]

The amounts of initial capital required even at this early stage tended to vary from business to business, with the amount required in retail trade being the smallest. Reports note for example the insubstantial nature of early shop buildings, which did not require materials or technology unfamiliar to traditional house builders, and the very small stocks, which reflected working capital constraints, but also the inability of African shopkeepers to obtain credit from Asian wholesalers—a source of considerable bitterness both at this period and later. Also, because small-scale retailing was possible on a minimal amount of working capital, it was the first sector of African small-scale enterprise to become crowded, with this 'crowding' often taking the physical form of the concentration of shops at market centres and communications centres in the Reserve.

Water-powered maize mills and particularly diesel-powered mills required a much greater initial investment in fixed capital, which is why such specific references as we have refer constantly to the owners as being chiefs and headmen or clerks, i.e. those Africans who had access to large and regular money incomes from the use (and abuse) of state power. This seems also to have applied, at least initially, to ox carts, and most of all to lorry ownership in the late twenties and early thirties (but probably not thereafter).[12]

However, both shop and maize mill owners had their money capital demands minimised at this period because so much of the trade conducted was in the form of direct barter. In the case of small-scale shops therefore small amounts of cash would be required for the retail purchase of tea (served brewed as refreshment, as well as in small unbrewed quantities), sugar (which could also serve both purposes), salt, soap, matches, kerosene and simple hardware goods. These would then be exchanged for maize, beans and other surplus food crops, as well as hides and skins, and (more rarely) milk and eggs. Small quantities of

11. P. Marris and A. Somerset, *African Businessmen: A Study of Entrepreneurship and Development in Kenya* (Nairobi, 1971), p. 189 and pp. 157–61. See for example KPAR 1927, p. 32.
12. See KPAR 1924, pp. 9–10; and 1926, p. 8; CKAR 1925, p. 16; and 1926, p. 14; NAR 1926, p. 5 and pp. 35–6; NKAR 1925, p. 12; and SKAR 1927, pp. 2–3.

these products having been bulked up in this way, they would then be sold for cash either to an Asian trader (for resale or transportation to a larger market), or—less frequently in these years—to a larger African trader/transporter.

In short, most of the small African shops in the Reserves acted as a low-level link in a chain of exchanges joining the African rural producer to a wider market. They were not always, at this period, the first such link, since in areas poorly served by shops there was still room for the itinerant African trader to bulk up products from neighbours and bring them to the shopkeeper. But as shops spread so they tended to come nearer to the cultivator and reduce the number of intervening links. The scanty evidence which we have suggests that most of the earliest African shopkeepers had themselves originally been itinerant traders, 'hawking' simple consumer goods in exchange for produce, either on their own behalf or as employees of Asian shopkeepers.[13]

Thus the exchange of simple manufactured commodities for agricultural produce yielded an aggregated set of exchange values which could be monetised through sale to a larger trader; the money so obtained could then be invested in further purchase of manufactured commodities, and (if one was fortunate) in expansion of the stock or in the transportation of produce.

Maize mills operated on a similar direct barter basis, though in this case of course a commodity (maize) was exchanged for a service or a labour process, the miller keeping a proportion of the maize brought as a charge for the service. (We should note incidentally that once diesel-powered mills became available they could be located with shops in market centres, rather than being con-strained by water sources. Thereafter there was some dual ownership of shops and mills, though this was probably rather limited up to 1930.)

Clearly success in the early days of shopkeeping and maize milling depended among other things upon a substantial advantage accruing to the shopkeeper or miller from the resale of the produce, and this advantage accrued where the charge to the cultivator in produce terms (measured in resale prices for the trader) for the goods or services sold was greater than the price paid for those goods or services by the vendor. In the case of maize milling (where the service sold is a labour process), the price would be the cost of wages, depreciation, etc. per unit of maize milled.

There are no empirical data available on Kenya on the extent of the gain from barter either for this period or later, but a fascinating study by Chipeta of the advantage accruing to diesel-mill owners from barter milling in Malawi does throw some light on the matter. In this study Chipeta attempts to measure what he terms the 'Gross Monetary Efficiency Ratio' (GMER) of 'customary money' to 'modern money' to grain mill owners in nine market centres selected from all

13. See FHAR 1924, p. 15; MasAR 1920 (unpaginated); and Marris and Somerset, op. cit., p. 62. SKQRs 1909 and 1911; and Fearn, op. cit., pp. 117–18.

Table VI:3. The relative advantage of maize grain and modern money payments to grain mill owners and customers

Area	Modern money cost of milling a tin of husked maize	Id. measure for maize grain payment	Number of units of (3) needed to fill 1 tin (four gals.)	Cost price of (4) (i.e. cost price of 1 tin unhusked maize)	Resale value of (4) (i.e. selling price of 1 tin of unhusked maize	GMER = (6)/(5)
1. Nkamanga	1s. 2d	14″ plate	21	1s. 9d	3s.–4s. 6d	1.7–2.6
		12″ plate	24	2s.	3s.–4s. 6d	1.5–2.3
2. Katete	1s	1/2 Part of long ruler dipped into tin	Whole length of long ruler dipped into tin	1s.	1s.6–10s.	1.5–10.0
3. Kavuzi	1s. 2d	1 part of graduated tin	14 Parts	1s. 2d	6s. 6d–8s	5.6–6.8
4. Chia-Benga	1s.	Small tin	10	2s. 6d	3s–3s.6d	1.2–1.4
5. Malikha	9d.	14″ plate	21	1s. 9d	3s.	1.7
		12″ plate	24	2s.	3s.	1.5
6. Chinani	9d.	Medium size tin	8	8d.	4s.	6.0
7. Nkanda	1s. 2d	—	—	—	—	—
8. Makwasa	6d.	14″ plate	21	1s. 9d	5s.–7s	2.9–4.0
		12″ plate	24	2s.	5s.–7s	2.5–3.5
9. Ngabu	10d.	14″ Plate	21	1s. 9d	5s.	2.9
		12″ Plate	24	2s.	5s.	2.5

Notes: (i)   1″ = One inch = 2.5 cms.

    (ii)   The Malawi pound (£) has parity with the £ sterling and is similarly divided into twenty shillings (s), each of which is subdivided into twelve pence (d).

Source: Chipeta., op. cit., p. 48. The exchange rate referred to in note (ii) is for 1970.

three regions (Northern, Central, Southern) of Malawi.[14] His results are shown in table VI : 3.

It will be seen that what is essentially being measured is the 'cost' to the women of paying for their milling by barter. Thus in Nkamanga for example (case 1), if a woman pays cash to have a tin of husked maize milled, she would be charged 1s 2d; if however she chooses to pay in maize she will be charged 1 tin of unhusked maize, the resale price of which (accruing to the mill owner and not to the woman) is—depending on the time of year—3s to 4s 6d. Thus the GMER (depending in this case on which of two measures for maize payment are used) falls in the range 1.7 to 2.6 or 1.5 to 2.3. It will be seen that the GMER varies markedly from region to region depending partly on the variable 'modern money' charges for milling, but mainly on the resale price of maize. Obviously enough, where maize prices are highest the GMER is highest and the loss to the women is not using modern money is greatest. As a result, as Chipeta notes, the GMER also varies within areas by season and with the weather, 'it being greatest when the supply of grain is low in relation to demand'. However a lot also depends on the measures of grain used,[15] and since some of the women in Chipeta's study had a choice between cash or barter payment, it is clear that some of them chose not to use the barter method when maize prices were high.

Chipeta also refers to data collected on the GMERs of fishermen near Lake Chilwa and of shopkeeper traders, but unfortunately does not present it, although he remarks that the gains from barter trading to both groups were considerable, and that in their case, as with mill owners, 'The decision to invest... may depend to some extent on the gain which they make in these transactions.'[16] He also suggests that at least some part of barter trading is 'forced' in the sense that it is a rational but costly adaptation to the difficulties of obtaining modern money for the crops: 'Women may have to carry on their heads maize to market places located far away. They may have to wait there a long time before their produce is bought.'[17]

Moreover, Chipeta's mode of measurement of the GMER understates the gain to the miller, in that the selling price of the service in modern money terms is used as the basis of comparison, rather than the cost of its provision to the miller. Clearly even the modern money charges would not be profitless. In addition Chipeta notes that 'the practice of accepting grain payments enables grain mill owners to use more of their existing capacity' with some saving in unit costs, but he does not attempt to quantify this saving.[18] Finally, if some or all of the maize gained is not simply resold but milled and resold *as maize flour* then

14. W. Chipeta, 'The Roles of Customary and Modern Money in the Rural Exchange Economy of Malawi', *East African Journal of Rural Development*, Vol. 3, No. 1 (1970) pp. 45–56.
15. Ibid., pp. 49–50.
16. Ibid., pp. 51–2 and p. 54.
17. Ibid., p. 51.
18. Ibid., p. 54. Chipeta himself makes this point, ibid, p. 51.

once again a measure of loss to the cultivator is not a true measure of the gain to the miller.

Now if these results may be obtained from a survey made in 1968, when agricultural production in Malawi was presumably a good deal more commercialised than in Kenya in 1930, it is not too much to assume that the GMERs of traders and millers operating in the earlier period were higher. In the first place there were fewer of them relative to the population and area of the Reserves, and competition was accordingly less severe. Furthermore communications in many parts of Kikuyuland and Nyanza were still very poor, and thus the cost in labour time to cultivators of carrying crops to the larger trading centres (where cash might be obtained) was accordingly greater. In addition cash needs were fewer and (partly because of the situation described above) the volume of cash transactions much lower, either than in Malawi in 1968 or than in Kenya even in 1940.

For all these reasons the 'choice' of mode of payment open to at least some Malawi women in 1968 would probably not have been open to Kenyan women forty years earlier, and thus much more barter trading would have been 'forced'. Guessing intelligently then we might put mean GMERs for African traders and millers in Kenya in the 1920s in the 6–10 range, rather than in the 1.5–4.0 range which seems to have predominated in Malawi. One would also expect of course that GMERs would fall through time, especially in retail trading, as the volume of cash transactions increased, as the level of competition among traders rose (capital constraints being so minimal), and as better communications and greater mobility made cultivators aware of relative prices. As I shall argue in the next section, there is quite a lot of evidence to support this hypothesis.

In the case both of maize milling and the preparation of jaggery from sugar cane, African businessmen were providing a labour process for cultivators which either allowed the expansion of labour time in cultivation, or increased the exchange value of the products produced. Without such services cultivators would either have had to undertake such processes themselves, with the use of a simpler technology, thereby expending quantitatively more labour time per unit of output, or they would have had to rest content with the sugar cane and unmilled maize. In the latter case they would have foregone the additional exchange value of maize flour over maize grain, and in the former case one further labour process would have been added to the preparation of beer—a labour process usually undertaken by women. The case of sugar cane is particularly interesting because, as we have seen from Peristiany and Wagner, beer was quite often exchanged for labour power to assist the family in cultivation and other tasks, as well as being used on ceremonial occasions or simply being sold for cash. Thus maize milling added exchange value to a surplus product, whilst sugar milling was part of the production process of a product (beer) which functioned from the point of view of the household partly as a surplus product with an exchange value, partly, as a 'wage good'. With the wage good so produced, households obtained labour power used partly for the production of the socially necessary product, partly for the production of the surplus product, though the proportions between these two types of labour time (socially necessary and surplus) cannot be determined.

Thus the introduction of an apparently simple innovation such as a maize or sugar mill produced a whole series of underlying shifts in the distribution of labour time and labour power, all of them tending to have a positive impact on agricultural productivity. Such services as these and the hiring of ploughs, which help either to release labour power for cultivation, or to lower the (labour time) cost of obtaining extra labour power for cultivation, or to add exchange value to the household surplus product, were all an essential part of the process of the commercialisation of small-scale agriculture which was beginning in earnest in the late 1920s. A similar release of labour time to cultivation was of course achieved by traders, and particularly their itinerant agents. The labour time that they expended in marketing would otherwise have had to be expended by the cultivators. However, the very limited number of traders in these years, their spatial concentration and the poor communications of the time must have made such a contribution minimal.

In all cases the businessmen involved obtained a share of the surplus product in return for the service, and as we have suggested from the analysis of the 'Gross Monetary Efficiency Ratios', this share was larger than would have been achieved under an alternative (hypothetical) set of circumstances, and almost certainly larger—at least in commodity trading, and probably in milling and transport as well—than was obtained in later years. To this degree the share so obtained was 'at the expense' of the cultivator.[19]

2. 1930–1940

In the previous section we traced the growth of shops, water-powered maize mills, carts and lorries owned by Africans in the Kikuyu and Nyanza districts, in Machakos and Kipsigis. Because of the interest taken in these palpable marks of 'progress' by a number of District Officers, it was even possible to attempt some form of tabulation of this growth toward the end of the 1920s.

However for the decade 1930–40 this becomes impossible despite the indirect evidence that all these kinds of African-owned enterprises were a good deal more abundant in 1940 than they had been in 1930. In fact the almost total

19. Though this certainly raises difficult theoretical questions, since it is arguable that the labour time 'saved' to the cultivator by these services enabled a volume of surplus product to be produced which more than offset the loss to GMERs. This is certainly unknowable, but is in any case less important than the fact that GMERs existed and were almost certainly large. It does however raise questions about exploitation in the sphere of circulation which are taken up later. See chapters XIII and XIV.

absence of estimates from the reports for this decade is a testimony to this growth, for as these 'new' phenomena of the 1920s became a regular part of life in the Reserves, so District Officers began to find them unworthy of note. And as businesses multiplied in numbers and location, even rough estimates became impossible. Thus in Kikuyuland throughout the decade Officers usually content themselves with remarks such as 'the number of native *dukas* continue of course to multiply'. While even in a district like South Kavirondo, where the sort of developments which in Central and North Kavirondo had taken place in the late twenties were more typical of the 1930s, the District Officer could content himself with the observation that 'Small native *dukas* are springing up all over the Reserve, the Kisii in particular have a mania for store/water mills.'[20] The slightly weary tone indicates that since most Officers moved districts very rapidly they came to expect such observations, having seen similar trends elsewhere. However there is another dimension to this change of tone, which is that by the mid-thirties the proliferation of African businesses, and in particular of African-owned shops acting as produce buying centres, was seen not as a mark of progress but as a problem, since by this time the Administration's 'new policy' toward African agriculture was in operation, and a central part of this policy was the attempt to reorganise marketing and to bring it under the effective control of the Administration. And the point of this in turn was to introduce a system of quality grading of crops, starting with maize but then taking in other crops.[21]

With the significant exceptions of cotton and wattle bark, the inspection centres were almost a complete failure, for the bulk of African produce marketed did not pass through them. Fearn holds that failure was due to the Administration's inability to win the co-operation of the Asian trader,[22] but this explanation does not strike to the heart of the problem. The idea behind inspection was to increase the proportion of African production going on to export markets, and to raise African incomes by improving the quality of produce marketed. In part this was to be done by offering better prices for the produce once it had passed inspection, and in part by forcing the African cultivator into local monopoly buying centres where sub-standard produce was unsaleable. Inspection failed because the price differential between inspection centres and other market outlets provided no incentive to go to such a centre (especially since each seller was charged a small fee for the inspection service) and the Administration never succeeded in eliminating these other outlets.

And this of course is where the 'problem' (as it was now seen) of the African *duka* arose. Most growers did not sell their produce direct to an Asian trader/

20. SKAR 1935, p. 12.
21. A fairly comprehensive account of the introduction of the system can be found in *DAR* 1936, pp. 92–100. See also Graham Gamble, 'Marketing of Native Produce', in E. W. Bovill and J. K. Matheson (eds.), *East African Agriculture* (London, 1950), pp. 224–6, and CPAR 1936, pp. 63–5.
22. Fearn, op. cit., pp. 156–7.

transporter, but to an African shopkeeper or produce buyer in the Reserve. It was on their co-operation much more than on that of the Asian trader that the efficacy of 'inspection' was reliant. So long as hundreds of such outlets existed and would in turn supply the Asian trader at prices below inspection levels, so long was inspection bound to be ineffective.

Moreover, much trade within the Reserves was 'subsistence marketing' and men and women looking for food in the markets had no interest in restricting their buying to a quality of maize or beans which the Kenya Farmers Association could get on to export markets, or which would allow the relatively high-cost settler producer to compete in domestic markets.

The Administration did its best in this regard. As soon as an Inspection Centre or market was so designated, local rules usually forbade the purchase of produce for a radius of several miles around (local rules varied between three and five miles depending upon the density of settlement and of markets). But of course without a positive army of personnel to enforce these monopolies they were widely breached. In response to these breaches, the Administration went in for a policy of fairly systematic harassment of African shopkeepers, principally by requiring shops in gazetted trading centres to be licensed, and denying licenses to those thought to be engaged in 'illicit' trading. All the evidence suggests however that these measures were just as ineffective as the local monopolies which had led to them, for the problem was on too large a scale for it to be effectively handled by an under-staffed district administration burdened with a myriad other tasks.[23]

Nonetheless, if, largely as a result of a change of administrative policies and the indifference produced by familiarity, we are denied even such scanty statistical data on the growth of African business as were available for the late 1920s,[24] this is compensated for to some extent by a set of interesting first-hand observations of the structure of trade in North Kavirondo provided by Wagner.

Wagner presents a fairly detailed description of the goods on sale, the mode of exchange and the sexual division of labour in trade in a market at Mbale, on the border of North and South Maragoli as it was in 1937. He also provides a sketch of increasing African involvement in the export trade in produce from

23. KAR 1934, pp. 18 and 31; and 1938, p. 27; FHAR 1934, p. 6; FHAR 1937, p. 24. See especially the cynical comments in NAR 1942, p. 9. Also NKAR 1936, p. 11; and 1938, p. 3. In Central Province the KCA became involved on the side of the persecuted traders, see FHAR 1936, p. 8.

24. This is not entirely absent. There are a scattering of numbers from various sources. Thus the number of shops in Machakos district rose from 85 in 1929 to 165 in 1932, with 35 of this latter figure being 'eating houses' and ten being butchers' shops. There were reported to be 201 Kikuyu-owned shops in Fort Hall district in 1936, but this probably only refers to shops in trading centres, and whereas there were reported to be 102 water-powered maize mills in North Kavirondo in 1927 the figure had risen to 314 by 1938. The 1938 North Kavirondo report also lists the presence of 3 'Overshot' watermills, 3 power-driven hammer mills, 17 ox carts (there had been 8 in 1937), 230 sewing machines and 2 lorries. Sources: *NAD* 1932, p. 56; Forbes Munro, op. cit., p. 171; FHAR 1936, p. 12; NKAR 1938, p. 9.

the district, and the development of a range of handicraft and artisan specialisms in the African population in the late thirties.

The market described by Wagner was one of sixty-four operating in the district in 1937, and was held weekly on a Saturday, apparently all the year round.[25] Women sold 'agricultural produce' in the market as well as pots, pipes, firewood, vegetable salt, dried fish and chickens, while men sold 'meat, livestock, baskets and quail cages, string, mats, ironwork, wooden objects, grindstones and grinders, and honey'.[26]

He also noted that as one would expect the market was at its busiest just after the two harvests of the year, i.e. after the long rain harvest (from July to October) and in January–February after the short rain harvest. At these periods not only were there more food crops for sale but demand for other goods was at its peak and with it the supply. Prices fluctuated accordingly. 'For sorghum they rose from 6 cents for one *enavodo* (standard measuring basket) soon after the 1934 harvest (August) to 12 cents in April–May 1935. Maize was cheapest in October (12 cents for one *enavodo*), rising by about 50% until the end of December.'[27] And this fluctuation extended to other products besides crops themselves. He quotes the number of pots on sale at Mbale falling from 120 in October 1934 to 'less than fifty' in December, with price falls of twenty to thirty per cent.[28]

He also observed the predominance of cash transactions in the market; cash was used in 'practically all market transactions', 'the only form of barter still practised to some extent being the direct exchange of various commodities (e.g. pots, tobacco, Luo mats) for maize.'[29] Now this observation is particularly interesting because it conflicts directly with Kenyatta's evidence for Central Province which dates from 1938: 'There are two ways of exchanging goods, one by barter and the other by money. The former is predominant, for the majority of people still adhere to the old form of exchanging one article for another.'[30] However Kenyatta's observation is couched in very general terms, and it may be that it is meant to refer not to contemporary practices in markets, but to barter between neighbours or friends.

We noted in the previous section that the profit accruing to a vendor of manufactured produce from barter trading with a cultivator derived from his capacity to resell the produce obtained—for cash—at a price in excess of that for which the cultivator could have obtained the goods for direct cash purchase, and it was also suggested that the bulk of the profit accruing to African retail shops in the 1920s came from this source. This would have meant that in the 1920s exchange chains were operated on a barter basis at the bottom (at the

25. Wagner, op. cit., vol. II pp. 166 and 168.
26. Ibid., p. 168.
27. Ibid., p. 169.
28. Ibid., p. 169.
29. Ibid., p. 169.
30. Jomo Kenyatta, *Facing Mount Kenya: The Tribal Life of the Gikuyu* (London, 1938), p. 61.

level of the cultivator and the shopkeeper or the cultivator and the itinerant trader) and on a cash basis at the top.

Now clearly this is a system that relies heavily on the cultivator's ignorance of relative prices, and/or his or her inability to reach towns, trading centres, etc., where cheaper cash purchases of products might be possible. One would therefore expect it to have broken down as cultivators became better acquainted with relative prices (through travel or by discussing prices with those who had travelled), as communications improved (thus lowering the cost in labour time to the cultivator of finding an alternative buyer), and as the number of shops and traders multiplied (which would have the same effect as improved communications). One might expect it also to have broken down from the top of the chain downwards: that African shopkeepers and produce traders would have demanded that produce purchased by Indians be paid for in cash, and would have purchased trade goods from them with cash. They themselves would then have faced the same demands from smaller traders supplying them, who would then have faced the same demands from cultivators. Once this had occurred one would then expect a 'lateral' spread of cash trading into exchange relationships between cultivators and local artisans in non-export markets and Wagner's evidence at least supports this speculation.

There would be a material gain to the cultivator in a switch to cash selling from barter, a gain accruing from the splitting of the act of exchange into two parts. In barter the exchange of the manufactured goods for the food crop occurs directly. In Marx's notation it is the relationship C−C, the simple exchange of one commodity for another without any form of mediation. In this exchange the party who is better informed about relative prices and can move the commodity to a cash purchaser stands to make a double gain. On the one hand the amount of grain he obtains for (shall we say) the amount of salt bartered, will exchange for more money than the salt cost him, even if he sells the grain immediately and in the same place. On the other hand, if he can move the grain perhaps (in Kenyan conditions) only a relatively short distance he may realise a further gain which would more than offset transport costs, and if he carries the grain bodily there may be very few or no cash costs.

If now the cultivator insists on cash purchase she cannot eliminate the second gain (which derives from what the economists are pleased to call an 'imperfect' market situation) but she can eliminate the first, because having obtained her money she can now 'shop around' for salt. By splitting the exchange into two parts, in Marx's notation C−M (commodity for money) and M−C (money for another commodity), money transactions allow the seller (in C−M) to have time before the second act of exchange. Insofar as this time is used for the comparing of relative prices and the purchase of the cheapest alternative, the adoption of money exchange is itself a factor helping to make markets more 'perfect'. This is the essence of what, in Marx's terminology is known as money's function as 'store of value'. The exchange value of the commodity sold is 'stored' in money until such time as the seller wishes to buy.[31]

Now in the Kenyan situation in the mid-thirties this switch from barter to cash transactions may have had very damaging effects for African retail traders, because they were throughout unable to obtain their manufactured goods on wholesale terms. This meant that as soon as the first gain accruing from barter was eliminated (by the elimination of barter itself), they were in trouble. Since they could not obtain their goods on wholesale terms, as soon as cash transactions became the norm they were unable to obtain a profit from selling to cultivators at cash prices significantly above the prices which they themselves had paid. This arose partly because cultivators were able to bypass them and go straight to the Indian shops where they could get exactly the same terms as African retailers, and partly because, even where this did not occur, the narrow range of goods for which there was any demand, and the proliferation of shops with the same goods, meant that price mark-ups had to be minimal or even non-existent if customers were to be attracted. In the days of barter the lack of wholesale terms for the African shopkeeper or itinerant hawker had mattered less, because profits could be made from the resale of the produce and from the ignorance of the cultivator about relative prices and/or her inability to shop around.

The switch from exchange carried out predominantly by barter to that carried out predominantly by money also accounts for a phenomenon appearing in Wagner's account of North Kavirondo, and confirmed for a later period by Fearn: the emergence of a group of African traders involved exclusively in the purchase and resale of agricultural produce.[32] These traders, as Wagner makes clear, operated entirely in cash, and made their profits from price differentials between different areas. At the time when Wagner observed them, these men were not in any way involved in retailing manufactured goods, an activity which was now the preserve of an apparently distinct class of traders whom Wagner hints, and Fearn confirms, to have been markedly less prosperous.

Frustratingly it is unclear when this division of labour in trade had come into being. But it would probably have been closely related to the switch over to money transactions in trade, which in Maragoli at least we must therefore date as having occurred before 1934. It may be that these more prosperous produce traders were those who had been in the shopkeeping or itinerant hawking business at an earlier stage, but who had realised that the maintenance of profitability involved a switch to an exclusive concern with the purchase and resale of crops where the form of profit was not threatened by money exchange.

The impossibility of dating either the emergence of this group in North Kavirondo or the movement to the predominance of money in exchange (at least in markets) is reflected in a general inability to attach a clear chronology

31. *Capital*, Vol. I, pp. 106–10.
32. Wagner, op. cit., Vol. II, pp. 171 and 172.

to this process in Kenya as a whole, a difficulty that is much exacerbated by the absence of any equivalent study to Wagner's for Kikuyuland in the thirties, or indeed in the twenties. It is almost certain that the process was markedly uneven, with the degree of monetisation probably being closely linked to the degree of commercialisation of agriculture (and thus the proportion of the surplus to the socially necessary product). One would therefore expect it to have been well advanced in Maragoli in the late thirties, because as we have seen this was the area which was producing most of North Kavirondo's maize surplus and had been doing so since the late twenties. On this basis too one would be very surprised if cash transactions were not totally predominant in Kiambu by the mid-thirties, and indeed they may have been so there from the mid-twenties.

One would also expect the spread of cash dominance to have been from south to north in both North Kavirondo and Kikuyuland, going along with the progress of commercialisation. Other powerful factors favouring 'monetisation' would have been the proportion of males in any area who were absent in wage employment and sending back cash remittances (we have seen that the proportion was thirty per cent or more in Maragoli in the late thirties), and the proximity to urban areas where cash transactions were universal. Beyond these obvious generalities we can say no more until further historical research has been undertaken.

Turning back to Wagner's specific observations of trade in Maragoli in the period 1934–8, we note that women appear to have dominated or perhaps even monopolised the sale of food crops in the market. Once again, as in the case of the emergence of a group of male produce traders not engaged in retailing, one wonders how long this had been the case. And in this case Hay's work in Kowe is suggestive.

We noted earlier that Hay characterised the period 1930–45 in Kowe as one in which a limited number of labour-saving technologies allowed the labour time invested in agriculture to be reduced, and to be invested in other activities: wage labour in the case of men, trade in the case of women. I suggested in presenting Hay's material that these findings had to be disaggregated by household, and that when this was done they amounted to the marginalisation of agriculture in the case of some households (i.e. households where the absence of male labour power was not compensated for by money incomes from wage employment sufficient to allow the hiring in of labour), and the increased commercialisation of agriculture in the case of elite households who had access to higher incomes from wages or salaries. Nonetheless there was a large group of middle-level households growing small surpluses of crops, and I suggested that it was mainly these households (in which male labour power supplemented women's efforts on the farm) from which the larger number of female traders came (though some trading may also have been done by women whose husbands were absent). In the case of Kowe an initial stimulus to this development came from the local goldmine market to which the women traded milk, fruit, vegetables, chickens and cooked food. But Hay makes it clear that even after the mine had declined this pattern of women's trade persisted, the women making trips to new markets which were opening up in the vicinity of Kowe in the 1940s.[33]

Clearly the shift of female labour time which Hay describes for Kowe had already occurred in Maragoli by 1934, and this should not surprise us. The limited improvements in the instruments and objects of labour on the farm which were occurring in Kowe in the 1920s and 1930s had also occurred in Maragoli and indeed were probably more advanced there. Maragoli, for example, had certainly entered commercial production of maize somewhat earlier than Kowe, and it probably had heavier rates of labour migration by the end of the thirties as well.

However it should be noted that this shift of female labour time into trading probably did not represent a deduction from time spent in cultivation. Rather it is likely that female labour time invested in agriculture was increasing in all households in this decade, except those households in which large amounts of peak period hired labour could be obtained. Even in those households where wives, completely unassisted, minimised labour input on their own plots to a subsistence level, it is likely that their overall input into cultivation was increased by part-time work for elite households and others. In short it is likely that the investment of labour time in marketing was a net addition to the total labour time of most women, occasioned partly by the desire to diversify the subsistence diet by exchanging one form of produce for another,[34] and partly by the social attractiveness of markets as a place for meeting people, exchanging news and gossip, etc. Meanwhile, it would appear that it was men in most households who sold the whole or the major part of the household's surplus product to the male specialist produce traders involved in the export trade.[35] In the case of Maragoli then a clear duality had evolved in the structure of the produce trade, reflecting both the control of the male household head over the surplus product and the concentration of women's trading into subsistence exchange of food crops, through the money mechanism.

Wagner also noted that the women in the Maragoli market sold pots and pipes as well as foodstuffs and chickens. Interestingly in this connection Hay mentions that in the period 1930–45 women shifted more and more labour time into craft production; and she mentions rope making and the making of pots and pipes for exchange as examples.[36] Since Wagner notes that 'Most of the products hawked on the market are sold by the people who have grown, reared, or manufactured them', it is too much to think that this is a coincidence. We are dealing

33. Hay, op. cit., p. 232.
34. This point refers back to one made earlier about the ambiguity involved in saying that the produce of the wife's plots was for the 'support' of herself and her children.
35. Wagner, op. cit., Vol. II, pp. 171–2.
36. Hay, op. cit., p. 232.

therefore with a comparatively recent change in the structure of production and trade and not, as Wagner seems to indicate, merely the introduction into trade of products traditionally manufactured by women.[37] By this I mean not necessarily that new pottery or pipe-making techniques had emerged, but on the contrary that because techniques were largely unchanged production was being increased by more women taking up potting, which must have meant some organisation of instruction in the craft and so on.

It may be noted too, in this connection, that pots are one of the commodities for which barter trading (primarily for maize it appears) remained common at Mbale, so it appears that some women must have felt able to obtain a greater quantity of maize for subsistence from the labour time spent in potting than they could obtain from its direct cultivation, and no doubt given the constraints of varied soil, rainfall and land availability on some women producers in some areas and households, this was the case. Clearly Ricardian 'comparative advantage' must work in some cases.

Finally Wagner's survey of trade and exchange relationships in Maragoli contains two further observations of particular interest. The first concerns the emergence of a group of independent artisans practising non-traditional skills and working on their own behalf. In a survey of adult male occupations in 'a headmanship' (i.e. a sub-location) in South Maragoli (probably in 1935) Wagner found twenty such men occupied as follows:[38]

Carpenters	10
Thatchers	3
Tailors	6
Cycle Repairers	1

In a 'Christian village' in Kimilili in North Kitosh apparently about the same time he found the following:

Tailors	8
Carpenters	2
Owner of a sawmill and timber workshop	1

37. Wagner's discussion of this is in fact somewhat ambiguous, and occasioned by his rather off-hand treatment of historical change. Thus his work contains an interesting and detailed discussion of pottery and pipe-making among the Logoli in particular, which was monopolised by women, and he notes that in the mid-thirties neither production techniques nor designs appeared to have changed from the pre-colonial period, whilst competition from imported pottery had not damaged the market for the pots. 'On the contrary', he says, 'it appears that the development of intertribal markets has stimulated the manufacture of pots for sale or barter, and that even more pots are made at present than in pre-European days.' And there the discussion finishes, without the implications of even more pots being produced for the production structure he had just discussed being explored. See Wagner, op. cit., Vol. II, pp. 11–14.
38. Ibid., p. 17.

What is particularly interesting about this is that in the case of the survey in South Maragoli Wagner interviewed a total of 444 adult men, so that these twenty independent artisans represented in 1935 a mere 4.5 per cent of the sample interviewed. Now this is in an area which was probably the most highly commercialised in North Kavirondo, and indeed one of the most commercialised areas in Kenya at this date outside of Kiambu. It seems likely therefore that at least in Nyanza the emergence of independent African carpenters and cycle repairers dates from the 1930s, and not earlier. In the case of tailors the matter is somewhat ambiguous, in that it is unclear how far, for example, the seventy-six 'sewing machines' being operated in Central Kavirondo by Africans in 1928 were those of independent proprietors, and how many were simply machines operated by employees of Asian shopkeepers. Wagner himself notes that 'The technical knowledge and skill required for all these new activities has been imparted by the industrial and handicraft departments of missions and government schools, and to a lesser extent by apprenticeships with Indian *fundis* in European townships or at Indian trading centres.'[39] But he does not indicate when any of these businesses were set up or became independent. More recent research however does tend to confirm that the emergence of this group of independent African artisans in Kenya dates from the 1930s.[40]

Despite the Administration's attempt to regulate marketing the structure of African trade and business in agricultural areas remained much as it had been in the 1920s, and the process of the quantitative expansion of a limited number of types of enterprises continued. However, there were two changes of major importance. Firstly there was the virtual universalisation of cash transactions in the market, certainly in Nyanza and Kikuyuland and almost certainly in Machakos and Kipsigis as well, with the damaging effects for African retail traders which we have already noted. It is probable that this led to the splitting off of produce trading from retailing not only in Nyanza, but in these other districts too. Secondly there was the emergence of a group of independent African artisans from the skilled ranks of the wage labour force into self-employment. These men practised new skills, and their numbers were to multiply in the years to come.

In addition a clear bifurcation of produce trading emerges in these years, with women being restricted to short-distance, 'subsistence' trading of produce for produce, or produce for handicrafts, and men monopolising the long-distance trade in the export of each district's surplus product. This bifurcation was the equivalent, in the sphere of exchange relations, of the control exercised by male household heads over the bulk of the household's surplus product with women being 'relegated' to control only over the 'subsistence product'. Since however

39. Ibid., p. 17.
40. See Kenneth King, *The African Artisan: Education and the Informal Sector in Kenya* (London, 1977), p. 103.

women's labour power appears to have remained predominant in all farm production at this time, the process of commercialisation would appear in general to have been appropriated by men at the expense of women.

3. 1940–1952

In commenting on the economic conditions for traders during the war years all the district reports have a marked similarity. All of them, as we have already noted, comment on the boom in demand for agricultural produce (and for other foods such as poultry and eggs) arising from military demand. In addition however nearly all of the wartime reports comment in general terms on the increase of purchasing power within the African districts arising not only from increasing farm incomes, but also from cash remittances received by families from army conscripts. From these observations and from the observed shortage of imported trade goods arising from wartime restrictions on shipping space, District Officers usually went on to formulate the most naïve monetarist theory of inflation, i.e. there was too much money chasing too few goods, so prices were rising.

They also had no doubts that at least some traders had benefitted enormously from this 'demand pull' inflation, in particular of course traders in agricultural produce, and above all transporters. The 'large profits' frequently, but vaguely, mentioned as accruing to transporters arose not only from increased demands for transportation as production and demand rose, but also because a great many lorries had been commandeered for military use at the beginning of the war, so that the supply of transport, particularly in African areas, had also been reduced. As early as 1939 the Fort Hall District Officer noted how lucky those traders were whose lorries had not been commandeered, since there was a demand for transport 'day and night', and wattle bark, for example, was being carried at the rate of Shs. 1/50 per mile.[41]

The Native Affairs Department *Reports* for the war years also put down the flood of post-war applications for produce-buying licenses and for transport licenses to the 'killing' made by the fortunate few who had held such licenses during the war.[42]

For the African retail trader it is more difficult to get a clear picture of the effects of the wartime boom. The Fort Hall report for 1942 explicitly links the boom in agricultural prices to the 'doubling' of the number of shops constructed from stone rather than wattle and daub, and the following year notes that there were 384 'stores' of this form of construction in the Reserve. After the war, in a number of districts, this originally spontaneous development was taken further

41. FHAR 1939, p. 3.
42. *NAD* 1939–45, p. 22.

and a number of local authorities demanded that all African shopkeepers operating in formally recognised market centres should have such 'improved' premises. However there is abundant evidence both from Nyeri and from North Nyanza that these structures became a major economic handicap to the traders involved since their profits were for years swallowed up by the need to pay off construction charges.[43] In addition the Asian stranglehold on wholesale buying, and the inability of the African shopkeeper to obtain his goods wholesale or to buy on credit, remained both throughout the war and afterwards, and was exacerbated at least up to 1948 by the general shortage of imported trade goods and by the tendency for Asian competitors to be supplied much more readily with what little there was.[44]

Both these handicaps generated immense resentment among African retail traders. There were various local authority and central government attempts to improve the situation, all of which appear to have failed. We shall come to this in a moment, but here it should just be noted that all these handicaps on the retail side of things probably meant that retail traders could have made profits during the war only if they were also, or primarily, involved in produce buying. But with the universalisation of money payments in these sorts of transaction, by the war years the prime need of a produce buyer was of course comparatively large amounts of working capital so that he could 'bulk up' produce for transport or for resale on a large scale. Since retailing was itself by this period unlikely to yield capital on the scale required, it is likely that the most successful African traders of the war years were those who had become more or less specialised produce buyers before the war and had built up capital by that specialisation. If such men owned retail shops or tea shops as well, this would have been in all probability a small sideline designed primarily to attract the produce seller to the premises, rather than to provide large profits.

The other great—if nominal—change in the lives of African traders introduced by the war, was the advent of the Maize and Produce Control in 1942. The new system, as it was supposed to work, is described in outline by Fearn:

> The maize sold to Control each season was brought in very small quantities to individual produce buyers in the trading centres and townships and African District Council markets of the province. The individual produce buyers were Africans in the A. D. C. markets[45] ...and Asian traders in the townships and trading centres. The African buyers at first sold to Asian buyers, but later sold direct to the Control ... produce buyers had to display the price on a board outside their *dukas* in relation to the varied small amounts that were marketed.[46]

43. FHAR 1942, p. 4; and 1943, p. 7; also *AAD* 1948, p. 50; and 1951, p. 61.
44. *AAD* 1949, p. 51; NKAR 1945, p. 2; FHAR 1947, p. 12; 1948, p. 10; 1949, p. 12; and 1950, p. 9.
45. The Local Native Councils became African Districts Councils in 1950. See next chapter.
46. Fearn, op. cit., pp. 160–2.

In practice however, when the free market prices were higher than those of the Control, or when local shortages provided the opportunity of large profits for the transporter who could move produce between surplus and shortage areas, produce buyers sold on to the 'black market' outside of 'controlled' channels. The mechanisms of this trade are not of course recorded in official sources, but one assumes it must have involved a good deal of selling, buying and transporting outside market hours, and particularly at night, and also possibly the opening up of secondary trading premises by produce buyers outside of licensed markets.[47]

It will be noted that Fearn says that African produce buyers sold to Asian buyers and transporters but afterwards sold 'direct' to the Control. In this regard it is interesting to note that in 1949 in North Nyanza the District Officer commented that the days of the 'secondary' trader in the district were numbered. By this he clearly meant that increasingly African produce buyers were also acting as transporters to the Control.[48] It is likely that this movement toward increasing African involvement in produce transport was greatly accelerated both in Central and Nyanza Provinces after the war. But if transportation during and after the war had been a very profitable business, it was also a very risky one, since road conditions made the running cost of transport so high. Fearn, for example, notes that Oginga Odinga's Luo Thrift and Trading Company based in Central Nyanza had bought 'five lorries and vans' from 1948 to 1953 and the depreciation rate on them had been 'in the realm of 50% per annum'.[49] Thus the reports from all districts from 1945 to 1948 speak of the failure of many African would-be transporters, as lorries (often bought second-hand from the military and in poor condition) broke down and could not be repaired or replaced because no allowance, or only an inadequate one, had been made for depreciation charges, repairs and maintenance. It was also alleged by traders themselves, and in one case, in an annual report, that in some cases where Africans were reliant on Asian mechanics, repairs were badly done or not done at all.[50]

It is equally clear however that some African trader/transporters came through these years, and by avoiding these sorts of mistakes or learning from them came to dominate produce transport within the African reserves. Only one year after an African Affairs Department *Report* had suggested that the failure of African transporters had returned the produce trade throughout Nyanza

---

47. Nor did evading tactics stop here. *DAR* 1949, Vol. II, p. 37 has the following entry: 'The export of produce was prohibited in many districts for the greater part of the year and produce inspection staff was largely employed on preventive measures. How difficult these measures are to enforce is exemplified by the following extract from the Meru Annual Report: "In spite of threats to his (the Produce Inspector's) person and the offer of large bribes, it was only when he was held up with a shot-gun that the produce got through".'
48. NNAR 1949, p. 20.
49. Fearn, op. cit., p. 191, n. 48.
50. Ibid., p. 190

Table VI:4. Turnover and trader commission of the leading African produce buyers in Nyanza for the 1954 season[51]

Trader	District	Turnover Value	Trader Com- mission	Comments
		£	£	
Sebi Saidi	NN	14,995	813	Buying maize at three markets and wimbi and paddy at two markets.
Leo Makokha	NN	6,837	376	Buying maize, paddy, mtama and wimbi at one market.
Jotham Lyadi	NN	5,923	326	Buying maize and mtama.
Joahana Wakwoba	NN	5,866	320	Maize only.
Tertio Ondari	SN	5,525	296	Maize and wimbi.
Simeon Wakesa	NN	5,502	300	Maize only.
Zadock Oloo	NN	5,475	303	Maize and paddy.
Morris Obava	NN	4,972	276	Buying paddy at one market and maize and cassava at another.
J. A. Ngeno	Ker	4,379	254	Maize only.
Grigori	NN	4,243	235	Maize and paddy.
Marach Atinda	SN	4,013	226	Maize and wimbi.
Benjamin Khakisia	NN	3,816	208	Maize only.
Andrea Khaomba	NN	3,597	197	Maize, mtama and wimbi.
J. Nyamochange	SN	3,372	173	Maize and wimbi.
Otundo Menge	SN	2,951	167	Maize and wimbi.
Clement Akwiri	CN	2,657	136	Maize and wimbi.
K. A. Cheruiyot	Ker	2,622	152	Maize only.
T. A. Tegutwa	Ker	2,561	149	Maize only.
Nyaega Kiyaka	SN	2,340	127	Maize and wimbi.
M. A. Chumo	Ker	2,252	131	Maize only.
Saulo Odera	CN	2,210	127	Maize, mtama and cassava.
G. K. Belyon	Ker	2,193	127	Maize only.
Abel Moseti	SN	2,182	119	Maize and wimbi.
C. A. Keter	Ker	1,981	115	Maize only.
William Tongi	SN	1,973	110	Maize and wimbi
Mathew Osoro	SN	1,917	106	Maize and wimbi.
Matatu Ombunya	CN	1,870	111	Maize, mtama and cassava.
Monyenye Menge	SN	1,792	100	Maize and wimbi.
K. A. Sitonik	Ker	1,791	104	Maize only.
M. A. Tlle	Ker	1,788	103	Maize only.
C. A. Langat	Ker	1,750	102	Maize only.
Jairo Kuome	CN	1,736	84	Maize, mtama and wimbi.
K. A. Cheptilmet	Ker	1,683	98	Maize only.
Washington Ondicho	SN	1,392	78	Maize and wimbi.
James Wambani	CN	943	55	Maize, wimbi and cassava.
Issack Wango	CN	872	49	Maize and mtama.
Oruka Bang'inya	CN	775	51	Maize, mtama and cassava.
E. Mugoma	CN	665	41	Maize, mtama and cassava.
Richard Ochola	CN	609	36	Maize, mtama and cassava.
Okudo Alaro	CN	485	28	Maize and mtama.

Notes:

1. The district abbreviations used in this table are:
   NN—North Nyanza
   CN—Central Nyanza
   SN—South Nyanza
   Ker—Kericho District
2. The traders named were licensed to buy only in one market, unless stated otherwise.

51. Source: Fearn, op. cit., Appendix E, pp. 263–4.

Province to the hands of Asians, the District Officer of North Nyanza was making his observations about the increasing degree to which African produce traders were bringing their produce direct to the Control and thus by-passing Indians.[52]

Some confirmation that this did indeed occur, and that a group of relatively prosperous specialised African produce traders with their own transport emerged after the war to successfully challenge the Indian trader, comes from Fearn's survey of African trade in Nyanza Province in 1954, the first systematic and quantitative piece of work on African trade in Kenya. Table VI:4 is his list of the forty largest produce buyers in the districts of Nyanza Province (which here includes Kericho) at that date. The figures in column three of this table can be compared with data provided elsewhere by Fearn of the 'average' trader turnover among the nearly 6,000 traders in the four districts of the Province in 1954.

These figures suggest that in trade, just as in agriculture, averages disguised the enormous differentiation which was such a feature of colonial economic development in Kenya. Thus the biggest traders in the four districts of Nyanza Province turn out to have turnovers (and one must therefore presume profits) ranging from five to seven times the average in North and South Nyanza and Kericho, to twenty-three times the average in the case of Central Nyanza.[53] It will also be noted that the biggest buyer, Sebi Saidi, operated in more than one market, as did one other, Morris Obava.

Even more significantly, in table VI:5 Fearn shows that by 1954 at least (and probably from 1950 onwards) African traders had attained a dominant position in the marketing of maize, and had ousted Indian traders from that position.

Unfortunately, Fearn does not make clear how much of the maize marketed by African traders in the Province was handled by these forty men, but the turnover differentials leave one with the distinct impression that this proportion must have been high. It is left unclear what proportion of these men were also transporters, but again one strongly suspects that this group comprised at least part of that category of African traders in the post-war situation who made a success of transportation while most of their compatriots fell, quite literally, by the wayside.

The 'average' trader turnover in the Province was so low, of course, because the bulk of traders were small-scale retailers, and Fearn presents clear confirmation of the continuing process of the marginalisation of the small retail trader which had begun three decades earlier with the decline of barter trading. He noted that by 1954

It seems doubtful (from the samples taken of prices paid by African traders

---

52. *AAD* 1948, p. 51; and NNAR 1949, p. 20.
53. Ibid.

Table VI:5. Delivery of bags of maize (200 lbs. each) to inspection centres in Nyanza in February 1955, showing the number of bags marketed by different agencies and the percentage of bags marketed by these agencies at each Centre.

Inspection Centre	Number of Bags (200 lbs.) delivered by					Percentage of Maize delivered by				
	African Traders	African Farmers	African Co-operatives	Asian Traders	Total	African Traders	African Farmers	African Co-operatives	Asian Traders	Total
Broderick Falls	32,834	1,205	9,401	21,804	65,244	50.3%	1.8%	14.4%	33.5%	100%
Butere	4,100		290	906	5,296	77.4%		5.5%	17.1%	100%
Kakamega	12,797		930	13,882	27,609	46.4%		3.4%	50.2%	100%
Kisumu	12,480			13,842	26,322	47.4%			52.6%	100%
Bungoma	18,373	2,411	4,658	5,147	30,589	60.1%	7.9%	15.2%	16.8%	100%

Notes:

1. The African farmers who delivered maize to Broderick Falls and Bungoma were 'Better Farmers' with a Good Husbandry Award. Possessing this Award they were privileged to market direct to an Inspection Centre and received the trader commission as well as the producer price.

2. These figures indicate that in 1955 the bulk of maize buying and marketing was in African hands.

3. These figures also show that only a small proportion of the maize delivered at Broderick Falls and Bungoma had been collected by co-operative societies, and this was the area of North Nyanza in which maize co-operatives were most active.

Source: Fearn, op. cit., p. 265.

for their stock, and prices at which they sold to consumers) if the average profit margin on all ranges of goods exceeded 15 per cent. On the £809 5s annual turnover [in North Nyanza] this would give an annual gross profit-margin of £121, roughly £10 per month. In the case of Central Nyanza traders this gross profit-margin would be as low as £13 per year, or just over £1 per month.[54]

Fearn's figures of the estimated gross income earned by farmers in the Nyanza districts confirm the relative decline of Central Nyanza as a surplus producing area compared with North or South Nyanza. Interestingly too the same table shows that the number of traders in Central Nyanza was almost double that in the other two districts, and their level of turnover was by far the lowest, being for example a mere ten per cent of that in North Nyanza.[55] I believe these two sets of findings are not unrelated. One can hypothesise that as Central Nyanza agriculture came under increasing subsistence pressure, and *per capita* agricultural surpluses declined, so proportionately more trade became 'subsistence trade' and more labour power shifted out of agriculture into trade in an attempt to gain higher returns. This would of course marginally increase the rate of decline of production on the land, and increase the competition for the circulating surplus.

Fearn indicates that most of the shops involved were not carrying any wider a range of goods than Wagner had observed in the mid-thirties (he enumerates kerosene, soap, cigarettes, matches 'and a few piece goods') and that the small profits involved had to be shared among more than one person since 'About 60 per cent of the traders interviewed in North Nyanza were aided by their relatives, and though licensed in the individual's name, these *dukas* are run as companies, or as partnerships as we would call them.'[56] He also indicates that in return for providing a contribution to an initial capital fund these relatives often wanted credit or goods at a cheaper price and 'Under such conditions trading is not profitable, and non-existent or low profits are not conducive to obtaining further capital, even from the same source.'[57]

Under such circumstances, it is understandable that many traders interviewed had found the K £500 or so of fixed capital they had had to invest in 'improved' stone shops to be a continual and heavy strain on their resources. 'In most cases, having expended £500 capital on permanent construction, they have little or no working capital left with which to engage in trade.'[58]

In addition to capital constraints, he found Nyanza retail traders still to be labouring under their long-time handicap of the lack of wholesale supply facili-

54. Ibid., pp. 182–3.
55. Ibid., Table 16, p. 182.
56. Ibid., p. 184.
57. Ibid., p. 185.
58. Ibid., p. 181.

ties. As we have already noted, this had been a problem for African traders in Kenya from the time of their emergence in the twenties, but it had been markedly exacerbated by the end of barter trading. In 1945, at a time when wartime rationing of shipping space and imports had still been in force, the Administration stepped into the situation and attempted to organise 'Group Buyers Organisations' of African traders, at first to take delivery of cotton piece goods supplied to them on wholesale terms through the wartime Import Controller, and then subsequently to purchase wholesale from European import/export firms whom the Administration attempted to persuade to move into the Reserves. All these attempts seem to have foundered on the same obstacles, which were firstly the unwillingness of many big import/export firms to move into the Reserves, and secondly the difficulty that such firms experienced when they did do so in extending credit to African traders. For wholesale purchase nearly always involved the extension of credit by the importer to the wholesaler who in turn extended it to the retailer, and African traders even when merged into groups had no assets with which to guarantee credit, and could not in these circumstances obtain limited company status. Moreover, Asian wholesalers appear to have responded to each of these threats to their hegemony by offering lower prices to African traders than could be got from the Group Buyers Organisation, and then when such ventures had collapsed returning to the former status quo. Such tactics continue to this day.[59]

Thus by the early fifties a comparatively clear picture of African trade and business emerges. It was for the most part concentrated on the classical middleman function—buying in order to sell—and its major profits (perhaps all its profits) came from the purchase and resale of African agricultural produce. Its most successful exponents were those who had managed to combine the capital resources to buy in bulk with the ability to transport the bulked produce. For this group, though bearing greater risks, were able to capitalise on the market imperfections of an agricultural system which almost annually produced surpluses in some areas and shortages in another. Moreover when they chose to sell there, they were also enabled after the introduction of 'the Control' in 1942 to take the largest share of the government's 'controlled' and 'guaranteed' prices. In undertaking these functions they of course helped marginally to reduce the discontinuities and rigidities in the fragmented agricultural markets of Kenya on which they relied, but as in the early fifties that fragmentation was still so marked and the number of 'transporter/traders' able to capitalise on it so few, comparatively large profits were still available.

It will be noted that one is essentially dealing here with a nascent form of

59. *NAD* 1939–45, p. 23; 1948, p. 49; and 1949, p. 51; FHAR 1947, p. 21; and 1948, p. 15; 1949, p. 12; and 1950, p. 14; KAR 1948, p. 5; NKAR 1946, p. 2. See also Fearn, op. cit., pp. 185–8. For continuation of these practices in the post-independence period see Jeffrey James Bucknell, 'An Appraisal of some of the Development Impacts of the Kenya National Trading Corporation' (University of Wisconsin, unpublished Ph.D., 1972), pp. 66–7 and 153–7.

'merchant capital', highly stratified even in its infancy, and at this time still firmly subordinated to Asian and European merchant capital (which dominated wholesaling of manufactured commodities and import/export respectively), but nonetheless showing the classical weakness of merchant capital vis-à-vis industrial capital. This weakness lay in its total non-involvement in the process of production. The African small-scale retailers, and even the more successful produce buyers, only entered into the economic process after the surplus product had been produced by cultivating households. Thus the size and the quality of that product were entirely outside the control of these small-scale merchants. Fearn attributes the problems of the small-scale retailer in particular to 'the limited extension of the range of consumer desires' (among cultivating households), but a much more accurate formulation of that blockage would relate it to the continued low levels of productivity of the labour power of which those households disposed. Unable (rather than unwilling) to do anything about this fundamental blockage, African merchants were necessarily engaged in a struggle over respective shares in the physical and monetised form of the surplus product once created. This indeed is a universal characteristic of merchant capital.

In the struggle the produce buyers were winning up to the early fifties because they operated at the point in the process at which cultivators turned their surplus product into money, and given the produce buyers' knowledge of supply conditions (the need of poorer households to sell immediately after harvest, the areas where gluts existed etc.), they could obtain proportionately large shares of the product for the money expended (and on reselling could make large monetary gains). The retail trader, however, only entered the picture *after* members of producing households had obtained the money for their produce, and in its monetised form the surplus product brought the cultivator a much greater choice of time and place of disposal. This meant that the retail trader had to be 'competitive' so far as the prices of his products were concerned. This we have seen he could not be (so far as Asian competitors were concerned) and in competing with a large number of other African retailers, supplied on identical terms and trading almost identical stock, he had to cut his mark-up to the absolute minimum. A situation approaching perfect competition in fact produced a small share in the surplus product both for individual retailers and for retailers as a group.

If merchant capital was able to play no part in altering the production constraints within which it had to operate, and could only squabble over the surplus product once created, the colonial state, as we have seen, had done something to raise the productivity of African agriculture. Its efforts were influential in raising the 'average' level of real farm incomes by about a hundred per cent between 1930 and 1952, in the face of increasing population pressure on the land and markedly unequal distribution of the land between households. For the poorest households the improvement was certainly much less, and may even have been wiped out by the wartime and post-war inflation.

Chapter VII

The Role of the Local Native Councils 1925–1952

In 1925 and 1926 the colonial administration set up in most of the agricultural districts of Kenya a very limited type of African local government—the Local Native Councils. For the most part they were nominated bodies consisting overwhelmingly of government chiefs and headmen. But a restricted form of election also allowed for the presence of what one officer called 'the [mission] educated young men and the young businessmen'.[1] The Councils were empowered to raise revenue in the form of a local 'rate' which in the beginning was set at Shs. 1 per hut and poll, and was collected with central government taxation. Toward the end of the twenties the rate rose to Shs. 2 in some districts and rose continually thereafter. In addition a certain amount of revenue deriving from the rent of trade plots and from fees for activities in the Reserves was transferred to the LNCs.

These Local Native Councils represented the colonial government's first attempt to provide an administrative agency through which a certain amount of African development could be secured, without the resources for such development having to be derived from central government revenue (most of which was expended in settler areas[2]). To secure central government control of their activities, District Officers acted as *ex officio* chairmen of the Councils, and it is abundantly clear from district reports that, certainly until the late forties or early fifties, no resolution which did not meet with their approval was put into effect, since they had an absolute power of veto.

Within this constraint, and those imposed by their limited revenue, LNCs proved themselves extremely successful in their allotted task, being an agency through which the energies of 'educated' and 'progressive' Africans emerging from the mission schools could be channelled, and acting first in opposition to, and then in co-option of, the activities of 'militants' associated with the Kikuyu Central Association and the Kavirondo Taxpayers' Welfare Association. In particular, they did much to expand the very limited educational facilities available to Africans through the provision of grants to missions for the payment of teachers' salaries, and later through the amassing of funds from which schools were built.

1. KAR 1925, p. 4. See also FHAR 1925, pp. 5–8; NAR 1925, p. 12.
2. For the structure of taxation in Kenya see E. A. Brett, op. cit., pp. 190–9.

They also encouraged a wide variety of 'progressive' activities in the Reserves, among which economic 'enterprise' and agricultural and pastoral improvements played a central role. The district reports do not, I think, give anything like a complete account of LNC activities, which included the construction of maize mills, small-scale dairies for the production of clarified butter (ghee), drying *bandas* (sheds) for hides and skins, the opening of demonstration plots and seed farms for the improvement of agriculture, the hire of European and African agricultural and veterinary extension personnel, and the provision of loans to prospective African businessmen. There is evidence of such loans being given for the construction and stocking of shops, the construction of maize mills, ghee separators and hide *bandas*, and the purchase of lorries.[3]

The district reports unfortunately do not show the precise mechanics of these processes. Thus we do not know whether LNC loans covered only fixed capital requirements for businesses, or whether part of current costs might be met as well, nor do we know anything about rates of interest and amortisation. In addition, though we are often told of LNCs 'constructing' maize mills or ghee 'dairies', we know little or nothing about the mode of contracting for such construction projects, nor how the projects, once completed, were managed. However, we do have clear evidence of ghee separators being constructed with LNC funds in the 1920s. and being turned over to private ownership and control in the 1930s.

In fact general evidence is not lacking that the Councils were an important source both of contracts and of credit for African businessmen from their found- ation, and that there was a very considerable degree of overlap between their membership and the first group of African entrepreneurs in the Reserves. This is in part because, as we have already observed, chiefs and headmen were them- selves so often in trade or business, and partly because District Officers made such an effort to ensure that the increasing number of 'mission boys' with busi- ness interests were represented on the LNCs. These 'mission boys' were seen by District Officers to be the progressive forces emerging in the districts. and were in any case, from the late twenties onward, those who stood for and ob- tained election to institutions in ever-growing numbers. This was at least in part because even more traditional Africans recognised that the LNCs required the presence of young modernists.[4]

It is not clear how far access to the LNC, either direct or indirect (through a friend, former schoolmate or relative) was the prerequisite of starting in business at all. It may have been so in some cases, particularly where the enterprise in

3. See, among a host of possible references, NKAR 1927, p. 29; SKAR 1927, p. 22; SKAR 1928, p. 24; KHOR 1929, p. 3; NKAR 1929, p. 7; FHAR 1931, p. 8; and 1932, p. 11; CKAR 1931, p. 16; KAR 1932, p. 4; FHAR 1932, p. 17; KAR 1933, p. 3; *NAD* 1934, p. 119; NKAR 1936, p. 36; *NAD* 1938, pp. 29 and 40; KPAR 1931, p. 6 and Appendix I; and 1930, p. 19; CPAR 1934, p. 43; and NAR 1938, p. 3.
4. FHAR 1925, p. 8.

question was one requiring a relatively large amount of initial capital. Thus, for example, the North Kavirondo district report for 1926 notes that Paul Agoi had set up a diesel-powered maize mill in the South Maragoli meat market. Lonsdale however reports that Agoi, who at this period was a headman (he was appointed chief of Maragoli in 1940), had already received a £20 loan from the Native Trust Fund to set up a water-powered mill (this seems to have happened in 1925).[5] Certainly LNCs attempted to intervene with legislation where they could to protect nascent African business. Thus the South Nyeri district report for 1925 notes that 'On the recommendations of the District Council (LNC) no further Mill Plots are to be issued to Indians, and every encouragement given to natives to erect Mills of their own', whilst in the same year the Fort Hall LNC passed a resolution to the effect that 'non-natives shall not be granted sites for flour mills in the Reserve'.[6] From the 1930s onwards we also have clear evidence of the provision of LNC loans for the purchase of lorries (up to 1930 it seems that the very few African-owned lorries in operation had not been purchased by LNC loans, but were mainly run by chiefs and headmen), but even in 1929 the District Officer in North Kavirondo was complaining of the LNC members in his district that

> The desire to vote themselves and their friends increased salaries and al-
> lowances has again manifested itself, and members still regard the Council
> funds as an inexhaustible reservoir upon which they can draw to finance
> personal ventures. Failure to negotiate loans of this kind leaves a feeling of
> actual grievance in their minds.[7]

This quotation brings out a further point about LNCs, which is that as well as being a source of capital for African business they were also a major source of wage and salary employment within the Reserves, both directly (through the clerical, agricultural, health and veterinary personnel they employed, as well as the unskilled labour employed on roads, bridges and other construction work) and indirectly (through construction contracts); and it is clear that where they could they gave preference to African personnel and contractors over Asian competitors. Moreover, there were some backward and forward linkages from LNC activities. One example of this was the quarrying and transportation of sand at Sagana in Fort Hall which serviced LNC construction projects as well as others, and a more subtle and complex instance of which is illustrated in the 1927 Fort Hall report. There it is noted that the LNC had built a number of houses for its clerks and other personnel in brick with *bahati* (i.e. corrugated iron) roofing. As a result, notes the report 'several natives' now want to build their own houses in this style, and in fact thirty-four such had been erected by

5. NKAR 1926, p. 28; and John Lonsdale, 'A Political History of Nyanza 1883–1945' (unpublished Cambridge Ph.D., 1964), p. 325.
6. NAR 1925, p. 20; and FHAR 1925, p. 27.
7. NKAR 1929, p. 11.

'natives of the Kihumbuini Mission'. As a result of this activity there was a 'brick-layer shortage' but twelve such were now being trained 'in the Reserve' (probably by a mission, but possibly by the LNC itself) and eight also at 'Fort Hall prison'. Further, 'All these are purchasing sets of tools out of their wages, so that they will be able to carry on their trades when the Government work is over.' Later reports make it clear that this expansion of a new form of construction then fed into the expansion of brickworks (some of which were apparently owned and run by African businessmen) and into the further expansion of sand and clay quarrying, both in turn generating more transport work.

The scale, but not generally the type of these activities undertaken by Local Native Councils (which became African District Councils after the war) expanded considerably through the 1930s and 1940s, as they raised their revenue and their expenditure, particularly in the area of school construction and education in general. In fact the business and employment generated by expanded LNC construction programmes did something to mitigate the effects of unemployment in the Reserves during the early depression years of the 1930s.

It is clear that we need to know far more than we do about this whole area of activity, about the details of its organisation, and about the scale and form of support to African business enterprise (both legal and illegal) which access to the LNC could give. Of course, throughout the colonial period the control of District Officers over the whole process was considerable, and they could and did use this control to prevent forms of support which they felt verged on graft or corruption, or on abuse of official positions. But there may well have been means of circumventing such control,[8] and in any case many District Officers took an altogether more sympathetic view, believing very firmly that it was a legitimate use of local authority revenue to encourage African 'enterprise' in this way. In one or two cases, this was explicitly related to the need to channel and encourage energies which might otherwise go into 'subversive' channels.[9] Not that the organisations regarded in this period as potentially or actually 'subversive' were in this respect very different to the LNCs. Lonsdale notes that among the activities of the Kavirondo Welfare Taxpayers Association were the following: organising ploughing matches, organising the first Nyanza Agricultural Show, building maize mills (an activity undertaken by its local branches), 'encouraging' shop-keeping, 'promoting' sales of hand gristing mills, providing bursaries for pupils at Maseno (Church Missionary Society mission school), appointing an African itinerant development officer to supervise tree planting and other agricultural activities, and the establishment of maize mills.[10] Even the distinctly more militant Kikuyu Central Association provided a range of very similar

8. See for example the very interesting eye-witness account of a meeting of the Central Kavirondo LNC in 1930 in Margery Perham, *East African Journey: Kenya and Tanganyika 1929–30* (London, 1976) p. 147.
9. See for example CPAR 1935, p. 24.
10. Lonsdale, op. cit., pp. 264 and 328.

services for its leaders and members, many of whom were engaged in trade and business.[11]

The expanding role of the Local Native Councils in Kenya in the decade 1930–40 has been touched on in dealing with the emergence of maize cultivation in Nandi, and in general in the discussion of the attempted regulation of marketing. As already noted, this involved the Councils in all agricultural districts in the employment of a staff of market inspectors, whilst the Administration's new policy for African agriculture also increased the LNCs' wage bill, since they were required to employ nearly all the 'native agricultural instructors' whose emergence in the 1930s marked the beginnings of agricultural extension for Africans in Kenya. In addition to all this, a parallel programme of 'improvement' in native livestock and dairy products required the employment of African 'veterinary' personnel involved in the management and supervision of ghee separators and creameries, hide drying *bandas* and stores, and stock inoculation and dipping programmes.

Aside from the employment derived from the funding of nationally-instigated programmes locally, Local Native Councils in the three Kikuyu districts, throughout Nyanza Province, and in such areas as Machakos, Teita and Kericho spent rapidly increasing amounts in the thirties on such local programmes as the construction of schools, clinics, produce stores (or 'godowns') and roads, and the payment of teachers' salaries in mission schools through payments of grants in aid.

In fact educational expenditure represented the biggest single claim on the budgets of LNCs in this period, both in the recurrent support of mission school budgets, and in construction programmes.[12] In Central Province, though, the latter was never as large as the Councils would have wished it to be, since all three Councils had land and funds to build secondary schools in their districts for which they could not get central government clearance.

As far as I am aware there has been no attempt to quantify the LNCs' share in total African wage employment in this period, and undoubtedly in absolute terms it was not large so far as the employment of unskilled labour was concerned. The latter was mainly restricted to occasional labour for local road construction and clearance, which was unpaid up until 1938.[13] However, there is no doubt of the importance of the Local Native Councils so far as the employment of better-paid African personnel was concerned, for in this period, and indeed for some time afterwards, the councils were the source of wages for most primary school teachers in rural areas, most African medical staff in rural

11. See for example FHAR 1927, p. 3; and NAR 1929, p. 12; also KHOR 1929, p. 25.
12. Specimen budgets and statistics on LNC revenue and expenditure can be found at intervals in appendices to Native Affairs Department reports from 1930 onwards. See for example *NAD* 1931 Appendix D; 1932 Appendix D; 1933 Appendices D and F; 1934 Appendices D and F; 1935 Appendix D; and 1938 Appendices A, D and E. See also Forbes Munro, op. cit., pp. 172–7.
13. FHAR 1938, p. 12.

areas, the majority of agricultural extension personnel, the majority of African veterinary personnel, and nearly all carpenters and masons employed for wages in rural areas. In addition they employed their own paid clerks, and provided travel and subsistence allowances for members of the Councils.[14]

In this chapter we are particularly concerned with their role in supporting African trade and business, but it is important to recognise that this function was inextricably bound up with those above for several reasons. The first might be called ideological, and concerned the image which LNCs had both in their own eyes and in the eyes of the colonial administration. They were seen quite explicitly as hubs of progress in the Reserves. As the thirties wore on, the LNCs in the most 'advanced' districts were increasingly dominated by educated Africans who saw their function as being to use Council resources to the limit in order to further African progress, and this broadly-formulated aim bound together ideologically such activities as health and educational provision, agricultural and livestock improvement and the support of African businessmen, particularly in their competition with Indians.[15] It cannot be overstressed that whilst individuals and groups among the educated Africans might disagree over the extent to which both LNCs and the colonial administration as a whole would support African progress so defined, they never disagreed over the definition. And this definition was implicitly petit-bourgeois in that the agent and beneficiary of progress and improvement was always the progressive, educated individual African. Thus for all the participants involved in this process, whether they were the teachers in the primary schools, the dressers in the LNC-funded dispensaries, the masons and carpenters building godowns or the Council clerk's house, or the trader applying for a loan, there was never any contradiction between demanding more 'progress' for one's fellow Africans and the pursuit of individual material advancement. Indeed the latter was seen as the explicit exemplification of what could be achieved by Africans with initiative and a progressive outlook. In successfully running a transport business or a school, in buying land, in growing large maize surpluses and in sending one's children to school, one was in one's own eyes a living refutation of the colonial stereotype of the 'backward native'. And politically one's aim was to reproduce oneself a million times over by making more of one's fellow-Africans 'educated', 'progressive', and 'advanced'. Hence the involvement in and demands upon the LNCs, the only institutions which at this period had capital funds at their disposal to be used for African advancement.

Aside from this ideological bond, these various activities of the LNC were bound together by the personnel involved. There is a great deal of evidence to suggest that the categories 'teacher', 'clerk', 'chief', 'headman', 'trader' and

14. *NAD* 1935, p. 69; FHAR 1931, p. 8; and 1932, p. 11. See also 'Memorandum . . .', op. cit., 1937, p. 31.
15. A particularly startling instance of this, and a harbinger of the future, is to be found in SKAR 1937, p. 8.

'LNC representative' were by no means mutually exclusive, in the sense that one man might be two or even three of them at the same time, and all of them at various times in his life. Moreover, at a time when all those who had received (say) four years of primary schooling and who were still resident in the district would be a tiny minority of the total district population, personal contacts and friendships between such men (often based on membership of the same mission community or school cohort, and often crossing political boundaries) would be an important factor.

The major change brought by the war years so far as Local Native Councils were concerned was the introduction of the Agricultural Betterment Funds with the Maize and Produce Control in 1942. We have seen that the funds were created by a cess on each bag of maize or other produce sold to the Control, and as a result of course the major maize producing districts, or certainly those which marketed large quantities of maize and produce through the Control, did best out of it, since the funds were credited to the account of the LNC of the district in which the produce was marketed.

Thus the Nyanza districts, and above all North Nyanza LNC, benefitted most from the Agricultural Betterment Fund. By the end of the war, in 1945, Agricultural Betterment Fund monies to the credit of the three Nyanza LNCs stood at £50,000, and by 1947 the district figures showed North Nyanza LNC to have £133,276, South Nyanza £36,797, Kericho district £32,260 and Central Nyanza £16,856 accredited to their respective accounts from the Agricultural Betterment Fund.[16]

The Kikuyu districts of course did much less well, since a much smaller proportion of their produce was ever marketed through the Control; but nonetheless their funds were sufficiently large that by 1948, for example, Fort Hall LNC had budgeted some £6,000 per annum from its funds to be spent on the terracing of land (though in practice most of it was not spent for this purpose, as discussed below), and as early as 1943 the same LNC had felt able to undertake all recurrent costs of primary education in the district (and not just to make grants-in-aid to missions for teachers' salaries), and had in addition undertaken the construction of a primary school of its own, which was opened in 1946.[17]

District Officers demonstrated a clear nervousness and apprehension about the uses to which the Councils would put their new-found wealth, and in the early years after the war, in particular, attempted to funnel most Agricultural Betterment Fund monies into the anti-soil-erosion measures on which the government was particularly keen at this time. There is clear evidence however that this was resisted, because of the general unpopularity of the 'communal' (i.e. unpaid) work which most of these measures entailed. Much more popular

16. *NAD* 1939–45, p. 18; *NAD* 1946 and 1947, p. 34.
17. FHAR 1943, p. 8; and 1946, p. 2.

uses of the funds, to which LNCs tried persistently to persuade their District Officers to assent, were all forms of educational expenditure,[18] loans both in cash and in kind to those farmers in each district designated as 'better farmers' by the Department of Agriculture (and which always included members of the LNCs themselves), improvements of LNC seed farms and demonstration plots and (in Central Province) 'manure schemes', whereby farmers were encouraged to fertilise their land organically by the LNC purchasing stocks and supplying them at below cost price to farmers.[19]

These grants and loans in cash and in kind, though they reached only a tiny minority of African farmers and never amounted to much more than K£50 per annum per farmer (in cash terms) over these years, did represent an important new stage in the development of African smallholder farming because they represented the first access to credit for African farmers, and therefore the first use of money as means of production which did not come from domestic savings or from off-farm earnings by household members.

Provision of agricultural implements either on free hire terms or by sale at sub-cost prices of course occurred before (we have noted the particular case of ploughs), but it seems that the scale and variety of such schemes expanded with the addition of Agricultural Betterment Funds monies. That expansion however was clearly not on the scale which at least some LNCs would have liked. In 1946, for example, the District Officer of North Nyanza reported that his LNC would have liked to have used the Agricultural Betterment Fund monies 'as a sort of land bank', but the old problem of African farmers lacking securable assets had prevented this. In view of the crucial role played by the Land Bank in the survival of settler agriculture through the depression, we have here yet further evidence of the economic shrewdness of the Kenyan petite bourgeoisie, and the eagerness which they learnt from their European mentors.[20]

Aside from this change in the scale of their finances, LNCs continued to play the same role vis-à-vis African farming, trade and business as they had always done. That is to say, they represented the interests of African traders against Indian competitors in the districts, and called in increasingly strident tones throughout the war and post-war years for the exclusion of the Indian trader from all intra-district trading. They resisted schemes by District Officers to restrict trading to designated centres or to reduce the number of traders so that turnover and profits per trader might be greater. They also continued to press

18. In fact, despite the Agricultural Betterment Fund, rapidly escalating educational expenditure after the war put many LNCs in debt. See *NAD* 1939–45, pp. 16–17 and 1946–7, p. 21.
19. See FHAR 1948, p. 12; and 1949, p. 11; 1950, p. 10; 1951, p. 11; 1952, p. 12; KAR 1948, p. 2; and 1949, p. 6.
20. NNAR 1946, p. 7. For the role of the Land Bank in the depression see above chapter III and van Zwanenberg, 'Agricultural History ...', op. cit., pp. 17–20.

for the right to grant loans and other forms of assistance to traders as well as better farmers.[21]

In addition particular LNCs attempted innovations in these years which were of marked significance for the future. In Central Province it was the Council representatives themselves who first pressed for the adoption of local bylaws which would have recognised the practice of irredeemable sale of land by one Kikuyu to another and would have created a register of such transactions through which purchasers could have proof of their 'titles'. Such rules seem to have been adopted first by the Nyeri LNC in 1943, but the Fort Hall LNC attempted to follow suit in 1944, only for the proposals to run into strong opposition when they were put to public meetings.[22] This innovation took place at a time when, with the enforced return of squatters from the Rift Valley, the absence of men in the armed forces,[23] and rapidly accelerating land purchase by all those who had done well out of wartime trade and employment conditions, the number and intensity of land disputes in Central Province (and apparently also in parts of North and Central Nyanza) had reached unparalleled proportions.[24] As the District Officer of Fort Hall himself noted, the promulgation of such rules was clearly in the interests of those who had accumulated large or larger landholdings by purchase or other rather more dubious means, and who wanted some guarantee of their title against the land-hungry.[25] The conflict in Fort Hall in 1944 was clear evidence that the LNCs had become the preserve of a particular privileged stratum of Africans in the Reserves whose interests could occasionally conflict with those of other sections of the African population whom they claimed to represent. That this privileged stratum of Africans suggested as early as 1938 an approach to landholding which was only to be adopted by the Administration after the outbreak of the Emergency (and which was in fact only given full support from 1955 onwards)[26] is a clear indication that this stratum cannot be seen merely as a creature of the colonial regime.

Almost from the time of their emergence, the privileged households of Kenya

21. *AAD* 1949, p. 17; NNAR 1946, p. 7; 1947, p. 3; and 1950, p. 4. However, the issue of restrictions on African trade and traders in the years immediately after the war (when a large proportion of the demobilized men returning to the Reserves seem to have wanted to enter commerce in one form or another), was probably a major cause of conflict between Africans and within LNCs. Where the latter were dominated by larger, established traders fearful of new competition, they seem to have been very willing to use licenses and minimum building or capital regulations to try and restrict access. See for example FHAR 1947, p. 6; and NAR 1946, p. 24.
22. NAR 1943, p. 2; FHAR 1944, p. 8.
23. See KAR 1943, p. 3. for a fascinating account of African servicemen attempting to use their European officers as contacts with the district administration in land matters. In this instance the 'government' was forced to declare 'a moratorium on land sales where serving officers were interested parties'.
24. See for example KAR 1945, pp. 2 and 6; *AAD* 1949, pp. 24–5; and *DAR* 1948, pp. 71–2.
25. See FHAR 1938, p. 7 referring to a combined meeting of LNCs in Central Province which suggested a register of all land transactions.
26. See the account in Sorrenson, *Land Reform...*, op. cit., pp. 52–71.

had a strong sense of their own interests and of the best means of advancing them. Sometimes this required support of the colonial administration, sometimes opposition to it; and the African petite bourgeoisie was continually divided upon this issue. Sometimes opposition to the Administration was couched in populist terms; this stratum saw itself and was seen by other Africans as being representative of 'the African people' as a whole. But even in the colonial period we can find instances in which the interests of this stratum and of other African cultivators were clearly and quite consciously opposed, and of these instances the question of land and land 'ownership' was the most persistent and important. In the end it produced the split between loyalists and forest fighters in Mau-Mau. For the most part the LNCs as institutions were clearly on one side of this divide, because their members were predominantly or entirely on one side of it.

Another interesting straw in the wind from these years also comes from the Fort Hall district. In 1943 in an attempt to control the black market in eggs, the District Officer declared a fixed minimum price for the sale of eggs in Nairobi and an attempt was made to restrict the right to sell in Nairobi to a number of selected sub-agents, all of whom were Indian. It is clear that profits from the sale of eggs were considerable in this period and this attempt to control the market appears to have run into fierce opposition within the LNC. It had in fact to be modified. By 1945 the LNC had granted its own monopoly for the purchase of eggs in the district for resale in Nairobi to an African 'Company' (the Agikuyu na Wanyona Wao), creating considerable opposition from three other Kikuyu 'companies' operating in the Nairobi municipal market. It is clear that the monopoly had operated in close conjunction with the Administration's 'control' policy on eggs whereby a minimum price was fixed for sales in Nairobi (an attempt to undercut the black market) but monopoly purchases within the Reserve were on whatever terms the company could negotiate. In 1946 however the demand for eggs appears to have been falling, and with the steam taken out of the black market the government abandoned its minimum selling price and the Agikuyu na Wanyona Wao Company lost its monopoly.[27]

Behind this schematic outline of the story found in annual reports there must have been a fascinating series of conflicts involving the government's Produce Control, Indian and African traders and conflicts among the African traders, with both the monopoly and other companies having their spokesmen on the LNC. What is significant is the attempt to use the power of the LNC to obtain monopoly status for a particular group of traders (albeit on a local scale),[28]

27. See FHAR 1943, p. 3; and 1946, p. 15.
28. Attempts of this sort by no means began in the forties. See for example the account of the 'North Kavirondo Chamber of Commerce' and its relation with the local LNC in Wagner, op. cit., Vol. II, pp. 175–6. There is no doubt that annual district reports alone are a woefully inadequate source for a history of the intra-African politics of the LNCs. I am sure that oral history, supported by a detailed study of LNC records, would reap a rich harvest of data showing the complexity and

for as we shall see this was an early example of what proved to be an increasingly popular strategy, particularly from 1963 onwards, when Africans came to have control of central as well as local government power.[29]

We see then that the LNCs were an arena of struggle among different groups within the African petite bourgeoisie, as well as a source of some power and resources which they could use or attempt to use against Indians and (occasionally) against other Africans. The addition of Agricultural Betterment Fund monies to the incomes of LNCs simply made them slightly larger 'honey pots' and therefore perhaps exacerbated conflicts and made their capture of even more significance for the stratum as a whole and for competing groups within it. In short, after the war, as before, the LNCs continued to function as a training ground for the African petite bourgeoisie, and taught important lessons about the uses to which governmental power could be put, as well as supporting and expanding the stratum through employment, contracts and (from 1942 onwards) the limited provision of credit. From our point of view, what matters is the central role which a 'state' institution could play directly in this process. It provided a limited but slowly expanding source of revenue which the African petite bourgeoisie could use to gain credit and contracts for their businesses, better-paid jobs for themselves and their relatives, and education for their sons, as well as a number of institutional and other supports to general agricultural and veterinary improvements, from which the petite bourgeoisie were in a strong position to benefit disproportionately. Needless to say, the salaries from the better-paid jobs so obtained could themselves also be a source of investment funds. As we shall see the lessons of the LNCs were not lost on the sons of these men when they in their turn came to obtain not local but central state power in 1963. Indeed in some ways the post-independence state in Kenya can be seen to be little more than the LNCs of old writ large.

We will now examine briefly the underlying pattern of resource transfer implied by this use of LNC resources. As noted earlier, LNC funds came overwhelmingly from a local authority rate levied on each 'hut' in the Reserve and collected with central government revenue. In so far as it was primarily through the sale of surplus food crops that African cultivators paid their taxes, then of course LNC revenue, just like central government revenue, represented a deduction from the monetary form of the surplus product. This deduction having been made, a proportion accrued directly to the petite bourgeoisie in the form of salaries, loans and contracts. In addition another proportion accrued indirectly to them through the greater use made by their children of educational facilities, and by them and their children of agricultural, veterinary and medical

---

constantly shifting bases of these disputes, and would throw much more light on the growth of the African petite bourgeoisie in Kenya.

29. See below, chapter XIII, but also Colin Leys, *Underdevelopment in Kenya: The Political Economy of Neo-Colonialism, 1964–1971* (London, 1975), chapter 5, pp. 148–69.

facilities. On the other hand, in so far as the use of all these facilities expanded through time, then their use was by no means totally monopolised by the group of African households forming the petite bourgeoisie at any one moment. On the contrary, expanded use of the facilities (particularly educational and 'business' facilities) was a prerequisite of the expansion of that stratum. Moreover, the salaries paid, loans made and contracts issued by the LNC all represented the creation of facilities (owned, eventually, by members of the petite bourgeoisie) which was the presupposition of the expansion or intensification of the labour time expended in cultivation. This is true whether we consider ploughs, maize mills, or shops, all of whose roles we have examined in earlier sections. The implication of this is that, looked at diachronically, the process of social stratification in a commodity-producing society and the process of raising the general level of productivity and income in that society are not antithetical but complementary. One does not occur at the expense of the other, but as a consequence of the other. That is, the rise in the level of general labour productivity is the prerequisite of an appropriation of a part of the surplus product so produced, by a section of the population. Once this has occurred, however, the appropriating stratum may feed back a part of the surplus so appropriated into investment which can further facilitate the increase in labour productivity and the surplus product, and thus increase the amount of resource appropriation. We should note here that the dynamic may be lost if the surplus product of production in area X with labour power Y is not fed back into that production process and that labour power, or if such feedback occurs on an inadequate scale.

Chapter VIII

Livestock, Money and Bridewealth
1905–1952

> The money-form attaches itself either to the most important articles of exchange from outside, and these in fact are primitive and natural forms in which the exchange-value of home products finds expression; or else it attaches itself to the object of utility that forms, like cattle, the chief portion of indigenous alienable wealth. Nomad races are the first to develop the money-form, because all their wordly goods consist of movable objects and are therefore directly alienable; and because their mode of life, by continually bringing them into contact with foreign communities, solicits the exchange of products. Marx, *Capital* Vol. I, p. 88.

The first part of this study was devoted to an analysis of the structure and development of agricultural production among the African people of Kenya. This was given priority because it has priority in the production structure of present-day Kenya, and because as agricultural production developed it gradually obtained hegemony over all other forms of African production, a hegemony which it still maintains.

The task of this chapter is to analyse the precise form which this hegemony had taken by 1952, and to do this with particular reference to the other major form of African production with which African agriculture coexisted over these forty-seven years—pastoralism, or animal husbandry. I shall therefore be concerned to elucidate schematically the ways in which the relationship between agricultural and pastoral production in the African areas of Kenya changed in this period, and the effects of those changes upon agricultural production and the social relations within which it was embodied. I shall not therefore be concerned with the effects of those changes upon the internal structures of the nomadic pastoralist economies, though these changes were certainly enormous, and merit the study which they are now beginning to receive.[1]

It will be noted that I have just spoken of 'relationships' between 'agricultural' and 'pastoral' economies, but in terms of the situation in 1905 this is a grossly inaccurate mode of conceptualisation. Indeed this conceptualisation was only

---

1. See especially Richard Waller, 'Uneconomic Growth: The Maasai Stock Economy 1914–29' (CPEK Paper, 1975).

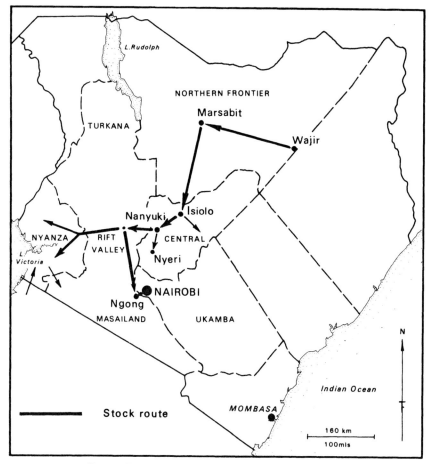

Figure VIII:1. Somali stock routes circa 1918.

made relevant by the changes between 1905 and 1952 with which this chapter is concerned.

In 1905 the East African Protectorate was predominantly an enormous expanse of open plateau grassland, with forest on the volcanic highlands which arose from it at intervals.[2] Across this plain, pastoral nomadic peoples of various types wandered in patterns determined by the distribution of rainfall and the availability of grazing. Conflicts—over grazing grounds, water holes or springs, or livestock—punctuated the relationships between different groups of these

2. The account which follows is based largely on evidence and memoranda given to the Kenya Land Commission, especially Vol. I on Kikuyu Province, but also parts of Vol. II on Masailand, Ukamba and the Rift Valley. But see also van Zwanenberg with King, pp. 79–87, 110–22, 145–82.

nomads at intervals, and were particularly severe during and after periods of drought or disease when grazing and animals were at a premium. On the higher ground above this plain lived more sedentary peoples whose women undertook a small amount of cultivation of cereals and pulses, but the bulk of whose land (itself always threatened with incursions by the nomads) was also devoted to the grazing of cows, sheep and goats.

Indeed, to have recourse once again to the dangerous device of the ideal type, the way to conceptualise a sedentary community in 'Kenya' in the pre-colonial period would be as a cluster of dwelling huts in a large open plain with perhaps an acre or two of land immediately adjacent to the huts under cultivation. Standing at the entrance to this hut cluster (which would probably be surrounded by some form of earthen wall or large thicket hedge) and looking to the horizon on all sides, one would probably see nothing but open grassland on which the livestock of the community would be grazing. From time to time pastoral nomadic people might cross part of this expanse and perhaps stop temporarily to graze their stock where the sedentary peoples had grazed theirs. If relationships were good, the two sets of stock might graze together, though with two sets of armed herdsmen/warriors looking on.

Presently the nomads would move on, leaving the sedentary community or household in sole sway once more over the surrounding grassland. At intervals this community would itself move residence, as its small cultivated area, having been cropped for three or four seasons, started to show declining yields, or as news was heard of better land within a short distance. However, wherever the dwelling units and the cultivated patches of the household or community might be, they would cover only a tiny fraction of the land over which the livestock would be allowed to wander for grazing.

In such a situation the distinction between the nomadic and sedentary peoples was one of degree rather than kind. The nomads grazed their stock over larger areas and moved their residence much more frequently. They did not cultivate, or did so only *in extremis* when drought or disease had so decimated their herds that the planting of a few millet grains or peas was necessary to stay alive. They lived in normal times almost completely on a diet of milk, meat and blood. The sedentary peoples grazed their animals over smaller and more defined areas, moved residence less frequently and, since they cultivated, mixed their diet of meat and milk much more with millets, pulses and vegetables. Since in general they had fewer livestock per head, losses due to drought or disease might shift their diet more markedly in the direction of vegetarianism, and keep it there whilst herds were built up again.

The distinction was also one of degree rather than kind, because groups of quasi-sedentary people and groups of nomads might speak mutually comprehensible languages or dialects and intermarriage might be frequent. If one wanted a label to apply to the entire economy of this region in the pre-colonial period, it would be 'pastoralist' not 'peasant', and this was true not only for large areas of eastern and north-eastern Africa, but for central Africa as well. It is important that this be grasped because far too often historical change in Kenya and elsewhere in Africa has been conceptualised as the 'transformation of a peasant society'. It would be more accurately conceptualised as the creation of a peasant society from a pastoralist one.

Perhaps the most important sign that these societies (whether nomadic or not) were all pastoralist was the status given to livestock as against food crops, and to animal husbandry as against agriculture. It is clear that for all the peoples of Kenya in the pre-colonial period the acquisition of livestock was the most important occupation. Cattle provided milk to drink and meat when they died; they were very rarely slaughtered. Their hides and skins were used to make clothing and house and floor coverings, and even their bones might be used for the carving of spoons and other implements. Sheep and goats also gave milk and meat, and their skins were used to make clothing.[3] These then were some of the direct use values of livestock in the pre-colonial period. They were of particular importance to the nomadic pastoralist people, who, since they did not cultivate, relied almost entirely on their stock to stay alive.

However, in addition to their direct use values, livestock of course had exchange value. The following exchanges were possible: exchange of livestock for food crops; for women (bridewealth); for land; or for artisan products or handicrafts (e.g. spears, shields, hoes, baskets, arrow heads, pottery, etc.).

It appears that the rates of exchange between livestock, food crops, land and artisan products were all generally in favour of the livestock owner. For example, when supplies of food crops and livestock were normal (i.e. drought or disease had not supervened) the livestock could command in direct barter a volume of cereals or pulses which were a product of more labour time than had been expended in rearing the livestock exchanged.[4]

In the case of land the reason for this was that up to 1905 (when land alienation to settlers began in earnest) land was in abundant supply everywhere in Kenya. As we shall see in chapter X, a number of other consequences followed from this simple fact, the most important of which was the vagueness of land tenure rules, or indeed the effective absence of such rules.

In the case of exchanges with food crops and artisan products the reason is somewhat different. Livestock was more desired than these other products because livestock and only livestock could be exchanged for women, i.e. in the case of virtually all[5] the peoples of pre-colonial Kenya, social norms specified

3. See Alan Jacobs, *The Pastoral Masai of Kenya: A Report of Anthropological Field Research* (cyclostyled report to the Ministry of Overseas Development, 1965?), p. 33, for the astonishing range of use values which cattle had for the Masai.
4. See Marris and Somerset, op. cit., p. 29 and the general account pp. 25–32, and also Miracle, op. cit., pp. 7–8.
5. Wagner for example noted that hoes formed part of the bridewealth in some cases (along with cows and goats), especially among the Logoli. However it is probable that this was a 'modern'

that bridewealth must be in the form of livestock, and no other products were acceptable. This meant that all men wishing to marry and have children had to have access to livestock. Had marriage been monogamous this need would have been restricted to young single men seeking their first and only wife. Since polygyny was the norm, the demand for livestock covered all men at all ages and stages.

Once a man had livestock he might marry. He might then have children, and if all or most of these children were girls he might gain more livestock (from in-coming bridewealth) with which he might acquire more wives, more daughters, more livestock and so on. In short it was this dual accumulation of livestock and wives through which nearly all men in pre-colonial Kenya measured wealth and social status.

Thus we may distinguish an 'exchange and accumulation complex' and a 'simple exchange complex'. In the case of the former, the aim was to exchange livestock for wives, and daughters for livestock, with the dual aim of accumulating both wives and livestock in ever greater numbers. It will be readily observed that this complex contains a massive weakness in the vagaries of biochemistry. Should a male household head by chance happen to have more sons than daughters by his wife or wives then his potential and actual bridewealth obligations (since fathers had variable but usually significant responsibilities to help their sons with bridewealth payments) would outweigh bridewealth income.

To guard against this potential or actual disaccumulation process therefore, the 'simple exchange complex' was brought into play. Here the aim was to exchange livestock for food crops, land or artisan products so as to consistently expand livestock holdings. Now it can readily be seen that so far as the sedentary (agricultural) pastoralists were concerned there was a potential link of some importance between these two complexes. If a man could exchange livestock for wives and for land at time X, he could expand his agricultural surplus with the labour of the wives on the land, and then exchange the food crops for more livestock at a more advantageous time Y^6 (say at a time when pastoral nomads were badly hit by drought or disease and the food crop/livestock terms of trade had turned 'abnormally' against them). It should be noted that in the pre-colonial situation the aim of these transactions was always to expand livestock holdings and the number of wives, not landholdings or the agricultural surplus.

In the light of this schematic discussion we may now consider how relevant or accurate were colonial descriptions of livestock as the African's 'money', 'currency', or 'capital'.[7] It will be noted that livestock was indeed a measure of

---

(i.e. twentieth-century) innovation coincident with the increasing importance of cultivation in Maragoli. It appears not to have occurred among the more cattle-rich Vugusu at the time of his study, which lends force to this speculation. See Wagner Vol. I, pp. 402, 429–33; and Vol. II, pp. 108–17.

6. See for example Marris and Somerset, p. 32 and pp. 39–40.

7. Virtually every European witness before the Kenya Land Commission asked to state the reasons

wealth, since (with some qualifications regarding the optimal constitution of herds) it was true that the larger the quantity of livestock a man had, the more wealthy he was deemed to be. This role of livestock as the measure of wealth was shared with wives, since other things being equal the more wives a man had the more wealthy he was deemed to be. However in practice neither of these *numeraire* were used separately. In precise terms a really wealthy man was one who had many wives, large herds and more daughters than sons. Measurement of wealth was therefore a multi-dimensional operation. Livestock also operated as a medium of exchange in that all other products which were exchanged with livestock were enumerated in terms of livestock.[8] Thus in the exchange of land for goats, or millet for sheep, so much land was deemed 'worth' so many goats, or so many baskets of millet were deemed 'worth' so many sheep and not the other way round. However this enumeration in terms of livestock applied as far as we know only to transactions in which livestock were actually involved. That is, separate equivalences were established if, say, millet was being exchanged for hoes, or beans for baskets. In this case enumeration would usually be in terms of either commodity interchangeably, i.e. either one basket equals four handfuls of millet or four handfuls of millet equals one basket.[9]

This invariant use of livestock as the *numeraire* in exchanges in which it was involved appears to indicate that livestock had moved some way toward fulfilling one of the prime functions of money—that of acting as a universal equivalent—but had by no means completed this process when colonialism supervened.[10] The reason for this incomplete development of the money form was probably the very narrow range of possible transactions in which most Africans could participate. Food crops, artisan products, land and women represented the total set of use values for which livestock could be exchanged (and

---

for 'overstocking' of African Reserves referred either to bridewealth or to the status of livestock as 'the African's money or currency'. See for example *KLC, E & M* II, p. 1393 (evidence of Sir Robert Shaw) and p. 1528 (evidence of 'The Public of Laikipia').

8. See for example *KLC E & M* I, pp. 172, 186, 224, 229, 231 and 344. Jacobs (op. cit.), p. 29 reports that 'Pastoral Masai do not as is commonly assumed measure wealth, status or position solely in terms of numbers of cattle. Indeed the term for wealthy man in Masai *enkarsisisho* means essentially a man with many sons and only indirectly implies that he may also have many cattle; for in Pastoral Masai society, a man with many cattle but few or no sons is a poor man in comparison to a man with many sons but a small number of cattle.' Clearly in a polygynous situation having many sons would not be incompatible with having as many or more daughters. Also one wonders about the 'implication' in *enkarsisisho* that a wealthy man had many cattle as well as many sons, for many sons and few or no daughters implies heavy cattle loss.

9. See for example Wagner, op. cit., Vol. II, p. 162. See also the evidence on pre-colonial markets of the coastal entrepôts of east and north-east Kenya contained in Peter Dalleo, 'Trade and Pastoralism: Economic Factors in the History of the Somali of N. E. Kenya' (Syracuse University, unpublished Ph. D., 1975), pp. 66–70.

10. Dalleo for example states of N.E. Kenya that 'during ... 1890–1920 except at the coast, cloth and livestock remained the major mediums of exchange', ibid., p. 70. The term 'universal equivalent' comes from Marx. See in particular *Grundrisse*, op. cit., pp. 142–6.

in addition livestock could be exchanged for other livestock). With such a narrow range of transactions there was hardly need for the emergence of a fully-fledged 'universal equivalent' with which to enumerate all transactions.

The centrality of livestock in the pre-colonial economy of both nomadic pastoralists and sedentary pastoralists therefore derived (a) from its multifarious use values and (b) from its being the only product which served both as a measure of wealth and medium of exchange. This latter point is of particular significance since there were other natural products which served as media of exchange (i.e. all products which were bartered) and one other (women as wives) who served as measures of wealth, but no other product combined both functions.

Ultimately then livestock owed its unique status as measure of wealth and medium of exchange to the bridewealth relationship, and this must now be examined, since in some ways it lay at the heart of the pre-colonial economy. Analysis is made difficult due to the highly emotive debates which have surrounded the question of bridewealth, which have involved colonial officials, missionaries, social anthropologists and more recently African nationalist scholars. I shall endeavour to treat the matter purely with regard to its changing 'economic' significance (in so far as in this historical context this principle of abstraction is meaningful).

Bridewealth

The mode of payment of bridewealth, the sources from which livestock could be drawn, and the rights which different payments were deemed to confer, all varied from people to people within Kenya in both the pre- and post-colonial periods, so any general description has necessarily to abstract from differences which, while important, do not greatly concern the issues with which I am dealing here. Essentially bridewealth payments (which would consist of sheep, goats, and cattle in varying proportions) were made by or on behalf of a man wishing to marry, usually to the father of the girl marrying, but sometimes to others of her older male relatives, notably the maternal uncle.

Such payments were made, from the point of view of those receiving them, as compensation for the loss of domestic and cultivating labour by the bride's family of origin, and for both parties (those paying and those receiving) as a public indication of the permanence of the union between the man and woman concerned. In particular, for the family making payments and for the male marrying, payment of bridewealth (or more accurately payment of particular parts of bridewealth) secured sexual access and control of childbearing (in the social anthropologist's jargon 'uxorial' and 'genetricial' rights) for a particular man with a particular woman which were, putatively at least, exclusive.

Payments normally took place over a long period of time, beginning before the wedding ceremony and continuing, in many cases, for as long as the woman bore children, since further payments would be forthcoming from the groom's family on the birth of each child, with particular importance (and therefore larger payments) attaching to the birth of the first child and/or the first male child. Should the marriage break up, the wife's family (and this usually meant her father) would be required to return all or part of the bridewealth payments, depending on the cause of the break-up. A childless marriage, which was always blamed on the wife, was almost invariably a cause of dissolution, and generally necessitated total repayment. Where however the blame for the break-up was unclear or could be disputed, then negotiations over the extent of repayment could be entered into, with each side obviously having an interest in pinning responsibility on the other. In practice, too, original payments were not fixed rigidly (though certain items might be for certain periods of time), and the matter was negotiated between representatives of the two families.[11] In this context it should be noted that where any part of the stock transferred was female (and some part of it nearly always was), transfer involved the rights to offspring as well as the original animal, and so (therefore) did repayment.

This implied that should a marriage last for any length of time and then break up, the wife's family could be faced with repaying a great many more livestock than they originally obtained, and conversely, of course, so long as the marriage remained in being the wife's father's herds were expanded by all the offspring which the goats, sheep, cows etc. had borne.[12] And indeed this is why in the precolonial period it was livestock alone which were acceptable in bridewealth payments, because given their power of reproduction the bridewealth livestock lasted through time along with the marriage and could therefore continue to act as its guarantor.

It will be seen then that a particular use value of livestock (its capacity to reproduce) made it uniquely suitable to act as bridewealth and to exchange for female labour power. It was also from this unique quality that its role as both measure of wealth and medium of exchange was derived. Livestock had therefore assumed some of the functions of money by the end of the pre-colonial period. Livestock was accumulated by means of the marriage of daughters, but since this method was not reliable it was supplemented by a series of exchanges of livestock with other products and with land, all with the aim of expanding livestock holdings and the number of wives. To this degree then Marx's general statement quoted at the beginning of this chapter is valid for Kenya, as are the somewhat looser assertions made by colonial officials and others about livestock being 'the African's' currency.

11. P. H. Gulliver, *The Family Herds: A Study of Two Pastoral Tribes in East Africa, The Jie and the Turkana* (London, 1955), pp. 223–43.
12. Wagner reports that among the Vugusu the recipients were entitled to keep the natural increase, even if the marriage were dissolved and the marriage cattle themselves returned (Wagner, op. cit., Vol. I, p. 444). In practice return of bridewealth stock after a long-lived marriage seems often to have evoked difficulties and quarrels. Knowing that this was the case of course gave the groom's kin an incentive to try and keep the marriage intact.

Livestock trading

In the discussion up to this point, we have treated 'livestock' as an undifferentiated entity, and indeed in a general analysis of its relationship to women, land, food crops and other products this was legitimate. However, different forms of stock were differently valued. Firstly, virtually all forms of cattle could be exchanged on advantageous barter terms of trade for sheep and goats. The reason for this seems to have been that both sheep and goats bred much more prolifically than cattle and were somewhat less susceptible to disease and drought—they could survive for example on a quality of grazing which would not support cows. They were therefore available in far greater abundance. In addition of course even poorly nourished cows had much higher milk yields than goats, and since milk was such a central part of the diet particularly of the nomads this was an important consideration. Among cattle, cows and heifers were generally more highly valued than male stock for the simple reason that they provided the milk and bore the calves which increased the herds. Waller quotes exchange rates of twelve sheep for one heifer and twenty-four sheep for a cow and a calf in Masailand in 1918,[13] and though ratios probably varied enormously with the availability of different types of stock and the quality of the particular animals being exchanged, there is no doubt that the large exchange differential did generally exist between cattle and small stock.

This hierarchy of valuations was also reflected in bridewealth payments. The numbers of sheep and goats transferred were often greater than the number of cattle, but in addition cattle were nearly always transferred at important stages in the process of betrothal and marriage. Thus it was nearly always cattle which were transferred for example when wives conceived or first children were born. Similarly, therefore, in repayment negotiations the return of cattle took first priority.[14] In this regard the greater natural longevity of cattle (if disease or drought did not intervene) and their less frequent calvings made them better bridewealth animals and made negotiations over offspring etc. somewhat easier. Among certain peoples in fact it was only the cattle portion of the bridewealth which was returnable.

Thus we must qualify earlier formulations in which the pre-colonial Kenyan economy was seen to revolve around the accumulation of livestock and wives. A more adequate formulation would be that it revolved around the accumulation both of wives and of herds of livestock in which cattle predominated, and in which, among the cattle, breeding and milk cows predominated.[15] Accumulation through trade could therefore take the form not only of the exchange of livestock for land, food crops and artisan or handicraft products, with the aim

13. Waller, 'Uneconomic Growth ...' op. cit., p. 7.
14. Among people rich in cattle or livestock generally, it was only the cattle which were returnable. See Wagner, op. cit., Vol. I, p. 442.
15. See Jacobs, op. cit., p. 30a, fig. II, showing that adult females made up 50% or more of all the Masai herds he surveyed.

of maximising livestock holdings, but could take the form of the exchange of sheep and goats for cattle with the aim of maximising cattle holdings, and the exchange of cattle with the aim of maximising holdings of heifers and milk cows. It should be noted that sheep and goats, far more than cattle, were the source of meat in the diets of both sedentary and nomadic pastoralist. Both sheep and goats were slaughtered and eaten for various ceremonial and sacrificial purposes. A man would therefore always wish to have substantial holdings of smaller stock along with his cattle.

Within the broad parameters set by the superiority of cattle over small stock, and cows over bulls and bullocks, specific exchange rates could change constantly with the impact of localised droughts or disease outbreaks, loss of livestock in fighting and so on. It will be readily observed, therefore, that opportunities existed for complex permutations of exchange, particularly for those who were able or prepared to move stock long distances to take advantage of shifting exchange rates. A man might choose at time and place X to exchange a herd of cattle constituted primarily of male stock for sheep and goats, in order at a later time and place Y to exchange these for a more desirable herd constituted primarily of young females. The difference between the more desirably constituted herd and the less desirably constituted one would be his gain.

Meanwhile, of course, those who had exchanged their sheep and goats for the cattle herd would already have made gains of their own, and would perhaps have moved on to reconstitute that herd more desirably in further exchanges.

But this account assumes that only livestock were being exchanged. Patterns could obviously become far more complex, even in the pre-colonial period, with the exchange of food crops or artisan products (pottery, iron work) being inserted alongside the livestock exchanges. In addition of course livestock exchanges would be far more fragmented than assumed in the first example. Thus one might for example have a pattern such as:

Exchange of sheep and goats for millet at place X, proceed to place Y (which might not be far distant) affected by drought, and exchange part of millet for cattle and sheep and goats at a better rate of exchange. Hear news that drought is even worse a little further on. Retain part of millet holdings, or return to place X to obtain more with part of increased stocks of sheep and goats. Make way to place Z, insist on millet/cattle exchanges only and specify type of cattle, or if exchange for sheep and goats demand even higher exchange rates. Return home with greatly expanded cattle, sheep and goat stocks.

Now clearly such patterns of trade entailed great risks, particularly in the pre-colonial period when attempts to move stock over long distances laid one open to stock theft (and death if one endeavoured to resist the theft), and attempts to drive too hard a bargain might produce the same result. The imposition of colonial rule, by reducing these risks somewhat, in fact stimulated this type of trading, at least for a short while. But even in the pre-colonial period it was clearly a widespread phenomenon, at first in very localised areas only, and then slowly becoming more organised and spreading over longer distances.[16] It should be noted of course that, like all forms of exchange, it was constrained within the overall parameters set by the production of livestock, food crops and artisan products. Within these parameters it acted only to redistribute a surplus product between households, and in fact to circulate that product in order to meet changing needs and patterns of consumption.

Two final points should be noted, before we end this schematic and necessarily simplified account of the pre-colonial period and proceed to analyse the changes wrought by colonialism. The first is simply that this economy had one over-whelmingly important presupposition on which its successful functioning depended, which was a continuing abundance of grazing land. This was so not only in the obvious sense that livestock require a certain area of land on which to graze. More importantly, under ecological conditions in which, with the failure of rain or the arrival of locusts, tens or hundreds of miles of grazing might very quickly be rendered unable to support a single animal, it was important that enormous areas of grassland should be available so that one could escape the effects of drought, locusts or disease even if they were quite widespread. In short a livestock economy under tropical conditions required a wide-open land frontier, and an effective scattering of people and animals over a huge expanse. In slowly but surely closing that frontier, colonialism in Kenya struck a blow at this economy which in the end undermined it totally. Animal husbandry as an activity remained, but in a totally different set of production and exchange relations.

The second point is that this economy was totally male-dominated. Herding and tending and trading of livestock were male activities, as were the fighting and raiding which often had livestock defence or livestock acquisition as their aim. Women were relegated to agriculture and to domestic work and child rearing, the term 'relegated' having the fairly precise implication that they had little or no contact with the product whose possession signified wealth and whose associated activities had high social status. The corollary of this of course was that agriculture as an activity had low social status commensurate with its secondary economic role. This norm was strongest among the nomadic pastoralists, but was also endorsed by the sedentary pastoralists whose womenfolk undertook cultivation. In the light of this one should not be too surprised at what happened when, under colonialism, agriculture began to predominate within African production: women increased their input of labour into cultivation in response to the new opportunities far faster and more markedly than men. This was in part because social norms changed rather more slowly than

---

16. See Waller, op. cit., p. 7, especially on the role of the Swahili in spreading the range of barter trading in the late nineteenth century. See also Miracle, op. cit., pp. 4–19 and Forbes Munro, op. cit., pp. 20–6.

economic reality, and the low status attached to cultivation remained even when households were obtaining larger and larger proportions of their subsistence and money incomes from that source. In part it was because, although the imposition of colonial rule diminished opportunities for some male activities vis-à-vis livestock (notably raiding and defence from raiding), for a while at least it increased the opportunities for others, notably stock trading.

When these opportunities began to diminish, men were left with a choice: to engage more fully in agriculture alongside women or to engage in wage labour. In earlier chapters I have suggested that this choice varied markedly from area to area and between households. But in general it can be said that whereas in the twenties the matter remained unresolved in most households, by the thirties increasing numbers of males in the more densely populated areas had made the choice for wage labouring. I will suggest in the next chapter that this was an economically rational choice given returns to labour time in agriculture and elsewhere, but what should be noted here is that, in once again 'relegating' women to labour input into agriculture where returns were lower, there was in fact a continuation, in another form, of the status and power hierarchy which in most households still identified agriculture as low status 'women's work'. Such a continuation of norms would not have been possible if economic realities (albeit very different ones) had not continued to underlie and support them, but nonetheless the continuation is notable and obviously had some effect in itself.

There was a continuation in another sense too. In the pre-colonial period male dominance over the primary measure of wealth and means of exchange— livestock—had been 'balanced' by the predominance of male labour input into the herding and rearing of stock. In the colonial period, as women's labour input into cultivation increased and livestock went into decline as a contributor to household income, women had an opportunity to increase their influence over decisions regarding the uses of household income, since their labour time became responsible for ever-rising proportions of it (at least until the thirties and the large-scale male conversion to wage labour). We have already suggested that a conflict over this took place in many households, but that by 1952 it had been resolved in favour of male household heads, who had secured largely unchallenged rights of disposal not only over the income accruing from wage labour but also over that part of household income which came from agriculture. In this successful male claim to ascendancy, the situation of the pre-colonial period when male household heads had also enjoyed almost total control over the wealth of the household (livestock) must have been of some help to the men, since it involved a presupposition that such control was 'right' and 'proper' and reflected the desirable ordering of things. There is some evidence that most wives were handicapped in family conflicts by the fact that they shared this ideology with their husbands.

We may now turn to a more systematic consideration of the changes brought to the 'sedentary pastoralist' peoples of Kenya (principally the Kikuyu, Machakos Kamba, Luo, Luhya and Kisii) by the imposition of colonialism and their conversion into what some observers have called 'peasant' people. In this analysis I shall be concerned primarily with three interrelated developments. Firstly, changes in the magnitude and organisation of the stock trade; secondly, changes in the uses to which stock were put by these peoples, and in particular changes in bridewealth; and thirdly (connecting the former two), changes in the money form.

The Somalis and the Origins of Long Distance Stock Trading

Up to about 1900 most trading with and for livestock was conducted over comparatively short distances and mainly engaged (on the sedentary pastoralist side) those peoples who lived on the borders of the open grasslands through which the nomads passed. In 1900–2 a major change occurred in this respect with the beginnings of long-distance stock trading by groups of Isaak and Herti Somalis.[17] The men involved seem all to have been soldiers, porters or personal servants who came into Kenya with the officials of the Imperial British East Africa Company and remained (occupying similar positions) when these officials became colonial civil servants with the declaration of the East African Protectorate in 1895. Between 1898 and 1900 a major series of famines and rinderpest outbreaks hit the Protectorate and decimated livestock holdings. These Somalis seized the opportunity afforded by this catastrophe to bring in livestock from the Northern Frontier Province of the Protectorate which was almost entirely inhabited by nomadic pastoral people (chiefly Somalis), and which had been hit by rinderpest somewhat earlier. Stock appears to have been barter-traded into sizeable herds in the Northern Frontier Province, brought down the Rift Valley and then bartered to the Kikuyu and Masai who were desperate for stock. We have to assume that at this period gains were made as specified earlier by the creation of more desirably constituted herds from less desirably constituted ones, but since we have no accounts of the Somali trade dating from this earliest period, this must be guesswork.

However, as former agents of the Imperial British East Africa Company and then of the Protectorate officials, these men had their homes in the tiny nuclei of wattle and daub huts which were at this period starting to function as the administrative headquarters of different districts. Many were also based in Nairobi, which mushroomed into existence as by far the largest urban centre in the up-country Protectorate between 1899 and 1903. They therefore pastured their herds in the grassland surrounding these settlements (in the case of Nairobi

17. As far as I am aware there has been no systematic published research on the origins and development of the Somali stock trade in Kenya. There are many scattered references to Somali traders and butchers in the early colonial reports, and in addition fragments of a history appear in the evidence given to the KLC, especially *E & M*, Vol. II. See especially pp. 1465–7, 1483–8 and 1643–9. In addition some remarks are to be found in Dalleo, op. cit., pp. 61–3 and Waller, pp. 7–8, 10–11 and 16–18. The map at the beginning of this chapter has been constructed from these fragments.

at a place called Mbagathi), and then at some time between 1900 and the start of the systematic colonial records (1906–7) appear to have gone into the butchery business, providing meat for the populations which were starting to build up first in the fledgling capital and then in the district headquarters. Thus in records pre-dating 1914, we hear of Somali butchers in Dagoretti, in Nyeri town, and in Kisii.[18]

Now of course the slaughter of sheep and goats, and very occasionally of cattle, for meat had gone on in pre-colonial Kenya, but this was done by the households wishing to consume, or in some cases by ritual or ceremonial experts. The slaughter of livestock for exchange was itself an unknown specialism in the pre-colonial period, and in addition these men sold the meat for money. They did not barter it, since their customers were the very first urban Africans (porters, the first generation of African administrative staff, and some unskilled labourers) who had access to the modern money form (actually rupees), and many of whom were, like the Somalis, 'aliens', i.e. Africans from other countries or British colonial territories drafted in to undertake necessary tasks in the skeletal colonial structure in the period before local collaborators were available.

Unfortunately, though something is known in general about the Somali stock trade (which continued, in changing forms, until after the second world war), almost no accounts are available of its detailed organisation, and in particular for this early period it is unclear what exactly the relationship was between the butcheries and the stock trade.

As early as 1914 a major threat to this newly established pattern of long-distance stock trading had begun to appear: European settler farmers in the Rift Valley. Alienation of land for settlement and plantation agriculture began in earnest in 1903, and by 1915 over five million acres of land in Kenya were formally in European hands.[19]

The initial effect of European settlement seems to have been to increase the demand for Somali stock, since the settlers required plough oxen, donkeys, and horses as well as cattle, sheep and goats. At this period these were obtained mainly from southern Ethiopia by the traders, collected on the Kenyan side of the Ethiopian border at Moyale and then trekked into the Rift Valley through Marsabit. Once again this trade seems to have been linked with the spread of Somali butchery businesses in the Rift Valley towns such as Ravine, Eldoret and Nakuru, which became the administrative and service centres of the settler areas.[20] Since we can once again assume that most settlers paid for their stock in cash, this must have given a further impetus to the monetisation of the trade.

Towards the end of this period settler attitudes to the trade and the traders

18. On Mbagathi see *KLC E & M* I, pp. 1168–71. See also Dalleo, op. cit., p. 134, SKAR 1911, p. 9, NAR 1912, p. 6. There were also Swahili and Nubian butchers in these early days.
19. See M.P.K. Sorrenson, *Origins of European Settlement in Kenya* (Nairobi, 1968), Appendix I, p. 296.
20. See Dalleo, op. cit., pp. 62 and 77.

began to change. By 1914 settler ranchers were being furnished or had furnished themselves with veterinary facilities, and had begun to dip and inoculate their stock, and in addition a number of the larger and richer settlers had imported pure-bred cattle, sheep and goats from Europe and had attempted cross-breeding with local animals to increase meat and milk yields. This meant that they had increasing numbers both of stock which had no natural immunities to local diseases and of stock which had been cleared of disease by dipping. In either case they did not welcome their animals coming into contact with local stock being trekked in large numbers through what were now their farms and estates to Kikuyuland, Masai or Nairobi. Since virtually all the farms were unfenced at this date, such contact was inevitable so long as the trade went on, particularly since the Somalis often stopped to graze their own herds at intervals during the journey (this of course became a source of grievance since it was now 'trespass' and 'theft' of grazing). The major source of worry was cattle disease, and in particular rinderpest, outbreaks of which were far more devastating than any other. A number of such outbreaks occurred on farms and ranches in the years before the war and brought agitation to have unrestricted trading of cattle in the Protectorate outlawed. The matter went into cold storage during the war, but immediately afterwards was renewed (partly as a result of widespread rinderpest outbreaks in 1919–20) and the Administration responded to it. The response was not in fact to stop the trading (an impossibility given the size of the colony, the small number of administrative officers, and the minimal policing—particularly in rural areas), but to place virtually all African cattle in near-permanent quarantine.[21] That is, the Administration placed slaughtering, dipping and quarantine stations on the major stock routes between different native reserves (as they had by now become), and forbade movement of any African-owned stock except through these stations. The two major stations were at Isiolo (on the exit point of the major stock route from the Northern Frontier Province into Kikuyuland and the Rift Valley) and at Ngong (on the exit point from Masailand into Kikuyuland and Nairobi). Sheep and goats could pass through after dipping, but cattle could only be passed through if slaughtered there.

The concentration by the Administration on Masailand and the Northern Frontier Province was by no means accidental. These were the two great areas of pastoral nomadism within the Colony and between them contained seventy per cent or more of the total African livestock holdings. From the first the Somali trade had revolved around these two hubs and then had gradually embraced Kikuyuland as well, and thus effective control over these two areas was the prerequisite of affording the settlers the protection they sought. In order to understand the changes which this intervention had brought about, I will attempt a schematic outline of the total structure of stock trading in the Protectorate around about 1914.

21. For a more comprehensive account of the origins of quarantining see Tignor, *The Colonial Transformation* . . ., op. cit., pp. 313–17.

We might begin a stock trading journey at Wajir in the north-east of the Northern Frontier Province. Here camels would be collected and trekked westwards to Marsabit, where they would be exchanged for heifers, sheep and goats with the Samburu, Rendille, Boran and other Somali nomads. The herd, now constituted overwhelmingly of heifers, sheep and goats, would then be trekked south to Isiolo. From there traders could either go south-east into Meru, or south to Nanyuki, where the route divided, going south into Kikuyu country at Nyeri or cutting due west and entering the southern Rift Valley at Thomson's Falls. From there one might go south past Nakuru, Naivasha and Escarpment, entering Masailand at Ngong, or cut further west through Njoro and Elburgon entering Nyanza Province through Kericho (if one was going south) or through Fort Ternan and Muhoroni on the way to Kisumu.[22] We shall however follow a herd to Masailand, where the following exchanges occurred:

A. *Exchange of heifers for bullocks:* Since the Masai, like all nomads, wished for a predominance of breeding and milk stock in their herds, exchange rates between heifers and male stock would generally be to the advantage of the Somalis.

B. *Exchange of heifers for sheep and goats:* Once again exchange ratios would be very favourable to the Somalis (for reasons noted earlier), and stress would be placed on obtaining good meat animals.

C. *Exchange of sheep and goats for sheep and goats:* The details of this are unclear, but it is probable that once again the exchange was of young breeding and milk females for males, and perhaps of kids and lambs for older males.[23]

Having now acquired an optimum meat herd, the Somali traders would proceed to the outskirts of Nairobi in order to dispose of it to butchers. It is clear that disposal was not necessarily immediate. There is evidence that herds were held on the outskirts of Mbagathi, or even pastured in Masailand proper, waiting for up-turns in meat prices. It is unclear whether these were herds already sold to butchers, or held off the market by traders, or both.[24]

It will be seen then that the exchange logic of this trade revolved around one simple fact. This was that the optimum constitution of a slaughter herd was almost the exact opposite of the optimum constitution of a breeding and milk herd, i.e. one was male and mature, the other was female (with a few good bulls) and young. Thus African pastoralists would accept high exchange ratios for male against female stock (in the case of both cattle and small stock) and through this the Somalis could obtain large numbers of slaughter stock for smaller quantities of female stock. The problem of course was to obtain the

22. I have pieced together these routes from data contained in UPAR 1906, p. 2; KisQR 1910, p. 2; KisuQR 1911, p. 6; SKAR 1912, p. 9; KAR 1915, p. 2; MasAR 1920, p. 7; FHAR 1920, p. 4; SKAR 1921, p. 14; KisuAR 1922, p. 27; as well as from data in Dalleo, Waller and *KLC E&M* II and Hay, op. cit., p. 177.

23. Exchange hierarchies are mentioned in Waller, p. 7 and more explicitly in Dalleo, pp. 16–18, 22–3, 72–3. See also MasAR 1921, p. 6, and Pamela and P. H. Gulliver, op. cit., pp. 59–60.

24. See MasAR 1923, p. 4.

female stock in the first place, and in this access to the Northern Frontier Province was vital, for in the much more arid conditions prevailing in this area the stock most prized by many nomads were not cattle at all, but camels. Hence if one could acquire camels (again, particularly breeding animals) heifers were obtainable at advantageous rates of exchange.

In the description of the trade routes (mapped on page 201) it was noted that choices of route existed at several points, and which of these were taken and by what proportion of the traders would have depended on news of exchange ratios passed among the traders by meeting and gossip *en route* and in their urban bases. Clearly these ratios would change constantly with weather and disease conditions in different areas, and also of course with the agricultural season. Just after a harvest, for example, any agricultural area would be a good selling ground.

It should be noted that as far as is known Somali stock traders only ever bartered stock for stock. If a sedentary pastoralist wanted stock from a Somali he either had to have stock to exchange, or money. They would not accept food crops or other products. Clearly this again meant a marked break with the traditions of more localised grain/stock barter trading and also acted as a pressure toward monetisation of the economy. It meant for example that there was an incentive to sell part of one's food crops at harvest, even if, in wanting to buy livestock with that money, one continued to demonstrate an allegiance to traditional norms of wealth.

Thus the emergence of long-distance stock trading based on the realisation of modern money profits in the meat market (primarily, at the beginning at least, the urban meat market) marked a rupture in the self-contained circuits of the pre-colonial stock economy. In that economy 'profit' had lain solely in the constitution of a more desirable from a less desirable herd, and wealth had lain in the possession of that herd and of wives. For the Somalis, there was profit proper, i.e. a net monetary gain which lay in the cash sale of a slaughter herd and there was 'modern' wealth in the possession of urban business premises, real estate, etc.[25] The conversion of one set of circuits into another was through barter trading based on two diametrically opposite conceptions of optimum herd structures.

This new long-distance stock trading coexisted with the old forms up to 1918, but it also influenced those forms. Both Newman and Hay confirm that in the years just before and during the first world war, longer-distance Kamba and Luo stock traders emerged, who also ended their chains of exchanges with money sales into the urban meat market. Interestingly enough, both authors also report that the men who first seized this opportunity to change the structure

25. Some of the Mbagathi Somalis owned boarding houses and made major contributions to the building of the first mosques in Nairobi. See A. H. Clayton, 'Labour in the East Africa Protectorate 1895–1918' (unpublished Ph.D., St Andrews University, 1971), p. 423, note 18.

of traditional trading were also some of the first in later years to take up plough cultivation, maize milling and shopkeeping, and in Kowe at least they were mainly the first generation of graduates from mission education.[26]

They were clearly attracted into the trade by its profitability and indeed there is fragmentary but persistent evidence of a sustained rise in the cash prices of all livestock from the turn of the century until 1918. This rise was of course primarily a sign of the continued predominance of pre-colonial economic patterns. The money prices of livestock rose so consistently because virtually all cash incomes whether they came from wage labour or from the sale of food crops and other commodities were used to purchase livestock. The number of households having such incomes increased markedly during the first world war, through conscription into the armed forces and the carrier corps, and also from food crop sales to the armed forces. In addition government intervention in the livestock market during the war drove up prices during that period.[27]

Above all in the early years of the century all the peoples of the East African Protectorate were attempting to build up their holdings again after the decimations of drought and rinderpest in the late nineties. We have already noted that Somali trading started in response to this demand, and since the Somalis themselves were an important force in monetising livestock transactions, one would expect the persistent demand, particularly for milk and breeding animals, to show itself in money prices. The livestock once acquired were used as they had always been used, for milk in the case of cattle, for milk and more occasionally for meat in the case of sheep and goats, but above all, in both cases, for bridewealth. It seems very clear for example that young unmarried males were the first category of Kenyan African males to seek out unskilled manual wage labour regularly, and that the prime reason for their doing so was to obtain money to purchase bridewealth stock. The imposition of a poll tax on unmarried males in 1910 (to supplement the hut tax which had been imposed on household heads in 1902) was undoubtedly a major factor starting this process, but it was the discovery that, with rising real wages before 1918, taxes could be paid and something remain for livestock purchases which kept these young men 'coming out', as the colonial records put it.[28]

We may now consider changes introduced into the pattern of stock trading after 1918.

Livestock Trading after 1918

In the immediate aftermath of the war, stock prices fell, with pastoralist areas being hard hit by droughts from 1918–21. This allowed grain producers to

26. See Newman, op. cit., pp. 4–5 and Hay, op. cit., p. 177.
27. For data on stock prices to 1918 see for example KisuAR 1912, p. 27, East African Protectorate, *Report of the Native Labour Commission* (NLC) 1912–13, pp. 233, 240–72; SKAR 1912, p. 5; 1916, p. 16; and 1917, p. 20; MasAR 1915, p. 3; and 1916, p. 4. See also Waller, op. cit., pp. 9–11 and Newman, p. 4.
28. See Hay, op. cit., pp. 172–3 and Clayton, op. cit., p. 102 and pp. 186–7.

benefit from much-improved terms of trade between stock and food crops, and we have evidence of advantage being taken of this by the Kisii of South Kavirondo in trade with the Luo of the lake shore, by the Abaluhya of North Kavirondo in trade with the Luo of Central Kavirondo, by the Kikuyu in trade with the Kamba and Masai, and by the Kisii again in trade with the Masai.[29]

In the light of developments in the late twenties and early thirties it is important to understand why, in periods of drought or locust infestation, stock prices or the barter terms of trade between stock and grain always favoured the grain producer. The reason was not simply, or perhaps even primarily, that when stock died nomadic people needed grain and other food crops to keep alive, since their stock rearing methods (particularly the stress on quantity rather than quality) allowed them some margin to weather all but the most protracted of droughts, especially by subsisting much more regularly on blood rather than milk. The much more important reason was that when grazing deteriorated the nomads fed cereals to their animals, particularly the cows.[30] Thus they tended to be wanting food imports in large quantities precisely at times (periods of drought etc.) when supplies were at a premium in the agricultural areas. Their tactic at such times was to attempt to dispose of less valued stock (small stock and bullocks) in much larger numbers in order to keep alive and productive the heifers, cows and the calves (their insurance for the future). These were only disposed of after periods of really prolonged drought when food crops were needed for human consumption as well as for the animals, and food crop traders were able to insist on obtaining heifers and cows for food. Things did not reach this pass in 1919–21, but they did in 1934, when in some pastoralist areas there had been continuous drought from 1928.

Although the evidence is fragmentary, it seems that both the barter and money prices of livestock went up in 1922–3, and continued reasonably buoyant thereafter until 1929, though it does not seem that money prices ever regained the levels of the war years, a sign that demand was probably not outrunning supply.[31] From the twenties, with the setting up of more and more quarantine stations, some statistics began to become available on stock movements, and table VIII:1 shows the number of sheep and goats leaving the Masai Province and the Northern Frontier Province on permits in the 1920s.

It seems reasonably clear that most of these sheep and goats found their way to Kikuyuland, along with an unknown quantity of illegal exports and a constant supply in unregulated trade from Machakos and Kitui. The marked

29. UPAR 1920, p. 43; MasAR 1920, p. 3; FHAR 1920, p. 6; SKAR 1918, p. 2; Hay, op. cit., p. 176.
30. Miracle, op. cit., p. 7. See also *KLC E & M* II, pp. 1490 and 1747; and *AAD* 1949, p. 52.
31. See Newman, pp. 4–5, and Waller, pp. 13, 17–19. Also *NAD* 1925, pp. 206–7; 1926, p. 35; 1927, p. 32; and the very interesting price index of Kitui cattle (1923–38) compiled by J. E. H. Stanner and reproduced in van Zwanenberg, 'Primitive Colonial Accumulation . . .', op. cit., p. 168.

Table VIII:1. Sheep and goats legally leaving Masailand and the Northern Frontier Province in the twenties[32]

Year	Masailand	Northern Frontier Province
1924	40,000	
1925	30,000	73,282
1926	31,412	37,312
1927		68,606
1928	27,777	80,015
1929	34,128	44,446
Totals:	163,317	303,661
Grand Total:	466,978	

variations in the supply from the Northern Frontier Province are to be noted and appear to have been almost entirely due to changing ecological conditions in that Province, the supply increasing when conditions were worst.

Now this was also the period when the cultivated area in Central Province first began to expand at a rapid rate, so that by 1931 a third (267,461 acres) of the cultivable land in the Province as a whole was under crops. All this land of course had been excised from the 'communal' grazing area, but at that date there was still just over double this amount (554,939 acres) still under grass, on which Fazan estimated there to be 109,251 cows, 46,303 bulls and bullocks, and 286,032 sheep and goats.[33] The marked discrepancy between this last figure and the export totals in table VIII:1 reflects both the proportion of the exported animals which found their way to other areas, and the fact that some of the sheep and goats in particular were slaughtered. It also reflects the gross under-estimation by Fazan of Kikuyu livestock holdings, a failure springing from the reluctance of all African livestock owners to have their stock counted (through fear of expropriation and/or taxation) and, in the particular case of the Kikuyu, from a failure to take into account the large number of animals belonging to men in the Reserve which were kept by friends or relatives who were squatters on farms and in forests, under the lending arrangements which were common at the time.[34]

In Nyanza Province, only eighteen per cent of the cultivable land in Central Kavirondo was under crops in 1931, and in fact nearly a million acres still remained under grazing compared with the mere 126,565 acres which were cultivated. This land was carrying 336,164 cattle and 381,389 sheep and goats, which meant that there was slightly more land per cow but slightly less per head of small stock than in Kikuyuland. In South Kavirondo less than ten per cent of the land

32. Sources: MasAR 1924–9, and *NAD* 1924–9.
33. Fazan, op. cit., pp. 984 and 986.
34. On this matter see *KLC E & M* I, p. 666 (evidence of Dr L. S. B. Leakey).

was under crops in 1931 and there were some 1,700,000 acres of grazing land available to support the 271,319 cattle and 201,068 sheep and goats which the Land Commission was told were in the possession of the district population at that date (6.3 acres for every cow and 8.5 acres for every sheep and goat). In fact only in North Kavirondo was there any hint of pressure on grazing land, and then only in the densely populated southern locations which had thirty-eight per cent of their total land area but seventy-seven per cent of their cultivable land under crops by the beginning of the 1930s. In the district as a whole less than twenty per cent of the land area was under crops and over a million acres were available to support a comparatively small livestock population of some quarter of a million cattle and some 15,000 sheep and goats.[35]

Even allowing for intra-district variations and for climatic changes which made land/livestock ratios virtually meaningless as fixed quantities, it does not seem that any of the districts of Kikuyuland or Nyanza were experiencing particular pressure on grazing by the end of the twenties, especially since in Kikuyuland in particular lending arrangements with squatters opened up large areas of the Rift Valley for extra grazing.

Farm incomes rising slowly from expansions of the cultivated area were generally invested in livestock, which continued to be used primarily for bridewealth. Virtually all the witnesses before the Land Commission took the view that this was the major use of livestock in 1931. Moreover, we have some evidence, certainly from the end of the 1920s, of the beginning of a rise in the amount of bridewealth. The Kiambu district annual report for example noted that bridewealth payments involved the transfer of between thirty and forty goats in Nyeri, but up to eighty in Kiambu, whilst in the same year the South Kavirondo District Officer put down the increasing scale of illegal stock movements into the district from Tanganyika and an increase of stock thefts to the 'steeply rising bride price'.[36]

Moreover it is clear that up to 1931 bridewealth payments were still made overwhelmingly in livestock. James Mukaa, testifying before the Land Commission about the situation in Ukamba, said that in that year 'typical' bridewealth in Machakos was thirty-five goats, two cows and one bullock, and in Kitui eight cows, one bullock and fifty goats, and when asked if money was ever substituted for any of these items he replied that this occurred only among the christianised minority of the population, and then only for part of the bridewealth. His view was in fact that 'some of them pay half in money, but the money is calculated at the market rate of the goats etc.'[37]

In short, up to 1930 the norms of wealth and the economic processes which had characterised the 'sedentary pastoralist' economies of pre-colonial Kenya

35. *KLC E & M* III, pp. 2214, 2258–9, 2352 and 2357.
36. KAR 1929, p. 8 and SKAR 1929, p. 43. See also *KLC E & M* I, pp. 667 and 689–90.
37. *KLC E & M* II, pp. 1338–9.

Table VIII:2. Exports of cows, sheep and goats from Masailand, Northern Frontier Province, Machakos and Kitui 1930–9

	MASAILAND		N.F.P.		MACHAKOS		KITUI	
Year	Cattle	Sheep and goats	Cattle	Sheep and goats	Cattle	Sheep and goats	Cattle	Sheep and goats
1930	10,388	32,208	—	70,295	—	—	—	—
1931	18,553	31,000	Nil	69,850	—	—	8,500	13,000
1932	15,672	48,575	Nil	68,160	—	—	19,500	71,000
1933	15,625	31,600	—	41,554	—	—	15,350	40,350
1934	11,117	21,904	—	58,152	3,525	37,235	—	—
1935	24,506	23,961	32	56,184	9,512	76,062	20,698	63,718
1936	8,532	14,448	679	67,499	10,520	49,243	—	—
1937	18,534	18,250	768	64,018	7,832	27,881	—	—
1938	—	—	530	58,459	29,745	34,358	—	—
1939	—	—	Nil	78,853	5,060	—	—	—

Sources: MasAR 1930–9; IsAR 1930–9; NAD 1932, 1933 and 1935; and Forbes Munro, op. cit., Appendix C.

still continued to predominate despite some movement in the direction of 'agriculturalisation' which had occurred over the decade in all areas, and most markedly in localised areas (such as Kiambu or southern North Kavirondo). In fact the slowly developing role of agricultural production had the initial effect of strengthening some of those processes, and in particular the centrality of bridewealth transfers. For with increasing female labour input into agriculture, women's labour power became increasingly prized by all household heads, and so its transfer became increasingly costly to effect. This is what lay behind the persistent rise in bridewealth payments, which was in turn a powerful factor in motivating unmarried young men to seek wage labour.

All this was to change in the 1930s and, in particular, in the 1940s, and the reasons for the change are perhaps predictable. On the one hand the area of available grazing began to decline much more rapidly as population increase, the Administration's production drive in the Reserves, and rising farm incomes (at least for the middle and large landholders) all stimulated increases in the cultivated area. The start of the change was the period of droughts and locusts from 1928 to 1934 when stock poured into the agricultural areas. Table VIII:2 shows the export of cows, sheep and goats from Masailand, the Northern Frontier Province, Machakos and Kitui for various years in the 1930s. It will be seen that counting only those animals which were moved on permits and for which figures are available, no less than 130,711 cattle and 778, 808 sheep and goats were exported from these four areas in the period from 1930 to 1935, when drought and locusts were at their worst. In the case of the figure for sheep and goats, which is certainly more reliable and comprehensive since it covers live animals (the figures for cattle include a majority of slaughter stock), the figure is almost double that of exports from Masailand and the Northern Frontier Province in the middle to late twenties. Moreover, even these figures are a gross underestimation of the amount of stock which was moved, the vast bulk of which went into Kikuyuland. This is because the official figures are most incomplete for Kitui and Machakos, from which the majority of the stock going into Kikuyuland probably came. In addition it is clear that there was a very large amount of totally unregistered export and import to which both the district reports of the period and the Kenya Land Commission *Report* bear witness. Dr Leakey, for example, in his evidence before the Commission, said

> the importation of goats and sheep from the Northern Frontier, from Kisii and from Masai to the Kikuyu country should be prohibited ... The annual number of goats and sheep from the Northern Frontier to the Kikuyu country is simply stupendous. I have had figures from Mr. Glenday for the Northern area; and goats are coming in from Masai at night, hidden under loads of skins on lorries etc. That is going on the whole time, and they are coming in from Kisii in truck loads.[38]

As noted in chapter IV, this occurred because the barter terms of trade between food crops and livestock turned savagely in favour of the Kikuyu and against the purely pastoralist peoples at about the same time that the depression drove down the money prices of these crops. The impact was most marked in Kikuyuland because it was surrounded on three sides by primarily pastoralist areas.[39] This massive influx of stock to the cultivating pastoralist areas went together with a further rise in bridewealth payments, and it is noticeable that this effect appears to have been most pronounced in the most agriculturalised and commercialised areas. Thus, for example, in the Fort Hall district report for 1932 it is noted that Kiambu bridewealth levels were notably higher than in Fort Hall, and as a result 'a large number of Fort Hall young women are married to Kiambu natives'.[40]

However this massive influx of livestock into the Central Province and (on a smaller scale) into Nyanza occurred coextensively with an acceleration in the rate of expansion of the cultivated area at the expense of grazing land, and this expansion continued after the 'stock boom' subsided from 1935 onwards. It took the form, as we saw, of massive extensions of the area under maize, wattle and cotton (in the case of cotton in Nyanza, in precisely those areas which carried the most livestock). Humphrey's survey of Nyeri in 1944 showed that some forty-one per cent of the total land area was under crops as against thirty-four per cent in 1931, and increases in other districts like Central and North Kavirondo, Kiambu, Fort Hall and Machakos were certainly greater through

38. *KLC E & M* I, p. 669.
39. UPAR 1929, p. 3 and NAR 1929, p. 5.
40. FHAR 1932, p. 4.

this period. Moreover a comparison of the cultivated area with the total land area of a district is severely misleading in that it suggests that all land not cultivated was suitable for grazing, whereas in fact the best grazing was precisely in those comparatively flat, well-watered areas which were most suitable for cultivation. Other areas unsuitable for cultivation because of their aridity, tsetse infestation or steepness could also only carry very few stock. In the case of Nyeri for example the situation in 1944 is probably best approximated if the grazing land and the cultivable land are treated as coextensive, in which case in that thickly populated district seventy-six per cent of the best grazing had disappeared under the plough and the hoe by that date![41]

Clearly in Central Province pressure was building up. The number of animals on the land probably at least doubled between 1930 and 1935 and the grazing land disappeared rapidly through the thirties. By 1938 in Kiambu there were reported to be 60,000 cattle, 130,000 goats and 30,000 sheep, nearly all of them grazing on the 47,000 acres of the Ndeiya area which the Kenya Land Commission had added to the district as a safety valve. This represented nearly three goats on every acre of land, whilst figures given to the Kenya Land Commission had suggested that a desirable ratio was approximately three or four acres to every goat.[42]

Once again it is likely that some relief was afforded by the pasturing of animals with squatters in the Rift Valley, and by making lending arrangements with Masai or other Kikuyu to use grazing land in Masailand or in Ukamba, but such arrangements must have become more and more difficult as in the late thirties settlers began to make more determined efforts to control the number of squatter stock. Ukamba came to be regarded as overstocked, and in 1938 was subject to the first major compulsory destocking compaign attempted by the Administration in the African reserves.[43] It only took a further increase of pressure to bring about structural changes, and in Central Province that further pressure appears to have come with the war years. For at one and the same time the high wartime prices called forth a further substantial increase in the cultivated area and settler farmers from the late thirties onwards began to substitute enforced repatriation of squatters and their stock for the limits on squatter stock holdings which had gone before but been widely evaded. In this situation two things appear to have occurred simultaneously: firstly, money began to be substituted for livestock in bridewealth payments on a large scale, and secondly, livestock holdings began to be treated primarily as a source of meat.

As far as the sources allow a chronology to be constructed, these processes

41. See above, chapter V, pp. 115–18 and Humphrey, 'The Relationship . . .', op cit., pp. 7 and 50.
42. KAR 1938, p. 8 and *KLC E & M* I, pp. 1007–8.
43. For the 'squatter stock' issue, see van Zwanenberg, 'Primitive Colonial Accumulation . . .' op. cit., pp. 507–17 and Frank Furedi, 'Kikuyu Squatters and the Changing Political Economy of the White Highlands' (CPEK Paper, 1975), especially pp. 4–6. For the Ukamba destocking campaign, see Forbes Munro, op. cit., pp. 217–23 and 227–42, and Tignor, op. cit., pp. 331–60.

appear to have got under way on a small scale and among a minority of house-holds in the early thirties. They accelerated slowly through the thirties and then massively in the forties. By the late forties and early fifties they were almost universal among the Kikuyu and appear to have been fairly well advanced in North and Central Kavirondo as well.[44]

We should now analyse the roots of these changes. We saw that, in the pre-colonial period, livestock had been both a measure of wealth and a means of exchange. With the monetisation of exchange relationships (which was almost complete in Kikuyuland, Machakos and Nyanza by the thirties), livestock lost its role as a means of exchange and became simply one of a widened range of commodities which exchanged through money. Like other commodities (notably food crops and some artisan products) it continued to be bartered in very localised exchanges occurring outside the market context, but by the thirties these were a small part of the total set of exchanges occurring in these 'heartlands'. Also by the thirties, livestock was no longer exchanged for land. This still appears to have happened in the 1920s, but by the late 1930s, in Central Province, North and Central Kavirondo at least, land purchase was being carried out almost entirely by means of modern money only.

It is not difficult to see why this should be. Unless a male household head was proposing to move his entire household elsewhere to obtain grazing land (which by the 1930s was virtually impossible, since the squatter option was closing), exchange of land for livestock would have been an irrational act, since he would have nowhere to graze them and disposal of part of his landholdings would make him less than ever able to do so.

It was true that there was still the option for some people of placing livestock in other areas through lending arrangements. But the stock was then at a distance and could not easily be utilised, and in any case it became increasingly unclear what one could utilise it for. As we have seen, the role of livestock as a means of exchange had been eroded, and in addition its range of use values had become somewhat reduced. New forms of house design made the use of cow hides for internal decoration unfashionable, and more importantly the availability and increasing use of cheap cotton clothing made sheep and goat skins and cow hides increasingly redundant for this purpose.

Bereft of its role as means of exchange (in which it had been replaced by modern money) and redundant in most of the agricultural areas as a source of clothing, livestock had, by the late thirties, two roles remaining: (a) to exchange for female labour (bridewealth) and (b) to be consumed as meat and milk.

Now through the late twenties and thirties, as we have seen, bridewealth payments increased, and given the changing production situation this was not at all surprising. For as the economies of the sedentary people moved more and

---

44. See for example Wagner, Vol. I, pp. 392, 402 and Vol II, pp. 108–17; Humphrey, *The Liguru...*, op. cit., p. 44; Kenyatta, op. cit., p. 67; and Fisher, op. cit., p. 16.

more towards agriculture, and as an increasing quantity of male labour time was devoted to working outside the holding, so female labour became increasingly vital to all households whether (in the case of richer households) to expand the marketed surplus or (in the case of poorer households) to maintain subsistence levels on smaller and smaller areas of land. At the same time that female labour time was becoming more and more central to agricultural production, livestock were becoming more and more marginal in production and exchange. The result was, as one might expect, that livestock became devalued relative to female labour. This was what was occurring in bridewealth 'inflation'.[45]

But of course there was a contradiction involved in such a process. The depreciation of livestock relative to women (the twin measures, it will be remembered of pre-colonial wealth) meant that ever larger numbers of stock had to be acquired for bridewealth, and this clearly was the prime motivation behind the influx of stock into Kikuyuland in the twenties and thirties, an influx which became a flood in the years from 1930 to 1935. But increasing quantities of livestock required increasing amounts of grazing land, and this as we have seen was in rapidly dwindling supply through the thirties. Clearly if this contradiction became acute it would have to be resolved, and in the forties it did sharpen to the point where a resolution was required—a sharpening produced, as noted, by a further increase of the cultivated area during the war and the return of squatter stock. The resolution was of course to substitute money for livestock in bridewealth payments, and this, a minority phenomenon in the thirties, appears to have become normal in Kikuyuland and increasingly so in North and Central Kavirondo in the forties and early fifties.

Interestingly enough, allegations by colonial officials that bridewealth transactions made African women little more than chattel slaves increased markedly once this substitution began to occur. For example, the Provincial Commissioner of Nyanza Province, reporting on the 'deterioration' of 'bride price' practices within the Province in 1948, said

> Today . . . the transaction is very nearly a sale, as the stock is not maintained, and may be passed on the same day as it is received, or even sold for cash. Particularly is this emphasized in the case of squatters living away from tribal control. By custom the bride price is distributed among close relatives for custody, but the squatter now keeps the entire proceeds and in many instances realises cash as soon as possible after receipt of the stock. Often the custom has so far deteriorated that bride price is paid in cash. This is surely a human sale.[46]

It was certainly true that cash substitution did strengthen the system whereby

---

45. Dr Leakey presented a not dissimilar explanation of bridewealth 'inflation' to the KLC as early as 1933. See *KLC, E & M* I, pp. 689–90.
46. *AAD* 1948, p. 53.

a man was primarily responsible for finding his own bridewealth from wage labour, trade or business etc., and conversely it tended to weaken traditions of kin contribution to bridewealth payments (and kin shares in receipts) which had precisely been the factor cementing this social nexus. Increasingly bridewealth transfers were of money from one man (the would-be husband) to one man (the father of the girl) who was primarily or solely responsible for repayment. In addition of course the situation in which girls' fathers had an incentive to marry them to those who could raise the largest bridewealth payments was continued, but now took the form (apparently much more abhorrent to missionaries and colonial officials alike) of calculation in pounds and shillings rather than cattle, sheep and goats.

Propaganda against the whole institution of bridewealth was stepped up, particularly by missionaries; but this had little effect. For most male household heads faced with static or even declining incomes as a result of land shortage and rising prices, women were still far too valuable an asset to waste, and indeed there is evidence that in the high inflation of the war and post-war years in Kenya bridewealth itself underwent a continued rise along with its monetisation. Thus, for example, the same African Affairs Department *Report* for 1948 which had quoted the Nyanza Provincial Commissioner's remarks on the deterioration of bridewealth practice also noted an increasing tension between 'the older and younger generations' in the post-war world as a result of 'the level of bride price'.[47]

A Case Study

There is one fascinating study of the causes and consequences of the monetisation of bridewealth in Kenya which concerns a somewhat later period and a different area: that of southern Kilifi district in the Coast Province. Since at least some of the processes directly observed here were undoubtedly occurring in Central Province and parts of Nyanza and Machakos in the forties and early fifties, but can only be inferred from colonial records, it is worth examining this study in some depth.

Parkin's study is of the social effects of copra production among a small group of Giriama households in the Kaloleni location of Kilifi district.[48] He begins by noting that the year 1944 was conventionally used as marking a dividing line between two economic 'eras' in the history of this area. Prior to this date most households had earned an income from the production and sale of palm wine obtained by the tapping of coconut palms. In a detailed description of the trade in palm wine, Parkin shows that large-scale accumulation either of money, palms or wine was not possible because of the labour intensity of the trade,

47. Ibid., p. 6.
48. David J. Parkin, *Palms, Wine and Witnesses: Public Spirit and Private Gain in an African Farming Community* (London, 1972).

the low levels of profit to be made in a highly localised and competitive activity, and the use to which the maintenance of a competitive position within the trade forced palm wine producers to put the wealth obtained. Since the production and sale of palm wine involved a large number of intermediaries—'tappers, carriers, loaders, transporters and sellers'—a large palm wine producer, or even a man hoping to expand his holdings of land and palms, had to maintain a regiment of poorer supporters, who undertook these functions and were also small-scale growers.[49] Winning of supporters might involve loans or gifts on special occasions, but its most important form was polygyny. By marrying many wives, some or all of whom would be the daughters or sisters of poorer men, a more successful palm wine grower assured himself of support and a labour force; but of course 'Apart from overloading a family estate with too many sons, this necessary heavy investment in local support inevitably diverted money from the purchase of more palms, so that rates of palm accumulation by individual families were slow.'[50] In short the absence of a really large market for palm wine, the perishability of the wine and the consequent difficulty of storing it or transporting it over large distances, the large number of producers and the mechanisms of maintaining a labour force through patronage and marriage links, all served to keep profits low and accumulation limited. To a very large extent the palm wine trade was a populist's dream, dominated by approximately equal small men and with a built-in mechanism (polygynous marriage, bridewealth transfers and equal division of land and palms among sons) which served effectively to check whatever tendencies there might be to differentiation.

However, from the second world war onwards this pattern began to change and the essential factor in that change was the opening up of an export market for copra. This occurred from 1950 onwards when, with the Korean boom, the demand for copra increased and the world price soared. This was reflected in local prices which rose from 9/70 per frasila in 1950 to 25/- in 1952. As a result of this boom, holdings of palms immediately increased their exchange value enormously, and the rewards for enlarging such holdings were considerable. This was especially the case as copra, unlike palm wine production, did not require each individual producer to engage a great deal of labour for preparation and marketing, the latter being done first by Asian businessmen, and then by a Cooperative Society.[51] As a result of all this, a small group of men (called 'accumulators' by Parkin) who had access to money from wage employment, or who had been in the copra trade as employees of Asians, began systematically to acquire land and palm trees on a much larger scale than their neighbours.

Since all their purchases were made in money, their activities began a mone-

49. Ibid., pp. 10-11.
50. Ibid., p. 11.
51. Ibid., p. 50.

*Table VIII:3. Livestock/cash composition of bridewealth transactions
undertaken in Kaloleni by living Tsakani men*

Year	All or mostly livestock[1]	Roughly equal livestock and cash	All or mostly cash[2]	Number of transactions
1920–9	2 (50%)	1 (25%)	1 (25%)	4
1930–9	5 (56%)	1 (11%)	3 (33%)	9
1940–9	5 (38.5%)	0	8 (61.5%)	13
1950–9	5 (14.7%)	3 (8.8%)	26 (76.5%)	34
1960–Mid-1967	2 (5.1%)	3 (7.7%)	34 (87.2%)	39
Total	19 (19.2%)	8 (8.1%)	72 (72.7%)	99

1. All but 3 are exclusively livestock

2. All but 5 are exclusively cash.

Source: Parkin, op. cit., p. 64.

tisation of the market in land, and the number of land and palm purchases and
sales with money expanded rapidly through the fifties and early sixties as other
farmers saw the profits to be made from copra, and endeavoured to follow the
early entrepreneurs. As the cultivated area expanded, grazing declined, and,
since livestock could not now be used to exchange with land, it was disposed
of, at first in 'inflated' livestock bridewealth and then by being eaten or simply
sold out of the area for cash. At the same time and for the same reasons, money
replaced livestock in bridewealth and money income from bridewealth was
itself invested in more palms and more land.[52]

Parkin provides the data shown in table VIII : 3 on the monetisation of bridewealth among twenty-six households in a small area of Kaloleni known as Tsakani. It will be seen from the table that the proportion of bridewealth transactions in Tsakani made 'all or mostly in cash' increased continuously from 1930
onwards, but accelerated markedly from 1940, and then even more markedly
through the fifties and sixties. As Parkin makes clear, the force behind this
monetisation was not some simple monetary determinism, whereby as cash
incomes from copra increased cash payments replaced livestock transfers. It was
intimately connected with the disappearance of grazing land, as Kaloleni
farmers began to concentrate on expanding their palm groves. But it was not
simply this either. Parkin describes the economic mechanism precisely:

> Though the scarcity of grazing land for cattle has been the ecological promp-
> ter of the switch to cash, the economic usefulness of cash is that surplus
> bridewealth (bridewealth not needed immediately or at all for the marriage

52. Ibid., pp. 52–4 and 62–5.

of a male dependent), can be used to buy palms. As the value placed on palms has risen, therefore, there has been a corresponding rise in the value of the increasingly monetised bridewealth. In other words the Giriama suffer from inflation.[53]

The reference to 'inflation' here is odd, because Parkin himself goes on to show that what was involved was not simply or even primarily 'inflation' but an actual rise in the 'real cost' of bridewealth payments. In Tsakani the average bridewealth payment between 1920 and 1940 had been about eight heifers and a bull. From 1940 to 1960 the rate had gradually risen to about twelve to fifteen heifers and a bull or its equivalent in palm wine. Since over this period the cash costs of these animals all rose together with their numbers, there had clearly been a real increase in bridewealth payments.[54]

Part of Parkin's confusion here derives from one of the central foci of his study, which is upon the response of the 'elders' of the community to the changes wrought by the rising group of 'accumulators'. He suggests that the elders had attempted to preserve the populist equality of the palm wine period by insisting that the new rich men, just like the old, should redistribute their wealth to the community through bridewealth payments and the provision of lavish funerals. Much of the study is taken up by the story of the attempts of the elders to insist on this, and of accumulator resistance to the old levelling mechanisms.[55] He considers that one outcome of the struggle (which he suggests that the accumulators were winning) was a general 'inflation' of bridewealth payments, since the elders' strategy was tending to backfire on the community as a whole, i.e. the standards of expenditure on funerals and bridewealth set by the accumulators had to be emulated by other household heads. They could afford the expenditures less, and often could only meet them by selling land and palms. When this happened, of course, the buyers were often the accumulators themselves.[56]

Concentration on the elder/accumulator struggle thus leads Parkin into explaining the bridewealth 'inflation' in Tsakani in terms of the strategy of the elders with its contradictory effects. But since such 'inflation' was not restricted to the Giriama, but had occurred (and would continue to occur) in areas where this sort of 'elder power' was not manifest, it seems a much less satisfactory explanation than the economic one we have posited, and which Parkin himself hints at elsewhere.

In particular, though his account provides no data directly on the rising value of female labour power, and indeed does not even provide an account of the division of labour in copra production, he does provide a comparison of the

53. Ibid., p. 65.
54. Ibid., p. 65 and especially tables 8 and 9, p. 66.
55. Ibid., pp. 25–9 and 63–86.
56. Ibid., p. 63 and pp. 100–1.

situation of women in inland Giriama country (away from the area of copra production), which in the light of our previous analyses is gratifyingly predictable. He says:

> In the open area of Giriamaland beyond the palm belt a wife or co-wife is entitled to her own garden (*koho*) in which she can grow crops to be used as she pleases provided she has done her share of cultivation in the main garden (*munda*) worked by all wives together. With the extension of the palm belt in Kaloleni, little land is available for any other than this larger 'husband's garden'. In Tsakani, figures show that, as the number of palms and people have increased fewer new wives have been allocated their own gardens. Crops from the communal main garden are in no way the property of an individual wife and are used either for subsistence or as the husband or his homestead head determines. Copra as a new crop, has always been the prerogative of men, who determine the use of cash earned from selling it. This is also the case with other even more recent tree crops such as citrus fruits and cashew nuts.[57]

Clearly a lot turns here on what is meant by saying that copra 'is the prerogative of men', and Parkin does not amplify, but the context suggests that male control over the income earned from copra sales had not been balanced by greater labour input into production. Otherwise this is an exact confirmation from field observation (dating from 1966–7) of processes which we have surmised from other sources had taken place twenty years or so earlier in more 'advanced' areas of Kenya.

Moreover, Parkin shows that the general trend of events in Kaloleni had been to the disadvantage of women, since the ever larger bridewealth payments, and the ever growing tendency for such payments to be used as investment funds for land and palms, had made it more and more in the interest of fathers to insist that their daughters remain in marriage. A particularly interesting change in the mode of payment of bridewealth reflects this.[58]

In the days when bridewealth had been in the form of livestock, among the Giriama, as among other peoples, payment had been in instalments often lasting over many years. With the monetisation of bridewealth however, Parkin noted a strong tendency for the time of payment to shorten considerably to the point where, at the time of the fieldwork, payment of an agreed monetary total was generally insisted upon very soon after the marriage had been contracted. One particular payment called 'the bull' (*ndzau*) had traditionally been transferred early on in the series of payments and assured the male and his family genetricial rights in the wife. Traditionally the 'bull' had been the animal which its name implies, but over time, and with the decline of livestock holdings, it had come to

57. Ibid., p. 72.
58. What follows is based on ibid., pp. 66–9.

be replaced by a certain quantity of palm wine. Once the 'bull' had been transferred the husband was able to lay claim to the paternity of any children, even
if the wife became pregnant or gave birth before the rest of the payments had
been completed, and then for one reason or another left her husband.

Parkin noted that at the time of his fieldwork more and more fathers of girls
would only accept the 'bull' of palm wine (interestingly this had not been
monetised) after all the cash bridewealth had been paid. And by 1967 this was
expected to have been done three to five months after the bride had taken residence in her husband's house. This ensured that should she leave her husband
before this time and be found pregnant, her family of origin could still lay claim
to the child. Parkin comments however that her father would only be likely to
make such a claim 'if the child is a girl', i.e. if she represented a source of future
bridewealth.

Otherwise the idea was simply to put pressure on the family paying to deliver
the whole amount quickly, and the reasons for this too were not in doubt:

> ...a wholly-cash bridewealth is useful to accumulators because it can be
> used, barring other expenses, to purchase palms and land. Its usefulness is
> enhanced if the accumulator receives the money, if not in one lump sum, then
> at least within a short time. Similarly, the loser who is obliged to sell palms
> and land in order to raise the cash to meet some exigency needs the money
> immediately: he has naturally been loath to dispose of such property until
> his resources reached a minimum, and now his need is desperate. The two
> needs balance each other, with the result that protracted payments for palms
> and land or bridewealth are discouraged by those to whom they are due.[59]

Not surprisingly there tended to be a spate of divorces in the early months of
marriage but very few thereafter, since pressure on a woman to stay with her
husband after the 'bull' had been delivered was strong, especially when her
father had already invested the money in palms or land or (if less fortunate)
had paid off a debt or mortgage with it. And here of course we come to the core
of the change made by the monetisation of bridewealth.

When bridewealth transfers had been in the form of livestock, the family
receiving payments had to be extremely careful about the use to which such
stock were put. Should they for example barter it for other animals or for food
or land, they could be faced with demands for the return of an animal of equivalent value in the event of the breakdown of the marriage. It seems that in many
cases there was an effective prohibition on the use of bridewealth livestock for
exchange purposes, at least in the early years of marriage and in the case of particularly important animals in the bridewealth, which were usually cows.[60] But
more importantly, such transfers operated in a context where livestock was the

59. Ibid., p. 66.
60. See for example Wagner, op. cit., Vol. I, p. 442, and Leakey, op. cit., p. 169.

measure of wealth as well as the means of exchange, i.e. in a situation where livestock exchanges were engaged in simply in order to obtain more livestock and/or higher value livestock. However in the changed situation of Central Province or Central and North Nyanza in the forties and fifties, or of southern Kilifi in the fifties and sixties, livestock was neither the measure of wealth nor the means of exchange, and money, though the means of exchange and the measure of wealth, had constantly to assume other forms in order to increase wealth, i.e. money had to be 'invested in' or take the form of land, coconut palms, coffee trees, pyrethrum bushes, lorries, stores or shop buildings, ploughs, insecticide sprays, cattle dips, fencing, etc. Money became the means, and eventually the only means, of obtaining these things, whose possession was in turn the means of obtaining more money. Livestock could be increased by exchange and by breeding, but money could only be increased by its more or less long-term alienation and metamorphosis into means of production. Thus the means of production in agriculture were becoming commodities.

The need to alienate money for prolonged periods of time so that investments could gestate, and the need to save and accumulate, increased the pressure which tied women to their husbands. It is not surprising that under these circumstances Parkin reports the phenomenon of women running away from their husbands to Mombasa and there becoming Moslems[61] (this section of the Giriama were mostly Christian). Other sources reveal that the adoption of the Islamic religion in an urban context was a way of placing cultural distance between the adoptee and the tribal environment from which she came, and we know from Bujra's work for example that many of Nairobi's prostitutes were at least nominally of the Islamic faith.[62] Interestingly, Parkin reports that when a woman left for Mombasa pressure was usually put on her to repay the bridewealth to her ex-husband's family, since her father might well refuse to do so.

An important theoretical point which emerges from this discussion is the precise theoretical status to be attached to the transfer of women through bridewealth. It is to be noted that though the loss (and acquisition) of labour power which was rising in value was the central force behind bridewealth increases, it was not labour power, as such, which was being transferred. That is to say labour power itself had not become a commodity under these circumstances since the women in no sense sold it as a commodity for a specified length of time before returning to their families of origin. On the contrary, under these circumstances labour power was only transferred with the transfer of labour, of the women themselves, for the largest part of their adult lives, until death. Was this then a species of slavery? Did bridewealth transfers represent payment for the person, body and mind, of the woman?

61. Parkin, op. cit., p. 71.
62. Janet M. Bujra, 'Women "Entrepreneurs" of Early Nairobi', *Canadian Journal of African Studies*, Vol. IX, no. 2, 1975, pp. 213–34. See especially p. 217 and pp. 226–9.

I think that even in its monetised form 'the bridewealth system' could not be equated with slavery, if only because the husband receiving the woman could not sell her again at will. If the marriage broke down the woman would return to her family of origin. The system came nearest to a form of domestic indentured labour in which the woman was tied to an occupation by a form of contract the terms of which were not controlled by her, and which normally lasted for life. At any rate, the formulation of a terminology is less important than the recognition of the change and greater unfreedom which became inherent in the bridewealth relationship with the commercialisation of agriculture. Except perhaps in the most prosperous households, the commercialisation of agriculture, the commoditisation of land, and the monetisation of bridewealth all reduced the independence and self-determination which women enjoyed within the household.

One can only regret that no study such as Parkin's is available for other areas of Kenya, either for the period before 1952, or indeed afterwards, so that one has to surmise from much more scanty data that very similar processes to the ones he described and analysed in Kaloleni had also occurred earlier elsewhere. There is no doubt that further work in oral history could reveal much more about it.

We may now turn to the other aspect of the transformation of the role of livestock which first took place in Central and Nyanza Province in the war years and afterwards. I refer to the contraction of the use value of livestock to the point where it became only a source of milk, and above all meat.

From Livestock as Money to Livestock as Meat: 1939–52

With the onset of war the colonial administration intervened in the livestock market in very much the same way that it had done in the markets for agricultural produce. A Meat Control Board was set up to purchase slaughter stock to feed both troops and civilians, and each area of the colony that had any considerable pastoral activity and was known as an exporter of stock was set a quota of animals to be provided. At first the system was to purchase livestock from African traders, which was then slaughtered and transported under the auspices of the Control. But from 1942 onwards buyers from the Control attended livestock sales and bought independently, bidding against local buyers.

In theory all livestock sales were carried out at recognised auctions, which were usually at quarantine stations, veterinary centres etc. For the most part therefore statistics in district reports tended to concentrate on sales to the Livestock Control (or Meat Marketing Commission as it later became), and thus for the war and post-war years they are less than usually indicative of actual trends. The reason for this is that from the very beginning the Control's buyers tended to offer prices which were consistently below those obtainable on the free or black market in meat. Thus, even when quotas were met, sales to the Control usually constituted only a small proportion of total sales even in offi-

*Table VIII:4. Cows, sheep and goats
passed through Isiolo quarantine
1939–52*

Year	Cows	Sheep and goats
1939	Nil	78,853
1940	1,679	91,113
1941	4,644	111,982
1942	7,392	199,745
1943	8,545	152,615
1944	950	5,157
1945	6,431	60,345
1946	630	62,707
1947	—	—
1948	—	—
1949	495	6,562
1950	555	35,687
1951	3,665	33,029
1952	525	52,264

Source: IsAR 1939–52.

cially recognised auctions. But in addition the volume of illegal selling appears to have increased markedly from the onset of war in response to a rising demand for meat in areas such as Nairobi, Central Province and North Nyanza. This demand in turn seems to have been generated by the increase in the incomes at least of larger farmers due to the wartime food demand, plus income from army remittances.

One indication of this demand in Central Province was the large increase in the number of livestock passing through quarantine in Isiolo from the outset of the war. The figures are shown in table VIII:4.

The large increases in the supply of livestock from 1940 to 1943 appear clearly in these statistics, and it is known that the largest proportion of these animals went to Nyeri for slaughter. For example, of the 78,853 sheep and goats which passed through quarantine in 1939, 48,426 went to Nyeri; while in the peak year of 1942, of the nearly 200,000 sheep and goats which passed through, 120,427 were bought by civilian traders, the bulk of whom were Kikuyu.[63] It is not to be supposed that a precipitate slump in demand occurred in 1944, as the figures might suggest. This fall appears to have been due partly to a cutback on sales by the nomads of the Northern Frontier district after the enormous demands of the first three years of war. But in addition, though the sources are somewhat demure about it, it appears that in this year the Livestock Control, unwilling to pay the prices which purchases in a free market demanded, began a policy of limiting all sales to a few official auctions in which it was the monopoly buyer.

63. IsAR 1939, p. 6; and 1942, p. 4.

Supplies dried up so completely that in the following year Kikuyu, Somali and other traders were allowed to re-enter the auctions. The supply immediately improved, but once again the Control's buyers obtained so little of it that in 1947 another monopoly was imposed. It apparently had precisely the same effect as the 1944 action with an immediate expansion of the black market, and livestock held back from official auctions. In 1947 for example at an official auction in Garba Tulla the Meat Marketing Board's buyer was offering Shs. 8 for sheep and goats, but no sellers would part at under Shs. 9/50, an indication of the level of 'black market' prices.[64] Finally after three years (1947–50) when official sales appear to have been derisory, the Kenya Meat Commission was persuaded to allow Kikuyu and other buyers to attend auctions, with the immediate improvement in supply shown in the figure for 1950-2.[65]

Much the same sort of evidence can be adduced from Kajiado district in Masailand, and indeed from other major stock districts, but this is perhaps unnecessary.[66] It is only important to grasp that the inability of any of the government buying organisations to compete with the free market prices is eloquent testimony to the buoyancy of the meat demand in Nairobi and Central Province, during and immediately after the war.

The District Commissioner in Kiambu complained in 1945 for example that:

However necessary the Livestock Control Regulations may be, the fact remains that they have interfered with the free purchase of stock from other districts. The Livestock Control can only supply the Kikuyu with a very small part of their mean requirements as gauged by pre-war standards and these have probably increased since the war. The result is that an illegal trade has sprung up with the Masai encouraged by the lack of meat and the consequent high prices available.[67]

And in 1949 the District Officer in Isiolo had much the same complaint about the Meat Marketing Board. He noted that nearly all its small-scale purchases from the district went straight to Nairobi whilst the 'great meat hunger' in Central Province was not being satisfied and the cash flow into Isiolo had consequently dried up.[68]

Nor was Central Province the only area afflicted with such a hunger. In 1948

64. IsAR 1947, p. 9.
65. It is clear that the official reports give only the briefest (and probably censored) glimpse of a fascinating story here. Even from this glimpse however it is apparent that there was some connection between the attempts by the Meat Marketing Board to operate a cattle purchasing monopoly, and growth in support for the Somali Youth League. For the latter see *AAD* 1948, pp. 4 and 5; and 1949, p. 3.
66. See KajAR 1942, p. 1; 1943, p. 2; 1946, pp. 3 and 10; 1947, pp. 5–9; 1948, p. 12; 1949, p. 9; 1950, p. 6; 1951, p. 14; and 1952, p. 15.
67. KAR 1945, p. 32.
68. IsAR 1949, p. 16.

26,917 'stock' (probably cattle) were slaughtered for human consumption in North Kavirondo. In 1949 the figure was 25,985 head, and by 1950 60,000 head of cattle were slaughtered in that district, of which 'many' were said to have been imported.[69] We know from Nandi district sources that many of these slaughter stock for North Kavirondo came from Nandi, and had done so since the thirties. The trade appears to have expanded during the war, when it was made particularly attractive by the low prices offered in the Nandi district by the Livestock Control. Moreover, a large part of this trade, even during the war years, seems to have taken a barter form, with slaughter cattle being exchanged for heifers, presumably at the normal high rate of exchange for the heifer vendors.[70] This is significant, because, as we have seen, traditionally heifers and cows in calf were the most prized of livestock and would not normally be disposed of except as a last resort. Yet this trade, though its magnitude cannot be discerned, seems to have reached very considerable proportions during the war, just at the period, as we have seen earlier, when North Kavirondo was experiencing its most rapid expansion of maize production brought on by high wartime prices. One may speculate that these two trends were not contradictory but connected. That is, as many sedentary pastoralist households in North Kavirondo entered commercial agricultural production on a comparatively large scale for the first time, and put large areas of former grazing land under the plough in order to monocrop maize, so they began to dispose of the breeding stock for whose offspring they knew they would have no grazing. This development did not go unnoticed. In 1948 for example the District Commissioner in North Nyanza drew attention to the 'disappearance' of stock from the district, which he attributed primarily to the high price of maize and the relatively small return from livestock in comparison with maize. He also noted that some male stock were also being disposed of, but this time into the Uganda market, where meat prices were higher than in Kenya.[71]

Some circumstantial confirmation of this train of speculation comes from the Nandi district itself. As noted the Nandi had been one of the peoples benefitting from this willingness to dispose of female stock, and through the thirties and the war years they continued to take full advantage of this trade. But by the late forties the situation in Nandi district itself was changing. As noted in chapter V, it was primarily in the war years and just afterwards that the sedentary pastoralists of Nandi district themselves started to go over to large-scale maize production. By the late forties, large extensions of the cultivated area and the beginnings of fencing had begun to eat into the district's grazing resources. Much still remained, but the District Officer was also worried by what was likely to happen when local authority bylaws passed in the Uasin Gishu and

69. NKAR 1948, p. 6; 1949, p. 5; and 1950, p. 7.
70. NaAR 1933, p. 35; 1943, p. 3; 1944, p. 2; 1945, p. 14; 1946, p. 8; 1948, p. 27; 1950, p. 27; and 1952, p. 23.
71. NNAR 1948, p. 49.

Trans-Nzoia districts came into effect. Under these bylaws (passed in 1947) both these settler districts intended to eliminate squatter stock on the settler farms within three to five years. Largely for political reasons, these bylaws were never fully implemented. But nonetheless much more stringent enforcement of livestock limitation rules by individual farmers began to produce a considerable drift of both people and livestock from the farms back into Nandi district from the late thirties onwards.

In response to the need to find grazing for the estimated 150,000 extra cattle which would be in the district when the influx was over, the District Officer attempted, through the Local Native Council, to place restrictions on the expansion of the cultivated area, while at the same time trying to persuade the Nandi to sell more and more of their stock so that 'overstocking' of the district might be avoided. The policy proved to be something of a success. In 1947, 6,041 head of cattle were sold at official auctions, though the Meat Marketing Board once again could only afford to purchase 1,218 of them. By 1949 sales had jumped to 10,473 head and the District Officer noted with jubilation that 281 of these had been heifers. By 1950, seventy auction sales had disposed of 16,744 slaughter stock; in 1951 the figure was 14,677; and in 1952, 17,522; and in all cases increased numbers of heifers were included in the livestock sold.[72] These figures of course only referred to official auctions staged under the auspices of the Meat Marketing Board, and did not include exports to North Nyanza.

This level of sales did not satisfy the Nandi District Officer, both because at the same time cattle were continuing to return from the farms in even greater numbers, and because with an estimated 145,000 head of cattle in the district in 1944, he did not believe that sales were sufficient even to take off the natural increase.[73]

This complex picture shows that district-level data are unable to define a process which was highly differentiated from area to area within districts and, ultimately, from household to household. In the years from 1945 to 1952, some Nandi households—those who had entered maize cultivation first and on a considerable scale—were seeking to dispose of their livestock holdings, including their breeding stock. A few of these were finding their way on to 'export' markets from the district, but the majority were probably being bartered internally with other households who were not involved in maize cultivation, or who were involved in it on a very much smaller scale and who still placed a premium on the amassing of livestock.

It is clear that North Kavirondo district had been going through a similar process in the thirties and early forties, and Kiambu and Central Province had probably commenced it in the late twenties, but with a marked acceleration

72. NaAR 1947, p. 5; 1949, p. 15; and 1951, p. 16.
73. NaAR 1944, p. 2.

and generalisation of the process in the thirties and forties. In essence the most progressive households ceased to treat livestock as a measure of wealth and a means of exchange and came to treat it as a source of meat. This usually involved either directly consuming more and more of one's own herds, as grazing land was put under cultivation, or more likely a more differentiated process: male sheep and goats were slaughtered and eaten; female sheep and goats were bartered for males which were slaughtered and eaten, or sold and the money used for buying meat; bullocks and male calves were either slaughtered and eaten or more likely sold for cash; and heifers and cows were either bartered for slaughter stock, or once again sold for cash.

In every area there would in the initial stages be other households keen to acquire the stock being bartered or sold. But as the process generalised, and more and more households in a district or location came to follow the progressives into commercial agriculture and expansion of their cultivated area, so livestock disposal had increasingly to take the form, first of export to more 'backward' locations within the same district, then to other more 'pastoralist' districts. This 'knocking on' process, which an accident of the colonial records has allowed us to observe in the case of North Nyanza and Nandi, must have occurred earlier within North Nyanza, and probably earlier still in Central Nyanza and Central Province. In Central Province a cautious guess would be that the process of stock displacement first began in Kiambu (specifically in southern Kiambu) and then spread north through the Province with breeding stock at first being disposed of between households but then being 'expelled' from the districts and the whole Province by way of Somali and other stock traders who would buy them or barter them for slaughter animals. The breeding stock so acquired could still be profitably exchanged with the Masai, with squatters (at least up to the thirties) and with the nomads of the Northern Frontier Province, all of whom still placed a premium on them and would in turn provide the slaughter stock in which the Kikuyu, the Abaluhya and large numbers of the Luo were now primarily interested.

It is certainly the case that by 1952, indeed by the late forties, the southern locations of North Nyanza, Central Nyanza district as a whole, Kiambu, Fort Hall and Nyeri had all come to be regarded as 'understocked', in that all were large importers of meat and milk, even though such grazing as was left (such as the Ndeiya area in Kiambu) might be full of animals. In the case of Central Nyanza for example, the District Officer reported in 1939 that the number of cattle within the district had fallen by 62,000 since 1928, and the number of sheep and goats had fallen by 544,386 since 1923.[74] And the bulk of the stock grazing on the remaining common land in Central Province in the late forties and early fifties probably belonged in large part to returning squatters who had nowhere else to put it.

74. CKAR 1939, p. 41.

There were other signs of this trend. In the 1920s and 1930s the milk cows of North Kavirondo had been able to support a large number of small ghee 'dairies' or separators, some run under Local Native Council auspices, others privately owned having begun as Local Native Council properties.[75] In the forties however this 'industry' (as the colonial records rather optimistically described it) went into a sharp decline and most of the dairies closed, so that in 1948 the handful remaining produced a mere 221 tins of ghee. By 1950 the ghee industry in Nyanza Province, in which at one time all three districts had shared, was almost totally dominated by production in South Nyanza, which in that year produced no less than 40,000 of the 41,869 tins which were produced in the Province.[76] South Nyanza was of course the one Nyanza district which at the end of the period under discussion still had quite a large part of its land area under communal grazing.

Conclusions

In 1905 the people and land of the East Africa Protectorate had been devoted overwhelmingly to the production and support of livestock. There is no way of knowing how many animals there were on the open pasturelands of the region in 1905, but in 1931, when figures were provided to the Kenya Land Commission (figures which were still being used as a basis for calculations in the mid-fifties), there were estimated to be five million cattle, nearly three million sheep and 4,300,000 goats in African hands, i.e. over twelve million animals, for a population estimated in 1931 to be about 4,100,000 people.[77] It is likely, at least judging from the evidence of African witnesses to the Kenya Land Commission, that by 1931 the livestock population was in excess of that in 1890 (i.e. before the droughts and rinderpest epidemics of the decade 1890–1900 decimated the herds). So if we placed the livestock population of nineteenth-century Kenya at between nine and ten million head in years of good grazing we would probably not be far wrong.

By 1952 livestock production had already been subordinated to agricultural production, and that production itself had become increasingly a form of commodity production in which a proportion of both input and output was bought and sold on the market. This subordination was expressed in the replacement of livestock as a means of exchange by coins and notes, and by its replacement as a measure of wealth by calculation in money terms.

These were changes at the level of exchange value. At the level of use value the subordination of the livestock economy took the form of its restriction to a source of meat and milk (rather than as a source of food, clothing and even of household utensils). But as always the use and exchange value dimensions of

75. Ghee is a form of clarified butter used for cooking, particularly by the Asian community in Kenya.
76. NNAR 1948, p. 7; and *AAD* 1950, p. 30
77. See *KLC E & M* III, pp. 3118–19.

economic change were intimately interlinked in that livestock's displacement as a measure of wealth and means of exchange made it markedly less useful to households.

The essential cause of that displacement had been the expansion of the cultivated area at the expense of grazing. This in itself however was motivated by the desire to obtain the new money form which from the beginning was the only permissible way of paying taxes, and then became a much more advantageous way to obtain imported manufactured goods (including cotton clothing) and certain important services (see the section of chapter VI relating to the decline of barter trading and maize milling).

With the increasing dominance of agriculture within the production structure of colonial Kenya, women's labour power, marginal in the livestock economy, came to occupy an increasingly central role and to rise in value relative to livestock, with which traditionally it had been exchanged through the bridewealth relationship. As a result the rate of exchange between women and livestock at first moved against livestock, and then bridewealth, as it was monetised, assumed a higher and higher monetary value.

Thus, as the grazing land on which the livestock depended declined, and as livestock ceased to be exchangeable either with women, land or other commodities, its value to the sedentary-pastoralists-turned-agriculturalists declined even further. Gradually therefore it was disposed of, a process which began in areas of Central and Nyanza Province in the thirties, and markedly accelerated in the early forties and fifties as the cultivated area underwent its last major expansion in those provinces. In disposing of breeding stock and buying in meat stock the Kikuyu, Abaluhya and Luo peoples, and then later the Nandi and Kipsigis, made a total break with the value system of the livestock economy, a break presaged by the other changes which had gone before.

As in the case of agricultural change, these processes were markedly differentiated and uneven both in spatial terms and, much more importantly, by household. Some households entered commercial agriculture earlier and used larger off-farm income sources to buy land and to put much larger areas of what had been communal grazing under cultivation. Within the now fixed boundaries of the African 'reserves', this act in itself put pressure on other households to follow suit or fall behind, and most, albeit in a staggered and uneven way which left a legacy of inequality, chose to follow suit.

We have seen that within households the net effect of this process was to increase the oppression of women, since they continued to provide the bulk of labour input into agriculture, lost control over any decision-making power in regard to the surpluses produced, and, through changes in the bridewealth relationship, became even more firmly tied into the household structure within which this oppression operated.

Chapter IX

The Creation and Differentiation of a Wage Labour Force 1905–1952

In earlier chapters the growth of wage labouring as a primarily male occupation has been treated peripherally from two related perspectives. Firstly we noted the impact on agricultural production within the Reserves of the permanent or temporary loss of male labour, and secondly we attempted to differentiate this impact by the interdependent criteria of size of landholding and type of wage or salaried employment undertaken, to show that it varied markedly from household to household. The broad conclusion drawn was that those households whose male heads took up 'better paid' waged or salaried employment were able to buy land, hire the labour to work an expanded cropped area, and thus increase farm income, as a result, primarily, of access to above-average off-farm income. Alternatively, in households where the male migrated to low-paid wage employment, the wife was left alone, unable to support her own labour power with that hired in, unable to purchase land, and possibly forced to sell it to meet subsistence requirements. She therefore tended to stabilise her labour input to a basic subsistence level, and where the holding size was too small (in conjunction with pre-1952 cereal yields) even to provide this, she might have to rely increasingly on the use of the market mechanism to obtain subsistence, and might even go over to part-time wage labouring on adjoining holdings. It was also suggested that even in 1952 a majority of households were not in either of these categories of 'richest' or 'poorest' but straddled between them in a finely-graded spectrum of holding and income sizes. Most of these 'middling' households maintained their male household head as an agricultural worker on the holding though his labour input remained consistently below that of his wife.

In this chapter the aim is to refine this picture a little further by giving a quantitative dimension to the extent of labour loss to African agriculture through labour migration, and by attempting to obtain a picture of the extent and form of income differentiation within the African labour force as it evolved over the period considered.

We must start with an attempt to estimate the size and growth of the African male wage labour force in Kenya over the period 1905–52. To do this it is clearly essential to establish firstly the number of adult African men in Kenya at any one time and through time, and secondly the number in wage employment at any one time and through time. Though simple in principle, this turns out to be almost impossible to achieve with any degree of accuracy until the 1940s.

Until 1948 there was no even remotely accurate census of the African population of the Colony; and until 1942, when regular labour censuses began, all labour statistics have to be treated with the greatest scepticism. Up until 1922 (when a Labour Section was set up in the Native Affairs Department of the Administration) there were no labour statistics worthy of the name. District Officers frequently provided figures for 'natives' working inside or outside their district or for men 'registering' for work inside or outside the district, or sheer guesses at the number of men from their districts working in towns or on settler farms. But the categories used were so varied, the frequency of presentation so random, and the basis of figures offered so flimsy, that it is impossible to obtain even the roughest picture of the overall situation from them.

Indeed, when the first of many Commissions of Inquiry met to consider the problem of the acute labour shortage which had arisen on farms and estates in the years before the first world war, many witnesses before the Commission complained of precisely this, saying that it was impossible to assess the extent of the labour shortage or the possibility of its being remedied because it was not known what the actual or potential African labour force was. The Commission itself did not attempt to present any statistics on the matter. In order to remedy the situation many Europeans called for the setting up of a State-run 'Labour Bureau' on the Rhodesian model, one of whose functions would be to collect such statistics.[1]

With the onset of war this idea (which was accepted in principle by the Administration) was shelved. But it came to fruition in a somewhat modified form in 1922 with the setting up of the 'Labour Section' referred to earlier. Prior to this (from 1919 to 1921), District Officers had been busy 'registering' all adult male Africans who from 1919 onwards were required to carry with them their 'registration card' or *kipande* as it came to be known. This card showed each man's name, age, the district, location and sub-location from which he came, and the date of commencement and termination of his last employment. When a man entered wage employment, his employer was supposed to sign him on, and then sign him off at termination. In each case the employer was supposed to enter the particulars on an employers' registration sheet or 'return', and send it to the Registration sub-section of the Labour Section of the Native Affairs Department monthly. It was an offence for an African male to be away from his home without his *kipande* in his possession, and an offence to be found out of employment with a *kipande* which was not signed off. It was also an

1. *NLC*, pp. 330 and 331.

offence for any employer employing more than five Africans not to maintain and return his registration sheets.[2]

Had this system worked, registration would have provided a complete record of African wage employment in Kenya from 1922 onwards. It did not work, for a number of reasons. Firstly, many employers found the completion of a monthly return an irksome business and many simply did not do so. The Registration Section reported in 1934 for example that between 1929 and 1933 only 66 per cent to 70 per cent of European employers and 35 per cent to 45 per cent of Asian employers were sending in returns.[3] Moreover, many of those who did send in returns did so either infrequently or incompletely. It was very common, for example, for returns to have fairly complete lists of engagements but very incomplete lists of discharges. Needless to say, legal sanctions were used much more frequently against African infractions of the Registration Ordinance than against European or Asian defaulters, most of the Europeans in particular getting off with an innocuous warning.

Secondly, in the early 1920s a High Court judgement determined that resident labourers on farms and estates were not 'servants' under the terms of the Masters and Servants Ordinance and thus need not be registered under the Registration Ordinance. As well as requiring amendments to squatter legislation, this decision meant that squatters did not appear in the registration statistics.

Thirdly, it is clear that African employees succeeded in evading registration, sometimes unilaterally, sometimes with the connivance of employers. Evasion took many forms, including obtaining several *kipandes* under different names, signing off from employment or obtaining a literate friend or relative to do so or simply getting an employer desperate for labour to wink at any anomalies on the card. It is impossible to say what the scale of evasion was, but it is certain that it was far in excess of the numbers of prosecutions brought by the Registration section for such offences.[4]

Fourthly, 'casual labour' taken on for less than thirty days to complete a specific task did not have to be registered. In addition domestic servants were separately registered, but this register started rather later and covered only the main towns of the Colony.[5]

This is one side of the equation. The other is the persistent underestimation of the population in the official population figures for the period up to 1948. It is possible to assess at least roughly the extent of this underestimation by projection backwards from the 1948 census, and this has been done by other writers. The effect is to reduce markedly the proportion of the total adult male population in employment from the levels shown in official statistics. My own

2. See Clayton and Savage, op. cit., pp. 131–4.
3. Van Zwanenberg, op. cit., p. 157.
4. See Clayton & Savage, op. cit., pp. 130 and 170 and Appendix II, table I, p. 199; also van Zwanenberg, op. cit., pp. 157–8 and 386–423.
5. Ibid., p. 125.

calculations for example showed that whereas official statistics have about twenty-eight per cent of adult males in employment in 1922 rising to thirty-five per cent in 1941, 'corrected' population figures reduced these proportions to thirteen per cent and eighteen per cent respectively. Continuation of these corrected projections into the post-war period showed the proportion of adult males in employment rising to about twenty-four per cent by 1952.[6]

But of course this procedure alone does not bring us much nearer the true picture, because, as already noted, the official employment statistics are themselves massively underestimated. As a prelude to discussing the extent of this underestimation it is worth restressing that the first major concern in this chapter is to clarify the extent of the loss of male labour to agriculture in the Reserves. In this context therefore, we may ignore squatter labour on settler farms, since nearly all these men had their wives and children with them, i.e. the entire cultivating unit had either been removed from the Reserves or had never been established there. Looking at the matter from the smallholding, as it were, we are concerned with all adult males permanently or temporarily absent either in work or seeking it. Now this latter qualification makes a very great deal of difference, since it is clear that, aside from the considerable under-enumeration of workers in employment due to employers' failures to fill in or complete returns, the mobility of the African wage labour force continually defeated the Administration's statisticians. That is, uncompleted or incomplete monthly returns and, even more noticeably, annual labour censuses, were simply unable to 'catch' a labour force which was continually and unpredictably mobile. Thus for example the Labour Department Annual Report for 1947 has the following entry, variants of which can be found in many of the other reports produced from the time of the department's founding in 1940: 'It is estimated that of the 281,000 men in employment at any one time, some 150,000 are in permanent employment outside the Native Land Units. The remainder average only 6 months work during the year, so that the actual number working outside Native Land Units during the course of the year was over 400,000.'[7]

To illustrate the problem with which the Labour Section of the Native Affairs Department and its successor the Labour Department was faced, it is perhaps worthwhile to construct an imagined, but I am sure not untypical labour migration pattern for an African male worker. We will set the date arbitrarily at 1937 and make the migrant in question a Kikuyu household head with his home in Nyeri district.

In March 1937, having helped his wife to get in the long rain harvest, he leaves for the North Nyeri farms where he signs on on a thirty day 'ticket'. He has worked there for nearly 'two tickets' (one 'ticket' of thirty days' work had to be completed inside a forty-two day period) when he hears that a Local Native

6. See van Zwanenberg with King, op. cit., pp. 7–8 and 12; and note 11 below.
7. *LDAR* 1947, p. 5.

Council building site in Nyeri township requires labour and is paying well. He therefore leaves the farm without having been signed off, but the literate son of a brother in Nyeri does that for him, and the farmer, not being particularly short of labour at this period, does not report the desertion (feeling in any case that the chances of the deserter being traced are rather slim). However, when he gets to town, our labourer finds that he has been unlucky. Many others have heard of the 'high-paid' labouring jobs available, and by the time he gets there all vacancies have been filled. It is now June, and he knows that his wife will be getting in the potato harvest, so he returns home to help her. He has been at home about a month when a neighbour, returning from a spell of work on the Thika coffee estates, reports that the coming year's coffee crop looks as if it may be particularly heavy and that owners are already looking for extra labour in anticipation of the harvest. He therefore sets off southward in July, this time taking the bus from Nyeri town and taking with him a load of wattle wood which he hopes to sell in Thika town, having also been told that charcoal is particularly expensive there at the moment. He arrives in Thika, makes a good sale of his wood to a charcoal vendor and goes to stay with a sister's son while waiting to hear what wage rates different estates are paying. In late July he obtains employment, and on the recommendation of a foreman, who comes from the same sub-location as himself, he is put in charge of a group spraying seedlings with insecticide. He is paid Shs. 5 a month over the minimum wage for this responsibility, and works two tickets at this wage, since he gets transferred from this position to another in which he also has limited charge over a group of workers.

At the end of September his sister's son in town comes out to the estate to tell him that there are a number of vacancies for waiters in the Norfolk Hotel in Nairobi and that a paternal uncle (with whom our labourer has always been friendly) has a senior waiter's job there, and might be able to recommend him. Excited at the possibility of a job which it appears will pay at treble the rate he is receiving on the coffee estate, our labourer sets off for Nairobi, only to be disappointed once more. Again he has received the news too late and all the vacancies have been filled. In this case, however, being somewhat nervous about repeating the procedure of the previous May, he has got himself properly signed off by the employer, and so, having stayed with his friend a while in Nairobi, he returns to the Thika estate in November when the harvest begins to come in. The predictions are proved correct and the harvest is an excellent one, and all estates are desperate to employ every picker they can obtain. This time therefore he is careful only to take employment on casual terms, i.e. he is paid daily on a piece-work basis at a set rate per tin (or *debe*) filled. He has had a great deal of experience as a coffee picker over the years, and reckons, correctly, that on a piece-work basis he may earn three or four times the money daily that he would on a monthly ticket. Moreover, being hired on this basis, he is free to leave at any time if he hears of a neighbouring estate paying better, and in fact he does this once before the end of the harvest in December.

At the beginning of January, he considers whether to sign on for another ticket with the estate to which he has transferred or to return home. He decides however that since he has now saved enough to pay the school fees of his two eldest sons and to pay his bus fare home, he will return home, though he has been half-hoping that further vacancies might have materialised in Nairobi, in which case he would have stayed.

He arrives home in mid-January only to find his wife worried about the likely size of the coming harvest, as the rains in his location have been very light. He also hears that school fees are to increase again. He therefore decides to go out to work once more and eventually obtains employment on a farm only about two miles from that which he had deserted some ten months ago. He is still on the farm in March when the harvest at home comes in again, but since it is poor, as his wife anticipated, she manages quite easily to get it in with the help of two neighbours and her two daughters.

If we now look at this hypothetical case history from the point of view of the labour statistics of 1937 we see that this one man has in the course of twelve months 'registered in employment' on monthly tickets on three separate occasions. Depending on the punctiliousness of his individual employers he might have appeared as 'signed on' once, twice or three times, or not at all. He would certainly not have been properly 'signed off' on one occasion, so unless the statisticians were able to recognise him in the coffee estate statistics or in the statistics of the 'second' North Nyeri farm, he might have appeared in the statistics as employed throughout the period on one farm. (All this would depend on the extent and the accuracy with which returns were filled in by his different employers.)

In addition of course he might have appeared once in the returns of the coffee estate for casual labour, but since these returns in particular were notoriously incomplete, precisely because of the high rates of labour turnover involved, it is unlikely that he would have appeared even once (and he would have needed to appear twice on the returns of two different estates for the statistics to be accurate).[8]

Thus the *kipande* was totally ineffective in achieving labour stability, and indeed over the years the knowledge of the migrant labour market acquired (often against their will) by the first generation of migrants led to a more genuinely voluntary pattern of 'playing' that market through short and long distance movement. Indeed had the *kipande* actually succeeded in its objective of enforced 'stabilisation', there is no doubt that many employers of labour would have been the worse off for it. When the Barth Commission sat in 1912–13, settlers and others had been preoccupied with the simple problem of obtaining enough labour by virtually any means, and having obtained it, keeping it.

---

8. Lest it be thought that this is an entirely hypothetical account, see the evidence of African witnesses in NLC, especially pp. 232–7.

Hence their preoccupation with 'deserters', and with holding men to contracts. But gradually through the twenties and thirties, as the labour force expanded, the problem increasingly became one of having labour available where and when it was most needed, i.e. increasingly labour shortages sprang not from any absolute lack of men looking for employment but from either the lack of labourers with the specific skills required, or (in the case of the bulk of unskilled labour) from the fact that men seeking work were not informed about or able to get to the places where vacancies were available.

This latter of course is an indication of a highly 'imperfect' labour market, and the effect of the *kipande* was if anything to make it even more imperfect than it might have been. By making it more difficult or at least more irksome and risky to leave one job when news of other vacancies came through, the Administration added one more difficulty to others (partial or unreliable information, slow and expensive transport, lack of temporary accommodation) which made being on the migrant labour market an uncertain and risky business.

We began this discussion with the question of the reliability or otherwise of labour statistics, and it is time to return to this issue. The unreliability of the figures prior to 1942 when labour statistics were based upon the registration system has been indicated. From 1942 onwards the registration figures were replaced by annual labour censuses, usually held in the November of every year, i.e. during one of the labour peak periods. However these censuses, just like the registration statistics before them, relied on the punctiliousness of the employer in filling in the census form and returning it to the Labour Department. Each employer was generally required to show the number of men, women and juveniles 'at work' in his enterprise on the day of the census, the number in each category 'employed' or 'on strength' (i.e. those working plus those absent sick or on leave and those absent without leave). He was also required to show the numbers employed on monthly 'verbal contracts', those on longer-term contracts and those employed on a daily paid or casual basis; and to provide an occupational breakdown.[9]

There is no doubt that the censuses, once perfected, provided a much more comprehensive set of figures on the size and structure of the African wage labour force than the registration figures had ever done, and this improvement in coverage is signalled by a sharp upward movement in the employment figures from 1941 to 1942 (an increase of some 60,000 in one year). On the other hand, for determining the number of African men away from home and on the labour market in any one year and over time, they are no more satisfactory than the registration statistics. For, like their predecessors, they provide no indication of the number of men who were away from home seeking work but not in employment on the census date. As we have already seen, Labour Department esti-

9. See for example *LDAR* 1948, p. 28.

mates for the late forties usually added another 100,000 men (about one third) to the totals of those in employment in order to provide an estimate of those on the labour market or the total 'labour force'.

What then can we derive from this statistician's nightmare? My own guess— and in the nature of things it cannot be any more than that—is that one needs to increase the registration figures prior to 1941 by at least fifty per cent in order to obtain figures for the total labour market (twenty per cent of this increase being to cover unenumerated employment and thirty per cent to cover men moving in search of work), and that one should add thirty per cent to the post-1942 totals to obtain comparable figures for this later period. In this way one obtains the series in table IX:1.

Treating these figures as indicative of trends but not of exact magnitudes, it appears from this table that the proportion of adult males in the labour force rose from about twenty per cent in 1922 to over thirty per cent thirty years later. In absolute terms this represented an increase of 139 per cent over a period when the adult male population as a whole rose by just over fifty-seven per cent. It must once again be emphasised that these figures are exclusive of squatter labour and so are no guide to the total number of Africans living and working outside of their area of birth.[10] In addition it should be noted that for purposes of continuity I have restricted the focus to civilian labour only. If one wanted a complete picture of all the men who left their homes and families in order to work for wages in the colonial period, then, aside from reliable statistics for the period 1905 to 1914, one would need to include the 70,000 or so men who were recruited into the armed forces (including the infamous Carrier Corps) in each of the two wars, and lived to be demobilised. Since these men either entered the civilian labour force after demobilisation or returned to cultivation, herding or other forms of self-employment, those remaining in the labour force would be comprised in the figures from 1919 and 1946.

From our point of view it would be important not only to have universal statistics of this sort, but to know where these men came from, since it is clear that the extent of labour migration varied greatly from area to area both at one time and through time.

Using the very fragmentary data which are available on this matter, and 'correcting' the figures in the same way as in table IX:1, it appears that Kiambu had some forty-three per cent of its adult male population in the labour force in 1928, falling to about thirty-nine per cent by 1933 with the onset of the depression. The figures for the other three districts for which a complete run

---

10. A figure for this could not be obtained simply by adding the number of squatters to the rest of the wage labour force, since at least from the 1930s onwards a whole generation of squatters grew up who had never been resident in the Reserves. In fact this was one of the main reasons for the intense resentment felt when from the late thirties onwards, the Administration started to 'repatriate' squatters to the Reserves.

Table IX:1.[11] *The Kenyan African wage labour market 1922–52*

Year	A Adult males away from home 'in the labour market' for some or all of the year	B Total adult males in population	A as % of B
1922	178,755	885,151	20.2
1923	207,495	898,630	23.1
1924	200,835	912,314	22.0
1925	228,576	926,207	24.6
1926	253,500	940,311	27.0
1927	221,839	954,630	23.2
1928	228,411	969,167	23.6
1929	240,114	983,926	24.4
1930	236,039	998,909	23.6
1931	212,210	1,014,121	20.9
1932	198,134	1,029,564	19.2
1933	211,628	1,045,243	20.2
1934	—	1,061,160	—
1935	—	1,077,328	—
1936	259,500	1,093,734	23.7
1937	274,500	1,110,390	24.7
1938	274,446	1,127,300	24.3
1939	—	1,144,467	—
1940	—	1,161,895	—
1941	312,000	1,179,589	26.4
1942	351,000	1,197,552	29.3
1943	356,516	1,215,788	29.3
1944	380,123	1,234,303	30.8
1945	375,406	1,253,100	30.0
1946	342,236	1,272,183	26.9
1947	378,403	1,291,556	29.3
1948	432,819	1,311,224	33.0
1949	405,344	1,330,892	30.4
1950	428,055	1,350,855	31.7
1951	415,204	1,371,118	30.3
1952	426,498	1,391,685	30.6

11. Notes to table IX:1: In column A, totals of men 'in the labour force' were obtained by increasing official figures for males 'registered in employment' by fifty per cent up to 1942, and by thirty per cent thereafter. No figures were published in 1934, 1935, 1939 or 1940. The figures in column B were obtained by projecting backwards and forwards from the figure in the 1948 census and assuming a 1.5% linear rate of growth of population throughout the period. This probably slightly overstates the rate of growth in the 1920s, is about right for the 1930s, but almost certainly understates the rate of growth for the 1940s. However, there is some warrent in recent demographic work on East Africa for the use of such a figure, and in any event, given the total uncertainty attaching to all these data certainly up to 1948, the percentages in column C do not purport to be more than rough orders of magnitude. For an outline of recent historical demography in East Africa see van Zwanenberg with King, op. cit., pp. 3–22.

of statistics is available are:

	1928	1933
Fort Hall	41.7%	30.4%
North Kavirondo	38.2%	35.8%
Machakos	18.2%	13.1%

As is well known, the proportion of adult males coming into the labour force from the most highly commercialised districts was well above the average for the colony as a whole. Thus for example in 1928, just before the depression, some twenty-four per cent of the colony's total adult male population were in wage employment or seeking it, but the figure for Kiambu is forty-three per cent, for Fort Hall nearly forty-two per cent, and for North Kavirondo over thirty-eight per cent.[12]

Whilst the figures up to 1942 are fragmentary, comparison of inter-war figures with the situation in the late forties and early fifties is also rendered very difficult by the way the published statistics are presented after the introduction of annual labour censuses. However, I have attempted a comparison of data on tribal groupings from 1933 and 1948. The data only allow comparisons to be made for the 'Kikuyu, Embu and Meru', 'Kavirondo, Luo, Kisii and Maragoli', and 'Kamba'. From these figures it appears that the number of men recruited from Nyanza, Central Province, Machakos and Kitui rose by 127 per cent over these fifteen years: from 172,864 in 1933 to 392,284 in 1948. In all the major recruiting areas the increases were considerable, being 129 per cent in the Central Province, 136 per cent in Kericho and Nandi, over 100 per cent in the three districts of Nyanza Province and no less than 303 per cent in the Machakos and Kitui districts.[13]

In fact these figures confirm a general quickening of the rate of entry into the migrant labour force in the thirties and forties compared with the earlier period, and the series for the Colony as a whole seems to indicate that this began in the late thirties with the recovery from depression, but became really marked from the onset of war.

Summing up, we may say that the labour statistics available for this period show a continual increase in the numbers of adult males in the migrant labour force, with the rate of increase being most marked from about 1938 to 1948. They also show that particular districts, notably all three Kikuyu districts, and Central and Northern Kavirondo, dominated the labour supply, with Nyanza Province in particular having over fifty per cent of its adult male population in or seeking wage employment away from home in 1948. Since this latter statistic included the population of Southern Nyanza which almost certainly had a lower

12. See *NAD* 1928, pp. 138–9; 1929, p. 117; 1931, p. 165; 1932, pp. 184 and 185; and 1933, pp. 172–3.
13. *LC* 1948, table 4.

proportion of its men 'out' even in the late forties and early fifties,[14] the district averages for North and Central Nyanza must have been well above this figure. In addition, it is probable that the late thirties and forties also saw an increasing contribution to the wage labour force by other groups, notably the Machakos Kamba and the Meru.

It is undoubtedly the case that were locational and sub-locational statistics available they would show even higher percentages of adult males in the labour force in some areas, with figures perhaps reaching sixty, seventy or eighty per cent of adult males by the late forties and early fifties. By this stage, of course, no household would be left untouched by the demands of the labour market, and many might have both the male household head and all adult sons missing for some or all of the year.

At this point we can turn away from the statistics and return our attention to the real process which they occasionally illuminate and often disguise. Firstly it should be noted that, constructing a rough chronology, the major labour-providing districts probably had some twenty-five per cent of their adult males in the labour market in 1918, thirty per cent by 1925, forty per cent by 1930 and (after falling back in the depression) fifty per cent by 1948. The implications of these statistics for the real situation were different at different stages. Up to about 1930 the majority of those in the wage labour force at any one time were unmarried men. Fazan, for example, in treating the Kikuyu labour situation in 1931 took the figure of 40,685 Kikuyu 'natives' registered in employment and immediately discounted half of it on the grounds that 'an enormous proportion' of those appearing in the returns as monthly paid labourers on farms were 'really squatters'. Having made this deduction Fazan concentrated his attention entirely on those working in townships (particularly Nairobi), on the railway, and genuine non-resident farm labourers working on farms and estates so near their homes that they might return each night or every weekend. He reckoned that the men involved totalled 21,316, which almost in passing he related as representing forty per cent of the '52,959 unmarried natives ordinarily resident in the reserve'.[15]

If Hay's findings in Kowe are typical for Central Kavirondo, the pattern there was very much the same as that suggested by Fazan's analysis of Kikuyu-land, with nearly all of the males who went on to the migrant labour market before 1930 being between fifteen and twenty years old at the time they left the area.[16]

---

14. An oblique confirmation of this is provided by the 1948 population census which showed that whereas 23.9% of the male population of the Luhya of North Nyanza were living outside of the district on the census date, and the proportion for the Luo of Central Nyanza was 16.4%, the percentages for the Luo and Kisii of South Nyanza were 11.35% and 11.9% respectively. See Fearn, op. cit., Appendix B, table 7, p. 239.
15. Fazan, op. cit., p. 996
16. Hay, op. cit., p. 172.

In time these men married, and in the case of North and Central Kavirondo most of them maintained their married household within the Reserve. In the case of Kikuyuland, this would probably have been the case as well, since by 1930 the flood tide of squatter out-migration had abated. It appears that most of these men did not give up the migrant labour market after marriage, but continued to 'play' it in very much the same way that they had learnt in their youth, certainly until they reached their forties or fifties.

It was the marriage of the majority of this pre-1930 generation of labour migrants which changed the structure of migration in the Reserves, for it meant that an increasing proportion of migrants through the 1930s and 1940s were heads of households leaving their wives at home in the Reserve for longer or shorter periods.

At this point it is worth referring back to the hypothetical labour migrant in 1937, described earlier in the chapter. In that account the open-endedness and indeterminacy of the migrant labour process was stressed, an indeterminacy based on the 'imperfections' in that market and on the persistent quest of all migrants to find a job which was just a little better paid than the last one: the attempt, in fact, to put together a chain of occupations in a way which would produce a gradually rising income with every link. The account also sought to suggest that such attempts could often meet with failure or frustration based on partial information, slow transport, and above all the tendency at the lower end of the market for there to be an abundance of men with broadly similar skills and experience, all on the look-out for the same sorts of opportunity.

From the point of view of a migrant's wife, one factor is worth stressing. If a woman's husband became a regular migrant after marriage, or if she married a man who was already a regular migrant, then she was generally forced to discount him entirely as a member of the household agricultural work force. It was true that a man might leave home for work on a farm, estate, mine or—occasionally—a factory very near by from which he might return daily or weekly. But there could be no guarantee that this pattern of migration might not turn very quickly into a pattern in which homecoming became much more infrequent. News of a slightly better paid opportunity on an estate a few miles more distant, or the chance of better 'pickings' at another estate at harvest might take him in the course of a few months or a year too far away for regular homecoming. This would particularly be the case if a man's wages would not support regular bus or lorry journeys (which in the 1930s and the 1940s were still relatively expensive), or if he preferred not to exhaust his savings in this way. The fact that periods of peak-period labour demand on farms tended to coincide with those on smallholdings in the same agro-ecological zone also meant of course that husbands might well be absent when their labour power would be most needed.

Frequent references by District Officers to men 'resting' in the Reserves are also I think very significant.[17] That is, as labour migration became a regular pattern of life for men, so (as our hypothetical case study suggested) the family holding became a place to which one returned in slack periods or whilst waiting for news of new and better opportunities. It is my view that, except in the very earliest years, very few labour migrants were ever 'target workers' in the sense that they left their homes with a fixed sum of money in mind, the obtaining of which would see them return home. Rather tax needs (initially) and then school fees, bridewealth or the cost of a bicycle provided a minimum income goal with which a man would leave home. But if, in the course of his sojourn, opportunities for earning money in excess of this minimum 'turned up', and if such opportunities seemed attractive in terms of the monetary return for the labour time involved, then a man would stay in the market. Indeed it is clearly by some such process that some of the young men who left Kowe in the twenties and thirties, presumably with some minimum of this sort in mind (probably bridewealth) ended up, in 'more than half' the cases staying away for fifteen or twenty years![18]

If nothing turned up, and if he was in a position to return home, then a man might do so. But it is my view that the timing of this return was only coincidentally synchronised with periods of peak period labour demand at home, i.e. homecoming was determined by conditions in the labour market, not by conditions in the household production unit. And this of course was why wives had to count their husbands out of that production unit once the decision had been made for them to enter the labour market. As already suggested in earlier chapters, this meant that as far as labour migrant households were concerned a great deal turned on the sort of income which the absent male head was earning, and the proportion of this which he was willing or able to remit home to his wife. The 'worst off' households were those with heads in permanent, semi-permanent or very regular off-farm employment, whose income and/or remittances were only sufficient to subsidise the recurrent costs of the household (clothing, food, school fees) but which were not sufficient to support 'capital investments' (land, buildings, hired labour). Households would be very finely differentiated according to what expenditure off-farm income made possible. Schematically one may identify (for purposes of exemplification only) the following sorts of distinction:
1. An income sufficient only to allow food to be purchased at times of harvest shortage.
2. An income/remittances sufficient to allow (1) above plus clothing.
3. An income/remittances sufficient to allow (1) and (2) above plus school fees for one child.

17. See KAR 1925, p. 8.
18. Hay, op. cit., p. 172.

4. An income/remittances sufficient to allow (1) and (2) above plus school fees for two children.
5. An income/remittances sufficient to allow (1), (2) and (3) above plus one hired labourer during harvest.

Clearly one may specify ever finer distinctions and I hope it is unnecessary to labour the point. At one end of the spectrum we have a man engaged in wage labour because the household landholding is simply insufficient to guarantee a subsistence for the labour power (mainly female) operating upon it, and at the other end one has a man earning sufficient to raise the subsistence standards of his household and to make the investments (in labour power and land) with which he can hope to raise that standard further.

This assumes a plurality of labourers, but of course within the working life of one man the aim would be to move from occupations allowing only situations (1) and (2) to occupations allowing situations of the type (4) or (5) or better. This was the aim with which men played the labour market. This was the basis on which it was rational to keep an eye constantly open for the job which paid a few shillings more a month, or to manoeuvre to obtain the overseer's post with a little more 'responsiblity' and money attached to it. But of course only a certain group of men were able to obtain jobs with the levels of earnings which would allow aspiration to situations (4), (5) and beyond. Those men were the ones who had a certain level of education which could get them a low-level 'white-collar' job (such as clerking or teaching) or those who possessed artisan or other skills (such as cart or lorry driving) which were in demand. At this point therefore we can turn to look at the income differentials of the African wage labour force in Kenya from its beginnings until 1952, for these data give firmer parameters to the discussion above.

Marked differentials in earnings seem to have emerged coterminously with an African wage labour force in Kenya. From the very first years of the East African Protectorate we can observe three groups of wage or salary earners who received incomes well in excess of the 'average' amounts which District Officers were so fond of quoting in their reports. These three groups were: chiefs, headmen and clerks recruited to staff the lower ranks of the colonial administration; those in positions of responsibility in which extra earnings came from showing oneself trustworthy—i.e. 'headmen' on farms and estates and trusted domestic servants; artisans and other men possessing particular skills, e.g. herdsmen and cart drivers.

The process by which the first chiefs, headmen and clerks were recruited to their positions in the colonial administration is fairly well known and I have discussed it in detail elsewhere.[19] All we should note here is that if a man, no matter how recruited, showed himself 'responsible' and 'efficient' (which in the early days usually meant only that he could collect his quota of taxes without

19. See my 'The Rise of an African Petite-Bourgeoisie . . .', op. cit.

violent opposition from his constituents) he could be well rewarded.

In addition to chiefs, headmen and clerks, whose wages, from 1905 to the end of the period under consideration, could vary from three to four times the minimum wage for unskilled labour up to twenty or twenty-five times that level, depending on their position and seniority, another group of comparatively privileged employees were those in positions of control within the labour force ('headmen' or 'overseers') and domestic servants.

But it is clear that among manual workers, it was certain sorts of artisans and skilled labourers who from the early days onwards enjoyed the greatest differentials.[20] In the South Nyeri Annual Report for 1929, for example, the District Officer pleaded for a rise in the salaries of chiefs and headmen, on the grounds that their wages had fallen behind those of skilled labourers: 'carpenters, masons, clerks, house boys, etc.'. He went on to give some examples: 'For instance at Karatina the local chief Karaithi with a population of over 6,000 souls gets Shs. 57/50 a month, while the dresser at the dispensary gets Shs. 90 and the native carpenter at the Council house gets Shs. 100.'[21] Or again, the Labour Inspectorate report for 1926 noted that of 13,788 men employed by the railways in Kenya at that date the vast majority earned the unskilled wage of Shs. 16 to Shs. 20 per month and rations, but skilled labourers, 'mainly artisans', could earn anything from Shs. 60 to Shs. 150,[22] and at the height of the depression in 1933 when some Meru labourers in the Thika district were employed on sisal estates for 'as little as Shs. 5 per month', 'experienced cutters and factory hands' were still cited as receiving 'Shs. 20 to Shs. 30 per month on average'.[23]

Throughout the entire period with which we are concerned there is no lack of impressionistic evidence of this sort to indicate persistent and large wage differentials in the African labour force, with district reports, Labour Section reports and then Labour Department reports all making general reference to these differentials. Indeed in 1938 the Labour Section report presaged its usual lists of 'average wages' in different sectors with the rather testy remark that 'It is quite impracticable to lay down a definite rate of wage as applicable to any particular employment',[24] since the differentials were so great even within what were, notionally, single occupational categories. And indeed this was the problem with most of the evidence in colonial records on this matter. For it makes general reference to differentials between 'skilled' and 'unskilled' labour, and may even provide the odd exemplification of wages for particular occupations — 'carpenters, masons, drivers', 'more trusted servants', 'headmen', 'senior

20. Ibid., pp. 9–16.
21. NAR 1929, pj 17.
22. *NAD* 1926, p. 72.
23. *NAD* 1933, p. 132.
24. *NAD* 1938, p. 118. For a general account of differentials in the African wage labour force, see Stichter, op. cit., pp. 229–44.

chiefs' and these examples show differentials ranging from as little as double or less than double the unskilled wage to twenty or more times this minimum. But this evidence is unsatisfactory because in using either very general categories ('skilled', 'unskilled') or even occupational categories ('chiefs', 'clerks', 'teachers', 'policemen', 'carpenters') it serves to disguise rather than illuminate actual situations. For almost universally throughout the African wage labour force in Kenya, in schools, in the Administration, on the railway, in industry, commerce and agriculture, wage levels were not differentiated by broad grades, or even by occupation, but in almost all cases differentiated according to the individual. An employer might employ twenty men nominally labelled 'carpenters', but they would be paid from as little as a shilling or two above the unskilled wage to perhaps ten or twenty times that figure depending on their level of skill, the length of time they had been with the employer, whether they had any duties or responsibilities apart from their own work, and even whether they were personally liked by the employer or not. As far as I am able to ascertain this was the case for virtually all occupations from the onset of the colonial period until the emergence of trade unions as effective forces in some sections of the wage labour force in the mid-1950s, and was certainly the case for the entire period with which we are concerned here.

It is true that from the mid-twenties onwards some sectors—notably the railways, the Administration and then (rather later) the mission schools—began to lay down 'grades' through which railway employees, chiefs, clerks, headmen and teachers were supposed to move in the course of a career, but salary levels within grades continued to vary so widely due to the large amount of discretion accorded to District Officers, mission authorities and railway management, that the *ad hominem* principle was not in practice abandoned.[25]

This means that in order to penetrate to the reality of the differentiation within the African labour force during the period under consideration, it is necessary to have fairly complete wage lists for labour forces in particular sectors (and in agriculture, probably for particular farms and estates) both at one time and through time, and this unfortunately we do not possess, since the necessary research has not been done. But nonetheless there are available a few scattered detailed listings of occupations and wages in particular sectors or areas, and these are illuminating. The earliest is from a survey of 21,000 labourers employed in Nairobi carried out by the Registration sub-section of the Native Affairs Department in November 1927. It is written up simply as a long list of occupations with minimum and maximum wages quoted in each case, as in table IX :2.

In general this table speaks for itself. It will be noted that with the exception of two 'ticket collectors' on the Railway, there is not a single occupational category with more than one man employed within it for which there is one

25. For the railways for example, see R. D. Grillo, *African Railwaymen: Solidarity and Opposition in an East African Labour Force* (Cambridge 1973), pp. 22–6 and 121–47.

Table IX:2. The Nairobi wage labour force, 1927

Occupation	Number employed (incl. govt. depts.)	Monthly rate of wage (Shs.)	
		from	to
Domestic Servants	3,633	10	150
Garden, fuel and rickshaw boys	2,458	10	60
Sweepers and Scavengers	448	10	65
Syces [grooms]	90	10	65
Male Nurses	8	25	70
Clerks and Telegraphists	129	24	416
Office Boys and Messengers	652	14	65
Shop and Store Attendants	704	10	75
Barmen	24	17	85
Bakers	53	16	80
Dairymen	72	12	42
Butchers	26	16	60
Tailors	121	17	140
Packers	12	21	40
Photographers' Assistants	7	25	140
Automobile Drivers	109	18	150
Tractor Drivers	25	16	60
Garage Assistants	118	15	75
Animal Transport Drivers	491	10	60
Herds and Cattlemen	86	4	36
Watchmen and Caretakers	120	15	80
School Teachers	22	20	90
Dental Mechanics	1	100	100
Barbers	1	34	34
Gun Bearers	26	60	100
Safari Porters	300	16	28
Skinners	12	40	60
Surveyors' Assistants	1	300	300
Surveyors' Chainmen	6	24	50
Coffee Pruners	12	12	60
Hide Graders	11	24	30
Newspaper Boys	20	14	34
Mechanics	14	24	130
Fitters and Moulders	105	12	120
Blacksmiths, Farriers and Wheel Wrights	22	16	110
Masons and Plasterers	57	20	150
Stone Dressers	21	24	75
Painters and Decorators	100	18	160
Carpenters	38	15	120
Furniture Polishers	10	22	145
Glaziers	5	26	30
Tinsmiths	51	16	160
Gangers	179	12	160
Navvies	6,618	9	75
Factory Hands	3	12	70
Sawyers	13	18	90

Occupation	Number employed (incl. govt. depts.)	Monthly rate of wage (Shs.)	
		from	to
Engine Minders	5	22	50
Printers and Printers' Machinists	68	6	125
Compositors	6	20	148
Linotype Operators	1	510	510
Book Binders	21	20	115
Oilers and Greasers	6	18	38
Crane Men	7	22	33
Saddlers and Shoemakers	37	8	180
Vulcanisers	10	14	200
Postal Clerks and Telegraphists	24	15	360
Postmen	1	60	60
Telegraph Linesmen	25	24	75
Railway in particular			
Trolley Boys	24	15	40
Ticket Collectors	2	50	50
Porters	148	20	30
Lamp Trimmers	90	20	52
Pointsmen and Flagmen	35	20	40
Keyman	6	16	84
Artizans [sic] including Fitters, Moulders, Carpenters, Painters, Apprentices	1,503	6	110
Military			
Rank and File	509	10	180
Porters	49	10	28
Artizans	2	50	60
Police			
Rank and File	449	24	98
Prisons			
Warders	135	32	76

Source: *NAD* 1928, p. 101.

wage rate, and this includes the dominant category of unskilled labour ('Navvies') in which the range from bottom to top is 1–8.3. There are some categories for which the ranges are small. These include Safari Porters (1–1.75), Skinners (1–1.5), Surveyors' Chainmen (1–2.08), Newspaper Boys (1–2.42), Oilers and Greasers (1–2.1) and Porters on the Railway (1–1.5), i.e. those categories which might at best be described as semi-skilled, and in which there were comparatively few men employed. The rest of the categories cover almost the complete range

*Table IX:3. Domestic servants in
Nairobi, 1934*

'Class of Servant'	'Average Wage' Shs.
Cooks	28/47
House Boys	17/90
Dhobis (washers)	25/00
Garden Boys	14/00
Shop Boys	21/00
Office Boys	20/00
Motor Car Drivers	50/00
Kitchen Boys	15/50
General House Servants	18/50
Ayahs (i.e. nursemaids) mostly women	34/00

Source: *NAD* 1934, p. 165.

of differentials from 1–2.8 (male nurses) to 1–24 (Postal Clerks and Telegraphists) with a concentration of categories in the range 1–5 to 1–10.

Of course this table tells us nothing about the distribution of individuals within the wage ranges for each occupation. A sensible assumption would be that a small minority of workers were at the top and middle of the ranges, with a concentration of workers nearer the bottom. It should also be noted that we are able to say with rare and gratifying certainty that the highest paid African worker in Nairobi in November 1927 was a linotype operator, paid 94 shillings more per month than the best paid African clerk.

Moreover some of the categories used are too broad to do justice to the range of actual jobs (and thus wages) which they encompassed. An obvious example is 'domestic servants'. The Labour Section of the Native Affairs Department provided the sub-categorisation of domestic servants employed in Nairobi in 1934 shown in table IX:3.

For reasons already stated I believe that the 'average wage' figures given here disguise wide deviations around them, even for each sub-occupation. In order fully to appreciate the extent of differentiation within the African wage labour force, it is necessary to have very well defined occupational categories and a listing of individual wages within each. For the period up to 1952 I have obtained two pieces of evidence approximating this ideal. The first is a labour census of the 14,115 men employed in the goldfields of Nyanza Province in October 1935 carried out by the Labour Section of the Native Affairs Department. Among the tabulations published from this census was that in table IX:4, showing wages by occupations for the entire workforce.

It will be seen from the last two columns of this table that almost ninety per

Table IX:4. Wages by occupational category: Nyanza goldmines and ancillary labour force October 1935[26]

Individual wages in shillings per month	Occupation Not Stated	Clerks	Office Assistants	Lorry and Motor Drivers	Blacksmiths	Carpenters	Masons	Other Skilled Labour	Police and Watchmen	Headmen	Surface Labour	Underground Labour	Labour not stated	Hospital Attendants	Compound Cooks	Domestic Cooks	Other Indoor Domestic Servants	Outdoor Domestic Servants	Fuel Cutters	Sweepers	Total	%
Wages not stated	2										15	3	20				2	2			44	0.3
1–9	46	5		2	2	1		79	33	89	2,134	597	317		17	1	37	10	31	15	3,216	22.8
10–14	51	5		6	9	2	1	18	23	64	4,833	3,659	242		10	9	55	14	331	5	9,448	66.9
15–19	4	8	2	1	1			9	30	23	161	270	23	5		13	34	2	8	13	637	4.5
20–24	1	1		2	5			3	4	9	94	68	3	3		18	28	2		2	302	2.1
25–29	1	9		5	2	3		6	7	3	30	24		6		14	18	2			124	0.87
30–34		2		6	2	16	5	3	4	2	39	18	2	2		16	9				141	0.99
35–39		4		3	1	7	2	3		2	17	7		3		2	2				56	0.39
40–44		2		3		7	1	2	1		14	5		2		3					43	0.30
45–49		5	1		2	7	3			2	18	2		2		2			1		40	0.28
50–59		2		5	3	2			1			1									21	0.14
60–69	1	2		1	1	6			3	3	8	2									25	0.17
70–79				1	1		2				5	2									12	0.08
80–89				1			1				1										3	0.02
90–100																					2	0.014
150																1					1	0.007
Total	106	45	3	36	29	51	15	141	106	197	7,369	4,658	607	23	27	79	185	32	371	35	14,115	100

26. Source: *NAD* 1935, p. 232.

cent of the workforce in the goldmines earned less than Shs. 14 per week in October 1935 with the bulk of these men (sixty-seven per cent of the whole African work force) in the Shs. 10 to Shs. 14 range. However, some 1,407 men, or ten per cent of the workforce, earned Shs. 15 or more per month, and this group, itself highly differentiated, could be regarded as the 'better paid' stratum of the force with the bulk of it (939 men) earning between Shs. 15 and Shs. 24 per month.

What is to be noted however is that virtually every occupational category is strung down its particular column from the bottom to the top of the wage scale, and this includes 'surface' and 'underground' labour, 'headmen' and 'police and watchmen' as well as more skilled categories like 'clerks', 'lorry and motor drivers', 'domestic cooks', 'other indoor domestic servants', 'carpenters', 'masons', 'blacksmiths' and 'other skilled labour'. Once again part of this differentiation is due largely to the fact that the occupational categories are very broad and thus disguise considerable occupational differences (e.g. 'underground' and 'surface' labour) or are simply residual (e.g. 'other skilled labour' and 'other indoor domestic servants'), but it is also clear that even apparently narrowly defined categories like 'masons', 'carpenters', 'blacksmiths', 'clerks', and 'domestic cooks' were highly differentiated.

Finally, to drive home the point I am trying to make, table IX:5 gives a list of wages paid to its workforce in Nairobi by the Railways and Harbours Board in 1947. This last is perhaps the most eloquent piece of evidence of all from our point of view. Note that in the first thirty-eight wage categories (Shs.18 to Shs. 56) the increase is by single shilling units in all but one case, and yet there is at least one man in every category. Up to Shs. 150 per month the wage categories do not rise by more than two to four shillings, and the 99.8 per cent of the men in the workforce who earned less than that were represented in every one of those categories. In fact fifty-five out of the seventy-six wage categories have less than one per cent of the workforce within them. The wage structure of the Kenya–Uganda railway was a finely-graded ladder, with the vast majority of the workers on the first few rungs (over fifty per cent of them were in the lowest three pay categories), but with the distance between each rung small enough to give every man some hope that he could climb, and small enough to keep him climbing once he had begun.

I feel sure that were detailed wage data for farms and estates available for the period 1905–52 they would show a very similar pattern to this, with the bulk of workers employed at any given time and through time being concentrated in the lower pay levels, but a not inconsiderable minority earning from 1.5 times the starting wage upwards. This minority would be highly differentiated internally but it would be spread across virtually every occupational category employed on the farm or estate. Certainly, this is very strongly suggested by the data on African wages in agriculture collected by the Committee on African Wages in February 1953. This was restricted to a survey of 2,895 workers on

*Table IX:5. Kenya Uganda Railway: African employees
distributed according to basic wage*

Basic pay Shillings	No. of employees	Basic pay Shillings	No. of employees
18	1,291	57	33
19	791	59	3
20	970	60	172
21	67	65	72
22	206	70	47
23	69	75	44
24	86	80	64
25	168	85	28
26	74	90	30
27	21	93	1
28	142	95	1
29	19	97	14
30	223	100	6
31	66	101	1
32	22	103	3
33	18	105	8
34	62	109	1
35	48	110	20
36	57	112	3
37	23	113	2
38	84	115	2
39	23	118	1
40	465	120	22
41	46	125	3
42	3	127	2
44	5	129	1
45	122	130	3
46	1	135	2
47	10	137	1
48	4	140	1
49	60	142	1
50	34	145	3
51	2	150	5
52	3	160	1
53	56	180	2
54	1	190	3
55	26	200	2
56	2	240	1
		Total	5,979

Source: C.H. Northcott, *African Labour Efficiency Survey (1947)* (London, H.M.S.O., 1949), p. 52.

Table IX:6. Average cash wages of ticket and monthly contract labour in non-plantation agriculture—February, 1953

Adult Males

Area	Average cash wage	
	Skilled workers (Sh. 50 and over)	Semi-skilled and unskilled workers (under Sh. 50)
	Shillings	*Shillings*
Kitale	75	22
Eldoret	88	22
Nakuru	87	27
Nanyuki-Nyeri	76	22
Nairobi (excluding Thika)	102	31
Highlands weighted average	85	25

Source: *Report of the Committee on African Wages (The Carpenter Report)* (Nairobi 1954) p. 35.

sixty-three farms, and excluded plantation labour. The Committee presented two tables showing the wage distribution of these workers, the first showing cash wages only, the second adding an imputed value for housing and rations provided by the farmer for his contract labour (tables IX:7, IX:8).

If we regard the top eight per cent of the distribution shown as representing the 'better-paid' workers, i.e. those earning more than Shs. 50 in cash or a real wage of Shs. 70 per month, then another table shows that once this threshold (Shs. 50 per month in cash) was passed, wages well in excess of it were available and that the 'average' differential between the highest and lowest paid labourers was 3.4 to 1.

To complete this review of the wage structure of the African labour force up to the early fifties, tables IX:9 and IX:10 show the distribution of earnings among 59,200 workers in private industry and 40,200 workers in the public services employed in the urban areas of Kenya, who were surveyed by the Carpenter Committee in July 1953. In the case of private industry, a breakdown by occupational groups was also provided, as in table IX:11.

It will be noted once again how nearly all the occupations listed cover a large number of the wage groups, with even the unskilled labour category covering half the groups. If one takes the top four wage groups in both sectors (from Shs. 150 to Shs. 399 in the private sector and Shs. 200 to Shs. 400 + in the public services) twelve per cent and thirteen per cent of the labour force respectively comprise this 'better-paid' category. In general, public service employment was better paid at this date than private industry, forty-eight per

Table IX:7. Cash wages of ticket and monthly contract labour in non-plantation agriculture—February, 1953

Adult Males

	Percentage of employees in specified wage groups						
Area	Shillings per month						
	10–14	15–19	20–24	25–29	30–39	40–49	50 and over
	Percentage distribution						
Kitale	3	43	19	15	11	4	5
Eldoret	—	31	38	12	10	3	6
Nakuru	2	13	21	17	28	8	11
Nanyuki-Nyeri	2	39	29	11	7	3	9
Nairobi (excluding Thika)	—	2	6	24	43	15	10
Highlands weighted average	2	24	22	16	21	7	8

Source: ibid., pp. 35 and 36.

Table IX:8. Total emoluments of ticket and monthly contract labour in non-plantation agriculture—February, 1953

Adult Males

	Percentage of employees in specified wage groups						
Area	Shillings per month						
	30–34	35–39	40–44	45–49	50–59	60–69	70 and over
	Percentage distribution						
Kitale	3	43	19	15	11	4	5
Eldoret	—	31	38	12	10	3	6
Nakuru	2	13	21	17	28	8	11
Nanyuki-Nyeri	2	39	29	11	7	3	9
Nairobi (excluding Thika)	—	2	6	24	43	15	10
Average all areas	2	24	22	16	21	7	8

Source: ibid., pp. 35 and 36.

Table IX:9. Private Industry—Distribution of employees by standard earnings (July 1953)

Urban area	Statutory minimum wage			Percentage of employees in specified wage groups — Shillings per month															Estimated total
	House Basic	allce.	Total	Under 50	50–54	55–59	60–64	65–69	70–79	80–89	90–99	100–149	150–199	200–249	250–299	300–399	400 & over	Total	Total employees
Nairobi	52 50	7 00	59 50	—	—	2	20	13	19	12	6	15	8	3	1	—	1	100	31,200
Mombasa	54 75	8 25	63 00	—	1	1	16	12	17	8	9	24	7	3	1	—	—	100	14,300
Nakuru	50 00	7 00	57 00	—	3	23	9	8	16	7	6	15	6	3	2	1	—	100	2,400
Eldoret	49 00	8 00	57 00	—	1	23	11	10	17	12	6	15	2	2	—	2	—	100	2,200
Kitale	51 00	6 00	57 00	—	—	30	26	9	6	6	4	13	2	2	1	1	—	100	1,400
Kisumu	47 00	5 00	52 00	1	24	24	9	8	10	5	2	10	4	1	1	1	—	100	3,800
Nanyuki	51 50	4 00	55 50	—	—	27	7	14	26	3	13	10	—	1	—	—	—	100	800
Nyeri	51 00	5 00	56 00	8	19	11	8	12	11	8	8	9	2	3	1	—	—	100	1,400
Thika	50 50	5 00	55 50	1	—	—	3	19	37	10	7	12	10	—	1	—	—	100	1,000
Ruiru	—	—	—	—	—	—	34	18	21	6	4	17	—	1	—	—	—	100	100
Kericho	—	—	—	18	36	14	4	2	5	4	2	8	4	1	2	1	—	100	600
All urban areas surveyed	—	—	—	—	3	6	17	12	17	10	7	16	7	3	1	1	—	100	59,200

Source: *ibid.,* p. 181.

Table IX:10. *Public Services—Distribution of employees by standard earnings (July 1953)*

Urban area	Statutory minimum wage Basic	Statutory minimum wage House Allce.	Statutory minimum wage Total	Under 50	50–54	55–59	60–64	65–69	70–79	80–89	90–99	100–149	150–199	200–249	250–299	300–399	400 & over	Total	Estimated total employees
									Percentage of employees in specified wage groups — Shillings per month										
Nairobi	52 50	7 00	59 50	—	—	—	6	6	16	11	11	24	12	8	3	2	1	100	19,400
Mombasa	54 75	8 25	63 00	—	—	—	—	—	28	12	10	28	11	5	3	2	1	100	8,500
Nakuru	50 00	7 00	57 00	—	1	1	8	6	25	6	10	20	12	6	3	1	1	100	3,200
Eldoret	49 00	8 00	57 00	—	—	6	8	16	19	12	8	17	7	5	1	1	—	100	1,900
Kitale	51 00	6 00	57 00	—	—	20	12	6	6	3	7	29	10	5	1	1	—	100	600
Kisumu	47 00	5 00	52 00	6	1	1	15	8	13	10	6	20	9	6	2	2	1	100	3,600
Nanyuki	51 50	4 00	55 50	—	1	5	6	14	26	7	2	22	10	5	1	1	—	100	700
Nyeri	51 00	5 00	56 00	1	1	1	11	6	11	4	5	38	10	8	2	2	—	100	1,400
Thika	50 50	5 00	55 50	—	—	1	2	4	19	6	7	26	14	13	3	5	—	100	200
Ruiru	—	—	—	—	—	—	12	11	5	8	4	50	3	6	1	—	—	100	200
Kericho	—	—	—	25	5	2	3	4	8	5	3	19	15	6	3	1	1	100	500
All urban areas surveyed	—	—	—	1	—	1	6	5	19	11	9	24	11	7	3	2	1	100	40,200

Source: *ibid.*, p. 181.

Table IX:11. *Private Industry—Distribution of employees by standard earnings in main occupation groups—all urban areas surveyed, July 1953*

Occupation	Percentage of employees in specified wage groups Shillings per month											Total employees	Estimated total employees
	Under 60	60–69	70–79	80–89	90–99	100–149	150–199	200–249	250–299	300–399	400 & over		
Clerks and Cashiers	—	—	4	3	5	25	27	15	9	9	3	100	2,400
Drivers	—	1	1	2	10	52	29	4	1	—	—	100	3,200
Carpenters	5	5	4	5	8	24	28	15	4	2	—	100	1,000
Motor Mechanics	10	10	9	9	8	25	15	10	3	—	1	100	1,100
Other Metal Workers	3	4	7	4	5	33	23	11	6	4	—	100	1,100
Masons	—	—	—	4	2	34	38	17	4	1	—	100	1,100
Painters	—	4	3	6	2	56	18	8	1	2	—	100	600
Printers	10	5	16	7	6	22	14	9	8	2	1	100	400
Tailors and Machinists	2	5	8	12	7	43	18	4	1	—	—	100	1,400
Cooks and Bakers	4	2	10	7	11	43	19	3	—	1	—	100	500
Other Skilled and Semi-Skilled Workers	2	18	13	11	9	23	12	7	3	2	—	100	3,400
Headmen	1	2	7	14	16	32	18	7	2	1	—	100	800
Watchmen and Guards	9	22	19	18	10	21	1	—	—	—	—	100	3,000
Office Boys	5	32	26	13	12	11	1	—	—	—	—	100	5,700
Labourers and Other Unskilled Workers	13	41	22	10	6	7	1	—	—	—	—	100	33,500
All Occupations	9	29	17	10	7	16	7	3	1	1	—	100	59,200

Source: ibid., p. 185.

Table IX:12. Approximate numbers of men in 'better paid' employment in the African wage labour force in Kenya 1922–1952

Year	Number of men
1922	17,900*
1923	20,750
1924	20,080
1925	22,850
1926	25,350
1927	22,180
1928	22,840
1929	24,000
1930	23,600
1931	21,220
1932	19,800
1933	21,160
1934	—
1935	—
1936	25,950
1937	27,450
1938	27,440
1939	—
1940	—
1941	31,200
1942	35,100
1943	35,650
1944	38,000
1945	37,540
1946	34,220
1947	37,840
1948	43,280
1949	40,530
1950	42,800
1951	41,520
1952	42,650

*1918 = 10,000?

cent of the labour force in this sector earning in excess of Shs. 100 per month, as against twenty-eight per cent in private industry.

If we take this rough similarity of the 'better-paid' proportion of the labour force surveyed in the Nyanza goldfields in 1935 and in agricultural and non-agricultural employment in the early 1950s as something of a guide, and suggest that some ten per cent of the African wage labour force at any one time could be regarded as markedly 'better-paid' then we obtain a rough and ready series as shown in table IX:12 giving the likely size of this group over the period for which we have constructed labour force statistics.

It must be stressed that this series is provided only so that the reader has some slightly firmer parameters on which to hang the discussion which follows. It should not be read as indicating anything more specific than that this group of relatively privileged African wage earners, itself highly differentiated internally, rose from something less than 20,000 men in the early twenties to something over 40,000 men in the early fifties. The figures are positively misleading in one respect in that they suggest that the employment of this category rose and fell with general employment, whereas there is quite a lot of evidence to suggest that employers generally tried to hang on to their more skilled or trusted workers in a depression, since they might be difficult to replace once an upturn came. [27] It is unlikely therefore that this category shrank with the onset of depression from 1930–5 as is suggested in the table.

If we now return to look at wage labouring from the point of view of the cultivating households from which these men were departing, we see how complex the picture has now become. I have very little doubt that it was this category of 'better-paid' men which broadly corresponded to the category of elite or privileged households in the Reserves which we have delineated from other points of view in earlier chapters. The correspondence is not total, both because there were in addition better-off businessmen and traders in independent employment, and because not all of these men would have been heads of households at any one time. I have already argued that at least from 1930 onwards it is probable that a majority of them were.

This means that the vexed question of the motives or causes of labour migration were rather more complex than is suggested in conventional treatments. Many observers at the time, and van Zwanenberg in particular since, have argued that the crucial relationship to examine in explaining the pattern and fluctuating magnitude of labour migration was the return to labour time in agriculture as against the return in wage labouring.[28] I have little doubt that in general terms this is true. But putting together the data presented and examined in this chapter with that on agriculture presented in previous chapters, we can now see that this relationship is not a simple bi-polar one, 'returns to labour in agriculture' versus 'returns to labour in wage employment', but a multi-variant one. At any given time the 'balance' between these two factors as assessed by a male contemplating migration would be a function of:
1. the level of the real wage which he might expect to receive,
2. the price of agricultural produce,
3. the size of the household landholding,
4. prevalent yields of the various crops grown.

If a man was migrating to better-paid employment, then he could hope to shift parameters (3) and (4) with investments in agriculture made with savings

---

27. See for example *NAD* 1931, p. 140.
28. Van Zwanenberg, 'Primitive Colonial Accumulation . . .', op. cit., pp. 215–17 and 'Conclusions'.

from wage income (mainly, at this period, investments in land and peak period wage labour), and to a very limited degree he might also hope to shift parameter (2) as well (through improvements in crop quality by greater labour input etc.). In the case of a man migrating to low-paid employment, I have already suggested that it was unlikely that he would be able to save enough to make these 'parameter shifting' investments. So for him wage labour was essentially a means of increasing the level of subsistence of the household, and in particular of making investments in the quality of the household labour power through education of his (male) children. The aim would be to gain marked increments in the subsistence level of a future generation, and to hope that they could make the parameter-shifting investments for their own households. The very poorest migrants might not even earn enough to do this, and remittances, if any, would go entirely towards the recurrent costs of subsistence (food, clothing etc.).

In short we may formulate the matter thus: the higher the wage income received, the more determinant was this factor alone in causing labour migration; the lower the wage income received, the greater the part played by other factors—notably the factors of yields and holding size—in causing labour migration. At the lowest level, a man left home because the directly consumed subsistence derived from the holding was inadequate to support him in addition to his wife and children.

However, the above formulation is misleading in that it is timeless and thus does not grasp the actual historical process, which certainly developed in stages. In addition, it is a formulation which presupposes that a migrant could know 'in advance' what level of wage income he was going to receive, and we have already suggested that the indeterminacy of the migrant labour market expressed itself in, among other things, the inability of the average migrant to have any such knowledge. A more complete if schematic outline of the actual development of labour migration looked at from the 'cultivating household' end of things would therefore be the following:

1. In an initial stage migrants are almost entirely single men and consist of the early generations of mission-educated men going to white-collar employment as clerks, teachers, etc., and a group of uneducated, unskilled men seeking ordinary manual labouring jobs principally in order to save money to buy bridewealth livestock. Some of this latter group however become long-term migrants and may acquire on-the-job training which enables them to move into more skilled or responsible wage categories. Very roughly this stage probably lasted from about 1905 to about 1930 in most areas, though it may have ended somewhat earlier than this (the mid-twenties) in the most densely populated areas such as south Kiambu or Maragoli.

2. With fixed reserve boundaries and a more rapidly growing population, pressure on land begins to build up, a pressure exacerbated by the unequal division of land, itself partly made possible by the much more rapid expansion of the cultivated area by some households, including the households of first

generation migrants as they begin to marry. The high-level, wage-earning migrants (including those working locally—chiefs, headmen, local teachers, etc.) become land-purchasing households. This in turn sparks off a second wave of migration by men already married, most of them seeking unskilled employment. Once again a minority with literacy or simple artisanal skills acquired in mission schools and elsewhere obtain better-paid employment, and copy the reference group of the earlier stage in the use of savings, i.e. land purchase, investment in ploughs, hired labour, or non-agricultural business, education for children. This stage, which takes the apparent form of a large quantitative expansion of the wage labour force, takes place from about 1935 onwards (after the depression has abated), accelerating rapidly in the late thirties and early forties. It in turn produces

3. a further wave of migration of men from households whose landholdings have become so small that, given current yields and crop prices, off-farm labour is necessary to maintain household subsistence. These men nearly all go, at least initially, to unskilled employment. In this case male migrants are responding to the fact that given holding sizes, fragmentation resulting from the land tenure system, and crop yields and prices, additional labour input into agriculture by them simply cannot yield a return commensurate with that from unskilled labour, even if, in the risky migrant labour market, long periods of unemployment are encountered annually. Clearly this situation approximates to the labour migration situation *par excellence* as defined by neo-classical economists, i.e. the situation in which the marginal product of labour in agriculture is zero or close to zero. But it is essential to note that it probably only came into being in the late forties and early fifties, referred only to a part or sub-group of migrants, and, above all, was the outcome of a particular historical process in which the effects of earlier labour migration in conjunction with other factors had played an important part.

In no sense are these stages simply sequential, at least within particular locations or districts. Rather, looked at from the point of view of households through time, a man who began as a single unskilled migrant in stage (1), might remain in the market in stage (2) as a married 'trained-on-the-job' artisan, and then might 'retire' to his home area to look after his larger-than-average holding and/or run his own off-farm business in stage (3), whilst his son becomes an educated first-time migrant in stage (3), leaving home to become a clerk or teacher. 'Privileged households' in fact built up a generational chain of male labour migration in which the aim, and sometimes the achievement, was to have each generation of migrants being higher earners than the last, and thus able to make bigger investments, buy more land, etc. And this of course is the underlying process which the simple arithmetical expansion of the total labour force, or of the better-paid labour force, suggested in tables IX:1 and IX:12 serves to disguise, for within both categories particular individuals and families were continually represented over the years.

Nonetheless the expansion process did involve new households being added to the male migration trend as pressures built up in the Reserves, and the general effect was to whittle away the 'middle categories' of households whose male heads remained at home on the land. This in turn increased the pressure on female labour power unless the migrant earned enough to replace or more than replace his own labour power by 'working with money' (as Kowe families put it very accurately). In the last stage, 'subsistence' migration, when the holding size did not warrant the replacement of the departing male labour power, and the wages earned did not allow it to be expanded, female labour input into the home plot might itself be minimised and resort be made to wage labouring for others.

Of course this process had by no means run its course by 1952 and it continued long afterwards with the squeezing out of male labour power from the

Table IX:13. Monthly wage rates in rupees, together with rations to their approximate rupee value, c. 1918 (shown as + RV)

Unskilled Labour			Domestic servants		Porters
Coast	Nairobi and Central Kenya	Rift Valley and Nyanza	Coast	Inland	
10 + RV 3–4	—	—	—	—	10 + RV 3–4
10–15 + RV 4–5	3–5 + RV 2–3	3–6 + RV 2–3	10–25 + RV 4–5	8–10 + RV 3–4	10 + RV 3–4
Local: 10–15 + RV 6–8	3–7 + RV 3–7	3–7 + RV 2–6	10–25 + RV 4–5	8–10 + RV 3–4	10–12 + RV 6–8 (Inland rate: 6–10 + RV 4–7)
Inland: 4–5 + RV 2–3					
Local: 12 + RV 7–8	4–7 + RV 3–7	4–7 + RV 2–6	12–15 + RV 5–7	8–10 + RV 3–4	10–12 + RV 6–8 (Inland rate: 6–10 + RV 4–7)
Inland: 5–8 + RV 2–3					(Inland rate: 8–10 + RV 4–7)
Local: 12–14 + RV 7–8	5–8 + RV 3–8	5–8 + RV 3–8	12–15 + RV 5–7	10–15 + RV 4–6	(Inland rate: 8–10 + RV 4–7)
Inland: 6–9 + RV 7–8	7–8 + RV 3–8	6–8 + RV 3–8	12–15 + RV 5–7	12–20 + RV 5–8	Carrier Corps: 5–6 + RV 3 (1915) to 10 (1918)

Source: A.H. Clayton, op. cit., appendix 1, p. 430.

smallest holdings into the lower end of the wage labour market (and eventually into the market for agricultural labour on other smallholdings). But nonetheless the essential dynamic or mechanism which linked agricultural production to labour migration and both to growing differentiation between households was established by that date.

It will thus be seen that the prime determinant of differentiation among cultivating households was the rate of savings and investment out of off-farm income, of which wages were in turn the major form. It is vital therefore to know the trend of real wages over the period, and the level of remittances and investment. In general the higher the level of real wages the larger the proportion of workers able to make remittances of some sort, and within the labour force at any one time, the higher the real wages of a worker or group of workers the more they could remit in absolute terms.

Unfortunately it is precisely these two dimensions which are the most difficult to establish for the period under consideration. Little or nothing of a quantitative nature can be established about the latter dimension, though a limited amount can be done in regard to the former. The scanty data series which can be constructed for money wages in the period have to be concentrated on the wages for unskilled labour: on the minimum wages in the labour force at any one time and through time. Since, as already noted, the majority of workers in every sector were concentrated in these lower ranges this provides a reasonable

Table IX:14. Direction of change of wages and prices 1901–16

(+ = increase; − = decrease; 0 = no change)

Year	Prices	Cash wages for unskilled labour
1901–2	0	0
1902–3	0	0
1903–4	0	0
1904–5	0	0
1905–6	0	0
1906–7	+	0
1907–8	+	0
1908–9	0	0
1909–10	+	+
1910–11	0	0
1911–12	0?	0
1912–13	+	+
1913–14	0	0
1914–15	0	0
1915–16	+	(− upcountry)
		(+ coast)

Source: Stichter, op. cit., p. 76.

Table IX:15. 'Average' wages of skilled and unskilled labour in shillings per month 1921–52

Year	Unskilled 'average'	Skilled 'average'
1921	10–14	40
1922	10–14	40
1923	10–14	40
1924	10–14	40
		(1924—'up to Shs. 60 Mombasa docks')
1925	10–14	60
1926	10–14	60
1927	12–16	60
1928	12–16	60
1929	up to 20 on the railways	60
1930	10–14	
1931	8–10	
1932	6–10	
1933	6–10	
1934	8–14	30–60
1935	8–14	30–60
1936	8–14	30–60
1937	8–14	30–60
1938	8–14	30–60
1939	8–14	30–60
1940	8–14	30–60
1941	10–16	80
1942	10–16	80
1943	10–16	80
1944	10–16	80
1945	10–16	80
1946	10–16	80
1947	10–16	80
1948	15–30	80
1949	15–30	100
1950	15–30	100
1951	18–40	120
1952	18–40	120

Source: Constructed from *NAD* 1923–39 and *LDAR* 1940–52

picture of the state of affairs for most working men. If one's primary interest is in the better-paid minority then such series are of more limited use. Nonetheless, they provide a starting point, and some relevant data are provided in tables IX:13–IX:16.

What can we make of these scrappy and disjointed data? On the whole it appears that from 1905 to about 1940 or 1941 real wages in Kenya showed an astonishing stability, i.e. money wages remained stable for long periods or rose

Table IX:16. Average retail prices of selected articles in Nairobi 1931–9 (shillings and cents)

	1931	1932	1933	1934	1935	1936	1937	1938	1939
Maize Meal	10	10	10	08	07	07	04.5	04	06+
Cotton piece goods	63	60	60	60	73	62	55	45	45
Rice	30	27	26	23	23	22	23	24	21
Sugar	27	29	25	26	14	15	16	16	18
Soap	82	40	32	28	25	24	26	33	30
Tea	1/30	1/50	1/73	1/60	1/89	1/79	1/99	1/93	1/37
Beer, local	1/33	1/33	1/26	1/24	1/23	1/22	1/20	1/12	1/24
Ghee	1/19	1/05	55	64	69	80	95	90	82
Salt	10	11	10	11	10	09	10	10	09
Total in cents	604	565	517	504	533	520	548.5	527	522

Source: Stichter, op. cit., p. 188.

Retail price index for African consumers (comprising food, fuel, soap, clothing and some household articles, and collected from thirty-seven representative dealers in Mombasa), base August 1939–100

December 1947–198
December 1948–207
December 1949–217
June 1950–224

Source: *Cost of Living Commission Report* (Nairobi 1950), p. 4.

very slowly, and when they did so these rises were offset by similar small rises in prices. The only apparent exception to this trend was during the depression from 1930 to 1935 when wage cuts were instituted in all industries up to a maximum of about thirty per cent. But if the data provided by Stichter are at all accurate, price falls over the period averaged out at over sixteen per cent, and even this figure may be an underestimate. If this is the case, then in general up to the onset of the second world war it seems likely that savings and investment ratios within the African wage labour force would have been a simple function of the level of money wages (i.e. real wages were rarely below and mostly above the level of money wages).

As noted, there are no data on these ratios before 1939, so we have to work with the earliest evidence we have on this matter which comes from Forrester's income and expenditure survey of 744 African households in Nairobi in 1957. Forrester tabulated her results by five income classes and she provides the data in table IX:17 on net investments in their home farms by male wage earners in each class.

Table IX:17. Incomes and farm investments of 744 African households in Nairobi, 1957

A Income class (shillings per annum)	B Percentage of workers in class	C Average income of class (Shs. per annum)	D Percentage of C invested in home farm
0–1,799	34.1	1,693	− 5.91
1,800–3,599	38.6	2,583	0.62
3,600–5,399	17.3	4,330	1.51
5,400–7,199	6.9	6,126	10.15
7,200–8,999	3.1	4,851	7.00

Source: Marion Wallace Forrester, *Kenya Today. Social Prerequisites for Economic Development* (Gravenhage, 1962), pp. 75–6 and tables I and II, p. 119.

Elsewhere she provides statistics on total remittances to rural areas by the workers, showing that they amounted to an average of sixteen per cent of total income in the top income class, eleven per cent in the fourth and third income classes and ten per cent in the bottom two income classes.[29]

This survey is almost certainly a poor guide to the situation prior to 1939, because it reflects the change wrought in the situation by the sharp fall in real wages between 1940 and 1952.[30] Nonetheless it shows that even poorer workers could remit ten per cent of their income to rural areas, while better-off workers invested seven to ten per cent of their average income in their farms, and only the poorest workers had any net disinvestment. My own guess is that a pre-war survey of this sort would have shown no urban wage earner actually disinvesting from the farm (though it may have shown many whose investments were minimal), and it would also have shown somewhat higher levels of total remittances, especially by poorer workers.

The implication of all this is that the 'better paid' workers in particular, whose numbers and earnings we surveyed earlier, had a consistent opportunity in the years from 1905 to 1939 to attain considerable savings and investment ratios. This was particularly true of those at the top of the wage distribution and those who could remain continuously in employment. On the whole it seems that these two characteristics overlapped, since employers were generally most keen to keep skilled, literate or responsible workers 'on the books' in bad times because of the difficulty of replacing them, and this was probably especially true of certain sorts of artisans who were continually in short supply throughout these years.[31]

29. Forrester, op. cit., table III, p. 122.
30. See *Report of the Cost of Living Committee 1954*, op. cit., pp. 7–8.
31. The Kiambu District Annual Report noted in 1916 that that there was 'an almost total lack of native artizans in the country' and commenting on the situation in 1935 the Labour Section said

In an earlier paper I have suggested that better-paid workers in Kenya before 1918 were able to make considerable savings from their wages, and that since most were single men looking for bridewealth this was the major factor in the 'demand pull' inflation in livestock prices for which we have abundant evidence in these years.[32] After 1930, and for reasons which I have already examined in detail, savings were gradually switched away from the acquisition of livestock to the acquisition of land, education for children and business interests.

Summing up, we may regard the late twenties and the thirties as the crucial time when the essential parameters of socio-economic differentiation among households were laid down in the most densely populated and agriculturally developed and commercialised areas of Kenya, i.e. the three Kikuyu districts, Machakos and North, Central and Southern Kavirondo. In this differentiation access to above average off-farm incomes (of which wage or salary incomes were the predominant form) played an absolutely crucial role. It will be remembered that according to Fazan the 'average' farm income in Central Province in 1931 was Shs. 202 per annum, and we provided 'corrected' calculations from Humphrey's 1944 data for Nyeri suggesting that the annual average farm income in that year was some Shs. 380. A minimal idea of what access to 'better-paid' wage employment meant to a cultivating household before 1945 can be obtained from the table below:

| | Household cash income from farm produce | Household cash income from wages, assuming one male wage earner in employment for | |
		A. Six months yearly	B. 12 months yearly
1931	Shs. 202	Shs. 360*	Shs. 720
1944	Shs. 380	Shs. 480†	Shs. 960

*Assuming one wage earner earning Shs. 60 per month } See table IX : 15
†Assuming one wage earner earning Shs. 80 per month }

We see then that in the first case (1931), depending on the amount of time which the wage earner spends in employment, the 'average' household could have increased its gross income 78 per cent or 256 per cent. In the second case (1944) the increases are 26 per cent or 153 per cent respectively. This is mislead-

'It was generally found that native artisans were incapable of carrying out any work except of a rough nature ... They were however offered employment freely, particularly by the mines. There were special opportunities for rough carpenters and blacksmiths. Brickmakers and bricklayers were also required but were not easy to obtain ... Rates of wages for native artisans varied from Shs. 30 to Shs. 60 per month.' KAR 1916, p. 40; and *NAD* 1935, p. 190. It should be noted that this latter quotation comes from a year in which the depression was still being felt in Kenya and in which the same report was noting the 'excess of supply over demand' for most labour including clerks or 'would-be clerks'. See also *LDAR* 1949, p. 10.

32. See my 'Rise of an African Petite-Bourgeoisie ...', op. cit., pp. 37–43.

ing in that it suggests that the gain to the household from the redeployment of part of its labour power into wage labouring might occur at the cost of a loss to agricultural output. Here it must be remembered that the income accruing to the household from agriculture was largely derived from female labour input even before the man left the holding. The crucial calculation for the household was therefore the ratio between the extra income to be obtained from wage labouring and the extra income which might have accrued in agriculture from the expenditure of the labour power redeployed to wage labour. There seems no doubt that at virtually all times such extra returns could not match those to be gained from redeployment to 'better paid' wage labouring, but that, in addition, as through time mean holding sizes fell, more and more males regarded the returns even from medium-range or low-paid wage employment as superior to those obtainable from deployment of their labour power in agriculture. In fact, the broad relationship was one in which the smaller the holding and the smaller the cash and subsistence income it gave, the lower the point on the wage range which would attract a man into the wage labour force.

There was a further point here. Clerks, teachers, chiefs, headmen, telegraphists, masons, carpenters , blacksmiths and mechanics were all in a position in which, saving illness or other misfortune, they could know in advance what their income would be for the coming twelve months. 'Better-paid' employment, as well as being more financially remunerative, was reasonably stable or secure. It hardly needs stressing after all that has been said in earlier chapters, that this was in marked contrast to agricultural incomes, which could vary widely from year to year. Thus the sort of ratios between farm and off-farm income cited in the example above might hold in one year, but be transformed in the next into ratios of 1:7 or 1:10, simply because a household's farm income had effectively disappeared. I am inclined to think that it was this factor, as much as the question of relative returns to labour time, which could make even relatively low-paid wage labouring a rational redeployment of labour time for many households, especially if the redeployment was to relatively low-paid employment outside of agriculture.

Of course this security depended on a man in wage labour making savings available to the rural household by way of investment or simple subsistence transfers in times of hardship, and the extent to which he could do this depended crucially on the proportion of his income taken up by his own subsistence, i.e. by the level of his real wage. In this connection it is important to note that throughout this period the vast majority of all wage earners obtained rations and housing or a housing allowance in addition to their cash wages, and the evidence suggests that up to 1939 these wages in kind, though meagre, were accepted and tolerated by workers in an effort to save as large a proportion of their cash wages as possible. After 1939, particularly in urban areas, food prices rose so rapidly and the housing shortage became so acute that many workers suffered a real fall in this portion of their wages, i.e. rations became more meagre, and where housing was not provided by the employer housing allowances did not keep up with free market rents. But this was predominantly a wartime and post-war trend.[33]

In short, the colonial period before 1939, and in particular the inter-war years, was a time of unparalleled opportunity when a minority of households who were able to obtain access to above average off-farm incomes were able, if they were determined, to generate quite considerable savings and investment ratios out of incomes which generally rose in real terms when they rose in money terms. There is no way now of knowing what those ratios were, but I suspect that figures of twenty or thirty per cent of gross income would not be far wrong. With the inflation of the war years, and the post-war period, this opportunity, though not irretrievably lost to others, became much more difficult to obtain because the money incomes required to generate the same sorts of savings ratios were much higher, and only the very top rungs of the African wage labour force could aspire to them. Meanwhile, more and more wage labouring became subsistence wage labouring designed to subsidise a household landholding which in an increasing number of cases was inadequate to the survival and reproduction needs of those dependent upon it.

If the inter-war years were the years of opportunity, then there was indeed a stratum of men who were able to take advantage of that opportunity, whose numbers we have tried very roughly to delineate. In seizing that opportunity they commenced a transformation of production relations in the Kenyan countryside which continues to this day. We have considered several aspects of that transformation already in previous chapters. In the following chapter we shall concentrate explicitly on the dimension of land ownership, and thus draw to a close this analysis of the African economy in Kenya before 1952.

33. See for example *LDAR* 1952, pp. 7–8.

Chapter X
Land and People

The study of the African part of the Kenyan economy before 1952 contained in the previous eight chapters has focussed in several different ways upon the process of socio-economic differentiation among African households. The general picture which has emerged—of differentiation rooted in multi-sectoral enterprise and accumulation from wages and salaries—is now beginning to be a part of the conventional wisdom of the new historiography of Kenya, which is why I have concentrated on its neglected background of production, consumption and circulation of products, and on some of its less well-known empirical dimensions, such as changes in the sexual division of labour.

In this chapter I wish to complete the account of this period by examining one important empirical dimension of the differentiation process which I have so far neglected—changes in land tenure and land use and the beginning of land accumulation. In addition I will present brief biographies of eighteen African men and their households whose lives were part of this process. This may help to ground in human experience what has hitherto been analysed in a very general and abstract way, and thus bring it more vividly to life.

1. The Land Question

Whilst changes in bridewealth practices, in the sexual division of labour, and the link between farm and off-farm income expansion were dimensions of the stratification process among Africans which received little or no attention in the colonial period, and have only begun to receive research interest now, the question of land and inequality of land ownership among African households engaged the attention of the colonial administration in Kenya constantly from the late twenties onwards. Predictably, therefore, it has also received much more attention in the modern academic literature.[1] It is because of the comparative

---

1. For the Kikuyu the standard account is in Sorrenson, *Land Reform* ..., op. cit., especially pp. 3–51, but see also Tignor, op. cit., pp. 307–9; Forbes-Munro, op. cit., pp. 200–7; van Zwanenberg, op. cit., pp. 192–217; M. P. Cowen with Frederick Murage, 'Notes on Agricultural Wage Labour in a Kenya Location' in *Development Trends in Kenya* (Centre of African Studies, University of Edinburgh, 1972); M. P. Cowen, 'Differentiation in a Kenyan Location' (PCSS, 1972); K. K. Sillitoe, 'Land and the Community in Nyeri' (*EAISR* 1963); and 'Local Organisation in Nyeri'

neglect of other dimensions of the stratification process that I have chosen to treat them in more detail in this work.

However, the colonial focus upon (at times, obsession about) 'the land question' was no accident. For land was perhaps the most important dimension of growing inequality among African households. Clearly the emergence of a smallholding agricultural economy meant that household incomes came to depend heavily on the size of the cultivated area, which in turn depended on holding size. This was especially so since a people being transformed from pastoralists to agriculturalists in a very short historical period did not have time to acquire the traditions of intensive land use which have long characterised, for example, the Chinese peasantry. This fact, together with the loss of labour power to wage labour, made African smallholder agriculture extremely 'extensive' in form, and thus tied total farm output and income very heavily to the size of the cropped area. We have already seen that by the early fifties small landholdings, together with a restriction to low-yielding, low-value cereals, had meant that many households could not obtain a subsistence from their land and had to resort increasingly to wage labour and a 'high risk' market strategy. How did inequality of land holding come about?

To understand this we must return again to the 'ideal typical' picture of the pre-colonial sedentary pastoralist economy which characterised the Kikuyu, Kamba, Abaluhya, Luo and Kisii peoples.[2] In a situation in which the total cultivated area was a minute fraction of the grazing area and in which accumulation of livestock and wives was the central norm of wealth, land tenure rules were extremely vague. In fact there were no land tenure 'rules' in any meaningful sense. A man setting up a household simply 'pioneered' an open stretch of land, set his stock to graze and allowed his wife or wives to choose a spot to cultivate. Generally speaking he would regard himself as able to utilise all the land over which his livestock grazed. He could cultivate it or build huts on it, as well as graze his stock on it, wherever he wished. If another man should desire to establish his household in the same area, he might seek to dispossess the incumbent by force. But more likely, since the land was so abundant, he would simply approach the incumbent for permission to use part of the land, and perhaps make an annual or occasional gift of livestock or produce as an acknowledgement of the favour done to him. His household would then commence to cultivate and graze their stock for as long as they wished, with no thought being given on either side to whether the rights of the 'second comer' were any different in kind to that of the pioneer. Clearly so long as land remained massively abund-

(*EAISR*, 1962); E. T. Atieno-Odhiambo, 'The Rise of the Kenya Peasant' (Historical Association of Kenya Conference Paper, 1972); and G. R. Lamb, 'Peasants, Capitalists and Agricultural Development in Kenya,' (PCSS, 1972).
2. The account which follows is constructed from evidence and memoranda to the Kenya Land Commission, especially Volume I (Kikuyu Province).

ant, any distinction beyond that of pioneer or second comer would have been redundant.

However, this description is misleading, in that it posits a Hobbesian world of atomised individuals or atomised nuclear households. In practice the peoples of East Africa roamed over its empty plains and through its forests in larger kinship units. In the case of the sedentary pastoralist peoples, these were generally lineage units, which were two or three generations deep, and might under certain circumstances (of which conflict against a common enemy was the most usual) be unified into larger clan or sub-clan groups under military leaders.[3] In pioneering or conquering a stretch of land therefore, leaders of these lineages or sub-clans might allocate different areas of the territory to constituent household heads, and would adjudicate any disputes which arose between such heads over grazing rights, livestock, water, etc. Nonetheless, once allocated its particular stretch of land (which might be roughly demarcated in a variety of ways),[4] each household head remained in occupation for as long as he wished, and made land use decisions in a largely or entirely independent way.

If conflict arose within a lineage or clan then a household head or heads might leave their land areas and pioneer new territory, thus themselves becoming founders and heads of new lineages, sub-clans, etc. Thus settlement spread by a process of kinship fission and colonisation, the one producing the other.

But there was also a third element in the pattern, which was one of regular conflict between lineages, clans and larger alliances of clans (which the colonial administrators termed 'tribes'). These conflicts, over livestock, water rights and grazing (but not over land as such) meant that any group might be dispossessed of its area of land by another, and might have to flee and colonise other land. Or it could find shelter with yet another group and obtain land use facilities by the very loose sort of tribute arrangements outlined above. Thus, aside from the massive abundance of land which made land tenure rules redundant, pre-colonial East Africa lacked, by definition, the essential prerequisite of anything which can meaningfully be termed a 'system of land tenure', namely a state. It is only by the imposition of a single set of civil rules backed by a monopolistic or at least predominant military force that widely recognised and obeyed rules of land tenure (or anything else) can come into being. Indeed the very concept 'land tenure' presupposes the legal and military apparatus of a state.

This simple point seems to have eluded completely the 1931 Land Commission in Kenya which devoted 1,200 densely-set pages of *Evidence and Memoranda* to trying to discover the 'pre-colonial land tenure system' of the Kikuyu and other African peoples of Kenya. In this attempt they would take for example evidence by Dorobo elders to the effect that they (the Dorobo) regarded all forest areas

3. See for example Michael Whisson, 'The Journey of the Jo-Ramogi' (*EAISR* July 1962) and Wagner, op. cit., Vol. I, pp. 22–7.
4. See the mass of evidence concerning '*itoka* lillies' in *KLC E & M* I. See also Fisher, op. cit., p. 179, and Wagner, op. cit., Vol. II, p. 84.

in which they hung their honey barrels as 'theirs' and took this to mean that among the Dorobo the land tenure rule was that where honey barrels were hung the forest was 'owned'. But aside from the arbitrary importation of Roman legal concepts of land 'ownership', the fact was that whatever the Dorobo might have felt about the matter they would frequently encounter other groups of people who ignored the honey barrel rule (since it was not their rule), and in that case fighting or negotiations had to be entered into.[5]

There is some evidence that in these cases negotiation was the norm and for a reason which was almost certainly of universal relevance, i.e. that the Dorobo and most other East African peoples did not look on land use in an exclusive way. Why should they have done? Consider the Dorobo for a moment. They were a hunting/gathering people living in the forest areas of the Aberdares, the Mau Escarpment and Mount Kenya. They lived entirely on a diet of honey, game meat and wild fruits and vegetables. Suppose now a group of Kikuyu people took up residence in part of the forest and began to cultivate. Sometimes after a period of fighting, but mainly it seems in order to avoid it, the Kikuyu transferred some sheep or goats to Dorobo elders as an acknowledgement of their hunting tradition in the area. Since the Dorobo did not herd, they then returned these animals to the Kikuyu group for safekeeping, perhaps taking a wife from among the daughters of the household or lineage colonising the land and returning the stock as bridewealth. If then times became hard or lean for the hunters they might return to the Kikuyu group for food, and having a preference for meat would eat some of their sheep and goats or ask for some more. Thus the hunters gained wives and some security against lean times, and the incoming Kikuyu gained some guarantee against molestation by a people whose fighting skills and poisoned arrows were much feared. None of this would prevent the hunter/gatherers slinging their honey barrels over trees on the land now utilised by the Kikuyu, nor would it prevent them from hunting over that land. Indeed, once friendly relations had been established then the Dorobo might be called in to exercise their hunting skills when a lion threatened livestock, or elephants were eating or trampling down the millet.[6]

It was this principle of non-exclusivity of land use which the Land Commission never managed to grasp. And their failure to grasp it meant for example that they constantly thought themselves forced to choose between directly conflicting Masai and Kikuyu accounts of how they had 'owned' the same stretch of land.[7]

In fact this latter formulation is a clue to the specific problems posed by much of the evidence given by African witnesses to the Commission, and strikes at the root of the essential change which came over patterns of land use and land

5. *KLC E & M* I, pp. 221–7, 230 and 1108.
6. Ibid., pp. 223–5, 227, 229, 231 and 430.
7. For such conflicting accounts, see ibid., pp. 233–41.

tenure with colonialism. The Land Commission was hearing evidence in 1931, in many cases from men who had known the pre-colonial land use pattern from direct experience. If for no other reason than this, its report and the three massive accompanying volumes of *Evidence and Memoranda* are a fascinating document for the historian, and one of the first exercises in 'oral history' which took place in the colony. However, the very circumstances under which the Commission heard evidence make its assessment extremely difficult.

The Commission was hearing evidence at a time when the settler presence was firmly established, squatters on settler farms and Crown forests had already begun to come under pressure to work longer and reduce their livestock holdings, and population increase and the uneven process of land acquisition by households was already beginning to build up pressure on land in certain parts of the Reserve. In short, all the witnesses before the Commission had lived through a period when a massive proportion of the best land in the region had been excised by a new state and handed over to white settler farmers and plantation owners. Many Africans made clear before the Commission that for them the novel aspect of this process was not that conquerors had come and taken land for their own use. To this, as we have seen, they had been accustomed. What was novel and produced great bitterness, was that the new white conquerors appeared to suppose that the rights of use conferred on them by victory were exclusive. These new men called themselves land 'owners', and forbade others to share the use of the land with them, or attached ever more stringent conditions to those whom they allowed so to share (whom they now called 'tenants' or 'squatters').[8]

Thus we may grasp the way those Kikuyu and other peoples who left the Reserve to go and 'squat' on settler farms in the Rift Valley saw their own activity. The new white conquerors had replaced the Masai in the rich grazing lands of the Rift Valley. However there were very few of them (far fewer than the Masai), and thus no doubt they would not mind if other men brought their herds and established or extended their households and lineages on the same land. The squatters were perfectly willing to accord the customary recognition of prior pioneer or conquerors' rights by gifts of livestock or crops. But it turned out that the new white conquerors preferred labour. This seemed reasonable, and since initially labour demands were very limited, they allowed plenty of time for men to go about establishing their households, building up their herds, acquiring wives, and so on.[9] Slowly however labour demands became more stringent, and in 1918 a minimum labour input (180 days a year for all adult males) was laid down by an Ordinance. In addition, in the twenties, some settlers began to restrict squatter livestock holdings or even to turn men off. Thus it was

8. Ibid., pp. 111–12, 130–1, 162, 188, 465–6 and 815–42, ('Memorandum on the Mission Estate at Kikuyu').
9. Wambaa and King, op. cit., pp. 1 and 4–5.

that squatters themselves, and through word of mouth, the Kikuyu in the Reserve, learnt that western concepts of land ownership had at their heart the notion of exclusivity. To own presupposed that there were others who did not own.

But by 1931 something else had also happened. Africans had come to conceptualise their own current and past land use patterns in terms of western concepts of land ownership and the subordinate concepts of land 'purchase', 'sale' and 'tenancy'. Thus the sort of transactions we have described in outline between the Kikuyu and Dorobo came to be conceptualised as the Kikuyu having 'bought' land from the Dorobo who had 'sold' it to them. Similarly those Kikuyu who had moved on to land as second or third comers after a pioneer group and had made recognition gifts now became 'tenants' who had paid 'rent' to 'land owners'.[10] And above all clans, lineages and sub-lineages came to claim that they were and always had been 'owners' of the land which their component households had occupied and used. However, because the prime use of land had traditionally been as grazing, with animals wandering free over large areas, the boundaries of the 'holding' of each household or each lineage or each clan had been very vaguely defined (if defined at all). Thus, as land shortage increased, land disputes over boundaries became endemic, and could not usually be resolved 'correctly' because for the most part 'correct' boundaries had never existed. Thus of course they were resolved in practice in favour of the strongest or most influential groups, those who enjoyed the patronage or support of chiefs, headmen and colonial officials.

Thus it was that the groundwork was laid for the eviction of 'tenants', as land which they occupied came to be claimed by other households claiming descent from pioneers or first comers, and that lineages and then households came to claim 'ownership' of land, and having claimed ownership, were able to sell and to buy from others who also 'owned'. These processes had already commenced in Central Province and in parts of North Kavirondo when the Land Commission commenced its hearings. But the significance of the conceptual change which had come over the way most Africans thought about land, a change which was the primary result of the Africans' drawing lessons and parallels from the material consequences of settler land 'ownership', seems completely to have escaped the Commission's members.

Indeed so ensnared were they in their own cultural and conceptual myopia that they asked questions which presupposed what had been historically created. Thus time and time again they asked African witnesses 'Who owned this (X) piece of land before the Europeans came?', and were surprised or irritated when representatives of two or three different groups claimed that they did.[11] None of the African witnesses took issue with the Commission's pre-

10. Among a host of possible references, see *KLC E & M* I, op. cit., pp. 5, 8, & 173, 145-6, 186, 1110 and 1111.
11. Ibid., pp. 222, 231, 590, 592 and 758.

suppositions because by this time they had no interest in doing so. If the land in question was occupied by settlers in 1931 then they hoped by claiming 'ownership' to get it back, and in the case of their own land in the Reserve they wanted title deeds to protect it from alienation.[12] In short they had learnt the new 'game' so far as land was concerned, and the concepts which underlay it. How far this unwillingness to challenge the Commission's presuppositions about the pre-colonial periods was conscious, and how far it reflected the complete change which had come over African conceptualisations of land, as the result of bitter experience, it is difficult now to say. Certainly there was no untruth involved in Africans claiming 'ownership', since in the pre-colonial situation various groups had utilised land in ways which Europeans could only have understood as a species of ownership, and in 1931 Africans had nothing to gain and a lot to lose in drawing attention to the fact that they had never traditionally had any concept of exclusive land use.

It was thus the change from simultaneous to exclusive land use which in general terms characterised the crucial transition in land tenure brought by settler colonialism. But in practice of course the situation varied from area to area and among the different peoples of Kenya, depending upon the precise form of their pre-colonial land use and land holding patterns, and, more importantly, on the extent of land shortage. The latter in turn depended upon the extent to which different peoples were affected by land alienation to settlers, as well as by their rate of population growth, and the speed of expansion of the cultivated area.

As is usually pointed out in the historiography of colonial Kenya it was the Kikuyu, and above all the Kiambu Kikuyu, who were most seriously affected by land settlement, in that the first major area of land alienated to farmers and plantation owners was that just north of Nairobi in what later became the Thika district. This land was, at the very least, land which the Kiambu Kikuyu had used in the pre-colonial period and constituted their area of natural expansion. In addition the Nyeri Kikuyu lost a large hinterland for expansion to the north. Other groups who lost their open land frontiers through land alienation to settlers were the Machakos Kamba, and the Kipsigis and Nandi of the Rift Valley, as well as the Masai.

The aspect of pre-colonial land holding patterns which is conventionally supposed to have had most significance for colonial developments was the extent of the control over household land use exercised by authorities other than the household head. In the ideal typical description of the pre-colonial situation with which this chapter began, it was noted that the pioneering of land with population expansion (which was probably the main mode of land acquisition in the pre-colonial period) was rarely if ever something undertaken by a single

12. Ibid., p. 203 and pp. 258–375. The demand for land titles had a long history. See for example KAR 1919, p. 13; and 1924, p. 2. Also KPAR (for nine months of 1921), p. 3; and 1924, p. 4.

household, but that kin groups of varying size and generational depth generally occupied a contiguous stretch of land. Such groups usually had leaders involved in military mobilisation, dispute settlement and ceremonial and sacrificial functions. Since every individual household head depended on his kinsmen for military and other support, and ostracism could mean hardship or death, then clearly he was constrained to act in ways (even in regard to household land) which might be regulated by this leadership. Thus disputes between neighbours over grazing or water might result in an adjudication which altered the land use pattern of one or both parties.

Like all ideal types, this description is historically static, as well as highly simplified. In one of the few pieces of historical reconstuction of the pattern of relationships between the household and wider kin groups in regard to land, Wagner presents the following three stages in the land holding pattern of the Logoli people of South Maragoli:

1. Land exceedingly abundant, South Maragoli is occupied by a series of small walled villages, occupied by the members of a single 'house' or 'lineage' (*enyumba*). The cultivated land surrounds the village *(amadala)*, and each household cultivates its strip and grazes the surrounding grassland as it pleases.

2. Population growth increases the number of *amadala*, and gradually groups of lineages tracing their origin to the same ancestor become more self-conscious 'clans' with the bigger clans at least defining their own clan territory. The most important expression of this expanded territorial consciousness is that men from other clans can only be invited to settle on clan land after the clan head (*eligutu*, pl. *amagutu*) has been consulted. In stage (1) above, members of a lineage of a different clan might obtain access to land within the broad purview of an *amadala*. Now some restriction is placed on this.

3. Still greater population pressure on the land, the very limited clan controls over household land use break down and land is bought and sold between household heads of different clans and lineages. Hence both clans and lineages as contiguous residential entities break down entirely.[13]

We see then a rather curious development, in which individual household heads throughout maintain great autonomy in land use and disposal, but such limited broader social controls as there are are first expanded from the lineage to the clan level and then collapse entirely. Very broadly, stage (1) above was predominant over South Maragoli until the onset of colonialism, stage (2) covered the period from 1890 or 1900 to the late twenties or early thirties, and stage (3) spread over the location from about 1930 onwards.

Interestingly enough something rather similar seems to have occurred among the Kikuyu. In the most thinly populated parts of what was to become Central

---

13. Wagner, op. cit., Vol. II, pp. 88–9 and 95–9. For later developments see Humphrey, *The Liguru . . .*, op. cit., pp. 17–27; and especially G. M. Wilson, 'Village Surveys, Bunyore, Maragoli, Nyangori, Tiriki, Boholo' (Kavirondo District Record Book, 1956).

Province, it appears that the initial Kikuyu settlement pattern might in fact have been individual households dotted thinly over the ridge and valley landscape. As settlement became denser, individual households banded together to lay claim to stretches of land, and once again the institutional expression of this banding was the emergence of a leader (*muramati*) who was usually the oldest surviving male descendent of the male ancestor to whom the male household heads banding together traced their origin. Once again the main power of the *muramati* so far as land was concerned was to place and enforce restrictions (in the name of the whole group) on the provision of land to other household heads outside the group. The group banding together in this way was called an *mbari* and the land over which it claimed jurisdiction *githaka*. Over time many *githaka* came to be coextensive with particular ridges, and encompassed both cultivated land and an area of surrounding grassland into which the *mbari* expanded its cultivated area as households multiplied. *Mbari* and *githaka* varied enormously in size, with the landholding size being a dependent variable of the size of social group designed by the term *mbari*. It appears that the kinship depth (real and fictive) of *mbari* varied from units much smaller than the Logoli lineage to others much larger than the Logoli clan. *Mbari* split up regularly of course as household heads quarrelled or went off to pioneer new land.

Once again, it seems that from the mid-twenties onwards household heads began to dispose of land by sale or to rent it to non-*mbari* members, and this practice increased rapidly in the thirties and forties. As a result, ever-increasing numbers of household heads looked to defend and expand their landholdings not by using the collective solidarity of the *mbari* to defend a given multihousehold 'territory' against other *mbari*, but by turning household holdings into totally independent 'freeholds' on the western model. This process was termed the 'individualisation' of tenure by colonial observers, and from time to time they attempted to arrest it and buttress the power of clan heads or *mbari muramati*. From 1952 onwards, however, it was systematically supported with a programme of land consolidation accompanied by the issuance of freehold titles to the consolidated household plots.[14]

This colonial conceptualisation of the matter is inaccurate in so far as it suggests that, prior to the emergence of land-purchasing elite households in Kikuyuland, Nyanza and Ukamba in the twenties and thirties, 'African land tenure' was not 'individual'. I have already suggested that in pre-colonial Kenya there could not be, by definition, any single system of land tenure over the entire territory since the territory did not exist in any political or legal sense. But it is striking that every monographic account which I have encount-

14. See Sorrenson, *Land Reform* . . . , op. cit., pp. 8–12, 28–33, 40, 47 and 52–71; *Report of the Committee on Native Land Tenure in Kikuyu Province* (Nairobi, 1929), pp. 5–11; and Sillitoe, 'Land and the Community . . . ', op. cit.; also M. P. Cowen with Frederick Murage, op. cit., pp. 52–3.

ered of the pre-colonial or early colonial land holding patterns of the different peoples of Kenya lays stress on the very considerable latitude in land use accorded to a household head once he was in possession of an area of land. That is, whether one is considering the Kikuyu, the Embu, the Meru, 'Abaluhya', Luo, Kamba, Gusii, Kipsigis, Nandi or Giriama peoples of Kenya, it seems that once in occupation of an area of land a household head very largely did as he wished with it.[15] Of course in the pre-colonial or early colonial period the culti- vated area relied heavily on the wife's labour, but the greatest part of the holding was in pastoral use, and it was the labour of the household head and that of his sons which went into this form of production. After the spread and commercial- isation of agriculture on the other hand, male right of disposal of the usufruct of the whole land (including its cultivated portion) was still successfully asserted. Similarly a man's ability to provide land for a sister or daughter's husband, for a friend from another clan or *mbari*, or even for a complete stranger, were generally not disputed, even if he might out of courtesy 'clear' the matter with a clan head or *muramati*.

This was the case in a situation of land abundance. As land became increas- ingly scarce, there were, as we have seen, attempts to restrict such rights of disposal to a broad range of real or fictive kin.

But in the end such attempts foundered on a central contradiction. For if a man supported his clan or lineage head in the attempt to prevent another house- hold head selling land to a stranger (who shall we say happened to be the highest bidder) and supported the assertion that sales should only be to clansmen or to fellow lineage members, then of course he had to accept that such restrictions did or should apply to him as well. As the practice of irredeemable purchase and sale spread, so more and more men became would-be buyers or would-be sellers, and thus their support for such restrictions waned.

The question of irredeemability was absolutely central here. As we have seen, pre-colonial practice had known the custom of making small 'presents' of beer, produce or livestock to a pioneer household or group of households in return for the unmolested use of a desired piece of land. Almost universally the practice seems to have been that if for some reason a pioneer household wanted this land back, they had simply to return the gifts made and they could reassume occupation. In a situation of land abundance this was of minor importance,

15. For the Kikuyu see sources above and also John Middleton and Greet Kershaw, *The Kikuyu and Kamba of Kenya* (London, 1965), pp. 45–50. Also Fisher, op. cit., pp. 200–3. For the Meru, see F. E. Bernard, op. cit., p. 61. For the Abaluhya, see Wagner, op. cit., Vol. II, pp. 75–99; and for the Luo see Hay, op. cit., pp. 102–4. For the Kamba see Forbes Munro, op. cit., pp. 14–15 and 201–7 and Middleton and Kershaw, op. cit., pp. 77–9. For the Gusii see Robert A. LeVine and Barbara B. Le Vine, *Nyansongo: A Gusii Community in Kenya* (New York, 1966), p. 10 and pp. 26–7, and also Robert A. LeVine, 'Wealth and Power in Gusiiland', in Bohannan & Dalton (eds.), op. cit., p. 521. For the Kipsigis, see G. W. B. Huntingford, *The Southern Nilo-Hamites* (London, 1969), p. 41; and Peristiany, op. cit., p. 133. For the Nandi, see G. W. B. Huntingford, *Nandi Work and Culture*, op. cit., pp. 57 and 58; and for the Giriama, see Parkin, op. cit., pp. 18–19 and 23–4.

since the wish or desire to redeem the land very seldom arose and if it did occur the household dispossessed had no lack of alternative opportunities. In fact they would usually be welcomed with open arms by other lineages or clans seeking military and other manpower.

Once land shortage set in, both the desire to redeem land and the difficulty of finding land elsewhere increased markedly. As a result a basic conflict of interest arose which expressed itself as a dispute over conceptualisation. Households which had received such small-scale tribute dubbed it 'rent' and called the in-coming households 'tenants', whilst the tribute-providers called the transfers 'payment' for the land and claimed to be 'owners'. However this is a rather schematic way of putting it. For in practice of course the people battling over conceptualisation and the people who made and received the original transfers were historically some distance apart. In fact the former were usually the descendants of the latter. The Kenya Land Commission ran into a welter of exceedingly complex cases in which claims and counter-claims of this sort were made, many of them going back into the mid-nineteenth century and earlier. Writing of the situation in Fort Hall as late as 1952, Fisher noted that in an attempt to reduce the number of land cases involving disputes over land transferred as part of bridewealth, the Native Tribunals had adopted a law that 'such gardens are irredeemable if the transaction took place prior to or during the 1898 famine. The ground on which this recommendation is based is that all rights of occupation and ownership must have accrued to the occupier during that long undisturbed continuity of occupation.'[16]

We can of course assume that this 'law' was brought in precisely because there were Kikuyu coming before the Fort Hall tribunals who did indeed deny that undisturbed occupation of a piece of land for half a century conferred 'all rights of . . . ownership'. My own view, as already indicated, is that any attempt by the historian to determine whether the original transfers were 'really' a form of rent or a form of land purchase is based on a false premise. For in the pre-colonial situation, conditions were such that the people involved had no need of such concepts because the distinction which they embodied was otiose. Land was abundant. People to work it and to defend the people and livestock upon it were scarce. Hence in the 'typical' situation there was no reason for second comers to suppose that they would be asked to leave and no incentive for first comers or pioneers to make such a request. The land which they all occupied was available to be put to the limited range of uses then open. This substantive situation would have been all that mattered to them. It only became necessary to distinguish between land 'owned' and land 'rented' when land became a commodity as a result of relative scarcity, and this itself came about

---

16. Fisher, op. cit., p. 203. Transfer of land as part of bridewealth seems to have occurred only exceptionally among the Kikuyu, and usually only when the family involved was too poor (in livestock) to do anything else (ibid., pp. 189–90).

through a change of land use (pastoralism to agriculture) and through the increasing commoditisation of agricultural production.

It is not difficult to see that patterns of land holding among the sedentary-pastoralist-turned-agriculturalist peoples of Kenya did not provide much of an impediment to the group of 'land accumulators' which began to emerge in real numbers from the mid-twenties onwards. We have already suggested who these people were and why and how they accumulated, and we shall look at some typical case histories in the next section of this chapter; but before we do this it is necessary to carry the argument one stage further. We have so far described how land was held, and suggested that even in the pre-colonial period the system of land holding was essentially 'individualist'—if by this we mean that the bulk of important land use and disposal capabilities lay in the hands of individual male household heads. We have also suggested that the one major capability 'missing' in the pre-colonial situation, i.e. the ability to transfer land permanently to the highest-bidding 'stranger', was institutionally difficult to resist once the economy had been monetised. However, this weakness of kinship group constraints on the land disposal powers of household heads would not have mattered if there had been no wish or desire to sell. Given that the desire to buy and accumulate land is now deemed to have been explained, what was the incentive to sell?

I think that the answer so far as the period from the mid-thirties onwards is concerned was very simple. Most sellers of land sold out of distress, i.e. they sold land to meet essential subsistence and other expenses when they had no other resources to meet such expenses. Given the extreme variability of natural conditions to which we have drawn attention before, it is not surprising that many households faced situations in which resort had to be made to land sales in order to meet subsistence requirements. Total harvest failure, or even a number of sub-normal harvests, could leave households with no other choice. If a decline in income coincided with a sudden need for a larger than average expenditure—funeral or wedding expenses, a rise in school fees for several children, bridewealth payments or even taxes—then the pressure to realise the land asset was increased. It is particularly significant here that over most of Kenya, as over much of Africa, rural households did not have access to money lenders (who in India or in pre-revolutionary China provided loans for just such purposes). Asian and African traders often provided credit to customers but this was in the form of delayed payment for goods or services received, not ready cash. Nor does there seem to have been any tradition of mortgaging land for money.[17] The absence (until the mid-fifties) of a legal title to individual tenure by African households, and the recognition in most 'traditional' land holding systems of 'redeemable sale', meant that for land accumulators out-

17. There were some exceptions to this in the Coast Province. Parkin for example makes mention of the practice: Parkin, op. cit., pp. 53–4 and 57–9. See also *NAD* 1935, p. 115; and 1938, p. 27.

right purchase was always preferable to any form of mortage.[18] If the buyer could get the seller to acknowledge (usually through a ceremony of transfer in front of witnesses) that the sale was an irredeemable one he could at least feel reasonably secure in his acquisition. Any transaction however in which the accumulator (buyer) acknowledged the potential redeemability of the land laid him wide open to litigation if the seller offered the return of the purchase price and he refused it. Since, as we have seen, tribunals could be got to take seriously redemption claims which were decades old and may have involved the parents or even grandparents of the litigants, the 'modern' land accumulators who emerged from the late twenties onwards generally tried to bind the seller as tightly as they could to a recognition of irredeemability, to protect their investment.[19]

In short the problem was that the 'livestock economy' of Kenya had indeed recognised some embryonic concept of land mortgage (in that on the very rare occasions when first-comer households wanted the occupancy of land which they had provided for second comers, they could apparently obtain this by a return of some or all of the gifts received). With the emergence of an agricultural economy in which exchange occurred through modern money, the development of this embryonic form of land mortgage was paradoxically blocked off by the absence of any legal household title to land in the Reserves, combined with the insecurity produced by the widespread legal use of precedents deriving from the earlier embryonic mortgage tradition to challenge household land rights. That accumulators in particular felt insecure in the face of such challenges is clear from the desire expressed in Local Native Councils from the mid-thirties to have some recognition of 'individual land tenure' (as it came to be called) combined with a legal moratorium on the use of challenges deriving from 'outworn custom'. The problem for accumulators was that however hard they attempted to 'tie in' sellers by ceremonial and other means to a public recognition of irredeemability they could never be absolutely sure (so long as the legal loophole remained) that sellers would not renege on commitments once their own economic position had improved and redemption was possible.

It appears then that most sales were distress sales deriving from hardship combined with the general absence of alternative methods of raising the cash required, such as usury or land mortgage. It is not to be supposed that 'natural' disasters alone pushed households into positions in which distress sales had to be made. By the forties and fifties, when a stratum of land-accumulating households was firmly established in Central Province, Nyanza Province and Machakos, the very inequality of land ownership, combined with population pressure and fixed Reserve boundaries, placed small landowning households in a vulnerable position. For, all things being equal, the smaller the landholding the smaller

18. See Sorrenson, *Land Reform* ..., op. cit., p. 63; and *AAD* 1950, pp. 10–11 and 20.
19. See for example Harry Thuku (with Kenneth King) *An Autobiography* (Nairobi, 1970), pp. 57–8.

the real and monetary farm income and the smaller the margin of safety. This was true both in the obvious sense that harvest failure would hit smaller land-holders harder and bring them nearer to malnutrition much quicker, but also in the sense that sudden comparatively large calls on cash resources were more likely to force such households into land sales. It is possible that there was some crucial minimum threshold of holding size (which would vary by area and by household with soil fertility, level of labour input, crop mix, etc.) below which land sales were likely to lead to further land sales, through a vicious circle in which sale of some land led to declining income with an increased risk of distress that would produce further land sales. It was clearly the attempt to break out of this vicious circle which sent male household heads from such households into the wage labour market in the thirties. But as I have already suggested in the previous chapter, male household heads taking to labour migration in these circumstances nearly always had to content themselves initially with unskilled work at the lowest end of the wage gradient. Whilst therefore departure of household heads and adult sons to wage labour might take the pressure of their subsistence requirements off the holding, it was un-likely to reverse the process of decline, unless some or all of them could get better-paid employment. Cowen has made a very similar point to this, and has reinforced it by relating it to the micro-economics of the farm:

> Engagement in wage labour by some family members reduces the real labour time for investment activity on the holding supplying wage labour. Where the required rate of investment for the expected increase in output is not satisfied, then the increase in cash consumption requirements cannot be met out of production for sale. Total output falls, and for the same number of family workers, Acreage Product of the Labourer (APL) falls, all relative to the levels of output and APL on the larger farm. The compulsion behind the search for wage labour is therefore reinforced.[20]

Or, in other words, with rising cash consumption requirements coming from household increase, and a widening of the range of consumer desires and possibilities, or both, such consumption requirements could only be met from a rising farm income if labour input on the holding is increased in those forms of 'investment' activity (irrigation or soil erosion prevention measures, con-struction of stores, fences, cattle leys and stalls) which promote income increase or prevent decrease. But once labour power begins to be lost to the holding through migration, the possibility of increasing labour input in this way becomes ever more reduced, and households look more to raise income through wage labour. But of course this produces no insurance against land sales if wage earnings are low and remittances small or non-existent, and such a situation is more likely to emerge at a time of falling real wages, as in the decade 1942–52.

20. M. P. Cowen, 'Differentiation . . .', op. cit., p. 16.

Nonetheless whilst distress sales of one form or another must have accounted for most land sales from the 1930s onwards in Central and Nyanza Province (as we have already seen, Parkin's work in Tsakani confirmed that this was the usual motivation for sales of land and palms there), there may have been another phenomenon operative in a slightly earlier period. The major period of migration of entire households from Central Province to the Rift Valley, Thika and North Nyeri as 'squatters' was the decade 1918–28. All the district and provincial reports for the early twenties from Central Province make note of the exodus and its swelling proportions, so that whilst there were probably less than 10,000 squatters on all European farms and estates before 1918, Native Affairs Department estimates for the late twenties generally put the figure at around 100,000 and the Land Commission put the figure at 150,000 in 1931.

I have already expressed the view that an unknown but probably considerable proportion of these migrants were large stock owners who were attracted to the Rift Valley because of the quality and extent of the grazing land available. Yet there were also those who were looking to build up their livestock wealth in the Rift Valley once they were there, though they may not have had a great deal of stock when they migrated.[21]

The land which had been occupied by these households was obviously available for use by others when they had left, and it is a matter of some interest how it was then transferred. Most available accounts, from Dr Leakey's observations on the Kikuyu economy to Wambaa's oral testimony, stress that many, perhaps the majority, of the squatters migrating were *ahoi* (or 'tenants'); so it might be supposed that the land in question would simply revert to the households of the *mbari* which had originally provided it. But this is to suppose that because the land which a household head left to go to the Rift Valley was not land of his *mbari* that he had no *mbari* land; and much of the testimony to the Kenya Land Commission makes plain that many pre-colonial *ahoi* were not poor men at all—quite the reverse. They were usually men who had taken up residence outside family land because they needed extra land resources to accommodate and expand their above-average livestock holdings.[22] If they were thus already resident outside their own family land before they went to the Rift Valley or elsewhere, they had probably already transferred land to a fellow *mbari* member on the sort of redeemable 'purchase' or 'mortgage' arrangement which we have discussed earlier. Indeed, as I have already suggested, for most of the initial squatters movement on to an area of prime grazing which had mysteriously become designated as a 'settler farm' was not seen as in any way different from previous household migrations. It was all part of the drive to

---

21. In addition to Rebman Wambaa's testimony on this, see Sillitoe. 'Land and the Community...', op. cit., pp. 1–2.
22. See *KLC E & M* I, pp. 167–70, 528–9, 589–92, 757, 885–7 and 1108–9. See also Fisher, p. 189.

expand the number of wives and livestock with their concomitant of increasing quantities of land for extensive use.[23] Similarly those households which migrated to farms without the benefit of pre-existing large stock holdings might have transferred *mbari* land with the aim of setting up a flow of stock gifts from the *mbari* to the settler farm to which they were moving, thereby creating the foundation of a herd to be expanded in their new home. In either case, whether one is concerned with the transfer of the 'original' *mbari* land of a rich *ahoi* who had already been resident elsewhere before becoming a squatter, or with the transfer of the *mbari* land of a younger household head looking to make his 'stock fortune' in the Rift Valley, an opportunity was available for men with large livestock holdings to turn these into land. At the point of transition between the livestock and agricultural economy (which in Central Province came around the mid-twenties or early thirties), astute men who saw the implications of the transition could obtain land from others who were still oriented to the pre-colonial wealth criteria and who consequently wanted to be squatters. This may explain the finding of a small survey of 'progressive farmers' in the Kangema location of the Kandara division of Muranga (formerly Fort Hall) district of Central Province, carried out in February 1973. Of the thirty farmers interviewed, twenty-seven had bought nearly all of their land. However, two had inherited all or most of their current landholdings from their fathers, and all of these men when asked how their fathers had come by the land, stated that they had been large stock owners and had turned their stock into land.[24]

It is likely that the period of accumulation by these means was comparatively short, and essentially ended when the squatter option closed down in the late twenties or early thirties. From this point onwards, to exchange land for livestock became an irrational act for those who had no means of finding extra grazing for the stock so acquired, and placing such stock with squatter friends or relatives became a more difficult business as a result of settler restrictions.

Finally and briefly it is worth pointing out that there was one other method of obtaining land in the colonial period which did not require there to be a 'willing' seller of any variety, and which did not indeed require selling or buying in any form. I refer to the use of coercion by chiefs and headmen to plunder land from others. One particularly blatant example of this emerged in the evidence given to the Kenya Land Commission. According to one Lewis Kaberere, his grandfather, Bere, a Dorobo hunter, had in the pre-colonial period transferred land to a group of Kikuyu whose descendants (in 1931) were constituted as the *Mbari wa Hinga*. As part of, or perhaps prior to this transfer, he had been 'adopted' by the Kikuyu involved, and a series of transfers of livestock appear to have occurred between the households who had entered the land involved (which probably lay between Fort Smith and the Nairobi river) and other

23. See Wambaa and King, op. cit., p. 2.
24. See below chapter XI, p. 369, and KAR 1934, p. 12.

households, descendants of Bere, who were now of course 'Kikuyu', being the offspring of Bere and a Kikuyu woman or women. At a certain point in this process (as often in oral testimony the chronology is vague), the community so established appears to have split, with some households (who Kaberere says were 'related' to the Paramount Chief Kinyanjui) refusing to make any further stock transfers when requested by the households descended from Bere. Fighting broke out, and Kaberere (the witness) and a number of other households were driven from the land by Kinyanjui's retainers and threatened with gaol by Kinyanjui if they protested.[25]

This example is particularly interesting. A number of Kiambu district and other reports for the early twenties make general reference to Kinyanjui's 'enormous land holdings' and either infer or assert explicitly that these were acquired by more or less coercive or illegal means.[26] But this example seems to show that land acquisition by Kinyanjui (which had certainly begun before 1914) was a somewhat different thing from the more modern land accumulation which began from the mid-twenties onward. For whilst Kinyanjui's own household no doubt did cultivate a larger than average holding, it is clear that the bulk of the land over which he exercised some form of control was not used for the expansion of cultivation by him (or, more precisely, by his wives) at all. Rather it was used politically as a way of winning or rewarding supporters, i.e. a man attaching himself to Kinyanjui either as a tribal retainer or unofficial agent, or who could lay claim to Kinyanjui's support by real or fictive kinship links, could hope to see his household and those of his relatives benefit by acquiring land at the expense of others. It is clear that the *Mbari wa Hinga* was just one of the many such claiming a 'relation' to Kinyanjui, and whether this relation was a real blood tie or purely fictive hardly matters in this context. What it implies is that in the Kiambu district by the late twenties (Kinyanjui died in 1929), the distribution of land among households was influenced by this factor among others. How far any trace of its influence could be seen in the present pattern of land holding there is impossible to say, and it would take a great deal of research to find out. We certainly know that some of Kinyanjui's close relatives lost land in court cases after his death,[27] but they must have been only a small proportion of the total set of households who benefitted from his enterprising style of administration. Certainly in this case, as in others like it in other parts of Kenya, a household which benefitted from a patron–client or kinship link with a powerful chief, and obtained a larger than average landholding in this way, could only have maintained this privileged position through time by means of other activities, above all by investing in the formal education which

25. *KLC E & M* I, pp. 223–5.
26. See for example DagHOR 1912, p. 18 and 1913, p. 20. For other evidence of Kinyanjui acquiring land and selling it to Europeans, see *KLC E & M* I, pp. 229, 231 and 735. See also the evidence adduced by Tignor, op. cit., p. 49.
27. Tignor, op. cit., p. 57.

would allow larger wage or salary incomes to be obtained and landholdings and other business investments to be expanded. At any rate, the use of official power to dispossess others of land, either forcibly or fraudulently, and the disposal of such land to relatives and clients, was a practice which continued throughout the colonial period, and indeed has continued into the post-colonial period. It has its modern counterpart in the methods by which politicians, civil servants and others obtained former settler farms in the Rift Valley after independence and then carved them up among 'relatives', and in the means by which some households investing in land-purchasing co-operatives in the Rift Valley ended up with land, while their fellow co-operators ended up with worthless pieces of paper.[28]

2. Some Case Studies

So far I have devoted a great deal of space to the thematic treatment of production in Kenya up to 1952 and the consequences of changing forms and relations of production for differentiation among households. At this point I wish to pull this data together, and give what has hitherto been a rather abstract and analytical discussion a certain colour, by presenting a number of biographical sketches of individuals who became 'upwardly mobile' (as the bourgeois theorists say) by these methods and mechanisms in the period being considered.

1. *Daniel Odindo: Businessman and Chief of Asembo Location (Central Kavirondo) from 1917 to 1931.*
Educated at Maseno Church Missionary Society school in Central Kavirondo which he appears to have entered in 1903. After leaving school in 1908, he worked at the District Office under District Commissioner John Ainsworth 'helping in the tax assessments, attending the district court and travelling with the commissioner on his tours of inspection'. Returned to his father's chiefdom of Asembo in 1912 and on his own initiative issued a Swahili 'Book of Instructions' to the elders of the chiefdom. 'They were to help in tax collection, in encouraging the planting of groundnuts, sesame and cotton and in the cultivation of bananas and potatoes to feed touring officials. All tribunal decisions were to be taken down in writing. He also demanded the full co-operation of the "clothed persons . . . men of sense". They were to lay out roads and to play at least as full a part in his father's councils as the elders. The various headmen were to make every effort to send their sons to school, to learn the "customs of the country". These customs were the customs of Europeans, and included the respectful gesture of doffing one's hat to a superior. He admitted that the Luo traditionally had good customs, but not this one. Finally, every-

28. See Leys, op. cit., pp. 89–93.

one must wear clothes; those without them had to meet with him each week to be taught the new customs. At these meetings they would discuss whether "the country is going backward or forward. With the government we can get experience and can push the country properly forwards."' Succeeded his father as chief in Asembo in 1917. From 1921 he ran a fish transport business supplying the Miwani sugar company inland from Kisumu with 2,000 dried fish from Lake Victoria monthly as part of worker rations. Resigned from his chiefship in June 1931 after his brother and cousin, who worked as baraza and location clerks in his chiefship, were prosecuted and convicted for misappropriation of public funds. Subsequently he himself was prosecuted for similar offences and convicted, being sentenced to eighteen months' hard labour.

2. *Yona Arao: Chief of Sagan and Kisumu from 1917 to 1950*

Also attended the Church Missionary Society School at Maseno, and was a classmate of Odindo's. Accompanied an early missionary, Archbishop Willis, to Buganda, and acted as his servant and teacher of the Luo language. Helped Willis translate the New Testament into Luo. Succeeded his uncle Ogola as Chief in 1917. Thus he denied the chiefship to his cousin *Joel Omino*, son of Ogola, who had been with him at Maseno. Omino himself subsequently became a schoolmaster at Maseno, the typist to the Young Kavirondo Association (first 'political' association in west Kenya, founded in 1921), clerk to the Local Native Council and Veterinary Department, and in 1961 the first African chairman of the Central Nyanza African District Council.

3. *Paul Agoi: Chief of Maragoli from 1940 to 1950*

Born in South Maragoli, and attended the local Friends Missionary Society school. On leaving school became a domestic servant with the District Commissioner and accompanied him on tour. Subsequently employed as one of the tribal 'retainers' of Chief Munubi of Maragoli, and was appointed headman after the first world war. Set up a water-powered maize mill (the first in North Kavirondo) with a loan of £20 from the Native Trust Fund administered by the District Commissioner. The mill started operating in 1926. Became Chairman of the North Kavirondo Branch of the Kavirondo Taxpayers' Welfare Association (which succeeded the Young Kavirondo Association in 1923), and in this capacity had 'a number of skirmishes' with the Administration. However, 'the granting of increased responsibility soon drew him over the uncertain boundary between opposition and participation. In the 1930s he was one of the most valued members of the North Kavirondo Local Native Council and president of the district's appeal tribunal. In 1937 he reached the apotheosis of colonial responsibility by entertaining the governor to tea. And by the time of his appointment to the chiefship in 1940 he appears to have concluded that real progress could come only in association with the government.'

John Paul Olola: Chairman and Founder of the Kisumu Native Chamber of Commerce.

Born in the Alego location of Central Kavirondo. Employed as a domestic servant by a European police officer 'in the early years of the century'. When with his employer in Mombasa he went to Buxton High School in his off-duty hours. One of the first Luo to have a good command of English. In 1913 became clerk at the government experimental farm at Kibos in Central Kavirondo, and then became a senior headman of the farm. Subsequently became an itinerant agricultural instructor, and in this position 'was one of the first Luo to be employed in a responsible position by a central government department'. Was very critical of the conservatism and ignorance of some chiefs in their attitudes toward agriculture. Set up a model farm on his own holding on which he grew cashew nuts, maize, sisal, oranges, guavas and pineapples and made daily meteorological recordings. A firm believer in individual private enterprise, and very hostile to attempted state regulation of agriculture, and to chiefs whose own business interests were supported and protected by the Administration. Set up the Kisumu Native Chamber of Commerce in 1927. In 1946 Olola helped Oginga Odinga to set up the Luo Thrift and Trading Corporation, a detailed history of which can be found in Odinga's *Not Yet Uhuru.*

5. *Canon Jeremiah Awori*

Awori was born in Samia in Central Kavirondo in 1895 at the same time that the bones of an early European missionary, Bishop Hannington, were being carried through Samia from Buganda on their way to Mombasa. He was therefore nicknamed *Mzungu* (European) by his family. His father, an elephant hunter of some repute who had come to Samia from Marach in North Kavirondo in 1890, died in 1910, and the young Awori was brought up by an uncle Ayienga. 'When the first missionaries sent to work in the Nyanza area came across the African boy named Mzungu and discovered the association of his birth with the remains of a missionary, the temptation to recruit him was too great to be resisted,' and Awori went to the Church Missionary Society mission at Butere in North Kavirondo in 1913 and was trained for the ministry by 1925. His eldest son W. W. W. Awori was a leading nationalist figure of the 1950s, and his other sons include an oil company personnel manager, a civil engineer, an F.R.C.S. Glasgow-trained surgeon, a lawyer, a bank executive and several primary school teachers. In addition, in gratitude to the care given him by Ayienga, and despite the latter's opposition to his own schooling and that of his own sons, Awori paid the school fees and other educational expenses of two of Ayienga's sons, one of whom was an MP in the first independent Kenyan parliament, and the other of whom is a sub-chief. In the early sixties Jeremiah Awori himself was still officially regarded as a progressive farmer, with some ten acres of land, and a cotton crop which required six labourers to tend.

6. *Kitadi Mwendwa*

Born in Kitui in the late nineteenth century, he left home 'when quite young' and became a government *askari* (guard or policeman) in 1903, and chief in 1904. His advice to his sons, recounted by M. K. Mwendwa, Kenya's Chief Justice, has become a well-known item of Kenyan historiography. He is said to have told them (in regard to the British) that Africans had to be 'like a reed in the water'. 'A reed in the water watches and when there is a fast flow of water it lies low and waits for calmer waters and then rises and breathes fresh air again and grows.' This collaborator's creed appears to have stood him and his family in good stead. Kitadi Mwendwa had seven wives and twelve sons, three of whom died when young. Of the nine alive in 1974, all had had some formal education and three of them had been to Alliance High School and Makerere College Uganda, and in 1974 were a Cabinet Minister, Chief Education Officer and Chief Justice respectively.

7. *P. J. Muinde and J. J. Nyagah*

P. J. Muinde, a Kamba, was born in 1920, went to Alliance High School and was a senior executive with the East African Railways and Harbours Corporation in 1974. His father was a stock trader, a convert of the African Inland Mission, and one of its earliest teachers, who had helped found a number of mission out-schools in Kamba country. He subsequently became a Local Native Council councillor and president of the African court. J. J. (Jeremiah) Nyagah was also born in 1920, attended Alliance High School and became a cabinet minister in 1974. His father, an Embu, left his home district in 1910 and walked to a sisal estate at Mazeras, near Mombasa, where he learnt to read and write. He returned to Embu in 1916 when he was one of only six literate members of the Embu people, and began work as a teacher for the Church Missionary Society mission. He worked as a teacher for the Church Missionary Society in Embu for twenty-two years and helped found much of the network of schools which spread literacy across the district.

8. *Simeon Kiplang'at arap Baliach: Chief of Longisa Location (Location 15) in Kericho District 1929–1958*

Born in 1892 in Mungango locality of Longisa location in the Sot division of Kericho district, and named Kimosop as a child. Both his parents died shortly after his birth, and he was brought up by an uncle's wife who treated him badly. When quite young he left home for Masailand, and became an overseer on a settler-owned ranch raising horses and ostriches.[29] He went on to join E

---

29. Before the first world war there were a number of ostrich ranches in Kenya, capitalising on a contemporary European fashion in women's hats and dresses. Most had disappeared by 1918 with the fashion.

company of the 3rd Battalion of the King's African Rifles (an all-Kalenjin company) in 1913, a decision which seems to have been partly motivated by the desire to acquire the military skills which would enable him to 'avenge the injustices' being inflicted on the Kipsigis people at that time by a particularly rapacious district officer. When war broke out he served in Voi 'Digoland' (the Coast Province), Tanga, Taveta and Kilimanjaro, and toward the end of the war was promoted to Regimental Sergeant Major. He continued in the Army reserve after the war and served in the Northern Frontier Province among other places. Throughout this whole period he appears to have been illiterate, but in 1926 whilst taking a letter from the Army Reserve to be read 'by the mission people' he found a Kipsigis preacher from Buret preaching to some labourers on the road. Arap Baliach was impressed by the preacher's neat attire and manner, and thus decided to join the Local World Gospel Mission as an adherent. He was baptised Simeon by them. In 1926 too, he joined the recently formed Kipsigis Local Native Council, and served on it until 1929, when he was appointed chief in Longisa Location after his predecessor had been dismissed for failing to turn out labourers for road work. He had married soon after the war and sent all his five sons to the Kabianga Government School. He seems to have been zealous as a chief in attempting to reduce stock thieving and in more or less coercing parents to send or keep their children at school, threatening them with forced sale of their stock to pay school fees. He also took strong measures against the Kipsigis custom of killing the children of women made pregnant before initiation and marriage, against the practice of ostracising women whose children frequently died (an ostracism mainly practised by other women), and the eating of animals which had died from unknown causes. He was one of the first Kipsigis to own a plough (which he seems to have acquired in the late twenties), and to build a house of 'modern' style, spacious, rectangular and with European-style doors and windows. When he first started work as a chief he earned Shs. 50 a month, but this was subsequently raised to Shs. 150, when the number of chiefships in Kipsigis was reduced to six. In addition to ox ploughing, arap Baliach was one of the first men in Sot division to fence in his land (probably in the 1940s), and just before his retirement led a group of Kipsigis pressing for the right to grow coffee. During the term of his chiefship he paid a wartime visit to Burma, and was awarded two merit certificates and a 'badge of honour' by the colonial administration. He was present at Jinja in Uganda in 1954 when Queen Elizabeth opened the Jinja power station and was presented to her. Predictably enough he was strongly anti-Mau-Mau throughout his period of office. One of his sons, Kabaliach, became clerk to his father, and was appointed headman after independence. It should also be noted that this account is drawn from Arap Baliach's brief biography written from interview sources by his grandson, Kipkoech Motonik arap Korir, and published in the Kenya Historical Review in 1974 when the latter was still a sixth-form pupil at Alliance High School.

9. *The Beginning of Plough Cultivation of Maize in the Buret Location of Kipsigis District (the account dates from 1958)*

'In 1931 a young, mission-trained Kipsigis in the vicinity of Cheborge in Buret Location acquired a plow and prepared about five acres of land for maize on the slope below his hut. Contravening accepted practice, he did not fence his newly planted fields. When his neighbour's animals wandered into the field, he threatened the owners with court action. Individually, and with the authority of the *kokwet* elders supporting them, they tried to persuade the young man to put a fence around his plot. They even offered to assist him in its construction. But he was adamant and suggested they could avoid difficulties with him if they planted their own plots of millet right up to the borders of his maize. In this way their animals would be kept out of his fields. The neighbours finally complied, and the following year—as was customary—they abandoned their plots after they had harvested their crops of millet. The mission-trained Kipsigis promptly extended his maize cultivation into the areas just cleared of millet. There were no grounds for objecting, for such fields were customarily abandoned and let lie fallow for several years after which they reverted to the use of anyone who wanted them for the planting of millet.

'By 1935 the young man had enlarged the area of his maize cultivation to something over 25 acres, fenced off the earliest areas of cultivation for a paddock —thus reviving the soil through natural manuring—and in subsequent years, by a judicious expansion of fencing, maize cultivation, and rotation of paddocks, he had amassed and enclosed between 250 and 300 acres of land. The pattern of permanent, individual tenure, which had in this particular case been established largely through use of the plow and cultivation of maize as a cash crop, soon spread throughout the Reserve until today there is virtually not a square foot of unclaimed land.

'Meanwhile the mission-trained Kipsigis had built two water mills for grinding maize, one on the river below his fields and another at Chemosit on the main road between Sotik and Kericho, some ten miles from Cheborge. He sold the maize he himself grew to Asian traders and to the tea estates. For grinding the maize of other Kipsigis he charged a fee in the form of a small percentage of the shelled maize. He bought a wagon for transporting his grain to the trading centers and markets and built a road to help him get it there. Later he acquired a truck for the transport of his grain. Within recent years he bought a passenger car and has built on the site of his old hut a brick house with several rooms and casement windows of glass and steel. He wears western suits, good shoes, shirts with neckties, and owns a warehouse and two general merchandise shops which are run for him by hired employees.

'He uses his money to educate his children and for the purchase of up-to-date equipment and farm machinery. The fruits of his enterprise are material comfort and prestige. The neighbourhood of which his farm is a part includes a high percentage of 'better farmers' (a term used by the District Agricultural Officer to designate and honour those who practise advanced methods of cultivation, house betterment, etc.) who have certainly learned from his example. And he is one of several outstanding Kipsigis leaders in the Reserve whose activities not only reflect the growing importance and use of money but who have served, by their example, to accelerate the tempo of emulation, to increase cash-mindedness, and to speed the drive for acquisition of Western commodities among their tribesmen.'

10. *Harry Thuku*

Harry Thuku's life story is one of the best known in Kenyan historiography, so only its outlines will be included here, primarily to exemplify a not unfamiliar transition from 'radicalism' to 'conservatism', and partly to show once again the sort of economic activities which distinguished virtually all the Kenyan petite bourgeoisie in the colonial period, whatever their political or official positions. Harry Thuku was born in the Kambui area of the Kiambu district in 1895, and was a part of the Mbari wa Gathirimu, a descendant of Gathirimu, one of the most powerful Kikuyu leaders of the mid-nineteenth century. He obtained instruction at the Gospel Missionary Society which arrived in Kambui in 1902, and to which Thuku originally went as a boy of twelve in an attempt to get a job to save up for 'a cloth'. He stayed at the mission from 1907 to 1911, and had a series of part-time jobs there, but also received a basic education, was converted to christianity and baptised. He went to Nairobi in 1911 to look for work but finding none went to jail for two years for attempting to forge a cheque. On release he worked as a hut counter in Suk and Turkana, and then as a compositor and machine-minder in Nairobi until 1917. This was followed by a spell as a Post Office telegraphist and despatch clerk also in Nairobi. It was in this period (1917–20) that he came into contact with a number of Indians, Bugandans and Swahilis in Nairobi who were interested in politics, and himself became politically active. In July 1921 he played a leading role in forming the East African Association, a pan-tribal grouping of mainly Nairobi-based Africans. The East African Association addressed itself to a range of African grievances of the period, notably land alienation, wage cuts introduced as a result of a currency change, and the *kipande* or registration system. After a number of speeches in which Thuku called for Africans to throw away their registration cards and containers, and said that communal or forced labour for the Administration should be refused, he was arrested. His arrest and detention in Nairobi police station led to a city-wide strike and riot by Africans in March 1922 in which twenty-one people were shot by police. Thuku then spent ten years in detention in various remote parts of Kenya, beginning in Kismayu in Jubaland (1922–5), and continuing, after brief periods at Lamu and Witu on the Coast, at Marsabit in the Northern Frontier Province. There he became a particular friend of the District Commissioner, Major Sharpe, who encouraged him to start farming on the good land immediately surrounding the station. 'The soil was good, and with his war-saving bonuses for initial capital, Thuku was soon farming four to five acres in maize and sweet potatoes. Labour was cheap, there was a co-operative Sikh who ground the maize into meal, and Thuku was soon making a nice little profit from his investment.' Out of the profits Thuku bought two horses, learned to ride them, and sometimes had them ridden in competition with some horses belonging to the District Commissioner. Sharpe also encouraged Thuku to take an interest in forestry and tree planting, and suggested that he take what he had learned back to Kikuyuland on his release. He was finally released from detention in December 1930, and he returned to his home at Kambui. Thereafter he tried to reinvolve himself in politics, but in the interval of eight years a new generation of African politicians had arisen, organised in the Kikuyu Central Association headed by Johnston (later Jomo) Kenyatta. Thuku seems to have been suspicious of what he took to be the 'disloyal' or 'unconstitutional' methods of protest which he thought the Kikuyu Central Association willing to use, and after an abortive attempt to set up his own counter-organisation he gradually faded out of politics, and became more and more interested in farming and the acquisition of land. He had been given some land by his brother Kigume on his return to Kambui and by 1935 he had some twenty-five acres and had turned *ahoi* off other land in his possession. Throughout the thirties and forties however he accumulated ceaselessly, buying even very small fragments if they were contiguous to his holding. In addition he built himself an imposing house with a tree-lined drive (Sharpe's teaching had stuck), and drove a car, first a Nash tourer, then a Dodge pick-up. His farm became a showpiece for the Agricultural Department. He practised crop rotation, and soil conservation, and was one of the first Kikuyu to take to the intensive stall-feeding and rearing of grade dairy cows. His increasingly rare entries into the political arena were usually in support of the Administration, though he remained a strong supporter of African educational progress. Once again, and very predictably, he was a fierce opponent of Mau-Mau in the 1950s, and his openly expressed loyalism (he broadcast against Mau-Mau on the radio) and his status as an early proto-nationalist led to several attempts on his life. Nonetheless he benefitted enormously from rewards to loyalists, being one of the first to have his considerable landholdings consolidated with freehold title deeds, and then entering coffee growing on a large scale, being exempted from the beginning from the limit of one hundred bushes which the Agricultural Department laid down as the initial allotment to growers. In applying for a licence to grow coffee, and stating that he would not accept the hundred bush limit, Thuku said 'I don't refuse to plant coffee but look at your hand—one finger is short, one thin, one fat, etc.—but all are different. The Government Agricultural Department is trying to make us all equal so I am not interested.' By the time of his death in 1970 he had fifty-six acres of land under coffee alone, his own coffee factory and his own nursery, and his wife—whom he had sent to England for two years' education with an agricultural bias—was well able to succeed him as farm manager.

1. *Two Kikuyu Students at Makerere College, Uganda in 1960* *(in the source used the students involved are anonymous)*

1. Born in Nyeri in 1939. His paternal and maternal grandparents were illiterate. His father however was a mission convert, probably with the Church Missionary Society, and was the first man in his part of Nyeri to receive a Standard VIII education. His mother had received a Standard VII education. Both parents had worked as mission teachers, and his father did so all his life. Up until the Emergency in 1952 this student's father had been a comparatively wealthy man, having not only his teacher's salary of Shs. 60 per month (in 1952) but also an income from 'farming, milk and agricultural product sales which were inflated by war time demand'. In addition, though the student's family were the only Christian family 'within four or five miles', his father had still been sufficiently cognisant of Kikuyu custom to become an *mbari muramati*. However, with the onset of the Emergency his father's loyalism made the family very unpopular and they were moved by the government to the Rift Valley where his father became a chief. Even there his house was burned down, but his chief's salary enabled him to sustain the loss. His father had two brothers, neither of whom had any education, though one of his mother's brothers was literate in Kikuyu and Swahili. Of the father's brothers one had his entire income in 1960 from a plot of land 'allotted' to him by the subject's father (presumably in his role as *muramati*), and the other was at that date a 'foreman' on a settler farm and 'owned' one hundred acres of land (which presumably means he was a squatter). In contrast, the subject's two brothers had both received some formal education, one having completed the school certificate and become a bank clerk, and the other (in 1960) still being in primary school. The subject made particular mention of the advantage he had received in school from having been tutored by his mother before he even began in the first primary class.

2. Born in Kiambu in 1936. This student's father was also a mission convert and this time the source allows us to identify the mission as the African Inland Mission at Kijabe. His father also received a Standard VIII education and was literate in Kikuyu, Swahili and English. His mother was literate in Kikuyu and Swahili. The student's father worked as an English translator at the Kijabe Mission until 1940, when he took up employment with the Forestry Department as a clerk and a guard. The Department made several plots of land available to him as part of his remuneration, and his mother began to work these expanded landholdings with hired female labour. They specialised in producing vegetables for sale in Nairobi. The student stated that prior to his father's change of employment and the access to land which it had brought, the family had not been noticeably better off than relatives, but from the forties onwards they were, and quarrels broke out 'perhaps' (according to the student) 'because [the new income] was not being shared enough according to traditional custom'. Up until this time the family had been based on their traditional land in Kiambu, but as a result of these quarrels his father moved his mother and the children

completely to the forest land in 1947. Unlike the case above, this student's father was a Mau-Mau sympathiser and was detained from 1952 to 1956. He appears to have been able to weather this, and by 1960 had been able to obtain an eighteen acre consolidated plot of land in Kiambu district producing tea and pyrethrum. It appears that all this student's family were African Inland Mission converts including all the brothers and sisters of his father and mother, most of whom had some education. The student himself had two brothers and nine sisters in 1960, all of whom had some formal education, the lowest level attained by any of them being Standard V. It is interesting to note that this complete immersion in a mission environment appeared in 1960 to have turned this student away from Christianity, principally it seems because his father, though a monogamist, had treated his mother very badly; by 1960 she had left him.

12. *Two Kikuyu Vegetable Growers in the Kiambaa Location of Kiambu district, near Nairobi.*

(Once again the men are anonymous in the source, simply being designated 'A' and 'B'.) The research on which the accounts are based was carried out in 1970–1.

'Farmer A is about seventy years old. (He was circumcised in 1922.) He started off life as a 'teacher', having attended Kiambaa primary school in 1917–20. But the pay was not good, and, dissatisfied with the meagre wages, he set out to make an independent living. He started farming with very little capital: "I . . . bought tomato seeds worth Shs. 5. When they grew, I did not sell the tomatoes. I took out the seeds and replanted them again. I got Shs. 4,000. I am prepared to buy one seedling for Shs. 2,000 if I know I will get more money out of it."

'So, with characteristic daring spirit, and great imagination, he set about growing vegetables and, more significantly, flowers, around the year 1924. It must be realized that even for an area as close to Nairobi as Banana Hill, this was a revolutionary thing to do at such a period. For a start, the road to Limuru had not even been built, and transport was on foot. And most people grew the traditional foodstuffs, not for sale but for consumption. Only as late as 1935 did the people of the area begin selling bananas along the Limuru Road as it was being constructed.

'. . . By all accounts of his neighbours, Farmer A was singled out as the one who introduced horticulture in the area. Farmer B learnt from him in 1934. His reputation was such that in the thirties and forties he was classified on a par with the richest Government officials of the time.

'Currently, Farmer A owns 9.5 acres. Although this is registered in his name, three of his sons have all built their houses on the farm—one a very impressive stone building, the others fairly modest wooden bungalows, well kept with clean flower gardens. Mr A is in the process of building his own permanent stone house. Thus, although Mr A has a wife and eleven children, the farm occupancy rate is higher than would be expected of a holding the size of 9.5 acres. Mr A does not own land elsewhere, either in the Rift Valley or in Riara Ridge. His land was inherited, and he has his title deed.

'Farmer B is about sixty years old and knows that he was born in 1910. Like Farmer A, he too went to Kiambaa Primary School, and then proceeded to High School till 1929, when he left because of lack of money for school fees. He too, started off as a teacher at a monthly pay of about Shs. 24.

'However, after teaching for ten years and farming on the side he decided to retire from teaching and take up farming full time. Meanwhile, he had learnt how to grow flowers from Farmer A and was growing various flowers such as roses and carnations by 1937. By this year he was also keeping pigs (which was illegal for Africans, but nevertheless profitable to sell to local butchers). By 1944, flower growing became such a hazard because of theft—thieves would invade the Shamba by night and transport the flowers to Nairobi—that Mr B has since concentrated on vegetables, notably strawberries, mushrooms and asparagus. Mr B keeps a ledger where he records in great detail the various crops he has grown and fertilizers he has used since 1934.

'Currently, Farmer B owns twelve acres in the sub-location, but has use of his brother's land of about three acres, and owns some shares in a Co-operative Farm in the Rift Valley, with six other partners. So in all, he uses about fifteen acres for his farming. His compound is immaculately clean—well mowed lawns and three impressive stone buildings, with electricity, telephone and a T. V. in his brother's house. His wife is a teacher, and helps with the farming. Besides farming, Farmer B keeps a little shop at Banana Hill, but he admits he is primarily a farmer'.

13. *Musa Nyandusi: Chief of Nyaribari Location, Kisii*

Musa Barare Nyandusi was educated at the Seventh Day Adventists' Mission in Kisii (Nyanchwa), and was made chief of Nyaribari Location in 1927, after working as a mission school teacher for several years. In 1926, he had been the first African in Kisii to open up a water-powered maize mill, and in 1930, encouraged by District Commissioner C. E. V. Buxton, he became one of the first Africans in Kisii to plant Arabica coffee on his land. His brother, Samson Ongaki was also one of the earliest coffee growers. The first ton of parchment coffee exported from Kisii district in 1937 all came from Musa's own plantation. In addition to his own coffee (and pyrethrum) growing activities, Musa was an enthusiastic supporter of African education, personally donating the land on which Kisii High School was built and playing a leading part in obtaining Local Native Council funding for five other primary schools in his location. By 1943 Nyaribari was the leading coffee-producing location in Kisii and in addition to being a large land owner, coffee grower, maize mill owner and running his own car and lorry, Musa became the Chairman of the Kisii Growers' Co-operative Society in 1946.

14. *D. L. Mutiso and David Kaindi of Machakos*

D. L. Mutiso from Mbooni location in Machakos district left school in 1928 and went to Murera sisal estate in Coast Province to work. He was taught to drive tractors and lorries, and after two years left to become a driver on a Nairobi building site. In the mid-thirties he returned to Mbooni and using a hired lorry began carrying wattle bark from Mbooni to Nziu. He estimated that he made a profit of Shs. 150 on every five-ton load. He left the wattle transport trade in 1943 and hired shop premises where he began a tailoring business which he claimed made him more profit than the wattle trade. When interviewed in the early 1970s he was the owner of a petrol station in Mbooni.

'David Kaindi, before becoming Chief of Mbooni, had worked as a houseboy, hide seller, Veterinary and Local Native Council clerk. As a clerk in the late 1920s, he used the money "for buying land because my father had very little. I bought land very cheaply and continued buying, some for Shs. 12, some Shs. 40, some Shs. 100. I bought a plough in about 1930 at Machakos ... I had been shown a plough by the people of Matungulu who were very clever when I was working for the Local Native Council." In his description, as of so many others, the change was dramatic. "When I began with the plough I had no profit but then I became a big farmer and was known, I sold maize to the Indians at Mbooni and Tawa." And it was from this basis that he branched out to become a shop owner.'[30]

30. Sources of biographies, by number:
 1. Lonsdale, op. cit., pp. 319–21 and CKAR 1929, p. 6.
 2. Lonsdale, op. cit., pp. 316 and 321–2.
 3. Ibid., p. 316 and pp. 324–6.
 4. Ibid., pp. 335–7 and Wagner, op. cit., Vol. II, pp. 175–6.
 5. B. E. Kipkorir, 'The Alliance High School and the Origins of the Kenya African Elite 1926–62' (unpublished Ph. D. thesis, Cambridge, 1969), pp. 107–8 and John Lonsdale, communication with the author.
 6. Kipkorir, op. cit., pp. 108–9.
 7. Ibid., pp. 109–10.
 8. Kipkoech Motonik arap Korir, 'An Outline Biography of Simeon Kiplang'at arap Baliach, a "Colonial African Chief" from Kipsigis', *Kenya History Review*, vol. 2, no. 2, 1974, pp. 163–73.
 9. Robert A. Manners, op. cit., pp. 505–7.
 10. Harry Thuku, *An Autobiography*, op. cit., and Kenneth King, 'A Biography of Harry Thuku', in K. King and A. Salim (eds.) *Kenya Historical Biographies* (Nairobi, 1971).
 11. M. Stanley, 'Heritage of Change' (EAISR Paper, June 1961), pp. 13–26.
 12. J. Karuga, 'Thresholds in the transformation of an economy—some preliminary thoughts on the structure of the Nairobi/Kiambu peri-urban zone: the case of Kiambaa Location', in *Strategies for Improving Rural Welfare* (IDS Occasional Paper, no. 4, 1971), pp. 208–15.
 13. William R. Ochieng, 'Colonial African Chiefs—Were They Primarily Self-Seeking Scound-

These cases all come from the increasing body of research in social history in Kenya, which has come to utilise biographical material based on personal recollection to an ever greater extent. It is not difficult to see why. Such accounts encapsulate a sense of development and change effortlessly, for they give a picture of the individual both adapting to, and making his own contribution toward the social change going on around him. In selecting from the material available I have chosen some extremely well-known cases (like the Awori or Mwendwa families and Harry Thuku) who, along with other families like the Koinanges and Waiyakis of Kiambu, the Boits of Nandi or the Ngairas of western Kenya (and of course the family of Jomo Kenyatta himself), constitute what might be called the topmost political and economic elite of Kenyan Africans.[31] But I have also included some lesser-known figures who nonetheless still enjoyed a position of some privilege in the colonial period, and whose offspring as a result often enjoy such privilege in present-day Kenya. Much more material of this sort needs to be gathered, and to be made as detailed as possible to shed as much light as possible on the mechanisms of upward mobility. But even with the material currently available it is not difficult to see the common strands running through much diversity.

Most obviously we see a universal factor of early access to formal education, usually through mission schools. The amount of education received does not have to have been great, and the earlier the period at which it was acquired, the less was necessary. Given such access, individuals then had opportunities to obtain the better-paid jobs which were available to Africans from the beginning of the colonial period, an opportunity strengthened by the fact that the very process of gaining an education often brought individual Africans into contact with Europeans (missionaries, district officers and others) who could continue thereafter to act as their patrons. Subsequently, having obtained the wages and salaries which by their size and their reliability would sustain an effort at saving, investments could be made in land and business. As we have already suggested, if the job in question was a chiefship or headmanship, or even a clerkship in local government or elsewhere, extra sources of income, more or less illegal but in certain circumstances winked at by colonial authority, were readily available.

What so many of these biographies point to is a sort of rugged individualism, a toughness, perseverance, and creative drive to take full advantage of the limited opportunities open to Africans in the colonial period,[32] even if the initial

rels?', in Bethwell A. Ogot (ed.), *Politics and Nationalism in Colonial Kenya* (Nairobi, 1972), pp. 59–60, and R. M. Maxon, op. cit.

14. Newman, op. cit., pp. 10 and 18.

31. Kipkorir, op. cit., p. 109. For some data on the wealth of the Kenyatta family, see John Barry, 'How Jomo's royal family grabbed the nation's wealth', *Sunday Times*, 17 August 1975, p. 5.

32. I have not included perhaps the most outstanding example of this yet recorded, the story of Mutisya Munge and Mwambetu Mutisya (his son) in the growth of Kamba wood carving. See W. Elkan. 'The Kamba Trade in Wood Carvings' (*EAISR*, 1958).

event which opened up that opportunity (access to formal education) often occurred more or less by accident. All these men would have pleased Samuel Smiles, and a certain pride in their own achievements is one of their most outstanding characteristics when one meets them. Moreover such men are often greatly admired in their own communities, and there is an almost universal desire to emulate them, a desire which in present-day Kenya fuels the demand for education facilities, and brings intense popular pressure on the government to expand employment opportunities for the educated. In addition, the experience of succeeding against the odds, by a mixture of good luck, initiative and ruthlessness, colours the attitude of most successful African families in Kenya to the poor. They very often see the responsibility of the poor as being to emulate the successful, and to make their way in the world by their own efforts, an individualistic attitude which is understandable among men who have themselves been born in poverty, or whose fathers were. They refuse to recognise that their own success (and that of thousands of others like them) has altered the conditions which made such advancement historically possible. I will discuss the theoretical grounds for this last assertion in later chapters; but here one may simply say that the widespread presence of this sort of attitude toward the poor among the elite of present-day Kenya (an attitude which I believe was present even in the colonial period but was temporarily submerged in the nationalist struggle) is one of the most marked aspects of present-day Kenya.

In speaking of the 'elite' of present-day or colonial Kenya, I wish to avoid the usual connotation of this term which suggests that what is being referred to is a very narrow stratum of extremely rich or powerful people concentrated in the capital city. Both now and at the end of the colonial period, virtually every small community in rural Kenya has or had one (and usually more than one) family whose relatively privileged position was recognised by relatives, friends and strangers alike. The household heads involved might be shopkeepers, primary school teachers, the local dispensary dresser, a successful trader, a civil servant or clerk, or a highly skilled and well-paid artisan, but almost invariably the greater wealth of their households would be signalled to all around by the quality of the houses in which they lived, the size of their landholdings, the clothes their families wore to church on Sunday, and the number of children they sent to school. From being in the earliest years of the colonial period a despised or feared minority of 'mission families' these households slowly became the 'reference group' for the entire African population, until today it is the aim of every household head to win such '*heshima*' (a Swahili concept combining notions of both honour and status) and to demonstrate it in these ways.

At a society level one may call this stratum what one likes. I have chosen the term 'petite bourgeoisie'. One may prefer 'middle class'. The terminology is less important than the recognition of the ubiquity of the stratum and its relative privilege. This petite bourgeoisie itself is highly differentiated internally by both wealth and power, with the Kenyatta family at one end of the spectrum, and a primary school teacher or shopkeeper and his family at the other. I wish to argue however that it is far less important to have an agreed terminology for the group as a whole, or indeed to find terminology to sub-divide the group, than to understand theoretically its mode of access to resources and the use to which it puts those resources. An understanding of this in turn leads on to a number of crucial issues affecting the likely pattern of development in Kenya and the limitations upon that development. Such an analysis requires the use of a Marxist perspective and ultimately the specification of classes and class relations in Kenya, but this, as a later chapter will argue, involves a rather different analytical procedure to that usually identified with Marxist 'class analysis' in Africa.

PART THREE

KENYA'S 'AGRARIAN REVOLUTION':
MYTH AND REALITY 1952–1970

Chapter XI

An 'Agrarian Revolution':
Agricultural Production and Rural Stratification in Kenya 1952-1970

1. Introduction

The following two chapters complete the description and analysis of social and economic change in Kenya up to 1970. In this narrative the onset of juridical independence for Kenya in 1963 is hardly mentioned, for the simple reason that as far as the issues dealt with in this chapter are concerned, Independence made little or no structural difference, there being (as indeed there was intended to be) considerable continuity of socio-economic trends from the colonial to the post-colonial period. The narrative is taken up to 1970 to demonstrate this point.

As against the detailed description of social and economic change in the period 1905–52 which has characterised Parts I and II of this book, these two chapters will only provide the most schematic description of general trends in the economy, and will instead concentrate directly on the impact of the trends and changes described, on differentiation among African households. The reason for this is two-fold. In the first place this period of Kenyan economic history is comprehensively covered in the secondary literature, and I have no wish to repeat the work of others.[1] In the second place I wish to argue that for all the apparent changes which came over the rural and urban scene in the period considered, so far as the pattern of differentiation between Africans is concerned the essential parameters had been laid down by 1952. After 1952 there was a speeding-up of the process of differentiation, particularly after Independence, when some African households gained privileged access to the resources of the state. With this speeding-up, there was also a widening of the relative gap between the richest and poorest African households, as some gained access to the very highest incomes and to forms of wealth which had previously been

---

1. See for example Sorrenson, *Land Reform* . . . , op. cit.; C. Rosberg and J. Nottingham, *The Myth of Mau Mau: Nationalism in Kenya* (New York, 1966); Judith Heyer, J. K. Maitha and W. M. Senga (eds.) *Agricultural Development in Kenya: An Economic Assessment* (Nairobi, 1976); Leys, op. cit.; Marris and Somerset, op. cit.; ILO, *Employment, Incomes and Equality: A strategy for increasing productive employment in Kenya* (Geneva, 1972) (hereafter '*ILO Report*'); Kenneth King, op. cit.

monopolised by Europeans and Asians. Despite this speeding-up and intensification of the process of differentiation, the mechanisms of income and wealth accumulation remained largely unchanged, and in particular the essential mechanism of using access to large off-farm incomes in order to save and invest in land, agricultural production and off-farm business remained the touchstone of accumulation and differentiation. It was for this reason that 'Africanisation' of large parts of the Kenyan state apparatus after Independence speeded up the process of differentiation in the countryside as well as in the town. This latter issue is considered from a theoretical point of view in chapter XIII, 'The State as Merchant Capital'.

In the two chapters which follow, therefore, I shall concentrate on the following empirical issues:
1. The description and analysis of inequality in landholdings, farm income and off-farm income among Kenyan households in the period considered.
2. Changes in the size and structure of the wage labour force in Kenya and the impact of these on inter-household stratification.
3. Changes in African trade and business in the period to 1970, and the impact of these on inequality.

Of these issues, (1) is dealt with in this chapter and (2) and (3) in the following chapter.

In order to set the discussion of issue (1) in some sort of context it is necessary to outline, however schematically, the changes which came over Kenyan agriculture between 1952 and 1970. Essentially these can be summed up as a process of land consolidation and enclosure on the one hand, and the adoption of new higher-value crops by African cultivators on the other (coffee, tea, pyrethrum and hybrid maize).

A subsidiary theme was the opening up of the former 'White Highlands' of Kenya to African cultivators by settlement schemes through which Africans were given access to land bought from departing European farmers. The largest of the settlement schemes was the so-called 'Million Acre' scheme begun in in 1962. Individual settlement schemes (for particular blocks of land within the million acres) were divided into two broad types, 'high density' schemes (in which the smallholder was supposed to attain a target income of between K£25 and K£70 per household, plus subsistence requirements and the repayment of certain loans made to him) and 'low density' schemes (in which the plot holder was set a target of subsistence, loan repayments and a minimum cash income of K£100 per annum). In practice, the high density schemes came to be peopled with landless households, many of whose heads had been active in Mau-Mau, while the low density schemes were mainly filled with households whose heads had considerable off-farm incomes, and who often already had land elsewhere.[2]

2. See John W. Harbeson, 'Land Resettlement and Development Strategy in Kenya' (*IDS*, Discussion Paper, 1967); and Gary Wasserman, 'Continuity and Counter-Insurgency: The Role of

African movement into the growing of high-value export crops, like Independence itself and the settlement schemes, were all stages in the demise of Kenya as a 'White Man's country'. The domination of the country's agricultural economy and its politics by a comparatively small group of European (mainly British) settler farmers came to an end. But they were also stages in the process by which a group of privileged Africans (politicians, civil servants and others) took over the position of Europeans in the 'large farm sector', and by which the position of European-owned commercial and industrial capital in Kenya was entrenched politically and economically, and gained the patronage and support of the new African rulers.[3] That support came at a price (in the form of shares in equity and other somewhat more dubious resource transfers), but to date it has been enthusiastic and unwavering. As self-made men, the leading politicians, civil servants and other sections of the petite bourgeoisie of Kenya were and are keen supporters of 'private enterprise'.

2. Trends in Production 1952–1970[4]

The simplest and most important trend shown by all the official agricultural statistics in this period is the startling growth in gross farm output and income on African smallholdings (including Settlement Schemes) in the period from 1952 to 1970. In the period 1958 to 1968 the gross farm revenue of African smallholders in Kenya grew from a little under K£8 million to over K£34 million, an increase of 425 per cent in a decade. The largest single item in this growth was coffee production, which was worth a little over K£1 million in 1958, and nearly K£8.5 million nine years later, when it accounted for over a quarter of gross farm revenue on smallholdings. By the late sixties production of arabica coffee on African smallholdings accounted for well over half of all Kenyan production, whereas in 1957 (when separate statistics for smallholder production began) it had accounted for just nine per cent. In absolute terms the growth was from something less than a thousand tons of clean coffee in 1955–6 to over 20,000 tons by the end of the 1960s.

There was a commensurate increase in the number of growers. Whereas at the beginning of the period under consideration only some 3,000 Africans were growing coffee on holdings covering some 11,000 acres (nearly all of them in Meru and Kisii where, it will be remembered, some limited experimentation

Land Reform in Decolonizing Kenya 1962–1970', *Canadian Journal of African Studies*, Vol. VII, No. 1, 1973, pp. 133–48.

3. See ibid.; and also Gary Wasserman, 'The Independence Bargain: Kenya Europeans and the Land Issue, 1960–62', *Journal of Commonwealth Political Studies*, July 1973. The full story is found in his Ph.D. thesis, 'The Adaptation of a Colonial Elite to Decolonization: Kenya Europeans and the Land Issue 1960–1965' (Columbia University Ph.D., 1972).

4. All data and statistics cited in the following section are drawn from *DAR* 1952–68.

with coffee growing by Africans had taken place from the 1930s), by 1968 there were over 133,000 licensed smallholder coffee growers in Kenya covering some 270,000 acres of land. By 1968 the bulk of them were in the Central Province; Kiambu, Nyeri, Fort Hall (now Muranga), Kirinyaga, Embu and Meru, with the main concentrations elsewhere being in Kisii district, and to a lesser degree Bungoma and Machakos. Of the 133,052 acres under smallholder coffee in Kenya in 1968 no less than 99,500 acres (over seventy-five per cent) were in the Central Province (which included at this date Meru and Embu districts) and over a third (48,400 acres) was in the three Kikuyu heartland districts of Kiambu, Nyeri and Muranga. In 1952 those three districts had not had a single acre under coffee.

Although the most startling change in African smallholding production (at least in terms of volume and value of output) was in coffee, this was by no means the only significant change. Smallholder production of pyrethrum flowers rose from considerably less than a hundred tons in 1952 to nearly 14,000 tons in 1968 when it was worth over K£2.5 million to growers. Official statistics show that nearly all the smallholder production came from the Central, Rift Valley and Nyanza Provinces, and in practice the bulk of the crop came from the highest altitude farms in Kiambu district, from Kisii (in the former South Nyanza district), and from settlement schemes in the pyrethrum area of the former settler Nakuru district in the Rift Valley. By 1968 African smallholders were producing ninety per cent of Kenya's total pyrethrum crop, whereas they had been producing just six per cent in 1957. In 1952 smallholder pyrethrum production had been restricted to a small area of Kiambu district.

Smallholders were not anywhere near to this level of domination of tea production by 1968, at which time they were producing only seventeen per cent of Kenya's total crop. Nonetheless, production of green leaf tea by smallholder growers had risen from less than a hundred tons in 1959 to over 5,000 tons in 1968. Once again the bulk of this production came from the Kisii highlands, the higher zones of the Aberdares in Kiambu, Muranga and Nyeri, and from the Rift Valley, notably the Kericho district.

In addition, from about 1960 onwards the introduction of grade cattle on to consolidated and/or enclosed African smallholdings (a process massively accelerated from 1963 onwards by stock sales from European settlers leaving the country) began to increase production and sales of milk and dairy produce from smallholdings. In 1967 an estimated 15,859,000 gallons of milk were sold off small farms (including settlement schemes), a figure which rose to 17,575,000 gallons in 1968. In 1968 total production amounted to some 60 million gallons, 42 million gallons of this coming from large farms; that is, small scale production accounted for some thirty per cent of the whole. Commercial production of milk on smallholdings had been negligible in 1952, was less than four per cent of total production in 1960, and only fourteen per cent of the whole in 1964, so the rapidity of growth through the sixties is clear.

Whilst the range of products produced by smallholders was expanded in these important ways, with significant results for the growth of farm output and earnings, there was nonetheless a continuity in other sectors of smallholder production. That continuity was most marked in the case of maize, which at the end of this period was still the dominant crop in the smallholder sector. In 1968 it was the third most important smallholder enterprise in terms of gross earnings after coffee and one other crop which we shall come to shortly. But in addition it remained the dominant staple crop for subsistence consumption, a severe shortfall of which could still lead to malnutrition (as it did for example in 1961 and 1966), and whose persistent and abrupt variations in supply from year to year were as much a cause of government concern in the late sixties as they had been in the forties, thirties or twenties.

In addition to maize, the production of fruit and vegetables, particularly in Kiambu, Fort Hall, Nyeri and Machakos (for the Nairobi market) and in Teita (for Mombasa), remained an important revenue earner for the small farm sector, and was supplemented by a post-war expansion of the canning industry and by the initiation of direct export flights to London for Covent Garden in 1958. The production of pulses and legumes also remained buoyant throughout the period, remaining like maize an important part of the subsistence diet with the sale of 'surpluses' off farm.

The production of cotton remained much the same difficult business that it had been up to 1952, with one significant change from about 1963 onwards, when in the face of a declining world price the Department of Agriculture once again began a campaign to expand production of cotton in the Kitui, Machakos and Embu districts of what was by this time the Eastern Province. Acreage under the crop in these areas rose from nil in 1961 to 500 acres in 1962, 4,000 acres in 1963 and over 25,000 acres by 1965. This expansion appears to have been heavily fuelled by loans to assist with cultivation and pest control, and seems to have been a response to worries among domestic textile manufacturers[5] about persistently declining production. There seems little doubt that the low returns per acre and per man hour to cotton on smallholdings remained the principal problem in expanding production of the crop (and indeed a late sixties' experiment with the production of cotton by groups of farmers on consolidated blocks — heavily backed by credit — seems to reflect this realisation). Post-war prices never reached levels which would remedy this defect, with the result that in both the Coast Province and the lakeside locations of Nyanza Province standards of cultivation remained poor, and Department of Agriculture campaigns for early planting and growth in pure stands met with little response.[6]

5. See *DAR* 1965, pp. 4 and 53; and 1966, p. 1. The marked expansion of manufacturing industry in Kenya, especially during the war, was of course an important new factor in the situation. For the beginning of a history of this, se R. van Zwanenberg, 'Industrialisation and the Growth of the Kenyan State 1929–52' (CPEK Paper, 1975).

6. *DAR* 1966, pp. 6, 10–11; and 1967, p. 16.

Wattle bark, the second largest small farm revenue earner in 1952 (after maize) underwent a marked decline in this period, largely brought about by counter-insurgency measures in Central Province from 1952. In order to build barracks, guard posts, counter-insurgency villages and other military installations, and to remove the cover from guerilla fighters, the British army cut down large areas of wattle trees within the Province. This process in itself produced a brief spurt in bark output in 1954 and 1955, but thereafter there began a more or less continuous decline in output, so that by 1966 the Kenyan Wattle Manufacturers' Association asked the Department of Agriculture to undertake a survey of wattle production to see how the '110,000 or 120,000 acres of trees which are needed to maintain an annual wattle extract of 20,000 tons per annum' could be kept in being. By the sixties the problem was not merely that of the tree destruction during the Emergency (had this been all, replanting by smallholders could have restored production fairly quickly). It was now compounded by prices for bark which fell as low as K£8 per ton (compared with over K£250 per ton at the height of the Korean boom), and by the consequent desire of smallholders to replace their wattle trees with tea, pyrethrum or even grass for intensive dairying. This price fall (there was a slight recovery at the end of the sixties) was due to the increasing replacement of leather by rubber and plastics in many commodities. The trend had become noticeable from 1955 but had been worsened by a scramble for a shrinking market in which Paraguay, Argentina and Brazil were Kenya's major competitors. A domestic result of this was that in order to prevent growers uprooting their wattle trees and dumping them on the market, the Department of Agriculture instituted a system of quota sales for each district, which were not supposed to be exceeded. Annual Reports from the early sixties onwards note persistent grower discontent with the size of the quotas, and a flourishing black market in permits for sales.[7]

The major change in the pattern of smallholder rice production occurred from 1959–60 onwards when the Mwea-Taberere settlement scheme in the Central Province took over from the Nyanza Province as the major area of smallholder production.[8]

Just as in the 1930s, it is important to recognise the hidden discontinuities behind the apparent continuity even of traditional crops. These arose from the much-expanded programme of agronomic research which was fed into the smallholder sector from the time that the Swynnerton Plan really began to bite.

7. See M. P. Cowen, 'Wattle Production ...', op. cit., pp. 90–107. The account presented of the decline here is an over-simplified one, since the matter is not central to my concerns. See for example Cowen's account of the attempt to concentrate the wattle trade in the hands of loyalists during the Emergency, Forestal's increasing switch to its own estate production during a boom in extract prices (1948–52) and then its attempts to restrict supply when from 1954 onwards world prices collapsed (hence the use of quotas, quality controls and price manipulation). See also *DAR* 1965, p. 13; 1966, p. 18; and 1967, p. 24.
8. See for example *DAR* 1961, pp. 2 and 19.

Table XI:1. Percentage of gross small
farm revenue accruing from the sale of
cattle and calves for slaughter 1958–67

Year	Percentage of small farm G.F.R. from slaughter cattle sales
1958	24.2
1959	22.1
1960	20.3
1961	16.9
1962	20.0
1963	19.3
1964	28.8
1965	30.5
1966	26.7
1967	26.9

Source: SA 1958–67.

Research into short-maturing maize varieties, a higher-yielding variety of rice, anti-rust strains of wheat suitable for growing on smallholdings, and improvements in the cotton varieties to give higher yields, were just part of a massively expanded programme of research. Nor was the effort restricted to improving seeds and seedlings. Research into fertilisers, insecticides (particularly for coffee and tea) and into optimum planting practices accompanied basic agronomic work, all with the aim of developing cultivating practices which would be simpler and easier for adoption by smallholders.[9]

This work was rewarded by the varieties of extremely high-yielding 'hybrid maize' which the Department at the end of the sixties felt confident would end Kenya's 'maize problem'. It seems that this did not happen, largely because massive upward shifts in the price of chemical fertilisers at the beginning of the seventies (hybrid maize required heavy applications of phosphate fertiliser for optimum yields) proved prohibitive for all but the wealthiest smallholders.

Nonetheless, it is important to stress once again that this input of mental labour was a prime factor in raising the productivity of physical labour power on smallholdings, and represented a powerful intervention by the State into the process of production on smallholdings.

One other trend in smallholder production in this period is particularly worthy of note. This is the important role played by the sale of beef cattle in the gross revenues accruing to smallholders. Table XI:1 shows the percentage of

9. Detailed accounts of agronomic research over these years are to be found in DAR 1952–68. For a general account see C.L.A. Leakey (ed.), op. cit., especially pp. 26–42 (on hybrid maize), pp. 68–74 (on sorghum improvement), 92–8 (on rust resistant wheat strains) and pp. 108–27 (on bean improvement). There are also accounts of soya bean, sesame, cotton and coffee improvement programmes.

gross small-farm revenue accruing from this source in the period 1958 to 1967. It will be seen that overall over a quarter of gross farm revenue in the smallholder sector came from this source in the period for which statistics are available. And in fact slaughter stock sales were throughout this period the second most valuable small-farm enterprise after arabica coffee. These statistics comprise only sales from agricultural areas, not Masailand or the North Eastern Province (as the Northern Frontier Province became) or areas such as Samburu or Turkana in the Rift Valley.

As we shall see shortly, the continually important role played by cattle sales in total farm income was not the result of high prices for beef, but largely reflects a gradually rising absolute number of slaughter cattle sales.

Official statistics show sales to the Kenya Meat Commission growing persistently over this period, but, just as in earlier periods, these sales were only a fraction of those into the free market. For example in 1967 and 1968 the Department of Agriculture estimated that between 950,000 and 1,000,000 cattle were slaughtered for beef, yet total deliveries of cattle to the Kenya Meat Commission from all sources in those years totalled 215,000 and 194,000 head respectively. That is, in the late sixties the Kenya Meat Commission was still only getting about ten per cent of all cattle slaughtered. Its share of the sheep and goat market was even smaller. In 1967, when total sheep and goat deliveries to the commission were some 59,000 head, the Department of Agriculture estimated that very nearly 3,000,000 sheep and goats had been slaughtered.[10]

The reason was familiar: the low prices offered by the Commission. An examination of official beef and mutton prices in the period 1961–70 shows that if inflation is taken into account they fell in real terms over this period.[11] Despite this, sales of cattle to the Kenya Meat Commission rose from 29,700 head in 1954 to 105,900 head in 1966, and mutton purchases only fell markedly from 1963, having remained steady before that. And this is a clue to the explanation of an apparent paradox which appears in this period.

The analysis in chapter VIII suggested that even before 1952 a gradually accelerating process was set under way in which, as the expansion of the cropped area cut into communal grazing land, livestock (having a reduced general utility) was either sold off or eaten. Would one not expect then that under the impact of the post-1950s agrarian revolution, with every inch of land being required for new cash crops or for dairying this process would have accelerated still further?

An interesting paragraph in the Department of Agriculture *Report* for 1968 does suggest that something like this was beginning to happen in some districts by that date.[12] Nonetheless, official statistics suggest that at the end of 1970

10. *DAR* 1967, pp. 34 and 36; and 1968, p. 29.
11. My calculations using price data in *SA* 1971, p. 84.
12. *DAR*, 1968, p. 27.

there were still 9.5 million cattle and nearly eight million sheep and goats in the nomadic pastoralist and smallholder areas of Kenya.[13] These figures suggest that, if those estimates provided to the Kenya Land Commission forty years previously were even remotely accurate, the number of such stock had actually risen in the intervening period. Even if we are generous to our own argument and hypothesise that the Kenya Land Commission figures were a gross underestimate, it is nonetheless clear that the absolute number of animals could not have fallen by much if at all over the period from 1930 to 1970. Even with three million animals being slaughtered yearly in the late sixties, the point had barely been reached where the slaughter of livestock had begun to exceed the natural rate of increase.

Looking at the figures a little more closely we see that in 1970 there were over a million cattle in Nyanza Province of which nearly half were in South Nyanza. There were 1.5 million cattle in the Rift Valley Province, of which nearly a million were in Kericho, and there was a similar number in Eastern Province where Kitui and Machakos districts between them had nearly 1,400,000 cattle, and over a million sheep and goats. There was almost the same number of cattle in these two Kamba districts in 1970 as there was in Masailand. The comparatively 'poor' provinces in terms of livestock were Central and Western Province, but even then the former still had over a million cattle, sheep and goats.

Certainly, as the Department of Agriculture suggested, these aggregate figures disguise changes in the constitution of Kenya's livestock herd (with increased numbers of grade and improved dairy cattle, and wool instead of hair sheep, particularly in the Central and Rift Valley Provinces),[14] but in 1970 the maximum number of such animals could not have exceeded 500,000. If this process of livestock disposal which we purported to observe in earlier periods was continuing, how do we explain the apparent buoyancy of livestock numbers?

A double explanation is possible. Firstly, there had probably been an absolute fall in livestock numbers in some areas (particularly in the Central Province) over the intervening period. But secondly, and much more importantly, it seems likely that the failure of overall livestock numbers to fall continuously in the post-1952 period reflects the very severe limitations on the expansion of effective demand for meat. That is, many Africans would have sold even more stock if incomes had been rising fast enough to allow consumers to eat meat as regularly and in as large a volume as they wished to. However, real incomes were not rising fast enough in urban or rural areas to allow such an expansion, and up to the mid-fifties, certainly in urban areas, they were probably falling. Thus, given the high rate of increase in livestock herds (with unregulated breeding) and the slow expansion of effective demand for meat, take-off rates barely kept

13. *SA* 1971, p. 90
14. *DAR* 1968, pp. 27–9.

up with natural increase. Faced therefore with a choice of selling to the Kenya Meat Commission at falling real prices, or into a rather higher-priced free market which nonetheless very quickly became flooded, many livestock owners decided to keep their animals as a source of milk, and (in the case of sheep and goats) of meat.

Now this in turn suggests two things. Firstly if there were these very real constraints on the expansion of demand for a much prized food-stuff, Kenya's 'agrarian revolution' must have raised the real incomes of rather fewer people than might be supposed from a casual reading of some of its more enthusiastic chroniclers. And secondly (to show the other side of the same coin) it suggests that many households in rural areas must at least up to 1970 have been completely untouched by the provision of the new farm enterprises which were at the centre of that 'revolution'.[15] Thus they had no incentive to get rid of their stock in order to plant coffee or tea, because local conditions did not allow such crops to be grown, or where they did some other constraint intervened. As we shall see shortly both circumstances were quite common; in fact up to 1970 they applied to the majority of households in Kenya's rural areas.

To sum up this initial section dealing with trends in production to 1970, table XI:2 shows the growth in cash revenue accruing to smallholder African producers in Kenya from the sale of crops and livestock products in the period 1956–67. It clearly shows a marked growth of the gross revenue accruing to African smallholders in the middle years of the period we are considering: a growth of nearly 600 per cent in money terms or of some 460 per cent in real terms in eleven years. The sharp upturn from 1964 onwards partly reflects the sharp increase in African output of coffee and tea as earlier plantings came into bearing, but above all it indicates the marked increase in revenue accruing from much greater sales of slaughter cattle. Revenue accruing from this latter source rose from K£2,184,000 in 1963 to K£7,091,000 in 1964, and rose continuously thereafter to K£8,109,000 in 1965, K£9,756,000 in 1966 and K£10,228,000 in 1967. This trend seems to have reflected a more buoyant demand for beef in the smallholder areas, a demand which may itself have been fuelled by increased incomes from coffee, tea and pyrethrum production.

This latter speculation brings us to the heart of the matter. For aggregate figures such as those in table XI:2, though useful for laying down rough parameters, are little or no guide to what was happening to actual farm incomes as a result of this 'revolution'. For this one has to examine the distribution of this gross farm output and income among the 1.2 million farming households which inhabited the smallholder areas of Kenya in 1970. This issue will be the central concern of the rest of this chapter.

15. The phrase 'agrarian revolution' is found in E. Clayton, *Agrarian Development in Peasant Economies: Some Lessons from Kenya* (London, 1964), chapter 3, pp. 32–55. See also H. Ruthenberg, *African Agricultural Production Development Policy in Kenya 1952–65* (Berlin, 1966).

Table XI:2. Total cash revenue accruing to African smallholders (including settlement schemes) from marketed crop and livestock products 1956–67 in current and 1956 constant prices (in Kenyan pounds)

Year	Total revenue to producers In current prices	In 1956 constant prices
1956	5,868,000	5,868,000
1957	6,926,000	6,718,000
1958	7,610,000	7,381,000
1959	8,350,000	8,099,500
1960	9,502,000	9,026,900
1961	10,380,000	9,549,600
1962	10,582,000	9,206,340
1963	12,387,000	10,652,820
1964	24,569,000	20,637,960
1965	23,801,000	18,564,780
1966	32,666,000	24,826,160
1967	34,036,000	23,825,000

Sources: *SA* 1960, p. 65; 1964, p. 60; and 1968, p. 75. No figures on cash revenue to producers are available before 1956, and separate statistics for small farm areas end in 1967. In order to construct a constant price series I had to use the Nairobi Cost of Living Index since this was the only one which covered this entire period, and actual constant price data do not become available in the published national accounts until 1964. Since the index was a weighted one for all consumer groups in Nairobi and covers a range of expenditures which most urban and rural Africans would not incur, its use deflates the growth of money incomes more than any specifically African index would do. On the other hand use of a 1952 base would have been rather more deflationary since there was quite marked inflation (about four per cent per annum) between 1952 and 1956. For the Nairobi Cost of Living Index see *SA* 1967, p. 158.

3. Production and the Pattern of Household Farm Incomes

A useful place to start such an examination is the process of land consolidation and registration which went along with this expansion of production, and in fact was the essential prerequisite of much of it. In particular, the introduction of coffee, tea, pyrethrum or dairy cattle on to a smallholding generally only occurred after that holding had been consolidated, though there was one significant exception to this in the case of the spread of arabica coffee in Meru district in the mid-fifties. This does not mean that consolidation always occurred as a result of direct administrative initiative. We have already seen that a group of enterprising pioneers in Central Province and elsewhere had built up consolidated holdings by a systematic process of land purchase even before the second world war, and some of these men (especially those who were loyalists in the Mau-Mau struggle) were often the first Africans entering coffee growing in the mid-fifties. In addition, as the Government-supported programme of consolidation got under way in other parts of Kenya, 'progressive farmers' often took the lead themselves in entering 'exchange groups' to consolidate fragments even before the Administration's consolidation and registration teams had arrived in a district.[16] Nonetheless, it was generally the case that consolidation, either officially or informally done, was a prerequisite of obtaining access to the high-value cash crops whose spread was in general carefully controlled by government. All things being equal, the sooner a farm, group of farms or district was consolidated the sooner it got into cash crop production.

Since the programme of land consolidation was largely a political measure intimately linked to the process of counter-insurgency during the Emergency, priority was of course accorded to the three Kikuyu districts. It was begun in earnest in 1956 and essentially completed by 1959, by which time nearly 780,000 acres of land had been consolidated out of a total of 999,000 acres of fragments farmed under the traditional tenure system.[17] With the completion of consolidation the number of coffee growers in Central Province began to expand rapidly.

However once the politically imperative case of Central Province had been dealt with, and the Emergency came to an end, the colonial and post-colonial regimes in Kenya put much less money and manpower into the process elsewhere, with consequent delays.

Until we have more evidence from research it is difficult to say what effect this slowing-down had on the spread of cash crops to other districts. We know that in Meru district smallholder arabica coffee growing became widespread (under the Administration's aegis) before the process of consolidation and registration of land was even begun, and indeed had a retarding effect on the latter for some time because farmers who had already planted coffee on their individual fragments feared the loss of crops and income from the process of consolidation.[18] (In fact it was probably this experience which made the Administration insist on consolidation before the issue of coffee seedlings elsewhere.) In addition there were districts such as Kericho, Nandi, parts of Elgeyo–Marakwet, Elgon Nyanza and Kisii where patterns of pre-reform land holding had largely been free of fragmentation in any case, so it was possible

16. See for example *DAR* 1958, p. 42; 1960, p. 39; and 1961, p. 52.
17. However after widespread protests it was found necessary to repeat the whole process in Fort Hall district. Reconsolidation was essentially complete there by 1962. See *DAR* 1960, p. 41; 1961, p. 54; and 1962, p. 64.
18. See Bernard, *East of Mount Kenya*, op. cit., pp. 101–7.

to go ahead fairly easily with enclosure of naturally consolidated household holdings. This happened very rapidly from the mid-fifties onwards, having begun on an informal basis among the most progressive households and locations as early as the 1930s in Kericho, Elgon Nyanza and Nandi.

These districts (Kericho, Nandi, Elgeyo – Marakwet, Elgon Nyanza—the most northerly part of the old North Nyanza—and parts of Kisii) were of course the ones whose pre-1952 pattern of commercialisation had been plough-based maize monocropping on an extensive basis. With enclosure, this type of production continued, but on the most progressive farms it became allied to intensive dairying with the use of grade and improved cows and to a lesser degree the raising of woolled sheep. The idea here was to replace the settler 'mixed farming' sector with production on very similar African land, and to restore soil fertility lost through maize monocropping by organic manuring.[19]

Nonetheless, whilst coffee growing spread rapidly in Meru district before land consolidation, and the relative absence of fragmentation allowed 'mixed farming' commercialisation to go ahead in the Rift Valley districts and elsewhere in advance of the formal programme, some districts did suffer delays in commercialisation because of the slowness of land consolidation. The most notable cases here appear to have been the Kisumu (old Central Nyanza) district and the most densely populated locations of what had been southern North Nyanza district. The lakeshore area of South Nyanza seems also to have been so affected.[20] Clearly a large part of these areas was and is not suitable for the growing of coffee, tea or pyrethrum in any case, and this applies particularly to the lakeshore areas of Kisumu and South Nyanza district where in 1970, as in 1952, cotton was the only remotely suitable pure 'cash crop' available. But there must have been some areas of Kakamega district (including Maragoli location) where the spread of coffee growing was held up by the slowness and lateness of land consolidation, and this is signalled in the official statistics by the doubling of the acreage under coffee in the district between 1965 and 1966 as progress began to be made in consolidation.

So inequalities were built into the process of post-1952 agricultural commercialisation by the unevenness of land consolidation, enclosure and registration which was its concomitant and (after the earliest years) its prerequisite. However, these may be regarded as 'leaps and lags' which may be overcome with time, and which give at best a temporary advantage to 'early starter' households

19. See *DAR* 1959, pp. 42-3; 1961, pp. 51-3; 1962, pp. 62-3; and 1966, p. 20.
20. See Ominde, 'Land and Population . . .', op. cit., pp. 317 and 327. See also T. Joseph Ogwang, 'The Politics of Land, Land Consolidation and Registration in terms of General Economic Development: A Case Study (Kojwach–Kowere, S. Nyanza, Kenya)' (University of Dar-es-Salaam, Political Science Dissertation, March 1972). Also R. J. Wilson, 'The Economic Implications of Land Registration in Kenya's Smallholder Areas' (IDS Staff Paper No. 91, Feb. 1971); and W. L. Sytek, 'A History of Land Consolidation in Central Nyanza 1956–62' and 'Social Factors in Luo Land Consolidation' (EAISR Papers, 1965).

and districts. Indeed by 1970–1, land consolidation and enclosure (though not land registration) was virtually complete in all the districts of Central, Eastern, southern Rift Valley, Nyanza and Western Provinces so that the basis for eliminating the spatial inequalities built into the unevenness of the process had been laid.

Much more central to the inequality involved was inequality in the size of the landholdings consolidated, and inequalities in natural resource endowment, and these are much more difficult to eliminate with time. Taking the latter first, it is obvious that inequalities of farm income between households on a national scale in Kenya are likely to arise from the fact that some households inhabit land which is not suitable for the growing of arabica coffee, tea or pyrethrum. If a household is restricted to growing cotton or low-value cereal and pulses on two or three acres of land in the lower drier areas of Central or Southern Nyanza, or in the semi-arid Kitui district, it is very unlikely that it will be able to raise its farm income substantially unless it can physically remove itself (perhaps through a settlement scheme) to land with a higher potential. In addition, even within a district or location deemed suitable for tea or coffee growing or for intensive dairying, particular households will have more or less access to the very best land, the best watered pasture, the less steep, more easily-worked slopes, and so on.

Taking the first dimension, which in gross terms is probably the most crucial one, we may give it a rough magnitude by asking how many land-owning rural households in Kenya in 1970 were not growing coffee, tea or pyrethrum, using hybrid maize, or rearing grade livestock. An approach to this question can be made via the estimates of crop areas and land use on small farms and settlement schemes in the 1969–70 season, contained in the 1971 *Statistical Abstract*.[21] This showed that in the agricultural districts of the Central, Western, Nyanza, Rift Valley, Eastern and Coast Provinces in 1970 there were 2,520,000 hectares of land under crops. In aggregate, coffee, tea, pyrethrum and hybrid maize formed the following percentages of the whole:

Crop	Thousands of hectares	% of total cropped area
Arabica Coffee	83.6	3.3
Tea	22.9	0.9
Pyrethrum	20.4	0.8
Hybrid or Improved Maize	166.4	6.6

From these figures alone, Kenya's much-trumpeted 'agrarian revolution' begins to come into some sort of perspective. In all, by 1970 somewhat less than twelve per cent of the cropped land in Kenya in 'peasant' hands was under high-value cash crops, or improved varieties of maize, which were at the heart

---

21. *SA* 1971, pp. 87–9.

of that 'revolution'. In addition, the cropped area itself, even in these agricultural districts (i.e. not including the areas of pastoral nomadism) was only thirty-seven per cent of the total land in use, there being nearly 7,000,000 hectares still under communal grazing, even in 1970. Of course this proportion varied markedly from district to district, around seventy per cent of the total land area in all three Kikuyu districts, for example, being under crops as against a mere 8.7 per cent in Elgeyo–Marakwet. Nonetheless, even within the cropped area, 'unimproved' (i.e. non-hybrid) maize and beans were still the dominant crops, encompassing half of the Kenyan total, with a large part of the rest being under other pulses and annual food crops. In short, even after Kenya's famous 'land reform' and the introduction of the new farm enterprises which went with it, the vast majority of smallholder land was still being used as it had been used in 1952, for the rearing of basic food crops and the pasturage of animals.

It is very difficult to turn these land-use proportions into proportions of farmers, particularly since after 1968 regular statistics of smallholder coffee growers cease. In 1968, there were 268,493 members in coffee co-operative societies, whilst at the end of 1970 there were 48,443 registered smallholder tea growers. There are no published statistics of the number of smallholder milk producers, but in 1968 there were 115,000 grade dairy cows on smallholdings in Kenya.[22] There is comparatively little overlap between areas of coffee and tea growing, but a considerable overlap between smallholder tea and pyrethrum production, and some overlap between both coffee and tea production and the ownership of grade cattle (64,000 of the 115,000 grade cows were in Central Province, the main area of smallholder coffee production). If then we said that there were probably 350,000 smallholders in Kenya in 1970 (including those on settlement schemes) who were involved in one or more of coffee, tea, pyrethrum and milk production, we would be erring on the side of generosity, whilst the addition of improved maize would probably bring the total nearer to 400,000. The ILO report stated that there were 1.2 million smallholder farmers in Kenya in 1971, so if we generously define 'progressive farmers' or 'farmers affected by the revolution in production' as all of those producing any quantity (however small) of one of the above five products, then the category of farmers involved embraces about a third of all smallholders in Kenya. Thus even before one considers such inequalities as those between large and small growers of these crops, one has already identified a relatively privileged category consisting simply of those farmers who grew any of them.[23] Up to 1970 a considerable majority of smallholders in Kenya were untouched by Kenya's agrarian revolution in the area of new high-value farm enterprises, though they may have experienced its consolidation and registration component.

We may therefore identify schematically four different types of farm which

22. *DAR* 1968, pp. 24 and 101; and *ES* 1972, p. 66.
23. For some reinforcing data on this see Heyer, Maitha and Senga (eds.), op. cit., pp. 195–9.

we might expect to find in Kenya's smallholding areas in 1970. Leaving aside the question of the indeterminacy of the categories 'large' and 'small' (which must of course be defined by reference to the local context and above all soil fertility) we might identify:

1. Large smallholdings with one or more of the new farm enterprises

2. Small smallholdings with one or more of the new farm enterprises

3. Large smallholdings without any of the new farm enterprises.

4. Small smallholdings without any of the new farm enterprises

Very generally, we would expect those households with the largest farm incomes to be in category (1) and those with the smallest farm incomes to be in category (4), with categories (3) and (2) having incomes in the intermediate range. We shall see that this was the case. On a national basis the absolute number of smallholders in categories (3), (2) and (4) far outnumbered those in category (1) in 1970, and do so to this day. Category (1) in fact roughly corresponds to our petite bourgeoisie which was the category which really benefited from the agrarian revolution. Category (4) were and are those who lost out, and their households provide a large part of the rural wage labour force.

4. The Distribution of Land and the Distribution of Farm and Household Incomes—Survey Data

The period 1952–70 is distinguished by the appearance of the first systematic studies of African agriculture and farm incomes. The first of these, an extremely ambitious sample survey of African agriculture, was carried out by the Economics and Statistics Division of the Ministry of Economic Planning in 1960/1, and formed part of the FAO's 1960 World Census of Agriculture. Bringing the first rays of hard quantitative light on to what had for seventy-five years lain in the gloom of small-scale social anthropological studies and agricultural officers' estimates, the survey covered 734,000 holdings or 7,389,000 acres in the areas of African smallholder agriculture. It estimated that there were a further 220,000 holdings (mainly in the Rift Valley and Coast Provinces) not covered by the survey, making the approximate total of all holdings in Kenya in 1960/1 about 950,000. For the purposes of the survey a holding was defined as:

> all land under the economic control of a selected farmer. It includes land over which the holder or farmer has individual cultivation or grazing rights as well as the land he owns. It excludes land that is leased to another but includes all land cultivated on behalf of the farmer by relatives (including his widow) or by unpaid or paid employees. All fragments of land under the control of the

Table XI:3. Analysis of proportion of arable land by size of holding in areas surveyed on holding basis

Percentages of all Land

District/Province	Size in Acres						
	Up to 2.49	2.50– 4.99	5.00– 7.49	7.50– 9.99	10.00– 14.99	15.00– and Over	All Holdings
Kiambu	65.6	57.1	42.0	45.8	37.7	24.0	42.5
Nyeri	70.6	56.0	46.5	44.2	33.9	30.8	50.1
Fort Hall	62.2	50.7	56.1	26.9	31.1	35.9	50.2
Embu	—	58.8	49.0	44.2	46.0	36.0	46.6
Central Province	65.7	55.2	48.4	42.3	38.7	29.8	47.0
South Nyanza	74.1	64.0	49.6	49.6	47.0	25.8	35.4
Central Nyanza	58.3	56.6	53.8	46.7	46.4	32.3	42.8
North Nyanza	69.3	57.0	54.3	61.3	41.3	36.6	46.7
Elgon Nyanza	49.8	66.2	52.7	42.1	37.1	26.6	30.8
Kericho	37.1	31.7	28.5	27.3	24.8	19.9	24.6
Nyanza Province	64.7	56.7	49.0	44.2	37.4	28.8	37.2
Nandi	45.1	19.3	18.2	19.3	15.2	11.0	12.7
All areas	65.0	55.8	47.9	42.5	35.7	26.9	36.8

Source: *Kenya African Agricultural Sample Census 1960/1*, part I, p. 27.

farmer are included even if the land is not being used for agricultural purposes.[24]

Data on holding sizes were collected for 509,800 holdings in the Central and Nyanza Provinces and in Nandi district. This showed the marked inequality in holdings which one might have expected (see table XI:4). In the area as a whole twenty-five per cent of all holdings (those of ten acres and over) covered sixty-five per cent of the land in use, whilst 50.7 per cent of the holdings (all those under five acres) covered just 15.6 per cent of the land in use.

The survey also revealed something which was to become commonplace in subsequent survey work on Kenyan, and indeed on East African agriculture. This was that, almost uniformly, the larger the size of the total holding the smaller the proportion of it which was cultivated; i.e. the larger the proportion

24. *Kenya African Agricultural Sample Census 1960/61* (Economics and Statistics Division, Ministry of Constitutional Affairs and Economic Planning, Nairobi, 196?), Part I, p. 15.

Table XI:4. Holding size distribution among smallholders in Kenya 1960

Size group in acres

District/ Province	Up to 2.49		2.50–4.99		5.00–7.49		7.50–9.99		10.00–14.99		15.00 and over	
	% of all holdings	% of all land	% of all holdings	% of all land	% of all holdings	% of all land	% of all holdings	% of all land	% of all holdings	% of all land	% of all holdings	% of all land
Kiambu	40.6	9.3	20.8	16.0	16.0	18.3	8.8	15.0	8.6	20.2	5.2	21.2
Nyeri	30.8	12.1	41.2	36.7	16.3	22.8	5.6	10.0	4.4	10.0	1.7	8.4
Fort Hall	44.8	18.6	33.7	35.7	14.3	26.1	3.6	9.0	2.8	7.4	0.8	3.2
Embu	0.3	0.1	35.6	18.0	33.0	26.3	15.1	17.9	9.1	16.6	6.9	21.1
Central Province	32.4	9.7	32.4	25.6	18.4	22.9	7.6	13.3	5.9	14.2	3.3	14.3
South Nyanza	17.6	2.6	26.3	8.7	16.9	8.5	7.4	6.7	6.7	6.6	25.0	66.9
Central Nyanza	31.5	5.3	27.2	13.8	12.5	10.6	6.5	7.8	9.8	16.5	12.5	46.0
North Nyanza	30.6	6.9	31.0	16.4	14.4	12.9	6.0	6.5	7.1	12.8	10.9	44.5
Elgon Nyanza	5.7	0.3	9.5	1.7	11.4	4.4	13.4	7.3	17.5	10.7	42.5	75.6
Kericho	3.7	0.8	13.9	5.4	19.5	11.9	18.9	15.0	31.0	36.5	13.0	30.4
Nyanza Province	22.8	3.5	24.8	9.6	14.5	9.5	8.7	8.1	11.7	15.0	17.5	54.3
Nandi	1.0	0.1	6.7	1.7	10.9	4.2	11.7	6.2	23.2	16.8	46.5	71.0
All areas	24.6	4.1	26.1	11.5	15.4	11.2	8.5	8.7	10.6	15.0	14.8	49.5

Source: ibid., pp. 20 and 21.

of it which was still under natural grazing. This point emerges clearly in table XI:3 covering the same districts.

This of course did not mean that smaller holdings had absolutely more land under crops than larger ones (in Kiambu for example a household with twenty-four per cent of a twenty acre holding under cultivation would have been working 4.8 acres, while a household working 65.6 per cent of a holding of 2.49 acres would only have had 1.6 acres under cultivation), but it did suggest that in Kenya, as in smallholding agriculture across the world, the smaller the holding, the more intensively it was worked.

One other finding is of central relevance to our concerns. The survey showed that again almost uniformly in the area surveyed, the larger the holding the larger the number of people dependent on it. This tendency opened up the possibility that even if the gross farm incomes of the largest holdings were larger than the smallest, and even if average gross farm incomes did rise with each landholding category, per capita farm incomes on the larger farms might be lower because the income would have to stretch further. Unfortunately the census itself does not throw any light on this issue, because no attempt was made to collect farm income data. However the census did provide two important clues to what the distribution of gross farm income per holding might be, in the distribution of crop acreages and livestock by holding size. As one might expect, its data showed that in virtually every case the larger landholding households had the bigger acreages under crops, and the larger number of livestock. All things being equal therefore, they certainly had the capacity to realise a larger gross farm income. Of particular importance here of course is the distribution of the new smallholder crops: coffee, tea and pyrethrum.

In the case of coffee in particular, growers in 1961 were quite heavily concentrated on the larger holdings. Nearly fifteen per cent of those holding over five acres of land, eight per cent of those with more than ten acres of land, and nine per cent of those with over fifteen acres of land were growing coffee in 1961 compared with only 2.6 per cent of those with less than 2.49 acres. In the case of tea, very few households at all were growing the crop in 1961, but once again 2.8 per cent of those with over five acres of land and 1.9 per cent of those with over ten acres of land were engaged in tea growing at this date, compared with a mere 0.1 per cent of those with less than 2.49 acres. It was much the same story in the case of pyrethrum, where 4.9 per cent of those growers with between 7.50 and 9.99 acres were engaged in growing the crop, compared with a mere 0.8 per cent of those households with less than 2.49 acres. Finally, in the case of commercial milk production the very small number of grade or exotic dairy cows on African smallholdings at this date was strongly concentrated on the larger holdings. In 1961 smallholder access to grade cattle and artificial insemination services was restricted almost totally to the Central Province with a marked concentration in Nyeri district. In Kiambu the largest farmers owned more of these rare beasts than any other group, whilst in Nyeri and Embu ownership was concentrated in the middle ranges with a tailing-off on the largest farms. The same was true in North Nyanza, but not in Nandi. These varied patterns indicate the different significance of holding sizes in different districts, and I shall attempt an explication and explanation of these differences later.[25]

For the moment, it should simply be noted that the very first systematic survey of African agriculture strongly confirmed the marked inequality in land holding whose creation we have attempted to trace through the colonial period. It also gave very good ground for supposing that this inequality would be reflected in an inequality of farm income; but it provided no direct evidence on this.

The Central Province Economic Survey[26]

Such evidence appeared for the first time in an economic survey of Central Province conducted by the Statistics Division of the Ministry of Economic Planning in 1963/4. The survey covered 900 households (or 0.32 per cent) of the *circa* 275,000 households of the Province in 1962. The sample covered a broad range of holding sizes from those owning less than one acre (about 10.5 per cent of the sample) to those owning over twenty acres (1.6 per cent of the sample) but for the purposes of tabulation, the survey report divided them into three 'strata': those owning less than four acres of land ('stratum 1'), those with four or more acres but less than eight acres ('stratum 2') and those with eight or more acres ('stratum 3'). Table XI:5 shows the absolute number of households in the sample in each stratum and the percentage of the total sample in each stratum by district of the province.

This is the final sample on which the income and expenditure figures which are the central focus of the *Economic Survey* were based. It is deliberately weighted in favour of larger land holders. The actual distribution of land among households in the originally selected 'primary sampling units'—which is a much closer reflection of reality—is shown in table XI:6. According to the report, stratum 1 households (40.5 per cent of all) operated thirty-two per cent of the total land cultivated, stratum 2 households (who were 28.4 per cent of the final sample) operated thirty-two per cent as well, while the stratum 3 households (thirty-one per cent of the final sample) operated thirty-six per cent of the total cultivated land. The average size landholding in each stratum by district is shown in table XI:7. The generally smaller overall size of holding in Kiambu district will be noted, a clear indication of the levels of population pressure there.[27] The crucial table for our purposes is XI:8, which shows the total value

25. For above data see ibid., Part I, text tables 49, 59, 75, 76 and 77, and Part II, appendix tables 34, 38, 51, 55, 68, 72, 85, 89, 127, 128, 141, 145, 158, 162, 179, 196 and 228.
26. *Economic Survey of Central Province 1963/64* (Statistics Division, Ministry of Economic Planning and Development, Nairobi, 1968).
27. In the 1962 census Kiambu district had an overall density of population of 1,082 p.s.m., Nyeri 806 p.s.m. and Fort Hall 586 p.s.m., *Kenya Population Census 1962* (Directorate of Economic Planning, Ministry of Finance and Economic Planning, July 1964), Vol. I, pp. 14, 18 and 28.

Table XI:5. Landholdings by strata, Central Province 1963. (1) Final sample

District	Stratum 1 — 4 acres	Stratum 2 + 4 to — 8 acres	Stratum 3 8 or more acres	Sample Total
Kiambu	108 (12%)	46 (5.1%)	51 (5.6%)	205 (22.7%)
Fort Hall (now Murang'a)	55 (6.1%)	38 (4.2%)	74 (8.2%)	167 (18.5%)
Embu	69 (7.6%)	44 (4.8%)	25 (2.7%)	138 (15.3%)
Nyeri	54 (6.0%)	33 (3.6%)	23 (2.5%)	110 (12.2%)
Meru	79 (8.7%)	95 (10.5%)	106 (11.7%)	280 (31.1%)
All districts	365 (40.5%)	256 (28.4%)	279 (31.0%)	900

Source: ibid., p. 6.

Table XI:6. Landholdings by strata, Central Province 1963. (2) Primary sample

District	Stratum 1 — 4 acres	Stratum 2 + 4 to — 8 acres	Stratum 3 8 + acres	Sample Total
Kiambu	3,473 (15.2%)	610 (2.6%)	265 (1.2%)	4,348 (19.1%)
Fort Hall	3,564 (15.6%)	852 (3.7%)	507 (2.2%)	4,923 (21.5%)
Embu	2,848 (12.5%)	821 (3.5%)	247 (1.1%)	3,916 (17.1%)
Nyeri	2,527 (11.0%)	518 (2.2%)	141 (0.6%)	3,186 (13.9%)
Meru	4,271 (18.7%)	1,556 (6.8%)	660 (2.9%)	6,487 (28.4%)
All districts	16,683 (72.9%)	4,357 (19.1%)	1,820 (7.9%)	22,860

Source: ibid., table 8, p. 7.

Table XI:7. Average size of holding (land operated) by strata (acres)

	Stratum 1	Stratum 2	Stratum 3	District Average
1. Kiambu	1.4	5.8	11.7	2.6
2. Fort Hall	2.9	6.9	18.1	5.2
3. Embu	2.8	5.6	14.5	4.1
4. Nyeri	2.5	5.1	12.1	3.3
5. Meru	2.7	5.2	11.1	4.2
6. All Districts				3.9

Source: ibid., table 28, p. 20.

Table XI:8. Value of agricultural production per acre of land operated

	Value of agricultural production (excluding livestock products) (Shillings)	Area of land operated (acres)	Average value of production per acre operated (Shillings)
1. Kiambu—			
1. Stratum 1	303	1.4	216
2. Stratum 2	741	5.8	128
3. Stratum 3	1,261	11.7	108
4. District	422	2.6	162
2. Fort Hall—			
1. Stratum 1	334	2.9	115
2. Stratum 2	585	6.9	85
3. Stratum 3	719	18.1	40
4. District	417	5.2	80
3. Embu			
1. Stratum 1	394	2.8	141
2. Stratum 2	595	5.6	106
3. Stratum 3	1,459	14.5	101
4. District	566	4.1	138
4. Nyeri—			
1. Stratum 1	811	2.5	324
2. Stratum 2	1,062	5.1	208
3. Stratum 3	2,068	12.1	171
4. District	907	3.3	275
5. Meru—			
1. Stratum 1	556	2.7	206
2. Stratum 2	640	5.2	123
3. Stratum 3	1,246	11.1	112
4. District	647	4.2	154
6. All districts	576	3.9	148

Source: ibid.. table 35, p. 25.

of all the crops produced by the households during the agricultural year of the survey. The value of production (including self-consumed production) is given in market prices then current but does not include income from livestock products. In addition the table shows again the average area of land operated by each stratum in each district, and from this the average value of production per acre.

It should be stressed that the figures in the left-hand column are the imputed cash value of all crop production (including self-consumed production).

Unfortunately there is no tabulation of total agricultural incomes (including livestock products) by stratum, though other tables suggest that inclusion of these items would raise the average agricultural income for all districts, which in table XI:8 is shown as Shs. 576, to Shs. 809.[28]

It is interesting to compare these figures with those for an earlier period which we reviewed in chapter V. In that chapter we recalculated Humphrey's 1944 estimates of crop yields in Nyeri and suggested that the cash value of agricultural production sold off the land in that year was Shs. 382. The figures in table XI:8 are for total production as we have said, so we must deduct from them an imputed value of home consumption. Once this is done we find that the average household in Nyeri in 1964 earned just Shs. 334 in cash from off-farm sales.[29] To this must be added Shs. 180 as the cash value of off-farm sales of livestock products (principally milk).[30] We thus arrive at a total figure of Shs. 514 as the average household cash income from farming in 1964, i.e. an increase of just Shs. 132 in twenty years. Since the index quoted earlier in this chapter suggested that the real value of money incomes fell sixteen per cent between 1956 and 1964, and since inflation was running at a somewhat higher rate than this in the late forties and early fifties, there can be no doubt at all that the real purchasing power of farm cash incomes had fallen over this period despite the onset of the 'agrarian revolution'. Moreover, as it happens, the Nyeri statistics give a somewhat rosy picture of the trend, since that district held a lead in coffee production and in particular in milk production in 1964 which pushed its average farm production figures up. Thus it will be seen that total crop income in Nyeri was more than double that in Kiambu and Fort Hall; thirty per cent larger than the Meru average and forty per cent larger than Embu. For the reasons given at length in earlier chapters it is important not to read too much into any one year's statistics, crucially determined as they are by climatic conditions. Nonetheless, the picture of the limited impact of Kenya's agrarian revolution on the generality of farm incomes built up through other sources seems amply confirmed here. This is particularly so if it is remembered that stratum 1 total production was always anything from ten to thirty per cent less than the district average, and that on all except the smallest farms direct consumption out of this production would be higher than on the larger farms. Thus to take an example: stratum 1 households in Kiambu had a total value of agricultural production of Shs.303 in 1964. If they were to attain to the standard of subsistence of the district population as a whole they would need to eat produce to the value of Shs. 276 of this,[31] leaving just Shs. 27 in off-farm sales. Even if one adds Shs. 50 to this for the value of milk or other livestock products, the average household with less than four acres of land in Kiambu would not have realised Shs. 100

28. *Economic Survey* . . . , table 33, p. 23.
29. See ibid., table 41, p. 31.
30. Ibid., table 38, p. 28.
31. Ibid., table 41, p. 31.

in cash from that land in this year. And it must be remembered that the stratum 1 category was a very broad one, embracing eighty per cent of all households in rural Kiambu, fifty-seven per cent of whom however were operating less than two acres of land, and twenty-six per cent less than one acre![32]

Clearly then most of the households in this stratum would not have obtained the district level average of subsistence, and indeed, unless they were adopting the 'high risk' market strategy of subsistence which we discussed in earlier chapters, they would not have had any off-farm sales at all. It is not surprising in these circumstances that this survey, like the census before it, found that the smaller landholding households worked their land far more intensively than the larger landholding households.

The survey results showed that in every case more labour power was applied per acre over the agricultural year on the small farms than on the larger, with the result that output per acre was always higher on the smaller than on the larger farms.[33] But of course greater labour input on the smaller farms, though absolutely necessary to subsist, did little or nothing to close the gap in farm incomes, because the larger farms, though having far lower output per acre, had a much larger gross output and could market more of it to increase their farm cash incomes. It is also important to note that although input of labour power per unit of land was higher on the smaller farms, total labour input was always higher on the larger farms. Moreover, the larger the holding, the more of this labour was hired labour.

However, whilst stratum 3 households hired a deal more labour than others, the level of labour hiring as a proportion of total labour input was quite low overall (five per cent) and thus family labour remained at the centre of production.[34] The survey results on family labour were interesting for their specificity, though predictable in their overall structure.

Firstly, levels of labour input by women were markedly greater than those of men (by about thirty per cent on average). Secondly, the discrepancy between female and male labour input was greater in Kiambu than in any other district, and within that district was greatest on the smallest holdings (women did sixty per cent more agricultural work than men on the stratum 1 holdings in Kiambu). This is a reflection of course of the large amounts of off-farm wage labour undertaken by men in Kiambu in particular. But above all there were very high absolute levels of labour input involved, particularly from the women, on all holdings. In the survey the work of one person in an agricultural pursuit for more than half a day was counted as one 'man day'. Work for more than one hour but less than half a day was counted as half a man day. Work for less than one hour was not counted at all.[35] Even allowing for the inflation inherent in this method of

32. Ibid., table 30, p. 21, also table 29, p. 20.
33. Ibid., table 37, p. 27.
34. Ibid., tables 18 and 19, p. 15. It was *c.* 13% on stratum 3 holdings.
35. Ibid., p. 14.

measurement, in the case of the stratum 3 households, for example, a total work load in 'man days' of three or four times the number of actual days in the year means that some part of every day was spent in agricultural activity by women on those holdings. In the case of stratum 1 holdings, a total of 324 man days worked by household members in Kiambu, 667 in Nyeri or 438 in Meru would have the same implication. It must be remembered that only agricultural labour is here being counted, i.e. no account is taken of time needed for domestic labour, child rearing, journeys to market, etc. This in turn carries a further implication. If the new enterprises being introduced as a result of land consolidation and its attendant pattern of more commercialised land use turned out to be more labour-intensive than previous smallholder enterprises (as was in fact the case), a family labour force, and especially female labour power, stretched already to this point would have a choice before it. Either the new enterprises could be substituted for old ones (which on the smallest holding would mean substituting pure cash crops like coffee, tea or pyrethrum for food/cash crops) or the total labour power at the household's disposal had to be increased, which in most cases meant hiring labour. But as the survey quite clearly showed, as of 1964 only the largest and (to a lesser degree) the middle-range households could afford to do this, so for the smallest landholding households the 'choice' was in fact no choice at all. Assuming that they had at their disposal holdings which were ecologically suitable for the new enterprises, they either had to divert virtually all their land and labour power to them or not have them at all.[36] In short, increases in household cash income from farming could only be obtained at the cost of being ever more reliant on the market for subsistence.

For the moment we shall complete this 'survey of a survey' by looking at the pattern of total household income among the 900 sampled households. There is an irritating gap in the *Survey* here because the statistics cease to be tabulated by the strata identified for the analysis of agricultural incomes. Instead the households are reclassified into seven income groups, as in table XI:10. As will be seen in the bottom row of the table, these income groups correspond to seven average holding sizes, but nonetheless the lack of continuity in categorisation means that certain sorts of comparison cannot be made.

The first and most important point to be made from the data in this table concerns the ratio of cash income from agriculture to total cash income, for all the income groups identified. I show this in table XI:9. Thus we see that in every case (in every income group and size category of landholding) household total cash income was at least double farm cash income, i.e. all the households in the sample were heavily reliant on off-farm income sources to obtain cash. Moreover, and perhaps unsurprisingly, the smallest holding households with the lowest overall income were most heavily dependent on off-farm income to

36. Aid by kin or neighbours always carried reciprocal obligations and did not usually mean a net gain in labour power.

Table XI:9.

A Income group* (Shs. per annum)	B Av. holding size	C Cash income from agriculture	D Total household cash income*
1. Shs. 0–1,000	3.3 acres	Shs. 109	Shs. 387
		ratio C to D (r) = 1:3.5	
2. Shs 1,001–1,500	5.3 acres	Shs. 252	Shs. 727
		r = 1:2.8	
3. Shs. 1,501–2,000	6.2 acres	Shs. 466	Shs. 1,060
		r = 1:2.3	
4. Shs. 2,001–2,500	8.2 acres	Shs. 560	Shs. 1,421
		r = 1:2.5	
5. Shs. 2,501–3,500	9.4 acres	Shs. 807	Shs. 1,990
		r = 1:2.5	
6. Shs. 3,501–5,000	10.0 acres	Shs. 1,262	Shs. 3,134
		r = 1:2.5	
7. Shs. 5,001 +	15.4 acres	Shs. 2,608	Shs. 7,871
		r = 1:3.0	

*Total cash income does not bring the households identified into their income group because the latter encompasses the imputed cash value of subsistence farm production as well.

get by, and in fact did not manage to do so even with off-farm earnings. On average they were Shs. 40 short of total expenditure at the end of the year. Unsurprisingly too, the largest single source of off-farm income in all income groups was wages and salaries (classified rather curiously in the Survey as 'Services'), with remittances (from household members employed outside agriculture) and 'manufacturing trade and transport' as the other major sources of off-farm cash income. Table XI:11 shows the percentage of total household cash income coming from these three sources by income group. Thus all households obtained between a quarter and a third of their total cash resources from wages or salaries (including part-time or occasional work by household members), whilst the smaller the holding and the lower the total household income, the higher the percentage of earnings from remittances and the lower the percentage from trade and business.

The total picture is one of 'bundled' or 'cumulative' privilege. Better-off households in Central Province in 1964 always had more land and more land cultivated, and more labour to work it (from household and hired sources), and more off-farm income and higher wages and salaries and more income from remittances and more income from trade and business than those in the next income category down.

Table XI.10. Receipts and disbursements per household by income groups: All districts (Shillings)

	Up to 1,000	1,001– 1,500	1,501– 2,000	2,001– 2,500	2,501– 3,500	3501– 5,000	5,001 and over	All groups
Receipts								
Cash receipts.								
Agriculture	109	252	466	560	807	1,262	2,608	354
Manufacturing, trade and transport	18	64	101	174	259	378	1,984	158
Services	125	241	281	506	581	1,020	2,527	459
Remittances	75	127	112	91	128	147	181	103
Other cash receipts	60	43	100	90	215	327	568	86
Total cash receipts	387	727	1,060	1,421	1,990	3,134	7,871	1,160
Consumption of own produce	340	482	645	707	891	961	1,355	517
Total receipts	727	1,209	1,705	2,128	2,881	4,094	9,226	1,677
Disbursements								
Enterprise expenditure	64	104	193	249	422	803	3,067	241
Household consumption								
Food	174	271	321	388	529	696	1,135	333
Non-food	178	339	505	622	829	1,134	2,350	493
Total consumption	352	610	826	1,010	1,358	1,830	3,485	826
Transfers (including money lent out)	3	8	22	23	51	76	138	23
Taxes	8	17	28	27	46	45	116	23
Total cash	427	740	1,068	1,309	1,877	2,754	6,806	1,113
Subsistence food	254	392	529	580	753	808	1,191	419
Subsistence firewood	86	91	116	128	138	153	165	98
Total disbursements	767	1,223	1,713	2,017	2,768	3,715	8,162	1,630
Surplus (+) Deficit (−)	− 40	− 14	− 8	111	113	379	1,064	47
Size of household (persons)	3.9	5.9	7.1	8.2	8.6	8.9	9.6	5.5
Size of holding (acres)	3.3	5.3	6.2	8.2	9.4	10.0	15.4	3.9

Gross income groups (Shs. per year)

Source: ibid., table 57. p. 44.

Table XI:11. Percentage of household cash income from different sources according to income group

Income group	Wages or salaries ('services')	Remittances	Trade and business
1	32.2	19.3	4.6
2	33.1	17.4	8.8
3	26.5	10.5	9.5
4	35.6	6.4	12.2
5	29.1	6.4	13.0
6	32.5	4.6	12.0
7	32.1	2.2	25.2

Table XI:12. Value of marketed and subsistence production as a percentage of total household income

Income group	%
1	61.7
2	60.7
3	65.1
4	59.5
5	58.9
6	54.2
7	42.9

Although agricultural production provided only a third or less of the total cash income of all households in the sample, one should not be misled by this into believing that agriculture as such was unimportant or marginal to the wellbeing of households in Central Province at this time. Not only on the smaller holdings is subsistence production a significant part of total income, but if one adds together the value of marketed agricultural production and the imputed value of directly consumed production in each income class, one finds that in all cases agriculture provides a substantial part of total income.

Moreover, as incomes and holding sizes rise, so the proportion of total agricultural output which is marketed rises. We see in fact that in the top two income groups (with average holding sizes of ten acres and 15.4 acres respectively) marketed production actually exceeds subsistence production, whilst in the two lowest income groups (average holding size 3.3 acres and 5.3 acres) households sold only a little over half of what they ate themselves.

It is possible that this latter finding is time- and sample-specific. Cowen in a later piece of work in Nyeri district concluded after a survey of coffee, tea and milk production on twenty-two holdings that 'it is the smallest and the largest

*Table XI: 13. Marketed production as a
percentage of subsistence production*

Income group	%
1	55.8
2	52.2
3	72.2
4	79.2
5	90.6
6	131.3
7	192.4

landholdings which register the smallest proportion of revenue from sales ...
there is no monotonic relation between the size group of holdings and the
proportion of consumption from directly consumed output'.[37] And he went
on to argue that, in the period 1965–75 in Magutu location, Nyeri, it was middle-
level households which had registered the fastest rates of growth of output and
of marketed output, thereby equalising the inter-household distribution of
farm income to some extent.

It is difficult to compare his findings with those from the *Economic Survey*
because the minimum and maximum holding sizes in his sample are markedly
smaller than those of the *Survey* (which it will be remembered was weighted in
favour of larger holdings). If the proportion of marketed to subsistence production were to be distributed in the manner graphed in figure XI:1 over the
size range one to fifteen acres (in Central Province), the *Survey* findings and
those of Cowen could be made compatible.

That is, one would expect to find in 1972, compared with 1964, that as a
result of a more rapid expansion of their coffee, tea and milk production and of
marketed production, holdings in the middle range of three to six acres had
higher proportions of marketed production than holdings in the range seven to
nine acres. This would be because they had not diverted labour power off the
land, or had brought labour power back to the holding, and if household
incomes were to rise through the use of this labour power, the smaller holding
had to be worked more intensively and higher proportions of output marketed
(even at the cost of depending more on the market for subsistence food as a
result of the diversion of land and labour power away from this form of production). At higher acreages farm cash incomes did not need to be expanded at the
cost of subsistence production, and thus, though the absolute value of marketed output would be greater, measured as a proportion of total production it
would be smaller. This pattern would be observed in the acreage range seven
to ten acres. Above this level a minority of still larger holdings would have land

37. M. P. Cowen and Kabiru Kinyanjui, 'Some Problems of Class Formation in Kenya' (cyclostyled
paper, IDS, Nairobi, March 1977), Section III, p. 12.

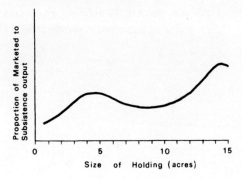

Figure XI:1. Proportion of marketed to subsistence output by size of holding, Central Province, 1963–70.

to spare for the continued expansion of cash crop production, and large off-farm income sources would make the regular hiring of extra labour no problem. On these, the very largest size holdings (ten to fifteen acres and upwards), the proportion of marketed to total production would rise again (despite the fact that the absolute level of subsistence consumption both by household and per capita would be larger than on smaller holdings). These, the really big households, are those who in both 1972 and 1964 had the best of all worlds.

The 1963 Central Province *Survey* showed clearly that off-farm income including wage and salary income and income from trade or business was of vital importance to all households. It was their major source of cash whether they were comparatively rich or poor. Although, given the continued importance of subsistence production, off-farm income was not the major contributor to total household incomes, it was by far the most important source of modern money. Moreover, off-farm income provided more cash for households than did agriculture, whatever the size of their farms, and however big their cash income from agriculture, as table XI:14 shows.

In my view this widespread reliance on off-farm income sources for cash is of vital importance from a number of points of view. Firstly, it is indirectly

Table XI:14. Proportion of farm cash income to total off-farm cash income

Income group	proportion
1	1:2.0
2	1:1.7
3	1:1.06
4	1:1.4
5	1:1.2
6	1:1.2
7.	1:1.8

indicative of the degree of diversion of household labour power away from the household landholding, and thus casts doubt on the status of these smallholders as 'peasants' as that term is understood by some authorities. Secondly, it is significant that the degree of reliance on off-farm income is greatest among the richest and poorest households, the one having to divert labour power away from the holding because it could make a greater contribution to subsistence elsewhere than in adding to labour input on already intensively worked land, and the other supplementing comparatively large farm incomes with even larger off-farm incomes.

The Nyanza Province Household Survey

These findings from Central Province are broadly confirmed by the *Rural Household Survey* of 900 households[38] in Nyanza Province carried out in May and June 1970. Partly modelled on the Central Province study, the Nyanza survey was much more narrowly an income and expenditure survey. Thus, income and expenditure data are not correlated with holding size, and there are therefore no data on output per unit of land. Nor are there any data on labour input or output per 'man' with which the Central Province results can be compared. Instead the tabulated data are disaggregated by district of the Province and by net income groups of households, with a strong stress on the components of gross and net household income, and on the composition of household expenditure. A final descriptive chapter also deals with capital investment and the accumulation of wealth. Although the data are not tabulated by holding size the survey report notes that the holdings selected covered the entire range from 0.2 to twelve hectares,[39] and we may safely assume a strong correlation between the income group data presented and holding sizes, though the precise 'fit' of this correlation must remain an open question.

The basic pattern of agricultural production in the Province in 1970 is set out in the two following tables. The dominant position of Kisii district stands out clearly in table XI:15, it being the largest producer of both food and cash crops, a testimony both to the ecological advantages of its highlands, and to the post-1952 expansion of export cash crops. Kisumu district households by contrast had an output of just over a third of that of Kisii and were the smallest producers both of food and cash crops. This confirms the long process of decline of this district which we traced in earlier chapters, and indeed another table shows that households in this district had by far the largest food deficit (an average of Shs. 283/4 or over a third of gross output) confirming the now established status of this district as a net food importer. Siaya (North Nyanza) households were also in deficit in this year, whilst both the Kisii and South Nyanza households

38. *Rural Household Survey Nyanza Province 1970–71* (Central Bureau of Statistics, Ministry of Finance and Planning, Nairobi, March 1977).
39. Ibid., p. 1.

Table XI:15. Value of farm production per household by district (Kenyan shillings per annum)

Commodity	District				Nyanza Province
	Kisumu	Kisii	S. Nyanza	Siaya	
Food, sugar and livestock					
1 Food and sugar	680.7	1,660.6	1,290.9	1,220.7	1,263.6
Cereals	267.0	688.7	292.6	548.8	452.0
Pulses	27.4	49.0	34.2	81.6	47.2
Roots and tubers	302.4	471.6	788.8	427.6	532.6
Other Vegetables	46.1	184.2	72.9	108.5	106.2
Fruit	16.3	206.4	58.5	34.1	86.2
Sugar	16.3	47.1	12.4	7.9	21.9
Nuts	5.2	13.6	31.5	12.2	17.5
2 Animal Products	181.5	365.3	372.9	275.6	314.1
Fish	6.4	0.0	55.1	6.8	20.4
Dairy Products	11.8	72.7	35.4	46.4	43.6
Livestock	163.6	292.6	282.4	222.4	250.1
3 Other Food	53.6	328.0	52.5	35.0	124.9
4 Total 1–3	916.1	2,353.9	1,716.1	1,531.3	1,702.6
Industrial crops					
5 Cash Crops	21.6	105.9	33.4	17.1	69.8
Tea	0.0	31.7	0.0	0.0	8.7
Coffee	0.0	70.9	1.2	0.2	20.0
Sisal	3.2	0.1	1.2	1.7	1.4
Pyrethrum	0.0	80.8	0.0	0.2	22.3
Cotton	2.6	0.0	28.1	13.6	12.5
Tobacco	0.9	0.6	1.1	0.2	0.7
Other	14.9	1.8	1.8	1.2	4.2
6 Other Products	17.5	1.8	5.4	12.2	8.1
7 Total 1–6	955.2	2,541.6	1,755.1	1,560.6	1,780.5
Number of Cases	144	190	201	171	706

Source: *Rural Household Survey . . .*, op. cit., table 4.2, p. 27.

were in surplus. The important part played by basic cereals (twenty-five per cent), roots and tubers (thirty per cent) and of animal products (17.6 per cent) in provincial output should be noted, as well as the stability of this structure across districts. In no case does 'cash crop' production exceed four per cent of

Table XI.16. Value of gross agricultural production and percentage of each enterprise in total output by income group
(Kenyan shillings per annum)

Type of Production	300–599		600–999		1,000–1,499		1,500–1,999		2,000–2,999		3,000 +		Nyanza Province	
	Shs.	%	Shs.	%	Shs.	%	Shs.	%	Shs.	%	Shs.	%	Shs.	%
Cereals	172.2	36.2	305.0	40.4	364.0	31.9	426.0	24.9	523.6	20.2	684.5	23.0	452.0	25.2
Pulses	17.2	3.6	27.3	3.6	37.6	3.3	44.1	2.6	54.9	2.1	76.9	2.6	47.2	2.6
Roots and Tubers	102.4	21.5	178.2	23.6	264.6	23.2	514.4	30.1	726.8	28.0	730.0	24.5	532.6	29.7
Other Vegetables	53.3	11.2	63.5	8.4	80.5	7.1	86.2	5.0	117.7	4.5	149.8	5.0	106.2	5.9
Fruit	23.7	5.0	46.9	6.2	37.0	3.2	90.2	5.3	121.1	4.7	115.0	3.9	86.2	4.8
Sugar	9.3	2.0	4.2	0.6	14.4	1.3	25.6	1.5	18.7	0.7	33.1	1.1	21.9	1.2
Nuts	1.1	0.2	5.9	0.8	20.1	1.8	21.0	1.2	20.2	0.8	18.8	0.6	17.5	1.0
Animal Products	55.6	11.7	69.5	9.2	137.8	12.1	371.5	21.7	762.5	29.4	826.8	27.7	324.1	18.1
Fish	7.7	1.6	5.5	0.7	6.2	0.5	10.1	0.6	32.5	1.3	67.9	2.3	20.4	1.1
Dairy	12.6	2.7	15.9	2.1	26.5	2.3	47.2	2.8	49.9	1.9	78.8	2.6	43.6	2.4
Livestock	35.3	7.4	48.1	6.4	105.1	9.2	314.2	18.4	680.1	26.2	680.1	22.8	250.1	14.0
Other Food	0.9	0.2	11.2	1.5	23.7	2.1	71.8	4.2	168.2	6.5	233.8	7.8	124.9	7.0
Coffee	29.4	6.2	15.6	2.1	24.7	2.2	25.8	1.5	21.4	0.8	15.9	0.5	20.0	1.1
Tea	0.0	0.0	0.0	0.0	0.0	0.0	2.5	0.1	9.2	0.4	4.8	0.2	8.7	0.5
Sisal	0.8	0.2	1.3	0.2	2.0	0.2	1.6	0.09	0.2	0.007	0.9	0.03	1.4	0.08
Pyrethrum	1.5	0.3	9.9	1.3	7.0	0.6	8.2	0.5	25.9	1.0	35.1	1.2	22.3	1.2
Cotton	5.8	1.2	10.8	1.4	9.8	0.9	10.0	0.6	12.8	0.5	30.1	1.0	12.5	0.7
Tobacco	0.1	0.02	0.2	0.03	0.6	0.05	0.6	0.04	1.1	0.04	0.6	0.02	0.7	0.04
Other	1.4	0.3	1.8	0.2	6.8	0.6	5.1	0.3	4.2	0.2	3.1	0.1	4.2	0.2
Other Products	0.3	0.06	4.3	0.6	9.7	0.9	7.2	0.4	6.4	0.2	19.6	0.6	8.1	0.5
Total	475.0	100.0	755.0	100.0	1,140.3	100.0	1,711.8	100.0	2,594.9	100.0	2,978.8	100.0	1,790.5	100.0

Source: ibid., table 4.5, p. 29.

gross output, and in two cases (South Nyanza and Siaya) it is less than two per cent of the whole. The particularly important role of livestock in the output of South Nyanza households should be noted (21.2 per cent)—an indication of the continued importance of pastoralism in this traditionally pastoral Luo district.

Moreover, as table XI:16 shows, this markedly subsistence-oriented production structure is also stable across income groups. Most high-income farmers in the sample concentrated their production on livestock and food crops just like their poorer neighbours. In fact the survey report noted a tendency for the proportion of 'industrial crop' production in gross output to fall with rising income, though of course rising in absolute terms; and though the sample was too small to allow a district breakdown of this trend, the authors expressed confidence that it also held for Kisii. The only other change of any real note is the tendency for the output of animal products and especially livestock to rise with income.

All these figures are of course inclusive of an imputed value of subsistence production. Table XI:18 shows the amount of this gross production actually marketed by farm enterprise and income group.[40] A comparison of this table with table XI:16 will quickly confirm the earlier impression of a provincial economy still strongly oriented to subsistence. Overall only some 17.6 per cent of the average household output of food crop and animal products found their way to market in 1970, and in no district did the value of marketed production exceed that of subsistence production. When the data are tabulated by income group, we obtain the results shown in table XI:17.

The contrast with the Central Province survey from seven years earlier could hardly be sharper (see table XI:13). Whereas that survey showed the degree of commercialisation of output growing with household income, the Nyanza survey shows an almost exactly opposite trend. What this suggests is

Table XI:17. Marketed production as a percentage of subsistence production

Income group	%
300–599	58.7
600–999	35.1
1,000–1,499	32.2
1,500–1,999	29.8
2,000–2,999	31.7
3,000 +	25.6
Provincial Average	26.4

40. These figures were calculated from table 4.5, p. 29 and table 6.6, p. 52 of the Survey. Only a tabulation of the proportion of marketed production in gross production by district and type of of crop (table 4.4, p. 28) appears in the Survey.

Table XI:18. Gross farm cash income by enterprise and income group: Nyanza Province 1970 (in Kenyan shillings per annum)

	300–599	600–999	1,000–1,499	1,500–1,999	2,000–2,999	3,000 +	Nyanza Province
Cereals	55.1	67.1	69.2	76.7	83.8	116.4	81.4
Pulses	3.1	3.9	4.2	4.9	5.5	7.7	4.7
Roots and Tubers	7.2	7.1	5.3	5.1	7.3	7.3	5.3
Other Vegetables	11.2	10.7	12.1	13.8	16.4	25.5	15.9
Fruit	1.9	0.9	2.2	2.7	2.4	4.6	2.6
Sugar	8.7	4.0	10.2	16.1	13.8	25.5	15.8
Nuts	1.1	5.0	16.7	18.1	4.7	16.3	10.0
Fish	7.5	5.2	5.8	9.6	31.5	58.4	19.0
Dairy Products	6.9	8.7	11.7	10.9	18.5	45.7	16.1
Meat	33.1	39.0	80.9	172.8	353.7	188.5	122.5
Other	0.8	4.0	6.2	6.5	10.1	16.4	8.7
All Food	136.6	155.6	224.5	337.2	547.7	512.3	302.0
Coffee	29.4	15.6	24.7	25.8	21.4	15.9	20.0
Tea	0.0	0.0	0.0	2.5	9.2	4.8	8.7
Sisal	0.8	1.3	2.0	1.6	0.2	0.9	1.4
Pyrethrum	1.5	9.9	7.0	8.2	25.9	35.1	22.3
Cotton	5.8	10.8	9.8	10.0	12.8	30.1	12.5
Tobacco	0.1	0.2	0.6	0.6	1.1	0.6	0.7
Other	1.4	1.8	6.8	5.1	4.2	3.1	4.2
All 'Industrial Crops'	39.0	39.6	50.9	53.8	74.8	90.5	69.8

Source: ibid, calculated from tables 4.5, p. 29 and 6.6, p. 52.

that in Nyanza Province just as in Central Province the poorest households had been forced into the 'high risk' market strategy whose structure and origins we examined earlier (in fact the poorest households in both Provinces marketed a very similar proportion of their output), but that on larger holdings in Nyanza neither the returns to food crop sales nor the returns to cash crops were sufficient to tempt even household heads on median holdings to market higher proportions of output, whilst on the largest holdings cash crop production could be introduced and expanded without any need for a reduction in subsistence output. To a degree of course this situation is self-reinforcing. Without a large urban market, and with the majority of provincial demand for food filled by domestic production, food markets are likely to be small and easily flooded especially at harvest time; hence returns will be low, especially if producers are at a distance from markets, and also have to bear transport costs out of low unit prices. Since in the Province as a whole marketed output of food accounted for 81.2 per cent of all marketed output, this self-generated 'blockage' of local food markets was a powerful factor in slowing down the commercialisation of agriculture.

However whilst food production dominated marketed production throughout the Province, a breakdown of marketed production by enterprise and income group shows some interesting variations (table XI:19).

Thus we see that the proportion of cereals in marketed production tends to fall with rising income, while the proportion coming from meat and dairy products rises. Similarly the proportion of marketed output from 'industrial crops' tends to fall with rising income, and this is notably the case with coffee, the most valuable of the industrial crops in the provincial sample as a whole. It is certain that behind these household figures there are considerable variations both within and between districts, but unfortunately the data tabulation in the

Table XI:19. Share of farm enterprise in marketed production by income group

	Household Income Group					
Enterprise (as percentage of marketed production)	300–599	600–999	1,000–1,499	1,500–1,999	2,000–2,999	3,000+
Cereals	31.4	34.4	27.9	19.6	13.5	19.3
Meat and Dairy	22.8	24.4	33.6	47.0	59.8	38.9
All Food	77.8	79.7	81.5	86.2	88.0	85.0
Coffee	16.7	8.8	9.0	6.6	3.4	2.6
Tea	0.0	0.0	0.0	0.6	1.5	0.8
Pyrethrum	0.9	5.1	2.5	2.1	4.2	5.8
Cotton	3.3	5.5	3.5	2.6	2.1	5.0
All 'Industrial Crops'	22.2	20.3	18.5	13.8	12.0	15.0

Source: ibid., tables 4.5 and 6.6.

Table XI:20. Proportion of livestock products marketed and value of marketed production by income group (in Kenyan shillings)

	Household Income Group					
	300–599	600–999	1,000–1,499	1,500–1,999	2,000–2,999	3,000 +
Dairy production	12.6	15.9	26.5	47.2	49.9	78.8
%Marketed	55	55	44	23	37	58
Value of marketed production	6.9	8.7	11.7	10.9	18.5	45.7
Livestock production	35.3	48.1	105.1	314.2	680.1	680.1
%Marketed	94	81	77	55	52	31
Value of marketed production	33.1	39.0	80.9	172.8	353.7	188.5

report does not allow comparable district figures to be derived. However, the impression is generally reinforced of the poorest households taking the risk of marketing more of their cereals output (another table in the report shows that the proportion of cereals and other food crops domestically consumed rises uniformly with income), whilst in Kisii in particular the smallest holdings devote proportionately more of their land and labour time to coffee production. Conversely, in all districts of the province livestock and dairy produce were the most uniformly commercialised of all 'food crops' (fifty-six per cent of the former and forty-three per cent of the latter being marketed in the province as a whole),[41] with the households on larger holdings with greater pasturage available dominating production as a whole and marketed production. Even here however it appears that the poorer households marketed much larger proportions of their total output, but because of much smaller livestock holdings were unable to compete in the market with the better-off households. Table XI:20 clearly demonstrates the pattern involved.

The important part played by livestock and animal products generally in the commercial production of Nyanza Province as a whole, and their dominant part along with cereals production in the farm cash incomes of all households, richer and poorer, demonstrate the fundamentally 'unrevolutionised' nature of Nyanza agriculture eighteen years after the Emergency and twelve years after the serious onset of the Swynnerton programme. This goes far to explain the aggregate figures of livestock marketed in table XI:1. It is certain moreover that in exhibiting this predominant 'subsistence' mix in output with marketed production still very much an appendage to subsistence, Nyanza Province was much more typical of Kenya as a whole (i.e. of the situation in the African

41. Ibid., table 4.4, p. 28.

farming areas of the Rift Valley and of Coast Province) in the sixties and early seventies than was the Central Province of 1963.

Agricultural Production and Household Income

Tables XI:21 and XI:22 show the structure of household net income among the sampled households by district and income group. An extraordinary stability across income groups is to be noted. In all cases 'net farm income' (the value of gross farm production minus farm production costs) dominates the incomes of all the households, with wage or salary earnings and remittances accounting for the bulk of the remainder. Interestingly remittances contribute more to total income than earnings in the two lowest income groups, and in the poorest households constitute nearly a sixth of total income. It is clear from table XI:21 that the bulk of the poorest households in this category of major remittance receivers were in Kisumu district. It is also notable that in Kisumu net farm income was a smaller proportion of total factor income than elsewhere whilst earnings were correspondingly more important here than in other districts.[42] It is also clear even from this data that both earnings and net business income rose faster than net farm income as total income rose.[43]

A comparison of the top row of Table XI:22 with table XI:12 (p. 342) reveals that agricultural production represents a somewhat larger part of total income among Nyanza households as a whole than among those in Central Province, though again the proportion among the poorest households in the two surveys is very similar. Since, as we have seen, a much smaller proportion of total production was marketed in Nyanza this comparison tells one little. In fact for a more illuminating comparison with the Central Province survey it is necessary to eliminate the subsistence production element and to look at the structure of household cash income. The four tables XI:23 to XI:26 analyse this structure in detail.

Although the net figures give a much more accurate picture of the 'year end' cash situation of the households, the absence of equivalent data in the Central Province survey means that comparison must be restricted to the gross cash receipts data. A comparison of tables XI:23–26 with tables XI:9 and XI:11 reveals that:

1. The proportion of gross cash receipts coming from wages and salaries ('earnings') was much higher in Central Province for all income groups except the richest. This undoubtedly reflects both the proximity of off-farm employment in Nairobi, and the greater availability of casual employment on other smallholdings, compared with Nyanza Province.
2. The proportion of all households' cash income coming from remittances is

---

42. This of course reflects the availability of wage and salaried jobs in Kisumu town, see ibid., p. 40.
43. Net business income rose by nearly 98% as income and earnings rose by over 96%. Net farm income rose 86%, ibid., table 5.2, p. 37.

Table XI:21. *Average amount of income per household by source and district*

DISTRICT

Source of Income	Kisumu		Kisii		S. Nyanza		Siaya		Nyanza Province	
	Amount K.Shs. p.a.	Share Percent	Amount K.Shs. p.a.	Share Percent	Amount K.Shs. p.a.	Share Percent	Amount K.Shs. p.a.	Share Percent	Amount K.Shs. p.a.	Share Percent
Net Farm Income	913.5	65.1	2408.0	85.6	1664.5	88.5	1510.6	76.7	1695.6	82.0
Net Business Income	32.2	2.3	64.9	2.3	22.4	1.2	120.5	6.1	57.0	2.8
Earnings from Employment	436.7	31.1	312.0	11.1	163.9	8.7	321.0	16.3	289.7	14.0
Rental and Income NEC	21.2	1.5	28.6	1.0	30.1	1.6	16.2	0.8	25.0	1.2
Total Factor Income	1403.6	100.0	2813.5	100.0	1880.9	100.0	1968.3	100.0	2067.3	100.0
Transfers Received	359.7	25.6	157.5	5.6	352.8	18.8	388.1	19.7	307.8	14.9
Remittances	214.9	15.3	35.7	1.3	215.6	11.5	165.0	8.4	155.0	7.5
Gifts	94.7	6.7	67.2	2.4	66.8	3.6	109.6	5.5	81.3	3.9
Dowries	50.1	3.6	54.6	1.9	70.4	3.7	113.5	5.8	71.5	3.5
Household Net Income	1763.3	125.6	2971.0	105.6	2233.7	118.8	2356.4	119.7	2375.3	114.9
Taxes	34.0	2.4	24.6	0.9	14.1	0.7	9.3	0.5	19.7	1.0
Transfers Given	62.0	4.4	162.9	5.8	207.9	11.05	92.4	4.7	143.3	6.9
Household Income less Transfers and Taxes	1667.3	118.8	2783.5	98.9	2011.7	107.0	2254.1	114.6	2213.7	107.1

Source: ibid., table 5.1, p. 36.; typographical errors corrected.

Table XI:22. Structure of household incomes by source of income and income group

Net income groups

Income Source	300–599		600–999		1,000–1,499		1,500–1,999		2,000–2,999		3,000 +		Nyanza Province	
	Amount	%	Amount	%	Amount	%	Amount	%	Amount	%	Amount	%	Amount	%
Net Farm Income	407.8	61.2	708.8	68.4	1,096.1	77.9	1,571.8	76.7	2,102.1	76.1	2,909.7	53.6	1,695.6	71.4
Net Business Income	4.6	0.7	15.5	1.5	23.6	1.7	22.6	1.1	48.0	1.7	212.1	3.9	57.0	2.4
Earnings	62.9	9.4	79.1	7.6	102.4	7.3	134.4	6.6	246.0	8.9	1,621.8	29.9	289.7	12.2
Rental and Other Income	3.8	0.6	6.9	0.7	11.2	0.8	16.4	0.8	38.9	1.4	50.4	0.9	25.0	1.1
Total Factor Income	479.1	71.9	810.3	78.1	1,233.3	87.6	1,745.2	85.1	2,435.0	88.2	4,794.2	88.3	2,067.3	87.1
Transfer Received	187.2	28.1	226.7	21.8	174.0	12.4	304.5	14.9	326.4	11.8	635.6	11.7	307.8	13.0
Remittances	109.1	16.4	106.9	10.3	73.9	5.3	142.1	6.9	192.2	7.0	403.7	7.4	155.0	6.5
Gifts	60.8	9.1	90.0	8.7	63.7	4.5	83.9	4.1	55.8	2.0	94.7	1.7	81.3	3.4
Dowries	17.3	2.6	29.8	2.9	36.4	2.6	78.5	3.8	78.4	2.8	135.2	2.5	71.5	3.0
Household Net Income	666.3	100	1,037.0	100	1,407.3	100	2,049.7	100	2,761.4	100	5,429.6	100	2,375.1	100
Taxes	−1.9	0.3	−5.5	0.5	−22.0	1.6	−24.0	1.2	−30.7	1.1	−54.5	1.0	−19.7	0.8
Transfer Given	−54.8	8.2	−55.2	5.3	−62.3	4.4	−177.9	8.7	−132.3	4.8	−257.9	4.7	−143.3	6.0
Household Income Less Transfers and Taxes	609.6	91.5	976.3	94.2	1,323.0	94.0	1,847.8	90.1	2,598.4	94.1	5,117.3	94.3	2,212.1	93.2

Source: ibid., table 5.2, p. 37.

Table XI:23. Household cash income in Nyanza Province 1970: A. Gross terms

| Income Group | Percentage of household gross cash income from: | | | |
	Earnings	Remittances	Trade & Business	Agriculture
Shs. 300–599	14.2	24.7	2.8	39.7
Shs. 600–999	14.4	19.4	7.6	35.5
Shs. 1,000–1,499	16.3	11.8	10.1	43.9
Shs. 1,500–1,999	14.8	15.7	6.7	43.1
Shs. 2,000–2,999	18.0	14.1	9.5	45.7
Shs. 3,000 +	46.6	11.6	16.5	17.3

Table XI:24. Household cash income in Nyanza Province 1970: B. Net terms

| Income group | Percentage of household net cash income from: | | | |
	Earnings	Remittances	Trade & Business	Agriculture
Shs. 300–599	21.0	36.4	1.5	31.6
Shs. 600–999	19.2	25.9	3.8	32.5
Shs. 1,000–1,499	24.0	17.3	5.5	42.9
Shs. 1,500–1999	22.8	24.1	3.8	50.3
Shs. 2,000–2,999	25.0	19.5	4.9	46.2
Shs. 3,000 +	59.3	14.8	7.8	14.0

Table XI:25. Ratio of gross farm cash income to gross household cash income

A Income group	B Cash income from agriculture		C Total household cash income
Shs. 300–599	Shs. 175.6	r = 1:2.5	Shs. 441.9
Shs. 600–999	Shs. 195.2	r = 1:2.8	Shs. 549.8
Shs. 1,000–1,499	Shs. 275.4	r = 1:2.3	Shs. 626.7
Shs. 1,500–1,999	Shs. 391.0	r = 1:2.3	Shs. 907.9
Shs. 2,000–2,999	Shs. 622.5	r = 1:2.2	Shs. 1,363.5
Shs. 3,000 +	Shs. 602.8	r = 1:5.7	Shs. 3,481.8

r = ratio of B to C.

Table XI:26. Ratio of gross farm cash income to total off-farm cash income

Income group	Ratio
Shs. 300–599	1:1.5
Shs. 600–999	1:1.8
Shs. 1,000–1,499	1:1.3
Shs. 1,500–1,999	1:1.3
Shs. 2,000–2,999	1:1.2
Shs. 3,000 +	1:4.7

higher in Nyanza Province than in Central Province for all income groups. This is a reflection both of the generally less commercialised structure of agricultural production and of the lower level of earnings in Nyanza, but it is also an indication of the greater prevalence of long-distance labour migration from the Province, since members of the family who were absent for most of the survey period were excluded from the household in the survey methodology.[44] Hence of course their earnings counted as 'remittances' from outside the household. The much greater importance of remittances in the income of Kisumu district households in particular indicates the high levels of migration from that district, which may also have been a factor in the low level of agricultural output there if the analysis proffered in earlier sections is correct. It is unfortunate that the sample size did not allow cross-tabulation of incomes by district and income group, since data of this type would have shed great light on this hypothesis.

3. The proportion of gross household cash income coming from trade and business is lower in all income groups in Nyanza Province compared with Central Province. Since a central hypothesis in earlier analysis was that the size and degree of differentiation of the off-farm small business sector in rural areas is a function to a large degree of the size of the marketed surplus in agriculture and of the degree of commercialisation in general (since the latter is expressed as an increase in both the size and the velocity of the circulation of money and commodities), this finding is the one which we would expect.

Despite these differences, table XI:14 and table XI:26 also show a marked similarity between the two Provinces at these two different moments in time, in that the farm/off-farm structure of cash income is extraordinarily similar in the two samples. In all cases (all household income levels) non-farm sources are more important than farming as sources of cash for the household. Moreover, in the Nyanza survey, as in Central Province, the importance of off-farm sources is greatest in the richest and poorest households, though this is more marked among the richest households in Nyanza (who received nearly five times more cash from off-farm than from farm sources) than it is in Central Province. Conversely, at the lowest income level the off-farm dependence seems to be slightly greater in Central Province than in Nyanza.

Given the lack of a breakdown of these data by district, any explanation of these differences must be speculative, but we may suggest that they are in different ways a reflection of the different level of agricultural commercialisation in the two provinces. In Nyanza the low returns available from the forms of commercialised production extant made it rational for the richest household heads (and others in such households) to direct their labour power overwhelmingly to off-farm pursuits, mainly to the higher-paid wage and salaried jobs which their education/training had made available to them, but also to various forms of off-farm trade and business (from which their gross monetary income

44. Ibid., paragraph 1.4, p. 1.

was almost double that of any other income group). It is also possible that such households preferred to use their land to maximise the directly produced portion of their subsistence rather than to expand off-farm sales, since off-farm pursuits made a relatively large and reliable cash income easy to obtain. Some circumstantial evidence in support of this hypothesis is that the average gross and net cash income from farming of this income group of households (with a net income of Shs. 3000 or more) in 1970 was actually lower than the average for the Shs. 2000–2999 income group, though the value of total farm production (in gross or net terms) was higher.[45]

At the bottom of the income gradient in Central Province precisely the opposite pressures were at work. Faced with higher population densities and greater subsistence pressure on the land than their Nyanza counterparts even seven years later, the poorest Central Province households were forced both to market more of their total output and to relieve subsistence pressure and bolster up household income by diversion of labour power off the land. Given the proximity of Nairobi and the much increased rate of casual labour hiring by better-off smallholders (as a result of the much wider and deeper spread of export cash crops), a labour demand was generated to match the supply. Of course both the demand and the supply were part of the same commercialisation/ differentiation process. The greater pressure on the poorest households in Central Province is implicit in the finding that, though marketing almost exactly the same proportion of their total output as their Nyanza Province fellows, their cash income from agriculture in 1963 was only some sixty per cent of that of the poorest households in Nyanza in 1970.

Other Studies

This heavy dependence of farm households on sources of off-farm income is widely reported in a large number of other economic surveys of smallholder agriculture which have taken place in Kenya since the early sixties. Most notably, it is reported in a survey of over 7,000 farms on both high and low density settlement schemes carried out by the Farm Economic Survey Unit of the Ministry of Agriculture in the seasons 1964/5 to 1967/8.[46] This survey showed that, irrespective of the size of farm, non-farm cash income always exceeded farm cash surpluses, usually by a substantial amount, and was the main means of paying back the loans made to farmers entering settlement schemes.[47] Since in 1967/8 only some forty per cent of all the farms in the survey had

45. See columns 6 and 7, table XI: 18 for the gross farm cash incomes in the two highest income groups. Other calculations not tabulated here show that the average net farm cash income of the Shs. 3000 + group was Shs. 381/4 and of the Shs. 2000–2999 group Shs. 455/6.

46. *An Economic Appraisal of the Settlement Schemes 1964/65–1967/68* (Statistics Division, Ministry of Finance and Economic Planning, Farm Economic Survey Report no. 27, Nairobi, 1971).

47. Ibid., p. 132, also p. 44.

a positive cash surplus from agriculture, without these off-farm incomes most of the settlers would have been heavily in debt. The major reason for the failure of farms of all sizes on the settlement schemes to reach their planned cash incomes was that crop yields per unit of land and levels of milk production were generally below those expected, and as a result a much larger proportion of total production on all farms (particularly of maize and milk) was directly consumed by those living on the land. As late as 1968 over sixty per cent of the total production on settlement schemes was maize and milk, and most of this was consumed on the farm.[48] The net result of this was that, though the subsistence levels of many farm families undoubtedly improved as a result of moving on to settlement schemes, the marketed surplus from production was generally below what had been expected.[49]

The main reasons officially given for the small marketed surplus and cash income from farming were: the unfamiliarity of many farmers with new enterprises (particularly grade dairy cows and new varieties of maize); a lack of capital resources to make the necessary supporting investments (such as grazing land improvement, fodder crops and feed for cattle, and fertilizer for maize); and, in the case of the small number of farms growing coffee, tea or pyrethrum, the labour constraint imposed by the high peak-period labour demands for these crops.

In essence all these constraints were different aspects of the same problem. In order to increase their expertise as farmers, settlers would have had to devote a larger part of their total household labour power to farming and to learning new techniques, which would have required a considerable amount of time. However to do this (and in particular the managerial expertise of the household head would be vital), labour power and labour time would have needed to be diverted from off-farm pursuits. However, for the smallest settlers (on the high density schemes), the problem was the familiar one of meeting existing cash expenditures (including loan repayments) before this diversion of intellectual and physical labour 'paid off' in terms of increased yields, marketed output and farm cash income. Since, as we have frequently said, under tropical conditions there can be no certainty that such a pay-off will materialise, the risk involved in such a diversion was considerable even if one believed that the increased yields and income (which would have to be greater per unit of labour time than in off-farm pursuits) were 'theoretically' available. Not surprisingly, therefore, most household heads, particularly on smaller holdings, weighed up the risks and decided against it.

On the larger holdings the situation was rather different but produced the same result. For even though cash surpluses from farming on the low density schemes were absolutely larger than from smaller farms with the same enter-

48. Ibid., pp. 124 and 55.
49. Ibid., p. 54.

prises, off-farm income sources were also markedly greater (indeed it was usually because they had these above-average sources of off-farm income from which to put down the ten per cent deposit on the purchase price and provide the minimum 'working capital' requirements, that most of these households had got on to the low density schemes in the first place). Thus a diversion of labour power (again particularly of the household head, but sometimes of other household members) back to agriculture would have required some realistic prospect of obtaining higher cash returns per unit of labour time in agriculture. As of 1967/8 neither the level of agricultural prices nor the range of farm enterprises available promised these returns.[50]

In the case of coffee, tea and pyrethrum (which as we have said were present only on a few settlement schemes even in 1968), higher gross returns were markedly reduced by higher costs, particularly for hired labour at peak periods on larger farms where total labour requirements outran family resources.[51] But the rational way for a high off-farm income settler to meet these labour demands was not to divert his own high-wage or high-salary labour power to the farm, but to use savings from off-farm income to buy in wage labour, while his wife gained the expertise required as farm manager. To put it another way, one hour of off-farm labour time for a highly-waged African could buy far more than one hour's agricultural labour time on his land. Given that no specific agricultural skills were required which could only be provided by him and not by a hired labourer, diversion of his own labour power would have been irrational under such circumstances, and generally did not occur.

The most important conclusion is perhaps the most obvious one. The principal constraints on the expansion of output in smallholder agricultural production in this period (and indeed both before and since) were land and labour power rather than fixed capital. As landholdings became bigger so both those constraints were relaxed, but the mode of that relaxation was in all cases the investment of savings from off-farm income. It was this which historically had allowed land to be accumulated through purchase, and it was this which from the commencement of the widespread use of hired labour (from the early sixties with the introduction of the new labour-intensive farm enterprises) allowed the labour power constraint to be relaxed on larger farms when family labour resources began to be stretched. Conversely, both these constraints operated most severely on the smallest landholdings, and in particular the heavy investment of female labour power on these smallest holdings did not allow much room for the adoption of new enterprises without cuts in an already slender subsistence (through a change in the crop mix) and greater dependence on the market. The initial step of redirecting departed male labour power to the

---

50. Ibid., pp. 96–7.
51. See also the very similar results to the above in H. W. von Haugiwitz with H. Thorwart, *Some Experiences with Smallholder Settlements in Kenya 1963/64 to 1966/67* (Munich, 1972).

holding (the only way that these households had of meeting the extra labour requirements) was a particularly risk-laden business in the case of coffee and tea production because both these tree crops took time to come into bearing, and their labour needs were heaviest in their immaturity, i.e. before they were yielding a return.[52] The poorest households did not have the resources to 'bridge the gap' which these simple agronomic facts implied.

A Qualification

The relationship between the size of holding and of the cropped area to gross farm output, cash income from farming, and above average sources of off-farm income, is one to be observed with impressive frequency from the commencement of systematic farm surveys in Kenya (and indeed in other parts of East Africa);[53] but it is nonetheless a relationship whose implications for household income distribution, and indeed the absolute level of household incomes, is heavily over-determined by local ecological conditions. It is not the case that over Kenyan smallholder agriculture as a whole, the larger the farm the larger the farm cash income and the larger the off-farm income. An underutilised large farm in the Rift Valley with a few acres of badly-tended maize and a number of unimproved cows, sheep and goats grazing on a large area of natural enclosed grazing, will almost certainly not have a larger farm cash income (whether measured on a household or a per capita basis) than a three or four acre intensively-cultivated market garden producing high value fruit, flowers and vegetables on the outskirts of Nairobi. Even within a small well-defined sample of farms having very similar soil, rainfall and market conditions, and similar farm enterprises, one may still find large farms with very small proportions of their land cropped, so that the area cultivated does not offset low yields. Thus farm cash income may be smaller on a large than on a small farm.

One important implication of this is that the levels of off-farm income which will divert household labour power away from agriculture and keep it there vary markedly from area to area of smallholder Kenya, depending on the ecological conditions and thus the range of possible farm enterprises available. The latter will also determine the amount of labour input which is required on the farm. In particular, farms situated in areas which are not suitable for coffee, tea, pyrethrum or intensive dairying may have markedly lower farm labour demands than more commercialised smallholdings and lower income thresholds for labour migration.

A clear example of such a phenomenon appears in Judith Heyer's work in the

52. See *An Economic Appraisal* ..., op. cit., pp. 91–2 and also Hans Ruthenberg, op. cit., pp. 18 and 46.
53. See my 'Economic and Social Inequality in Rural East Africa: The Present as a Clue to the Past' (Swansea CDS Monograph no. I, 1977) and the works cited therein.

semi-arid Masii location of Machakos district (1962–3).[54] Her work showed that, with the extreme variability of returns to labour in these conditions, the limited range of low-value farm enterprises available, and the failure of the introduction of cotton to provide any higher returns, off-farm employment was extremely attractive even at the lowest end of the wage labour market. And the release of labour power into that market from the farm household was made possible because, even with seasonal peaks, the overall labour input required on the farm was well within the compass of the women and children remaining behind. Hence at the time of her study some sixty-seven per cent of Masii's adult males were in the off-farm labour market.[55]

Nonetheless, despite variations from area to area, which make it important to specify very exactly the ecological, farm enterprise and marketing situation within which the comparison is being made, it remains the case that within similar agro-economic zones the larger the holding the larger the cropped area, the larger the cropped area the larger the gross farm output, the larger the gross farm output, the larger the absolute level of output marketed, and the larger the amount of output marketed the larger the household cash income from farming. In addition off-farm cash incomes usually rose with farm incomes, so that the best-off farm households (from the point of view of cash income) usually had the largest off-farm cash incomes as well. Thus overall the larger the holding the larger was the total household income and the larger the per capita income from all sources, despite the fact that the larger holdings nearly always had larger households upon them.

This appears clearly in table XI:27 which shows the distribution of average per capita income by holding-size groups in Central Province in 1963, and of average per capita income by income group in Nyanza in 1970.

Conclusions from the Surveys
Thus the close relationship between above-average farm incomes from larger holdings and access to above-average off-farm incomes, and the importance of

54. J. Heyer, *The Economics of Small-Scale Farming in lowland Machakos* (IDS Monograph, Nairobi, 1967).
55. Heyer's study of Masii is one of the most careful and detailed pieces of farm survey work undertaken in Kenya to date and provides some very interesting findings. In particular, from the point of view of this work, it provides confirmation of the weakness of cotton as a smallholder cash crop deriving from its low yields and returns per acre and its low returns to labour. It also confirms the importance of windfall returns to food crops in times of shortage (as well as the converse of this— the drive for security in marginal farming conditions) as a factor entering into smallholder calculations of the relative attractiveness of maize and other food crops vis-à-vis cotton. Above all it shows the innumerable ramifications of the inherent unreliability and riskiness of farming in areas like Masii, and the importance of the quality of labour input (rather than the quantity) in explaining differences in performance of similar sized farms with almost identical enterprises upon them. See Heyer, op. cit., especially pp. 55–82.

Table XI:27. Per capita incomes in Central Province and Nyanza

CENTRAL PROVINCE 1963			NYANZA PROVINCE 1970		
Holding size group	Household size (persons)	Per capita income (Shs. per annum)	Income group (Shs. per annum)	Household size (persons)	Per capita income (Shs. per annum)
3.3	3.9	186	666.3	5.2	128
5.3	5.9	204	1,037	7.2	144
7.1	7.1	240	1,407.3	7.0	201
8.2	8.2	260	2,049.7	7.0	293
9.4	8.6	335	2,761.4	8.4	329
10.0	8.9	460	5,429.6	12.2	445
15.4	9.6	961			

Sources: Central Province figures calculated from *Economic Survey*, table 57, p. 44, and Nyanza Province figures from *Rural Household Survey*, table 5.2, p. 37 and table 2.2, p. 13. Both sets of figures are for gross income and include an imputed value of subsistence production.

off-farm income to both the richest and poorest households (for different reasons) emerge as the predominant findings of the farm survey data which began to appear in Kenya in the sixties. On the whole they provide confirmation (though only indirectly) of the sort of mechanisms of differentiation which I have attempted to lay bare in the earlier historical analysis. Any explanation of 'rural', 'agricultural' stratification in Kenya cannot be separated from the explanation of all income and wealth inequalities there, since the very category of 'off-farm income' points us in the direction of the explanation of wage labouring on other smallholdings, and into the agricultural and non-agricultural labour market in general. This in turn has one important theoretical implication which is worth taking up at this point.

A number of recent analyses of 'peasant economies', most notably that of Shanin, have been based on the work of A. V. Chayanov on the Russian peasantry.[56] They have sought to generalise his findings to other areas and periods from that in which it was formulated. I do not wish here to enter into a detailed discussion of Chayanov's theory or its adaptations, or indeed its accuracy even for the Russian peasantry which it purported to analyse. I simply wish to note that at the heart of Chayanov's theory and its modern variants is a simple assumption of a conceptually and spatially isolated 'peasant economy' in which the only alternatives before the household are the use of its labour power in cultivation on the peasant holding or 'leisure'. However, as far as the Central Province and large parts of the Nyanza Province, Machakos and the Rift Valley were concerned, the emergence of smallholding agricultural production was

56. A. V. Chayanov, *The Theory of Peasant Economy* (Homewood, 1966) and T. S. Shanin, *The Awkward Class: Political Sociology of Peasantry in a Developing Society. Russia 1910–1925* (Oxford, 1972).

almost coterminous with the expansion of off-farm labour opportunities on settler farms and in non-agricultural pursuits. Thus most households have from the very beginning operated with three 'choices' for the use of their household labour power: its use on the holding, its use off the holding, and 'leisure'. Since, as I have argued, the historically crucial determinant of holding size was access to off-farm income (or more exactly the level of off-farm income to which a household had access), there has never, in Kenya, been any simple way that the size of farm income could be derived from the demographic characteristics of the farm household (in the way the Chayanovians attempt to do).[57] To be sure, larger holdings in Kenya often have larger households resident upon them, but those larger households do not generally have lower dependency ratios, i.e. fewer children in proportion to adults (usually quite the reverse). Historically, in the most commercialised zones holdings became large because off-farm incomes (earned by the household head) were large, and as a result larger families could be supported upon them. So in this case the holding size is the 'independent' and the household size the 'dependent' variable and not the

57. It is this 'demographic determinism', and the theory of cyclical mobility of peasant households based on it, which is at the centre of the Chayanovian model of a peasant economy. It almost invariably leads on to a denial of the possibility of a cumulative pattern of stratification or differentiation among peasant households. To show that, in a particular set of circumstances, the autonomy of the household as a production and consumption unit does not hold, and that patterns of differentiation can indeed be cumulative because household income is not primarily determined by the household's agricultural labour resources, is to successfully demonstrate the irrelevance of the Chayanovian model to that particular set of circumstances. It is not necessary for such a demonstration to deny, as Cowen attempts to do, that there is any force at all to the Chayanovian concept of the relative autonomy of the peasant household. This argument is only necessary if one wishes to argue, as Cowen seems to do, that peasants are a source of 'surplus value'. See Cowen and Kinyanjui, op. cit., pp. 18–38, esp. pp. 28–9. A central plank in such a demonstration is the argument that the bulk of 'middle peasants' in Kenya do not in practice have any choice as to whether to expand commercial production for international capital, because given their land resources, refusal to expand would entail a fall in real incomes. However, this seems to involve an elementary confusion of use and exchange values. It is true for example that if milk prices fall relative to maize prices, and a peasant on a medium-sized holding has switched into commercial milk production at the expense of maize, household real cash incomes will fall if milk production is maintained, and will fall even further if milk production is reduced in response to declining prices. If, in addition, total milk production is reduced so sharply that on-farm consumption falls with sales, then the real level of subsistence of the household will fall for a while. But if land and labour power is then switched back into maize and (say) the production of vegetables, then subsistence and real farm money incomes may rise again. This of course is quite apart from the possibility of adjusting by transferring labour power to the off-farm labour market. It is certainly the case that on small peasant holdings (two acres and below), the diversion of labour power off the farm may allow a very small holding to remain viable as a source of subsistence for part of the household. Thus down to a certain size threshold, smallholdings give the peasant as worker some autonomy as a worker, and off-farm employment gives him and his household some autonomy as a peasant household. The crunch comes of course when holdings become so small and exhausted that, even with part of the household's subsistence pressure removed, it is unable to support the rest. In such circumstances without a rise in off-farm real wages, the household is impoverished, and must attempt to sell all its labour power.

other way round. In short, wherever else the Chayanovian model may hold, it does not hold in Kenya, nor I suspect in a large part of sub-Saharan Africa.

5. The Distribution of Land and Farm Income and the Distribution of Off-Farm Income: A Closer Look

Up to this point we have seen that the farm economic survey data which began to emerge in the sixties provide strong support for the hypotheses (deriving from historical material) which have been developed in earlier chapters to explain the mode of differentiation of African households in Kenya. This support is only circumstantial. It derives from the repeatedly observed correlation between holding size, above average farm cash incomes, and above average off-farm incomes. The precise causal hypothesis, it will be remembered, is that off-farm income is used as the primary source of savings, and from these savings investments are made in a variety of economic ventures, of which the purchase of land, support investments for agricultural production, and other forms of trade and business are all different varieties.[58]

The problem with obtaining more than circumstantial statistical evidence on this is that, in order for this process to be observed directly, very detailed household budget studies would be required for a variety of households in a large number of areas, and covering a long period of time. One is here concerned not simply with transactions and resource transfers over one agricultural season, but over the whole economic life of a household, as its income sources alter, occupations are changed, gross household incomes rise (or fall) and investments are made. In the simplest case this means that one would be involved in charting the economic profile of a household for at least as long as its male head was economically active and the household intact as a land holding unit and as a quantum of labour power. One would also be involved in watching changes as that quantum was altered and sons or daughters left to set up or join other households. A particularly important dimension here would be the economic links between kin-linked households, and the extent to which they were able to remain single or closely-connected production and/or financial units after residential fission had occurred.

For a variety of reasons, reliable household budget studies of smallholding units even for a single year present very many and severe methodological

58. Thus, for example the *Central Province Economic Survey* is not a great deal of help since, although it shows that the principal source of capital investment on farms was 'savings', it does not show where these came from. Interestingly it does show that after savings, money income from bridewealth was the next most important source of capital, ibid., pp. 36–8. Though the *Nyanza Household Survey* has a special chapter on the acquisition of 'wealth' or 'capital assets' this is restricted to an attempt to measure the size of asset acquisition by income group rather than to trace sources of saving. See *Rural Household Survey . . .*, op. cit., pp. 58–63.

difficulties in Kenyan conditions, so that data of the type we are seeking are not to be expected.

Somewhat stronger circumstantial evidence in support of our central hypothesis comes from the work of Michael Cowen. In a pioneering study conducted in two sub-locations (Gaikuyu and Gatei) of Nyeri district, Cowen collected data on a number of households operating holdings of more than seven acres and on the households of labourers working on these holdings in the agricultural season 1971–2. In December 1972 he presented a preliminary analysis of findings on thirteen 'farmers' (those holding seven acres or more in 1971–2) and thirty-one 'labourers' in Gaikuyu sub-location alone. It is to be noted that nearly all these 'labourers' (all of whom were male) also held land in 1971–2, but in every case much less than the farmers. Table XI:28 shows the occupational pattern and the mean income from wages or salaries of the farmers vis-à-vis the labourers over the years 1922 to 1943. Cowen's own comments on this table are: 'No statistical significance is intended, but the series of case studies do show the earnings of the present group of labourers widening [*sic* —'falling' would be more accurate] relative to those of present farmers especially during the 1930s.'[59]

Of course not too much should be read into these findings, since they cover a tiny sample in a particular area, and necessarily Cowen had to rely on the memories of informants for occupational and wage data from the past. But nonetheless, the extent to which the present-day farmers had persistently earned off-farm incomes well in excess of the present-day labourers is impressive. Once again, the sheer extent of off-farm working in both groups should be noted. It is difficult to be precise because age data on the household heads interviewed do not appear in the paper, but in 1943 for example it appears that no less than seventy-one per cent of the 1972 'labourers' were in off-farm employment for some or all of the year, as were nearly seventy per cent of the 1972 'farmers'. It must be stressed again therefore that what was vital in the pattern of differentiation in rural Kenya was not the fact that household heads left the holding to work, but what they did and how much they earned once they had left.

Direct evidence in support of the hypothesis also comes from a survey of a small sample of 'progressive farmers'[60] which I undertook in the Kangema location of the Kandara division of Muranga district in Central Province in February 1973. The mean size of holding of this group of thirty farmers was very nearly eighteen acres. Seventy per cent of them were engaged in coffee growing, forty-three per cent were growing tea, all of them had hired casual labourers over the previous twelve months, and twelve of them employed 'permanent' labourers (i.e. labourers not paid by the day or on a piece-work basis, but

59. M. P. Cowen, 'Differentiation . . .', op. cit., p. 19. The table is from p. 18.
60. I asked to interview thirty 'progressive farmers' and left the choice of these thirty up to the Divisional Agricultural Officer. I wished to see what sort of people counted as progressive farmers in the eyes of the local administration.

Table XI.28. Occupational and income profiles of 'farmers' and 'labourers' in Gaikuyu sub-location, Nyeri, 1971. Wages of shown in Shillings, by month, for each year, and the jobs refer to the men who were in wage employment, or trading during each particular year given below.

LABOURERS:

1922	Shs.	1929	Shs.	1936	Shs.	1939	Shs.	1943	Shs.	1949	Shs.
Cook	20	Cook	50	Supervisor	225	Supervisor	225	Supervisor	225	Supervisor	225
Labourer	6	Herdsman	7	Shamba boy	6	Askari	40	Woodcutter	100	Woodcutter	150
		Herdsman	10	Cook	30	Shamba boy	30	Batman	60	Cook	180
				Messenger	20	Shamba boy	15	Askari	50	Houseboy	70
				Labourer	12	Shamba boy	6	Agric. Instructor	40	Houseboy	68
				Labourer	8	Labourer	20	Houseboy	40	Clerk	50
				Labourer	8	Labourer	6	Shamba boy	35	Shamba boy	45
						Labourer	6	Shamba boy	30	Shamba boy	15
						Labourer	3	Dobie	25	Agric instructor	48
								Labourer	10	Headman	70
								Houseboy	8		
								Labourer	25		
Mean Income	13		22		44		39		39		92

FARMERS:

1922	Shs.	1929	Shs.	1936	Shs.	1939	Shs.	1943	Shs.	1949	Shs.
Supervisor	20	Househoy	50	Houseboy	70	Supervisor	150	Supervisor	300	Supervisor	410
Herdsman	10	Cook	60	Artisan	150	Army		Askari	56	Assistant Forest Ranger	80
Herdsman	6	Artisan	45	Tractor Driver	20	Artisan	300	Army Driver	80	Driver	400
		Labourer	12	Artisan	45	Artisan	45	Vegetable Farming	300	Trader	300
										Trader	155
Mean Income	12		42		71		165		184		270

Source: Cowen, 'Differentiation ...', op. cit., p. 18.

employed for a regular wage and resident on the landholder's property). Nineteen of the thirty farmers interviewed had labour costs in excess of Shs. 2,000 per annum and twenty-four had labour costs in excess of Shs. 1,000.

There was strong evidence too of these farmers as land accumulators. Twenty-eight out of thirty had bought some part of their current holdings for money, and twenty-three out of thirty had obtained the majority of their current holdings in this way. Ten had holdings made up entirely of land they had bought. In contrast, twenty-four of these farmers had never sold land at all, and, of those who had, three had sold plots totalling less than two acres. Eight of the farmers had bought more than twenty acres of land up to 1973, and fifteen had bought ten acres or more up to that date. They could recall a total of fifty land purchases of which seventy per cent were in the period 1951–65 and fifty-eight per cent in the nine years 1956–65.[61]

No less than twenty-eight out of the thirty male heads of household involved had held a non-farm wage or salary occupation during their economically active life, and a list of the jobs held in February 1973 or 'the last job held' before February 1973 appears in table XI:29. It will be seen that thirteen of the male household heads were actually in full-time off-farm employment at the date of the survey.

These twenty-eight farmers can be roughly divided into two groups. The first, and largest, comprises the teachers, chiefs, sub-chiefs, civil servants and skilled artisans, who were among the better-paid of African employees. This group comprises eighteen of the thirty farmers interviewed (sixty per cent), who are representatives of what might be called the quintessential 'petite bourgeoisie' of Kenya. This group would be even larger were we to add to it the baker, the electrical engineer, the office boy, the prison guard, the mission station 'labourer', the settler farm carpenter and the domestic servant.

There would be a strong case for doing so in all these cases because all the seven men involved had ended their period of paid employment in the 1940s or 1950s when the wages which they were receiving at the time were well above the prevalent levels for unskilled labour received by the majority of African workers. Thus for example E. M. K. was receiving his Shs. 42 per month in 1942, and K. N. his Shs. 75 per month in 1955. If we do add in these six cases as coming from the second stratum of African employees, still comparatively well-paid in their time, then the 'petite bourgeoisie' category is expanded to twenty-five

61. The findings here are somewhat at odds with those of Karuga on Kiambu. He observed no tendency toward polarisation of land holding sizes through land purchase. It may be that this difference is due to Kiambu's present-day status as almost a 'dormitory suburb' of Nairobi where agriculture is increasingly a secondary activity (most of the land sales he recorded seemed to be for house plots or trade premises). It may also be a function of the very high price of land in Kiambu which gives modern-day accumulation there a high 'opportunity cost' even for the richest, given the much lower price of land in the Rift Valley and elsewhere. See J. G. Karuga, 'Land Transactions in Kiambu' (IDS Working Paper 58, August 1972).

Table XI: 29. Off-farm occupations and incomes in Kangema location, Murang'a, 1973.

Household head	Size of holding (Acres)	Job in Feb. 1973 or 'last job'	Wage or salary (Shs. per month)
O.M.N.	8.2	Teacher	840
M.K.	3.2	Baker[+]	28[+]
N.G.	17.1	Sub-chief	590
G.G.	18.0	Sub-chief	270
L.K.	4.9	Sub-chief	425
T.M.	10.0	Chief	n.a.[+]
W.G.	6.75	Teacher	500
C.M.K.	9.3	Chief	1,340
N.W.	16.0	Office Boy[+]	30[+]
E.M.	3.0	Ran own Lorry Business[+]	n.a.[+]
A.N.	12.5	Garage Mechanic[+]	400
M.W.	7.7	Ran own shop	12
J.M.	2.0	'Engineer' East Africa Power and Light Co [+]	50[+]
M.A.	6.2	Teacher	640
K.N.	10.5	Labourer at Mission Station[+]	75[+]
M.M.	9.6	Machine Operator, Sweet Factory, Nairobi	250
E.M.K.	16.2	Prison Guard, Nairobi[+]	42[+]
M.K.G.	35.0	Agricultural Assistant	600
S.N.	45.0	Casual Labourer, Settler Farm[+]	8[+]
M.G.	22.0	Civil Servant, Public Service Commission	3,000
P.K.	70.0	Chief[+]	890[+]
N.M.	34.0	Cook in European Home[+]	300[+]
B.W.	43.8	Teacher	670
H.N.	12.0	Carpenter, settler farm[+]	50[+]
J.M.W.	42.0	Teacher	600
N.K.	21.5	Domestic Servant	30
E.K.	15.0	Assistant Education Officer	1,500
J.K.	7.6	Sub-chief	600

[+] Indicates that the job was not held in February 1973. Wages quoted are those received at the end of the employment period.

out of these thirty progressive farmers, or over eighty-three per cent of the whole sample. This still leaves us however with five apparently discrepant cases.

Three of these exceptions were more apparent than real. One of the household heads in the sample was a woman, S. W., who was the recently widowed wife of a primary school teacher, managing a fourteen-acre holding which had mainly been obtained by land purchase out of her husband's savings. Another, E. M., had been employed as a casual labourer and then as a lorry driver on the same settler farm from 1920 to 1950. In 1950 he had begun his own transport business, which had collapsed in 1953. He said he found it 'difficult' to remember how much he had earned from the business before its collapse; he seemed to recall it with some distaste, and it was impossible to ascertain his level of earnings from it. But in view of the data on the marked profitability of the transport business in the post-war period cited in chapter VI, it seems likely that these earnings were considerable. The third apparent exception, M. W., had had wage employment, but only for six months in 1951, when he sold beer in a bar. He had been one of four partners in a clothes shop since 1960, but claimed this only earned him Shs. 240 per annum on an initial investment of Shs. 2,500. It is possible that for one reason or another he was understating these earnings.

There were however two genuine and important exceptions to this general trend of above average off-farm earnings by these 'progressive farmers' in Kangema, S. N. and W. M. Moreover, the accounts given by these men of how they had obtained their land were remarkably similar. They both explained that they had inherited large amounts of livestock, particularly sheep and goats, from their fathers who were 'rich' in this respect. S. N. for example obtained the bulk of his holding in 1946 for 200 goats valued at Shs. 13 each at that time. Before that he had been a squatter on one or more settler farms (1930–43). Prior to obtaining the first part of his holding (in 1955), W. M. had been a stock trader, and in 1973 he was one of ten partners in a shop at Kiriani market. He made it clear that since he had obtained the money to start buying his land (by the sale of stock), all his on-farm investments had been made purely out of farm income. One interesting point emerges here. It seems to have been possible even in 1946 to find some landholders in Kangema who were willing to exchange land directly for stock. Ten years later it was clearly not possible, and W. M. had first had to monetise his stock holdings before he could move into land.

One other important point emerged from the survey. Asked the question 'How have you obtained most of the money which you have invested on your land since you started farming?', eighteen out of the thirty farmers stated that most of the money had come mainly or solely from the reinvestment of farm income, and nearly all the others stated that investments had been made from both salary and farm income, often stating that they were unclear about the proportions. In fact the general pattern which emerged in supplementary discussions outside the questionnaire framework, was that off-farm income usually provided the savings from which land was bought, and large-scale investments (such as the purchase of a grade cow) were made. However, the aim of nearly all farmers was to meet the bulk of recurrent farm costs (including hired labour, which was invariably the largest single recurrent cost) out of farm income. Off-farm sources were used only as a 'fall-back' if, for example, a bumper harvest required a larger amount of hired labour than had been expected, or a cow died and needed to be replaced, or veterinary or other fees proved higher than expected.

Such a fall-back was only available to those who still had regular sources of off-farm income at the time of the survey, and thirteen of the thirty farmers were not in this category. At the time of the survey then, these farmers had no choice

Table XI: 30.

Household head	Type of off-farm Investment	Total investment up to Feb. 1973 (Shs.)
L.M.	Taxi Gitugi-Muranga Road	8,000
O.M.N.	General store, Kamune Market	36,000
A.N.	Boarding house, Muranga	10,000
S.N.	General store, Ichichi	40,000
B.W.	'Hotel' (i.e. bar and tea room), Kiriani Market	12,000
N.M.	General store, Tutho	5,000
M.G.	Shop and bar in Githiga, shop in Kahuti and several (unspecified) businesses, Nairobi	'A lot'
M.K.	Fifty ordinary shares in Kenya Breweries Ltd.	n.a.
M.M.	100 shares in Kenya Transport Ltd, Nairobi	2,500
G.G.	Butchers shop, Ichichi	800
C.M.K.	Two shops, one in Kangema, the other in Kiriani	36,000
N.W.	Transport business (1946)	2,700 ('failed')
M.K.G.	General store in Gitugi and another in Nairobi	20,000
S.W.	Boarding house, Muranga	1,400
E.M.	Transport business in Rift Valley. Collapsed with Emergency	3,000 plus running costs
M.W.	Clothes shop	2,500
W.M.	Building and shop, Kiriani	3,000

but to make investments out of farm income, unless they could get access to official or other credit sources. They generally pointed this out, and went on to complain about the difficulty of obtaining government credit.[62]

In addition to investments in farm enterprises, seventeen out of the thirty farmers used savings for off-farm investments. Table XI : 30 shows who these seventeen were, the nature of their investments and their estimates of their total investments off the farm up to the time of the survey.

Interestingly, only five of these seventeen were in receipt of off-farm wages or salaries in 1973, but those who were were among the biggest investors (notably O. M. N., B. W., M. G.—who both as a salary earner and as a businessman was in a different league from the rest of the households in the sample—and C.M.K.). Moreover, of the other big investors in this list, one—A. N.—had made his investment while he was still a well-paid garage mechanic in Nairobi and the other two—M. K. G. and S. N.—had made their investments with other partners (S. N. with nine others and M. K. G. with three others) and the figures quoted refer to the joint investment. Their individual shares were undoubtedly much smaller. All the other investments were of comparatively small amounts, and in nearly all cases were made when the farmers involved had had access to wage or salary incomes.

62. For the skewed availability of smallholder credit in Kenya, see Heyer, Maitha and Senga, op. cit., pp. 208–11. See also J. Heyer, 'Smallholder Credit in Kenya' (IDS Working Paper 85, 1973).

A fairly coherent pattern emerges then from this survey. All but two of the households picked out by the local agricultural administration as 'progressive farmers' had had access to above average off-farm wage or salary incomes at some point in the past, and this access had been vital both in the purchase of land, and in investments in other forms of business enterprise. Twelve of the farmers were still using savings from wages or salaries as back-up funds for farm investments in 1973; eighteen were not, but of these, thirteen had no choice in the matter.

What this shows, as one might have deduced from earlier analysis, is that a smallholder in a comparatively highly commercialised area of Kenya in 1973 could continue a heavy involvement in the 'new' farm enterprises (coffee, tea, dairying) once farm output and income were high enough to allow savings to be made; but, with a few rather peculiar and interesting exceptions, he could not hope to gain access to the amount of land which would make the necessary levels of output, income and savings possible, unless he had or had had (at some point in the past) access to above average wage or salary incomes. Very often savings from this source had also been used to make other forms of investment, but in a surprising number of cases (thirteen out of thirty in this sample) this had not happened, and household heads had remained content with farm investment and other forms of investment, notably in education for their children. This may have reflected the fact that, certainly in the post-war period, really profitable investments in off-farm trade and business were only open to the particularly well-off. Men like M. G., who come from the elite of Kenyan African salary earners in the post-Independence period, could mobilise resources on a scale not open to most even of the better-off smallholders.

One final point should be made. Within this sample there was no simple correlation between the size of off-farm income and the size of holding. The second largest landholder in the sample for example, S. N., was one of the household heads who had never had access to a large wage or salary income, whilst the largest landholder—P. K.— had a significantly smaller salary income on his retirement than M. G. or E. K., both of whom had much smaller holdings. Partly this is a question of time and the cost of land. In many respects what mattered in Kangema, as in many other parts of Kenya, was not so much the absolute level of wage or salary income, but the time at which it was acquired, the length of time for which it was available, and the price of land over that period as a proportion of that income. With land shortage escalating land prices very rapidly through the sixties and seventies, the 'land purchase' power of nominally higher salaries in the early 1970s was probably less than that of smaller money incomes obtained in the 1940s and 1950s.

In addition, access to above average off-farm income was a major determinant of the intensity and effectiveness with which land could be worked (through wage labour, fertiliser, insecticides and other infrastructural investments) and above a certain size threshold this probably mattered more in determining gross

372 Class and Economic Change in Kenya

farm output and income than mere holding size. Nonetheless, the essential point remains. For it can be no coincidence that, left to apply their own criteria, the local agricultural administration came up with a sample of progressive farmers, who, with three exceptions, had holdings at least three times the mean size of holding in Muranga district in 1973, and at the top end thirty times the mean size. They were clearly aware that in order to be a comparatively successful smallholder farmer in Kenya in 1973, as for decades before, an above average-size holding was by no means a sufficient condition, but it was nearly always a necessary condition. For this reason, if no other, to lay bare the mechanism by which land was acquired is to reach to the heart of differentiation in rural Kenya.

6. Conclusions

The supposed 'agrarian revolution', which followed land consolidation and enclosure in Kenya from the mid-fifties onwards, had by 1970 touched only a minority of the smallholding households of Kenya in any way. At least two-thirds of them continued to combine the raising of grains and pulses together with traditional stock rearing on more marginal land, just as they had done in 1952 (and this included the bulk of the holdings on the high density settlement schemes). Even within those areas where the new crops would grow and intensive dairying was taken up (Central Province, Kisii, Kericho and Nandi), it was generally only the larger farmers who could spare the land and obtain the labour power to enter into the new enterprises on a scale which had an appreciable impact on farm output and income. It is very difficult to specify the holding size threshold below which the new enterprises were unviable, because so much depended on soil fertility and other ecological conditions. But in the more densely populated areas of Central Province, highland Machakos, Central Nyanza and southern Western Province it is doubtful if many holdings below the three-acre threshold were greatly touched by the new enterprises.

In the less densely populated districts of the Rift Valley, such as Kericho, Nandi and West Pokot, mean holding sizes were much larger, and far larger proportions of holdings were still under grazing. Even here however it is likely that in the introduction of grade dairy cows and the expansion of milk production (the dominant form of commercialisation after enclosure), access to off-farm income to make the investments in the cattle and the ancillary services was a prime factor differentiating 'progressive' households from others.[63]

Thus two broad groups of households made up the category of those left out in the cold by the 'agrarian revolution'. Within the most densely populated parts

63. See for example *Some Economic Case Studies of African Farms in Rift Valley Province 1961* (Farm Economics Survey Unit Report No. 13, April 1963), p. 26 and pp. 40–58, and *Some Economic Case Studies of Farms in Nandi and West Pokot Districts 1963–64* (Farm Economics Survey Unit Report no. 23, December 1965), pp. 19–47.

of Central Province, the Kisii Highlands, Central Nyanza and the southern locations of Western Region, households on the very smallest holdings, even on land suitable for tea, coffee or pyrethrum production, could not enter on any scale into the production of these crops without diverting land and labour power away from subsistence production. Yet others were on land such as the coastal lowlands of central Nyanza, where these crops would not grow in any case, and where the Administration before and after Independence could still find nothing better than cotton as a 'pure' cash crop. All these smallholders were in the range of holdings of three acres or less in size, and many had less than two acres. They could be categorised together with those households with rather larger holdings but on agriculturally marginal land, such as those analysed in Masii by Heyer, and those found in large numbers in Kitui, lowland south Nyanza and parts of the Coast Province. For them too, production remained concentrated on low-value food crops because the only available alternative, cotton, could not match the returns even from maize and pulses.

The second broad group of households left out were those on large, and even reasonably fertile holdings in the Rift Valley which might be ten or fifteen acres or more, which, though not matching the holdings of better-off neighbours, could have yielded a far greater return except that capital constraints (due to lack of a sufficient level of off-farm income or no such income) kept development to a minimum, and meant that grazing was used for unimproved stock while a small proportion of the land remained under subsistence maize and pulses.

Thus those left out were those with the ecological opportunity but without the land, capital or labour power to take advantage of that opportunity (Central Province, Kisii, Machakos highlands and parts of Central Nyanza), those without the ecological opportunities and without enough land to make up for yield deficiencies by the size of the cultivated area (lowland Machakos, Kitui, other parts of Coast, Nyanza lowlands), and those with the land and the opportunity, but essentially without the capital (Nandi, Kericho, West Pokot).

Common to all of them was the marked narrowing of alternatives due to lack of access (either in 1952–70 or before) to sufficiently large sources of off-farm income. With such sources land could be bought, labour hired and capital invested in the 'home' area, or, if the latter was poor or semi-arid, better land could be bought elsewhere. It was thus the 'elbow room' given by access to above average off-farm income (particularly wages and salaries) for which it was so prized. Failing access to it, the only alternative was the diversion of labour power off the holding into low-paid off-farm employment to take the subsistence strain off the holding and perhaps raise household subsistence levels a little. But of course there was always the hope that the latter form of adaptation to rural poverty (what might be called migration out of poverty into poverty) could be turned into the former by upward mobility off the farm. The aim of every migrant was to turn 'average' or 'below average' off-farm earnings into 'above average' earnings, and thus start on the path of accumulation which he had seen others tread.

Thus Kenya's much-touted 'agrarian revolution' did little or nothing to alter the patterns of differentiation which had been operating among Africans in Kenya before its onset. In fact, being, as Cowen has quite correctly pointed out, simply a response to, or a copying of, the mechanism which a nascent petite bourgeoisie had been using to improve its own position well before 1952, the 'revolution' simply fed into that mechanism, since to take advantage of it households had already to be in a comparatively privileged position.

This chapter, though concerned overwhelmingly with agriculture and rural-based households, has pointed us constantly off the farm, to the urban labour market and to the wage labour market in the rural areas. Whereas up to 1952 trends in the wage labour market were primarily explicable by agricultural change on the smallholding, after 1952 to a very large degree trends in agricultural production became the dependent variable controlled by the off-farm labour market. The reason for this is very simple. By 1952 the smallest and poorest households in Kenya had already adopted the strategy of reliance on off-farm (comparatively low-paid) wage labouring. The task of the agrarian revolution, if it was genuinely to help the poorest, was to get that labour power back on the farm. This it never succeeded in doing, because the prerequisite of a major rise in household income from the new enterprises was land, which the poor did not have, and 'bridging' savings (while new investments were maturing), which they did not possess. On the other hand the largest and richest households had sources and levels of off-farm income which (in terms of return to labour time) even the new farm enterprises could not match, so they opted for a hired labour strategy on the farm. Clearly these two sets of circumstances meshed somewhat, in that the poorest households could also divert labour power on to the holdings of the better-off as well as into the towns and cities, and indeed did so. Thus, in very different ways, the prospect of these two very different groups of households continued to be determined by the off-farm labour market. With population growth and increased pressure on the land, together with continuing land purchase by the better-off, the number of poor households sending one or more, usually male, members into the bottom levels of the off-farm labour market multiplied, whilst in general the better-off households kept their male heads in that market until retirement.

All this implies that the social and political stability of Kenya continued to be heavily dependent, after Independence as before it, on the rate of expansion of off-farm income opportunities, and especially such opportunities as would provide the means of saving. It is to this aspect of matters which we look in the next and final empirical chapter, which deals with trends in the wage labour market and in off-farm trade and business in the period from 1952 to 1970.

Chapter XII

Wage Labour and 'The Informal Sector' 1952–1970

1. Discovery of 'The Informal Sector'

If both rich and poor households in Kenya's rural areas continued to look to the off-farm labour market for the resources to begin accumulation and upward mobility, their prospects, and the prospects of the ever-increasing numbers of poor households whose minimal or non-existent land resources left them no choice in the matter, were to be crucially determined by the rate of expansion of off-farm employment. Study of this question is hampered by the meaninglessness of the statistics of recorded employment which are to be found in Labour Department Reports and Statistical Abstracts of this period. A large part of the history of off-farm labour in this period is the story of how the State first panicked over what it initially conceived as a massive problem of 'unemployment', and then came to understand that to some extent the problem was that it knew little or nothing about a great deal of off-farm employment which existed. This is the history of the discovery of the by now famous 'informal sector', culminating in the ILO's report on Kenya *Employment, Incomes and Equality*, published in 1972.

There is a sense in which, as Professor Palacky said of the Austro-Hungarian Empire, had the 'informal sector' not existed, it would have been necessary to invent it. The nature of that 'necessity' can be seen in table XII:1 which compares the amount of officially 'recorded' employment of African males in the period 1952 to 1970 (as determined by the annual labour censuses or 'enumerations of employees' as they became after Independence) with the estimated number of Africans males of working age in the population in those years.

It will be seen from the table that throughout the entire period 'recorded' employment was never much more, and usually rather less, than a quarter of the total adult male labour force. Moreover, the picture is one of a more or less continuous fall in this proportion from 1957 onwards, with the slight rally in 1964 being almost entirely due to a change in the mode of collection of labour statistics. On the assumption that the population growth projections used are underestimates for the later period, the picture presented here is the rosiest

Table XII:1. 'Recorded' employment of African males and estimated numbers of African males of working age in Kenya 1953–70

Year	A Recorded employment[1]	B Males of working age[2]	C A as % of B
1953	357,870	1,426,684	25.1
1954	390,949	1,467,781	26.6
1955	—	1,510,063	—
1956	426,520	1,553,563	27.5
1957	440,995	1,598,316	27.6
1958	431,886	1,644,358	26.2
1959	435,221	1,691,726	25.7
1960	460,719	1,740,459	26.4
1961	432,961	1,790,596	24.2
1962	430,793	1,842,177	23.4
1963	400,549	1,893,758	21.2
1964	462,061	1,946,783	23.7
1965	457,243	2,001,292	22.8
1966	470,499	2,057,328	22.9
1967	488,516	2,114,933	23.1
1968	480,516	2,174,151	22.1
1969	496,970	2,235,037	22.2
1970	512,938	2,297,618	22.3

1. Figures for 'recorded' employment come from the annual labour censuses and enumerations of employees carried out by the Department (from 1965 Ministry) of Labour. There was no census in 1955, and from 1964 the coverage of the census was widened so as to embrace more of the employment in small private sector establishments. The sharp increase in employment 1963–4 is mainly a reflection of this. There was also a widening of coverage in 1954, and the figures for 1953 and 1954 are not strictly comparable. The census was supposed to cover all establishments in the public and private sector (including domestic employment), but excluded all self-employment inside and outside agriculture, and the armed services. Adult male employment was always about 80% of total African employment, which in turn was usually about 90% of total recorded employment. Female employment usually accounted for some 15% of total African employment, and employment of children the remaining five per cent. In later years recorded child employment fell somewhat and that of adult males and females rose slightly. From 1966 the Department of Labour ceased to publish separate statistics of African employment, and the figures for 1966–70 are derived from *Statistical Abstracts* (which continued to provide data on total African employment) with the proportions of adult male employment estimated on the basis of the 1965 figures.

2. 'Males of working age' refers to all males between sixteen and sixty years. The 1962 census was used as a base, with the figure obtained being projected backwards and forwards on the assumption of a constant rate of population increase of 2.8%. It was found that the figures obtained fitted reasonably accurately at both ends of the projection if compared with the 1948 and 1969 census data. Comparison with the 1969 census was made difficult by the fact that the oldest age category identified in that census was fifty years and over. It is however to be noted that were the 1962 figure to be projected forward at the rate of 3.3% to 3.5% per annum (the sort or recent population growth suggested by the ILO on the basis of the 1969 census), the projection would have considerably exceeded the total adult male population of Kenya (including non-Africans) as recorded in that census. This suggests either that the 1962 figures are underestimates, the 1969 ones overestimates, or that the ILO's view of the sixties' rate of population growth was too extreme. Nonetheless, there is no doubt that the simple projection procedure used here does tend to understate the adult male population in the later period (after 1962) and probably overstates it slightly for the earlier years.

possible one, and the fall in the number of African men finding recorded wage employment after 1957 was probably more precipitate than that shown.

This was what one might call the 'official' position of the Department of Labour until 1966. Reading the Department's reports the picture which emerges is of some 400,000–500,000 African men in Kenya working full- or part-time for wages, another 1,000,000 to 1,350,000 working on their smallholdings or in other forms of self-employment, and a few in the armed forces. It is only in 1966 that it is openly admitted that 'as a measure of obtaining information on gainful employment ... (the Enumeration of Employees) ... has diminished over the past few years because of the widening front of economic activity brought about by the Development Plan'.

That is, up to 1966 the official estimates of the size of the 'unemployment problem' among Africans was based on the belief that the annual labour census captured all or nearly all of the remunerative off-farm employment which was available. Hence, if a man had little or no land, did not work in his own business, and did not appear in the statistics of recorded employment, it was thought that he at least, and probably his family as well, were not merely unemployed, but destitute. This view, linked to a vulgar Marxist interpretation of political instability (destitute people are revolutionary people) produced much 'concern' about 'unemployment', especially in the wake of Mau-Mau.[1]

This conceptualisation also determined the way in which the size of the 'unemployment' problem was calculated, up to about 1966. That is, one took the number of adult Africans, deducted recorded employment and the estimated number of smallholders, and everybody else was deemed unemployed. Needless to say this often produced a frightening picture of the size of the unemployment problem. Dalgleish for example estimated that there were some 245,000 adult African men who were surplus to the economic requirements of the smallholder areas but unable to find employment, and this was from the 'major tribes' (i.e. the Kikuyu, Embu, Meru, Nyanza tribes and the Kamba) alone.[2]

I do not wish to suggest that the problem of 'unemployment' in the fifties and sixties in Kenya existed only in the eyes of the Administration and was generated by a mixture of inadequate statistics and a faulty understanding of the African part of the Kenyan economy. On the contrary, I shall argue that the problem which appeared to the Administration as 'unemployment' was real enough; indeed it was a product of the central structural contradiction in the Kenyan economy in this period, a contradiction which had begun well before the Emergency but which worsened markedly after it. The problem was wrongly conceptualised, but it existed. The belated official discovery that many Africans, with little or no land, and not appearing in the formal employment figures, were occupied, and in some cases gainfully occupied, made the so-called informal

1. *LDAR* 1958, p. 4; 1959, p. 3; and A. G. Dalgleish, 'Survey of Unemployment' (Nairobi, 1960).
2. Ibid., p. 15.

sector spring statistically into being overnight—to be precise, in 1967, when the official reservation expressed about the employment statistics in 1966 was followed up by the first survey of wage employment in non-agricultural rural occupations, which revealed 60,000 Africans (mainly men) working in 55,000 different rural establishments.

This sudden official discovery of what came to be known as the 'informal sector' (or rather part of it, since its urban dimension remained undetermined until the ILO report in 1972) is of importance because from the point of view of the historian it is extremely frustrating. Clearly these 60,000 rural, non-agricultural employees, and the 100,000 to 125,000 people whom the ILO estimated were employed in the urban informal sector in Kenya in 1970, did not spring from nowhere. They had been building up over time, as Africans found and exploited a demand for goods and services which could bring them a livelihood off the land, however precarious that livelihood might be. And yet the very mode of conceptualisation of the African part of the Kenyan economy on which employment statistics had for so long been based masked that development so perfectly that years, probably decades, of its development are lost in the published sources.

2. Origins of 'The Informal Sector'

Yet there is a clue to the likely onset of the expansion of the informal sector, and that clue arises from the structural problem which, however confusedly, the Administration perceived. As population pressure on land in the Reserves grew with accelerating population growth, and as the ongoing process of stratification turned that pressure into an impoverishment of those who lost out in the land scramble, so it became ever more necessary for the poorest male labour power to find an outlet elsewhere and for its subsistence pressure to be taken off the land. And yet, as we have seen, at the very same time the rate of expansion of 'formal' employment was slowing down, and for a time (the three years before Independence) it was falling absolutely. In short, more and more people were chasing proportionately (and sometimes absolutely) fewer and fewer jobs. In this situation the only solution was the expansion of other forms of self-employment and wage employment—an expansion which because of the way the employment censuses were compiled went unrecorded by them. But when did this happen and what did it entail? The question of time may be considered first.

Between the census years 1948 and 1969, the total adult male African population of Kenya rose by 84.5 per cent whereas formal sector employment rose by only 39 per cent. In absolute terms this meant that whereas in 1948 the potential 'reserve army of labour' of men competing for waged or salaried employment was some 950,000 men, in 1969 it was well over 1,900,000. The proportion of this potential constituency which would actually enter the off-farm labour market was of course determined by conditions on the land, but with such a slow rate of expansion of formal sector employment (a little over 1.8 per cent per annum on average over the two decades from 1948 to 1969), the slightest deterioration of those conditions was likely to send a volume of labour power into the off-farm labour market which the formal sector would not be able to absorb.

To take a concrete example: if during the year 1967/8 rural conditions had deteriorated just sufficiently to send a mere 1.5 per cent of men of working age into the off-farm labour market for the first time, this would have been enough to absorb the entire increase in formal sector jobs in that year (18,017) and still leave nearly 6,000 men without employment. Moreover, this is a conservative example in that, as table XII:1 shows, the year 1967/8 saw an unusually large increase in formal sector employment. In many other years increases were much smaller than this, or non-existent. The previous chapter tried to demonstrate that over the period 1952–70 pressure on the poorest households was more than enough to induce annual rates of entry at least as high as this into the off-farm labour market, especially from the most densely populated areas. In 1964, for example, the Central Province *Economic Survey* showed that nearly forty-one per cent of the households in Kiambu, eighteen per cent of those in Fort Hall, fifteen per cent of those in Embu and nineteen per cent of those in Nyeri were not working any land at all, whilst twenty-six per cent of households in Kiambu with land were operating less than one acre.[3] Certainly, the continued domination even of recorded employment by the peoples of the most densely populated districts is striking. In 1960, for example, 32.2 per cent of all Africans in employment were from the Central Province, 33.2 per cent were from Nyanza, and the bulk of the remainder from Machakos and Kitui.[4]

In the light of such trends the failure of the rate of expansion of formal employment to match the rate of population growth meant that an ever-increasing proportion of the potential reserve army became an actual reserve army, i.e. entered the labour market for all or part of the year in search of (in the majority of cases) unskilled employment. Table XII:1 suggests that formal employment as a proportion of the total adult male population fell more or less continuously in the post-war period, from about thirty per cent in 1947–8 to about twenty-two per cent in 1970, and behind these figures lies another very important trend in this period—a rising intensity of exploitation of labour power, especially in the urban private sector.

3. Labour Productivity and Employment Growth

A greater intensity of exploitation of labour power in a situation of growing labour abundance is not as contradictory as it may appear. Indeed, as Marx

---

3. *Economic Survey* . . ., op. cit., tables 29 and 30, pp. 20 and 21.
4. *LDAR* 1960, p. 3.

makes clear in Volume I of *Capital*, a large and growing 'reserve army' is often the prerequisite of greater exploitation, as it helps, through fear, to ensure the docility and pliability of the work force in employment.[5]

However, this schematic description, though capturing the essence of the labour situation in Kenya in the post-war period, does scant justice to the complexity of the actual process, which was complicated—so far as formal sector employment was concerned—by a two-stage development. In the first place the Emergency itself produced an artificial labour shortage in the period 1952 to 1956 which drove up wages in urban and rural areas.[6] From 1956 onwards the labour shortage which had resulted from the mass repatriation of Kikuyu, Meru and Embu people to their own districts, or from their incarceration in labour camps, began to diminish with the easing of the Emergency, and by 1958 the stream of labour power into the labour market had become a flood, bringing with it fears of 'unemployment', as we have seen.[7]

From 1957–8 therefore there began a second stage in the development of the post-war labour market, a stage which was of great complexity. That complexity was the product of the interaction of a number of factors. These were:
1. the increasing 'surplus' of labour which slowed down the rate of increase of wages—particularly for the unskilled,
2. a reorganisation of the labour process on some settler farms and in some factories in which existing labour forces were used more efficiently and, on some large farms in particular, machinery was substituted for labour,
3. a run-down of the settler mixed farm sector as Independence under black majority rule approached. This run-down began in earnest in 1960, and reduced reported African employment in agriculture from nearly 270,000 in 1960 to less than 203,000 in 1965. Thereafter employment in this 'large farm sector' declined further (though more slowly) as farms were excised from it and turned into settlement schemes,[8]
4. a rapidly growing unionisation of the African labour force particularly in urban employment which began in earnest from the late fifties.[9]

Essentially it was the combination of factors (2) and (3) which was respons-

---

5. Marx, *Capital*, Vol. I, pp. 427–47 and 628–48.
6. See *LDAR* 1954, p. 13; 1955, pp. 7–8.
7. It is perhaps worth making clear the nature of that concern. Dalgleish spelt it out explicitly. He noted that in the late fifties in the settled areas there was a 'more than usual amount of potential labour wandering round the farms, plantations and the forest estates ... [looking for work]. Not unnaturally with memories of the days immediately prior to the declaration of the Emergency possibly revived by the political events of January [the Lancaster House Conference on Independence—G.K.], this movement has been responsible for much anxiety locally.' Dalgleish, op. cit., p. 15.
8. See *LDAR* 1960–5; also *SA* 1960–70.
9. For an account of this see Alice H. Amsden, *International Firms and Labour in Kenya 1945–70* (London, 1971), especially pp. 30–82; also Richard Sandbrook, *Proletarians and African Capitalism: The Kenyan Case 1960–1972* (Cambridge, 1975), pp. 28–48.

ible for the painfully slow rate of increase of formal sector employment in the period, whilst factors (1) and (4) were to some degree in conflict and were conjointly responsible for a rather curious trend in wage rates. Very broadly, their effect was to widen the gap between the wages of unskilled workers in urban and rural areas and those of skilled or white-collar employees. That is, in the former case unionisation was not sufficient to offset the depressive effect of the ever-growing reserve army on wage rates (unions were in any case weaker among the unskilled, particularly in rural areas, partly of course because of the leverage given to employers by the existence of the reserve army and the weaker bargaining position of the workers). In the latter case, workers, particularly in the corporate sector of private industry and in the public sector, were able to use unions much more effectively to partially insulate themselves from the effects of the reserve army on wages. This was partly because of the support given to unions of the skilled and the white-collar workers by governments both before and after Independence,[10] and partly because the workers involved had attained a level of skill and/or socialisation into the labour process and consequent levels of productivity which made them worth higher wages to employers. We shall take these two issues in turn, treating first the trend of labour use in the economy, and then the pattern of wages and wage inequality.

Labour Productivity

Predictably, the tendency toward more efficient labour use, both on farms and in factories, was given its initial impetus by the Emergency. Faced with a temporary cessation of the stream of low-paid labour power, settlers, plantation owners and others were forced to reorganise their labour process to make fuller use of the labour power they had.

A good example of what this implied comes from the Labour Department *Annual Report* for 1954 in which it is reported that 'The subject of productivity was well to the fore during 1954 . . . the widespread shortage of labour served, as possibly no other circumstances could, to focus attention upon the economies possible in the use of African labour and upon the part which management itself could play in raising productivity . . .'[11] Among the examples of actions taken to maintain or increase productivity with reduced staffs, the same report mentioned the use of cash incentive schemes, the supply of hot meals at midday, the replacement of obsolete plant, the adoption of work study techniques by 'one large Nairobi firm', and the setting up of a committee in the sisal industry to study employment conditions and productivity.

From late 1956 labour supply began to return to normal, but this occurred at a time when world prices for agricultural products began to fall with the end of the Korean war boom. In addition the improved labour productivity achieved in

10. Amsden, op. cit., esp. pp. 104–59.
11. *LDAR* 1954, p. 16.

manufacturing industry during the earlier years of labour shortage slowed down the rate of expansion of employment after 1956.

Thus the Department of Labour's 1957 *Report* tells us that in the agricultural sector jobs became more difficult to obtain toward the end of the year, and as a result 'there was evidence of increased willingness among labour to work longer hours and employers found it easier to introduce new conditions of service, including incentive bonus schemes'. The same report instanced as examples of such schemes a daily cash bonus for production in excess of a fixed norm, and the setting of two agricultural tasks per worker per day ('each requiring about four hours work, with payment at overtime rates for the second task').[12]

By 1960 the motive for the increase of productivity was no longer any form of labour shortage—indeed by this time, as we have seen, mass 'unemployment' was the worry—but 'the widespread trade recession'. This, as the 1960 *Report* noted, 'together with increasing demands by trade unions for higher pay, compelled both urban and rural employers to give more attention to . . . productivity . . . From the manufacturing industries in particular, frequent reports were received of improved techniques leading to increases in output, or of employers reducing their establishments while maintaining production standards. The farm labourer, increasingly conscious of the threat of unemployment, was also reported to be working more effectively.'[13]

I have quoted and cited Department of Labour reports at length because it is important to grasp how far the attempt to raise labour productivity and to 'economise on labour' was part of a conscious government policy and programme.[14] Without further research it is impossible to say whether it was a stimulus to employers' own efforts in this direction or simply a response to their known desires. It may be that there is no aggregate answer to this, some employers being a lot more conscious of the need to raise labour productivity than others, who needed government prodding. Nonetheless it is significant that the stress on productivity fades away (at least in published reports) from 1960 onwards. The Department clearly became aware of the contradiction involved in expressing concern at the unemployment problem on the one hand, and on the other running a campaign which was designed to exacerbate it. And with the changing political climate from 1960 onwards, it became inadvisable to be seen to be contributing, however indirectly, to damaging African welfare.

It is one thing to point out how far the drive for productivity was a conscious policy, and quite another to assess its efficacy. The general impression one gets from the reports is that incentive schemes and reorganisation of the labour

12. *LDAR* 1957, p. 10.
13. *LDAR* 1960, p. 8.
14. In 1957 for example the Labour Department actually organised a conference of employers in Nairobi on the subject of productivity (*LDAR* 1957, p. 9). In fact the Department had shown a consistent concern with low productivity since the end of the war, see for example *LDAR* 1946, p. 5; and 1949, p. 10. See also Northcott, *Labour Efficiency Survey . . .*, op. cit. (1948).

process to increase output and per capita productivity were a good deal more effective in manufacturing industry, where employers could control the labour process much more completely, than they were in agriculture. As early as 1955 the Department noted that 'In rural areas, the raising of individual productivity presents special problems not associated with urban employment—in particular, that of maintaining close supervision over widely dispersed labour forces, and, perhaps even more intractable, that of breaking down the tradition of short working hours.'[15]

It appears that this latter 'problem' was partly solved with the expansion of the reserve army from 1956 onwards. The 1958 *Report* for example tells us that

> The surplus of labour helped employers to exercise greater selectivity in engaging workers; at the same time labour forces were reduced and increased output was often achieved from the smaller, and better supervised number of employees. In agriculture there was a trend to longer working hours and a move away from the long established custom of a four or five-hour working day.[16]

And by 1960

> In general agriculture, the normal working hours varied between five and six per day, for a six day week. However, it was noticeable that many employers were attempting to lengthen the working day in anticipation of upward trends. They were assisted in this by the prevailing free supply of labour —those in employment being prepared to work longer through fear of losing their jobs![17]

The celebratory exclamation mark notwithstanding, it is almost impossible to assess the quantitative effect of these measures in the agricultural sector on employment there, for the simple reason that they would have begun to bite most from the late fifties and early sixties (at the period of the most marked labour surplus after the Emergency) which happens to coincide almost perfectly with the period of rapid run-down of settler agriculture (particularly the mixed farming sector) as it became obvious that black majority rule was on the way. Hence any effect productivity improvement might have had on agricultural employment was overwhelmed in the aggregate statistics by the precipitate fall in agricultural employment from 1960 resulting from the flight of settlers and their capital.

Manufacturing
It is clear that improvements in labour productivity begun in the manufacturing sector in the late fifties have had a marked impact on the rate of expansion of

15. *LDAR* 1955, p. 10.
16. *LDAR* 1958, p. 9.
17. *LDAR* 1960, p. 8.

employment in that sector, and it also seems that the main mode of achieving this increase in labour productivity was not so much the increased mechanisation of industry as reorganisation of the labour process with essentially the same technology. Given the very low levels of labour productivity from which most firms were starting, simple reorganisation of the labour process could have disproportionately large effects on productivity and slow down very markedly the rate of labour hiring by making much more effective use of the existing labour force. These forms of reorganisation were in turn made possible by an 'improved' management and supervision of the labour force.

This conclusion is supported by Howard Pack, who analysed sources of productivity growth in a large number of different manufacturing firms in Kenya.[18] He showed that increases in labour productivity had come almost totally from the improved utilisation of existing plant and machinery, and from increased mechanisation of ancillary processes such as delivery, loading and unloading, and filling operations within the factory. He found very little evidence of increased mechanisation of the production processes as such, which in all the plants visited were a good deal more labour-intensive than alternative processes in use internationally. The main reason for the failure to install more 'capital-intensive' processes up to the time of his survey (1971) was that the volume of production required to meet the current domestic demand did not, in the managers' eyes, justify the initial capital outlay involved. And in any case, because current production processes were comparatively so labour-intensive, quite considerable gains in output and productivity could be made 'simply as a matter of reorganisation of production and better training and supervision'. He provided some examples:

A typical change involved a simple rearrangement of the position of two processes within the same plant. A worker who had formerly been idle half the time (evenly spaced over the day) was more fully employed when the two processes converged on him. In addition to these types of completely disembodied change, there were some that could be called slightly embodied in so far as they were implemented with internally produced 'equipment' containing material and labour worth less than K£50; nevertheless they increased productivity noticeably. The archetype of such innovation occurred in a fruit processing plant in which crushed fruit had formerly been packed into cans one by one. The manager had the machine shop bore twelve holes, each the size of a can top, into a sheet of metal, one worker pushed the fruit through the holes until the cans were full. The manager estimated that this increased output per worker at this point fourfold and this was undoubtedly true when the older process was observed in another plant. Many similar tales about

18. Howard Pack, 'Employment and Productivity in Kenyan Manufacturing', *East African Economics Review* (New Series), Vol. 4, no. 2, Dec. 1972, pp. 29–52.

very simple reorganisation and inexpensive internally generated devices could be spun.[19]

Pack also found that many of the firms he visited had considerable underutilised capacity (a finding echoed by the ILO report a year later).[20] As demand and output grew 'both labour and capital utilisation increased', and thus 'output growth can ... occur with little, if any, change in ... labour input: hence productivity, measured as output per employed worker, will grow rapidly despite the absence of any capital deepening'.

Moreover Pack gives evidence that older-established firms in Kenya had chosen to install more labour-intensive equipment than that technically available, and that the main motive for this and for the previous toleration of low levels of productivity had been the low level of wages in Kenya, and the belief by firms that they could compensate for any lack of skill in the work force by closer supervision. Hence, as Pack argued, when wages rose, or even when managers expected to be faced with demands for wage increases, the relative labour intensity of the production process was utilised to ensure that growth in productivity matched or more than matched wage increases. As Pack neatly puts it,

Wage levels ... influence the initial choice of technique. Once installed, equipment is used increasingly intensively, as is overhead labour. Value added thus increases as demand grows; but if wages were constant, the profit share would grow rapidly. In a highly unionised sector, also characterised by racial differences between workers and management, it is naive to expect that workers will not insist on a share in this increase in value added. Thus wages will follow the growth of productivity, but one cannot infer from this correlation the existence of increasing capital-labour ratios (other than that reflecting changes in the utilisation rates) which augment the productivity of labour. This implies that the estimated elasticity of substitution is really a distribution (or bargaining) parameter rather than a rigorous production parameter.[21]

19. Ibid., pp. 38–9.
20. *ILO Report*, pp. 182–4.
21. Pack, op. cit., pp. 42–3. This is not to deny of course that there were highly capital-intensive manufacturing processes in Kenya in 1970 (e.g. oil refining) or to suggest that industrial processes were as labour-intensive as some technically feasible alternative could have made them. There was even evidence of automation in some areas of manufacturing being increased to save on expensive supervisory labour. But it does mean that there was no general tendency to substitute capital for labour, and no general tendency for foreign capital to employ more capital-intensive techniques than local capital. Indeed in some industries precisely the reverse was the case. For data on this see *ILO Report* pp. 446–52, and for the dubious inferral of capital-labour substitution from aggregate economic data see J. K. Maitha, 'Capital-labour Substitution in a Developing Economy: The Case of Kenya', *East African Economics Review*, Vol. 5, no. 2, Dec. 1973, pp. 43–51.

Table XII:2. Output, employment, and output per worker in Kenyan manufacturing

Year	Output at factor cost (K£ millions)	Employment (thousands)	Output per worker (K£)
1955	17.44	55.2	316
1956	18.18	55.4	339
1957	19.80	57.0	347
1958	20.52	55.6	369
1959	20.23	53.7	376
1960	21.62	52.3	413
1961	22.73	42.6	534
1962	23.04	45.3	509
1963	24.38	40.7	599
1964	33.74	49.1	687
1965	37.45	52.1	718
1966	41.90	52.4	800
1967	45.19	56.8	796
1968	50.06	58.2	860
1969	57.19	57.1	1002
1970	62.16	61.3	1014

Sources: *SA* 1960, 1964 and 1971.
From 1964 a new series of employment and GDP statistics was begun. Figures below and above the line are not strictly comparable.
N.B. Over the period, output grew by 256%, output per head by 221%, but employment by only 11%.

This represents fairly accurately the process in Kenyan industry which produced such startling growth in labour productivity and such a slow growth in total employment over the late fifties and sixties. Table XII:2 shows the value added in this sector from 1955 to 1970, employment within it, and the increase of value added per worker over the period.

To sum up, in agriculture 'recorded employment' fell over the period partly because of productivity improvements, but mainly because of the simple decline of the sector (particularly its mixed farm component) before Independence, and its partial dismantling and neglect afterwards. In manufacturing the slow rate of increase seems mainly to have been due to improvements in labour productivity induced largely by organisational changes within the labour process. It is likely too that a similar process to that observed in manufacture applied to certain sections of the construction industry, to the public utilities (such as electricity and water supply), and perhaps to some sections of commerce and service industry. Harris and Todaro, for example, generalise their argument on productivity growth to cover the whole of private sector employment,[22] as

22. J. R. Harris and M. P. Todaro, 'Wages, Industrial Employment and Labour Productivity:

did a number of other economists seeking to explain the slow growth of employment in Kenya.

In virtually all cases the argument was that more efficient labour use had been forced on employers by rising wages, and that this pressure was greatest in the most unionised sectors. It seems from Pack's account that in manufacturing at least a dialectic operated whereby increased wage claims brought about increased intensity of exploitation of labour, which in turn, being reflected in increased output and profits, called forth the demands for more wage increases. Generalisation of this finding to other sectors must await further empirical research. Given the shortcomings of economic data in Kenya it certainly cannot be generalised simply on the basis of a priori reasoning using capital/labour ratios and estimated elasticities of substitution.

One question which emerges is why, faced with rising wages, did employers not simply use the rapidly growing reserve army to keep wages down by increased labour turnover? One answer to this must certainly have been union pressure, but another I think was that some part, perhaps a large part, of the increased productivity forthcoming from reorganisation of the labour process was dependent for its efficacy on the stabilisation of the labour force. Much of the benefit obtained from the 'training' of workers (even if this training only consisted of a certain dexterity in a simple task) could be lost if the worker left employment, and the more labour time and money invested in this improvement of labour power, the greater the loss would be. Hence, so long as productivity increases outpaced wage increases, it was in the interest of the employer to keep workers on the books, and the more 'efficient' they became the more this interest was strengthened.[23]

It is interesting to note in this connection that Labour Department reports explicitly date the increased stabilisation of the work force in Kenya to the post-Emergency period of the late fifties and early sixties, when, with the sudden expansion of the reserve army, it was reported that many more workers feared to leave their jobs in case of displacement. In 1962, for example, employers covered by the census reported only 132,000 engagements over the year, which was eighty-three per cent of the 1961 total and fifty-six per cent of the 1960 figure, and in 1963 in reporting that overall employment had fallen by 7.9 per cent and the wage bill had risen by three per cent, the report went on to note that turnover had continued to decrease 'and thus employment opportunities open to work-seekers were reduced more than the fall in the level of employment would itself suggest'.[24]

There is no doubt that the urban labour force in Kenya as a whole did begin

---

The Kenyan Experience', *East African Economics Review*, Vol 1, no. 1, 1969, pp. 29–46.

23. In the case of a great deal of service employment of course (from domestic service, vehicle repair and maintenance to 'up-market' hairdressing or shop work), 'socialisation' of the worker into the occupation was the main factor raising productivity.

24. *LDAR* 1962, p. 3; and 1963, p. 2.

to stabilise from the mid-fifties,[25] though this process was restricted almost entirely to African male workers. It did not mean that men brought their families to urban areas. Except for a tiny band of the salaried elite this did not really begin to happen until the early seventies. Thus despite the Carpenter report's recommendation that urban minimum wages should be fixed at levels which would support a man and his 'family',[26] it seems either that despite rising wages men preferred to restrict urban subsistence consumption to themselves and 'remit' such savings as they could to rural areas, or that real wages did not rise fast enough or to levels at which movement of the entire household to an urban domicile could be contemplated.

Nonetheless, it was the conventional wisdom of all commentaries on employment trends in Kenya at least from the mid-fifties in the post-war period that rising wages were primarily responsible for the slow growth of formal employment. The general mechanism posited was that outlined by Pack. i.e. that as wages rose, through union pressure, or as employers feared that they might, greater stress was placed on productivity.

Sometimes commentators drew the conclusion that if employment was to be increased wages had to be held down[27] (this was the philosophy behind both Tripartite Agreements). Sometimes they went further and called for curbs on the unions (a position which the post-Independence government also came to endorse and act upon). None of these policies had much impact on the rate of growth of employment.[28] Though increased exploitation of labour power may initially have been in response to or in anticipation of wage rises, yet stability of wages or even falls in real wages did not reverse the process. On the contrary, once employers found they could obtain higher output with the same work force for very little cost, the process tended to be cumulative, and to a degree became independent of the trend of wages.

Wages and Earnings in the Formal Sector

What was the trend of wages over this period? Table XII:3 shows the average earnings of Africans from 1955, and the real value of those earnings as from 1958.

It will be seen that average earnings increased by over 247 per cent in money terms between 1955 and 1970, and by 127 per cent in real terms between 1958 and 1970. Employment by contrast was a mere eight per cent higher in 1970 than it had been fifteen years earlier, and most of that increase occurred in the years

25. See for example Josef Gugler, 'Urbanisation in East Africa', in John Hutton (ed.), *Urban Challenge in East Africa* (Nairobi, 1970), pp. 1–26.

26. See Carpenter Report, op. cit., pp. 70–85.

27. See for example Dudley Jackson, 'Economic Development and Income Distribution in East Africa', *Journal of Modern African Studies* (JMAS), Vol. 9, no. 4, 1971.

28. The Tripartite Agreements for example simply had the effect, in the private sector, of 'bringing forward' hiring which employers would have done in any case. See *ILO Report*, pp. 534–5.

Table XII:3. Earnings, employment and per capita earnings, African labour force, 1955–70

Year	Total African earnings (K£ mil)	Total African employment	Average African earnings (K£ per annum)	Real value (K£ per annum)
1955	29.3	558,000	52.5	
1956	30.3	540,000	56.1	
1957	33.5	554,800	60.4	
1958	33.5	534,700	62.3	62.3
1959	34.6	537,400	64.4	63.7
1960	38.3	560,900	68.3	66.2
1961	40.2	529.800	75.8	72.0
1962	42.1	525,400	80.1	73.6
1963	45.5	480,700	94.4	86.8
1964	59.9	522,400	114.7	104.3
1965	66.7	527,800	126.4	107.4
1966	78.0	529,000	147.4	120.9
1967	86.7	547,300	158.4	126.8
1968	94.0	559,000	168.2	132.8
1969	101.1	582,000	173.8	137.3
1970	109.6	600,700	182.5	141.4

Sources: *SA* 1955 to 1971. 'Earnings' include all cash payments, including basic salary, cost of living allowances, profit bonus, together with the value of rations and free board, and an estimate of the employer's contribution toward housing. They do not include non-cash items such as pensions, gratuities, passages, uniforms or employers' contributions to the National Security Fund or private provident funds.

In order to obtain the 'real value' of earnings, I deflated them using 'Wage Earners Index of Consumer Prices' which is available from 1958 to 1970. For some details of this index, see SA 1961, p. 109.

'Employment' is of course 'recorded' employment, and there is the usual change of coverage at 1964.

1968 to 1970. Indeed total African employment only surpassed its 1955 level in 1968.

The trend of average earnings, suggestive though it is, is less important from our point of view than the trend of earnings among different groups and strata of African workers. The best place to begin an analysis of this is through the sectoral distribution of earnings. Table XII:4 shows average per capita earnings in six major sectors of the Kenyan economy in the period 1955 to 1970. In the public sector, the trend was as shown in table XII:5. From these figures, we see that the differential between rural and urban earnings levels was enormous throughout the period, and indeed got worse over the years. Table XII:6 expresses average earnings in agriculture as a percentage of earnings in the other six sectors in 1955 and in 1970. This uniform worsening of the position of agricultural workers vis-à-vis other workers was due of course to the fact that average earnings in all other sectors rose faster than those in agriculture. Thus whereas they rose by 93 per cent (in money terms) over this period in agriculture, they rose by 110 per

Table XII:4. Average per capita earnings in six major sectors (Africans and non-Africans) 1955–70 (in K£)

YEAR			SECTOR			
	Agriculture	Manufacturing	Building and construction	Transport	Commerce	Other services
1955	38.7	161.2	133.9	78.4	268.9	95.9
1956	40.8	164.3	149.2	75.4	282.1	113.4
1957	41.8	177.2	169.4	92.6	302.5	132.0
1958	43.3	185.3	157.8	87.9	318.7	139.6
1959	43.3	188.1	153.4	96.2	325.3	151.2
1960	46.0	204.6	151.7	101.3	322.3	155.0
1961	48.8	218.9	173.2	112.5	340.3	159.5
1962	47.3	205.3	174.6	108.8	350.5	166.6
1963	56.1	223.3	186.8	143.2	354.6	202.0
1964	62.8	248.5	184.8	131.3	379.8	152.4
1965	62.7	263.0	206.9	167.7	415.1	152.8
1966	72.3	299.6	242.7	212.6	440.3	157.3
1967	72.4	299.2	229.9	129.3	503.5	182.2
1968	71.0	324.7	254.1	156.7	519.9	202.4
1969	72.7	341.5	312.9	143.5	492.8	212.1
1970	74.6	407.8	334.8	165.8	605.5	227.1

Sources: *SA* 1955 to 1971. For the definition of 'earnings' see notes to table XII:3.

cent in transport, 136 per cent in the public sector, 137 per cent in the recorded services sector, 153 per cent in manufacturing, 125 per cent in commerce and 150 per cent in building and construction.

These differences were not correlated in any simple way with productivity increases. It is true that in manufacturing there was a startling rise in productivity, as we have already seen (value added per worker increased by 221 per cent over this fifteen-year period), but in agriculture, in which earnings only rose by 93 per cent over these years, value added per worker also went up by 243 per cent, and in fact this sector fared better than any other over the period as a whole, so far as this crude measure of productivity goes. It is true that a large part of this rise occurred in the period 1966 to 1970, and thus owes something to a change in the coverage of the statistics. But even up to 1965, for which period there is a run of more or less consistent figures, per capita output rose by 98 per cent and earnings by only 62 per cent.

In other sectors, changes in employment statistics and in the measurement of GDP make it wise to restrict comparison to the period 1964 to 1970. Here the figures show that in the public sector, as well as in transport, communications, building and construction, the rate of growth of earnings always outpaced

*Table XII:5. Average per capita
earnings in the public sector (Africans
and non-Africans) 1955–70 (in K£)*

Year	Public Sector
1955	98.5
1956	116.1
1957	116.8
1958	129.4
1959	132.4
1960	142.5
1961	160.3
1962	155.5
1963	161.1
1964	159.9
1965	185.9
1966	197.1
1967	209.3
1968	215.0
1969	220.0
1970	232.7

Sources: *SA* 1955 to 1971. 'Public Sector' here includes all Kenyan Government and parastatal employment, and civilian employment in the Defence forces. It excludes the East African Railways and Harbours, and all East African Common Services (later East African Community) employment.

*Table XII:6. Average per capita earnings in agriculture as a
percentage of average per capita earnings in six other
sectors 1955 and 1970*

	% in 1955	% in 1970
Commerce	14	12
Building and Construction	28	23
Manufacturing	24	18
Public Services	39	32
Other Services	40	33
Transport	49	45

that of per capita output. Only in commerce, where output rose 113 per cent and earnings by only 59 per cent, was the position reversed.[29]

29. However a significant measure of doubt attaches to all these figures. They are based on tables of GDP by industrial origin and on figures of earnings and employment by sector which vary constantly and inexplicably almost from one *Statistical Abstract* to the next. Also there were major

This tends to show that, as in manufacturing, workers could only turn productivity rises into earnings increases if they were strongly and effectively unionised. Strong unionisation was a feature of the 'formal sector' work force in the larger, commercial, construction and service sector firms (as well as manufacturing firms) whose workers found their way into the statistics of recorded employment, and this was also true of a great number of the white-collar employees in the public sector. Unionisation began in these areas of employment from the late fifties, and unions in these sectors have continued to exercise not inconsiderable bargaining power since Independence, despite quite stringent legal and institutional curbs on unions, because they have enjoyed the general support of the regime in their wage claims (indeed this has been an important part of the way in which unions have been incorporated into the state apparatus). More weakly-unionised workers, such as those in agriculture and in wholesaling and retailing, have not been able to turn productivity increases into wage increases.

So much for sectoral distribution of earnings. We may now turn to the distribution of income among workers in Kenya as a whole over this period. One would expect that there would be a strong interaction between these two (sectoral and income group) measurements of income distribution, and indeed this is the case. We shall begin with data on earnings differentials among African workers in urban employment (which data is much more abundant), and then go on to consider the distribution of earnings within agriculture. Tables XII:7 and XII:8 give a breakdown of all African men in 'regular' employment in the public sector and in the urban private sector into seven earnings groups in the period 1963-9, for which a consistent data series is available. The earnings groups were originally enumerated in pounds per annum, but I have converted them to shillings per month for ease of reference and comparison.

Two points will be immediately apparent from these tables. Firstly the persistent rise in money and real wages in these sectors over this period is reflected in the general upward shift of workers through the earnings categories. Thus, for example, whereas sixty-three per cent of workers were earning less than Shs. 200 per month in 1963, this proportion had dropped to less than a quarter in 1969. All other categories had increased over the period, so whereas less than thirty per cent of workers in these sectors were earning more than Shs. 200 and less than Shs. 398 in 1963, nearly half were doing so at the end of the decade. The largest single increase was in the two categories covering the range from Shs. 600 to Shs. 998 per month, where the numbers quadrupled over the period from 5,461 in 1963 to over 23,000 in 1969.

changes in categorisation in 1964 and 1966. In particular from 1966 the SAs stopped categorising GDP in agriculture by large and small farms and the figures for 1966–70 thus undoubtedly inflate value added by including small farm production. Thus a comparison of per capita earnings in the large farm sector from 1968–71 with per capita marketed production in that sector shows the former actually outpacing the latter in this period. See *SA* 1972, pp. 212 and 220; and *ES* 1972, p. 56.

Table XII:7. Numbers of African males in seven earnings groups 1963–9 (includes all public sector 'regular' recorded employment and all private industry and commerce except agriculture)

Earnings Group	1963	1964	1965	1966	1967	1968	1969
Up to Shs. 198 per month	140,619	177,626	155,111	117,104	79,716	70,520	70,395
Shs. 200–Shs. 398 per month	64,123	85,733	98,327	109,363	123,504	143,124	129,102
Shs. 400–Shs. 598 per month	9,590	14,835	20,713	32,518	37,080	39,227	43,810
Shs. 600–Shs. 798 per month	3,806	5,301	6,561 ⎫	13,471	18,027	20,009	23,542
Shs. 800–Shs. 998 per month	1,655	2,651	3,613 ⎭				
Shs. 1,000–Shs. 1,498 per month	1,635	3,298	2,669	7,106	8,293	9,446	11,572
Shs. 1,500 + per month	436	1,150	3,911	4,777	4,753	5,470	6,874

Sources: *SA* 1963–9.

Table XII:8. Percentage of African males in seven earnings groups 1963–9 (includes all public sector 'regular' recorded employment and all private industry and commerce except agriculture)

Earnings Group	1963	1964	1965	1966	1967	1968	1969
Up to Shs. 198 per month	63.3	61.1	53.3	40.8	29.4	24.5	24.7
Shs. 200–Shs. 398 per month	28.9	29.5	33.8	38.1	45.5	49.7	45.3
Shs. 400–Shs. 598 per month	4.3	5.1	7.1	11.3	13.7	13.6	15.4
Shs. 600–Shs. 798 per month	1.7	1.8	2.3 ⎫	4.7	6.6	7.0	8.3
Shs. 800–Shs. 998 per month	0.7	0.9	1.2 ⎭				
Shs. 1,000–Shs. 1,498 per month	0.7	1.1	0.9	2.5	3.1	3.3	4.1
Shs. 1,500 + per month	0.2	0.4	1.3	1.7	1.8	1.9	2.4

Sources: ibid.

In the top three earning categories (all those earnings Shs. 800 per month and more), the rise in numbers reflects not only wage rises, but the process of 'Africanisation'—a process which seems to have begun to accelerate from 1966 onwards—three years after Independence. The fifteen per cent of African wage

Table XII:9. Africans other than resident labourers,
employed in non-plantation agriculture 1953

Wage Group (Shs. per month)	% of work force
30–4	2
35–9	24
40–4	22
45–9	16
50–9	21
60–9	7
70 +	8

Source: *LDAR* 1953.

and salary earners (some 42,000 people) in these three categories were part of the African income elite of Kenya at the end of the period covered in this study. Indeed they were by far the largest part of it, the number of independent African traders and businessmen earning these levels of income from their enterprises being very small. They represented those who had unambiguously gained from Independence, and those to whose standard of living virtually all other Africans aspired.

The second and more obvious point is the high level of earnings inequality within this category of male African full-time workers, overwhelmingly in urban areas. Whereas those earning Shs. 600 or more per month were a mere fifteen per cent of the whole in 1970, over eighty-five per cent of workers earned less than this figure, and seventy per cent earned less than Shs. 400 per month. And yet this total category (male workers earning over Shs. 200 per month), massively internally differentiated as it was, was itself a privileged category of sorts.

Most notably, in 1970, there were still 154,000 agricultural workers who were earning less than this amount, as were 16,500 workers in manufacturing, 6,000 workers in building and construction, 13,700 workers in commerce (most of them in the retail and wholesale trade) and over 80,000 in service occupations.[30]

Moreover, even these low-paid groups were themselves markedly differentiated. If we take agricultural workers in this period, just as in the years prior to 1952 it is clear that the agricultural wage labour force on large farms continued to be highly and minutely stratified. One may compare the two sets of figures given in tables XII:9 and XII:10, one taken from the beginning of this period, the other from its end. Thus in 1970 the best-paid workers (the farm foremen and clerks) were earning a little over three times the wage of an unskilled male worker, and over four times that of an unskilled woman worker. Unfortunately

30. *SA* 1971, p. 203.

Table XII:10. Wage rates on mixed farms negotiated between the Kenya Plantation and Agricultural Workers' Union and the Kenyan Farmers' Union 1970

Category of worker	Wage (Shs. per month)
Unskilled Females under 18	41
Unskilled Males under 18	56
Unskilled Females over 18	60
Unskilled Males over 18	86
House Servants and Cooks	114
Section Foremen	128
Farm Artisan	135
Tractor Driver	143
Combine Harvester Driver	188
Lorry Driver	194
Farm Foremen	255
Farm Clerk	266

Source: *MLAR* 1970

we are not told how many people fell into each of these categories, but we do know from another source that in 1970 there were still over 100,000 workers in agriculture earning less than Shs. 100 per month, while fewer than 15,000 workers in that sector (much fewer than ten per cent of all agricultural workers) were earning more than Shs. 200 per month.[31]

The latter set of wage statistics is particularly interesting in fact, because it represents the start of an attempt by the agricultural workers' union to introduce coherent wage rates into the mixed farming sector, in place of the individualistic structure of wages which had characterised the sector from its origins. A similar initiative had been made on coffee and tea plantations by the same union a few years earlier.

But, as Leitner shows, the attempt has been a complete failure and in 1972 as in 1922 it could still be reported that

wage rates paid in the four branches of agriculture (sisal, tea, coffee and mixed farming) differ remarkably: up to 100 per cent for the same type of work. The task allocation and the combination of various wage rates are left

31. *SA* 1971, p. 203. Earnings are not strictly comparable with wages because the former include such items as cash value of rations and housing as well as the basic wage. As far as one can judge the 1953 and 1970 agricultural wage data are directly comparable, and they appear to show that over the period the wages of the better-paid farm worker rose more than those of the ordinary labourer. Thus whereas the top of the wage distribution in 1953 was Shs. 60 per month and above, with only eight per cent of the labour force getting Shs. 70 or more, in 1970 the best-paid agricultural workers were getting from Shs. 180 to Shs. 260, a minimum increase of 157% and a maximum of 271% or more. At the bottom of the scale however, adult labourers' wages had only risen from Shs. 45 to Shs. 86 in seventeen years, i.e. by slightly over 90%.

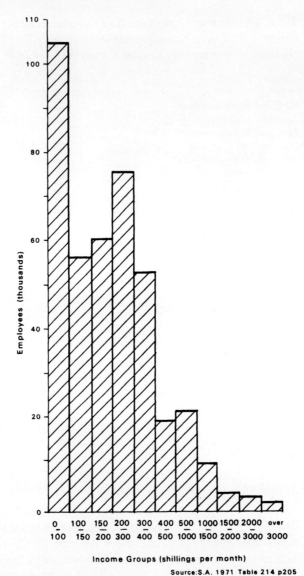

Figure XII:1. The wage structure of the formal sector labour force, 1970.

to the discretion of supervisors and managers. Although the workers offer increasing resistance to this organisation of the work process, it has been altered neither by collective agreements nor by the law.[32]

32. Kerstin Leitner, 'The Situation of Agricultural Workers in Kenya', *RAPE*, no. 6, May-Aug. 1976, pp. 34–50. Quotation is from p. 39.

It is also clear that the prime reasons for the failure of agricultural workers to raise their real wages to any significant extent, and of the continued minute fragmentation of the work force, have been the power given to employers in the agricultural sector by the existence of an ever-growing reserve army, and the chronic weakness of the Kenya Plantation and Agricultural Workers' Union (KPAWU) which in 1972 still had only 25 per cent of all agricultural workers as members. That weakness is in part a reflection of the labour supply situation (and the rapid labour turnover it induces, since many employers simply turn off workers who strike or protest against their conditions in any way) but also reflects the domestication of the Union's leadership by the powerful African politicians and civil servants who now own many former settler farms.[33]

In short, as the bar chart (figure XII:1) powerfully demonstrates, the African wage labour force in 1970 was, as it had been in 1952, and indeed as it had been since its origins, a massively and ubiquitously differentiated entity. There had been change since 1952, but that change had mainly taken the form, at least up to 1970, of a persistently widening gap between the better-paid highly unionised workers in the urban areas and the rest; non-unionised and unskilled workers in urban areas came a long way second, and the mass of agricultural workers (with the exception of a small elite group) a long way third.

4. 'The Informal Sector' Revisited

Having set it in its proper historical context, we may now return to a consideration of the 'informal sector' with which we began. In the case of Kenya at least that sector is clearly a residual category. It consists of all forms of wage employment and of self-employment which do not find their way into the labour censuses. At its simplest therefore the sector comprises:

1. All forms of wage employment and self-employment in urban areas not included in the enumerations.
2. All forms of non-agricultural employment and self-employment in rural areas not so enumerated.
3. All full or part-time wage employment provided on smallholdings and settlement schemes.

It will be noted therefore that, at least as defined by the ILO at the end of our period, the 'informal sector' did not comprise self-employment on smallholdings and settlement schemes. This was not always the case. In the rather confused official attempts to come to terms conceptually with the nature and extent of the 'unemployment' problem in Kenya in the early sixties, self-employment on smallholdings was occasionally counted as part of total 'employment' and deducted from total 'unemployment'.[34] This did not help matters greatly,

33. Leitner, op. cit., esp. pp. 43–50.
34. See Dalgleish, op. cit., pp. 12–15.

because quite clearly the 'employment problem' in Kenya, if there was one, consisted essentially of finding productive and remunerative occupations for men and women who did not choose to expend any or all of their labour power on their household smallholding, or who did not have access to such a holding. The essential problem of measurement was not in the first instance that of determining the size of 'employment' or 'unemployment' at all. It was that of determining the size of what I have in earlier sections called the off-farm labour market. How many people were and are there in Kenya who are seeking or in off-farm employment for all or part of any given year, and in particular how fast is the sub-group of off-farm work-seekers growing?

How many of these people actually find such employment, and how fast all forms of off-farm employment opportunities are growing are essentially secondary questions. Even the ILO report, though it approaches the matter a good deal more systematically than the Kenyan Labour Department, is somewhat frustrating in this respect, because it concentrates so exclusively on the size and rate of expansion of unenumerated off-farm jobs. In their treatment of rural areas in particular, the ILO team assume that off-farm employment opportunities (either on other smallholdings or in non-agricultural rural enterprises) expand with the labour force, so that every man or woman is expanding as much labour power off the smallholding as they wish. This may be the case, but there is no necessity for it to be so, and their data on urban areas suggest that it was not the case there at the beginning of the 1970s, i.e. that at any one time about ten per cent of males and twenty-three per cent of females in urban areas were unable to find remunerative employment of any sort.[35] There is no reason why there should not have been men and women in exactly the same situation in rural areas, but who were resident on the holding and helping around the place. These people would therefore be 'employed' on the holding, but a large part of their labour power would go unused for substantial periods of the year (at all periods in fact except those of 'peak' labour demand such as a harvest), i.e. they would be in 'disguised unemployment'.[36]

Interestingly enough the ILO report did not consider the size of the disguised unemployment problem in rural Kenya, though it would certainly be necessary to establish this, in order to know the size of the total off-farm labour 'market' at any one time.

Noting this shortcoming therefore, what was the size and scope of the 'informal sector' in Kenya at the end of the period being considered? The ILO report estimated the following to be the situation in 1969:

35. *ILO Report*, table 15, p. 56.

36. In fact G. D. Gwyer has suggested that the 'imperfections' of the labour market for smallholder farm labour in Kenya produce precisely this result (i.e. the coexistence of shortages of labour in one area with underutilised labour in another, not knowing about the opportunities, or unable to move). Because of staggered harvests and other types of peak period labour demand in Kenya agriculture, this is a major problem. See G. D. Gwyer, 'Labour in Small Scale Agriculture. An Analysis of the 1971 Farm Enterprise Cost Survey and Wage Data' (IDS Working Paper no. 62, Sept. 1972).

1. *Rural areas* Employed full or part-time on other smallholding or settlement schemes as agricultural labourers—450,000 to 500,000. Self-employed or wage employed in non-agricultural rural based enterprises (mainly small-scale manufacturing, commerce and service enterprises)—106,000.
2. *Urban areas* Total informal sector employment in the major towns of Kenya (estimated—data are only available for Nairobi)—100,000 to 125,000.[37]

Now in 1969 total enumerated employment was 627,200, so that at the very least total unenumerated employment was its equal, and on the maximum estimates was well in excess of it (731,000). It can be safely assumed that the vast majority of the labour power being expended in this sector was African, and most of it male, so very roughly one can say that about twenty-five per cent of the adult African male population of Kenya earned part or all of its livelihood in the informal sector by the end of our period.

We thus need to consider two aspects of this sector as important for our concerns. Firstly, when it originated and how fast it had grown, and secondly what the distribution of income was within the sector. This is obviously particularly important since all the income distribution data which we have looked at to date has concerned enumerated employment only.

As far as the question of origins goes it is clear that there can be no single answer. Chapter VI of this work in particular is concerned with tracing the origins of small-scale wholesale, retail, service and manufacturing enterprises in rural areas which provided informal sector off-farm employment in rural areas. We know from survey results that there were some 55,000 of these establishments in rural Kenya in 1967, and employment within them was broken down as follows:

Forestry and charcoal burning	1,400
Fishing	6,100
Quarrying	1,606
Manufacturing	11,800
Building and Construction	2,400
Commerce	22,600
Transport	1,400
Other Services	13,300[38]

Unfortunately there are no statistics equivalent to these before 1967, so we have here a single beacon in historical darkness. Fearn's survey showed that in 1954 there were 5,631 licensed traders in the rural markets of Nyanza Province including Kericho.[39] If one assumed, not unreasonably, that there would be somewhat more than this in Central Province at that time (say 8,500), and allowed another 5,000 for all other parts of Kenya, this would suggest that there were

37. *ILO Report*, pp. 38, 39 and 54.
38. *MLAR* 1967, p. 2.
39. Fearn, op. cit., p. 176.

some 20,000 such establishments in the country at the end of 1954. I believe this estimate to be generous, so it is clear that the most part of the growth to the 1967 total occurred between 1954 and 1967. There is no doubt whatsoever that the number of such enterprises coming into being in that short period were considerably in excess of the number which had been founded and survived between 1915–16 (when businesses owned by Kenyan Africans first came into being in southern Kiambu) and 1954.

Beyond this it is difficult to go. It will be observed that over forty per cent of all the small-scale rural businesses in Kenya in 1967 were in 'Commerce', and it can safely be assumed that the vast majority of these were the small retail shops which are the hallmark of every African market centre. Marris and Somerset in 1966, just like Fearn in 1954, noted the heavy competition and the small turnover and profits of these businesses, and that the competition was largely due to the small initial capital requirements which could easily be assembled out of the incomes of a group of even comparatively poor households. We can therefore assume that expansion of this sector (with ever greater pressure on profit margins) was a feature of the fifties and sixties, and indeed this is confirmed, impressionistically, by Sandberg's work on Meru district.[40] It will also be noted that the second and third largest categories are 'other services' (twenty-four per cent) and 'manufacturing' (twenty-one per cent), and in fact these three categories put together accounted for most part of the employment in the rural non-agricultural 'informal sector'. It is almost certain that the bulk of the businesses in these latter two categories would be artisan businesses of various types. This is obviously so in 'manufacture', but would probably also be the case in 'other services' where most of the services involved repair and maintenance of various types. Kenneth King has confirmed here that the large-scale spread of artisanal skills among African men in Kenya was essentially a post-war phenomenon. He says:

... from as early as the 1920s the impact of the immigrant Indian artisan society had been making itself felt, and as ... with oil-lamp making certain Indian artifacts had become entirely an African preserve by the late 1930s and 1940s. The adoption of such Indian skills by Africans turning to self-employment was however still on a rather small scale. For one thing there was no shortage of openings for employment in the expanding European and Indian industrial sectors during and after the Second World War, and with the circulation of money in the rural areas still artificially restricted by the controls on African enterprise and particularly on the cash crop production of coffee and pyrethrum, little incentive to set up as an artisan in the smaller provincial and district township was offered. Several factors combined in the

40. Audun Sandberg, *Individualism and Collectivism in Development Planning* (cyclostyled paper, Bergen, 1971), p. 21. See also Ichirou Inukai and Jasper A. Okelo, 'Rural Enterprise Survey in Nyeri District, Kenya' (IDS Miscellaneous Paper, Feb. 1972).

late fifties to speed the development of an artisan society in rural and urban areas. For one thing the wholesale evacuation of Kikuyu from their urban employment into detention probably had an impact on self-employment—particularly in the rural areas—that has been so far neglected in the literature. Very large numbers of those taken out of circulation for four years (1954–58) had been employed in the Indian fabricating sector in Nairobi; and when they were finally released from detention it was extremely difficult for many of them to get passes to return to the city without long delays. They were under pressure instead to return to their villages, and lacking any other means of income, they began in many instances to practise as best they could by themselves the skill on which they had previously been employed. The Emergency thus acted as a forced decentralisation of skill from Nairobi to the rural areas.[41]

Moreover, the general trend of King's whole analysis is to suggest that not only did the expansion of African artisan businesses in the rural areas only really get under way in the late fifties but also that the rate of expansion has continued to rise since. In particular King opines that there was an enormous expansion in the numbers of young men looking for apprenticeships and employment in the late sixties when the first wave of students from the greatly expanded post-Independence primary school population hit the labour market.[42]

It is possible to build a not-dissimilar chronology for the urban informal sector. The ILO report for example suggested that

> Until about 1960, the urban informal sector was comparatively small by the standards of other African countries because of the shortage of labour in Kenya and the restrictions on informal sector activities, particularly in Nairobi. But with rapid migration after Independence, growth in the informal sector accelerated, though as far as we can judge more in numbers employed than in output. Limited resources and continuing restrictions on activities inhibited the expansion of output at the same time as the family base of most informal sector operations enabled, or perhaps more accurately compelled, the informal sector to continue to absorb labour, even if at low incomes. The result was a process of rapid 'involutionary' growth in which the number of people in the sector increased faster than incomes, adding to the numbers of the working poor, if not to unemployment.[43]

We may turn finally to employment on small farms and settlement schemes. It was in 1966 that the Labour Department first reported that there were some 100,000–130,000 people employed on small farms in Kenya outside the settlement schemes. In addition the same report noted that there were 15,000 workers

41. Kenneth King, op. cit., p. 103.
42. Ibid., pp. 107–8.
43. *ILO Report*, p. 94.

on settlement scheme farms but they were included in the annual enumeration (there had only been 6,800 reported agricultural labourers on settlement schemes in 1964). By 1967 there were reported to be no less than 284,700 men and women employed full- or part-time for wages on African smallholdings, not including the settlement schemes. By 1969–70 the official statistics showed there to be 378,100 men and women employed as agricultural labourers on small farms and settlement schemes, of whom some 186,000 were employed regularly and 192,000 on a casual basis.[44] It is clear that these rapid increases are due almost entirely to dawning official awareness, and a consequent greater coverage of the statistics, as the issue was more systematically investigated with each annual survey. They are very little guide to the actual historical process of the expansion of this type of employment.

Cowen's work on Nyeri is explicitly concerned with this issue. He suggested that agricultural wage labour on smallholdings there had virtually emerged twice. It had first appeared in the mid-twenties when the *athomi* ('those who had gone to C.M.S. Tumu Tumu from and after 1916') began to plant potatoes, wattle and wheat on a scale which introduced marked labour peaks into the agricultural cycle. The quantity of labour required at these peaks, and certain impediments which prevented Christians making full use of traditional communal labour practices (most notably the fact that being in permanent off-farm wage employment themselves they could not reciprocate) made them introduce wage labouring into the district.

This initial introduction of wage labouring was a minority phenomenon, and tended to decline in the late thirties and forties, before being completely disrupted by the Emergency. The reasons lay in potato blight attacks, bird attacks on wheat (with increasing numbers of children at school the fields could not be adequately guarded) and the decline of wattle, which in any case was not a particularly labour-intensive crop.

The second and much larger 'wave' of labour hiring in Nyeri came with land consolidation in 1958–9, and above all with the new labour-intensive enterprises such as dairying and tea growing which followed on land consolidation particularly on the larger farms.[45] There is no reason to suppose that Cowen's findings for Nyeri are not typical of all other areas where the new farm enterprises were introduced, as well of course as the settlement schemes where coffee, tea, pyrethrum growing and dairying were introduced later than in the 'Native Land Units' (as the Reserves had now become). If this is the case one would expect the expansion of labour hiring to have got under way in the late fifties and early sixties and to have expanded through the sixties as more and more particularly of the more prosperous smallholders moved into the new enterprises and expanded production. It is difficult to be more specific than

44. *LDAR* 1964, p. 4, *MLAR* 1966, p. 2 and *SA* 1971, p. 206.
45. M. P. Cowen with Frederick Murage, op. cit., p. 40.

this but it is clear that this phenomenon (the hiring by Africans of other Africans as agricultural labourers), which had probably not embraced more than 20,000 or 30,000 such labourers in the whole of Kenya in the entire period from 1918 to 1960, probably expanded five-fold in the period from 1960 to 1965 and then doubled again between 1965 and 1970. If there was one aspect of the 'agrarian revolution' which was revolutionary (in the sense that it altered the social relations of production in the Kenyan countryside profoundly), it was this.

In the previous chapter I estimated that there were probably some 900,000 to 1,000,000 smallholder households in Kenya (out of 1,200,000 altogether in 1971) who were left out in the cold by Kenya's agrarian revolution. Either for one reason or another the land which they farmed was unsuitable for the new enterprises, or they did not have enough land to take up the new enterprises without putting their basic subsistence at risk. If the ILO report is correct and the actual number employed on small farms and settlement schemes in Kenya in 1970 was nearer to 450,000 than to the 378,000 of the official statistics,[46] then it is clear that it was to this newly available form of activity that many of these households diverted their labour power. It was not the case that a precise half of the households who failed to benefit from the agrarian revolution sent some of their members into this new labour market. Both the new employment opportunities and the households needing them were spatially concentrated, so that in some areas the poorest households might have all their adult members in off-farm employment (including employment on other farms), whilst in other areas off-farm employment opportunities might not be close at hand and so more labour power would remain under-employed on the home holding.

In addition one household might have different members in each of the labour markets we have identified, e.g. a son and a daughter in the urban informal sector and a mother and father in part-time employment as agricultural labourers. I am inclined to believe, moreover, that the type of labour market to which a household sent its labour power was a good indication of its relative prosperity, i.e. a poor household would be involved almost entirely in the urban informal and/or rural informal labour markets, while a more prosperous household would be far more likely to have its labour power concentrated in the higher-income occupations of the urban formal sector and to be hiring in the labour power of the poorer households. The ILO report provides strong support for the proposition that the poorest workers are heavily concentrated in the rural and urban informal sector (see table XII:11).

It will be seen that on average in 1969 the lowest-income earners in Kenya were wage labourers on small farms (K£38 per annum or a mere Shs. 63 per month), wage workers in the urban informal sector (K£40 per annum or Shs. 66 per month), wage workers in the rural non-agricultural informal sector (K£45 per annum or Shs. 75 per month) and then the self-employed in the urban

46. *ILO Report*, p. 38.

Table XII:11. Average[1] incomes of selected groups in rural and urban areas 1969 (K£ per annum)

	Adults	Men	Women
RURAL			
Wage employment[2]			
Large farms[3]	68	73	46
Small farms[3]	38	41	34
Non-agricultural enterprises[4]	45	47	34
Self-employment			
Smallholders[3]	113	—	—
Owners of non-agricultural enterprises[4]	130	—	—
URBAN			
Wage employment[2]			
Formal sector, Nairobi[3]	443	471	297
Statutory minimum wage in the formal sector, Nairobi[3]	—	106	84
Informal urban[5]	40	—	—
Self-employment	60	—	—
Informal urban[5]			

1. There are often wide variations in earnings around the averages shown. This applies particularly to smallholders.
2. Regular employees.
3. Source: *Statistical Abstract* and *Economic Survey*, 1969 and 1970.
4. Source: *Survey of non-agricultural rural enterprises*, 1969.
5. Mission's estimates.
Source: *ILO Report*, p. 77.

informal sector (K£60 per annum or Shs. 100 per month). All these groups earned on average considerably less either than the formal sector average wage or smallholders or owners of rural non-agricultural enterprises.

However, these averages themselves disguise enormous internal variations, and in particular both the smallholder average and the urban formal sector average are pushed up markedly by the presence of comparatively small numbers of high-income earners within the group. The same report reckoned for example that there were some 225,000 smallholders with incomes in excess of K£200 per annum (Shs. 333 per month), and some 144,000 households in urban areas (most of them in formal sector employment) earning Shs. 300 or more per month before tax and over 100,000 earning over Shs. 500. This figure of 225,000 accords well with our own estimate of the proportion of all smallholders (about twenty per cent) who did benefit from the agrarian revolution.

In addition, it is clear that the incomes both of those owning rural small businesses and of those owning such businesses in urban areas were enormously widely dispersed around the mean, with the owners of more prosperous businesses being able to earn three or four times the average earnings of workers in low-paid formal sector employment, especially services.[47]

47. See for example Kenneth King, op. cit., p. 124.

Nonetheless, for the vast majority of wage workers in the informal sector at any one time, earnings are generally lower than they would be even in the lower reaches of the formal sector, and markedly lower than those who employ them. Of the 731,000 men and women who were working in the 'informal sector' in 1970, it must be doubtful whether more than 50,000 to 100,000 had incomes in excess of Shs. 200 per month in 1970, and nearly all of these would have been employers while most of the rest would have earned well below Shs. 100 per month.

Of these the largest single group were those men and women who worked as full- or part-time agricultural labourers on the smallholdings of others. For these workers their cash wages rarely constituted their total income, either because, as part-time workers, they were also gaining a part of their subsistence from directly consumed production from their own land, or because they would obtain food and accommodation from the smallholders employing them, in addition to their wages. Nonetheless that there should be 400,000 or more men and women in Kenya in 1970 all working for cash incomes of less than Shs. 100 per month, and in many cases (particularly in the case of the women) for less than half of this, suggests how minimal were the alternatives for the productive use of their labour power. I have already suggested why so many household members on the smallest holdings should choose to work on the holdings of others, and there is no need to repeat those arguments here. The important point is to recognise that for many the choice was and is only one between greater and lesser poverty.

The same observation applies to many of the wage workers in the urban informal sector and in non-agricultural rural businesses. Earnings here might have been a little higher than in agricultural labouring, and even where they were not there was the hope of upward mobility into a business of one's own.

Until we know a lot more about the micro-economics of the informal sector it is difficult to be more precise than this. I feel certain that such studies will show the prospects for advancement to be much greater in some parts of the sector than others (which is one of the reasons why, except as a residual official category, the 'informal sector' is really not a single sector at all), but I very much doubt whether such research will reveal either the existence or the prospect of much except grinding poverty for the majority of those employed by others in most parts of the sector. With the significant but still untypical exception of a narrow stratum of employers and the self-employed in certain occupations, the so-called 'informal sector' in Kenya, just as in other parts of Africa, is a collective description of a motley assortment of activities which the reserve army of the unemployed undertakes in order to keep itself alive whilst waiting and hoping for the economic system of which it is a part to provide the more remunerative occupations which will make upward mobility a possibility.[48]

48. See for example Chris Gerry, 'Poverty in Employment: A Political Economy of Petty Commodity Production in Dakar, Senegal' (Leeds University Ph.D., 1979).

Perhaps the most eloquent evidence that this was and is the case was the response to the two Tripartite Agreements of 1964 and 1970, in which employment was expanded by set amounts in both the public and private sector by government fiat. On both occasions people were invited to come forward and register as 'unemployed' so that jobs could be allocated on the basis of priorities laid down by the government. In 1964 205,000 people registered within two weeks, and in 1970 registration was closed after four days by which time 290,911 people had come forward![49] Even if it was the case, as the Labour Department claimed and the ILO report repeats, that some of the people registering were not genuinely unemployed, but were registering simply to get 'better jobs', there could hardly be stronger proof of the existence of a large number of workers in Kenya whose incomes were inadequate by their own standards and who were looking to get into those upper echelons of 'formal sector' employment where wage levels allowed some saving and investment to be undertaken.

In short, the 'informal sector' is a place where people go whose only options are even worse, in the sense that the alternative uses of their labour power open to them would yield an even lower rate of return per unit of labour time than does employment in that sector. Nor is the 'informal sector' a new phenomenon in capitalism; on the contrary it is invariably present at that stage of capitalist development in which the supply of labour power is out-running the rate of capital accumulation and employment growth, as Gareth Stedman Jones' work on Victorian London demonstrates.[50]

What is the overall picture of income distribution in Kenya which emerges from this analysis? In a purely static sense, this is well summed up in the ILO report's outline of income groups and their socio-economic characteristics reproduced in table XII:12. But this is a distinctly inadequate conceptualisation of the matter, even from a static point of view. For a relational analysis shows that to a very large extent the incomes and employment of groups (5), (6) and (7) are dependent upon the incomes and employment of groups (1), (2) and (3). That is, the very nearly 1,500,000 households in categories (5) and (6) in the table earn their incomes on small farms owned by households in groups (1), (2) and (3), or on large farms owned by households in group (1), or they work in the urban informal sector and are dependent to a large extent upon demand generated by urban households in groups (1) and (2).

It is true that the total income distribution pattern of Kenya is not exhausted by this relationship between groups (1), (2) and (3) on the one hand and groups (5) and (6) on the other. Group (4), for example, contains the remains of the rapidly eroding group of middle-level smallholders who are heavily involved in cash cropping and neither hire in nor hire out significant quantities of labour

49. See *LDAR* 1964, pp. 3–4; and *MLAR* 1965, p. 2; and 1970, pp. 2–5.
50. Gareth Stedman Jones, *Outcast London: a study in the relationship between classes in Victorian Society* (Harmondsworth, 1976).

Table XII:12. Household income distribution by economic group and income size 1968–70

Economic group	Annual income (£)	Number of households[1] (thousands)
1. Owners of medium-sized to large non-agricultural enterprises in the formal sector of commerce, industry and services; *rentiers*; big farmers; self-employed professional people; holders of high-level jobs in the formal sector.	1,000 and over	30
2. Intermediate-level employees in the formal sector; owners of medium-sized non-agricultural enterprises in the formal sector; less prosperous big farmers.	600–1,000	50
3. Semi-skilled employees in the formal sector; prosperous smallholders;better-off owners of non-agricultural rural enterprises; a small proportion of owners of enterprises in the formal sector.	200–600	220
4. Unskilled employees in the formal non-agricultural sector; significant proportion of smallholders; most of the owners of non-agricultural rural enterprises.	120–200	240
5. Employees in formal-sector agriculture; a small proportion of unskilled employees in the formal sector; better-off wage earners and self-employed persons in the informal urban sector; a small proportion of owners of non-agricultural rural enterprises.	60–120	330
6. Workers employed on small holdings and in rural non-agricultural enterprises; a significant proportion of employed and self-employed persons in the informal urban sector; sizeable number of smallholders.	20–60	1,140
7. Smallholders; pastoralists in semi-arid and arid zones; unemployed and landless persons in both rural and urban areas.	20 and less	330
Total		2,340

[1]Very approximate.

Source: *ILO Report*, p. 74.

power. It also contains those owners of rural small businesses who depend on the demand generated by all classes of smallholder but above all of course by the most prosperous. Similarly group (7) consists of those groups who are truly 'marginalised' in a social and economic sense, i.e. those who for one reason or another play almost no role in the functioning Kenyan economy as it now operates. Nonetheless, it remains significant that what might be called the 'income situation' of most households in Kenya in 1970 (1,800,000 out of 2,300,000) was defined by this crucial employment and income linkage between the rich and better-off on the one hand and the poor and very poor on the other.[51] For this implies that the prospects of the 'working poor' in Kenya (as the ILO report called them) were, are and will be for the foreseeable future dependent on the rate of expansion of the employment and income of groups (1), (2) and (3) in this statistically identified income hierarchy. At its crudest what it means (if we use the ILO figures) is that the creation of one job or one income source in groups (1) to (3) creates very nearly five jobs or income sources for the poor and very poor in groups (5) and (6). Thus the crucial key to the future prospects of the Kenyan economy, and indeed to the likelihood of political stability there, is the speed at which higher-income occupations can be created.

However, to understand the issue dynamically, we must go beyond the 'economic groups' identified in the ILO table, and look at the matter from a historical point of view. Here the whole trend of our analysis has been to suggest that categories such as 'big farmers' and 'holders of high-level jobs in the formal sector' (group (1)) are very largely coterminous, as are such categories as 'intermediate level employees in the formal sector' and 'less prosperous big farmers' 'prosperous smallholders' (group (3)). Moreover the latter category ('prosperous smallholders') may also encompass a large number of 'better-off owners of non-agricultural rural enterprises' (also in group (3)).[52] That is, the 'annual income' figures in column two of table XII:12 are misleading in that they suggest that each household has one income of this average level if it is in one of the occupational categories identified in the group. But in reality the same households may fall into two or even three of these categories, and may thus have double or treble the average group income identified. Income distribution in Kenya is even more unequal than this table suggests.

Aside from employment and income provided by local subsidiaries of multi-national companies in Kenya (which accounts for a small proportion even of formal sector employment, or even formal sector employment in manufacturing), most other income and employment in urban and rural Kenya is provided directly or indirectly out of the investment and consumption expenditure made by an elite of high-income wage and salary earners in the public and private sector. It is to membership of this stratum that all aspire either for themselves or for their children, and it is on its rate of expansion that much else turns. To complete this chapter, therefore, we must look at this issue.

The best way to approach it is via the growth of employment, and in a sense to retrace steps taken earlier in this chapter. Table XII:13 shows the growth of recorded employment in the private sector (excluding agriculture) and in the public sector from 1952 to 1970. It shows clearly that the very slow rate of

51. For a more detailed analysis of this see my 'Modes of Production and Kenyan Dependency' *RAPE*, no. 8, Jan-April 1977, pp. 56–74.
52. Marris and Somerset found that most of the African businessmen they interviewed also owned land, and that in general the more prosperous their business, the bigger their landholdings. Marris and Somerset, op. cit., pp. 118–20.

*Table XII:13. Employment in the private sector (excluding agriculture) and
in the public sector, and rates of growth of employment in both sectors 1952–70*

	Private sector	% rate of growth (annual)	Public sector	% rate of growth (annual)
1952	152,600		115,600	
1953	150,700	− 1.3	134,500	16.3
1954	172,900	14.7	148,400	10.3
1955	191,600	10.8	175,600	18.3
1956	193,500	1.0	168,000	− 4.5
1957	194,000	0.3	167,000	− 0.6
1958	186,000	− 4.1	157,700	− 5.6
1959	185,100	− 0.5	160,100	1.5
1960	189,000	2.1	161,400	0.8
1961	170,800	− 9.6	166,600	3.2
1962	167,400	− 2.0	168,500	1.2
1963	164,100	− 2.0	159,500	− 5.3
1964	191,300	16.6	182,000	14.1
1965	191,500	0.1	188,200	3.4
1966	197,000	2.9	200,400	6.5
1967	212,700	8.0	212,100	5.8
1968	211,500	− 0.6	221,900	4.6
1969	210,800	− 0.3	237,600	7.1
1970	215,300	2.1	248,000	4.4

Private Sector—Overall Growth of Employment 1952–70 = 41.1%
Public Sector —Overall Growth of Employment 1952–70 = 115%
Private Sector—Overall Growth of Employment 1964–70 = 12.5%
Public Sector —Overall Growth of Employment 1964–70 = 36.3%
Source: *SA* 1954–70.

growth of employment in the private sector outside of agriculture (about 2.2 per cent per annum on average) has to some degree been counterbalanced by a much higher rate of expansion of public sector employment (over six per cent per annum over the entire period). The net result of this was a change in the balance of recorded non-agricultural employment. Whereas in 1952 public sector employment accounted for only forty-three per cent of the whole, and even at Independence was only forty-nine per cent, by 1970 it accounted for nearly fifty-four per cent of total recorded employment outside of agriculture (and this trend has continued, so that by 1975 for example the proportion was very nearly fifty-five per cent).[53]

It is difficult to know how far this reflected conscious policy, but whether conscious or not it is of considerable importance because its implication is that the Kenyan state has (deliberately or otherwise) taken upon itself a greater

53. *SA* 1976, p. 263.

and greater share of the burden of satisfying the expectations and ambitions of its population.

To recapitulate: it is in the higher reaches of 'formal sector' public and private sector employment that the wages and salaries are earned on which are based the investment and expenditure funds on which such a large part of the rest of Kenya's population is directly or indirectly dependent for their more meagre incomes. Politically these positions represent the 'honey pot', the major source of investment funds with which families may start on the path of upward mobility trodden by so many since the beginning of the colonial period. Competition for such positions is therefore intense, and there is hardly a household in Kenya which is not striving to advance one or more of its members. Great sacrifices may be made, principally to provide higher and higher levels of education, especially for male members, in order to succeed in this goal. With population growth since 1962 running at well over three per cent per annum, and the vast majority of Kenya's African population now well aware of how accumulation of wealth and upward mobility is achieved (the long historical process outlined in this book has not been lost on them), the rate of expansion of high or above-average income opportunities is the central determinant of political stability in Kenya. It is difficult to believe that those who control the state apparatus there are not well aware of this, and indeed there is very strong circumstantial evidence to suggest that they are.[54]

Given the trends toward more intensive exploitation of labour power in the private sector (which indeed is the normal response of capitalism to a rapidly swelling reserve army), the rate of expansion of employment in that sector is not, and is unlikely to be, sufficient to provide anything like the number of such opportunities required to keep the situation stable. The state must therefore step in and try to fill the gap.

The next stage in the analysis opens before us. If the state is to expand employment, and in particular 'better paid' employment, at anything like the required rate (and it is the weakness of this analysis and the nightmare of Kenyan politicians that the precise magnitude of that rate is unknowable), then it must find the funds to underpin both the volume of employment which already exists and its expansion. In short the state must, for the foreseeable future, expand its payroll and its wage bill at a fairly rapid rate. Where does it currently find the money to fund public sector employment, and what are its prospects of expanding those funds? The answer to these questions necessarily takes us into theoretical as well as empirical terrain, and this is explored in the next chapter.

---

54. Some of the strongest being the tone of President Kenyatta's preambles to the two Tripartite Agreements. See *ILO Report* p. 529.

PART FOUR

CLASSES, EXPLOITATION, AND THE ROLE OF THE STATE IN KENYA: A THEORETICAL ANALYSIS

Chapter XIII

The State as Merchant Capital

The last chapter ended with the State wage bill in Kenya having been provisionally located as one important source of the savings and investment which Africans use to accumulate land and other business interests, and so commence or continue on the path of upward mobility. It also ended with a question as to how the State obtained the money to finance this ever-growing wage bill. At the empirical level this is easily enough answered. The National Accounts show that the Kenyan government, like all other governments, obtains its revenue from direct and indirect taxation, from borrowing, and (to a much lesser extent) from the profits and dividends it obtains from the enterprises which it owns or has shares in.

To pursue the matter further at this empirical level would not take us very far. For it is at this point, at the question of the source and uses of government revenue, that a mass of theoretical issues are opened up. Categories like 'taxation', 'borrowing', and 'profits and dividends' are monetary categories. They operate in a world in which the goods and services, the 'commodities' being produced in an economy have 'already' been turned into money, or at least, whether turned into money or not, are potentially measurable in money. They have a price, irrespective of whether, at any given point in time, that price has yet been realised.[1] Similarly, categories like 'saving' and 'investment' are also monetary categories which direct our attention to the increase of monetary aggregates rather than to the real processes (changes in production and in production relations) which investment may bring about.

In short, if this study is to do more than describe an income distribution using statistical aggregates, if it is to proceed beyond the empirical identification of a mechanism of accumulation, it must be concerned to elucidate the 'deep structure' of class relations, or relations of exploitation, within the Kenyan economy through which this accumulation is made possible. This chapter and the one which follows constitute an attempt to do this.

The State in Kenya stands at the focal point of a network of exchanges between commodities and money which link together producers and consumers within Kenya and the Kenyan sub-system of world capitalism to that world system. I intend to argue in this chapter that the State's wage bill, and indeed nearly all

1. Marx, *Capital*, Vol. I, pp. 95–6, 117–24.

of its current expenditure, is financed directly or indirectly out of the price mark-ups between the buying and selling of commodities. I will then go on to draw out some of the implications of this for the rate of expansion of the wage bill, but I will also endeavour to show that to some degree this in its turn is partially dependent on the uses to which the investment funds derived from that wage bill are put. In passing I will also endeavour to determine, albeit roughly, the size of those investment funds.

In order to understand the way in which the State in Kenya has taken on some of the functions of merchant capital,[2] it is probably best to start where we have started throughout this analysis: on the rural land holding. In the account which follows, for the sake of simplicity I speak as if all such households produced a product surplus to their subsistence needs, i.e. as if all rural households in Kenya sold off their land a volume of produce which enabled savings and investments to be made out of the money received. In reality only some households are in this position. Very many use all the money received to buy in means of subsistence. In their case the produce sold off does not represent a 'surplus product' in the sense in which I shall use the term from now on.

Let us start with a highly simplified (indeed counter-factual) situation in which there is only one harvest and it occurs at one point in the year. Part of that harvest is directly consumed by the households which produced it, and the rest is sold off the land. The produce sold off is divisible into two broad types of crop. On the one hand there are food crops consumed within Kenya; on the other hand there are export cash crops (such as cotton, coffee, tea and pyrethrum) which are mostly exported either in their natural form or in some partly worked-up state.

State Marketing Boards in Kenya purchase a proportion of the domestic food crops (probably the smallest part of the total sold off the land), and virtually all the export cash crops. In the case of the former (handled by the Maize and Produce Board) the crops are re-sold, generally to urban consumers, at a certain price mark-up. Urban consumers do not simply pay a price equal to the producer price paid by the board plus its costs and profit margin. They also have to pay for the commission of the wholesalers and retailers through which the board operates. In theory these commissions are fixed by the board, as therefore is the consumers' price.

In the case of the export cash crops two different sorts of arrangements are entered into. In the case of pyrethrum, for example, state agencies buy the crop from farmers and place it on the world market directly. In the case of tea or

<hr>

2. Strictly speaking of course it is simply wrong to talk about the State 'as' merchant capital since capital as an economic form presupposes private ownership. In addition, as the subsequent argument will show a lot hinges on the phrase 'directly or indirectly' in the first paragraph above. I should also add that the economic functions of the State in Kenya identified in this chapter are not its only economic functions, nor are its economic functions its only functions. They are simply those which are most important from the point of view of the analysis being undertaken here.

coffee, the crop is bought from the farmers and sold at a mark-up to private export firms.[3]

Here then is the way in which the State's agencies, the marketing boards, operate classically in the role of merchant capital. They buy in order to sell, and these agencies cover their costs (including their wage bills) and make a profit out of the difference between the price which they pay to producers and the price at which they sell. It seems that the largest part of the earnings made in this fashion goes to cover recurrent costs (especially wage bills), but in addition they finance investment in storage and transport facilities, and a proportion of their earnings goes into central government revenues. It is to be noted that in the case of the export cash crops state marketing boards are in theory and in practice monopoly purchasers. In the case of food crops the boards are in theory monopolists, but in fact a large part of the crop is sold privately in large numbers of rural and urban markets.[4] At times of normal supply the consumer price set by the boards can act as some sort of ceiling on 'free market' prices, but in times of shortage, as the 1966 Maize Commission of Inquiry made clear, demand (especially in rural areas) generally far outruns the boards' stocks and so the free market price can rise to a large multiple of the official price.[5]

If this was all there were to it, the matter would be very simple. For here is the very simplest case of the State deriving revenue directly from a classical merchant or middleman role. However, the proportion of state revenue coming from the activities of marketing boards is quite small (a maximum of two per cent in 1970 rising to 2.5 per cent by 1974), and the proportion either of public sector employment (less than seven per cent in 1969) or earnings (less than six per cent in 1969) for which they account is also tiny.[6]

It is therefore the indirect reliance on middleman or merchant income which is of far greater quantitative importance to the revenue of the Kenyan state, and this must now be examined. Let us take the scenario with which we started a little further. Let us suppose that all rural households have sold the proportion of the total harvest which is to be exchanged for money, and the crops are now in the hands of the buyers who have laid out money for them. In the case of the food crops they may be sold to consumers in their natural unprocessed form, or they may be partly processed before sale (e.g. maize flour). In the case of processed foods of all types consumed domestically, the State levies an indirect tax, which is incorporated in the price which the manufacturer charges the consumer. In the case of export crops sold to private exporting firms, there is an

3. Though there are considerable differences between coffee and tea with the marketing of the former being much more closely controlled by the Coffee Marketing Board. The Tea Board of Kenya is in fact not really a marketing board at all. For a comprehensive account see Heyer, Maitha and Senga (eds.), op. cit., chapter 10, especially pp. 338–50.
4. See ibid., pp. 323–7.
5. See *Report of the Maize Commission of Inquiry* (Nairobi, 1966), p. 7.
6. *SA* 1971, pp. 164, 188 and 196; and 1976, p. 237.

export tax which is incorporated in the price which the export firm charges the foreign importer. In addition, money now being in the hands of farming households, they will proceed to make purchases of commodities which will either have been manufactured in Kenya (in which case they will have an indirect tax incorporated in their price) or have been imported (in which case they will bear both an import duty and an indirect tax). Thus, irrespective of where in the process of buying and selling payment of tax to the government is actually made (in the case of manufactured goods, for example, payment to the State is usually made by the manufacturer), it is the final consumer of imported goods, of domestic manufactures or of exports who ultimately meets the tax bill. In Kenya the majority of final consumers are either rural households or urban workers. In the case of exports, given the structure of Kenya's export trade, the final consumers are either capitalists (industrial raw materials) or workers (means of consumption) in Europe and North America.

In the case of rural households in Kenya, indirect taxes on manufactured commodities (irrespective of whether these be used as means of production or means of consumption) are a factor in the determination of the exchange value of agricultural commodities. By acting on the price of such commodities this taxation may affect the amount of labour time (embodied in commodities) which the rural producer receives for the labour time he invests in the commodities sold. They may also affect relative exchange values among different manufactured commodities and therefore exchanges of labour time between different groups of workers. In either case the importance of indirect taxes for the Kenyan state is very considerable. In 1970 indirect taxes accounted for forty-three per cent of total current revenue and by 1974 that figure had reached nearly fifty-four per cent.[7] They were and are the largest single source of government current revenue. In essence indirect taxes are of course a form of price mark-up. They may be seen as a charge levied on producers and consumers (ultimately final consumers) for maintaining the political and economic order within which exchanges occur.

The other major sources of government current revenue are direct taxes—taxes on income and capital. Here it is clear that the majority of income earners in Kenya derive these incomes from buying and selling commodities. In the case of rural households, of course, the sellers are also the producers. But in addition there are a large number of wage and salary earners working for enterprises (retailing, wholesaling, transporting, insuring, exporting) whose income essentially comes from charges levied on commodities in their journey from producer to final consumer. What the State is doing in this connection is to help set the level of charges made by these intermediaries by being a partial determinant of the size of their wage bill. Income taxes levied on public employees are of course an accounting exercise. The State must have revenue from elsewhere large

7. *SA* 1971, p. 164; and 1976, p. 237.

enough to pay its own wage bill excluding that part of the wage bill taken up by the taxes which it collects. In 1970 direct taxes of all types accounted for thirty-five per cent of all current state revenue in Kenya, and the proportion was still just over thirty-four per cent in 1975.[8]

All in all, direct and indirect taxes in Kenya account for between eighty and ninety per cent of total current revenue (from which the bulk of the wage bill is paid), and I have suggested that the vast bulk of this is derived indirectly from price mark-ups on 'already' produced commodities. In addition a very small proportion (one to two per cent) comes directly from such mark-ups. In the case of sellers who are also producers (rural agricultural households), both the tax structure and the activities of the marketing boards help determine the exchange value of their labour time embodied in the commodities sold. In the case of workers in private manufacturing industry, direct taxes determine the size of the wage bill (and therefore help determine the volume of commodities and of labour time required to meet the wage bill), and indirect taxes determine the exchange ratios between the commodities produced by different groups of workers and thus the proportion between wage-producing labour time and surplus labour time in each industry.

Let us now consider the modes by which the State might increase its revenue. Clearly it may do so purely in the sphere of circulation and prices by: raising its mark-up on export crop prices; raising its mark-up on internal food crop prices; raising indirect taxes; or raising direct taxes. I wish to follow through the logic of each of these mechanisms of raising government revenue one by one.

Suppose, somewhat improbably, that Kenya were unilaterally to raise the price of its coffee and tea on export markets. Since most of the consumers of these commodities are in western Europe and North America, the initial effect would be to raise the wage bill in these capitalist heartlands. The heartland importers may react by substituting other sources of supply, or there will be a rise in the price of labour power in the heartland. If other sources of supply are substituted then the effect of the price increase on revenue will very soon be wiped out by declining sales.

Let us assume, more realistically, that Kenya has not raised prices unilaterally but has done so in the wake of price increases imposed by much larger producers of these commodities. Given that Kenya is a tiny producer—on a world scale—of all its export commodities except pyrethrum, it can normally only increase prices markedly under these circumstances. In the simplest possible case, the price of labour power in the heartlands will rise across all sectors, including sectors exporting to Kenya, and this will be reflected in a rise in the prices of Kenya's imports, unless real wages in the heartland fall; or profits in the heartland fall; or the productivity of labour power in the heartlands rises to offset or more than offset the rise in its cost.

8. Ibid.

In the real world the general tendency is for prices to rise immediately in order to offset increased costs, and for wage policies and attempts to increase labour productivity to lag somewhat behind this initial effect. That is, the initial effect of a large rise in costs is usually inflationary, but if sustained the secondary response of capitalism is to attempt to lower real wages and increase productivity. The success of capital in the heartlands in achieving these latter objectives (and thus the issue of whether increased prices for peasants and workers in a satellite mean lower standards of living for metropolitan workers) depends overwhelmingly on the class struggle within the heartlands. The initial effect, however, if Kenyan price rises are simply part of a general rise in world prices (which they are almost certain to be), is likely to be inflationary, with that inflation producing a 'clawback' in import prices. Increased import prices of course mean that revenue increases from export price mark-ups are likely to be short-lived and will not provide much of a sustained base for state saving and investment. That something like this does indeed occur can readily be deduced from Kenya's experience in the post-1973 'commodities boom' in world markets.[9]

Not dissimilar considerations apply to the alternative of raising the mark-up on domestic food crops. A rise in such prices will generally affect urban wage bills and profit margins. Once again the initial effect is likely to be inflationary, though, given the success of manufacturing industries in Kenya in raising labour productivity in the recent past, it may be that such increases will be absorbed rather more quickly in increased labour productivity, i.e. an increase in the exploitation of labour power but no necessary fall in real wages. The problem here is that a large part of the urban labour force is not employed in high-productivity manufacturing industry, and outside of this sector real wages are already abysmally low. A rise in food prices could therefore be politically explosive, even if it were not particularly inflationary. If it were inflationary in those sectors which supply government agencies, then of course the 'clawback' mechanism would operate.

An increase of indirect taxes faces two main problems. The major structural one is that many rural households have some 'space' into which to retreat from involvement in the money economy, and in addition the 'informal sector' (in which indirect taxes are widely evaded) can act as an alternative source of supply of commodities whose prices rise markedly through tax increases. If such increases are large-scale and across the board, rural households have the alternative of minimising purchases of manufactured goods, and (in the case of food products) substituting increased direct consumption for market purchases.

9. See the appendix to this chapter. This same argument applies equally well to increases in export taxes, in fact of course increases in such taxes by the Ministry of Finance are locally analogous to an increase in export prices by marketing boards. They are simply two mechanisms to achieve the same result, though export taxes cover commodities (e.g. re-exports) not in the purview of marketing boards.

Urban households without any access to rural producers (and these are few) may switch demand to the urban informal sector where substitute untaxed commodities may be produced.[10]

Direct tax increases face similar difficulties. Direct taxation is most effective where the working population is entirely or predominantly wage-earning and where the labour market is sufficiently regulated for payment of taxes before wages are received to be the norm. In a situation in which the majority of labour power is still expended on the smallholding or in unregulated employment, earnings or incomes are extremely difficult to assess accurately, and are subject to enormous fluctuations. Large increases in direct taxation of smallholders will thus generally lead to widespread evasion and/or a shift of labour time out of production for the market. Direct taxation is a much more potent weapon in the case of those in higher-income regulated employment in urban areas, but in Kenya this advantage seems to be offset somewhat by the inefficiency and corruptibility of the tax authorities, which makes it easy for high-income earners in particular to evade payment partially or totally.[11]

None of this is meant to suggest that the State is unable to obtain any increase at all in its revenues by intervention in the price structure. It can of course gain some increase in this way and frequently acts to increase its revenues not by massive across-the-board increases (which is what is posited above), but by small increases either in direct taxation or in the prices (taxes and duties) of particular commodities, particularly those whose price elasticity of demand is not very great. The logic of consequences described above rather suggests that a consistent and sustained increase in revenues and in capital accumulation out of those revenues is not likely to come from these mechanisms alone, given the marginal situation of the Kenyan economy in world capitalism, and the internal structure of that economy. The central weakness of the internal structure from the point of view of capital accumulation is simply that labour power within it is not predominantly a commodity.

The beauty of the mature capitalist mode of production as an agency of capital accumulation is the following. Since the vast bulk of labour power is a commodity, the control of wages represents effective control over the bulk of consumption within the economy. Since the worker cannot live on the single commodity (or more usually, tiny part of a commodity) which he produces, he or she must continue to sell his or her labour power, and must exchange the money form of that labour power for other commodities to live. Thus if, over the long term, the productivity of labour power is increased and real wages rise (i.e. the rate of relative surplus value is either stable or increases) it is possible simultaneously to expand output and consumption of that output. Thus an

---

10. Just as the same logic applies to export taxes as to marketing board mark-ups, so the same broad logic of consequences applies to increases of import duties as to rises in indirect taxes.
11. See *ILO Report*, p. 272.

upward spiral is set in motion in which increased capital accumulation (out of rising relative surplus value) produces both increased output per worker, and increased consumption (out of rising real wages) and this 'calls forth' yet greater capital accumulation and yet more output. The heart of the matter is that the process of consumption (the 'appropriation of nature')—both in its productive and its unproductive forms—takes the monetary form of 'effective demand'. Without money both as means of production ('capital') and as means of consumption ('wages') the mature capitalist mode of production can neither produce nor consume.

In Kenya, by contrast, some part of production (especially in agriculture) still takes place without need for money either for means of production or labour power, and more importantly a great deal of consumption is possible without money (directly consumed subsistence production of the rural household, some part of which may also find its way to urban workers). In short a block is placed in the way of the Kenyan state as an agency of capital accumulation, both because a part of 'domestic demand' falls outside the monetary sphere and is therefore not controllable within the realm of circulation (in which the State is largely active), and because the Kenyan state does not control demand for exports, because that ultimately depends on the process of capital accumulation (and thus of labour productivity and the class struggle) within the capitalist heartlands.

How is this block to be removed? How could the Kenyan state become a more effective agency of capital accumulation? The answer is clearly implicit in this critique of its current role. The State must endeavour to increase the volume and quality (in terms of labour time directly and indirectly embodied) of the commodities which are produced within Kenya. It must endeavour to increase the production of use values, and of use values with a higher exchange value, if sustained capital accumulation is to occur. It cannot depend on price manipulation.

Put more simply, this means that the volume of agricultural and industrial output must be increased, and that in both sectors the type of commodities produced must embody more labour time (be more complex or 'worked up' commodities which will call forth a greater exchange value). What are the prospects of this occurring? In order to examine this question we must backtrack a little to the observation made at the end of chapter XII.

There I suggested that the State's wage bill is one of the prime sources of investment funds used by the petite bourgeoisie in Kenya. Use of savings from above-average wages and salaries for investment purposes is a hallmark of that stratum, and the expansion of the wage bill (in higher wages and salaries and in an increasing number of such wages and salaries) one of its major modes of expansion. I also suggested that relative to the other major mode (access to such salaries in the higher reaches of the private sector), the public sector was and is growing in importance.

We may now return to this issue but from a slightly different perspective. I have argued above that expansion of the revenue upon which the public sector wage bill is based has been and will be difficult unless real output and labour productivity in industry and agriculture can be raised. At this point however the argument comes full circle. For I wish to argue that one of the main hopes for the latter occurring is the use of investment funds from this wage bill in ways which will revolutionise production inside Kenya. It is probably the case that the size of the investment funds available from the public and private sector wage bill is substantially greater than that which the State invests directly in its so-called 'development expenditure'. In what follows I therefore proceed in two stages. Firstly, I shall be concerned to show empirically that such funds are available and even on conservative calculations considerable. In the second stage I shall consider some of the contradictions which would be likely to emerge were such revolutionising investments to be made by the petite-bourgeoisie and to be supported by the State. Those contradictions themselves elucidate the central dilemma of the Kenyan political economy, and of those who control the State there.

To take the empirical issue first, we have argued that the State is the source of a large privately-utilised investment fund through its wage bill. We must now attempt to quantify this, and by far the best source for doing so is the Kenya Government's Report of the *Commission of Inquiry (Public Service Structure and Remuneration Commission)* (known as the Ndegwa Report, after its Chairman). This report surveyed wages and employment in the Kenyan Civil Service (including teachers), the para-statal corporations or 'Statutory Boards', and local government; and the employment of Kenyan nationals in the East African Community Organisations such as the Railways and Harbours, Posts and Telecommunications and the East African Airways. Table XIII:1, derived from the report, shows the growth of the total public sector wage bill from 1959 to 1970.[12]

The particularly sharp rise in the period after Independence stands out clearly. In the four years from 1959 to 1963 the average annual increase in the public sector wage bill was some 7.9 per cent but from 1964 to 1970 it was 14.2 per cent. moreover this trend has continued at an ever-accelerating rate. In the period from 1971 to 1975 the wage bill rose from K£86.7 million to K£156.8 million, an increase of eighty-one per cent in four years, or an average increase of 20.3 per cent per year. Moreover, this scale of increase cannot simply be put down to the effects of the two Tripartite Agreements since though there were large rises in both 1964 and 1970, there were as large or larger increases in subsequent years.

Of course not all of this wage bill was paid to Africans, since as late as 1969 there were still substantial numbers of Europeans and Asians employed in senior

---

12. The *Report*'s data (p. 27) covered the decade from 1959. The figure for 1970 is taken from *SA* 1971, p. 196.

Table XIII:1.

Year	Public sector wage bill (K£ mil)
1959	30.7
1960	32.3
1961	37.3
1962	37.1
1963	37.8
1964	42.9
1965	51.4
1966	58.0
1967	62.9
1968	67.1
1969	71.9
1970	79.4

Table XIII:2. Changes in average wages of Africans and in overall average wages in the Kenyan public sector 1959–69 (1964 = 100)

Year	Africans	Total public sector
1959	53.0	81.4
1960	57.5	85.0
1961	63.8	94.7
1962	68.0	94.1
1963	78.4	100.5
1964	100.0	100.0
1965	114.9	115.8
1966	121.0	122.6
1967	123.7	125.7
1968	129.8	128.2
1969	132.6	128.2

i.e. Average wages of Africans in the public sector increased by 150.2% from 1959 to to 1969. Average wages in the sector as a whole rose 57.5% in the same period. Source: *Ndegwa Report*, p. 31.

state posts. In that year, for example, when the average public sector wage was Shs. 504 per month, there were 1,048 employees earning over Shs. 4,000 per month of whom no less than 649 were Europeans and only 289 were Africans.[13]

Nonetheless, in sheer quantitative terms Africans did dominate employment within the sector (being 226,000 of the 237,600 employees in 1969), and in addition African wages within the sector rose far faster over the period surveyed by the Ndegwa Report than the wages in the sector as a whole, as table XIII:2 shows.

13. *Ndegwa Report*, pp. 30 and 36.

Table XIII:3. Distribution of wage employment by income group, Kenyan public sector 1975

Income group (Shs. per month)	No. of employees	% of all public sector employees
0–99	2,767	0.9
100–149	1,779	0.6
150–199	6,664	2.1
200–399	67,347	21.6
400–599	95,166	30.6
600–799	48,182	15.5
800–999	32,789	10.5
1,000–1,499	24,764	8.0
1,500–1,999	14,364	4.6
2,000–2,999	11,387	3.7
3,000 +	7,030	2.3

Source: *SA* 1976, p. 295.

Thus the public sector wage bill has risen considerably since Independence, reflecting both a rapid rise in employment in the sector (far faster than the private sector),[14] and a general rise in earnings, especially at the higher levels where both Africanisation and an expansion of employment has taken place. Though Africans within the sector as a whole have raised their earnings continually in real and money terms, there is still of course massive inequality of earnings within the sector as table XIII:3 shows.

Now if we were to consider the whole of the public sector wage bill as an investment fund it would be enormous. For example, in the period 1964–9, it amounted to K£356.2 million, or nearly three times the Kenyan government's total development expenditure in this period (K£119.1 million).[15] Of course one cannot do this, since the bulk of these wages, particularly at the lower levels, would have been expended on subsistence, and would not have led to saving or investment at all. We must therefore try and estimate some 'investment coefficients' (however approximate) for the wage bill.

One method of approaching this problem is through the scale of remittances from urban 'formal sector' employees (i.e. roughly the public sector plus most of the enumerated employees in the private sector outside of agriculture) to rural areas. One of the most thorough pieces of work on this matter was undertaken by

14. In the nine years from 1966 to 1975 employment in the private sector (outside of agriculture) rose by 43%, or at an average rate of 4.8% per annum. In the public sector it rose by 71%, or at an average of 7.9% per annum. See *SA* 1976, p. 263.
15. Republic of Kenya, *Development Plan 1970–74* (Nairobi, 1969), p. 54. Total public sector capital expenditure in this period (1964–9) amounted to K£80,100,000 so the total public sector wage bill was over four times this figure.

Johnson and Whitelaw[16] in December 1970 when they interviewed 1,140 African males in Nairobi in 'middle and low income' occupations. They found the average level of remittances in the sample to be twenty per cent of total earnings, though this was patterned in a rather odd way. They found that: 'The coefficients on income suggest that T/Y [income transferred as a proportion of income earned] declines with income up to Shs. 881 per month, then increases up to Shs. 1,363 and declines thereafter.'[17] Or, in other words, up to the income level of Shs. 881 (in December 1970) income increases tended to be spent on improving living standards within the town. Above this level more could be spared for remittances, and over Shs. 1,363, incomes were large enough to allow more to be remitted in absolute terms though as a proportion of total income remittances fell.

However, one cannot even take remittance levels as investment coefficients, because only a part of remittances go to investment in any form at all. Thus Johnson and Whitelaw's survey suggested that most of them went for 'school fees', 'expenditure on the farm' and 'payment of taxes', and of these, only the first and second could be regarded as 'investment' of any sort.

Another method of attempting to arrive at an investment coefficient for the public sector wage bill is by looking at the expenditure patterns of households. In the Central Province *Economic Survey* for example, capital expenditure accounted for 5.4 per cent of average household income in the sample and in the Nyanza Household Survey the figure was three per cent.[18] In the 1963 survey of 'African Middle Income Workers in Nairobi' the Ministry of Finance and Economic Planning's team of researchers found that remittances exclusive of school fees totalled ten per cent of the average income of the 324 households in the sample. In addition they found that about one per cent of the average income of their households went on 'lending', and another 1.7 per cent on 'gifts'.[19]

Out of these snippets of discrepant data it is difficult to produce any coherent picture, but if we assume that the difference between the level of remittances found by Johnson and Whitelaw in 1970 and those found by the survey of middle income workers in 1963 reflects both a change of definition (incorporat-

16. G. F. Johnson and W. E. Whitelaw, 'Urban-Rural Income Transfers in Kenya: An Estimated Remittance Function' (IDS Discussion Paper 137, 1972).

17. Ibid., p. 6.

18. *Economic Survey* . . ., op. cit., (table 49, p. 37. and *Rural Household Survey*, op. cit., p. 59.

19. *The Pattern of Income, Expenditure and Consumption of African Middle Income Workers in Nairobi* (Ministry of Finance and Economic Planning, Nairobi, 1964), pp. 13, 24–5 and 29. This percentage agrees very closely with Grillo's figures derived from a survey of African railway employees in Kampala in the same year (R. D. Grillo, op. cit., p. 49). It may be that Johnson and Whitelaw's markedly higher figure reflects the fact that they included school fee payments as part of remittances, whilst the 1963 survey in Nairobi did not. The position with Grillo is unclear, though it is clear that his remittances did not include money transferred for house or farm investment in rural areas, whereas Johnson and Whitelaw's figures do include expenditure on the 'maintenance of the farm'.

ing school fees in the former but not in the latter) and also the rise in real incomes for some sections of the urban work force which occurred in these years, then we may be able to map some rough parameters. In her account of remittances and of 'the urban workers' investment in the tribal areas' Marion Forrester showed that the two top income groups of workers in her sample invested seven per cent, and the second highest income group 10.5 per cent of their wages in such rural investments as house building, land purchase and livestock.[20] Moreover it is clear from Grillo that substantial investments of this sort are made in addition to remittances.

If, then, to be conservative, we said that in 1970 about a quarter of actual remittances (i.e. about five per cent of wages) would represent investment in any form (not counting school fees as investment in 'human capital'), and in addition we assumed that a further five to ten per cent would go in rural and urban investments not included in remittances, we would not I think be far wrong. We would be saying that between ten and fifteen per cent of the total wage bill in Kenya was used for investment, and for lack of an alternative we would also assume that this percentage was distributed equally between the public and private sector (or that at least the discrepancies between the two sectors were not sufficient to make this a wildly inaccurate assumption). I am inclined to think that the upper figure is preferable to the lower, because, in my own experience, respondents persistently understate their incomes and expenditure in income surveys, and that in particular, for various reasons (the most common being the very understandable one that their financial affairs are their own business) they persistently understate their margin for saving, which is what we are especially interested in here.

Returning now to the public sector 'investment fund' and its likely size, we see for example that in the period 1964-9 (when the total wage bill was K£356.2 million), if investment had proceeded at ten per cent per annum it would have amounted to K£35.6 million over this period, if at fifteen per cent, the investment fund from the public sector alone would have amounted to K£53.4 million. This latter figure represents some forty-five per cent of total government development expenditure over the same period, or sixty-six per cent of total public sector 'official' capital investment.

But of course this is only part of the picture. If the same proportion of the private sector wage bill is also invested, then the total investment fund generated out of wages would be even larger. Between 1964 and 1969 the total wage bill in the public sector and the private sector (excluding agriculture) was K£862.6 million. Ten per cent of this if invested — K£86.2 million — would have exceeded total public sector capital expenditure over the same period, and fifteen per cent (K£129.4 million) would have been in excess of all public sector development expenditure.

20. See above, chapter IX, p. 275-6 and *Rural Household Survey*, op. cit., table 7.4, p. 61.

426 Class and Economic Change in Kenya

Very little faith can be placed in the rough investment coefficients developed above, because the data on which they are based are so scanty. But for the total (public and private sector) wage bill, they would have to be very much over-estimated for us not to be dealing with what are, within the parameters of the Kenyan economy, very large amounts of money. My own feeling is that if anything this coefficient range is rather underestimated, because with a rise in real incomes one might expect the rate of savings and investment, especially in the highest income ranges, to rise somewhat faster than incomes. According to the ILO report some twenty per cent of all households in Nairobi earned about fifty per cent of all income, whilst in 1964 Berg-Schlosser was reporting that 2.2 per cent of all income earners in Kenya as a whole earned more than twenty-five per cent of the total income.[21] Taking the ILO's less extreme and probably more accurate estimates as not untypical of the situation in Kenya as a whole in 1970, then those twenty per cent of households would only have had to save and invest twenty per cent of their total income for ten per cent of the total wage bill to have been invested. If they were to save thirty per cent, then the fifteen per cent level would be reached by their activity alone, and this is on the totally unrealistic assumption that the other eighty per cent of income earners did not save or invest at all. In fact from the evidence of remittances alone, it can be seen that even the poorest households strive with might and main to put something aside from immediate consumption expenditure (even if most of this 'saving' is in the end only delayed consumption).

In short it seems very likely that at least fifteen per cent of the total public and private sector wage bill goes to what might be called (at the risk of perpetu-ating a fashionable term) and 'informal' investment fund to fuel the commerciali-sation of agriculture and the expansion of trade and business enterprises out-side of agriculture. In addition it is clear that the bulk of this fund is in the hands of comparatively few people. If we take the top twenty per cent of income earners as controlling most of it, then in 1970 we would be dealing with some 80,000 people out of a total adult population in Kenya of nearly 5,500,000, or a total adult male population of over 2,600,000 (assuming most of those involved to be male), i.e. a mere three per cent of the whole.

It is also to be noted that, just as in the public sector, the private sector wage bill outside of agriculture is derived in good part from income earned in the realm of circulation. In fact in 1970 over sixty per cent of it was accounted for by commerce (i.e. wholesale and retail businesses) and transport and service industries.[22] Thus the largest part of this total investment fund is, at the mone-tary level, obtained in activities which are not directly involved in expanding the stock of use values within the economy, and to this degree is entirely subject

21. *ILO Report*, p. 75; Dirk Berg-Schlosser, *The Distribution of Income and Education in Kenya: Causes and Potential Political Consequences* (Munich, 1970), p. 18.
22. Calculated from data in *SA* 1971, pp. 197–8.

to the sort of contradictions which have already been identified for the public sector wage bill and investment fund.

But as already stated, the resolution of this contradiction lies in part in the use to which the investment fund is put. If it is utilised primarily for investment in agricultural and non-agricultural commodity production, then it may certainly help to increase the production of real use and exchange values within the Kenyan economy, and at the same time raise the productivity of labour power there. If however it goes primarily into commercial ventures and into service activities of various types, then it will simply contribute to the exacerbation of that contradiction. Such scanty evidence as we have suggests that the latter is the case, and that the bulk of 'informal' investment (i.e. outside the corporate private sector and the public sector) does not go into the expansion of agricultural and manufacturing output.[23] However, in the absence of anything like adequate data on this (which is simply one aspect of the largely unexplored economics of the 'informal sector') it would be unwise to draw too many conclusions from it.

What one can do is to consider some of the possible consequences which would follow if the investment fund were utilised in a productive fashion, and indeed, less hypothetically, one can look at some of the consequences which seem to have arisen already because it is not being so used. To take the latter issue first, we have suggested that the essential contradiction in Kenya is that, in order to maintain political stability, employment and the wage fund (which increasingly has meant public sector employment and the public sector wage fund) have had to be expanded at a rate which, while still inadequate to absorb the ever-swelling reserve army of labour, is dependent on revenue whose expansion is held within fairly well-defined limits by the rate of expansion of real output within the economy. If this wage fund is not simply to be expanded by inflationary means, i.e. by printing money—which of course is no expansion at all—then the real product of the economy must be expanded. I have already suggested that one possible way of doing this is to use the wage bill 'investment fund', whose size I have attempted roughly to determine, but it also seems that to date this has not occurred, because the bulk of this 'informal' investment has not gone into productive activity, but into activities within the realm of circulation.

There is one other possible solution to this contradiction, which is to close the gap between domestic production and domestic consumption by external borrowing, and this, we are unsurprised to find, is precisely what Kenya has been doing, and doing to an ever-increasing extent. As the appendix to this chapter indicates, Kenya's balance of trade worsened slowly through the late sixties, and then very rapidly in the period from 1972 to 1975. Until about 1972, a negative balance of trade had been balanced by a strong inflow of foreign

23. See for example Leys, op. cit., pp. 148–69.

capital which was mainly private foreign investment. From 1972, partly in response to Kenya's rapidly worsening balance of trade, private foreign investment tailed off, and the Kenyan government was forced to fill the gap by increasing amounts of direct borrowing.

It appears from the ILO report and from the 1970–4 development plan that at least up to 1974 Kenya's broad strategy was to meet the State's recurrent expenditure (including the wage bill) out of domestic revenue, and to rely almost entirely on foreign capital inflows (including aid flows) to fund development expenditure. As a number of commentators have pointed out, such a strategy is possible in the short term, but in the face of an ever-worsening balance of trade it is difficult to sustain, because private foreign investors and the commercial markets for government borrowing become worried about credit-worthiness and either cut down lending or demand harsher terms. The end-result is of course a situation in which amortisation and interest payments build up to a point where repayments are well in excess of receipts with the effect on the overall balance of payments and need for yet further indebtedness so familiar in Latin America. Indeed, there are signs, as the ILO report pointed out, that Kenya has already started on this path.[24]

The persistently worsening balance of trade and the need to fill the gap by ever greater amounts of government borrowing are simply the phenomenal form, the mode of appearance, of the underlying productivity problem sketched out in this chapter. The solution to the spiral of indebtedness is an increase in the quantity and complexity of the commodities produced in Kenya by means of capital investment. At the level of economic logic, at least, the solution to Kenya's problem is nothing less than industrialisation—the industrialisation of agriculture, and the raising of labour productivity outside of agriculture by increased capital intensity of non-agricultural production.

Such a 'solution' begs all sorts of questions about the presence of an 'initial' market large enough to make such increases in output worthwhile, about the possibility of capital accumulation within Kenya on the scale required, and about the social and political consequences of such a strategy. Each of these issues would require a volume to itself. But it should be noted that unless the quantity and exchange value of real output in Kenya is raised, the Kenyan state and the petite bourgeoisie which dominates it are likely to find themselves faced with a structural problem of increasing severity. And I wish to outline as clearly as I can what I take this problem to be. It involves nothing less than the whole economic mechanism which brought this stratum into being and keeps it expanding.

Kenya has a high level of population growth, running at at least three per cent per annum at the present time. The degree of commercialisation of agri-

24. *ILO Report*, pp. 279–81 and 569–72. See also Richard Theuman, 'Political and Economic Consequences of Kenya's Development Strategy' (USSC Paper, 1971).

culture and of consequent rural stratification in that country to date, though limited, has been and is sufficient to render increasing numbers of people either landless or (more commonly) in control of such a small amount of land that total household labour power cannot be produced and reproduced upon it. The result is a continually expanding reserve army of labour. The private sector has taken advantage of the existence of this reserve army to exploit its labour force more effectively and to raise their productivity. The resultant 'employment gap' has been partly filled by the so-called 'informal sector' and partly by an accelerating expansion of public sector employment. From the point of view of political stability it is particularly important that the number of 'better paid' jobs, from which savings and investments can be made, should be expanded and the 'educated unemployed' (often produced by immense consumption sacrifices within the household) bought off. To keep the political system stable this must continue to happen, and given the rate of population growth and the ever-increasing number of households entering runners in the 'education race' it must happen at an accelerating rate, at least in the immediate future. Yet this may not be possible unless real output within the economy can be expanded. However, the short-term effects of the use of either state investments, foreign private investment or the informal investment fund to do this, would be likely to expand the reserve army even more, as the exodus from the land accelerated, and labour was shed in large-scale agriculture and manufacturing.

There is a further point too. Should either the State's formal 'development' plans or 'informal' investors (the biggest of whom are often politicians and state officials) go over to this strategy, they might come into conflict with international capital. With 'proletarianisation' continuing on an ever greater scale, the latter would lose the subsidy to its wage bill from direct consumption which has undoubtedly been a factor aiding profitability, and would have to meet the full costs of the subsistence and reproduction of the working class (i.e. the wage bill would become coterminous with 'variable capital' in Marx's sense). This would only be acceptable to international capital if labour productivity, output, and demand, were expanding fast enough in the same situation to offset the loss to profits sustained by this change.

But this is to pile speculation upon speculation. What can be said with more certainty is that the contradiction outlined above has already entered the realm of appearances in the increasing concern about the expansion of 'employment', and will also take other apparent forms, of which difficulties in expanding the State's revenue sources, and difficulties in simultaneously expanding the State's payroll and maintaining real wage increases and differentials at the top levels are just two. It may even be that the tendencies toward the reduction of differentials within the public sector observed by Cowen are a partial expression of the contradiction manifesting itself.[25] But of course the contradiction does not

25. See Cowen and Kinyanjui, op. cit., pp. 8 and 23–7.

lie in reality at the level of 'revenue' or 'the wage bill' or 'employment' or 'differentials' or 'inequality'. It lies rather in the low level of productivity of labour power in Kenya, which in its turn reflects the historical absence of that process of capital accumulation whose history is the history of class stuggle and rising living standards in the capitalist heartlands. To borrow the polemical formulation of Geoffrey Kay, the essential contradiction facing the Kenyan petite bourgeoisie is not the product of their country having been too exploited by capitalism, but on the contrary the product of its not having been exploited enough.[26] Since by its very origins and attitudes this stratum looks to capitalism for development in Kenya, it may one day be faced with a choice; either to attempt to carry through to its conclusion a capitalist revolution in production there, or to remain an increasingly indebted appendage to the world system, faced with ever-worsening political difficulties internally. In short the petite bourgeoisie of Kenya, in order to keep its gaudy caravan on the road, must constantly attempt to universalise itself within its domain. This is impossible, since, as I will attempt to show further in the next and final chapter, it owes its existence to a form of resource transfer (exploitation) of other classes in Kenya.

---

26. Geoffrey Kay, *Development and Underdevelopment: a Marxist Analysis* (London, 1975), especially chapter 5, pp. 96–124.

Appendix to Chapter XIII

The World Commodity Boom and Kenya's Balance of Payments

Up until 1971, Kenya's post-Independence balance of payments had been in credit, due partly to earnings from invisible exports such as transport and tourism, and above all, to a rising amount of long-term private foreign investment. In 1971 the situation changed dramatically. Private foreign investment fell for the first time since 1965, but above all the trade deficit (the second row in table XIII:4) widened to the point where it could no longer be offset by the combined effect of 'invisibles' and foreign investment. This was due to an increase in imports (from K£158 million to K£197.7 million), whilst exports rose only fractionally (from K£108.8 million to K£110.9 million). According to the Kenyan government's *Economic Survey* in 1972, thirty per cent of the rise in imports was due to inflation in the West. There was also a six per cent devaluation of the Kenyan pound in 1971 due to the turmoil in the international monetary system occasioned by the large U.S. balance of payments deficit.[27]

The major part of the increased deficit was due to a rapid growth in capital formation, and a consequent large increase in the imports of fuels and other chemicals, metals, transport machinery and capital goods for agriculture and industry. This was the continuation and acceleration of a long-term trend. End-use analysis of imports showed that over seventy per cent of them in the period 1966–71 were intermediate and capital goods for use in the private and para-statal sector.[28]

So if, even before 1971, Kenya's balance of trade gave cause for concern, her performance in attracting private foreign investment had been outstanding, and earnings from transport and tourism also helped convert the trade deficit to a balance of payments surplus. Moreover, it could be argued that even the trade deficit gave cause for hope, in that it was in large part a reflection of a sustained growth in productive capacity and output, especially in manufacturing.

Thus when from 1972–3 the world prices of some of Kenya's major exports began to rise, and when in addition she was able to obtain volume increases in most of her exports as well, it might have been thought that she would have been able to eliminate or at least reduce her balance of trade deficit.

27. *ES* 1972, pp. 22 and 30–1.
28. Ibid., pp. 26 and 32–9.

Table XIII:4. Kenya balance of payments 1964–71 (K £ million)

	1964	1965	1966	1967	1968	1969	1970	1971
Current Account Balance	17.5	0.2	− 6.6	− 21.5	− 14.4	− 2.9	− 16.6	− 51.4
of which:								
Visible balance	− 9.4	− 19.4	− 26.7	− 37.5	− 37.0	− 31.1	− 50.2	− 89.2
Invisible balance	26.9	19.6	20.1	16.0	22.6	28.2	33.6	37.8
Long-term capital movements	− 15.6	8.1	14.7	16.5	15.6	20.2	29.2	21.9
Current and long-term balance	1.9	8.3	8.1	− 5.0	1.2	18.3	12.6	− 29.5

Source: *SA* 1972, p. 47.

Table XIII:5. Quantities of principal overseas exports, 1971–5

	Unit	1971	1972	1973	1974	1975
Coffee	Tons	56,426	63,142	75,317	71,680	67,615
Tea	,,	33,508	47,126	51,472	49,595	52,547
Petroleum Products	Million Litres	1,145	1,129	1,219	1,259	1,016
Pyrethrum products	Tons	2,676	3,358	3,438	4,566	4,906
Meat products	,,	7,180	10,208	6,336	6,564	8,123
Sisal	,,	34,713	38,764	44,800	72,070	42,717
Hides and skins	,,	8,271	10,522	8,226	9,082	11,940
Soda ash	,,	149,904	144,717	201,880	139,510	78,481
Cement	,,	331,689	372,208	432,694	490,651	510,470
Maize (raw)	,,	12*	8*	199,544	44,681	118,570
Canned pineapples	,,	10,805	9,734	13,352	8,663	19,990
Butter and ghee	,,	227	1,979	1,860	1,147	637
Beans and peas	,,	8,059	21,268	16,283	10,408	15,977
Cotton (raw)	,,	4,606	4,266	4,780	3,318	3,008
Wool	,,	1,313	1,605	1,498	1,343	1,979
Animal feeds	,,	21,566	39,403	29,711	9,292	12,298
Cashew nuts	,,	10,604	15,540	9,368	20,350	14,297

*Consisting of small shipment of 'special purpose' maize.

Tables XIII:5–XIII:7 show (1) the volume trends of major Kenyan exports 1971–5, (2) the unit price trend of the same items, and (3) an export price index from 1972–5 using 1971 as the base year. As will be seen the latter index rose from 111 to 196 in the period, and the non-oil items rose from 112 to 173.

Unfortunately the trend of import price increases was even more impressive as tables XIII:8 and XIII:9 indicate. Whereas export prices rose seventy-seven per cent (non-oil items fifty-four per cent) in these four years, import prices rose

Table XIII:6. Overseas export prices, 1971–5 K Sh./Unit

	Unit of Quantity	1971	1972	1973	1974	1975
Coffee unroasted	kg	6.92	7.84	9.50	10.71	10.41
Tea	kg	7.09	6.99	6.59	7.82	8.73
Petroleum products	1,000 lt	154.94	158.44	155.64	416.00	623.64
Maize	100 kg	. .	. .	56.02	74.40	79.07
Meat and products	kg	10.20	9.55	11.88	13.75	12.33
Pyrethrum extract	kg	149.79	148.52	164.10	192.20	223.49
Sisal	100 kg	87.29	106.70	213.20	470.56	343.76
Hides and skins, undressed	kg	5.90	7.18	12.61	9.78	9.07
Wattle extract	kg	1.58	1.62	1.91	2.12	2.46
Soda ash	100 kg	24.82	26.74	27.89	38.76	60.00
Cement	100 kg	9.44	10.55	11.86	16.25	21.02
Beans, peas, etc.	kg	1.13	1.04	1.44	2.97	2.24
Cashew nuts, raw	kg	1.41	1.35	1.30	1.59	1.59
Wool	kg	4.00	4.60	10.76	10.31	6.97
Animal feed	100 kg	39.59	30.03	64.80	63.88	59.84
Cotton, raw	kg	5.13	5.70	5.74	6.85	8.53
Pineapples, tinned	kg	1.78	1.89	2.22	3.26	3.57
Butter and ghee	kg	8.17	7.67	7.44	8.00	8.98
Wattle bark	100 kg	58.68	54.54	51.90	66.42	79.61

Table XIII:7. Price indices of exports, 1972–5

			1971 = 100	
Exports	1972	1973	1974	1975
Food and live animals	106	122	142	150
Beverages and tobacco	106	101	92	132
Crude materials, inedible	110	157	204	183
Mineral fuels	101	109	222	309
Animal and vegetable oils and fats	100	114	172	225
Chemicals	133	148	195	245
Manufactured goods	113	143	170	209
Machinery and transport equipment	113	133	157	193
Miscellaneous manufactured articles	112	148	163	200
All exports	111	126	171	196
Non-oil Exports	112	129	161	173

Source: *ES* 1976, pp. 66 and 71.

112 per cent and even non-oil items rose 182 per cent. Note however that the real deterioration in the balance of trade only set in in 1974. From 1971–3 inclusive, the price increases of non-oil exports and imports (and indeed the overall index) just about kept pace. As from 1974 however, as table XIII:10 shows, the

terms of trade turned violently against Kenya. This was not simply a reflection of the massive oil price rises in 1973–4, for the prices of all other major imports (apart from beverages and tobacco) turned up sharply in 1974 too. Indeed while the net barter terms of trade on all items deteriorated from 98 to 85 in this

Table XIII:8. Total imports, 1971–5, by broad economic category (K£ thousands)

	1971	1972	1973	1974	1975
1. Food and Beverages	19,100	19,173	21,569	24,467	20,751
Primary	4,817	4,709	6,681	4,418	6,367
For Industry	1,251	2,455	4,815	2,619	4,667
For Household Consumption	3,566	2,254	1,866	1,799	1,700
Processed	14,283	14,464	14,888	20,049	14,385
For Industry	4,812	3,873	4,672	7,630	8,608
For Household Consumption	9,471	10,591	10,216	12,419	5,777
2. Industrial Supplies (Non-Food)	70,437	66,035	84,507	145,443	99,818
Primary	5,884	4,952	5,307	9,288	7,660
Processed	64,553	61,083	79,200	136,155	92,158
3. Fuels and Lubricants	16,933	20,542	23,120	81,147	95,036
Primary	13,193	14,816	17,904	67,461	87,242
Processed	3,740	5,726	5,216	13,686	7,794
Motor Spirit	630	1,230	1,036	2,125	884
Other	3,110	4,496	4,180	11,561	6,910
4. Machinery and other Capital Equipment	31,874	36,107	40,607	39,642	57,755
Machinery and other Capital Equipment	29,234	32,976	37,754	36,115	53,215
Parts and Accessories	2,640	3,131	2,852	3,527	4,540
5. Transport Equipment	35,663	26,290	24,440	41,362	43,959
Passenger Motor Vehicles	6,657	5,945	4,650	9,300	5,788
Other	12,678	9,496	8,914	12,081	18,171
Industrial	12,345	9,273	8,768	11,826	17,951
Non-Industrial	333	223	146	255	220
Parts and Accessories	16,328	10,848	10,876	19,981	20,000
6. Consumer Goods not elsewhere specified	24,750	21,576	23,352	33,178	29,293
Durable	6,533	4,510	5,143	6,957	5,014
Semi-Durable	10,667	8,955	9,317	15,034	12,523
Non-Durable	7,550	8,111	8,893	11,187	11,756
7. Goods not elsewhere specified	1,305	1,368	495	1,121	685
TOTAL	200,064	191,091	218,089	366,361	347,296

Table XIII : 8 (Contd.)

	Percentage Shares				
1. Food and Beverages	9.5	10.0	9.9	6.7	6.0
2. Industrial Supplies (Non-Food)	35.2	34.6	38.7	39.7	28.7
3. Fuels and Lubricants	8.5	10.7	10.6	22.1	27.4
4. Machinery and other Capital Equipment	15.9	18.9	18.6	10.8	16.6
5. Transport Equipment	17.8	13.8	11.2	11.3	12.7
6. Consumer Goods not elsewhere specified	12.4	11.3	10.7	9.1	8.4
7. Goods not elsewhere specified	0.6	0.7	0.2	0.3	0.2
TOTAL	100.0	100.0	100.0	100.0	100.0

Source: ibid., p. 66.

Table XIII:9. Price indices 1972–5

			1971 = 100	
Imports	1972	1973	1974	1975
Food and live animals	113	139	183	176
Beverages and tobacco	113	125	131	164
Crude materials, inedible	117	129	153	180
Mineral fuels	116	125	394	518
Animal and vegetable oils and fats	95	102	179	232
Chemicals	102	139	248	260
Manufactured goods	110	128	188	216
Machinery and transport equipment	116	127	153	184
Miscellaneous manufactured articles	111	122	177	208
All imports	112	128	201	237
Non-oil imports	111	128	179	202

Source: ibid., p. 67.

Table XIII:10. Terms of trade, 1972–5

			1971 = 100	
	1972	1973	1974	1975
All items	99	98	85	83
Non-oil items	101	101	90	86

Source: ibid., p. 68.

Table XIII:11. Kenya balance of payments 1972–5 (K£ million)

	1972	1973	1974	1975
Current account balance	− 24.3	− 46.8	− 114.3	− 76.7
of which:				
Visible balance	− 65.9	− 54.7	− 161.0	− 134.2
Invisible balance	41.6	7.9	46.7	57.5
Long-term capital movements	32.8	53.1	85.8	62.9
Current and long-term balance	− 9.0	6.3	− 28.5	− 13.8

Source: *ES* 1976, p. 20.

one year, even non-oil items fell from 101 to 90. They fell again (to 86) in 1975, and almost certainly fell again in 1976. Thus, leaving oil aside, we see the 'claw back' mechanism working extremely effectively in 1974–5, more than compensating for any small gains that Kenya may have made in the period 1971–3.

The predictable effect of all this on the balance of trade is shown in table XIII:11 (row two). But once again the full impact on the balance of payments was reduced because of a continuing good performance on invisibles, and (a new factor) because of very considerably expanded borrowing by the Kenyan Government.

The crucial figures here are in row four of table XIII:11. The persistent, if unsteady, rise in long-term capital investment shown there had been going on continuously since 1965. Around 1972 there was a marked change in its composition. Prior to that date, long-term borrowing by the Kenyan government had not exceeded K£5,200,000 annually, and never constituted more than thirty per cent of the total flow of capital to Kenya, most of which was private direct foreign investment. In 1972 the government borrowed K£15,100,000 in order to reduce the balance of payments deficit. In 1973 government net borrowing rose to K£16,800,000 then to K£21,800,000 in 1974 and to K£36,100,000 in 1975. In 1975 government borrowing exceeded private long-term foreign investment (K£24,300,000) which had fallen heavily between 1974 and 1975. In short the Kenyan government was increasingly being forced to borrow in order to reduce the balance of payments deficits originating in the worsening balance of trade. By 1975 these deficits could not be covered by invisibles and private foreign investment alone.

So the Kenyan state has managed to compensate for trade difficulties (whose roots lie in the productivity problem analysed in chapter XIII) by considerable inflows of private foreign investment and more recently by increased government borrowing. Both of these expedients involve the storing up of future troubles in the form of interest and amortisation payments, repatriated profits and so on. Already they involve the Kenyan government in the provision of very generous 'incentives' to investors by way to tax relief, investment grants, guaranteed protected markets, and so on,[29] and they also involve a considerable burden to the present balance of payments as a result of transfer pricing and profit repatriation.[30] These negative present and future effects of foreign private investment and borrowing will only be offset if the capital involved yields increased output and exports and/or reduced imports on a scale which will more than counterbalance future balance of payments losses through profit repatriation and repayment of loans. The precedent of Latin America[31] does not suggest that the likelihood of this is very great.

29. See Theuman, op. cit., pp. 9–10.
30. *ILO Report*, pp. 454–5 and table 4.3 in Leys, op. cit., p. 137.
31. See Lawrence Whitehead, 'The Trade and Aid Relationship in Latin America', in Barbara Ward, J. D. Runnalls and Lenore d'Anjou (eds.), *The Widening Gap: Development in the 1970s* (New York, 1971), pp. 213–34.

Chapter XIV

Classes and Exploitation:
An analysis of Kenya and some views of Marx

In this final chapter, I wish to draw together and make more explicit some of the theoretical implications which have been implicit in the analysis offered in the previous chapters. The central issues considered are the relationship between Marxism and bourgeois stratification theory and the form of 'class analysis' which can be offered for a country like Kenya. The issues dealt with in this book are treated in much neo-Marxist and Marxist-influenced work on Africa under the rubric of 'class formation'. I believe this to be fundamentally mistaken because it involves conflating Marxist class analysis with bourgeois stratification theory, and thus mingles what Marx called the 'realm of appearances' with 'the realm of reality'.

Clearly if we observe any society at a moment in time or through time we may also observe forms of socio-economic inequality, and we may characterise or measure these with reference to any number of criteria separately or in combination. Among such criteria would be firstly monetary income, secondly non-monetary income, thirdly wealth in money or in other forms (e.g. land or capital), and fourthly education.

In addition one might wish to know how forms of inequality are observed and conceptualised by those within the society concerned, and in that case one might prepare questionnaires to try and discover 'subjective' images of different-iation or stratification within that society. One might then go on to describe norms of social status for that society based on these subjective data, and per-haps relate such norms to the objective factors listed above.

Now bourgeois social science is engaged in doing all these things, though from varying perspectives and with varying foci. Thus, for example, neo-classical economics is generally more concerned with the first and third items in the 'objective' list, while sociologists tend to concentrate rather more on the second and fourth items in the objective list and on the subjective, 'social status' side of things.

All of these things are of interest and are more or less useful for a variety of purposes, including 'policy making' purposes. None of them has anything to do with Marxist class analysis. The primary focus of Marx's work was never classes in the above sense; he was never a 'sociologist of class' and on the whole I believe he would have treated such a sociology with some scorn, regarding it as dealing only with the realm of appearances.[1] The primary focus of Marx's mature work (in which I include the *Grundrisse*) was production and production relations. It is clear that Marx believed that in commencing the analysis of any society one should always endeavour to discover the following (and probably in the sort of order outlined below):[2]

1. What is being produced (in terms of use values)?
2. Is what is being produced being exchanged (i.e. do the use values also have exchange value)? And if so are all the products which are being produced being exchanged, or only part of them?
3. Are there products being produced in order to be exchanged, i.e. is there commodity production? If so does this apply to all the products being produced or only to some of them, i.e. is there universal commodity production?
4. Is money used in the exchange of commodities? If so is it used in all such exchanges (is it a 'universal equivalent') or only in some of them?
5. Are means of production as well as final products produced as commodities? i.e. are land, tools, machinery, and raw materials bought and sold with money, and in the case of those which are produced (tools, machinery, raw materials) are they produced as commodities, i.e. produced in order to be sold?
6. If there is commodity production, and a universal equivalent (money) and if means of production are also commodities, is labour itself a commodity, i.e. is it bought and sold for money?
7. If labour is bought and sold for money, is it the human being which is bought and sold (slavery) or only his or her labour power, i.e. his or her strength, energy, intelligence but not the total person?

In *Capital* Volume I what Marx essentially does is to show that:

1. All societies depend on the production of 'use values' (or useful products) for the obvious reason that this is how human beings eat, shelter and clothe themselves. However in the very simplest societies (hunting-gathering societies) this 'production' may be restricted to taking what is naturally given in the environment, rather than expanding use values through the reworking of the products of nature with labour.
2. All societies which produce beyond a bare subsistence minimum will commence to exchange products (use values will acquire exchange value). At first this will be in the form of direct barter, but as the range of such exchanges expands one product will come to act as mode of enumeration of the exchange value of all other products, i.e. one product will come to perform the function of money. However, the fact that products may exchange without means of money serves as the basis for the distinction between exchange values of products and their prices. For a variety of reasons prices may sometimes be an accurate measure or reflection of exchange values and sometimes not.

1. The perspective offered here is essentially taken from Göran Therborn, *Science, Class and Society: On the Formation of Sociology and Historical Materialism* (London, 1976).
2. What follows is based mainly on the *Grundrisse*, expecially pp. 83–108.

3. There are two possible forms of universal commodity production. In the one case each individual product is produced by one (or a number) of individual producers who own their own means of production and sell their products on the market, using their income from sales to buy other products which they require from other producers. Marx calls this type of commodity production 'petty' or 'simple' commodity production and its distinguishing characteristic is the universalisation of exchange relations. That is, each individual producer is dependent on a dense network of exchanges in order to survive and to obtain means of production for his own work. (In this case we may conceptualise the 'individual producer' either as a single individual or a household or family.) The second type of commodity production is capitalist commodity production (or in Marx's terms 'the capitalist mode of the production of commodities') in which, as in petty commodity production, all products are commodities, including means of production, but in which in addition labour power has itself become a commodity. That is, the major part of petty commodity producers have been dispossessed of their own means of production, and now have only their labour power to sell in order to survive. The purchasers of this labour power are the group of people who own all the means of production in society, and Marx calls these people the 'bourgeoisie' or the 'capitalist class'. He calls those who have only their labour power to sell the 'proletariat', or the 'working class'.

So it is only at this point that classes make their appearance in Marx's analysis at all, and then only as a particular outcome of a change in the manner or mode of production which has had certain consequences for the division of labour in society. And in fact if Marx has any continuing interest in delineating social groups throughout his analysis, it is only in this regard, i.e. with reference to the changing division of labour in production. However it should be noted that Marx's method of delineating both modes of production and their changes involves the continual use of ideal types, and of what might be called an historiological mode of analysis. That means, for example, that the petty commodity mode of production in the pure form in which Marx outlines it has never existed, and probably will never exist, and this is equally true of the capitalist mode of production as he outlines it. In the former case for example we are asked to imagine a world in which individual producers owning their own means of production concentrate solely and exclusively on the production of one commodity, all of which they sell in order to buy commodities from others. One implication of this is that such producers are entirely dependent on the market for their subsistence, since even in the case of agricultural producers on their own smallholdings we are invited to posit onion producers who produce only and exclusively onions, and carrot producers who produce only and exclusively carrots. Similarly in the case of the capitalist mode of production we are asked (in Volume I of *Capital*) to envisage a world in which this mode of production exists everywhere. Thus for example there are no imports from or exports to underdeveloped or peasant economies because there are no underdeveloped or peasant economies.[3] The class structure of society in this world is entirely exhausted by the delineation of the working class on the one hand (those selling labour power and without means of production) and the capitalist class on the other (those owning all means of production and purchasing labour power) because there is nobody else.[4]

Now Marx's justification for making such breath-taking abstractions was two-fold. On the one hand it was necessary to make such abstractions in order to distinguish clearly concepts of use value, exchange value, value, surplus labour and surplus value. This is an aspect which I shall not treat here since it is extensively discussed in the appendix to this book. And secondly, Marx believed that though at the time he wrote an ideal typical capitalist mode of production such as he had created was not found in its pure form anywhere (not even in Britain, the most advanced capitalist country of the period), nonetheless over time reality would come to approximate ever more closely to this ideal type. That is, capitalism would expand to the point at which it was a world-wide system of production, and in doing so would destroy all other modes of production. Similarly within capitalism he envisaged that all petty commodity producers would be eliminated, leaving only wage earners on the one hand and capitalists on the other. It should be noted here that for all these reasons, it is totally irrelevant to suggest that Marx's class analysis has been disproven because, for example, there are more 'white collar' workers, or the proportion of manual workers in the population of Britain, Germany or the U.S.A. has fallen, or because fewer and fewer people classify themselves as working-class in surveys. Marx's 'working class' or 'proletariat', just like his 'capitalist class' is an analytical abstraction. In Marx's central analytical perspective a university professor is as much a part of the working class as a miner (providing neither of them own shares), since they have in common the characteristics of selling their labour power and not owning means of production.

This simple fact has been obscured by two major factors. Firstly it has been obscured by an analytically subsequent distinction between productive and unproductive labour in the capitalist mode of production made by Marx. The validity of this distinction has been hotly debated,[5] but it is clear that, whether valid or not, this was simply a distinction within the working class, not a distinc-

---

3. This restriction is relaxed in Vol. III of *Capital* (see especially pp. 237–40) with logical implications for value analysis which have never really been fully explored. For the restriction itself see Vol. I, p. 581, note 1.
4. Again this restriction is relaxed in Vol. III, but no systematic exploration of the implications of this relaxation for class analysis is attempted. Marx may have intended this exploration in the uncompleted chapter LII.
5. See for example Ian Gough, 'Marx's Theory of Productive and Unproductive Labour', *New Left Review*, no. 76, Nov.–Dec. 1972, pp. 47–72; John Harrison, 'Productive and Unproductive Labour in Marx's Political Economy', *Bulletin of the Conference of Socialist Economists*, Vol. II, no. 6, Autumn 1973.

442   *Class and Economic Change in Kenya*

tion between the working class and something else. Secondly it has been obscured by the fact that, having elaborated his basic underlying model, Marx went on to relate it more and more closely to actual historical situations, pointing up points of convergence and divergence between his model of the capitalist mode and reality (specifically nineteenth-century British reality), and drawing out implications from both convergence and divergence. When he begins to do this in *Capital*, and more especially in other more polemical or political writings, Marx is apt to switch to a use of the term 'working class' which has rather more in common with its usage in British and other sociological writing, i.e. he uses it to refer to manual, and particularly industrial manual workers. The reason for this was that, at the time when Marx was living and active as a theorist and revolutionary, the major part of the analytically-defined (labour-power-selling, non-means-of-production-owning) 'working class' was actually industrial manual workers (both skilled and unskilled). But this, though important politically, was a contingent historical fact, and one which the very structure of Marx's underlying model would have suggested was likely to be transient. Thus the increased occupational and status differentiation of the working class through time, far from disproving Marx's theory, is precisely what one would expect if, as his model suggested, more and more different occupations were to be proletarianised.

This discussion may seem to have taken us very far from our primary concerns, but it has been necessary to show both that Marx's class categories were the outcome (and an analytically secondary outcome) of his method, and that they have nothing in common with bourgeois social stratification theory or with the income distribution analysis of neo-classical economics. What then is the central characteristic of classes in Marx's analysis? In essence the answer to this question is simple. Classes are those groups in society which either exploit or are exploited by other groups. A further implication of this is that classes in themselves are of little interest. What is important is their relationship. Marx is, if anything, a theorist of class relations, not a theorist of classes.

In order to obtain a clearer idea of what is meant by saying that, in Marx's model, classes are those groups which exploit or are exploited by other groups, it is necessary to return again to the fundamentals of the model. I have already noted that Marx asserted that all societies which have obtained a minimal level of development will be able to produce a surplus product, i.e. a product in excess of immediate subsistence needs. This surplus product, whether we conceive of it as being of the individual producer, household or entire society, can be used in a variety of ways. It may be traded for other products. It may be used for investment or it may be consumed, in excess of subsistence needs, by a privileged group. In the simplest case, if we imagine a petty commodity producer of carrots, he directly consumes those carrots which he wants for subsistence, and then sells the rest. With the money so obtained he may then: buy a hoe (investment); and/or pay taxes to the State or rent to a landlord (this may allow luxury consumption to occur if there are enough producers who have a considerable surplus product and only comparatively few state officials or landlords); and/ or he may buy bread.

It is to be noted however that if the producer's entire surplus of carrots goes to the purchase of other subsistence goods, then this is not a 'surplus' product in Marx's sense.

In order therefore for exploitation, in Marx's most theoretically central sense, to occur, it must not merely be the case that a relatively small number of people appropriate a part of the surplus product which others produce, but in addition the exploiting class must control the conditions under which another class can produce. The reason for this is quite simple. Let us suppose that we have petty commodity production, in Marx's 'pure' sense. Suppose now that a group of merchants interpose themselves between those petty commodity producers who are selling and those buying. Suppose, in one sector, that the merchants buy carrots at ten shillings per bag, and though competing against each other all manage to sell the carrots to consumers at twenty shillings a bag. This in Marx's view does not constitute 'exploitation', for a number of reasons, all of which focus on the impossibility of deriving an 'objective' standard to determine what the producers of the carrots 'ought' to have received. For if the merchants are competing against each other (i.e. there is no monopoly), then then incapacity of individual producers to obtain more than ten shillings a bag, and the ability of the merchants to obtain a selling price of twenty shillings a bag are both indications that the minimum handling, transport costs etc. which the merchants have to meet if they are to fulfill their function, and the carrots reach consumers, come to ten shillings a bag. A moment's thought will reveal that this could be the case (assuming some competition between merchants) even if the mark-ups were much in excess of this (e.g. a producer price of ten shillings a bag and a resale price of £100), since once again it may be the case that the producers in question are in a very remote area with very high transport costs etc. Moreover, should this resale price be 'excessive', given reasonably competitive markets the merchants would not be able to sell the carrots for £100, i.e. they would be 'undercut' by others. If they can sell at this price in a competitive market, then it is probably an indication that the resale price is not excessive, but in accord with real costs.

In short, Marx, along with the classical, and indeed neo-classical economists, accepts the view that with competitive markets it is impossible to derive any criteria of 'excessive' mark-ups or 'sub-normal' prices which do not reflect some arbitrary notion of a 'just' or 'fair' price. This is always on the assumption that one is dealing with petty commodity production in which individual producers own their own means of production, and that there is competition between merchants. It should also be noted that in circumstances where, for example, carrot producers note that carrot selling prices are below those for potatoes, they may switch to potatoes, or, if they feel prices to be too low for all products sold, may increase that portion of their land and labour time devoted to directly consumed subsistence production, i.e. they may withdraw partially or totally from the market. Such switches would of course cut supplies of certain products and cause producer prices to rise.

This situation can be contrasted with the situation under slavery, feudalism or capitalism. Let us take ideal typical feudalism as an example. If we assume a situation where the serfs on the lord's manor own no land at all, but are allowed to keep a proportion of what they produce on the lord's demesne as their subsistence, then it is to be noted that the serfs literally cannot live unless they work for the lord, and the lord has the power to determine what part of the serf's total production is to go to their subsistence, and, constrained only by the need to keep the serfs alive and capable of working, he may raise or lower this quantum at will. Thus if he wishes to accumulate faster in order to build a new castle or equip an army, he may squeeze his serfs harder. The lord's economic power thus derives from his ownership of the means of production (in this case primarily land), and from the fact that therefore the serfs (in contrast to the petty commodity producers vis-à-vis the merchant) have no way of 'withdrawing' from his control, since they cannot subsist unless he allows them access to 'his' land. If we considered plantation slaves without land of their own, then exactly the same situation would apply. It should also be noted that this is a far better means of control over producers than a monopoly (set up by a state or by agreement among private merchants), since even in this case some of the petty commodity producers would still have the alternative of retreat into subsistence production open to them, and monopoly purchasing power is of little use if supplies of the commodity monopolised are cut drastically or disappear.

This is the essential reason why Marx reserves the concept of exploitation (and thus exploitation of one class by another) to situations in which one class, by owning the means of production, can determine both the conditions under which another class can produce and the level of that class's subsistence. It is of course his contention that under capitalism the capitalist class has exactly this form of control over the proletariat, but that under capitalism that control takes the form of the ability of the capitalist class to determine the value of the labour power which the working class sells.

In the light of these considerations I intend to argue that if one restricts oneself to African production, circulation and consumption patterns, both in the colonial period and subsequently, then there was and is no class exploitation in Kenya in Marx's most analytically central and 'deep' sense, since the situation in Kenya approximates much more closely to the petty commodity producer/merchant situation than to the exploitation situation underlying ideal typical feudalism or capitalism.

This has important implications for class analysis. The essential feature of Marx's class analysis of capitalism as it appears in Volume I of *Capital* is a posited symbiosis of value categories and class categories which can be diagrammatically represented thus:

VALUE CATEGORY	CLASS CATEGORY
Source of Surplus Value	Proletariat (working class)
Mutually Exclusive	
Appropriators of surplus value	Bourgeoisie (Capitalist class)

Now in the Kenyan case one can substitute for 'source (appropriators)' of 'surplus value', 'source (appropriators)' of 'surplus labour', and indeed one must do so.[6] But no real progress is made with this procedure because a much more substantial problem remains. This, very simply, is that the categories 'source of surplus labour' and 'appropriator of surplus labour' are not mutually exclusive for large sections of the Kenyan population. This is simply another effect (in class terms) of the failure of labour power in Kenya to be transformed into a commodity. It is these issues which we shall pursue further in the next section.

Labour Categories and Class Categories: The Problems of the Kenyan Case

The following labour situations are to be found in Kenya:
1. A peasant who has worked his own land with his own labour moves to another area to work for a capitalist farmer. He obtains no land from the farmer to work on his own behalf, and obtains a cash wage for his work. However, his wife remains behind in his area of origin and works a plot of family land. His wife and children obtain the bulk of their subsistence from this land, and may also supplement their income by the sale of surplus food crops or export cash crops. The migrant helps his wife to employ casual labourers on the home plot by remitting part of his wages home.
1a. The same situation as (1) above, except that the migrant works in a manufacturing plant or in a mine.
2. A peasant who has worked his own land with his own labour migrates to work for a capitalist farmer. In this case the farmer provides the migrant with land to cultivate for himself. His wife and family join him on the land provided, and the family gives up whatever land rights they possess in the area of origin.
3. A migrant obtains a better-paid job in manufacturing, commerce or in state or private bureaucracy and he and his family become entirely dependent on this

6. See Appendix, pp. 456–61.

income for their livelihood. All rights to land are given up, and the entire family takes up permanent urban residence.

4. A male family head, or more commonly a female family head or sibling with no access to land, or with access only to a small plot of land inadequate to provide a subsistence for him or herself and dependents, works part-time for a neighbouring peasant farmer. This peasant farmer may well be the 'wife' of situation (1).

It is very difficult to determine with any accuracy the numbers of workers in each group, partly because of the usual shortcomings with labour statistics in Kenya, especially problems of coverage and reliability, and because the statistics are not collated by these categories. However, in 1970 in Kenya 644,500 people were employed in the public and private sectors combined, including large farms and plantations, but excluding employment on small farms and settlement schemes and excluding the self-employed and 'family workers' in urban areas and 'all activities in rural non-agriculture'. Of these about 120,000 were classified as 'high and middle level manpower' and would undoubtedly fall into category (3). If, arbitrarily we say that a further twenty-five per cent of workers on large farms were squatters who would not have been enumerated, i.e. some 44,647 workers, this constitutes the size of category (2). All the rest would fall into categories (1) or (1a). In addition there were some 311,000 people employed on small farms and settlement schemes, in 1970. Of these 168,000 were classified as 'regularly employed' and 142,400 as 'casual employees' and virtually all would fall into my category (4). In addition, the ILO report on Kenya quoted survey figures suggesting that some 80,000 workers were employed in 'small rural non-agricultural enterprises' in 1969. These workers, together with the 85,000 workers whom the ILO reckoned were employed in unenumerated urban employment at that date, are probably best included as part of category (1a).

Thus the total categorisation would be as shown in table XIV:1. The important thing to note is that the employment in category (4) is largely made available by the income of those employed in categories (1), (1a) and (3). In the case of category (3), even those who do not depend on land for part of their subsistence or current income often own land as an investment, and some of Kenya's richest men are polygamous, having 'families' in town and a wife or wives and children in the country managing landholdings. In the case of those in categories (1) and (1a) the labour power hired is largely to replace that which has departed to work elsewhere. In the case of category (3) far more than this is hired.

The theoretical problem touched on at the end of the previous section, i.e. that the categories 'source of surplus labour' and 'appropriator of surplus labour' are not mutually exclusive in Kenya, is generated by cases (1) and (1a). On the one hand the worker on the capitalist farm or in the factory or mine is a source of surplus labour for the owners of these means of production, but on the other hand as the juridical owner of the home farm he is the 'appropriator' of the surplus labour of others, usually those in (4). Moreover, insofar as part of the worker's subsistence in (1) or (1a) is supplied by the home farm, the total cost of his labour power, as well of course as the cost of the reproduction of labour power, i.e. of his children, is not met by the wages bill, but is supplied in part by the product of the direct labour of his wife/wives, and by the labour of those whom he hires.

Cases (2) and (3) are rather less troublesome from the Marxist point of view. Case (2) is essentially that of squatter labour and the labourers in question are unambiguously a source of surplus labour for others. Even here there can be complications in that, historically, it was not unknown for squatters to hire in labour on their own farms. However, since the squatter labour system has now been dismantled with the run-down of settler farming, and since the theoretical problem from this point of view is not significantly different from that posed by (1) and (1a), we can ignore this phenomenon in the following discussion. Case (3) is in part the classic proletarianisation of *Capital* Volume I, bringing with it the conversion of labour power itself into a commodity and the transformation of surplus labour into surplus value. We have already noted that the theoretical problem here is to explain why this development has been so limited in Kenya.

It is (1) and (1a), the typical cases of present-day Kenya, with their con- comitant case (4), which constitute the central theoretical problems. How are we to come to terms with them, in the context of the theoretical body of Marxist concepts already developed?

The essential problem is this: in the classical model of capitalism developed in *Capital*, and in the remarks on pre-capitalist economic formations found in the *Grundrisse* and elsewhere, Marx always assumes that the components 'socially necessary' labour and 'surplus labour' can be unambiguously identi-

Table XIV:1. Occupational structure of African households in Kenya, 1970

Category	Definition	No. employed 1969–70
1.	Agricultural employment for a male, 'home plot' retained for wife and children	178,589
1a.	Non-agricultural employment for a male, 'home plot' retained for wife and children	466,264
	Sub-total	644,853
2.	Squatter agricultural employment, 'home plot' on hiring farm	44,647
3.	Higher-paid non-agricultural employment, usually in urban areas. Wife and children dependent on wage earnings alone	120,000
4.	Employment of the landless or of 'poor peasants' by other smallholders	311,000

Sources: *SA* 1972, tables 220, 222, 227 and 234b. Also *ILO Report*, pp. 39 and 54.

fied. In the case of mature capitalism, and working at the aggregate level, the socially necessary labour time is that consumed in the production of wage goods, whilst the surplus labour time is that devoted to the production of expanded means of production and of non-wage, 'luxury' goods consumed by the capitalist class and others. Similarly under feudalism, the surplus labour time is that worked on the lord's *demesne*, whilst the socially necessary labour time is that worked by the serfs on their own land for their own subsistence.

However in the Kenyan case, the socially necessary labour time is extremely heterogenous. Some of that labour time (taken in the aggregate) is worked in Kenyan factories, some of it is worked in artisan workshops and some is worked on 'peasant plots'. For in all these cases goods are being produced which will enter into the socially and historically given subsistence of the labourers and their families found in (1) and (1a), and indeed into the subsistence of the workers in (2), (3) and (4) as well.

We see a similar heterogeneity if we examine the concept of 'surplus labour' in Kenya. The products which are surplus to the subsistence needs of Kenyan workers are once again produced in factories, on peasant plots and in small-scale artisanal workshops. It is not possible analytically to distinguish a body of socially necessary labour time which can be delimited spatially, temporally, or sectorally (as for example the concept 'wage goods production' distinguishes it) and set apart from surplus labour time. In the real process the same forms of concrete labour performed by the same labourers in the same locations may be both necessary and surplus, and neither the form of concrete labour involved (planting, weeding, spinning, canning, carving), nor the spatial locations of that labour (on peasant plot, capitalist farm or estate, or in the factory or workshop), serves to label it as necessary or surplus. Moreover, not even the product, use value, itself can be so used. It may seem, for example, that all the labour time going into the production of coffee or tea in Kenya is part of the surplus labour time, since nearly all of these products are exported rather than domestically consumed. But the coffee that is picked by the labour of the poor widow, old man, or dispossessed sibling working for a nearby rich peasant is for him or her picked as part of the socially necessary labour time, since he or she is only working because they are landless, or, more commonly, because their land is inadequate to provide the level of subsistence to which they are accustomed—their 'socially given' level of subsistence.

What produces this heterogeneity? Why is it impossible meaningfully to formulate concepts of socially necessary and surplus labour at the disaggregated level? The answer is provided by money. Money is indifferent to the concrete form of labour whose product it monetises, and to the form of use value for which it is exchanged. It is the role of money to aggregate the heterogenous, by purchasing the means of life for its owner, and the means of production, capital, for those who have accumulated enough of it.

Since it is money which has played a central part, both as means of exchange and as finance capital, in the peculiar form of incorporation of the Kenyan economy into the world capitalist system, it is also money which has dissolved the distinction 'socially necessary' and 'surplus' labour at the disaggregated level. These two forms of labour can nowhere be distinguished in, as it were, their 'natural' form; only their results can be distinguished, and only then in the aggregate. It is because we observe that there are those in Kenya who have access to money accumulated in the form of capital, living alongside those who only have access to the most basic means of subsistence, part or all of which have been purchased by money, that we can validate the concepts of surplus and socially necessary labour. Put simply, if there were not surplus labour time being worked in Kenya it would not be possible for money to be accumulated and to become capital. We must look for exploitation then not in the direct relation of surplus labour appropriator to surplus labour source but in the capacity of various strata to accumulate money in the form of capital.

To put this more concretely: we cannot take the worker in a Coca-Cola plant in Nairobi, measure the amount of surplus labour which he provides for the Coca-Cola Corporation and then offset this against the amount of surplus labour his wife, as manager of his home farm, pumps out of the six agricultural labourers she hires. We can derive no calculus which will differentiate the 'net exploiters' from the 'net exploited'. This is so for two reasons. Firstly, because value relations, or more generally labour time relations, do not manifest themselves directly in this way at the disaggregated level; and this is true universally. Secondly, in the particular context of Kenya the non-homogeneity of surplus and socially necessary labour, which is made possible and sustained by the role of money, renders such a calculus both impossible and unnecessary. For the rate and scale of accumulation of money and of capital, through money, by particular individuals and strata is the necessary and sufficient condition of identifying their essential class position. Very simply, those who can accumulate money and capital on any scale at all must be in control of part of the product of Kenya's surplus labour. The more and the faster they can accumulate, the greater must be their share of surplus labour.

But who are 'they'? Which groups benefit by obtaining a disproportionate share of the monetised surplus product? We may identify three groups initially. They are:

1. Merchant capitalists proper, i.e. those who buy and sell the agricultural surplus product, and accumulate through the classic circuit $M - C - M^1$. These are both foreign-owned import/export firms, and on a smaller scale African and Asian merchant capitalists operating in the domestic market, and (in a few cases) in the international market too.

2. The best-paid public sector employees, and especially officials in the state and para-statal sector who obtain access to the surplus product in the form of the wage fund, which in its turn, is derived from that product, through the mechanisms outlined in the previous chapter.

3. To a much smaller extent, domestic retailers and wholesalers dealing with rural households as initial purchasers of output and suppliers of consumption goods. Since in this sector the situation approximates to perfect competition (especially in retailing and crop purchase), the share of the surplus product appropriated by small-scale merchant capital is very small.

However, precisely because appropriation and accumulation by these methods is comparatively inefficient, groups (2) and (3) have also used capital accumulated in this manner to move into agricultural production on a larger scale and to set labour power to work. State officials in particular have moved into large-scale farming in taking over settler farms in the Rift Valley,[7] whilst in addition, as we have seen earlier, they have taken the lead in land purchase, commercial production and the hiring of labour power in the smallholding areas. It is because the latter process is so ubiquitous, extending well down the public sector wage hierarchy and also embracing wage earners in the private sector (some of whom are industrial workers) that the problems for class analysis examined earlier have arisen. The future pattern of the class structure in Kenya, as much else, will be crucially determined by how far this use of capital, accumulated primarily in the realm of circulation, to commercialise agricultural production and to stratify the countryside, will be carried. As I have already argued this is essentially dependent on how severely the limits on accumulation within the sphere of circulation (and of expansion of the wage bill) will be felt by those who benefit from it, and by those whose role it is to keep the political system stable in order that this accumulation can go on.

Accumulation out of a surplus product produced in manufacturing industry also goes on within Kenya, though this does not involve the appropriation of 'surplus value' (see appendix). The prime beneficiaries of this are of course multinational companies but some nationals (mainly big state officials, politicians and managers with shares in equity) also benefit. The wage bill here, at least at the higher wage levels, also helps to fuel the process of commercialisation and stratification in agriculture.

Whilst the complexities of the Kenyan case make it impossible to utilise the concept of class developed in Volume I of *Capital*, in which classes (or rather two classes, the proletariat and the bourgeoisie) are identified with reference to their diametrically opposite roles within the production process alone, it is possible to develop a Marxist form of class analysis for Kenya (and perhaps for other parts of sub-Saharan Africa too) based on the slightly more inclusive concept of the mode of appropriation of the surplus product. This second level concept of class (which Marx outlines in the incomplete fragment of Chapter LII of Volume III of *Capital*, and which he essentially borrowed from Ricardo) is probably generalisable to a greater variety of empirical instances than the severely abstract class theory of Volume I, because in bringing in ground rent as

7. See Leys, op. cit., pp. 89–92.

a particular mode of appropriation of surplus value under capitalism and tying this criterion to a particular class ('landlords'), it opens up the possibility of relating class structure to the sphere of circulation in addition to the sphere of production.[8] This does not mean, as Marx indeed makes clear at the end of this fragmentary chapter, that every different type of revenue justifies the creation of a different 'class' to appropriate it, but it does point to the possibility of conflicts of interest between different appropriating groups (between those appropriating in production and those doing so in circulation, and indeed between groups appropriating at different points in the production and circulation process).[9] My own view is that conflicts within the sphere of circulation may be particularly severe in a situation where the bulk of labour power is not a commodity, because different groups are squabbling over a cake whose absolute size they find difficult to expand. On the basis of these reflections, and to end this study, I wish to suggest that one might approach the delineation of the class structure in Kenya using this criterion of the mode of appropriation of the surplus product in the following fashion.

In the first place, this criterion must be divided into two: first the appropriation of the product through the process of its production; second the appropriation of the surplus product through the process of circulation. Individuals and certain occupational categories, e.g. high-level state officials and politicians, will qualify as beneficiaries by both these latter criteria, which means of course that they cannot be regarded as mutually exclusive. In fact the limits of class power and domination in Kenya are defined by their conjoint use. That is, the richest in Kenya are those who both employ those whose labour produces significant proportions of the surplus product, and who receive a disproportionate share of the product when it is monetised and circulated, whilst the poorest are those whose labour produces little or no surplus product, i.e. most or all of those whose labour time is expended in the pursuit of a basic subsistence, and who receive little or nothing of the monetised surplus product when it is circulated through the State and private capital.

In this process access to the State is in fact vital, since it is the State which controls the circulation and monetisation of the bulk of the surplus product in Kenya, and in this respect acts as a form of merchant capital. Historically in Kenya, privileged access to the monetised form of the surplus product, especially the State's wage fund, was the means by which labour and means of production, especially in agriculture (but also elsewhere) were acquired by the African petite bourgeoisie. This in turn allowed the surplus product to be expanded, and for the petite bourgeoisie to take a part of that expanded product both through the production process and through the circulation process. By this 'straddling'

8. I refer here to the money rent paid by the capitalist farmer or industrialist to the landlord (what Marx calls 'capitalist ground rent') which is in Marx's terms 'but an excess over average profit' (*Capital*, Vol. III, p. 796).
9. Industrial capitalists, merchant capitalists, bank capitalists etc.

'African' capital accumulation was (and is) mainly carried on in Kenya.

However, whilst it is access to the surplus product both in production and circulation, principally through the State, which defines the position of the richest Africans in Kenya, and the total absence of such access which defines the poorest, there are a significant number of other groups coming between these two extremes whose position can be illuminated by use of the two criteria separately. That is to say, there are some groups which contribute significantly, in terms of labour time and labour power, to the creation of the surplus product but receive a disproportionately small share of its monetised form, the most numerous of this category being the middle-level smallholders and sections of the urban and rural wage labour force; and others who contribute little or nothing to the creation of the surplus product but who receive a disproportionately large share of its monetised form. This category would include small groups of highly-paid service workers in urban areas, workers and executives for finance and merchant capital, and large numbers of middle and senior level state and para-statal officials.

This is the position considered, as it were, from the point of view of personal income and wealth and of shares in the production and circulation of the surplus product. But from the point of view of the Marxist, a further cross-cutting criterion should be noted, and this is the distinction between productive and unproductive labour. If we define productive labour as labour which produces and transports the subsistence and surplus product of Kenya, and unproductive labour as including that which wholesales and retails that production and undertakes the financial transactions which purchase and sale on any large scale require, as well as labour involved in maintaining the social formation (for example, the police and the army), we may distinguish:

a. those who have large shares in the monetised surplus product and use that share to purchase means of production, raw materials and instruments of labour for productive labour and indeed to hire the labour power itself, e.g. local industry shareholders, 'rich peasants', owners of big farms and plantations;

b. those who have large shares in the monetised surplus product and use that share to employ unproductive labour, e.g. hairdressing salons, boutiques, or safari lodges;

c. those who labour productively on their own behalf, e.g. self-employed artisans and the bulk of 'middle peasants';

d. those who labour unproductively on their own behalf, e.g. self-employed hairdressers, shoe shiners or tourist guides;

e. those who are hired to labour productively for others, e.g. landless labourers, poor peasants, plantation workers, urban industrial workers, transport workers and workers in small scale manufacturing; and,

f. those who labour unproductively for others, e.g. assistants in boutiques, waiters in tourist hotels and safari lodges.

It is clear that there can be and are considerable differences in earnings and income in the last four groups determined by their relative shares in production and/or distribution of the surplus product, and that indeed there will be similar differences inside groups (a) and (b) as well, though here the differences will be between the rich and the very rich rather than as in (c), (d), (e) and (f) between the middle income groups and the poor.

I think it is the constant need for one to use the criteria of production of the surplus product and of relative shares in its monetised form conjointly, and the way such conjoint use illuminates the structural situation of the rich, the poor, and the middling groups in Kenya's distribution of income and wealth, that justifies theoretically the view not only that Kenya's ruling class is a petite bourgeoisie, but that Kenya is predominantly a petit-bourgeois society and economy. For it is the hallmark of the petite bourgeoisie that their position within an economy cannot be grasped simply by reference to their role in production alone, or their role in circulation alone, precisely because they are so frequently involved in both dimensions. Moreover, they can rarely be charac-terised simply as 'exploited' or 'exploiters'. They frequently occupy both posi-tions with reference to different classes (which is why their politics are shifting and prone to oscillate between left and right). The difference in Kenya, and in many other parts of the Third World, is that a section of the petite bourgeoisie, having gained control of the State, approximates much more closely to the situa-tion of 'pure' exploiters than any petite bourgeoisie does in advanced capitalist situations. Nonetheless, though it approximates to this situation in Kenya, it is still an open historical question whether the state petite bourgeoisie in particular will attempt to convert itself into a fully developed bourgeoisie (a 'national bour-geoisie') by using its dominant position within the sphere of circulation (through the State) to convert to primary exploitation within the process of production (i.e. by employing productive labour power on a large scale).

As the previous chapter tried to make clear, I do not think that the issue of whether they will or will not do this is as easy to resolve as a lot of theorists appear to suppose. I certainly do not think that in any simple sense it is structur-ally or historically precluded. A great deal of this book has demonstrated how historically the Kenyan petite bourgeoisie was both a product and an agent of the change and development of production (especially agricultural production). I see no reason to suppose *a priori* that this process has ended. Indeed, in trying to outline the kinds of contradictions which are inherent in the attempt to accumulate within the sphere of circulation in Kenya, I suggested one reason why the state petite bourgeoisie in particular might be forced to attempt to intervene much more forcefully in the process of production of all commodities within Kenya, thus raising the possibility of conflict with international capital. However, there is another 'variable' in this situation, far more important than any actions by the Kenyan petite bourgeoisie, which is the trend of profitability and the class struggle within the capitalist heartlands. This may lead to invest-ment switches toward the Third World which, if they affected Kenya, could alter production relations there much more quickly and dramatically than anything which the state petite bourgeoisie could attempt alone. Whether this is possible or likely I cannot say, and it would require an in-depth study of the world system (which we do not have) even to begin to determine it. One thing is certain. Kenya is an integral part of the world capitalist system, and the implications of this are that its development prospects are strongly over-determined by those of the system as a whole, and that autonomous development (even of a capitalist sort) in even partial opposition to international capital would be bought at a high price for the bulk of Kenya's people. The petite bourgeoisie will therefore only embark on such a course (with all its economic costs and political risks) if the political risks of continued dependency seem greater.

To return to the theme of class analysis which is at the heart of this work: if one took each of the six classes identified above, treated their members as individuals, and looked at them from the point of view of bourgeois stratification theory, i.e. from the point of view of the relative sizes of their money incomes, landholdings, capital assets, level of education etc., one would observe very considerable inequalities not merely between these classes, but between individuals within them. Thus for example in class (a) one could have a clerical worker in a large commercial concern in Nairobi buying twenty acres of land in Kiambu, hiring ten agricultural labourers every year and owning a few shares in a brewery. One could also have a senior politican owning huge tracts of land in the White Highlands, hiring hundreds of agricultural labourers, running a tanker fleet and owning London real estate. Thus the classes (a) and (b) for example could be ranked into several strata in conventional stratification theory using educational, income or life-style criteria. The same would be true of classes (c) and (d) and even of classes (e) and (f) who are certainly the most exploited of Kenya's people.

The search for such stratification criteria, however useful and necessary for political purposes, should not be confused with Marxist class analysis. Indeed the term 'class analysis', a modern coinage, is severely misleading. For in seeking to disaggregate any society into social or economic groups, the Marxist is not (or at least should not be) concerned with these groups *per se*, but with isolating the mechanisms by which the products of labour power either in their natural or monetary form are transferred between groups, and by which accumulation of money and the means of production is accomplished. This may involve placing in the same class (e.g. those producing the surplus product, those hiring productive labour, those accumulating through production, those accumulating through circulation) men and women whose monetary wealth, life-styles, and political positions are enormously varied. Having accomplished this intial and fundamental analysis of classes at the level of the 'deep structure' (to use loosely a term from Chomsky) of production relations, one may then (a logically and theoretically subsequent step) go on to look at the implications for politics and for political strategy made by differences induced by wealth and lifestyle and (in the African case) by tribal identity, regional origins, etc. Differences in the degree of exploitation may be of importance here too.

This book has in essence been restricted entirely to a 'stage one' analysis of Kenya. It has been concerned to illuminate the modes and mechanisms of the creation and appropriation of a surplus product in Kenya and to identify those groups or classes related through these processes. It has said nothing, and was not conceived as saying anything, about 'class consciousness', political loyalties and ideologies, or other forms through which self-conscious group identities are formed in Kenya (such as 'tribalism').

I believe that Marxist work on Africa has been hopelessly ensnared by attempting simultaneously to grapple with what is often called the 'objective' structure of class and production relations and the 'subjective' structure of consciousness, ideology and political factions. The beginning of clarity is to sort one out clearly from the other, and at least to get the objective questions posed in a clear fashion. It is my hope that this book has achieved that and perhaps a little more, and above all that it has pointed to the importance of disentangling Marxism or historical materialism from the stratification theory of bourgeois sociology. For in my view a persistent conflation of these two entirely different theoretical problematics has been the principal hallmark of much neo-Marxist work on Africa.[10] Once the distinction between the deep structure of production relations and what Marx would surely have regarded as the 'realm of appearances' dealt with by stratification theory has been clarified and held firm, then Marxists are free to do productive and flexible work on African realities. They can also make much more profitable use of the empirical work of bourgeois scholars, because they can treat it on its own terms (as dealing with an important but secondary level of reality) without becoming entangled in such tedious and theoretically confused questions as to whether part-time low-income smallholders are a 'poor peasant class', or state officials earning more than K£10,000 per annum are a 'bourgeoisie', or part-time workers in import substitution industries a 'proletariat'. All this reflects an inadequate grasp of Marxism, and deflects attention from much more important questions, such as the likely pattern of development of an economy such as Kenya's, which only an analysis of the dynamics of underlying production relations is likely to reveal.

---

10. See for example Peter C. W. Gutkind and Peter Waterman, *African Social Studies: A Radical Reader* (London, 1977), especially pp. 226–94; also nearly all the work of Cliffe, Saul and Arrighi and others in the 'early 'Dar es Salaam School', a representative selection of which is found in G. Arrighi and J. S. Saul (eds.), *Essays on the Political Economy of Africa* (New York, 1973). See also Issa Shivji, *Class Struggles in Tanzania* (London, 1976); and M. Mamdani, *Politics and Class Formation in Uganda* (London, 1976). For a wider range of literature on Central and West Africa, see my 'Concept of Class and the Study of Africa', *The African Review*, no. 3, 1972, pp. 327–50—an article which itself exemplifies this confusion perfectly.

Appendix

Values, Prices and the Analysis of Underdevelopment: A Guide for the Unwary

The discussion which follows is peripheral to the main themes of this work, which is why it appears as an appendix. However, since much Marxist and neo-Marxist work on Africa has been and is being predicated on the relevance or potential relevance of 'value analysis' to the African situation, I hope that the anguished process of theoretical exploration through which I have gone over the last five years will be of help to others. This is not to say that I hold my current view to be simply and indelibly right and authoritative. The issues in-volved are far too complex for anyone to feel this. But I do think that the discussion which follows may help others to avoid some blind alleys whose murky confines I have spent a great deal of time exploring.

The purpose of this work as originally conceived was to 'found class analysis in Africa in the value domain', something which I took to be the prerequisite of a 'thorough-going Marxist analysis'[1] as against the theoretically muddled 'neo-Marxist' approach which in my view distinguished much of the writing on Africa of the late sixties and early seventies. I have already stated in detail the way I came to reconceptualise the 'class analysis' side of things, as a result of some in-depth study of Marx. I wish to deal here with the value domain question.

My starting point was the discovery that Marx's model of universalised petty commodity production in Volume I of *Capital*, out of which he built his concept of 'value' (as distinct from 'use value' or 'exchange value'), was not a form of petty commodity production which was ever likely to be encountered in the real world. In this model the division of labour in production had developed to a point where every petty producer devoted all his labour time to the production of one and only one commodity. In such a situation all commodity producers, though owning their means of production, are entirely dependent on the market for subsistence, i.e. they sell the whole of their own production on the market and buy in the whole of their subsistence with the money obtained. In such a situation the labour power embodied in commodities has a value, i.e. it takes a certain amount of labour time to produce and reproduce it, and that labour time is itself embodied in commodities. By measuring the amount of labour time em-bodied in the commodities which all the petty commodity producers consume

1. The quotations are from earlier drafts and papers which I hope and intend shall never see the light of day.

456

as subsistence, one can determine the value of their labour power. Since all commodities produced in this situation are produced by labour time which has a value, they themselves have value, and that value is (in principle) determinable. Since in the model thus set up the ratios in which commodities exchange (their money prices) are deemed proportional to the labour time embodied in them, the amount of labour time (or more exactly socially necessary 'abstract' labour time) embodied in each commodity is 'revealed' through its price, i.e. a commodity with three hours of socially necessary labour time exchanges with a commodity which has two such hours embodied in it in the ratio of three money units to two.

Thus, this model of petty commodity production is exactly that: an abstract, analytical model created for certain theoretical purposes; and all sorts of problems arise if any simple attempt is made to apply it to a real situation. For example, it is wrong to speak of an actual 'peasant' economy as an 'example' of petty commodity production, because most peasant households are distinguished by the fact that they do not produce a single commodity (they usually produce a variety of agricultural commodities); and above all a considerable part of their labour time is not spent in the production of commodities, i.e. peasants produce part or all of their own directly consumed subsistence from their own land and sell only a 'surplus'. Strictly speaking, therefore, within the structure of Marx's model, their labour power cannot be 'valued' since it does not depend entirely upon the market for its production and reproduction.

The issue of course is whether there is any merit or point in 'speaking strictly' in this case. If a large part of reality cannot be accommodated within the structure of a model because of the strictness and peculiarity of its parameters, is there not some merit in stretching or bending those parameters so as to accommodate reality within them? I shall argue that there is not.

Marx set up his model of petty commodity production as a logical tool designed to show that whereas the concept of value merely presupposed universalised commodity production, the concept of surplus value presupposed the specifically capitalist production of commodities. That is, in the model of petty commodity production set up, the labour time of all producers has a value, and thus all commodities have value. Nonetheless, since they own their own means of production all producers may, if they wish, produce only a quantity of commodities equal to the value of their own labour power, i.e. they can choose to produce only such commodities as embody the amount of socially necessary labour time equal to the amount of such labour time as they require for their own subsistence.

Another way of putting this is to say that as long as the producers own and control their own means of production they can determine the intensity of application of their own labour power. They work for as long and as intensively as they require to produce the commodities which will enable them to procure the means of their own reproduction.

Under capitalism however labour power itself has become a commodity, the intensity of application of which is controlled by the capitalist class, and it is this latter point, as much as the former (labour power becoming a commodity) which distinguishes capitalism. Of course this control over labour intensity is only possible because labour power is a commodity. But the crucial thing is that the 'working class' (as the direct producers have now become), having sold their labour power for a certain period of time, do not control how much is produced in that time. It thus becomes possible for the capitalist class to ensure that the working class produces a product in excess of that which it needs for its own reproduction, and this product embodies surplus value. Marx conceptualises the surplus product so produced as 'surplus value' because

1. it is a product in the form of commodities, and
2. the socially necessary 'abstract' labour embodied in it has a determinate value, and
3. that value is a surplus over the subsistence needs[2] of the proletariat which produced it.

Now note that within the logical transition between the two models (petty commodity production and capitalist production) the crucial changes are that

1. labour power which had a determinate value under petty commodity production has now realised that value, i.e. it is actually being bought and sold as a commodity; and
2. the existence of a surplus product is now logically necessary within the structure of the model since the capitalist class cannot itself expand net investment or even subsist without such a product; and
3. the intensity of application of labour power is now controlled by the capitalist class (since they own the means of production) and is no longer controlled by the direct producers.

Now Marx never confused this logical transition (and the formal models of petty commodity and capitalist production which are necessary to its location) with the actual historical process of transition. In historical reality labour power only became a commodity when the direct producers had their own means of production expropriated, and, given that the dominant form of petty commodity production prior to the emergence of industrial capitalism was smallholding agricultural production, this is not at all surprising. For in general peasants, so long as they maintain control of their own land, will continue to produce at least part of their own subsistence directly, if only out of considerations of security. Generally they can only be made to give up this theoretically inconvenient practice by being forced off their land, and thus in reality the creation of the actual conditions which will justify the use of the concept value is generally coterminous with the creation of the conditions which justify the use of the

---

2. The volume of commodities equal to those 'subsistence needs', includes those means of production required to produce wage goods, as well as the wage goods themselves.

concept surplus value; whereas in logic the value of labour power may be 'created' under pure petty commodity production, and 'realised' under capitalism, in reality its creation and realisation are coterminous and occur alongside the creation of surplus value. I therefore take the view that if we are interested in the analysis of the real world, use of the concepts of value and surplus value should be restricted entirely to those situations in which all, or the overwhelming majority of producers, are a 'proletariat', totally without means of production of their own, and in which all or almost all products produced are produced in factories owned by a capitalist class in which the expropriated working class sells its labour power.[3] Trying to 'bend' the concepts to fit situations in which the dominant form of production is actual 'impure' petty commodity production is to confuse a logical form with a substantive reality, and infringes the strict conditions laid down by Marx for the use of such concepts.

One form of 'bending' is to argue that, as peasant ('household') production becomes more and more specialised, more and more of household labour time is devoted to the production of commodities, and that, for small peasants in particular, a stage may be reached where the household is almost totally dependent on the market for its subsistence.[4] In this situation is it not permissible to speak of the 'value' of the peasant's labour power and thus of surplus value? In my view it is not. For though, as indeed I have argued in this work, situations such as this were and are met with in Kenya, and indeed in many other parts of the world where peasant agriculture has been commercialised, in practice whereas some peasant households are in this situation others are not, and in fact the largest landholding households who produce a disproportionate share of all agricultural commodities also produce a larger part of their own subsistence directly. Thus overall a large part of the total labour power expended in Kenya is produced and reproduced out of directly consumed production. So long as this is the case, there can be no justification for the use of the concepts 'value' and 'surplus value'. Indeed, it was precisely because Marx was aware that actual historical forms and patterns of transition were inordinately complex and varied that he tried to lay bare their essential results. This required stress on the logic of transition and the structural changes which such logic revealed. In all cases therefore where the matter is unclear or ambiguous it seems better to err on the side of strictness and caution.

A more difficult question emerges in the case of industrial workers in Kenya. Many of these men are working for profit-making capitalist enterprises, but

3. For a powerful argument in support of this position (though focused on a rather different debate) see Robert Brenner. 'The Origins of Capitalist Development: a Critique of Neo-Smithian Marxism', *New Left Review*, no. 104, 1977, pp. 25–92.
4. This is essentially what is attempted by Cowen and by Banaji. See Cowen and Kinyanjui, op. cit.; and J. Banaji, 'Modes of Production in a Materialist Conception of History', *Capital and Class*, no. 3, Autumn 1977, pp. 1–36.

many of them are also using savings from their wages to expand household landholdings. Usually this means that a worker's wife and children will obtain part of their subsistence from directly consumed production, and the worker himself may do so at intervals. If we take the strict view that until workers and their families are entirely dependent upon wages for their subsistence it is not appropriate to speak of value or surplus value in Kenya, we seem left with the paradox that in Kenya profit is produced without surplus value. This paradox is merely apparent. For so long as workers produce a product in excess of that which they consume as subsistence, i.e. so long as there is a surplus product, then the essential prerequisite for the existence of profit is fulfilled. The fact that the labour power of the working class involved is not produced and reproduced entirely by means of commodities simply means that this process cannot be measured or enumerated in terms of 'values', i.e. in units of socially necessary abstract (or 'simple') labour time. The profit in question still has its origins in the expenditure of labour time and of excess labour time. But the formal conditions which allow this exploitation to be conceptualised in a certain manner are not met. What is essential is that one be able to show that without a concept of surplus labour (and thus of a physical surplus product) it is impossible to explain the existence of profit (as distinct from a particular rate or level of profit), and that in particular the existence of profit as such cannot be explained simply by reference to the excess of selling price over (money) costs of production. The demonstration in Volume I of *Capital* that if labour power is purchased at its value there could be no profit without surplus value, and Sraffa's more recent demonstration of the logical contradiction inherent in the neo-classical theory of profit as the marginal product of aggregate capital, are both in their way potent demonstrations that without some concept of a surplus product— the product of surplus labour—the existence of profit must be mysterious or inexplicable.[5]

The whole issue of values and value analysis is a fascinating one, and recent debates upon it have many profound implications, even for the Marxist analysis of advanced capitalist economies. But from the point of view of this particular study we may leave the matter there. The concepts 'value' and 'surplus value' are seen to presuppose the existence of fairly strictly defined conditions which are not met with in Kenya, since it is not a fully developed capitalist mode of production, but rather a subordinated production system integrated into the world capitalist system in a manner which has not yet reproduced a fully developed capitalist mode of production locally. This need not inhibit the development of a theory of exploitation suitable for Kenyan conditions. But clarity about the meaning and limits of value theory is the prerequisite of such development. The starting point of such clarity is the recognition that in a real world where com-

5. Marx, *Capital*, Vol. I, especially pp. 156–76; and P. Sraffa, *The Production of Commodities by means of Commodities* (Cambridge, 1960).

modities exchange through money, and where relations of production assume the apparent form of monetary relations, rates of exploitation are necessarily unmeasurable.[6] A level or rate of exploitation, whether expressed in terms of value and surplus value or in terms of labour time and surplus labour, can only be shown logically to be a prerequisite of sustained accumulation (I attempted such a demonstration in chapter XIII). It is not, and by the very nature of commodity production could not be, an empirical datum.

6. Though of course it is theoretically necessary to be able to demonstrate that (a) in a simplified model of a commodity-producing economy, it can 'in principle' be measured, and that (b) as each of the simplifying assumptions are dropped and the model approximates closer to reality, there is no logical change which would make such measurement logically impossible. This is essentially what Marx attempted to do in Parts I and II of Vol. III of *Capital*, and it is one of the central issues in current debates on Marxist economic theory. See Ian Steedman, *Marx after Sraffa* (London, 1978); Bob Rowthorn, 'Neo-Ricardianism or Marxism?', *New Left Review* no. 86, 1974; Maurice Dobb, 'The Sraffa System and Critique of the Neo-Classical Theory of Distribution', in E. K. Hunt and Jesse G. Schwartz (eds.), *A Critique of Economic Theory* (Harmondsworth, 1972), pp. 205–21. Also, A. Sen, 'On the labour theory of value: some methodological issues', *Cambridge Journal of Economics*, Vol. 2, no. 2, 1978, pp. 175–90 and J. Harrison, P. Armstrong and G. Glyn, 'In Defence of Value—A Reply to Ian Steedman', *Capital and Class*, no. 5. Summer 1978, pp. 1–31.

Bibliography

Only the most important primary and secondary sources used are listed below. For fuller referencing and a more complete range of citation, see footnotes.

I. Primary Sources

A. Kenya National Archives (unpublished sources)

1. Annual and Quarterly Reports for the following districts, c 1907–52, or as available:
   Kiambu
   Fort Hall
   Nyeri (South Nyeri)
   North Kavirondo (Nyanza)
   Central Kavirondo (Kisumu or Central Nyanza)
   South Kavirondo (Nyanza) or Kisii
   Nandi
   Nakuru
   Uasin Gishu
   Wajir
   Garissa
   Isiolo (earlier Bulesa district)
   Masailand (1919–39), later Kajiado District (1940–52)
2. Provincial Commissioners' Annual Reports, c. 1907–38
   Ukamba Province ⎫ Provincial boundaries redrawn and
   Kikuyu Province ⎬ Province retitled at various dates
   Central Province ⎭ —see maps
   Nyanza Province
   Rift Valley Province
   Naivasha Province

B. Published Departmental Annual Reports—Kenya Colony

The following were consulted as dated:
Department (later Ministry) *of Agriculture* 1911–70
Department of Native Affairs (later African Affairs) 1923–55

Department (later Ministry) *of Labour* 1942–70
Blue Books 1919–39
Trade Reports 1929–40

C. Published Commission and other official Reports —
Kenya Colony

1912/13 *Report of the Native Labour Commission*
1925 *Report of the Economic and Finance Committee on Native Labour*
1927 *Report of the Labour Commission*
1929 *Report of the Committee on Land Tenure in Kikuyu Province*
1930 *Report of the Committee on Native Land Tenure in the North Kavirondo Reserve*
1934 *Kenya Land Commission: Report* and *Evidence and Memoranda* (3 volumes)
1937 *Memorandum on Native Agricultural Development in the Native Reserves*
1943 *Food Shortage Commission of Inquiry Report*
1945 Humphrey et al., *The Kikuyu Lands*
1946–8 *Reports on Native Labour Census*
1946 *Economic Survey of Resident Labourers*
1947 Humphrey, *The Liguru and the Land*
1948 *African Labour Efficiency Survey*
1950 *Geographical and Tribal Studies* (East African Population Census 1948)
1950 *Cost of Living Commission Report*
1953/5 *East Africa Royal Commission Report 1953–1955*
1954 *Report of the Cost of Living Committee*
1954 *Report of the Committee on African Wages*
1959 *The Patterns of Income, Expenditure and Consumption of Africans in Nairobi 1957/58*
1960 A. G. Dalgleish, *Survey of Unemployment*

D. Commission and other official Reports: Republic of Kenya

Economic Surveys (annual 1960–77)
Statistical Abstracts (annual 1955–76)
1963 *Kenya African Agricultural Sample Census 1960/61*
1964 *Kenya Population Census 1962*
1964 *The Pattern of Income, Expenditure and Consumption of African Middle Income Workers in Nairobi, July 1963*
1966 *Maize Commission of Inquiry: Report* and *Evidence* (3 volumes)
1968 *Economic Survey of Central Province 1963–64*
1971 *An Economic Appraisal of the Settlement Schemes 1964/65–1967/68*
1971 *Kenya Population Census 1969*

1971   *Report of the Public Service Structure and Remuneration Commission 1970–71 (Ndegwa Report)*
1972   *Employment, Income and Equality (ILO Report* on Kenya)
1977   *Rural Household Survey Nyanza Province 1970–71*

II. Secondary Sources

A. *Unpublished Ph.D. Theses* (for origin see footnotes).

J. J. Bucknell, 'An Appraisal of some of the Developmental Impacts of the Kenya National Trading Corporation'
A. H. Clayton, 'Labour in the East African Protectorate 1895–1918'
P. T. Dalleo, 'Trade and Pastoralism: Economic Factors in the History of the Somali of N. E. Kenya 1892–1948'
M. J. Hay, 'Economic Change in Luoland: Kowe 1890–1945'
B. E. Kipkorir, 'The Alliance High School and the Origins of the Kenya African Elite 1926–1962'
J. Lonsdale, 'A Political History of Nyanza 1883–1945'
S. H. Ominde, 'Land and Population in the Western Districts of Nyanza Province'
S. B. Stichter, 'Labor and National Development in Colonial Kenya'

B. *Unpublished Papers and Reports* (for origin see footnotes)

M. P. Cowen with Frederick Murage, 'Notes on Agricultural Wage Labour in a Kenya Location'
M. P. Cowen, 'Differentiation in a Kenyan Location'
M. P. Cowen, 'Wattle Production in the Central Province: Capital and Household Commodity Production 1903–1964'
M. P. Cowen and Kabiru Kinyanjui, 'Some Problems of Class Formation in Kenya'
J. Fisher, 'The Anatomy of Kikuyu Domesticity and Husbandry'
F. Furedi, 'The Kikuyu Squatter in the Rift Valley 1918–1929'
F. Furedi, 'Kikuyu Squatters and the Changing Political Economy of the White Highlands'
F. Furedi, 'Olengurone in Mau Mau Historiography'
A. Jacobs, 'The Pastoral Masai of Kenya: A Report of Anthropological Field Research'
J. G. Karuga, 'Thresholds in the Transformation of an Economy: Some Preliminary Thoughts on the Structure of the Nairobi/Kiambu Peri-Urban Zone'
R. M. Maxon, 'Cash Crop Innovation among the Gusii in the 1930s'
M. P. Miracle, 'Economic Change among the Kikuyu 1895 to 1905'
J. Newman, 'First Steps in Rural Capitalism: Machakos before the Second World War'

I. D. Talbott, 'The Politics of Agriculture: Rural Development Planning in Kenya in the 1930s'

R. Theuman, 'Political and Economic Consequences of Kenya's Development Strategy'

K. K. Sillitoe, 'Land and the Community in Nyeri'

R. Waller, 'Uneconomic Growth: The Maasai Stock Economy 1914–29'

Rebman W. Wambaa and Kenneth King, 'The Political Economy of the Rift Valley: A Squatter Perspective'

W. E. Whitelaw and G. F. Johnson, 'Urban-Rural Income Transfers in Kenya: An Estimated Remittance Function'

R. van Zwanenberg, 'Industrialisation and the Growth of the Kenya State 1929–52'

C. *Journal Articles and Published Papers*

J. Banaji, 'Modes of Production in a Materialist Conception of History', *Capital and Class*, no. 3, Autumn 1977

Brighton Labour Process Group, 'The Capitalist Labour Process', *Capital and Class*, no. 1, Spring 1977

J. M. Bujra, 'Women Entrepreneurs of Early Nairobi', *Canadian Journal of African Studies*, vol. IX, no. 2, 1975

W. Chipeta, 'The Roles of Customary and Modern Money in the Rural Exchange Economy of Malawi', *East African Journal of Rural Development*, vol. 3, no. 1, 1970

F. Furedi, 'The African Crowd in Nairobi: Popular Movements and Elite Politics', *Journal of African History*, vol. XIV, no. 2, 1973

J. R. Harris and M. P. Todaro, 'Wages, Industrial Employment and Labour Productivity: The Kenyan Experience', *East African Economics Review* (new series), vol. 9 no. 1, 1961

Kipkoech Motonik arap Korir, 'An Outline Biography of Simeon Kip-lang'at arap Baliach, a "Colonial African Chief" from Kipsigis', *Kenya History Review*, vol. 2, no. 2, 1974

L. S. B. Leakey, 'The Economics of Kikuyu Tribal Life', *East African Economics Review*, vol. 3, no. 1, 1956

K. Leitner, 'The Situation of Agricultural Workers in Kenya', *Review of African Political Economy*, no. 6, May–Aug. 1976

R. A. LeVine, 'Wealth and Power in Gusiiland', in P. Bohannan and G. Dalton (eds.), *Markets in Africa* (Evanston, 1962), pp. 520–36.

R. A. Manners, 'Land Use, Labor and the Growth of a Market Economy in Kipsigis Country', in Bohannan and Dalton, op. cit., pp. 493–517

H. Pack, 'Employment and Productivity in Kenyan Manufacturing', *East African Economics Review* (new series), vol. 4, no. 2, 1972

C. Palloix, 'The Internationalization of Capital and the Circuit of Social Capital', in H. Radice (ed.), *International Firms and Modern Imperialism* (Harmondsworth, 1975), pp. 63–88

N. Swainson, 'The Rise of a National Bourgeoisie in Kenya', *Review of African Political Economy*, no. 8, Jan.–April 1977

R. L. Tignor, 'Colonial Chiefs in Chiefless Societies', *Journal of Modern African Studies*, vol. 9, no. 3, 1971

R. M. A. van Zwanenberg, 'The Agricultural History of Kenya to 1939', *Historical Association of Kenya Papers*, no. 1, 1972

D. Books

A. H. Amsden, *International Firms and Labour in Kenya 1945–70* (London, 1971)

F. E. Bernard, *East of Mount Kenya: Meru Agriculture in Transition* (Munich, 1972)

E. A. Brett, *Colonialism and Underdevelopment in East Africa: The Politics of Economic Change 1919–39* (London, 1973)

A. H. Clayton and D. C. Savage, *Government and Labour in Kenya 1895–1963* (London, 1974)

E. Clayton, *Agrarian Development in Peasant Economies: Some Lessons from Kenya* (London, 1964)

H. Fearn, *An African Economy: A Study of the Economic Development of the Nyanza Province of Kenya 1903–1953* (Nairobi, 1961)

M. W. Forrester, *Kenya To-day: Social Prerequisites of Economic Development* (Gravenhage, 1962)

R. D. Grillo, *African Railwaymen: Solidarity and Opposition in an East African Labour Force* (Cambridge, 1973)

P. H. Gulliver, *The Family Herds: A Study of Two Pastoral Tribes in East Africa, The Jie and Turkana* (London, 1955)

H. W. von Haugwitz with H. Thorwart, *Some Experiences with Smallholder Settlements in Kenya 1963/64 to 1966/67* (Munich, 1972)

H. Heyer et al., *Agricultural Development in Kenya: An Economic Assessment* (Nairobi, 1976)

G. Kay, *Development and Underdevelopment: A Marxist Analysis* (London, 1975)

K. King, *The African Artisan: Education and the Informal Sector in Kenya* (London, 1977)

C. L. A. Leakey, *Crop Improvement in East Africa* (Farnham Royal, 1970)

R. A. LeVine and B. B. LeVine, *Nyansongo: A Gusii Community in Kenya* (New York, 1966)

C. Leys, *Underdevelopment in Kenya: The Political Economy of Neo-Colonialism 1964–1971* (London, 1975)

P. Marris and A. Somerset, *African Businessmen: A Study of Entrepreneurship and Development in Kenya* (Nairobi, 1971)

K. Marx, *Capital* (3 vols.), translated by Moore and Aveling (Moscow, 1965–8)

K. Marx, *Grundrisse*, translated by Martin Nicolaus (Harmondsworth, 1973)

K. Marx, *Pre-Capitalist Economic Formations*, translated by Jack Cohen, introduction by E. J. Hobsbawm (London, 1964)

J. F. Munro, *Colonial Rule and the Kamba: Social Change in the Kenya Highlands 1889–1939* (Oxford, 1975)

G. Muriuki, *A History of the Kikuyu 1500–1900* (Nairobi, 1974)

Oginga Odinga, *Not Yet Uhuru* (London, 1967)

B. A. Ogot (ed.), *Politics and Nationalism in Colonial Kenya* (Nairobi, 1971)

S. H. Ominde, *Land and Population Movements in Kenya* (London, 1968)

D. J. Parkin, *Palms, Wine and Witnesses: Public Spirit and Private Gain in an African Farming Community* (London, 1972)

J. G. Peristiany, *The Social Institutions of the Kipsigis* (London, 1939)

C. G. Rosberg and J. Nottingham. *The Myth of 'Mau Mau': Nationalism in Kenya* (New York, 1966)

D. H. Ruben, *Marxism and Materialism: A Study in the Marxist Theory of Knowledge* (Hassocks, 1977)

H. Ruthenberg, *African Agricultural Production Development Policy in Kenya 1952–1965* (Berlin, 1966)

R. Sandbrook, *Proletarians and African Capitalism: The Kenyan Case 1960–1972* (Cambridge, 1975)

M. P. K. Sorrenson, *Land Reform in the Kikuyu Country: A Study in Government Policy* (Nairobi, 1967)

P. Spencer, *The Samburu: A Study of Gerontocracy in a Nomadic Tribe* (London, 1965)

P. Spencer, *Nomads in Alliance: Symbiosis and Growth among the Rendille and Samburu of Kenya* (London, 1973)

G. Therborn, *Science, Class and Society: On the Formation of Sociology and Historical Materialism* (London, 1976)

R. L. Tignor, *The Colonial Transformation of Kenya: The Kamba, Kikuyu and Maasai from 1900 to 1939* (New Jersey, 1976)

G. Wagner, *The Bantu of Western Kenya: with Special Reference to the Vugusu and Logoli*, Vols. I and II (London, 1970)

G. Wasserman, *Politics of Decolonization: Kenya Europeans and the Land Issue 1960–1965* (Cambridge, 1976)—consulted as a Ph.D. thesis—see footnotes

R. D. Wolff, *The Economics of Colonialism: Britain and Kenya 1870–1930* (New Haven, 1974)

R. M. A. van Zwanenberg, *Colonial Capitalism in Kenya 1919–1939* (Nairobi, 1975)—consulted as a Ph.D. thesis—see footnotes

R. M. A. van Zwanenberg with Anne King, *An Economic History of Kenya and Uganda 1800–1970* (London, 1975)

Index

478   *Index*

Sesame, *see* Crops
Settlement Schemes, 357–60
Shanin, T.S., 362
Sheep, *see* Livestock
Siaya, 345, 353
Sim-Sim (sesame), *see* Crops
Sisal, *see* Crops
Socially necessary product, 37, 37n8, 39,
    42, 43, 44, 45, 54, 97, 111–12, 115, 124,
    127, 133, 152, 175, 178, 224–5
Somalis:
    butcheries, 213
    Mbagathi, 213, 213n18, 216, 216n25
    settlers, 213–14
    quarantines, 214
    Youth League, 235, 235n65
Sorghum, *see* Crops
Sorrenson M.P.K., 196, 213, 280, 288,
    292, 315
South   Kavirondo,   *see*   South   Nyanza
South Nyanza:
    agricultural statistics, 26, 41, 45, 81–2,
        132–3, 346, 348
    bridewealth, 220
    coffee, 79–80, 82, 102, 318, 351
    cotton, 74, 78–9, 327, 373
    labour migration, 250–1
    land reform, 326–7
    livestock, 220, 239, 372
    Local Native Council, 194
    maize, 26, 41, 45, 81–2, 132–3
    trade and business, 40, 161, 170, 182,
        185, 218
South Nyeri, *see* Nyeri
Squatters, 17–19, 33, 45, 49–50, 91, 99–100,
    154, 154n84, 219, 223, 243–4, 248,
    248–10, 284–5, 294–5, 446–7
State:
    and African agricultural development,
        59–60, 79–80, 82, 101–6, 109–10,
        155, 170–1, 316–21, 325–8
    borrowing, 427–8, 430–7
    and capital accumulation, 419–26
    and circulation of commodities, 414–47
    and depression, 57–61
    and direct taxation, 413, 416–17, 419
    and employment, 406, 408–10
    and indirect taxation, 413, 415–16,
        418–19
    and informal investment fund, 421, 423–7
    as merchant capital, 413–19

and settlers, 57–8, 59–61
wage bill, 421–3
weakness of, 420
Stichter, S.B., 58, 150–1, 255, 273, 275
Stock trade:
    accumulation, 204, 207–9, 217, 220–1,
        225, 238
bridewealth, 203–4, 207, 217, 220
    depression, 59, 107, 221–2
    Masailand, 208, 212, 214, 215, 218–19,
        221–2, 235
    Nandi, 236–8
    Northern Frontier Province, 212, 214–16,
        218–19, 221–2, 234–5
    North Nyanza, 236
    pre-colonial, 208–10
    quarantine, 214
    routes, 201, 212, 212n17, 215, 215n22
    settlers, 213–14
    Somalis, 20, 212–17
Sugar, *see* Crops
Surplus labour, 445–9
    and surplus value, 445, 456–61
Surplus product:
    in agriculture, 21, 28, 32, 34, 37, 39,
        42–5, 50, 54–5, 69, 85–7, 93, 97,
        106, 111–12, 123, 125, 130, 143–4,
        152, 175
    and capital accumulation, 419, 420,
        449–52
    and circulation of commodities, 21, 32,
        34, 53, 107, 168, 172–3, 198–9, 209–10,
        414–19, 426–7, 451–2
    definitions, 39, 414
    in Marx, 152, 442–3
    and the State, 414–19, 420–6, 428–9,
        451–2
    and surplus value, 458, 460
    and taxation, 153, 198, 415–19
    and traders, 31–2, 165, 168–9, 169n19,
        170–1, 174, 176–7, 187
    and women, 54–5, 85–7, 93, 100, 106,
        123, 125, 128–9, 143–4, 176–9, 224–5
Surplus value, 445, 457–61
Survey of Unemployment 1960, 377, 380, 397
Sweet potatoes, *see* Crops

Taxation:
    direct taxes, 413, 416–17, 419
    hut tax, 25, 29, 61, 61n13, 153, 217
    indirect taxes, 413, 415–18